Amiche

Theo

Copyright © Theo 2025

All Rights Reserved

No part of this publication may be reproduced, stored in a retrieval system, or transmitted in any form or by any means, electronic, mechanical, photocopying, recording, or otherwise, without the written permission of the author or the publisher.

DEDICATION I
ACKNOWLEDGEMENTS II
ABOUT THE AUTHOR III
CRADLE OF HUMANITY (HISTORICAL AND GEO-POLITICAL CONTEXT) 1
A HUMBLE BEGINNING 15
    A Change is Gonna Come (Sam Cook) ....
MY MOTHER'S BACKGROUND 24
    The Most Beautiful Girl in the World (Prince) ....
UNION OF SOULS 37
    Can't Help Falling In Love (Elvis Priestley) ....
TENDER TRIALS 43
    Superstition: When You Believe In Things You Don't Understand (Stevie Wonder) ....
AN UNUSUAL ENCOUNTER 68
    Sweet Child O'Mine (Guns n Roses) ....
CARING FOR THE OTHER MOTHER, NATURE 74
    Heal the World (Michael Jackson) ....
FROM RED TERROR TO RED CARPET 78
    Living on a Prayer (Bon Jovi) ....
KINGS AT HEART 135
    Stand By Me (Ben E King) ....
MOVING PICTURES 157
    Tunnel of Love (Bruce Springsteen) ....
FLIGHTS OF HORROR... 177
    Come Fly With Me (Frank Sinatra) ....
THE GREATEST GIFT 201
    Another Brick On The Wall (Pink Floyd) ....
UNITED IN HARDSHIP 213
    Glory Days (Bruce Springsteen) ....

TALKING HANDS 236
    Painter Man (Boney M) ....

CITY OF OPPORTUNITIES 249
    I Can See Clearly Now (Johnny Nash) ....

PARTY OF ONE 277
    Winds Of Change (Scorpions) ....

DERAILED BY SUCCESS 315
    Highway To Hell (AC/DC) ....

FREEDOM AT LAST 352
    Jailhouse Rock (Elvis Presley) ....

THE LAST MILE 380
    One Way Ticket (Eruption) ....

RECYCLED CONFLICT 430
    War Pigs (Black Sabbath) ....

THIRD TIME UNLUCKY 463
    Every time You Go Away (Paul Young) ....

WRITTEN IN THE STARS 505
    Fast Love (George Michael) ....

AN UNEXPECTED ENCOUNTER 572
    What's Going On? (Marvin Gaye) ....

END OF THE ROAD 582
    Dance with My Father Again (Luther Vandross) ....

PAYING IT FORWARD 588
    I'll be there (Michael Jackson) ....

THE BIG MESSAGE 593
    We Are Family (Sister Sledge) ....

BLURB 601

Dedication

To my father Yosief, my mother Hewan, my brothers Kaleb, Simon, Biruk and Alazar and all those who supported us in our harshest times.

Acknowledgements

My father Yosief, my mother Hewan, my wife Helen, my children Delia and Rakieb, and my friend Sesen.

About the Author

AMCE: Automotive Manufacturing Company of Ethiopia.

Back in the 1930's Fiat introduced in Ethiopia the first truck model in history. The success lead Fiat to open assembly plant in Addis Ababa in 1970 with the collaboration of both governments at the time.

Theo Solomon, nicknamed Amiche, was born in Eritrea in the early 1970s and raised in Ethiopia during a time of transition from monarchial rule to military governance. His childhood was a tapestry woven with threads of struggle and resilience.

The nickname "Amiche" was given to him and many other Eritreans born and raised in Ethiopia from 1970 onwards. Sarcastically derived from the acronym AMCE, which referred to an Italian automotive assembly company in Addis Ababa, the name became synonymous with Eritreans like Theo—born (or "assembled") and raised in Addis Ababa, the capital of Ethiopia.

In the heart of the Horn of Africa, amidst the tumultuous winds of political change, young Theo Solomon's story began. His childhood was a tapestry woven with threads of struggle and resilience.

Theo's father, Yosief, a man dedicated to civil and humanitarian service, stood as a beacon of compassion in a sea of turmoil. His mother, Hewan, with her unwavering love, provided solace amid chaos. Together, they nurtured Theo and his siblings through the uncertain landscape of their homeland.

As the shadows of communism loomed over Ethiopia and Eritrea, imposing rigid ideals on the impressionable youth, Theo and his brothers embarked on a journey marked by hardship and adventure. They traversed contrasting landscapes of poverty and luxury, experiencing the extremes of destitution and abundance.

Amidst the relentless cycle of violence and misfortune that plagued his family, Theo emerged as a beacon of creativity and self-reliance. With ingenuity born of necessity, he crafted pathways to survival, safeguarding the lives of his loved ones in the face of adversity.

Familial and political upheavals posed stark challenges to Theo's youth, threatening to tear his family apart. Yet, with the unwavering courage of his mother and the extraordinary resilience of his father, they weathered the storms that raged around them. Their bond, fortified in the crucible of adversity, emerged unbroken and unyielding.

Theo's journey as a young person was one of defiance against despair, a narrative of triumph over tragedy. The world bore witness to the astonishing resilience of a family that defied the odds, navigating through unfathomable trials unseen by many.

Transitioning to a new chapter in the United Kingdom, Theo carried with him the values instilled by his family and the lessons learned during their darkest hours. With a wife by his side and two teenage daughters to guide, he embarked on a journey of gratitude and service, paying forward the support and kindness extended to them in their times of need.

The legacy of Theo Solomon, born in the crucible of political upheaval and tested by the fires of adversity, shone brightly in the enduring power of hope and resilience. In a world marked by turmoil and uncertainty, his story stood as a beacon of light, illuminating the path for those who dare to tread the winding road of survival and redemption.

CRADLE OF HUMANITY

Historical and geo-political context of Eritrea, Ethiopia and Tigray (region)

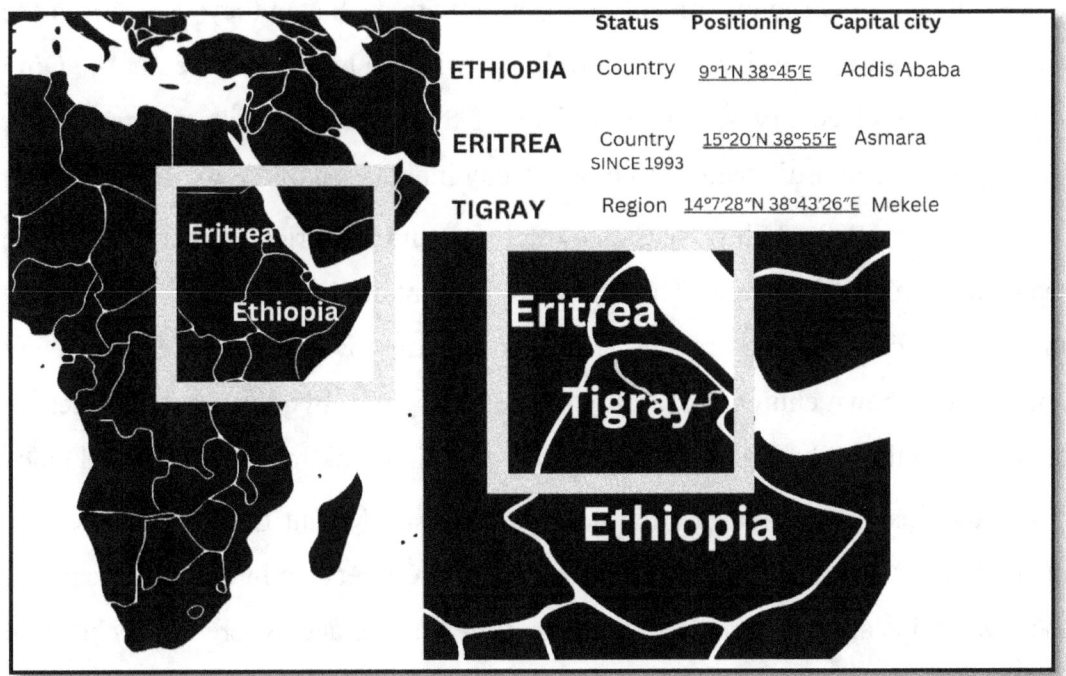

In the heart of the Horn of Africa, also known as Eritrea and Ethiopia, as well as neighbouring Somalia and Djibouti, lies a land teeming with ancient mysteries and whispers of the origins of humanity. This region, rich in both archaeological treasures and spiritual significance, holds the key to unlocking the secrets of our shared past.

Amidst the vast expanse of the Horn of Africa, particularly in the Eritrean and Ethiopian highlands, where the scent of some of the richest spices and the most beautiful precious stones can be found, lies the site of one of the most remarkable discoveries in human history—Lucy, the oldest human fossil ever found. Lucy, a distant ancestor who walked the Earth over three million years ago, offers a tantalising glimpse into our evolutionary past, a reminder of our humble beginnings in this ancient land.

The archaeological wonders of the Horn of Africa paint a vivid picture of a time long forgotten, when early human settlers roamed the vast savannas and lush forests, forging the foundations of civilisation with each step they took. From the ancient rock art of the Tigray region to the prehistoric tools unearthed in the Omo Valley, every discovery serves as a piece of the intricate puzzle that traces our journey from primordial beings to modern-day inhabitants of the world.

The Great Rift Valley casts geographical and historical marvels over the majestic Semien Mountains. The echoes of ancient civilisations resonate through the craggy cliffs and deep ravines. Here, among the towering obelisks of Aksum and the rock-hewn churches of Lalibela, the legacy of a bygone era still lingers, a testament to the enduring spirit of humanity that first took root in this sacred land.

In the heart of Eritrea, nestled near the majestic Mount Emba Soira, lies the ancient town of Qohaito. From the moment explorers set foot in this historical site, they were instantly transported back in time to a place where the echoes of civilisations past still linger in the air.

As one wanders through the rocky terrain, remnants of a once-thriving community can be found. The rock art that adorns the cliffs tells tales of people who called this land home since the fifth millennium BC. Intricate symbols and drawings depict hunting scenes, sacred rituals, and daily life, offering a glimpse into the rich culture of the past.

The town of Qohaito itself stands as a testament to resilience, having survived through centuries of change and turmoil until the sixth century AD. Its ruins whisper stories of battles fought, trades made, and lives lived within its walls. Just a stone's throw away from the ancient town is a small successor village, where the descendants of those who once inhabited Qohaito continue to thrive. As time stood still, the traditions and heritage held dear were passed down through generations.

The rock art, the ruins, and the village—all are threads woven together in the intricate tapestry of Eritrea's history.

But it is not just science that points to the Horn of Africa as the cradle of humanity; it is also the spiritual connection that binds the people of this land to their ancestors and the divine forces that shaped their destinies. From the mystical journey of Queen Sheba's dervishes to the ancient biblical stories of Christianity and the Coptic Orthodox Church, the spiritual landscape of Eritrea and Ethiopia is alive with the echoes of a time when gods and mortals walked hand in hand.

As the winds of time sweep across the arid plains and verdant valleys of this ancient land, one thing remains clear: the Horn of Africa is not just a place on a map, but a sacred realm where the threads of our shared humanity are intricately woven. It is here, in the shadow of towering mountains and beneath the watchful gaze of ancient gods, that our story began—a story as old as time itself, waiting to be discovered and retold for generations to come.

Therefore, as the sun dips below the horizon and the stars twinkle in the velvety sky, we are reminded of our humble origins in this cradle of civilisation, where the past and the present converge in a timeless dance of wonder and awe. In the Horn of Africa, where the whispers of Lucy, the pilgrimage of Queen Sheba, and the echoes of ancient civilisations linger, the story of humanity unfolds—a tale as old as the rocks that guard our secrets and as enduring as the spirits that guide our souls.

In the heart of the tumultuous region lies a land steeped in history, its significance resonating far beyond its borders. From ancient times, this land has been a battleground, a melting pot of civilisations and beliefs, each vying for dominance over its sacred soil. The winds carried whispers of past conflicts, ancestral claims, and defiance against invading forces.

Amidst this backdrop of strife, the people of the land stood resilient, their identities forged in the fires of adversity. They are proud and fierce people, their actions shaped by an unwavering quest for truth and a determination to hold onto their heritage amidst the chaos that engulfed them.

The landscape itself bore the scars of countless battles, its rugged terrain a testament to the enduring spirit of its inhabitants. From the ancient ruins that dotted the countryside to the bustling markets of its cities, every corner of the land exuded an air of defiance and resilience.

Despite the looming clouds of colonial invasions that threatened to engulf their homeland, the people of the Horn of Africa refused to bow to despair. They drew strength from the tales of bravery and sacrifice that echoed through generations; their resolve remained unshakeable in the face of adversity, ensuring these precious lands remained uncolonised.

The people of the Horn of Africa, united by their beliefs and traditions, have withstood their past filled with adversity and uncertainty. They knew that the only way forward was to stand together, united in their struggle for identity and freedom.

The Horn of Africa, with its rich tapestry of culture and heritage, stands as the source of various civilisations in sub-Saharan Africa—a land where time seems to stand still amidst towering mountains, endless water resources, and rugged landscapes.

Tucked away in the northern reaches of Ethiopia is the region of Tigray, a land blessed with more than 3,000 years of history. It is here that the remnants of the Aksumite civilisation stand proud, a testament to a glorious past that once rivalled the great empires of Rome, Persia, and China. The ancient city of Aksum, nestled in central Tigray, served as a beacon of trade and power in its heyday, its influence reaching far and wide.

The land itself seems to speak of a time when Ethiopia was known as Abyssinia, a land shrouded in mystery and legend, mentioned in the sacred texts of the Bible and the Quran, and the site of the first discovery of coffee beans.

But perhaps the most enduring legacy of Tigray lies in its unique writing system, the Gəʽəz/Fidel script, a remnant of an ancient civilisation that still thrives in modern-day Ethiopia. The alpha-syllabic Aksumite writing and numerical system have stood the test of time, a living link to a past where Africa was not just the cradle of humanity, but also of literacy and culture.

Venturing further into the Wollo region, one encounters the marvels of Lalibela, where churches carved from solid rock stand as a testament to the ingenuity and faith of the inhabitants. These UNESCO-registered heritage sites, with their intricate carvings and timeless beauty, serve as a reminder of the rich cultural tapestry that weaves through the fabric of East African civilisation.

Through the ages, Tigray has been a sacred land, a place where the seeds of Abrahamic religions were first sown in Africa. Christianity found its foothold here before the 4th century, followed by Islam in the early 7th century, shaping the religious landscape of the region for centuries to come. The fusion of these faiths with the ancient writing and numerical system of Ge'ez and the Ge'ez calendar has preserved a wealth of religious and cultural artefacts that document the rich history of Ethiopia and its enduring spiritual institutions.

As the stars twinkle overhead and the ancient stones of Aksum and Lalibela stand silent vigil, one cannot help but feel the weight of history pressing down. Tigray, the birthplace of renowned heroes and brave souls, with its ancient wonders and timeless beauty, stands as a living testament to the enduring spirit of Africa — a land where civilizations rise and fall, but the echoes of the past never truly fade away.

In the heart of the Horn of Africa, where the lands of Eritrea, Tigray, and central Ethiopia converge, lies a tapestry of intertwined histories and complex relationships among the various tribal and ancestral communities. These regions, sharing commonalities in language, religion, and traditions, have woven a rich cultural fabric that celebrates wisdom and heroism yet also hosts the shadows of periodic rivalries that have evolved into modern conflicts, defining the lines of their differences.

The shared histories of these communities, where tales of ancient migrations and settlements are interwoven with legends of shared heroism against invaders, tell of those who defied the odds to protect their people. The bonds forged through common rituals and beliefs are vividly portrayed in colourful ceremonies where songs and dances echo through the valleys, celebrating the resilience and spirit of the tribes.

But beneath the surface of harmony lies the undercurrent of occasional rivalries that emerge, fueled by territorial disputes and power struggles — often caused by wrongful miscalculations made by politically unqualified monarchs and community leaders. What once were friendly competitions and displays of strength now morph into political conflicts that draw outside interests seeking to exploit the strategic importance of the region in the wider world context. Foreign powers and internal factions vie for influence, manipulating the tensions between the tribes for their own gain. As the stakes rise, the once familial ties between the communities strain under the weight of mistrust and betrayal. The lush landscapes that once symbolised abundance and prosperity now bear witness to the scars of conflict, with villages burned and fields left barren by the ravages of war, supported financially and politically by the same forces they once fought against together.

As the differences reach a climax, the conflicts that once simmered beneath the surface erupt into open warfare, engulfing the lands in a maelstrom of violence and bloodshed. The once vibrant communities find themselves torn apart by divisions that threaten to erase the bonds forged over centuries of shared history. And as the sun sets over the rolling hills, casting a golden glow over the land, new chapters begin almost every decade in the history of the people of Eritrea, Tigray, and central Ethiopia — chapters defined by conflict that further fractures their resilience, keeping communities in a constant cycle of deprivation and poverty.

The historical context of Eritreans living and working in the neighbouring Tigray region during the reign of Emperor Haile Selassie is a fascinating reflection of the socio-political intricacies that characterised the Horn of Africa during the mid-20th century. This period was marked by significant shifts in political power, social dynamics, and economic strategies, within which the Ethiopian empire sought to consolidate its territories, including Eritrea. Until the elections of a new Eritrean Assembly in 1952, the Unionist Party held the largest number of seats, but not a majority. The party thus formed a government in coalition with a Muslim faction, which was adopted by the Eritrean Assembly on July 10, 1952, and ratified by Emperor Haile Selassie on August 11 of that year.

The act of federation was ratified by the emperor on September 11, and British authorities officially relinquished control on September 15. Eritrea, then the 14th region of Ethiopia, is located at the tip of the country, north of Tigray, and borders the Red Sea on its entire eastern shore.

The positioning of Eritreans in high-ranking roles within Tigray could have been multifaceted in its motivations and implications. On one hand, it may have been a strategic move by the Ethiopian government to integrate Eritreans into the broader administrative and social fabric of the empire, thereby promoting a sense of unity and cohesion among the diverse ethnic groups within its borders. This could have been seen as a way to strengthen the central authority's influence over Tigray and other regions by leveraging the expertise and loyalty of Eritrean professionals. On the other hand, the prevalence of Eritreans in such positions might have been a testament to the individual qualifications, skills, and competencies they possessed, gained from the presence of more advanced educational facilities due to the colonial status of Eritrea at the time. These skills were recognised and valued in the region of Tigray and beyond.

The socio-political dynamics of the era were indeed complex, influenced not only by internal policies and ethnic relations but also by the broader geopolitical landscape, including the intensification of the Eritrean independence war and other tensions of historical and global context. This sheds light on the intricate tapestry of Ethiopian and Eritrean history, marked by periods of collaboration and conflict. It underscores the profound impact of individual and collective actions on the shaping of regional and national identities. The struggle for independence from colonialism and self-determination in various African countries, as well as shifts in global economic paradigms, had a profound impact on shaping the new regional alliances. Understanding the roles that Eritreans played in Tigray during Emperor Haile Selassie's reign requires a nuanced appreciation of these multiple layers.

I was born into an Eritrean family who lived and worked in Tigray, like many others, during Emperor Haile Selassie's rule amid these geopolitical changes. My father's story is a testament to the power of community engagement and cross-cultural understanding, particularly in regions marked by complex socio-political landscapes. In Tigray, a region known for its rich history and cultural heritage within Ethiopia, the presence of intellectual Eritrean civic workers and business owners, especially in cities like Adigrat, a town north of the regional capital Mekelle, underscores the interconnectedness of people in northern Ethiopia. Despite historical tensions and scepticism from local communities towards Eritreans, my father's role exemplifies how individuals can bridge divides and foster a spirit of cooperation and mutual respect.

Most of the businesses in Tigray, including utility supplies, transport service provisions, and wholesale trade, were owned by Eritreans. My father, a community development civil servant with a huge interest in working to uplift the lives of many farmers and rural communities from natural and geopolitical adversities, had a significant role in both the local and Eritrean communities in Tigray. He used his position for good humanitarian causes.

The significance of my father's work in leveraging his influential position for humanitarian causes cannot be overstated. By collaborating with Tigrayan community leaders and scholars, he not only contributed to addressing immediate social, political, and environmental challenges, but also played a part in building a foundation for relative peace and understanding between Eritreans and Tigrayans, as well as the broader Ethiopian regions. This collaboration likely helped to mitigate scepticism and build trust among native Tigrayans, showcasing the potential for unity and collective problem-solving despite historical grievances.

Through his humanitarian work and good relations with both communities, my father demonstrated that diaspora members could serve as bridges between cultures, contributing valuable perspectives and resources toward the resolution of complex issues. His legacy serves as an inspiring example of how individual commitment to cross-cultural dialogue and community engagement can lead to meaningful change and foster a sense of belonging and cooperation among historically divided groups.

Some of the main challenges the Tigray region was facing at the time were desertification, food shortages, and political instability. My father played a major role in coordinating efforts to prevent the escalation of these man-made and natural adversities.

As a devoted leading civil servant in the agricultural and community development sectors, my father mobilized local, governmental, and international efforts to educate communities on the prevention of desertification. He also coordinated resources to build irrigation systems to grow food and terrace mountains to prevent landslides. He worked on large projects alongside aid agencies such as USAID to combat the rapid desertification affecting the Tigray region, which left thousands in need of food aid as their arable lands were washed away due to aridity and the fast-expanding sub-Sahara desertification affecting many Horn of Africa regions.

The political landscape of Ethiopia since the mid-twentieth century has been fraught with tension and unrest for decades, deeply influenced by both natural and social instability. This volatile environment has provided fertile ground for the emergence of various resistance groups, particularly in Tigray and Eritrea. These groups have been driven by a commitment to fight for what they perceive as justice for their constituents, who have suffered under policies and actions—or lack thereof—attributed to the central government. The discontent in these areas is rooted in a complex history of resistance against central authority, which has often been perceived as oppressive and neglectful, especially in the face of natural calamities that exacerbated the locals' hardships.

One of the core beliefs among the rebel factions in Tigray and Eritrea was the accusation that the Ethiopian monarchy, and later the derg, a military regime that overthrew the emperor, were deliberately exacerbating the suffering of the northern Ethiopian population. This population has a historical reputation for resisting central government rule, contributing to a cycle of mistrust and antagonism between the regions and Addis Ababa. The rebels argued that this neglect was not just administrative incompetence but a calculated move to weaken historically resistant populations. As a result, the regions witnessed an escalation in armed resistance, with skirmishes and light-armed conflicts becoming increasingly common between the Tigray and Eritrean rebel groups and central government forces.

The Ethiopian government's response to these groups was initially one of dismissal and denigration. Referring to them as bandits or small-time anti-social elements, the government was slow to recognise the political motivations and the depth of support for these rebel groups among the local populations. This failure to acknowledge the groups as legitimate opposition with genuine grievances allowed the conflict to fester and grow, contributing to a protracted struggle that has had significant humanitarian and political ramifications for Ethiopia. The journey towards recognising and addressing the root causes of this unrest has been long and fraught with challenges, underscoring the complex dynamics at play in the country's political landscape.

The Eritrean independence movement, which formally started in the deserts of Sahel in the 1960s, represents a pivotal moment in Eritrea's pursuit of autonomy. This political movement was characterised by a strong-armed resistance aiming to establish Eritrea as a sovereign nation independent from Ethiopian rule. The struggle extended beyond local borders and garnered substantial backing from foreign nations, who viewed Eritrea's cause as part of broader geopolitical strategies or as a moral duty to support self-determination. Islamic countries like Sudan and Egypt, which had a historical rivalry with Ethiopia over religious dominance and the use of the Nile River, became direct sponsors of the resistance. The global aspect of this partnership was crucial in providing moral, material, diplomatic, and military support to the Eritrean fighters.

This broader historical narrative, combined with the personal sacrifices made by Eritrean families—including my father's brothers joining the armed resistance—adds a deeply human dimension to the independence movement, as it does to many Eritrean and Tigrayan families. These personal stories of sacrifice highlight the widespread commitment to national identity and independence among Eritreans, making the struggle intensely personal and reflective of the broader societal commitment to the cause.

The resilience and determination embodied by the Eritrean independence movement are symbolic of a people united by a common purpose: the belief in their right to self-determination and independence. Despite the challenges of facing superior military forces and navigating limited resources, the enduring spirit of the Eritrean people shone through. The eventual attainment of independence in 1993 was not just a political victory but a triumph of the human spirit, marking the culmination of decades of struggle, immense personal sacrifices, and a testament to the power of solidarity among Eritreans.

My father's story within this context is a powerful reminder of how individual efforts can contribute significantly to healing divides, fostering understanding, and building stronger, more resilient communities even in the most challenging circumstances.

My father's story is not just inspiring; it's a beacon of hope in a world often divided by insurmountable barriers of ideology and ethnicity. His commitment to pacifism and humanitarian efforts, despite the swirling vortex of political and ethnic tensions, serves as a powerful testament to the strength of human compassion and the impact of individual actions on broader societal issues. His ability to remain ideologically neutral and approachable in such situations underscores a profound understanding of humanity's shared values and the importance of focusing on common goals for the greater good.

The respect and admiration my father garnered from all sides were clear indicators of his success in forging paths of communication and understanding among conflicting groups. This ability to serve as a messenger of peace, facilitating the negotiation for the safe passage of aid, the release of prisoners, and the stabilisation of conflicts, especially in famine-stricken areas, highlights a rare and invaluable skill set. It's a role that demands not just deep empathy and resilience but also a strategic and thoughtful approach to problem-solving under the most challenging circumstances.

Amidst the tumultuous echoes of political unrest and personal vendettas, there stood a man of unwavering conviction and integrity—my father. His commitment to peace and humanitarian causes was unwavering, even in the face of insurmountable challenges that threatened to tear both his family and his noble mission apart.

In the hostile regions filled with power struggles and deep-rooted rivalries, my father emerged as a beacon of hope and wisdom. His words carried the weight of experience; his actions spoke of compassion and understanding. He was a leader not by title but by virtue—a man who selflessly dedicated himself to the service of others.

As the political landscape grew more treacherous, personal animosities towards my father encompassed our family like a suffocating miasma. Yet, my father remained steadfast, his resolve unshaken by the storms that raged around him. He continued to advocate for peace and humanity, extending a hand of reconciliation even to those who sought to see him fall.

But in his unwavering commitment to his cause, my father unwittingly became a sacrificial lamb in a game of power and deceit orchestrated by those he once served. Betrayed and forsaken, he stood alone against a tide of injustice, his voice silenced by the very forces he had fought so tirelessly against.

And so, it was in the shadows of his sacrifice that the true extent of his legacy shone the brightest. His dedication to peace and development, and his unwavering spirit in the face of adversity, became a beacon for those who had witnessed his plight. Though he paid the ultimate price for his beliefs, my father's legacy lived on—a testament to the enduring power of a single individual to make a difference in a world fraught with turmoil and strife.

My father's legacy was undoubtedly one of unwavering dedication to alleviating human suffering and promoting peace. Through his actions, he demonstrated that it is possible to transcend political and ethnic divides, making significant strides toward stabilising communities in crisis. His life's work serves as a powerful reminder of the impact one individual can have on humanity, inspiring others to pursue a path of peace, understanding, and humanitarian service, regardless of the obstacles that may arise.

In the heart of a tumultuous era, my father was a man whose resilience and unwavering sense of justice sculpted a legacy that transcended the confines of time and circumstance. My father, to many, bore the weight of multiple man-made atrocities orchestrated by those consumed with their political pursuits, heedless of the carnage left in their wake.

Despite the shadows of suffering that lingered in his past, this man's resolve to shield his loved ones from the repercussions of his battles stood as an unyielding testament to his character. Through the trials of mental and physical captivity endured under the oppressive fists of various regimes, his spirit remained unbroken, his determination etched with the steel of unwavering conviction.

From the depths of adversity emerged a beacon of hope—a father whose sacrifices were not in vain. His children, inspired by his indomitable spirit, carried forth the torch of his legacy, illuminating a path of righteousness and compassion in a world darkened by greed and malice. His actions, though unquantifiable by wealth or numbers, reverberated through the annals of time, shaping a society built on the principles he so fervently defended.

The man, my father—a victim of tyrants and oppressors—stood as a symbol of resilience and grit. His legacy is a testament to the enduring power of the human spirit. In his name, his family and the society he helped shape continue to thrive, guided by the light of his unyielding determination and selfless love. And thus, his story transcended the boundaries of mortality, eternally etched in the fabric of a world he fought to protect.

A Humble Beginning

A Change is Gonna Come

My father, Yosief Solomon, came from a humble peasant family and had a truly inspiring life journey. He showed remarkable determination and resilience in changing his own life and that of others.

Born in 1946, he grew up in a rock-barren mountaintop village called Kakibda, in the Seray region of Eritrea, some 60 km south of the Eritrean capital, Asmara, where there were no schools or social and economic structure. My father decided to pursue education, demonstrating his thirst for knowledge and personal growth. Coming from a large family during a very difficult time for rural Eritreans—who faced continued neglect by the Ethiopian government and Italian colonialists—my father seemed to understand from his early life that he needed to break free from the terminally unsustainable lifestyle he and his family were living.

The tale of my father's childhood, marked by the arduous 18 km journey to and from primary school each day, paints a vivid picture of resilience and dedication. It wasn't just a physical trek across the landscape to the town of Duba-ruba; it was a symbolic journey of commitment, embodying a profound respect for the value of education. This daily odyssey, undertaken out of sheer necessity, speaks volumes about the lengths to which he and his brothers were willing to go for the sake of learning. Such experiences undoubtedly laid a strong foundation for the values he held dear.

This journey through childhood wasn't merely about overcoming physical distances; it was an early lesson in perseverance, time management, and the importance of education. Imagine the break of dawn, the cool morning air, and the determination in each step towards Duba-ruba, a town that symbolised not just a place of learning but a beacon of hope—a promise of a better future through education. These walks were not just physical trials but were instrumental in shaping his character, instilling in him a sense of purpose and an undying belief in the power of education.

Reflecting on my father's story offers a profound lesson for current and future generations about the value of education and the sacrifices many have made—and continue to make—to access it. It serves as a powerful reminder of the lengths to which individuals have gone, and continue to go, to seize opportunities for learning and growth. My father's journey from home to school in Duba-ruba is a testament to his unwavering commitment to education, a legacy that undoubtedly influences his perspective on life and continues to inspire those around him.

Embarking on this journey to retrace my father's steps from his birth village, Kakibda, to Duba-ruba was a profound way to connect with my heritage and understand the struggles endured by previous generations. The 18-kilometre trek, traversed each way, is not just a measure of distance but a testament to the resilience and determination of my father and his siblings. Walking the same route, feeling the sharp, uneven rocks underfoot, and navigating the hills and mountains offers a tangible link to the past, bringing to life the stories I grew up hearing.

The physical challenges of this journey, compounded by the lack of proper nourishment and suitable footwear, highlight the hardships my father and his siblings endured in pursuit of education. It's a stark reminder of the value placed on learning and the sacrifices made to attain it—to survive in the 21st century's modern living. In today's world, where education is more accessible, understanding the lengths to which previous generations in Eritrea and other parts of the world went to achieve this fundamental right is both humbling and inspiring.

Reflecting on this experience, it's clear that the endurance required for such a journey goes beyond physical capabilities—it speaks to a mental and emotional strength that is deeply ingrained in my family's legacy. This pilgrimage not only pays homage to my father's perseverance but also serves as a powerful personal reminder of the importance of resilience, gratitude, and the pursuit of knowledge, regardless of the obstacles in our path.

The legacy of a village chief, particularly one as illustrious as my grandfather, carries a profound narrative of resilience, vision, and transformative leadership. His dedication to valuing family, education, and the advancement of civilisation within his community paints a vivid picture of a person who was not only ahead of his time but also deeply committed to the welfare and progress of his people. The emphasis he placed on education, advocating for both vocational and academic pursuits, underscores a fundamental belief in the power of knowledge and skills as catalysts for change. This progressive mindset, rare in times and settings where short-term needs often overshadow long-term visions, set the foundation for a legacy of empowerment through education.

My grandfather's history as an advocate and activist, with his aggressive efforts to uplift his village, serves as a testament to the role individuals played in shaping the destinies of their children and the community they led. By representing his village in various settings and tirelessly working to better the lives of its inhabitants, he demonstrated the impact of strong, benevolent leadership. His advocacy went beyond mere words; it was a series of actionable steps that provided tangible opportunities for his children, setting a precedent for future generations. The ripple effect of his vision is evident in the professional paths pursued by his descendants, showcasing the enduring power of education to elevate individuals and, by extension, their communities.

The loss of a mother at an early age is an unimaginable challenge, yet it is a reality that many, including my father, have faced with resilience. The departure of my grandmother due to an endemic illness when my father was just a boy could have been a point of despair, but it became a catalyst for a future filled with dedication and commitment. This transformation from grief to determination was not just a testament to my father's character but also an inspiring narrative on the power of the human spirit and the ability to find strength in adversity—whether in man-made or natural adversities.

My father's journey from the depths of loss to the heights of personal and familial achievement underscores an important life lesson: it is not the tragedies that define us but how we respond to them. His dedication to improving the family's life in the wake of such a profound loss demonstrates an unwavering commitment to not just survive but thrive. This resolve likely served as a guiding light for my father's family, setting a foundation of resilience and hope for future generations.

Drawing inspiration from such a remarkable familial heritage, my father's family journey is a beacon of hope and a clear illustration of the transformational impact of education. The legacy left by my grandfather and carried forward by my father and his siblings highlights the profound influence that one person's vision can have on the trajectory of many lives. It serves as a powerful reminder of the value of investing in education and the potential it has to empower individuals, uplift communities, and bridge the gap between present challenges and a brighter, more civilised future.

Moreover, my father's story is a poignant reminder that behind every challenge lies an opportunity for growth and betterment. It teaches us that the human spirit is incredibly robust and capable of overcoming even the most daunting obstacles.

My father's life is a legacy of perseverance, showing that with dedication and commitment, it is possible to forge a path of success and fulfilment despite the odds. Through his actions, my father has imparted invaluable lessons on the importance of resilience, the power of a positive outlook, and the significance of family as a source of strength and inspiration.

My father and some of his brothers managed to complete their primary school education in Duba-ruba and progressed to study further in a high school in a nearby town as resident students, where some adopted vocational learning, and others continued to graduate and became professionals in various fields.

My grandfather is said to have had a special place in his heart for my father. This was further demonstrated by the special arrangements he made for him alone. He encouraged my father to pursue further education by arranging an adoption with a close family member who lived in Ethiopia's Shoa region, where educational opportunities were more available. There, my father attended high school and continued his studies in community development at Jima Agro College. He furthered his education by obtaining an advanced diploma in similar fields at the American University of Beirut, Lebanon, showing his commitment to learning and growth.

In the quiet moments of dusk, my father's eyes would light up as he spoke of Beirut, the city that once shone brightly like the Paris of the Middle East. It was a place of luxury and modern elegance during the 60s, where my father spent three fleeting years. Beyond the realm of academia, Beirut offered him the best times of his life—memories he cherished with deep ardour.

His tales painted vivid pictures of bustling streets lined with lush palm trees, vibrant markets filled with the aroma of exotic spices, and dazzling nightlife that never seemed to end. In his memories, Beirut was a symphony of cultures, a melting pot of traditions that intermingled effortlessly under the Mediterranean sun.

But as swiftly as the tides turned, Beirut's glory was overshadowed by the dark clouds of civil unrest in the 80s. The picturesque cityscape was marred by the scars of war, its vibrant spirit shattered by the violence that tore through its heart, a violence that continues to affect the city to this day. The memories of Beirut, once a sanctuary of joy and laughter, now mingled with sorrow and grief in my father's soul.

Despite the passage of time, the wounds of Beirut's destruction still lingered, a poignant reminder of a city that once stood as a beacon of hope in the region. As my father reminisced about his days in Beirut, his voice carried the weight of sorrowful nostalgia, a bittersweet melody of love and loss.

And so, in the soft glow of twilight, I listened to my father's stories of Beirut during my growing years—a city that lived in his heart as a testament to a time of beauty and resilience, forever etched in the tapestry of his memories.

It was the year 2005, and I had just arrived in Beirut for the annual Middle East IT exhibition. I was running a small logistics business that connected me with major computer exporters in Dubai, and I was offered free travel vouchers by one of the exhibitors. I was excited to learn about opportunities and trends in the shipping industry. But what made this trip even more special was that I was going to visit my father's alma mater, the city, and the American University of Beirut. My father had always spoken about his time at AUB with nostalgia, and I was eager to see the campus and relive some of his memories. I was determined to find Beirut's landmarks where my father had taken pictures and replicate his photographic adventures.

Following an evasive security check that included a manual search and an extensive documentation process, I walked into the heavily fortified university, filled with a mix of emotions. The architecture, the atmosphere—everything seemed so familiar yet so different. I was greeted by a friendly staff member who offered to take me on a tour of the vast campus. We walked past the iconic clock tower, the beautiful gardens, and the historic buildings. I couldn't help but feel a sense of pride knowing that my father had studied here.

The highlight of my visit was yet to come. My guide led me to the university's archives, where I was able to flip through my father's yearbook from his time at AUB. As I turned the pages, I came across a picture of my father, a young man with a bright smile and a determined look in his eyes. I couldn't believe how different he looked from the father I knew. I felt a lump form in my throat as I realised that this was a side of him that I had never seen before. The yearbook also showed records of my father's prized achievements in amateur photography and sport. It had the photograph of a flying rooster, a masterpiece my father shot with his Leica camera.

The photograph, taken in one of the squalid neighbourhoods of 60s Beirut, was shot by my father under mysterious circumstances—why the rooster was flying perpendicularly so high in what looked like a rather unprovoked backdrop. The hazed image of two young girls in the background painted a much deeper story into the life and culture of Lebanese people.

Over the years, the picture has attracted various comments and depictions from professionals and others, but to our family, it was a masterpiece—a source of pride that made an important part of the collection of our family's visual stories.

One fateful day, as we arrived home from school, we were greeted by an unusual sight—the framed photograph of the rooster was missing from its designated place on the wall. Panic ensued as one of my brothers, Simon, with tears streaming down his face, declared that we had lost our beloved rooster.

"Lost our rooster?" exclaimed our mother, who was busy in the kitchen preparing a delicious meal. "But we don't have a rooster, dear. There are chickens in the backyard, but they belong to our neighbours."

We were perplexed by our mother's response, unable to understand why she didn't share our distress. We tried to explain that it wasn't a live rooster, but the framed picture that had disappeared. However, in our haste and emotional state, our words came out in a jumble, only adding to the confusion.

As the commotion continued, Simon, the second eldest and known for his keen eye, suddenly spotted the missing rooster. It was lying on the floor, its frame slightly cracked but otherwise unharmed. Relief washed over us as we realised our precious rooster had not been lost but simply made an accidental landing on the floor.

With a chuckle, our mother bent down to pick up the fallen rooster. "Ah, I see now," she said with a smile. "You were talking about this handsome fellow all along. I must admit, I was quite puzzled by all the fuss over a rooster that we didn't even own."

We laughed at the mix-up, our worries now turned into amusement. My mother carefully placed the rooster back on the wall, making sure it was securely fastened this time. The incident became a cherished memory—a tale we would recount with fondness for years to come. And amidst our laughter and shared memories, our family found solace in knowing that sometimes, the most cherished things in life are the ones that make us laugh the hardest.

I remembered well the description and date on the back of the photograph, which read, "Yarmout Road, Beirut, July 1964." With determination, I found the street where the photograph was taken. Little had changed in the street's layout, but it was still recognisable.

But the most surprising discovery was yet to come. As I continued to flip through the yearbook, I came across pictures of my father participating in boxing matches. I couldn't believe my eyes—my father, a boxer. He had never mentioned this to us, and I had never seen any evidence of it. I felt a mix of emotions—excitement, curiosity, and a hint of embarrassment. How could my father keep this a secret from us for so long?

I spent the rest of the day exploring the campus, taking in the sights and sounds of the university. I couldn't help but wonder what other secrets my father might be hiding. As I left the campus, I felt a sense of gratitude towards my father for sharing this part of his life with me. I realised that there was so much more to him than I had ever known, and I was excited to learn more about his past. The visit to AUB had been a life-changing experience, one that had opened my eyes to the complexity and richness of my father's life.

His decision to return home and serve the environmentally challenged communities of Ethiopia, particularly Tigray, where he had worked for some time after graduating from Jima University and before going to Beirut, speaks volumes about his character and dedication to the community.

His first graduate job was as coordinator of a USAID-funded forestation project around the Adigrat area of the Tigray region, later moving to the capital, Mekelle, as regional director of the Agricultural Department under the National Office of Agriculture. This was a remarkable achievement for his hard work. My father made significant contributions to combating environmental issues and promoting sustainable practices.

The northern part of Ethiopia, which included Wollo, Tigray, and parts of Gondar, was facing rapid desertification, characterised by famine, displacements, and natural and political changes, which ultimately led to political unrest and rebellion by various groups against the emperor's rule. My father continued to work in different civil capacities in the Tigray region until he was transferred to other locations in 1983. He holds a special place in the hearts of many Tigrayans who worked with him and recognised his services and achievements.

My Mother's Background

The Most Beautiful Girl in the World

My mother's background is quite different from my father's but equally fascinating. Born into a wealthy and privileged family in the affluent district of Geza Banda in Asmara, Eritrea, in 1949, she grew up surrounded by aristocracy and a luxurious upbringing. Her parents, who owned several properties and land, held a high position in the societal hierarchy.

My mother, Hewan, is the eldest of ten siblings. She carried the weight of responsibility with poise and unwavering dedication. From a young age, her tender heart and unwavering faith shone brightly, earning her the adoration of her parents and the respect of the entire community.

My mother's selflessness knew no bounds; she stood by her mother's side, a pillar of strength, aiding in the upbringing of her younger siblings. Her days were filled with nurturing love, guiding her brothers and sisters with unwavering care and compassion. Such was her devotion that even her father, a man of stature and influence, sought her counsel above all others in matters of great importance, entrusting her wisdom and intuition with reverence.

My mother, tall and light-skinned, beautiful inside and out, is a person whose kindness and grace enveloped the family and beyond, leaving an indelible mark on all who crossed her path. She was not just a daughter or a sister; she was a beacon of light in the darkness, illuminating the lives of those she so lovingly touched.

My mother's father, Stefanos, fondly known as 'Goita Papa' or 'Goitapa'—meaning 'King & Father'—was a commanding figure. Born in the early 1930s in Adi Teklay, Hamassien region, on the outskirts of Asmara, to a peasant family, his powerful and defiant characteristics as a young man, followed by his strong presence and authoritative speech, made him a well-respected figure who could get things done efficiently. Considering my father's humble origins, this shows how diverse backgrounds can come together to shape a family's history.

Goitapa was a truly larger-than-life figure, both in stature and in personality. Standing at nearly 2 metres tall with a straight, upright posture, his physical presence alone was enough to command attention. His influence extended beyond his physical attributes, as he was a well-connected businessman, advocate, and community leader. His demeanour, with a stern face—often not answering back to greetings and rarely smiling—further added to his unique persona. These traits, combined with his confidence and belief that he could rule the world, made him a formidable figure in his community.

Goitapa's lifestyle and choices reflected a deep respect for his roots and traditions. Despite his white skin appearance, he didn't try to imitate white culture, which was quite common at the time, a colonial heritage that everyone adopted. Instead, he embraced his own culture and traditions in many aspects of his life.

As colonialists influenced Eritreans' lifestyles in the bustling cities, where modernity was rapidly creeping in, Goitapa stood out like a relic of the past. While everyone around him was embracing the colonial lifestyle—with tailored suits and foreign ways—he remained steadfast in his traditional practices.

Goitapa remained rooted in his heritage, honouring the wisdom of his ancestors and the beauty of his culture. His food preferences were traditional, favouring a simple charcoal-baked wholemeal barley bread and spicy vegetarian stew over European food. His clothing choices were also traditional, opting not to wear European clothes. Even when it came to healthcare, he preferred using herbs and traditional medicines over European-manufactured ones when he fell ill.

This adherence to tradition and cultural practices, even in the face of societal pressures, speaks volumes about Goitapa's character and his commitment to his heritage.

Goitapa's unique style and daily rituals further highlighted his distinct personality. His traditional white attire, known as 'eje tebab' or 'kdan habesha', and preference for locally handmade leather sandals, along with the fact that he never wore socks, show his commitment to local products and perhaps a certain level of comfort with his own culture and environment.

He always carried a leather-clad stick or whip with him wherever he went. This stick, which he used to wand on people to emphasise emphasise his points, became a symbol of his power. His use of the stick, not just as a symbol of power but also as a tool to assert his authority, further emphasised his dominant personality. It's interesting to reflect on how his reputation preceded him, making people in Asmara wary of crossing his path or asking him to wait in a queue.

As I found myself becoming Goitapa's closest aide later, I witnessed his grizzled behaviour and unyielding principles. One day, we were in the midst of a heated court dispute over the fair use of a flour mill he had installed in his village—a crucial source of livelihood—between his community and a neighbouring village. The proceedings were led by a young high court judge, who presided over the case with stern determination. As the judge began to announce his decision, Goitapa's face darkened, his weathered hand gripping the leather stick tightly. In an unprecedented display of fury, he rose from his seat, his eyes ablaze with defiance. Without a moment's hesitation, he confronted the judge and the jury members, his voice booming through the courtroom, hitting the court's desks hard with his stick.

As though overseeing the courtroom, in what resembled Al Pacino's motivational speech from the film *Scent of a Woman*, Goitapa took control of the room. "I will not stand for this injustice!" he thundered, the force of his words echoing off the walls as he delivered his evidence in a loud and commanding speech. With a resolute stride, he brandished his stick—a silent but powerful threat hanging in the air—as he presented his argument in an eloquent and powerful manner.

The atmosphere tensed; the judge was visibly taken aback by the sudden display of defiance. In that charged moment, it became clear that Goitapa's unwavering resolve would not be swayed. With a steely gaze, he dared the panel members not to uphold their decision, knowing that he would stop at nothing to fight for what he believed was right. Goitapa also called the young judge immature and unfit for the position he held.

As the tension reached its peak, the judicial panel members, struck by the sheer force of Goitapa's conviction, relented. The judge's gavel fell, and the decision was overturned in his favour and that of his village. Amid the palpable relief that swept through the courtroom, I glimpsed a sense of quiet triumph in Goitapa's eyes—a testament to his unyielding spirit in the face of adversity.

As we left the courtroom that day, I knew that I had borne witness to a force of nature, a man whose legacy would endure long after the echoes of his righteous fury had faded. This was a clear example of his strong will and commitment to his community at a time when Eritreans were under the strict, iron-fist rule of the communist government.

Goitapa's daily routine of walking to all his destinations within Asmara, and sometimes making a 21 km trek to his village, Adi Teklai, were evident sources of his physical strength and healthy lifestyle. He shaved his head and face daily due to his belief that hair was a harmful growth that harboured lice. This was quite unique and speaks to his strong convictions. His approach to hair was the same for his boys. Everyone sported monk-style short hair under his strict orders. He called hair and nails 'toxic growths' that need not stay in the body. These details paint a vivid picture of Goitapa as a man of strong presence, deep cultural roots, and unique beliefs.

Goitapa's assertive personality and commanding presence certainly made him a formidable figure. His dislike for queues and direct approach to addressing issues, even in formal settings like a court, show his determination and fearlessness.

Goitapa painted a vivid picture of a man deeply committed to his community and unafraid to challenge authority. His life seemed to be a testament to the power of conviction and the impact one person can have on their surroundings.

Goitapa's influence and impact on his community were truly remarkable as a self-made king who commanded respect and admiration from everyone, especially the young, to whom he gave life opportunities, small gifts, and blessings. His symbolic presence and the love he received from people of all ages highlighted his charismatic leadership. His role as an informal community moderator showcased his commitment to helping others. He used his influence to assist with personal and familial problems, secure school places for children, provide housing for families, and address various socio-economic challenges under the openly oppressive and bureaucratic administrations governed by the monarch and, later, the military regime. His efforts to stop unlawful evictions, provide financial assistance, and mediate marriage and other social affairs further demonstrate his skills and dedication to his community.

As an informal arbitrator, Goitapa's rulings were widely accepted without challenge, reflecting the trust and respect people had for him. His decisions were seen as balanced and unbiased, with a focus on upholding family values that benefited children and mothers. This is a testament to his fair and compassionate leadership.

Goitapa's influence extended even to formal legal proceedings. If someone in the community disobeyed his decision and sought formal court intervention, Goitapa would ensure that his decision was upheld because the judges would approach him for advice. This shows his authority and the respect he commanded in both his community and public offices.

Goitapa's approach to community justice not only expedited the resolution of disputes but also helped maintain harmony within the community. Goitapa's story is a powerful example of leadership and the impact one person can have on their family and the wider community. His life and impact on his community are a powerful reminder of the difference one person can make in the absence of an effective and affordable legal system.

Goitapa's status as a self-made king, judge, and wealthy aristocrat was indeed intriguing. His natural strength and belief, coupled with the privileged position he held as a *banda* (moderator working for the emperor and colonial Italians), played a significant role in shaping his identity. As a shadow member of the *mahber shimagle* (Eritrean National Assembly), he worked to resolve the Eritrean independence question with the Ethiopian central government. He also served as an operative for Italian businesses. All these roles—being a public servant and businessman—required a skill set of good knowledge and personality. Having no formal educational background is a reminder of how some individuals can be born leaders and achieve so much through determination and experience.

It is believed that, for their services, *bandas* were rewarded with land and money from the emperor, while the Italian colonialists also paid them lavishly for their role in helping integrate their colonial ideology with the locals. *Bandas* were also committed to maintaining the delicate relationship between the occupying colonialists and locals, ensuring resources were not over-exploited, basic human rights were upheld, and services and infrastructures were delivered.

The National Assembly, a group of elite Eritreans selected and approved by the emperor, comprised influential individuals who played a pivotal role in maintaining a balance between the quest for independence by younger Eritrean intellectuals, the unwelcome Italian colonialism, and the various socio-political unrest brewing in Eritrea's streets. For their useful role, members of the National Assembly gained various privileges, including access to land and property developments and direct contact with representatives of the emperor, enabling them to influence policies and administrative decisions. The Italians also offered the *bandas* business opportunities, membership in Italian cultural and social institutions, clubs,

European education for their children, and healthcare in local and overseas facilities.

Among Goitapa's high-profile encounters in Eritrea's power corridors while serving as an adviser in the National Assembly, his meeting with Queen Elizabeth of Great Britain and the Commonwealth during her visit to Asmara in 1965 stands as a poignant symbol of cultural recognition and respect, resonating deeply within the annals of Eritrean history.

As a distinguished figure among the Eritrean elite, Goitapa's presence at the dinner hosted in the Queen's honour at the royal palace was not just a formality but a significant moment that bridged two vastly different cultures. The striking image of Goitapa, adorned in traditional Eritrean attire amidst a sea of Western formal wear, caught the Queen's attention, underscoring the rich cultural tapestry that Eritrea boasts.

Queen Elizabeth's request to meet Goitapa, whom she described as an "interestingly unique gentleman" with whom she wanted to be photographed, was more than a mere diplomatic gesture; it was an acknowledgment of the importance of preserving and respecting cultural identity. Through the medium of a translator, the young Queen's interaction with Goitapa transcended the barriers of language and culture, highlighting her appreciation for the diverse heritage represented by Goitapa's presence. The exchange was emblematic, showcasing the Queen's openness and respect towards Eritrean traditions and the broader significance of cultural diversity on the world stage.

The unplanned and controversial decision by the Queen to meet only Goitapa outside the strictly choreographed state protocols, leaving other high-ranking dignitaries, including the emperor's son, raised a few jealous eyebrows, remaining one of the main highlights of the Queen's historic visit.

Goitapa's recounting of his meeting with the Queen, aided by a translator, was filled with reverence and awe. It was evident that the conversation was not merely about pleasantries but touched upon deeper, more meaningful subjects that left a lasting imprint on him. The way he described the Queen's demeanour showcased a leader who was not only regal but profoundly wise and compassionate. This encounter was a revelation for Goitapa, opening his eyes to the values and legacy of the British monarchy.

The gift of a chronograph pocket watch from the Queen to Goitapa was laden with symbolism, representing the timeless nature of cultural exchange and the enduring links forged between individuals from disparate backgrounds. This moment between Goitapa and Queen Elizabeth is symbolic of the potential for mutual respect and understanding between different cultures, serving as a reminder of the importance of embracing diversity. Such encounters underscore the rich tapestry of human history and the unifying power of recognizing and honouring our cultural differences.

Goitapa treasured the pocket watch, wearing it daily and showing it off at every opportunity, telling its story and how he had impressed the Queen to win the gift.

The story of Goitapa and his mechanical watch is as heartwarming as it is amusing, serving as a delightful anecdote about the connections we form with the objects in our lives. Goitapa, with a blend of innocence and wonder, believed his watch to be more than just a timekeeping device; to him, it was a conscious companion intricately linked to his very soul. This belief was reinforced by the watch's peculiar behaviour of stopping whenever Goitapa fell ill and couldn't wear it. Little did he realise that the watch's need for movement to remain functional was the real reason behind this phenomenon.

Mechanical watches, unlike their digital or quartz counterparts, operate through a complex system of gears and springs, all powered by the motion of the wearer. This intricate mechanism, known as 'the movement', requires regular motion to wind the mainspring, which in turn keeps the watch ticking accurately. When Goitapa was bedridden, and the watch was left untouched in his pocket, the lack of movement caused the watch to stop, a common characteristic that he misinterpreted as a sign of empathetic connection.

In a modern twist on the age-old connection between health and technology, Goitapa lived as a man who placed his trust in an unusual health monitor: his watch. He believed that if his watch stopped ticking, it was a sign that he too was not in optimal health—a belief that led him to view his wellness through the lens of his watch's activity.

As he lay resting a few weeks after receiving the precious gift from the Queen, his watch ceased its usual rhythmic ticking. Interpreting this as a reflection of his vitality, he concluded he must be unwell. It was a charming yet misguided correlation that overlooked the simpler explanation: watches, like the one he wore, need movement to operate, and without it, they naturally come to a halt. This oversight led him to a false assumption about his health, tethered to the stillness of his timepiece.

From that moment on, Goitapa was convinced that the watch held a mystical connection to his well-being. He would proudly display it, telling anyone who would listen of its miraculous powers. Everyone around him, captivated by his conviction and charisma, indulged him in his belief, never daring to correct or educate him. Goitapa remained steadfast in his conviction that it was no ordinary watch, his trust unwavering as it ticked on—a symbol of hope and connection to his well-being. When he sometimes felt unsure about his health, he would monitor his pocket watch's functionality to confirm his own health status.

Often, the misconception was cleared up by unlikely saviours: when Goitapa felt unnecessarily ill for an extended time, his children, who were aware of the simple solution, wound the watch and shook it discreetly—not as a diagnostic tool, but as a mechanical necessity. By winding the watch and giving it a gentle shake, they not only brought the watch back to life but also dispelled their father's unfounded health concerns.

This charming story not only highlights Goitapa's endearing belief in the animate nature of his beloved timepiece but also sheds light on the magic of mechanical watches. Their reliance on human movement fosters a unique bond between the watch and its wearer, a bond that, in Goitapa's case, transcended the mechanical and ventured into the realm of the spiritual. While the true reason behind the watch's behaviour might be rooted in physics, adding a layer of enchantment to the relationship we share with the objects in our lives reminds us of the joy and wonder they can bring.

Motivated by a life-changing experience of a twenty-minute meeting with Queen Elizabeth, Goitapa expressed a strong desire for me and his other children to pursue our education in England, specifically to become maritime lawyers. He saw this as an opportunity, especially for me, to imbibe the values, rigour, and excellence that he believed the British education system represented. The encounter with the Queen wasn't just a personal milestone for Goitapa; it became a catalyst for envisioning a future that was broader, richer, and more ambitious for those he cared about. His insistence on studying in England was not just about the prestige of the British legal system but a testament to the profound impact that one meeting had on his worldview and aspirations.

Goitapa's story is a testament to his ability to navigate complex personal, social, and political landscapes while maintaining a strong family presence. He managed to leverage his connections and position to accrue wealth and social status for himself and his family. His connections with government officials, rulers, and police commanders in both the old and new governments further underscored his influence and reach.

His death in 1987 from complications related to gangrene following a small fracture on his toe and his reluctance to take pharmaceutical antibiotic treatment marked the end of an era. His legacy, however, lives on in the stories and memories shared by those who knew him.

It's also interesting that Goitapa preferred to stay away from the camera and interviews despite his dictator-like character. This adds another layer to his intriguing personality. While it might make it challenging to have visual memories of him, the vivid stories and memories paint a rich picture of his life and character. These oral histories are a valuable way of preserving and sharing his legacy.

My grandmother, a tall woman who stood upright at all times in posture and resilience, was an incredibly strong and resilient matriarch. Raising a dozen children single-handedly, enduring the strong personality of Goitapa, and maintaining a household is no small feat. Her dedication to her family and her ability to keep them healthy and well-fed speaks volumes about her strength and determination.

When Goitapa, the patriarch of the family and respected figure in town, passed away unexpectedly, all eyes turned to his widow, Zenu. It was now her responsibility to manage the myriad of affairs that once fell under Goitapa's domain.

From the intricate management of familial relationships to overseeing the recovery of the extensive family estate confiscated by the government, my grandmother took on each task with a sense of purpose and determination that commanded respect from all who knew her. Her ability to navigate complex issues with grace and precision was a testament to her sharp decision-making skills and deep knowledge of the law.

As she dove headfirst into the role of Goitapa, my grandmother quickly became the linchpin that held the family together. Her presence at community gatherings and meetings with government officials solidified her reputation as a force to be reckoned with. The community marvelled at her poise and eloquence, realising that my grandmother was not just carrying out her duties but excelling in them beyond measure.

Through all the challenges and obstacles she faced, my grandmother remained steadfast in her commitment to upholding the strict family values that had been instilled in her by Goitapa. Her ability to manage such a wide array of responsibilities flawlessly was a true reflection of her strength of character and unwavering dedication to preserving the legacy of her late husband.

In the end, my grandmother Zenu's remarkable journey as the new Goitapa was not just a tale of succession but a testament to the power of women's resilience and leadership in the face of adversity. She had proven herself to be a beacon of strength and inspiration for the entire community, forging a path forward with grace and fortitude that would be remembered for generations to come.

Her skills as a great cook and housekeeper, along with her strong sense of family unity, earned her respect in her community and neighbourhood. Her religious devotion and service to the church, especially her efforts to help the poor and feed the hungry, show her compassionate nature and commitment to helping others until she died in 2014 due to age-related health complications. Her life was a testament to the power of resilience, hard work, and compassion.

Born into a lineage deeply ingrained with values of education and discipline, my mother's siblings rose to the pinnacle of success, each excelling in their chosen professions. From an early age, the siblings were nurtured in an environment that prioritised learning and growth. Their parents instilled a passion for knowledge that burned bright within each child. As they grew, it became evident that they were destined for greatness.

Some of my mother's siblings possessed a natural talent for structural engineering. Their creations revolutionised the telecom and oil rigs in Norway, where they now live with their families, making them household names in the engineering world. Others pursued careers in veterinary medicine, specialising in advanced treatments that saved countless lives. Their success was a testament to the values instilled in them by their parents – hard work, dedication, and a thirst for excellence. Together, they formed a formidable force, each contributing their expertise to shape the future of society.

As I looked upon their achievements, I understood the power of a strong upbringing and unwavering values. It was a legacy that would ripple through the ages, inspiring generations to come to reach for the stars and achieve greatness.

Union of Souls

Can't Help Falling In Love

In the backdrop of Asmara, a small modern city built by Italians nestled among lush, paved streets, lies the heart-warming tale of my parents' union—a story that intertwines tradition, culture, love, and an unprecedented bond.

It all began on a breezy summer evening when the sun was setting, casting a golden hue over the city square. The air was filled with the aroma of spices and laughter, signalling the start of the Orthodox New Year festivities.

My parents' story is a testament to the enduring power of tradition, the richness of culture, and the depth of true love—a union that transcends time and space, an unbreakable bond forged in the flames of destiny. To this day, their love continues to bloom, a beacon of hope and inspiration for generations to come.

My mother, the eldest among 10 siblings, had a privileged upbringing in a large house in Geza Banda, Asmara, thanks to her father's wealth and status. The fact that she and her siblings received an education in prestigious Italian schools around Asmara laid a strong foundation for their future endeavours. Although she had to leave school at 18 to marry my father, her ability to speak, read, and write Italian showcases the lasting influence of her education. Despite the interruptions in her academic journey, she was always curious and kept herself up to date with world affairs, technology, and science. Her early education undoubtedly left a significant impact on her life and skills.

My parents were selected by their respective communities to be part of a reconciliation through marriage to end a rivalry—or, rather, a long-term dispute—between their ancestral villages. Although it is unclear to me what caused the bitter rivalry between the two villages, which are some 100km apart, legend has it that my two grandfathers decided to end the generations-old bloodshed by uniting the communities through skilful traditional diplomacy. It is believed that the two chiefs of their respective communities decided that the only way to ensure lasting peace and reconciliation was through the age-old tradition of a matrimonial union between young members of their communities. It was necessary to ensure that the blood wasted in the conflict was replaced by a shared new generation. The continuity of a mixed future generation would eliminate the feelings of vengeance on each side and promote a brotherhood founded in blood.

My parents were chosen, but they were not consulted beforehand, as marriages were arranged in those times. Despite the circumstances surrounding my parents' union, their story reflects a fusion of history, tradition, and the complexities of relationships that transcend social and economic boundaries. This blend of backgrounds and circumstances likely shaped their journey together in unique and unexpected ways.

The exchange of contributions from the wise men at the top of their communities was carefully considered to ensure the continuity of their status and hierarchy in future generations to come.

In 1966, my parents were treated to a grand wedding attended by dignitaries, both local and colonial, highlighting the significance of this union. The lavish gifts and support showered upon my parents, from land to furniture and money, symbolised a strong start for their family.

Growing up as young children, we always asked my father to repeat the tale of seeking out our mother at her Italian school before they were formally introduced. He would patiently follow from afar, watching her on her way home, and their eventual introduction and marriage painted a picture of a love story that transcended initial circumstances.

A few weeks after my parents were introduced to each other, my father's best friend also took a sudden interest in one of my mother's friends, Asmait. With subtle charm and affection, the two men, pushing their bikes, began to shadow the two girls, watching from a distance as they playfully walked home from school.

My father was the architect in this twisted game of love. Together, they would lurk in the shadows, their eyes following the unsuspecting girls like predators on the hunt. After slow progress that took weeks, one day, my father approached my mother with a gentle proposition, suggesting a double date—a seemingly innocent outing that would bring the two couples together under the guise of friendship.

Free to start their romantic lives, they embarked on their first date—a visit to the iconic Odeon Cinema, along with the other couple, to watch the classic Bollywood film *Mother India*. Behind closed doors and hidden glances, a clandestine affair unfolded, weaving together the lives of two families in a tangled web of secrets and desires.

Mother India unfolded before their eyes, weaving a tapestry of emotions that resonated deeply with their budding romance. The epic film, first for her, captured my mother's heart with its poignant storyline and haunting melodies, evoking a sense of nostalgia for a bygone era. It also touched on my father's past with its desperate stories of poverty, hardship, family separation away from home, and reunion.

However, as the intricate plot of *Mother India* unfolded on the silver screen, the afternoon passed seemingly fast. My mother and her friend, exhausted from a long day of school and a fast-approaching family curfew, found themselves struggling to stay awake and asked to go home. Despite their best efforts to remain, the relentless pull of the curfew proved too strong to resist.

Realising her predicament, my father looked at her tenderly, understanding her fatigue. Without hesitation, he gently took her hand and led her out of the cinema, leaving behind the captivating long tale of *Mother India* unfinished. In a funny twist to the events surrounding the double date, my father's friend reluctantly stayed behind, insisting on getting his money's worth of viewing, risking his love affair through his misguided priorities that placed money above his romantic commitments. His companion stayed to finish the film. However, despite the rocky start, their relationship blossomed, and they were later married.

Walking under the settling sun, my parents shared a quiet moment of understanding and connection. The unspoken bond between them grew stronger as they navigated the bustling streets of Asmara, lost in their world of shared experiences and newfound emotions.

The echoes of *Mother India* lingered in my mother's heart for her lifetime after that fateful afternoon. She would often retell the tale of their first date with a sparkle in her eye, reminiscing about the moments that had shaped their love story.

As my siblings and I drifted off to sleep each night, my mother's melodic voice would fill the room, recounting her version of *Mother India* with such passion and emotion that we felt transported to a time long gone. Each night, we would select a chapter from the long *Mother India* story we wanted to hear, and my mother would customise it to make it age-appropriate, narrating her own version. The strains of the film's iconic theme song, 'Dunya Mein Hum', became a lullaby that lulled us into dreams filled with visions of romance and sacrifice.

Despite never getting the chance to finish watching *Mother India* together, the film remained a cherished memory for my parents, etched forever in the fabric of their love story. As I grew older, I came to realise that some stories are not meant to be completed but rather cherished for the moments they create and the memories they inspire.

The blend of tradition, romance, and commitment in their journey formed a unique and heartfelt bond that has withstood the test of time. My mother always shyly contested my father's skewed version of the first few days of their love, particularly how my mother's eyes would anxiously search for him while he hid behind corners during his stalking adventures. There were also unconfirmed tales in my father's versions about my mother leaning on his shoulder during their first date when they watched *Mother India*. My mother shyly denied all the stories every time my father deliberately mentioned them in various dramatic versions, laughing at her reactions. My father would describe his stylish looks, likening himself to Elvis Presley, and his love for suede shoes and rock 'n' roll music when he told us how he got my mother to like him.

These became some of the funniest stories we had throughout our childhood. It is charming how the tale of my father seeking out my mother at her Italian school and their eventual courtship has become a cherished part of our family folklore. The playful disagreement between my parents about the romantic details adds a delightful touch to our family story.

These bedtime stories, filled with humour and differing perspectives, brought laughter and warmth to our childhood. It is wonderful to have such anecdotes that blend tradition, humour, and a touch of romance, creating lasting memories for me and my family to treasure.

The intertwining tales of my parents' lives, from the arranged marriage aimed at fostering peace between rival communities to the romantic gestures that followed, add a rich and captivating layer to their relationship. The symbolic gesture of matching children from both communities to solidify the newfound peace demonstrated a unique blend of tradition and effective reconciliation.

My mother, a beautiful woman and a young bride, inherited the distinct features of her father. She was significantly taller than the average woman, with her natural beauty wrapped in soft brown skin that had all the hallmarks of a well-nourished and happy upbringing. My father, more light-skinned with glossy black hair that shone like a raven's feather, was the counterpart to her in this beautiful union. The five sons, each a unique masterpiece, were crafted from the blend of our parents' lineage and their ancestors' stories.

The long journey of my parents' married lives started in Tigray, where my father was already working before their marriage. They expanded their family in testament to their commitment and love for each other, welcoming their first son,

Kaleb, a year after their marriage, and then adding four more boys—Simon, Theo, Biruk, and Alazar—each year thereafter. This painted a picture of a bustling and growing household.

The rapid expansion of my family reflected the joy and blessings that each child brought into our parents' lives. It's a beautiful portrayal of familial love, growth, and togetherness that created a vibrant and lively home environment for all of us.

Together, the five brothers made up a kaleidoscope of colours and features—a living testament to the beauty of diversity and the strength of family ties that bound us together, transcending differences and uniting us in a tapestry of love and kinship. Despite our differences in appearance and behaviour, our bond was unbreakable, a testament to the unbreakable thread of brotherhood that bound us together.

Tender Trials

Superstition: When You Believe In Things You Don't Understand

In the heart of Tigray, nestled amidst the rugged terrain and rolling hills, lay the town of Selekleka. It was here, in this remote town, that my parents embarked on a new chapter of their lives following their marriage. My father, a recent graduate already deeply involved in environmental projects in the area, welcomed my mother with open arms as they arrived in the small town.

As a newly married Eritrean couple starting life in Tigray, the people welcomed my parents with open arms, their kindness and generosity leaving a lasting impression on my parents' hearts. As the seasons passed, my parents immersed themselves in the rich culture and traditions of Tigray, learning the intricate art of weaving from local artisans and savouring the flavours of traditional dishes passed down through generations. Their love story unfolded against the backdrop of Tigray's beauty, strengthened by the bonds of friendship and the unwavering support of the community.

When they look back on those years spent in Tigray, my parents do so with deep admiration and love for the place that shaped their lives in ways they never imagined. The memories of the kindness and friendship they received from the people of Tigray remain etched in their hearts, a testament to the enduring power of love and community.

My parents were greeted by a warm and welcoming community. Friends and town residents alike came together to celebrate their union, showering them with congratulations and well-wishes for their new life together. The air was filled with excitement and a sense of belonging as the townspeople brought gifts and blessings to the newlyweds, embracing them as one of their own.

Selekleka, a town known for its simplicity and humble way of life, stood in stark contrast to the bustling city where my mother had grown up. Coming from an affluent background, the transition to a place with no facilities and limited amenities was a stark change for my mother. However, the beauty of Selekleka lay not in its material offerings, but in the genuine warmth and hospitality of its residents.

Despite the stark differences in upbringing and surroundings, my father had a plan in place to ease my mother's adjustment to life in Selekleka. The proximity of Asmara, a city less than 200 km away, provided a sense of comfort and closeness, as my mother knew she could easily visit whenever she felt the need to reconnect with her family and her city. Regular trips to Asmara in my father's open-top Toyota SUV became a source of solace for my mother, allowing her to navigate the transition and slowly embrace the charm of Selekleka.

Amid this new beginning, my mother found solace in the presence of other Eritrean working families and people from different parts of Ethiopia who had made Selekleka their home. The community was a diverse tapestry of individuals, including teachers, doctors, and nurses, all of whom extended a warm welcome to my mother, embracing her into their close-knit circle.

Days turned into weeks and weeks into months as my parents settled into the rhythm of married life in Selekleka. The simplicity of the town began to weave its magic on my mother, gradually easing her longing for her previous life. The rolling hills that surrounded Selekleka whispered tales of resilience and beauty, painting a serene backdrop for the new life that was unfolding.

Amidst the rustic charm of Selekleka, my parents discovered a sense of peace and tranquillity that transcended material comforts. It was in the simplicity of everyday life, the genuine connections forged with the townspeople, and the shared moments of laughter and joy that my parents found true happiness.

My parents' love story continued to unfold through the highs and lows, the challenges and triumphs. They stood united, a testament to the enduring power of love and the resilience of the human spirit.

As the days turned into weeks and the weeks into months, my parents embraced each new dawn with a sense of purpose and gratitude. They revelled in the small blessings that surrounded them. Despite the material challenges that life presented, they faced each obstacle with unwavering optimism and a deep-seated faith in the goodness of the world.

Soon after my mother became pregnant with the family's first child, a shadow fell upon our family. Whispers of an unseen force known as the evil eye began to circulate among the townspeople. The residents had been disturbed by the arrival of a nomad tribe called the 'kalicka', known for their tales of evil powers, particularly targeting the most beautiful women. Rumours of beautiful women hiding and wealthy men paying money and possessions to stop being caught by the evil eye spread like wildfire, creating an atmosphere of fear and superstition.

My father, a pragmatic man with a sceptical view of anything beyond the tangible world, brushed off the rumours of the evil eye as mere superstition. He found it hard to believe in the existence of an unseen force capable of causing harm based on envy or admiration, dismissing them as fanciful tales meant to amuse or frighten.

One incident, however, shook my father's disbelief to its core. A local elderly woman, known for her uncanny ability to sense hidden truths and secrets, approached my parents in their home. With a knowing look in her eyes, she offered them cryptic blessings, hinting at unseen dangers and urging them to stay vigilant against the evil eye's gaze. She advised them not to make eye contact with any stranger, as evil might enter her soul through the rays of vision.

Despite my father's initial scepticism, the encounter left a lingering sense of unease in his heart. He couldn't shake the feeling that perhaps there was more to the town's superstitions than met the eye. However, determined not to let fear dictate their lives, my parents continued to embrace their new surroundings, immersing themselves in work, socialising with the friendly townsfolk, and embarking on leisurely drives in their dusty open-top Toyota Land Cruiser around the town. When they went out and about, my mother felt uneasy with the sight of the weirdly dressed kalicha men and women, who had long dreadlocked hair and looked as though they were drenched in dirty engine oil. They sat by the road in small groups, drumming and singing hymns while begging for food and change.

Against the odds of my father's hopes and his attempts to relieve my mother of her fears of the kalichas, my mother, a vibrant and spirited woman, was afflicted by the evil eye—a curse that had long been whispered about in hushed tones in the town. The effects of the evil eye were swift and merciless, causing my mother to suffer from epilepsy-type fits and other psychotic illnesses that threw our parents' peaceful existence into turmoil.

My mother, a kind and gentle soul, found solace in the prayers of the priests and monks who resided in ancient monasteries around Tigray. As the seasons changed and, unable to get any help from medical facilities in hospitals in Asmara, she became increasingly drawn to their spiritual teachings and rituals, seeking guidance and protection in the face of the mysterious illness she was suffering from.

Still in her late teenage years, my mother began experiencing frequent seizures, the intensity of which seemed to shake the very foundations of my parents' home. The seizures came unpredictably, striking her in various settings and leaving her and all our extended family grappling with the fear and uncertainty that they brought. It was a relentless battle that my mother fought with all her strength, but the burden of her condition weighed heavily on both of them.

Despite the darkness that threatened to engulf my parents, they refused to be consumed by despair. They clung to each other with fierce determination, their love serving as a beacon of light amid the storm. Together, they faced each day with courage and resilience, their unwavering faith in each other and a higher power sustaining them through the darkest moments.

As the seasons changed, they navigated the stormy seas of my mother's pregnancy, seeking solace in the simple joys of life – a shared meal around the hearth, a happy moment looking forward to the arrival of their first child, reflected in their home. Their love for each other grew stronger with each passing day, a testament to the unbreakable bond that held them together. Frequent trips to medical centres and churches in search of a cure for my mother's illness and to ensure her pregnancy was not in danger became commonplace.

My mother gave birth to a healthy first child, Kaleb, despite a difficult pregnancy filled with obstacles, pessimistic prenatal medical advice, and uncertainty regarding the child's health before and after birth.

After the arrival of their first child, it was this light that guided their path through the darkness, leading them toward a future filled with hope and endless possibilities. And as they stood side by side, my parents knew that, no matter what challenges lay ahead, they would face them together, with their hearts entwined and their spirits unyielding.

As time went by, my parents embraced each new day with renewed vigour and optimism, their hearts filled with gratitude for the simple blessings that surrounded them. In the end, it was not the presence of darkness that defined their journey, but the light that shone within them, guiding their path toward love, courage, and unbreakable faith.

With the arrival of their first child, my parents continued to embrace their newfound sense of life and purpose. They emerged from the storm stronger and more united than ever before. The whispers of the evil eye faded into the background, replaced by the resounding chorus of a newborn's cry and resilience that echoed through their home. With hope and determination, they were confident that my mother's illness would somehow come to a happy end through medical means and her strong spiritual belief. They never imagined that this would be a lifelong challenge they would have to endure.

As a young child, I witnessed my mother experiencing seizures at home, on the street, in the market, and even inside church. During these episodes, a ventriloquist male voice speaking in an unknown, bush-like language would emanate from her. The reliance on prayers and support from those around her to help her regain consciousness and continue with her daily life showcased the strength and resilience she possessed.

My father, who mostly worked out of town, had to grapple with the worry of my mum's well-being, and managing these circumstances presented a significant challenge. The need to be constantly vigilant, especially when he was away and unable to assist in case of an episode, would undoubtedly have added a layer of concern and responsibility to his life. Despite these challenges, the support and care provided by friends and the community played a crucial role in helping them navigate through these difficult times.

The narrative surrounding my mother's belief that she was afflicted by the evil eye, which led to her battle with epilepsy and the quest for a cure, added a poignant and mystical dimension to her journey. The decades-long struggle with both mild and severe seizures, particularly at her happiest moments – such as when she attended weddings, her children's birthdays, and other social gatherings – alongside the diverse treatments sought in hospitals, both at home and abroad, reflect the depth of her quest to find relief. As my parents welcomed more children into our humble home, my mother's illness cast a shadow over our once peaceful existence.

The turbulent winds of politics swept across Ethiopia in 1967, toppling Emperor Haile Selassie from his throne and ushering in a ruthless military regime, plunging the country into chaos and war. Amidst the upheaval, my parents tirelessly sought a cure for my mother's ailment, but the unrest of the revolution created insurmountable barriers. Roads closed, movements were restricted, and sanctuaries like churches and monasteries transformed into battlegrounds, making every journey fraught with danger. Specialist hospitals, essential for my mother's treatment, lay in remote cities, their doors closed to them by the turmoil of the times.

Faced with an uncertain future, my parents made the difficult decision to relocate to the town of Adigrat, seeking better medical care for my ailing mother. The promise of more advanced facilities offered a glimmer of hope in the darkness as we embarked on a new chapter in our quest for healing amidst the harsh realities of a war-torn land.

My parents' visits to numerous holy waters, monasteries, and spiritual healers across Ethiopia in search of a remedy for her epilepsy speak to their unwavering determination to find relief and solace. These quests included driving and walking through hostile terrain and crossing war fields, with bullets fired at them. In some instances, they faced near-death experiences while escaping gun-toting rebels or government soldiers engaged in battle. There is no doubt that my father's position as a senior field worker helped ease some of the logistical challenges, including well-coordinated intelligence and armed escorts that ensured their safety.

The blend of medical treatments and spiritual endeavours highlights the lengths to which my mother went in pursuit of healing and respite from her condition. This amalgamation of conventional and spiritual healing paths underscores the complexity and depth of my parents' journey toward finding peace and a cure.

In the heart of a tumultuous time, my parents welcomed my four brothers and me into this world, each birth a testament to their unwavering love and hope. I, the third among my siblings, grew up in the shadow of their sacrifices, benefiting from the privileges bestowed upon my older and younger brothers.

Our family was a product of revolution, our home a sanctuary amidst the chaos and uncertainty of the political landscape. From a young age, I witnessed the resilience of my parents as they navigated through personal trials and societal upheavals, their dedication to us unwavering despite the challenges we faced.

Life for us was a journey woven with dramas, twists, and turns, each thread telling a story of perseverance and strength. The struggles of our past moulded us into resilient individuals, bound together by a shared history of hardship and triumph.

As the son of revolution, I carry within me the echoes of a turbulent time, a reminder of the resilience and determination that runs through my veins. Our family's journey continues, marked by the indomitable spirit that defines us, propelling us forward amidst the uncertainties that lie ahead.

After working in various departments and positions around the country, my father was unexpectedly assigned a daunting task – to lead a community resettlement and integration project following the catastrophic famine that ravaged the northern regions in the mid-1980s.

But fate had a different plan in store. A revelation came, leading to a pivotal decision to relocate the settlers to regions where customs and beliefs intertwined harmoniously. The government finally acknowledged the importance of respecting cultural boundaries in the face of unrest.

As communities from the famine-affected areas were forced to resettle in the more fertile lands of western Ethiopia, my father was tasked by the government to mobilise and convince communities who were reluctant to leave their ancestral homes in Tigray, Gonder, and Wollo regions. Metu, the capital of Illubabor, a western Ethiopian province, served as the base for this mission, which he had not been a part of planning. True to my father's work experience and knowledge of the rural communities' cultures and beliefs, the project had a profound and diverse effect as conflicts were imminent due to disputes over origins and land ownership. My father always said it was like planting a time bomb that would explode unexpectedly. True to his prophecy, some 40 years later, after the settlers had called their new locations home, daily mass killings in the name of reclaiming ancestral lands from settlers have become very common. The communities who were forced to accept the settlement orders at gunpoint at the time are now reclaiming their land under the new Ethiopian Ethnic Federalism political system, which constitutionally allows communities the full right to evict settlers.

As the ethnic ancestral landowners continue to reclaim their lands through various means, often quoting ill-conceived and thoughtless rights, they frequently do so in the form of extrajudicial, brutal mass killings of tens of thousands, with guns and machetes supplied by the government in the name of self-defence. When the current government came under pressure from the global community to stop the killings, a new rebellion to liberate the occupied lands began to ferment, giving rise to new waves of armed resistance in almost every region of Ethiopia, threatening the unity and integrity of its nationhood today.

Before the abandonment of the resettlement projects in the Gambella region due to irreconcilable cultural differences with the settlers, the project was later moved to the Oromo regions. My father's task was to navigate the challenging terrain of the tropical forest and bridge the cultural gaps between the indigenous Agnawk tribes and the new settlers. My father was paired with a local driver named Galore, a man of slender build and towering stature, typical of the Agnawk tribes. Galore possessed not only exceptional driving skills but also a deep knowledge of the communities in Gambella, Illubabor.

Galore's demeanour was as striking as his physical appearance—polite, well-behaved, and unwaveringly committed to the success of the relocation project. His soft-spoken manner belied a reservoir of wisdom accumulated from years of traversing the rugged landscapes of western Ethiopia.

The lush greenery of the Illubabor region enveloped the duo as they ventured into remote villages, where village chiefs guarded their traditions and resisted the resettlement plans. My father's diplomatic and humanitarian skills were put to the test as he engaged in dialogue with these leaders, seeking to find common ground amid differing perspectives.

Galore's presence proved invaluable during these negotiations, serving as a bridge between my father and the Agnawk communities. His ability to navigate local customs and traditions with grace and respect smoothed the way for productive conversations, fostering understanding and cooperation.

As the days turned into weeks, my father and Galore forged a bond that transcended their roles as government official and local driver. Their shared mission to bring about positive change in the lives of the displaced communities united them in purpose and determination.

Through Galore's eyes, my father gained a deeper appreciation for the rich tapestry of cultures that thrived in Illubabor. The rhythmic beats of traditional drums, the vibrant colours of tribal garments, and the earthy aroma of roasting coffee beans became familiar sights and scents, blending harmoniously with the natural beauty of the region.

Despite the challenges they faced, my father and Galore remained steadfast in their resolve to implement the government's orders, which my father could not oppose openly. Together, they navigated the intricate web of relationships and dynamics that defined the communities of Illubabor, earning the trust and respect of those they sought to assist.

The turning point came when a group of village chiefs from around the region, who had vehemently opposed the resettlement plans, had a change of heart after a lengthy conversation with my father's team. The chiefs, who represented their communities, recognised the potential for conflicts between the newcomers and their people, as there were already similar problems with settlers who had fled South Sudan, driven out of their villages because of the brutal war for independence.

The wise chief's words reflected the spirit of the land, whispered in every rustle of the wind. A clash was brewing between the settlers and the guardians of tradition. The government's relentless determination to push ahead with forced resettlement plans had angered the chiefs, who, often governed by land rules rather than law, stood firm in their resolve to protect their ancestral lands.

As tensions mounted, my father, a skilled civil servant, found himself caught in the middle. While he stayed to continue working on other community projects, his driver, Galore, remained by his side. The weight of the unsettled atmosphere hung heavy in the air as they laboured under the curious gaze of the tribespeople.

As a colleague very close to my parents, Galore was aware of my mother's frequent illnesses when she visited my father in Illubabor. Galore sometimes drove my parents to hospitals and emergency units when my mother encountered seizures. He also travelled with them to distant monasteries and holy waters in search of a cure.

Galore was known for his kind heart and unwavering dedication to helping those in need. He often went out of his way to assist others, but when he saw the suffering etched in my mother's daily life when she visited my father one summer, Galore couldn't contain his concern any longer. He approached my father, his eyes filled with empathy, and shared his belief that there might be a healer capable of easing my mother's pain. With a mix of hope and apprehension, he sought my father's permission to investigate further.

Days passed, filled with anticipation and uncertainty, until Galore finally returned with news of the healer's whereabouts. Without hesitation, he offered to accompany my mother to meet this mysterious healer, eager to provide any assistance needed.

With my father's reluctant approval, the journey began. The air was heavy with the unknown, each step echoing the weight of their fragile hopes. Galore's determination and kindness guided them through winding paths, leading them closer to a chance at healing and unravelling a tale of compassion and perseverance in the face of adversity.

The quest to seek the help of a master of all evil eyes in a remote village near the South Sudan border, legendary advice from Galore, was somehow vivid. Galore arranged with another local guide, and they started driving to the healer's village. The five-day challenging trek through the dense tropical forest of Illubabor, relying on horses and long walks to reach the traditional healer, had a sense of adventure and desperation in the quest for a cure.

As they entered the secluded village nestled within the dense forest, an eerie aura enveloped them; the air was laced with an unsettling stillness, broken only by the occasional rustle of leaves. Following the guide's directions, my parents and Galore sought out the renowned healer, rumoured to possess mystical powers.

My parents' hearts pounded with trepidation as they finally laid eyes on the healer. He stood before them, a towering figure with a hunched back and a face that bore the marks of age and wisdom. My father's description did not do justice to the sheer otherworldly presence of the healer. His skin was weathered, his features resembling that of a wild canine, while his sharp front teeth jutted out menacingly in a horizontal display. The sight sent a shiver down my father's spine, but he steeled himself, for his wife's life depended on him.

With a voice as deep as the roots of the ancient trees, the healer beckoned them forward. As they watched in awe, he began to chant incantations, his hands moving with a grace that belied his rugged appearance. Slowly, a soft glow enveloped my mother's form. At that moment, as my mother's fever broke and her eyes opened, my father realised that appearances could be deceiving and true magic resided in the most unexpected of places.

Upon meeting the healer, whom my father described as the most unpleasant-looking figure, with a frightening appearance likening him to a hybrid of a human and a wild dog, my mother's immediate connection and admiration for the healer's handsome features created a stark contrast in perceptions. The eerie familiarity and communication in an unknown language between my mother and the healer, both in male voices while my father sat listening terrified, had an element of mystery and intrigue to the encounter.

The ventriloquist-styled conversation between my mother and the healer was an out-of-world experience my father couldn't come to terms with for the rest of his life. It was interpreted as the evil inside my mother negotiating with the healer about exiting her soul. My father insisted on leaving immediately during that session, but things were out of his control, and he had to settle and face what was unfolding in front of him.

My mother kept telling my father that she had never felt so peaceful in her life and had never seen a handsome man like the healer before. My father's confusion grew even bigger, but he was somehow convinced something unexplainable but good was happening, which may lead to my mother's eventual healing. He felt very positive about the whole healer experience because none of their previous shallow visits to monasteries and holy waters were filled with such drama and mystery.

My father didn't understand what was going on while my mother kept a closed mouth, staring at the healer, fixated with a smile, and the ventriloquist's aggressive voice almost initiated every conversation in a bush language, which resembled the voice that came out of my mother's soul during her frequent seizures. It was as though she didn't want to miss any of the 'quality' time she was spending with the healer. My mother ignored my father the entire time, even when he talked to her. She was busy healing.

The ventriloquist's voice had always been the biggest challenge for my mother's science-led doctors, as those symptoms never existed in any of their medical books.

The blend of physical descriptions, reactions, and the mysterious communication between my mother and the healer was a fascinating and somewhat surreal picture of their first encounter with traditional non-faith-related healing practices.

The experience is shrouded in an air of mystique, adding a layer of complexity to my religious mother's journey in seeking a remedy for her condition. Her thoughts were filled with a sense of betrayal to her one God, who would not approve of the healer, but her decisions were driven by desperation, and there was no going back from that point.

After spending the day sitting outside the healer's hut, surrounded by native villagers, and visiting the nearby fields and forest, my father insisted it was time to leave before darkness fell, as they had to reach the nearest town where they had left their car before continuing their journey back to the capital, Metu. My mother was not happy with my father's suggestion and asked him what the hurry was about, expressing her wish to stay with the healer longer. My mother couldn't help herself, telling my father several times how handsome the healer looked, resembling St. Gabriel, as she knew from local artists' depictions of the saint on church walls. It is a common tradition in our society to liken a handsome male to Jesus or one of the angels, and a woman to the Virgin Mary.

After receiving my father's message through the guide, the healer agreed to their request and advised that it was best for them to leave. He went to his hut and returned with a small package wrapped in a second-hand plastic sachet, placing it firmly in my mother's right palm and squeezing it, as if marking its importance.

As my mother held the parcel in her trembling hand, a strange sensation washed over her. It felt as though a thousand icy needles pierced her skin, sending shivers down her spine. The energy within the parcel was sharp and intense—indescribable yet palpable.

My mother's eyes widened in astonishment as she felt the same chill radiating through her. She couldn't find the words to express the mix of feelings flooding her senses. Was it a blessing or a curse wrapped within that enigmatic gift?

The healer gave my parents strict instructions not to share the package or show it to anyone, and that my mother must apply the contents to her skin with a daily pea-sized amount until it was finished. He also reassured my mother not to worry and said that her long ordeal would be over from that moment on. He added that he identified with the evil that possessed her and even reconstructed the sequence of events about how, where, and when the evil spirit had possessed her. His description of events took my mother back to a time and place she was suddenly familiar with. She saw that moment in a flashback, as if it were being played on a screen. The healer remarked that the evil spirit that had possessed her was a very cowardly one, targeting unsuspecting, innocent young women.

My father placed the mysterious package in his rucksack, where he carried snacks, water, and other essentials, including his old, full-metal, brown leather-clad Leica camera. They expressed their gratitude and respect for the healer and bid him farewell.

Before leaving the premises, my father reached into his bag and took out his camera, which he carried 'religiously' everywhere, especially when travelling. He asked the healer to take a photograph of him with my mother. In my father's mind, this was an opportunity to capture another historical moment to add to his prize-winning photographic collection. Capturing the healer with his unique appearance through his lens was a photographer's dream moment. Through the translator, the healer agreed to be photographed but strongly insisted that only one shot be taken.

My father asked my mother, Galore, and the local guide to pose by the healer's side for what was expected to be an epic picture. While there, he took multiple shots of that same pose with his brown leather-covered, full-steel Leica 35mm roll monocular camera. They thanked the healer again for his kindness and left the village.

My parents had a profound experience with the healer. The practice of using traditional healing methods and the belief in the evil eye are deeply rooted in many cultures around the world. The evil eye is often thought of as a curse, believed to be cast by a malevolent glare, usually given to a person when they are unaware.

Many cultures believe that receiving the evil eye will cause misfortune or injury, and they use various forms of amulets or rituals to protect against the harmful effects. To my mother, this was a reality she had to live with.

The healer's instructions to my mother—to apply the contents of the package on her skin and not to share or show it to anyone—suggested the personalised and confidential nature of the treatment, which is quite common in traditional healing practices. It was important for her to follow the healer's instructions if she believed in the efficacy of the treatment.

The discrepancy in the healer's appearance and the bush language, being the official medium, were the highlights of the trip that were engraved in my father's mind forever.

The sense of peace my mother felt after visiting the healer was an essential part of the whole experience. Emotional and psychological states can significantly impact physical health, and feeling peaceful can be beneficial in any healing journey.

As they made their way back home to Metu, my mother couldn't shake off the feeling of unease about the mysterious package and its magic power to heal. She remembered holding the bag closely, agreeing with my father's previous comments about it feeling 5 kilos heavier than before the mysterious package had been placed in it. Despite their curiosity, they decided to trust the healer and keep the contents a secret until they reached home.

Once they arrived home, my mother wasted no time unpacking the package, which was approximately 10 grams in weight. She carefully unwrapped the parcel, her hands trembling with anticipation, a faint energy she couldn't explain inside. She found a pasty solution. The dark green herbal ointment looked like a thick paste, with no significant colour, texture, or smell to suggest its usefulness.

As she applied it to her arm, she felt as though a laser beam had ripped through her skin. She cried out in intolerable pain and fainted when my dad rushed into the bedroom where she was. What my father saw as he entered was unforgettable. She was shaking and crawling on the floor while a strange, distressed mixture of voices filled the room. Confused, my father thought he had lost her. There were no written instructions or references to explain what he was witnessing, and he wasn't sure if this was another epileptic episode or a new phenomenon. My father's eyes held a haunted glint as he described the scream and agony of pain, likening it to the torment of acid searing through flesh. The healer had not told them what reaction to expect. My mother regained consciousness after about 10 minutes.

My mother crawled and sat in the far corner of the room, her brows furrowed in confusion, unable to recall the horrifying event my father spoke of. My father's hands trembled, his voice quivering with raw emotion as he painted vivid pictures with his words.

As the tale reached its chilling conclusion, my mother's eyes widened in disbelief, a faint glimmer of recognition flickering across her face. But my father remained steadfast, his gaze fixed on my mother. And in that moment, my father realised that some change—good or bad—was coming to their lives.

The resemblance of the mixed voices my father heard, one belonging to the healer and the other which he always heard when my mother fainted from her seizures, was another horrifying incident he couldn't explain. The voices sounded as though the two were fighting inside my mother's body.

The following morning, my mother looked fine, liberated, and happier than she ever had before. She slept that night as though she hadn't slept her entire life. She was full of optimism and peace, craving the medicine again.

Before going to work that morning, my ever-curious father decided to check the mysterious package that was tucked away at the deep end of my mother's bedside table. Intrigued, he gingerly picked it up and inspected it closely. He couldn't shake off the feeling that there was something strange about it.

Unable to resist his temptations, my father decided to open the package and see what was inside. To no surprise, he found a small pasty compound that looked like an extract from plants, with no smell or aroma. Unsure of what it was, he cautiously touched it with his index finger to see if there was any reaction. To his relief, nothing happened. He then applied a small amount on his arm, and again, nothing happened. It was as if he had rubbed lotion on his skin.

Curiosity turned to concern, and my father put the package back before leaving for work, with a strict written warning not to use the medicine in his absence.

Despite my father's warning and the piercing pain she had felt the night before, my mother couldn't resist the urge to apply the mysterious medicine again. She carefully applied it to different parts of her arms over five days, sitting on her bed each time and feeling a burning sensation that would occasionally make her faint for a few minutes. There were no witnesses to account for what may have happened when my mother used the medicine for consecutive days while my father was at work.

In a gripping and mysterious scene, tinged with the unknown and perhaps even the supernatural—especially in the absence of a family member—the imagination can conjure a myriad of scenarios.

In the quiet, close-knit, gated community built for government officials, where every neighbour knew each other, a casual over-the-fence chat between my parents and a neighbour took an unexpected turn, hinting at an underlying story filled with distress.

The neighbour, who lived in the villa attached to my parents', spoke with carefully chosen words, yet casual in delivery, and suggested sounds she heard during those mornings—double-pitched, multi-directional voices of two males, one of whom seemed to be in dire straits or trapped. This evoked a vivid and unsettling image in both my parents' minds. This level of distress went beyond the ordinary, hinting at an extraordinary journey my mother took unconsciously.

Such intrigue, born from a seemingly innocuous conversation, can alter perceptions and dynamics within a close-knit setting, leaving an indelible mark on the collective memory of the neighbourhood.

My parents' response to the neighbour's account was equally fascinating. My mother, especially, chose to ignore the story, yet acknowledged it as scary. This opened a realm of speculation for my father, who wondered if she had been using the medicine in his absence contrary to my mother's assurance she was only using it while he wat at home. Was my mother's dismissal a way to protect herself or others from the truth, or the weight of the experience? Or perhaps, it was her method of coping with an event too complex or painful to revisit.

It's not uncommon for individuals to downplay or sidestep discussions about experiences that are deeply personal or troubling, especially when these experiences are linked to the superstitious world.

My mother's story, with its blend of the mundane and alarming, underscores how mysterious events can ripple through the lives of those involved, leaving imprints that are interpreted and remembered in varied, sometimes conflicting ways. It also highlights the human propensity to seek explanations for the unexplained, to fill in the gaps of understanding with speculation, and to grapple with the discomfort of not knowing. The delicate balance of keeping the story indoors requires careful handling, as people, with little or no understanding of these superstitious events, may confuse the possessor with the possessed.

Being at the centre of such unresolved stories, it is not difficult to imagine how my mother must have felt. In the end, what remains is a tapestry of narratives, each offering a glimpse into the complexities of human experience, perception, and resilience.

As the days passed and the talk surrounding the medicinal stories died down, my parents began to notice the changes. The burning sensation was intense, but after each application, my mother felt a surge of energy and a renewed sense of vitality. She started to see visible changes in her energy levels, which were notably reflected in her face and skin, both of which appeared more radiant with each passing day, revealing her true beauty, seemingly restored to life.

By the end of the five days, my mother's transformation was nothing short of miraculous. She looked like a woman reborn, her face glowing with freshness and hope, and her motivation and zest for life had increased significantly. The years seemed to melt away, and she felt as though she had shed the weight of nearly two decades.

With newfound confidence and a renewed sense of self, my mother stepped out into the world, ready to embrace a new chapter in her life. The mysterious medicine had given her a second chance, a new lease on life she had never thought possible.

In a society where visiting healers is considered against Orthodox religious teachings, my mother's edited version of the story about her healing spread to her closest friends and family members. People began to seek out more information about her cure, but it was all kept in strict secrecy. Rumours swirled that my mum's miraculous healing came about through prayers, and no one found out where it had really come from or what it involved. Nor did anyone learn the instruction given by the healer.

In the end, it didn't matter where the medicine came from, as long as God enabled it. What mattered was the hope and joy it brought to my mother, a reminder that sometimes, God's miracles come in the most unexpected ways.

As my mother moved forward, leaving behind the shadows of the past, she knew that she was ready to face whatever the future held, with courage and grace.

In the days that followed, my mother felt the reassuring presence of God in her life. This made her more dedicated to His service, and she kept herself close to Him, as if she didn't want to leave Him for fear of being attacked again. And though she never fully understood how the healing came about, she was grateful for the gift of healing God had somehow brought into her life.

As for the mysterious package, its contents remained a mystery to my parents. But it didn't matter anymore, for what truly mattered was the gratitude they felt for the healer's hospitality, kindness, and assurance, as well as the beautiful memories they captured with my father's camera. As they looked back on their time at the healer's cottage, they knew that they had experienced something truly magical and unforgettable.

The incident that unfolded one evening, weeks after the visit to the healer, was nothing short of a mystical enigma, one that would leave an indelible mark on the family's memory. My father, a man of science and a fervent believer in the tangible, found himself grappling again with a reality that defied explanation.

Weeks passed after the historical visit to the healer, and life went on as normal. My father continued travelling and working around the Gambella region, which has striking tropical forest landscapes, rivers, and wildlife—fueling his appetite for his favourite hobby, photography. He shot hundreds of pictures with his Leica camera, capturing nature and humanity during his trips for work.

My father was always eager to see prints of the shots, as he prided himself on being a semi-professional photographer. It was easy for him to prove, with many award-winning photographs to his credit. He developed his slides in a makeshift darkroom at home and sent them to local studios for printing.

One day, he picked up the many black-and-white prints on his way home from work. That evening, my mum had prepared food for friends who came for a meal and a few rounds of drinks over a card game.

During one break, my father pulled out the large envelope containing the newly printed photos and spread them on the table, inviting his friends to share in his passionate works. My father excitedly explained the places and circumstances behind some of the interesting shots as his friends continued to express their admiration for his skills and love of photography.

In the middle of this "show-off" moment, my father froze in disbelief and confusion upon pulling out one photograph. His friends looked on in awe as he remained speechless, staring at the photo from different angles. My father then began searching through the pile frantically, grabbing more photos, leaning back in his chair with his mouth and eyes wide open, looking more confused and lost. He shuffled the photos quickly and aimlessly while his friends sat, bewildered and waiting for some explanation for his sudden and strange change in behaviour.

After a long silent wait, my father's friends' patience wore thin, and he finally told them not to mind him and to just continue playing cards. The guests insisted that he couldn't simply dismiss what they saw on his face and that he owed them an explanation. My father silenced the conversation by telling them he couldn't find some important photographs and that the studio might have them. He said he would check with the studio the next day, effectively silencing their curiosity.

Despite my father's efforts to calm the situation, he couldn't help himself, panicking and intermittently taking out some of the slides to find what he was missing. Showing a real sign of dissatisfaction, his friends exchanged glances and agreed to continue the card game, leaving my father to sort out his problem, whatever it may have been.

The photographs, developed from a roll that captured the lush vibrancy of tropical nature, also bore witness to an event that transcended the ordinary. Among these images were the ones intended to immortalise the visit to the healer, a pivotal moment in their lives, which harboured a mystery that challenged the very essence of my parents' beliefs.

The absence of the healer's image in the photographs was a mystery that could not be easily dismissed. It was as if the very fabric of reality had been altered, leaving behind no trace of the healer's physical presence. In an era long before the world knew of digital editing and printing, this inexplicable phenomenon sparked a flurry of questions and theories in my father's mind. Was it a mere trick of the light, perhaps a flaw in the development process? Or, was it conceivable that the healer possessed an otherworldly ability to evade capture by the lens, a manifestation of powers beyond the grasp of the material world? These questions swirled in my father's mind, propelling him into a realm of wonder and speculation.

My father waited until the visitors had left and then showed my mother what he had discovered. The already highly mysterious healing journey, which had left my parents with unexplainable, life-changing encounters, took a completely new and even more otherworldly turn when they checked the photos my dad had taken of my mum with the healer.

The monochromatic pictures showed only my mum, Galore, and the guide standing in the front yard of the healer's hut, everything beautifully captured—except the healer. In his place was a hollow space, with a blurred background of trees and shrubs.

The mysterious absence of the healer in the photographs, as preserved in a family album, opens up a fascinating corridor into the realms of unexplained phenomena. It is intriguing to consider why the healer would be missing from these visual records. This phenomenon could be attributed to various factors, ranging from the technical to the mystical.

From a technical standpoint, early photography had its quirks and challenges. Long exposure times were required, and any movement could result in ghostly images or complete erasures. However, to have the healer absent suggests something more mystical. It is possible that spiritual beliefs played a significant role. In many traditions, healers are believed to possess unique energies or are considered to be in close communion with spiritual realms. It was sometimes thought that a camera, in capturing one's image, could also trap a person's soul or essence. Perhaps the healer, or the community at large, held such a belief, leading to a deliberate choice to ensure the healer's physical absence from photographs to protect their spiritual integrity.

Moreover, the healer's absence in these photographs adds an element of mystique and reverence to his persona. It emphasises the healer's transient, perhaps ethereal, nature in the physical world, suggesting a being more attuned to the spiritual realms than to the mundane. Such an omission could have elevated the healer's status in the eyes of the community, embedding him more deeply into the folklore and collective memory of the village.

This phenomenon underscores the complex interplay between cultural beliefs, the mystical, and the advent of photographic technology. It invites us to reflect on how we document existence and how some individuals, by virtue of their spiritual or social roles, transcend traditional modes of representation, leaving behind a legacy shrouded in mystery and inviting endless speculation. In the days that followed, the incident became a topic of spirited discussion within the family.

My father, despite his initial shock, began to view the photographs not as a source of bewilderment, but as a gateway to a deeper understanding of the mysteries that lie beyond the veil of the known. The experience served as a reminder that the world is replete with wonders that defy rational explanation, inviting those who encounter them to look beyond the surface and consider the possibility of the extraordinary. While this story remained a closely guarded secret, it enriched the tapestry of our family's history, weaving into it a thread of the mystical that would forever colour our perception of reality.

There are no pearls of wisdom or knowledge in the world to explain what may have happened inside the 35mm camera, so my father was right to just leave it where it was.

This changed my father's outlook forever. He didn't know what to believe or worship. He lost all sense of his own being and everything he thought he knew. The theories about who controls our souls and our bodies—was that God's play, or was it something unexplained? It changed his perspective forever, and he couldn't get it out of his head for the rest of his life. He was left with mixed, contradictory theories of conspiracies and beliefs he could neither follow nor reject.

My father couldn't process all the phenomena he encountered, which failed to explain themselves with all the deep mysteries embedded in the experience. From the looks of the healer, and what my mum thought of him as an extremely attractive man, to the bush language my mum used to communicate with the healer and her full understanding of his entire conversation, the medicine and its reactions—everything else about it deserved answers that could not be found. To my father, the circumstances involving the disappearance of the healer from the photos were the mother of all illusions. My father could only liken it to a Hollywood horror sci-fi story he had never watched but had experienced himself.

My mother's eventful life was filled with flashes of episodes of illness, hope, despair, love, and endurance. She finally had a profound experience with the healer that changed her life for the better.

The healer remains a deep mystery to me and my family. Although I don't understand how the practice of using traditional spiritual healing methods and the belief in the "evil eye" are deeply rooted in many cultures around the world.

An Unusual Encounter

Sweet Child O'Mine

The unique dynamics of my family's generational overlap are a testament to the rich and complex tapestry that makes up family histories. The story of my mother and grandmother giving birth around the same time, almost in parallel, paints a vivid picture of a time when life was governed more by natural rhythms and less by the calculated decisions that modern conveniences allow.

This phenomenon in our family, where uncles and nephews are of the same age, creates a unique familial relationship that blurs the traditional lines of generational hierarchy. Instead of the conventional roles dictated by age, our family experienced a more peer-like relationship with our uncles and aunts. This led to a rich, shared experience that strengthened familial bonds in different ways, fostering a sense of camaraderie and collective growth among the members of the family who are contemporaries.

Moreover, our family story highlights the importance of understanding and appreciating the nuances of family history. It serves as a reminder of how societal norms and practices evolve, impacting family structure and dynamics in profound ways. The closeness in age between myself and one of my uncles, my elder brothers, and my uncles — merely three weeks apart — is a beautiful illustration of the interconnectedness of life's cycles and the unexpected ways in which families grow and bond together. It's a unique heritage that adds depth and colour to my family narrative, one that is rich with stories of coincidences, close-knit relationships, and the enduring strength of familial ties.

My birth story is quite unique and memorable! I was born during the hot season of May 1970 in the serene town of Adigrat, Tigray. I, the third of five precious boys, emerged into the world with a touch of tragedy but a sprinkle of resilience.

Born at home, Mamma Silias, the trusted midwife, cradled me in her skilled hands, guiding me into existence with a grace that belied the sombre undertones of my birth. The room, filled with hushed whispers and soft prayers, bore witness to the delicate dance of life and destiny. The warmth of family and community wrapped me in a cocoon of love; the walls of our home echoed with the laughter and mischief of my older brothers, painting a vibrant backdrop to my early days.

The story of Mamma Silas, a traditional community midwife, weaves an intriguing tapestry in the fabric of many a childhood story, highlighting the invaluable role these figures played in the early days of life in various cultures. Mamma Silas, with her imposing presence and years of experience, was a cornerstone of wisdom and care in her community. Midwives like her are often unsung heroes, bearing witness to the first breaths of generations and guiding new mothers through the labyrinth of postnatal care with a blend of ancient wisdom and practical advice.

Mamma Silas, with her unique blend of character and expertise, represents the enduring impact of traditional midwives who continue to play a crucial role in many societies around the world. Reflecting on the role of Mamma Silas and countless other traditional midwives enriches our understanding of the diverse tapestry of childbirth practices globally. It reminds us of the importance of preserving these traditions while embracing advances in medical care. Their stories, filled with affection, laughter, and sometimes mishaps, are a testament to the human touch that remains at the heart of the birthing experience. In celebrating figures like Mamma Silas, we honour the blend of tradition, care, and community that shapes the beginning of life's journey.

When mothers give birth, a heart-warming tradition blossoms amongst close friends and families. Whenever a baby is welcomed into the world, the community rallies together to support the family in their time of need, overwhelmed with the demands of caring for the newborn while also tending to her other children.

Recognising the mother's struggles, families, friends, and neighbours stepped in without hesitation. They took turns looking after older children, ensuring they were nurtured, entertained, and supervised.

As traditionally done, a group of mothers organised a meal train, delivering delicious homemade dishes for my mother each day. This act of generosity not only relieved my mother of the burden of cooking but also provided her with nutritious meals to replenish her energy, indirectly fulfilling the newborn's nourishment needs through adequate breastfeeding.

In the absence of her mother and close family members due to travel difficulties caused by the war, my mother relied on the generous support from friends and neighbours. Through their collective efforts, they not only lightened the family's load but also strengthened the bonds of camaraderie that held their community together. Their actions showcased the power of unity and goodwill in times of need, leaving a lasting impression on all who witnessed their selfless acts of kindness. Such stories remind us of the unpredictable and sometimes comical nature of life's most significant moments.

The tradition of gathering around new mothers to celebrate with a feast of 'ga'at', a nourishing porridge, and roasting coffee beans highlights the communal spirit and the importance of food and aroma in marking life's milestones. These practices not only provide physical sustenance but also weave a sensory tapestry that embeds itself in the memory, strengthening the bonds of communities and families. The burning of 'Etan', a natural gummy essence derived from special trees, with its antibiotic properties and pleasant aroma, symbolises the blending of practicality and tradition, embodying the community's wishes for health and well-being for the newborn.

Amidst the backdrop of a simpler time, when the world was humbler and the bonds between people ran deep, mothers found themselves giving birth without the careful planning that modern mothers often undertake. One child after another, they brought into the world with strength and resilience that was both awe-inspiring and humbling. My mother gave birth to three boys in less than three years. Each birth was a testament to the unyielding power of motherhood, and as her brood grew, so did the love that filled her heart. Yet, with each new arrival, my young mother faced the daunting challenge of providing nourishment for her precious babies because of the mysterious illnesses she was suffering from.

In a time long past, where the pace of life was slower and the worries of contamination or other effects were unheard of, the act of breastfeeding others' children was a testament to the unbreakable spirit of motherhood. It was a practice that defied societal norms and expectations, rooted in a deep understanding of the calm and unspoken strength that flowed through the hearts of these remarkable young women. Theirs was a world where the undefined tone of love and compassion reigned supreme, where the act of nurturing and caring for each other's children was a natural and beautiful expression of the unyielding bonds that tied them together.

I have heard from other mothers who fed me from their breasts while my mother struggled with my two older toddler brothers, who dominated the fight for this vital produce, as they both were breastfed until the age of three.

The story of Mamma Silas and the unexpected encounter shortly after my birth unfolds like a tapestry rich with cultural intricacies and familial bonds, reflecting the depth of tradition that accompanies the arrival of a new member into the world.

I heard this story many times from several families and friends later in life, recounting what they witnessed from first-hand experience. It is customary for families and friends to surround new mothers in large numbers to celebrate new births, eating 'ga'at', the traditional porridge made from wheat flour and spice-infused butter. To keep the social atmosphere warm, they roast fresh coffee and burn 'Etan' to fill the room, chit-chatting and laughing with a pleasant aroma, while also disinfecting the room.

In the peaceful hush of the dimly lit room, where the soft glow of a lone lamp danced across the walls, I found myself nestled at the edge of the bed, hidden beneath layers of cosy blankets. My mother, exhausted from the long night's events, had finally succumbed to a nap, her gentle breathing a soothing melody in the room.

Amidst the whispered conversations of well-wishers and visitors who gathered silently, ensuring that both mother and baby rested peacefully, there was a sudden shift in tranquillity. Mamma Silas, the formidable old midwife known for her ample curves and gentle demeanour, had arrived for the routine first-week health check.

The room, already filled with occupied seats, left Mamma Silas with limited choices of where to sit. With a graceful yet cumbersome movement, she settled herself on the side of the bed where I lay, unaware of the impending mishap.

As Mamma Silas positioned herself, her weight shifted, causing a moment of disarray. In an unexpected turn of events, her considerable frame shifted just so, and before anyone could react, I found myself enveloped between the folds of her majestic, oversized posterior.

As the moments ticked by, the room remained shrouded in silence, broken only by a sudden scream. The tranquillity was shattered as my mother woke up from her short nap, her eyes widening in shock at the sight before her. With a gasp, she hurriedly rushed to extricate me from my precarious position, my nose slightly askew and my head bearing a subtle deformity from the unusual ordeal. Mamma Silas, realising what had transpired, rose with apologetic bemusement, ensuring that my unexpected encounter with her big booty had caused no harm. Using her skills, she carefully and delicately remoulded my nose and skull back to their original form.

At that moment, amidst the unusual turn of events, there was a collective release of laughter that filled the room—a light-hearted end to what could have been a moment of chaos. As the story was retold for years to come, I would always be known as the baby who briefly disappeared into the depths of Mamma Silas's curves.

Despite the bizarre circumstances that led to these comical mishaps, I found myself chuckling at the memory as I grew older. The sight of my slightly mishap features served as a reminder of that fateful day under Mamma Silas's oblivious watch. However, amidst the laughter, I remained a normal kid, revelling in the joys of childhood and the innocence of playful escapades.

The anecdote about Mamma Silas might initially bring a smile or a chuckle, picturing the scene of a well-meaning visit turning into a humorous mishap. However, it underscores the intimate, personal care that midwives provide, often becoming part of family lore and cherished memories. Their visits are not just medical check-ups but are imbued with a sense of warmth, reassurance, and a deep connection to community traditions.

Mamma Silas, through her inadvertent action, becomes a memorable part of my life's story, illustrating how moments of vulnerability can foster a sense of connectedness and shared history within a community.

Caring For the Other Mother, Nature

Heal the World

My father's commitment to environmentalism and his proactive approach to involving the community, including his own family, in conservation efforts is truly commendable. It's heart-warming to hear how these collective efforts not only helped the environment but also fostered a sense of unity and support among the communities we lived in.

The experiences we had as a family and community, from planting trees to building terraces to prevent soil erosion in Tigray, are valuable lessons in sustainability and community engagement. These memories are a testament to the positive impact one person can have on their community and the environment.

The initiative my father took to allocate small plots for community gardening is a wonderful example of grassroots environmentalism. It's a sustainable way to encourage local food production, teach agricultural skills, and strengthen community bonds. My father's approach of rewarding the best yields and sharing tips on vegetable growing not only promoted healthy competition but also ensured knowledge transfer and self-sufficiency within the community.

As a young child growing up in the town of Adigrat, Tigray, I had the privilege of experiencing weekends of community service like no other. When I was young, my father, a dedicated environmentalist and community builder, would load my siblings and me onto his trusty Toyota pickup truck and whisk us away to his projects scattered across the picturesque villages of the region.

The sheer excitement of these trips was enough to make any child's heart race with anticipation. The dusty roads winding through rolling hills, vibrant greenery stretching as far as the eye could see, and the warm, welcoming faces of the villagers waiting for our arrival painted a picture of community spirit and togetherness like no other.

Arriving at the projects, we were greeted with the sights and sounds of a bustling village in motion.

When we arrived in the early morning hours of those weekends, the sound of drums and joyful chants filled the air. The villagers eagerly anticipated our arrival, usually on a fleet of five to ten pick-up trucks, and they stood in full force at the edge of the mountain, a sea of faces illuminated by the flickering torches held high. When the skilful drivers struggled to drive up the rocky and rugged mountains, the villagers helped by pushing or lifting the pickups to free them from being stuck.

Men, women, and children alike were decked in their traditional attire, their eyes shining with excitement as they waved tree branches in unison, creating a rhythmic rustling that seemed to echo through the entire valley. The scene was reminiscent of a rock band stepping onto the stage, the energy palpable and infectious.

As we approached, the villagers' chants grew louder, filling the air with a melodic hum that seemed to reverberate in the very bones of those present. The air was filled with the scent of wood smoke, a heady sign that added to the sense of anticipation and celebration.

It was a moment of unity and joy, the coming together of two worlds in a harmony that transcended cultures. Men and women worked tirelessly to plant trees and build terraces, their laughter and chatter mingling with the rustling of leaves and chirping of birds. Young girls bustled around makeshift outdoor kitchens, kneading dough for bread and roasting corncobs over open fires, filling the air with the irresistible scent of homemade goodness.

Despite our tender age and limited physical capabilities, my siblings and I dove headfirst into the tasks at hand, eager to lend a helping hand wherever we could. Whether it was offering a supportive word to village children or attempting to plant a tiny sapling with all determination, our presence served as a symbol of hope and solidarity for the communities my father tirelessly served.

As the day wore on, the sun dipped lower in the sky, casting a golden hue over the landscape as the villagers gathered to share a meal and rest after their hard work. Platters of freshly baked bread, roasted corn, and other local dishes adorned the communal table, inviting us to partake in a feast of flavours that only the land of Tigray could offer.

After finishing our task and before sitting for meals, my father would gather the villagers under the ancient Teek tree at the centre of the village. With a gentle smile and a commanding presence, he would share his knowledge, weaving intricate tales of nature and agriculture that captivated the listeners.

But the true magic of these weekends lay in the moments of connection and reciprocity that transcended words. Before leaving, the generous villagers would load our pickup truck with an abundance of gifts—from farm-fresh eggs and plump chickens to sacks of wheat, barley, and charcoal, ensuring that our family was well taken care of in return for our contribution to their community projects.

I remember watching in awe as my father distributed essentials like oil and paraffin for lanterns—practical items that held immeasurable value to those in need. My father's actions spoke volumes, demonstrating his commitment not only to environmental conservation but also to the well-being and empowerment of the villagers he served.

These weekends spent immersed in the beauty and warmth of Tigray's communities left an indelible mark on my young heart, shaping my understanding of the power of unity, generosity, and selfless service. As we drove back home, the setting sun cast a warm glow over the landscape, a tapestry of humanity woven with threads of kindness, resilience, and the unwavering spirit of community.

Before leaving the village, my father and his colleagues would educate the villagers about the importance of planting trees on mountains to combat soil erosion. He spoke of how the roots of the trees would anchor the soil, preventing it from being washed away by rain or blown by fierce winds. And among all the trees they could have chosen for this purpose, he explained why the majestic eucalyptus tree stood out. With its long-reaching roots and leaves imbued with medicinal properties that could cure colds and serve as alternative antibiotics if utilised correctly, the eucalyptus tree became a symbol of resilience and healing.

My brothers and I, along with the other village children, sat enthralled at our father's feet, absorbing his teachings like thirsty soil drinking in the rain. Through his lessons, we gained a profound understanding of the intricate dance between nature and humanity. Our minds expanded, our curiosity sparked, and our connection to Mother Earth deepened with each passing day. It was a priceless education that went beyond textbooks and classrooms, nurturing our intellectual growth and shaping our reverence for the natural world.

Years later, as I delved into the archives to uncover the extent of my father's work, I was astounded by the magnitude of his impact. His dedication led him and his devoted team to plant millions of trees across the chain of mountains that connected villages in a span of five years. But it wasn't just about the numbers; it was about the transformation of the landscape and the preservation of the land's integrity. They had painstakingly terraced more than fifty kilometres of rugged terrain, all by hand, carving out steps and pathways to prevent soil erosion and safeguard the future of the village and its people.

Upon visiting, in my later years, some of the communities my father helped develop, I stood on one of those terraced slopes, gazing at the lush greenery and feeling the earth beneath my feet. I understood the legacy my father had left behind. It was a legacy of knowledge, stewardship, and unwavering commitment to the land, knowing that his spirit would forever be entwined with the very soil he had dedicated his life to protect.

From Red Terror to Red Carpet

Living on a Prayer

In the dusty streets of Mekelle, our lives as a young family began amidst the turmoil of political upheaval. It was 1975, and I was just five years old when my family moved to the capital city of Tigray after my pre-school year in Adigrat. The transition marked the start of a new chapter in my young life, one overshadowed by the ever-present spectre of political uncertainty that still lingers in the Tigray region to this day.

My father, a dedicated civil servant, had been promoted and transferred to Mekelle due to his prestigious appointment as the head of the regional agricultural office. Little did I understand at that tender age the gravity of the historical events unfolding around me. The Derg, a military junta, had deposed Emperor Haile Selassie, plunging the nation into a maelstrom of chaos and fear. Political allegiances became a matter of life and death, and our family found itself caught in the crossfire of a revolution in its infancy.

Mekelle town painted a picture of turmoil and distrust, with whispers of dissent and fear echoing in the wind. The once-colourful markets now stood as sombre reminders of a bygone era, overshadowed by the oppressive presence of military rule.

Tigray is a land of rugged mountains and proud people, a region etched with a rich history and a resilient spirit. But amidst its stunning landscapes, a shadow loomed over the land – the Tigray People's Liberation Front, a group born out of grievances and seeking humanitarian and economic freedom, had developed into an organised resistance. As the rest of Ethiopia embraced the dawn of a new political era with relatively less resistance, Tigray found itself caught in a complex web of loyalty and dissent. The Liberation Front, with its bold defiance, stirred the embers of resistance, refusing to yield to the winds of change blowing through the nation.

My parents, stalwart pillars of resilience, bore the brunt of the political storm with stoic determination, as some of their friends and family members were either detained or killed for their political activities or simply for being Tigrayans or Eritreans. My parents' unwavering commitment to their social and governmental duties continued to strive in the face of uncertainty, navigating the tumultuous waters of our childhood with newfound courage. The Derg's erratic leadership changes only added to the air of confusion that enveloped the towns of Tigray like a shroud.

In a realm of confusion and bloodshed, the oppressive regime cast a dark shadow over the native Tigrayans. As the wicked Derg conscripted the young for the newly formed security apparatus called 'yehizb dirijit,' meaning "people's organisation," which served as the eyes and hands of tyranny, fear and mistrust wove their way through the once harmonious communities.

Many prominent figures in the community had fallen victim to the indiscriminate and ruthless cadres, leaving families with nothing but grief. Determined to seek justice and end the bloodshed, many young local community members embarked on a perilous journey to join the resistance in the mountains of Tigray.

The killings by the communist cadres were not limited to Tigrayans. Eritreans were equally under the watchful eyes of the cadres, meaning they, too, were hunted and killed in front of their families and at their places of work. Some of my father's close friends and work colleagues were murdered without warning. Almost all of my family's friends had either been killed or fled to join the rebels in Tigray and Eritrea. Some decided to cross the border to Sudan to find new lives as political refugees in other countries.

Therefore, my life as a young boy in Mekelle unfolded against the backdrop of a nation in turmoil. It was a time of loss and upheaval in the months and years that followed. Through the lens of a child's eyes, I witnessed the worst of human suffering, with bodies of dead people on our streets and news of those killed and mourned by my parents. As I look back on those tumultuous days, I am reminded of the indomitable spirit that carried us through the storm, emerging stronger on the other side.

In the rugged terrains of Tigray, where the echoes of war reverberated through the hushed valleys, my father continued his perilous journey to finish the work he had started. Despite the turmoil gripping the region, he remained steadfast in his mission to oversee the urgent environmental projects he had initiated, covering positions voided by the deportation of his 'imperialist' American friends.

My father was not just an ordinary man; he was a beacon of hope, a guardian of the environment, a protector of the land. He dedicated his life to preserving the natural beauty and fertility of the Tigray region, but his commitment went far beyond just leading projects, planting trees, and terracing mountains. His passion for environmental work ran deep, so deep that he was willing to risk his own life to save others.

The changing climate in sub-Saharan Africa had taken a toll on the once-lush farmlands, causing erosion and threatening the livelihoods of thousands. However, my father refused to stand idly by and watch as his trees and mountains suffered the consequences of brutal natural and human errors. He knew that the key to reversing the devastation lay in reforestation and sustainable land management. So, he took it upon himself to lead the charge, rallying the local communities to continue the permanent life-saving missions in the face of what might have been a short-lived civil war.

Despite the dangers that lurked in the treacherous terrain of the mountains, my father forged ahead. He braved steep cliffs, unpredictable weather, and unforgiving wildlife and landmines, all in the name of a greater cause. His selfless determination inspired those around him to stand tall and fight against the impending crisis amidst an unforgiving civil war.

As the days turned into weeks and the weeks into months, my father worked tirelessly, organising tree planting and mountain terracing, while also delivering food and medicines to those communities he was helping. My father's spirit remained unbroken, fuelled by the smiles of gratitude on the faces of the villagers whose lives he was touching.

At times, land mines exploded, killing my father's colleagues. Tanks and warplanes swept through the villages he was visiting, threatening to undo all his hard work in an instant. The raging bullets tore through the walls of the huts he slept in during his rounds. The villagers looked on in despair, praying for my father and his colleagues' lives, unsure of how to combat the destructive force of man and nature.

My father stood firm, with determination. Without a second thought, he threw himself into the heart of his projects, anchoring the trees with his own body, shielding them from the wrath of the elements. The villagers watched in awe as their protector braved the tempest, his very existence a testament to his unwavering dedication. They even wrote a traditional song for him that became the theme of their project. The trees my father helped plant and the terraces he built stood tall and proud, their roots deep in the earth, thanks to the sacrifice of one man who believed that his life was not dearer than those he sought to save.

My father became a symbol of hope, a reminder that one person's courage and determination could change the course of history.

My father knew that as long as he had the support of the communities he had devoted his life to protecting, there was nothing he couldn't overcome. For in his heart, he carried the spirit of the land, a spirit that would never be extinguished if someone was willing to fight for it.

Each trip from his office in Mekelle to the capital, Addis Ababa, and the remote sub-regions of Tigray was fraught with uncertainty. My father's trips were made in various modes depending on his destination. He drove his 1960 VW Beetle to attend meetings and compulsory communist indoctrination workshops in Addis Ababa. The journeys to his environmental projects in rural Tigray were always completed in his open-top Toyota HJ45 Land Cruiser and on the blue and red 175cc Suzuki all-terrain bike he inherited from his American friends.

The roads of Tigray, once bustling with life, now bore the scars of conflict, lined with remnants of a once-thriving infrastructure and burnt tanks, Soviet-made Ural and AMCE trucks. Yet, undeterred by the dangers that lurked at every turn, my father pressed on. His determination to ensure that the environmental projects he had poured his heart into continued to flourish superseded the constant threat of peril that loomed overhead.

Each journey was marked by near-death experiences, a testament to the precarious nature of his mission. Yet, his resolve remained unshaken, a beacon of hope amidst the chaos that engulfed Tigray. As he navigated through the war-torn region, his unwavering dedication to his cause illuminated a path of resilience in the face of adversity.

Amid an era devoid of mobile phones, where communication resided within the limitations of rare landlines, my mother's heart bore the weight of unease each time my father embarked on a journey. The urban landscape had been scarred by the ravages of war, rendering the infrastructure fragile and unpredictable. In these times, the safe return of a loved one was not a guarantee but rather a sincere hope that lingered in the hearts of those they left behind.

As my father set out on his trips to his environmental projects in rural Tigray, my mother's eyes mirrored a mosaic of emotions—pride in his resilience and dedication, coupled with the sombre realisation of the dangers that lurked in the shadows of the war-torn region.

Each tick of the clock echoed the cadence of worry in my mother's heart. In a world where a simple delay could mean much more than just a missed appointment, she paced the streets to church and the floors of our humble abode, her thoughts drifting to the dangers that awaited beyond our doorstep. My mother's heart leapt in trepidation with every hour that passed until my father's return. For in a world where communication was scarce and danger abundant, our family love had bridged the gap, guiding him home safely once more after each trip.

Therefore, in an age where electronic communication was but a distant dream, the bond between a husband and wife stood as a testament to the resilience of the human spirit, transcending barriers and conquering fears amidst the ruins of a war-torn world.

In the heart of Eritrea, where the dust of war had also settled upon every surface like a heavy shroud, families were torn apart by the chaos of conflict. The political landscape was a battlefield, with shifting allegiances and fractured loyalties between the various Eritrean rebel groups and the government, leaving no one untouched. Amidst the thud of boots on barren ground and the distant echoes of gunfire, the people of all corners of Eritrea found themselves caught in a storm of uncertainty and fear.

As independence fighters surged through the region, their control tightening like a noose around the struggling government, the fabric of society began to unravel. The once vibrant Italian-built cities and traditional villages now stood desolate, haunted by the shadows of those who had fled or fallen. Foreign mercenaries from far-off lands prowled the alleys, their presence a chilling reminder of the stakes at hand.

Communication lines connecting Eritrea to the rest of the world had been severed, leaving families stranded in a void of silence. For Eritrean families who lived away from their homes, the weight of separation from loved ones bore down upon their shoulders like a mountain of sorrow. Unable to reach families and friends, my parents, who resided in Tigray for many years and were cut off by war, felt the ache of uncertainty gnawing at their hearts.

Rumours swept through the land like wildfire, carrying tales of tragedy and triumph in equal measure. Some whispered of family members lost to the conflict, their names added to the growing list of casualties. Others spoke of brave souls joining the fight, their voices raised in defiance against tyranny. Still, more stories emerged of those who had fled, seeking refuge in foreign lands where the promise of safety beckoned like a distant beacon.

As days turned into weeks and weeks into months, my parents found themselves adrift in a sea of worry. Each sunrise brought fresh fears; each sunset carried the weight of unanswered questions. With no way to reach out to their families, my parents felt a sense of helplessness settle over them like a dark cloud.

In the dusty lands of Tigray and Eritrea, the echoes of war reverberated through the hearts of the people, growing louder and more desperate with each passing year. The once vibrant villages now lay in ruins, a haunting reminder of the devastation inflicted by the communist regime's relentless pursuit of control. False convictions, fueled by an insatiable thirst for control, had plunged the region into a never-ending cycle of violence and suffering.

As the conflict escalated, the regime made a fateful decision to invite foreign powers into the fray. The Soviets and Cubans, drawn by the promise of influence and domination, descended upon the war-torn lands like vultures, their presence casting a dark shadow over the already beleaguered communities. What was once a regional conflict now morphed into an international proxy war, with the fate of countless lives hanging in the balance.

Amidst the chaos and bloodshed, the true horror of the foreign intervention began to unfold. The soldiers, clad in unfamiliar uniforms, swept through the villages with ruthless efficiency, their actions driven not by compassion or justice but by a cruel sense of superiority. Rape and looting became commonplace, the innocence of the innocent shattered by the inhumanity of those who claimed to be their saviours.

In the heart of a war-torn Tigray, where the cries of the oppressed blended with the rumble of distant explosions, there stood a man who defied the darkness that enveloped the communities he served. My father, a beacon of hope amidst the chaos, whose dedication to the communities he served knew no bounds. The verdant hills and terraced fields he nurtured with tender care were but a fraction of his legacy. In a time when war crimes stained the land, perpetrated by both local factions and ruthless foreign mercenaries, my father rose as a stalwart defender of human rights and a champion of discipline and the rule of law.

My father's unwavering commitment led him to confront the perpetrators of atrocities and challenge the corrupt army officials who tarnished their uniforms with the blood of innocents. His brave stand earned him enemies among the powerful military, political elite, and cadres who sought to maintain their grip on power through fear and manipulation.

Yet, my father's influence and popularity in the communities he served could not be extinguished. With a neutral political stance and genuine compassion for the suffering of the people, he used his position to advocate for the oppressed and negotiate for the passage of much-needed aid and resources to the environmentally deprived areas neglected by the authorities.

However, my father's acts of compassion and righteousness incited jealousy and suspicion among some high-ranking conspirators in the regional political powerhouse who viewed his actions as a challenge to their authority. False accusations began to circulate, painting my father as a double agent, a traitor who consorted with rebels and exchanged information with the enemy.

The whispers of treachery reached the ears of those in power, and soon, my father found himself under the watchful gaze of spies and informers. They trailed his every move, monitoring his interactions and scrutinising his motives. The fact that he ventured alone into the rural hinterlands without seeking military escort only fuelled the rumours of his supposed immunity to rebel attacks, further deepening the shadows of doubt that loomed over him.

Despite the mounting pressure and the shadow of suspicion that darkened his every step, my father remained resolute. He continued to live up to his commitments to environmental missions while standing for justice and truth, fighting for the voiceless and the oppressed, even as the walls of deceit and betrayal closed in around him.

Despite my father's pure and neutral intentions, his reputation among the fierce Eritrean Liberation Front was tainted. They accused him of collaborating with and working for the very government they fought against, mistaking his humanitarian efforts for treachery.

In a war-torn land rife with despair and tragedy, my father stood as a beacon of hope amidst the chaos. Forced by circumstance to work as a government official, he bore the heavy burden of not only providing for his own family but also caring for the families of his fallen brothers and friends, victims of the harsh reality of war. With unwavering determination, he took on the role of a fatherly figure to those who had lost everything.

Amidst the rubble and ruins, my father's unwavering presence brought a ray of light to those plunged into darkness. His days were spent tirelessly juggling bureaucratic duties and acts of compassion, offering financial and moral support to the families left without guardians, including his brothers and several friends. He was the only hope for many families, offering support in difficult economic and humanitarian situations in a society torn by war, grief, and desperation. Through his actions, my father became a symbol of resilience and compassion, a guiding light in the midst of turmoil. Though the scars of war may never fully heal, his legacy of kindness and generosity will forever be etched in the hearts of those he touched.

As the years passed, our humble abode became a sanctuary for the orphaned and abandoned, a safe haven in a world filled with uncertainty. My father's selflessness knew no bounds, as he used his position to extend a helping hand to many families.

As whispers of betrayal spread from all sides, including accusations of fostering the families of colleagues who had abandoned their children to join the wars in Tigray and Eritrea, my father found himself isolated, defenceless, caught between loyalty to his government, his people, and the families he helped.

In the face of adversity and danger, my father's unwavering commitment to his principles shone like a beacon in the night, guiding those who had lost their way back to the path of righteousness. And though his enemies sought to tarnish his name and drag him into the depths of mistrust, my father's legacy of compassion and courage would endure as a testament to the enduring power of hope in the face of despair.

The sun began to set on my father's humble humanitarian work as he found himself amidst the chaos of accusations from warring factions. The air crackled with tension, carrying whispers of revenge from all directions. He was ordered not to travel to the communities he had known for many years. Some of his projects were finished, while others were left incomplete. The government declared they would not be responsible for his death if it happened. That was another way of saying, 'We will kill you if you keep going, and we will make it look like an accident.' It was a stark warning that demanded attention.

To my father's disadvantage, the crackling of the old radio set in our home filled the air with propaganda, its static-laden voice amplifying the discord that had engulfed the region. The Tigrayan rebels' propaganda station extolled my father's virtues, painting him as a beacon of peace and goodwill in a sea of turmoil. They hailed his efforts in aiding the war-torn communities with his humanitarian and environmental works, even going so far as to suggest peace talks led by his gentle hand, a notion that both honoured and burdened him. The very fact the rebels labelled my father as a good person was enough to raise suspicions that he was sympathetic, and in some ways, suggest he was regularly and informally in touch with anti-government forces.

Yet, amidst the broadcast of praise, there lurked a darker shadow. The Eritrean freedom fighters' radio waves carried venomous words, branding him a traitor to his people and their cause, a pawn of the oppressive government they despised. Their accusations cut deep, for my father's heart yearned only for harmony and relief for those caught in the crossfire of a conflict not of their making.

The dichotomy of these narratives, one showering him with accolades and the other tarnishing his name, created a whirlwind of confusion and fear within himself and the government. The historical hostility between the two factions amplified the tumult surrounding my father, for he stood at the confluence of their disdain, a solitary figure in a storm of opposing ideologies and ethnic divisions.

As the wars escalated, so did the pressure on my father. Some low-ranking but influential military commanders in the region, who blamed everyone but themselves for their failure, grew suspicious of his intentions and affiliations. They began to view him with wary eyes, unsure of where his allegiance truly lay. The frequent mention of his name over the airwaves for various reasons fuelled the flames of uncertainty, painting a target on his back that he could not erase, no matter how fervently he tried to remain impartial and neutral in the chaos that threatened to consume him. The conflicting narratives wove a tapestry of despair around him, blurring the lines between friend and foe, ally and adversary.

Amidst the echoing cacophony of propaganda and accusations, my father stood as a solitary figure in a land torn asunder by strife and discord. The once-proud beacon of hope and compassion now found himself trapped in a web of betrayal and manipulation, his very existence a bargaining chip in a game of power and control that threatened to shatter the humanitarian projects he had advanced over several years, which required continuation to achieve their full goals.

The rumours and uncertainty about my father worried my mother, who was struggling with her own predictability. Her worries etched deep into her weary eyes. The constant mention of my father's name by the warring rebels and in the government's media had crept into her every waking moment, a haunting reminder of the fragility of our lives. To win their own political games, each warring party painted a skewed picture of my father that would upset the other.

As my mother grappled with the daily battle of raising five children while fighting the constraints of her epilepsy, her faith became her sole refuge. She sought solace and resolution in her prayers, leaning on her God for strength in the face of impending turmoil.

The looming fear of a life without my father weighed heavily on my mother's shoulders, especially in a land where she had no immediate family and no hope or way of returning to Asmara. The thought of navigating Tigray's harsh realities alone was a daunting prospect, made even grimmer by the power of those who accused my father unjustly.

Despite her unwavering love and determination, my mother knew that no amount of preparation could shield her from the storm brewing on the horizon. And so, she braced herself for the unknown, her unwavering resilience a testament to the indomitable spirit of a mother's love in the face of adversity.

The air was heavy with fear as my parents navigated the treacherous life in Tigray. The once bustling roads now lay barren, closed off, and heavily fortified, cutting off any hopes of escape to the relative safety of the Sudanese border. My parents were trapped, caught in the crossfire of lies and spiteful accusations that could have fatal consequences.

The government's desperation was palpable as it clung to its last shreds of authority, determined to crush any form of opposition, armed or unarmed. The military regime, teetering on the brink of defeat from all fronts, including a fierce border war with neighbouring Somalia, resorted to unimaginable brutality in a final bid for survival.

The 'red terror' was unleashed upon the people of Ethiopia, a wave of violence that surpassed all bounds of humanity. The streets ran red with the blood of those who dared to challenge the iron-fisted rule of the regime. Firing squads carried out executions in broad daylight, their ruthless efficiency leaving a chilling spectacle for all to see. Bodies were displayed on the main streets of cities and towns, a grim reminder of the consequences of defiance.

As a child, aged just seven, I was a silent witness to these atrocities. Every day, as we made our way to school and back with our older schoolmates, we would be herded like cattle by brutal soldiers, their faces devoid of compassion, their hands stained with the blood of innocent people. We witnessed young people being shot at and their bodies left on the streets under the hot sun. Children, too, were not spared from their cruel machinations, forced to bear witness to acts of unspeakable horror.

In the heart of the Mekelle town square, a place of profound sorrow loomed every day. It was the haunting stage where the chilling acts of the red terror took place. It was a macabre theatre where the cruel hand of fate sealed the lives of up to thirty souls each day. The mood was heavy with dread, the ground stained with the blood of innocents, all against the backdrop of a terrified and motionless crowd.

During morning rush hours, the rumble of military trucks reverberated through the square. A convoy of dark Soviet-made vehicles arrived, bringing with them prisoners shackled in their tattered clothing. They were pushed out onto the square, their eyes haunted and their spirits broken, forced to face the finality of their twisted fate.

A short, bearded cadre with eyes devoid of humanity stepped onto the stage, his voice cold and commanding. He delivered a short, venomous speech, a litany of propaganda and slogans designed to justify the abominable acts about to unfold. The crowd stood silent, a captive audience to the horrors that were about to be unleashed.

The prisoners, lined up against the grim wall, their faces etched with resignation, awaited their inevitable demise. As the condemned souls stood with heads held high, the history of their dissent was recounted — a twisted narrative of betrayal and defiance against the oppressive regime. Each word spoken was a jagged blade, cutting through the last shreds of hope that clung to their hearts.

A well-rehearsed admission followed, extracted through fear and coercion, a final act of submission before the ultimate act of brutal finality. The young executioners raised their weapons, the barrels cold and unforgiving, aimed at the hearts of the condemned.

The sound of gunshots pierced the morning silence, the echoes ricocheting off the walls of the square. The air was thick with the scent of gunpowder and fear, a chilling reminder of the unforgiving grip of tyranny.

As the lifeless bodies crumpled to the ground, the onlookers remained frozen in shock and horror, their souls stained by the atrocities they had witnessed. The haunting stage stood as a grim monument to the cruelty and inhumanity that had taken root in the heart of Mekelle.

As the last shots were fired and the smoke cleared, the square lay silent, save for the quiet sobs of those left behind. Families, torn apart by the ruthless hands of fate, stood in stunned disbelief, their grief raw and uncontained. They were not only robbed of their loved ones but also forced to pay for the bullets that snuffed out their lives, a final indignity heaped upon their shattered hearts.

Each body was left with a placard, a macabre introduction to the world of their made-up crimes. Some bore names familiar to the spectators — neighbours, teachers, and friends. Others were strangers, ordinary people caught in the merciless grip of tyranny. The bodies were left until sunset for everyone to see and 'learn'. Families would sit by the side of the bodies until they were allowed to collect and take them home to begin mourning.

In the aftermath of the bloodshed, a heavy silence descended upon the square, a silence broken only by the hollow sound of shoes against the cobblestones. As the sun dipped below the horizon, casting a blood-red glow over the stage of death, the echoes of the Red Terror resonated through the heart of Mekelle — a chilling reminder of the darkest depths to which humanity could sink.

Years after the aftermath of the massacre, the true scale of the horror was revealed. The Red Terror campaign had claimed up to a quarter of a million lives in just a few months — a staggering toll that left scars on the collective memory of each town. The spectre of those dark days lingered, haunting the streets and homes where once laughter had reigned.

My parents were bound by love and courage, ready to face whatever trials lay ahead. In a land torn apart by violence and fear, they started discussing my mother's action plans based on hypothetical scenarios of my father's disappearance. Each passing day brought with it a new wave of terror, a new reason to fear for my father's life. With all his friends and colleagues killed or fled, the walls seemed to close in on him, suffocating him with the knowledge that there was no way out — no escape from the horrors that surrounded him.

It was an ordinary morning — or so we thought. My father, a stern yet caring man, kissed us goodbye as he left for work. Little did we know that it would be the last time we would see him, the last time we would hear his voice calling out to us, the last time he would walk through that front door.

My mother, ever intuitive and sensitive to the energy around her, felt something ominous in the air that day. She decided to seek solace in the church, her refuge in times of unease. She sat there in silent prayer for what seemed like an eternity, as if trying to ward off the impending storm that loomed over our household.

Meanwhile, in our absence, a new housemaid had joined our household. Young and timid, she stood outside, tears streaming down her face, unable to contain her emotions. It was as if she felt the guilt of bringing the demons to the family in the weight of the impending tragedy that was taking place on her first day with us.

As the school day came to an end, we returned home, unaware of the darkness that had descended in our absence. The sight that greeted us was harrowing. Our usually composed mother stood outside, her eyes bloodshot and filled with a mix of fear and despair. And there, next to her, stood my father's driver, holding his coat in trembling hands.

In an instant, my mother's world shattered. The driver's presence with the coat triggered a wave of panic and disbelief. The dreadful thought that my father had met with a tragic end coursed through her veins, causing her to collapse right there on the doorstep. Neighbours, quick to respond, rushed to her side, mistaking her distress for one of her epileptic episodes.

Carrying her inside, they laid her down, surrounded by a circle of worried faces. The coat, a silent witness to the turmoil that had unfolded, lay abandoned on a nearby chair. The driver, distraught and lost for words, hesitantly revealed the chilling truth — my father had been forcibly taken by plain-clothed men from his office in a white Fiat 124 car, and his whereabouts were unknown.

The weight of the news bore down heavily on the onlookers, the gravity of the situation sinking in with each passing moment. The neighbours, bound by duty and compassion, faced the grim task of delivering the devastating revelation to my mother. How do you tell someone waking up from epilepsy that their pillar of strength, their source of light, has been ripped away from them without warning?

It wasn't clear if my father had been kidnapped by rebel groups or detained by government agents.

As my mother regained consciousness, her first words trembled with anguish and disbelief. She desperately inquired about my father, her voice cracking with emotion. In her mind, the assumption of his demise lurked ominously — the idea of his body being the only tangible evidence of his fate.

And so, our once tranquil home was plunged into a nightmare, a labyrinth of uncertainty and fear. The search for my father, the quest for answers, had just begun, shrouded in a veil of mystery and dread. As we grappled with the unknown, the echoes of my mother's anguished cries reverberated through the walls, a haunting reminder of the fragility of our existence in the face of unforeseen tragedy.

As the news of my father's disappearance spread through the town, a sombre group of women, friends of my mother, gathered around the family home. They came with heavy hearts, their eyes filled with silent tears, their faces etched with worry. It was as if they were attending a mourning ceremony, for in their hearts, the absence of my father felt like a death sentence.

My mother, a woman of quiet strength, bore the weight of her husband's disappearance with a grace that belied her inner turmoil. She clung to her children, seeking solace in their presence while grappling with the agonising uncertainty of her husband's fate. She longed to reach out to her parents to seek comfort in their words, but the distance between them felt like an insurmountable chasm. That, too, was not possible as Eritrea remained cut off from the rest of the country.

In a politically depressed society where the support of men in times of crisis was laden with consequences, only women dared to stand beside my mother in solidarity. They braved the unknown, venturing out into the town in search of any shred of information that could shed light on my father's whereabouts. The days turned into weeks, and still, there was no word of his fate.

The neighbourhood was shrouded in heavy silence, broken only by the hushed conversations of the women gathered at our household. Each passing day deepened the sense of loss that hung over them like a pall, a constant reminder of the gaping void left by our father's absence. The women clung to hope like a fragile thread, each holding on to the belief that their friend's husband would return home safe and sound.

However, as the days turned into weeks, doubts began to gnaw at their faith. The authorities remained tight-lipped, offering no solace or reassurance. It was not uncommon for captives to disappear into the shadows, their presence hidden from the world. The uncertainty weighed heavily on the hearts of those left behind, a sense of foreboding that refused to be ignored.

And so, the days stretched into an endless expanse of waiting, of hoping against hope for a miracle that seemed increasingly unlikely. My mother's eyes reflected the pain of a woman caught in the grip of a nightmare—her spirit unbowed, but her heart heavy with the burden of uncertainty. Her epilepsy was triggered by the constant psychological storms brewed by the new worries, becoming more frequent. The neighbours had the added task of looking after us, cooking for us, and helping with all household chores to support the young, inexperienced housemaid. They became parental figures in a true reciprocation of my parents' kind and sociable behaviour.

In the days and weeks that followed my father's disappearance, our once peaceful abode became a haven for chaos and fear. Soldiers and cadres, clad in their menacing uniforms and armed to the teeth, descended upon our home like a swarm of locusts in search of clues to unravel my father's alleged crimes. Each raid was more brutal than the last, leaving behind a trail of destruction and heartache.

The first time they came, it was like a storm raging through our humble dwelling. They stormed in unannounced, their heavy boots thudding against the floor as they tore through every corner of our home. The children's bedrooms, once filled with laughter and toys, were now tossed asunder in their relentless quest for evidence. They even invaded the sanctuary of our bathrooms, ripping through cabinets and drawers in their zealous search.

The soldiers' presence was suffocating, their expressions masked by hardened resolve and suspicion. They wielded their weapons with an air of authority, intimidating us with their mere presence. As they ransacked our home, their lack of direction became apparent. It was as if they were on a wild goose chase, tearing apart everything in their path without a clear objective in mind.

Outside, the jeeps lined our driveway like ominous sentinels, a constant reminder of the looming threat that hung over our family. The soldiers dug up the garden, uprooting flowers and plants in their pursuit of hidden caches of weapons or covert messages. Even a disused doghouse was not spared, dismantled in a futile attempt to uncover any shred of incriminating evidence.

When the soldiers finally deemed their search complete, they left no stone unturned. They pillaged our belongings with no regard for sentiment or value. Our treasured family albums and slides, my father's prized photographic works filled with precious memories captured in time—including the original 'flying rooster' and other credentials—were callously ripped from their shelves and walls. My father's academic papers, meticulously organised and vital to his projects, were scattered like confetti. Children's exam certificates and trophies were confiscated, never to be returned, and books that held the wisdom of generations, including Bibles, now lay strewn across the floor, their pages crumpled and torn. Even our music cassette player and tapes were taken without explanation, never to be seen again. Some of the tapes had recordings of our first cry, our first songs, and various audible memories my father created and treasured for our future. They were all gone.

In the aftermath of the raids, our home stood as a hollow shell of its former self, robbed of its soul, warmth, and past. Each passing day brought with it a sense of uncertainty and dread as we grappled with the unknown fate of our father and the harsh reality of living under the watchful eyes of those who sought to tear us apart.

As the soldiers departed, their jeeps laden with the spoils of their search, we were left in a state of shock and devastation. The once cosy confines of our home now lay in ruins, a stark reminder of the tyranny that had befallen us. My mother wept silently, her eyes weary from the constant barrage of intrusion and violation. The children clung to her, our innocence shattered by the brutality of the world outside our doorstep.

Weeks had slipped through our fingers like grains of sand, leaving behind only the ache of uncertainty and fear. My mother and her children were trapped in a relentless search for my father, a search that seemed to lead nowhere but to the cold, lifeless bodies of the victims of the red terror.

As the days stretched into weeks and the weeks melted into months, attending red terror-killing squares to search for my father became a grim routine. The once dreaded gatherings now beckoned us like a haunting spectre, a relentless reminder of our unanswered questions. We would stand in line with other families, our eyes scanning the faces of the dead, searching for any trace of my father. The stench of death clung to the air, mingling with our desperate hope and suffocating us with its dread.

The bodies kept lying in rows, a macabre display of the horrors that had befallen Mekelle city square. Some were mangled beyond recognition, their faces twisted into grotesque masks of agony. My mother and her children would comb through the corpses, our hands trembling as we lifted the blood-soaked placards to read the names. Each name was a dagger to our hearts, a reminder of the countless lives that had been stolen by the merciless hands of the red terror. But my father's name never appeared, not among the living nor among the dead.

As the weeks turned into months, a sense of futility settled over us like a shroud. In the midst of our despair, a ray of hope pierced through the darkness in the form of a few kind-hearted officials who had known my father. They whispered news of his existence under enemies lurking in the shadows of power, ready to strike at any moment. My father's gentle demeanour and friendly nature had made him a target, a pawn in a deadly game of politics and betrayal.

My mother clung to these officials like a lifeline, their words offering a glimmer of hope in the vast ocean of despair. They provided us with scant details, vague hints of my father's possible whereabouts. Each lead was like a fragile thread, easily broken, but we clung to them with desperate determination, unwilling to let go of the faint hope that flickered within our hearts. His closest friends in high government positions kept their lips tight for fear of repercussions. The news of his existence was less important than the fate awaiting him in a land where those who fell into the brutal hands of those merciless killers were forgotten.

Therefore, the search continued, a relentless pursuit of the truth in a world shrouded in lies and darkness. My mother stood on the precipice of uncertainty, our spirits battered but unbroken, our resolve as unyielding as the steel that forged our souls. In the midst of this turmoil, we clung to the memories of my father, a beacon of light in the midst of the encroaching shadows, guiding us through the long, harrowing seasons.

In the quiet neighbourhood we lived in, a sense of familiarity was ever-present. Strangers greeted each other with warm smiles, and every face held a story to tell. One day, the routine walk my mother took to the church for her daily prayers was interrupted by the unwavering presence of a young man who seemed to shadow her steps.

As my mother navigated the familiar path to the local St Michael's church, she couldn't shake the feeling of being watched. Glancing over her shoulder, she noticed a young person, a figure she recognised from the neighbourhood, following her every move. Unease settled in her chest, quickening her prayers and pace until she reached the sanctuary of the church gates.

Stepping into the hallowed space, the young man hesitated, lingering outside as if held back by unseen forces. My mother finished her prayers, comforted by the calm serenity of the church walls, only to find the young man—who was a newly recruited cadre—waiting for her return. With a cautious whispered greeting, he approached her, urging her to follow him discreetly to a more secluded area on the side of the church.

Apologies tumbled from his lips, knowing how my mother was scared of his presence. He explained his connection to my father, a respected figure in the community who had extended a helping hand to the young man and his family. Gratitude shone in his eyes as he recounted how my father had paved the way for his job at the Department of Agriculture, guiding him and paying for him to obtain a driver's licence, eventually elevating him to a driver position after his initial employment as a car washer.

The young cadre, one of many who seemingly joined the revolution only to stay alive, spoke of love and admiration for my father, his voice filled with sincerity as he revealed that he felt compelled by a sense of moral duty to convey a message to my mother—one concerning my father's whereabouts. There was a vulnerability in his demeanour, a stark contrast to the imposing figure that had followed my mother earlier, revealing a depth of gratitude and respect that touched my mother's heart.

The young cadre's figure seemed less imposing, more human, filled with gratitude for the guidance he had received. My mother, with a newfound perspective on the familiar faces that surrounded her in the neighbourhood, carried the message of love and kindness back home—a testament to the power of benevolence in even the most unexpected encounters. Amidst the shadows of uncertainty and fear, a glimmer of hope emerged in the form of the young cadre. His words pierced through the veil of anxiety that shrouded my mother's heart as he stood before her, offering a lifeline of reassurance.

With eyes brimming with empathy, the earnest young man spoke of a connection to my father that transcended prison walls. He spoke of daily glimpses, fleeting yet profound, that offered solace in the midst of chaos. Working within the confines of the main prison, he became a silent guardian, a beacon of support for my father in his darkest hours.

As he relayed his encounters with my father, a vivid portrait unfolded before my mother's eyes. She could almost see the prison offices where her beloved husband was brought for daily questioning—a place fraught with tension and uncertainty. Yet, amid it all, there was a glimmer of humanity, of connection forged through shared prayers and unspoken understanding.

In the cadre's words, my mother found a newfound strength, a belief in the resilience of her husband's spirit. The young cadre's gentle assurances painted a picture of survival against all odds, a testament to the enduring power of hope in the face of adversity. As the echoes of his promise lingered in the air, a sense of calm descended upon my mother—a fragile yet undeniable peace born from the knowledge that her husband was alive and, against all odds, unharmed.

Under the dim glow of the sun on that cloudy day in the disenchanting dark of a politically depressed city, the young cadre—his eyes reflecting the turmoil of divided loyalty—could not promise certainty to my anxious mother. Yet, in his voice, carried the unwavering conviction that her husband, a political prisoner, would endure the harsh tides of captivity. With a resolve tempered by defiance, he assured her that they would be reunited and that hope would prevail in the face of adversity.

With a gravity-laden warning, the young cadre implored my mother to guard their secret meeting, as the repercussions of their communication might have heavy consequences for both of them. As their clandestine encounter ended, the young cadre pledged to be the emissary of any message the mother wished to impart to her captive husband.

My mother, her spirit buoyed by the fleeting encounter, entrusted the young cadre with a message of unwavering strength and resilience. She relayed to her beloved husband that our family endured, united in prayer and unwavering faith in his safe return. In the final moments of their covert meeting, the young cadre—his voice a wellspring of solace and reassurance—spoke words that shimmered with the promise of divine protection. With a quiet certainty that cut through the veil of uncertainty, he shared with my mother a whispered assurance that her husband's life was not in imminent peril. And with a heavy heart laden with unspoken words, he bid her farewell—a parting marked by the weight of unshed tears and unspoken fears.

In the eerie stillness of the church backyard, as the young cadre melted into the shadows, my mother was left with a glimmer of hope she couldn't share with anyone—a fragile hope in the vast expanse of uncertainty. And as she cradled the words of promise in her heart, she found solace in the belief that her husband, a beacon of kindness in the face of aggression, was being watched over by celestial guardians in the midst of darkness.

As the rain started to drizzle, a silent testament to the enduring strength of the human spirit, my mother clung to the whispered assurance of the young cadre—a fragile ember of hope amidst the engulfing shadows of tyranny. And in that fleeting moment of connection, a bond that lasted for a very long time was forged—unbreakable in the face of adversity, a testament to resilience in the darkest of times. In the weeks and months that followed, the young cadre continued to deliver short exchanges of messages between my parents. It even went to the extent of suggesting to my father to scribble a small message in his handwriting to reinforce my mother's trust with visual evidence of his existence.

In the heart of Mekelle City, where chaos and conflict brewed like a storm on the horizon, our family navigated the turbulent waters of a nation torn by political upheaval. Eighteen months had passed since the disappearance of my father, a shadow cast long over their once-serene existence. War had descended upon the city's outskirts like a relentless plague, echoing through the streets with the deafening symphony of gunfire and the ominous roar of warplanes overhead.

In the shadow of oppression, the streets whispered tales of disappearances. People vanished silently, leaving only empty spaces and quiet despair. The government and rebels played a cruel game of cat and mouse, snatching innocent souls without a trace of mercy. Homes became haunted by absences, offices haunted by unanswered questions. Years passed, but the truth remained buried in unmarked graves—a grim testament to the atrocities committed. Among the forgotten faces, the military regime's ruthless hand left a trail of sorrow, staining the land with the blood of the young. In the silence, their voices cried out for justice, echoing through the dark corridors of memory.

Schools, once bustling with the laughter of children, now stood silent and deserted, their doors shuttered against the violence that encroached upon their walls. The outskirts of the town bore the scars of battle, with fighters launching sporadic attacks that sent tremors through the fragile peace that still clung to the town.

Amidst the chaos that gripped the country, one beacon of hope flickered faintly on the horizon. My father, imprisoned unjustly during the tumultuous times of the Red Terror, found a glimmer of solace as the political landscape shifted. With the promise of a potential transfer from the informal secret prison managed by cadres to a more formal petitionary facility governed by the Department of 'Justice'—where visits from family members and improved living conditions awaited—a ray of light pierced the veil of uncertainty that had clouded our lives for so long. My father was relocated to the main prison known as 'Carcelli,' nestled among the shadows of long-term inmates bearing the weight of their misdeeds.

It all felt like a miracle. In a land where carnage had reigned and humanity ceased to exist, with all those taken by the cadres never returning, my father was being protected by a divine shield and remained to live to see the sun again.

This act of compassion from the officials and the fact that he remained alive spoke volumes of their regard for my father—a testament to the enduring innocence that transcended the confines of prison walls. The winds of change whispered promises of justice and redemption in the post-Red Terror era, as the regime sought to rectify the sins of the past and hold accountable those who had wielded power with impunity.

As weeks turned into months, a momentous occasion unfolded for our family. Our mother was granted the precious gift of reuniting with her beloved husband for the first time since his imprisonment. Clutching tightly to clothes, blankets, and other essentials, she embarked on the weekly pilgrimage to the prison, her heart heavy with a mixture of trepidation and longing.

In the bleak expanse of the prison yard, under the watchful gaze of stern guards, families reunited in a fragile embrace that transcended the confines of their surroundings. Children laughed amidst the solemnity of the occasion, their innocent voices a balm to the wounded souls of those imprisoned unjustly.

As my father adjusted to the routine of life behind bars in his new home, he found solace in a newfound sense of purpose. Within the prison walls, he embraced the camaraderie of a gardening and carpentry club formed by fellow inmates. Together, they planted vegetables for the prison officers' kitchen, flowers for gifts and bouquets, maintained the greenery in the prison yard, and crafted musical instruments as well as souvenirs—each one a token of love and connection he could offer during our visits.

In the heart of a tumultuous time, my father remained locked within the confines of Carcelli for what seemed like an eternity, with another eight months passing by in the relentless cycle of Sundays spent visiting him. The backdrop of violence and unrest painted a grim picture, yet amidst the chaos, a subtle shift occurred. My father witnessed several violent attempts by rebels who stormed the prison to free their comrades. Many innocent, politically unaffiliated inmates were killed in the crossfire.

The once dominating presence of the red terror had faded, replaced by an uneasy calm, as many chose to flee the country, while others defiantly joined the rebel cause until there was no one left to detain or kill.

For my mother, the burden of holding our family together weighed heavily on her shoulders. Though she refused to voice her struggles, her unwavering faith and silent prayers became her solace. With no support from her family and the memory of luxuries long gone, she navigated the challenges of daily life with a quiet strength that inspired awe. Her fainting fits became a weekly phenomenon that our neighbours grew accustomed to. We reached out for help whenever my mother fell in the house.

In a time when kitchen utilities and washing machines were but distant dreams, and unable to afford a house helper, my mother became a pillar of resilience. She cooked, cleaned, and cared for her children with a tenderness that knew no bounds. And amidst her own trials, she found the capacity to extend her kindness to those within the prison walls who had no family to lean on.

My mother, once the cherished daughter of a wealthy family, basking in the luxury of her surroundings in Asmara, had cruelly been led down a path she could never have imagined. She bore the weight of this transformation with a grace that belied the turmoil within her heart. Every day was a battle, but she refused to let the darkness consume us.

Our home was once filled with the aroma of Sunday Italian feasts and the chatter of guests. Now, a shadow of despair had descended upon the household. Once bustling with life and laughter, our home now stood silent, a stark reflection of the tightening grip of poverty that had enveloped our lives. Once a beacon of vibrant energy and prosperity, our home now stood shrouded in the hushed whispers of poverty and the struggle for survival. The walls that once echoed with laughter and pride now absorbed the weight of uncertainty and hardship. It was a stark reality that none of us could have ever imagined would befall our family.

To buy essentials, my mother had secretly pawned all of her jewellery and other valuable belongings, including a set of precious gold wedding gifts my father had bought for their wedding. In Eritrean tradition, selling wedding jewellery is a mark of ultimate financial desperation, kept secret from society.

In the heart of this lonely home stood a woman of unparalleled strength and unwavering resilience—my mother. She held the fraying threads of our existence together with a fierce determination that bordered on the miraculous. With no income to speak of and no financial support in sight, she became the pillar that supported us in the face of adversity.

Despite our circumstances, my mother ensured that her children were not aching with hunger. She toiled tirelessly to put food on the table, even if it meant sacrificing her share. Her hands, weathered and worn, worked ceaselessly to cook meals that brought a fleeting sense of comfort and nourishment to our weary souls.

But it wasn't just us that she tended to. My mother's compassion extended beyond the confines of our small abode, reaching out to my father and his destitute inmates. She prepared extra portions of food and ventured out into the unforgiving streets, carrying heavy loads of sustenance to those who had hit rock bottom. The generosity that flowed from her stirred a glimmer of hope in the hearts of those who had all but given up. My mother became a secret messenger of hope and news of existence between some inmates and their families, who for months and years had never known where their loved ones were. My father passed names of secretly detained inmates from his previous detention centres, and my mother would find their families and let them know of their location. In that way, my parents became messengers of hope, connecting those separated by the cruelty of the system.

In the chaos and despair of a war-torn region, the prison stood as a grim reminder of the government's neglect. Inmates languished within its walls, their basic needs unmet as the authorities turned a blind eye. It was in this bleak setting that my mother, a beacon of compassion in a world consumed by darkness, became a lifeline for those imprisoned souls.

As families struggled to reach their loved ones, trapped in the city by violence and lack of transport, my mother took it upon herself to ensure that no one went hungry or without essentials. Every day, she would gather provisions and make her way to the prison, a glimmer of hope in the desolate landscape.

Stepping through the imposing gates, she was met with faces worn by hardship and suffering. Yet, her presence brought a spark of light to their eyes, a fleeting moment of respite from their harsh reality. With unwavering determination, she delivered food and sanitary items, offering a touch of humanity in a place devoid of compassion.

As the days turned into weeks and then months, my mother's visits became a source of solace for the inmates and their guards. Sometimes, she made multiple deliveries in one day—feeding the inmates first, and then the stern-faced guards, softening their attitudes by injecting some humanity they had lost in their profession. She baked sweets and brought flasks of coffee and tea for the prison guards to share. In return, the guards slowly showed their respect, changing their overall attitude towards inmates and visitors, confirming the old saying: "The best way to a man's heart is through his belly."

In the darkest of times, my mother's kindness shone brightly, a beacon of love guiding those lost in the shadows, both inside and outside of the prison walls. And so, in a world torn apart by strife and indifference, my mother stood as a testament to the power of humanity—a guardian angel for those who had been forsaken by society and a messenger of God in the absence of worldly hope.

As the months stretched into years, my mother's unwavering spirit remained unbroken. She faced each sunrise with a quiet resolve, never letting despair cloud her vision of a better tomorrow. The sacrifices she made and the tears she shed in the silence of the night all bore witness to the depth of her love for her family.

Amid our trials, my mother emerged as a beacon of strength and resilience—a guiding light in the enveloping darkness. Her unwavering faith in better days ahead fueled our determination to rise above our circumstances and reclaim the vibrancy that once defined our home.

And so, as I look back on those turbulent days, I am reminded of the indomitable spirit of a woman who refused to let poverty snuff out the light of hope. My mother's legacy of courage and compassion will forever be etched into the tapestry of our lives, a testament to the power of love in the face of adversity.

The graceful figure of my mother, once a passionate hostess who delighted in preparing sumptuous meals, now moved through the dimly lit rooms with a weariness that weighed heavily on her shoulders. The vibrant colours that once adorned the walls had faded, and the once-filled dining table sat empty and deserted, a cruel reminder of better days long gone.

As the days passed, the impact of poverty became more pronounced, affecting every aspect of our existence. Food quality diminished, and the once-plentiful provisions dwindled, leaving our family struggling to make ends meet. Yet, amidst this bleak backdrop, a glimmer of hope shone through in the kindness of our neighbours.

Despite facing their own hardships, the neighbours extended a helping hand, sharing whatever they could spare to alleviate the burden of poverty that hung over our household. During festive occasions like Christmas, Easter, and New Year, the neighbours would arrive bearing trays of food, a gesture of solidarity that bridged the gap between despair and hope.

However, the true test of resilience came when our family home, a symbol of privilege and stability, was forcibly taken away by the government. The grandeur of the three-bedroom villa gave way to the harsh reality of eviction, leaving our family displaced and vulnerable.

With no income and severed familial ties, my mother embarked on a desperate quest to find a new home for her five young children. The search led her to a humble two-room house with basic amenities, a stark contrast to the comfort we once knew. The absence of a proper kitchen and the necessity of fetching water from a public source underscored the harshness of our new reality.

Despite the hardships, the community spirit prevailed, with our new neighbours stepping in to offer assistance and support. The collective effort to endure the daily challenges of poverty brought us closer together, forging bonds of solidarity in the face of adversity.

The humble farmers' generosity knew no bounds. Members of the community my father served to protect their land shared their crops with us and became pillars of strength in times of adversity. As word spread like wildfire through the communities about my father's detainment, the village members came together to show their solidarity and support for my father and his family during this trying time. Baskets of eggs, live chickens, corn cobs, and even sacks of wheat and barley were brought from far and wide, each gift a testament to the bond of loyalty for my father.

Some villagers travelled for days, crossing mountains and valleys, their donkeys laden with the precious cargo of grains and charcoal. They arrived at our doorstep, weary yet determined, their faces etched with lines of resilience and hope. The sight of their offerings brought tears to my mother's eyes, overwhelmed by the outpouring of love and compassion from the villagers.

The villagers, comprised of farmers and priests, men and women, some carrying very young infants on their backs, gathered around our home. A sea of faces reflected pain and sorrow, yet they were united in their purpose. The villagers sat down with my mother to offer their support and prayers, their hearts heavy with sorrow yet ablaze with a flicker of hope. The priests turned their gaze towards the heavens, their voices rising in a prayer, a plea for my father's freedom.

"Why have you forsaken one of your own, dear God?" cried out one priest, his voice trembling with emotion. "Have we not served you faithfully? Has he not served you enough through us?"

Communication became a luxury in this new world of deprivation, with even basic amenities like a phone line out of reach for the struggling family. The poignant image of our mother using a neighbour's phone, two blocks away, to stay connected with the outside world epitomised the resilience and resourcefulness required to navigate life on the margins.

Amid scarcity, a peculiar addition appeared in our meagre diet – Soviet military rations with Russian instructions printed on their covers, a symbol of sustenance amid scarcity. The unappealing packaging and bland taste of the field food were transformed into a means of nourishment under the loving guise of our mother, who saw beyond the surface to ensure her children's well-being.

In a quaint home nestled among several neighbours, my mother held a peculiar rule: conceal the origins of our packaged meals. Every package that arrived had its cover ripped off and placed on plates, a secret preserved from prying eyes. "God doesn't approve of flaunting our blessings," she'd murmur, her voice a blend of warning and reverence. We, her children, obeyed, lips sealed with the weight of her words. Neighbours and visitors remained oblivious to our culinary misadventures, shrouded in mystery. Curiosity lingered, but fear of sinning, of defying my mother's wishes, kept us silent guardians of our household's hidden secrets.

Through the vivid tapestry of our daily struggles and victories, a tale of resilience, community, and the enduring power of familial love in the face of overwhelming adversity lives. Our mother emerges as a beacon of strength, a testament to the indomitable spirit that thrives even in the darkest of times. Amid poverty and despair, our family found solace in the bonds that hold us together, illuminating the path forward with hope and courage.

In Asmara, where my mother's family lived, her father, a prominent figure in Eritrean society, had lost his entire wealth to the new government's nationalisation programme, which banned private ownership of land and property. Their extravagant lifestyle, once boundless, is now a distant dream. The political winds began to shift, casting dark shadows over their once-bright existence.

My uncles, on both sides of my parents, were once pillars of strength, their voices ringing with defiance against the oppressive regime that gripped our homeland. But one by one, they vanished into the shadows, fleeing to distant lands or joining the valiant resistance fighters.

Separated by fate and distance, my mother clung to hope, her heart heavy with worry for her beloved siblings. Amid the chaos, a risky lifeline emerged – human traffickers who braved the dangerous journey across the Sudanese border. For a hefty price, they became messengers of news, carrying letters that bore the weight of life and death. Through those secret messages, my mother learned of the ebb and flow of life in Asmara. Some letters brought tears of joy as she heard of those who survived and those who bravely stood against tyranny. Others brought sorrow, revealing the tragic fate of those lost to the cruel whims of fate.

My mother learned to embrace her new reality and to find joy in the small moments of connection and camaraderie. The grandeur of her past life faded into insignificance, replaced by a newfound resilience that bloomed in the harshest of conditions.

And so, in the flickering light of her humble abode, my mother clung to these letters, each word a lifeline connecting her to a past she feared she might never see again. The distant whispers of her brothers echoed in the silence, a bittersweet reminder of the bonds that even the darkest of times could not sever. As the years passed, communication between Asmara and Mekelle became a distant memory, a luxury my family could no longer afford. My mother's once-vibrant world faded to grey, her spirit battered by the harsh realities of her new life without her family and my father.

The bond between my parents, a tapestry of love woven with threads of sacrifice and resilience, held firm against the trials of separation. Each Sunday visit became a lifeline, weaving moments of togetherness amidst the harsh reality of their circumstances. My father sent gifts, crafted with care and shared with love in his carpentry club, which served as a tangible reminder of his enduring presence in our lives. His carpentry products filled our home, from candle holders and chopping boards to musical instruments and carvings shaped into animal characters.

In the backdrop of uncertainty, my mother found a tribe of steadfast friends who stood by her side through thick and thin. Together, they formed a support system that served as a beacon of hope in the darkest of times. Their collective efforts, from assisting with meals for the prison mates to offering practical help in any way they could, underscored the power of community in times of adversity.

Through the lens of hardship and resilience, the story of my family unfolded with poignant grace. Each character played their part in a narrative that spoke of love's resilience in the face of adversity, of strength found in the unlikeliest of places, and of a bond that transcended walls and boundaries. Amidst the trials of separation, the enduring thread of love wove a tapestry of hope that carried us through the darkest of days.

In the prison cells where my father was detained, the air was thick with tension, with no access to news from the outside. It had been nearly two and a half years since my father had been taken away, and every day of his detainment was shrouded in mystery and fear.

In the heart of the nation, turmoil brewed as the regime's governance crumbled. Whispers of uncertainty filled the air, painting a canvas of political chaos. The government resembled a ship adrift in a turbulent sea. Each day brought forth a new decree, a fresh wave of radical changes that left the populace reeling. Military barracks echoed with the shuffling of troops, while civilians braced for the unknown. Amidst the tumult, alliances shifted like sand in the wind, leaving a bewildered populace in its wake. The government had lost its way, dancing to the erratic tune of uncharted waters.

It was amidst this unpredictability that, one evening, a sudden bombshell of news emerged in Carcelli prison as my father was told he had been selected to attend an important meeting the next morning. No further details were given, except that he had to be in his best clothing and show the proper 'manners'. Throughout his detention, my father had been taken to different locations for interrogation, and he thought this one was just another of the same trips. Curiosity engulfed him as to why he was being dressed up for this one.

The morning of the meeting arrived swiftly, and my father was escorted into a fully covered prison van, his heart filled with heavy uncertainty. As dusk settled, the city felt even more tense with the presence of extra military personnel and hardware in every corner.

As the vehicle rumbled through the dusty streets, my father couldn't shake the feeling of impending doom that hung in the air like a heavy fog. The journey seemed endless, each passing moment filled with dread and anticipation. Finally, the truck came to a stop. Blindfolded, my father was led into a building, separated from two inmates. The sound of people and hushed whispers echoed around him. He was ushered into a solitary confinement cell, where he sat in silence, his mind racing with questions and fears. The hours passed slowly, the weight of the unknown pressing down on him like a suffocating blanket.

My father was no stranger to the knowledge of inmates being taken away under different disguises, never to return to their cells, but the fact he was instructed to dress up gave him some optimism and hope. Then, as if from a nightmare, the deafening sound of a military helicopter landing nearby shattered the stillness, signalling his imminent departure to the unknown. The air hung heavy with anticipation as my father sat frozen in fear. The once tranquil surroundings now echoed with the menacing whirl of the military helicopter near him. His heart raced, mirroring the thunderous blades slicing through the air.

As he thought of being ushered towards the metal beast, the chilling rumours of punishment flashed before his eyes. Would he too meet the same fate, thrown out into the abyss for crimes he didn't commit?

After a long silence, my father heard a gentle whisper of men mentioning his name, planning the timing of his transfer to the next room, the auditorium. After a few minutes, uncuffed and unfolded, guided by the new men, my father was led to the main auditorium of the city hall, where a gathering of government officials awaited Mengistu, the military ruler's arrival, with a mixture of trepidation and anxiety.

The hall was surrounded by hundreds of soldiers loyal to Mengistu, with heavy machine guns strapped onto their shoulders, resembling soldiers well-prepared for war, standing among the audience with revolving eyes.

There was a sea of faces, some familiar, others new, all bearing the weight of past mistakes and uncertain futures. With no clue as to why he had been brought there, my father's eyes searched for a glimpse of familiarity in the sea of strangers, a lifeline in the storm of uncertainty.

As Mengistu, a short man in military uniform who had arrived in the giant Soviet-made helicopter, ascended the stage, the room fell silent, only to be broken by thunderous applause. His presence loomed large, casting a shadow of unease.

As Mengistu took the stage, his presence commanding and imposing, a sense of foreboding settled over the room like a dark shadow. Mengistu's words cut through the tense atmosphere like a sharpened blade, his accusations and condemnations landing like blows on the already fragile spirits of his officials. He spoke of betrayal and incompetence, corruption and greed, painting a stark picture of a government in shambles, teetering on the brink of collapse. Each word he uttered pierced the air like a dagger, accusing and condemning. The officials, once proud, now wilted under his gaze, their faces a portrait of guilt and fear.

Mengistu stood as a colossus against a crumbling backdrop, the precursor of a reckoning long overdue. His words of betrayal and incompetence dripped from his lips like poison, staining the very fabric of the government. Corruption and greed, he spat, had woven a web of deceit so intricate that collapse seemed inevitable. He warned that those liable for the suffering of his soldiers would meet their deserving fate on that day. Mengistu, known for his routine execution of officers he deemed inefficient or corrupt, was a highly feared figure.

My father's heart sank as he listened to Mengistu's words, knowing that the fate of some officials hung in the balance. My father had never met Mengistu before, nor had he attended such a highly charged, tense meeting in his lifetime. Piles of handguns and Kalashnikov rifles, with thousands of bullets, lay near the stage where Mengistu sat. They were taken by his soldiers from the army officers who attended the meeting, a measure taken to prevent sudden attempts to attack him in that tense moment.

Accusations of heinous crimes tainted the once-peaceful atmosphere. My father found solace in the fact that he had been far away when the alleged crimes took place. The weight of innocence lifted his burdened heart as he embraced the serenity of solitude. But as the speech drew to a close, a glimmer of hope flickered in the darkness. Mengistu's intentions were clear: he sought to cleanse the ranks of the corrupt and rebuild an autonomous regional government worthy of the people's trust.

Mengistu chaired the meeting by sitting next to one officer, Colonel Hailu Jima, Chief Commander of the army's northern division, in charge of all living and non-living things in Tigray and Eritrea. He was from the same officers' batch as Mengistu, as were most of the leadership at the time.

In Tigray, amidst the turbulent and shifting political landscape, Colonel Hailu Jima was a decisive figure. His presence in the high-ranking echelons of Mengistu's inner circle was not merely a consequence of loyalty and trustworthiness but a testament to his strategic insight and unwavering dedication to the regime he served, as interim governor of the Tigray region in the absence of a trusted civilian to take the role.

Mengistu's heart was heavy with the weight of his soldiers' despair, revealing the devastation at the frontlines. He knew he had to act swiftly. He had just finished a rare and dangerous visit to the frontline, where he listened to the grievances of the soldiers and low-ranking officials. Their eyes were filled with despair, their voices tinged with anger as they blamed their losses on the corrupt army and civilian officials who demanded their sacrifices without accountability.

Mengistu, a man who had climbed the ranks from a lowly officer to a controversial leader, felt a fierce determination burning within him. His hands clenched into fists as he vowed to implement immediate actions to root out the corruption that had infiltrated their ranks.

Earlier that year, in a mysterious game of bribery and betrayal by high-ranking government generals, the Eritrean independence fighters managed to gain undeterred access to the military airfields at Amara airport, destroying the entire airborne fleet, which included jets and helicopters. They also stole several pieces of equipment and fuel, significantly reducing Mengistu's capacity to fight.

In the hours that followed the start of the meeting, a wave of sudden announcements of change swept through the regional leadership, as new faces replaced the old, bringing with them a promise of redemption and reform. Mengistu asked questions and ordered the immediate detention of some of the army generals. In some cases, he called officials by their names and insulted them for their incompetence, belittling and humiliating them by ordering them to go home and help their wives with housekeeping, as they were not fit for the manly positions they held.

The heavy air in the grand hall was thick with tension as Mengistu's booming voice echoed off the walls. His face contorted in fury, emphasising the gravity of his words. Among the sea of faces, my father stood with a mix of disbelief and a flicker of hope igniting within him.

Mengistu, the formidable leader, declared that only a select few could be trusted to navigate the complexities of the war in Tigray. Surprisingly, my father was chosen, his past transgressions seemingly erased by Mengistu's newfound vision for unity and progress. Despite never having met Mengistu before, my father's dedication to his work, integrity, and unwavering commitment to growth had not gone unnoticed.

As Mengistu replaced his incompetent generals with other low-ranking loyalist officers to reinstate the chain of command in the war operations, new officials, who had been driven by bus from other regions the day before, were given different roles in various civic departments. However, my father's role was both new and heavy; he was named the governor of the Tigray autonomous administrative region. It was as if Mengistu had just decided to make Tigray autonomous without consulting anyone, with my father as the highest authority on the land, tasked with implementing Mengistu's unwritten manifesto.

My father was now in charge of the region's civilian and political structures, a position of authority and responsibility, yet devoid of direct military involvement. It was a twist of fate that took everyone by surprise, including my father himself. Therefore, amidst the chaos of war and political intrigue, my father found himself thrust into a new chapter, where forgiveness and redemption paved the way for unexpected opportunities and challenges ahead. Mengistu's belief in placing an ethnically and politically neutral person to bring civil order and cooperation was the consequence of repeated failures and betrayals by previous officials, many of whom were native Tigrayans removed for their atrocities as double agents. In the eyes of Mengistu and other high-ranking officials, only one man could fit that profile—my father.

After meticulously selecting a new team for the important task ahead, Mengistu dismissed the rest of the attendees, ordering the arrest of some officers and leaving only those he deemed essential for the extended meeting. With a commanding voice, he began to give firm orders and instructions, his words laden with the weight of responsibility and expectation.

As the meeting progressed, the newly selected team members found themselves bombarded with questions and comments, each vying for attention and recognition. To my father, it felt like the most challenging mass job interview, as Mengistu asked questions testing their efficiency and willingness to live up to their new responsibilities.

Amidst the sea of voices, there was one figure who remained silent, watching with a sense of unease. This was my father, a man of few words and unfamiliar with such high-pressure environments.

Curiosity sparked in Mengistu's eyes as he turned his attention to my father, asking him with an intimidating attitude, "What is your name and ethnicity, you 'ferenj'?" Sarcastically referring to him as a white man because of his fair skin, Mengistu inquired, his tone sarcastic yet inquisitive. My father hesitated momentarily before revealing his name, a sense of apprehension lingering in the air. It became apparent at this point that Mengistu had nominated my father, a man he hadn't even met before, for the highest role in Tigray to fix all the millennia-old problems.

To everyone's surprise, Mengistu's expression softened as he continued to ask my father why he wasn't talking or asking questions. My father whispered his name, which Mengistu recognised. "Ah, I should have known. You are my top man here, and I have heard commendable things about you; I have every reason to trust you." Mengistu praised, instilling a sense of pride and responsibility in my father's heart, as Mengistu exemplified my father and shared some of his achievements and dedication to civil service. To my father's surprise, Mengistu asked him where he was working at present and if he was ready to relocate immediately, a testament to his unawareness about my father's status. My father, bewildered and unprepared for the question about his current occupation, only answered the latter, confirming he was ready to relocate as needed. In silence, he added to himself, "Yes, relocating from prison to home first would be great."

Mengistu thanked him and promised that his office would swiftly replace his current position to ensure no gaps were left. Moving on to the next person, Mengistu continued his shabby mass job interview with others.

Mengistu had entrusted my father with a pivotal task: to clear the corruption and bureaucracy plaguing the civilian offices reporting directly to him. He assured my father of his support and protection, offering him the opportunity to join the communist party through an enlightenment course and training. My father was taken aback by the sudden turn of events but vowed to work with unwavering trust and dedication.

The meeting stretched late into the night, with Mengistu exuding an air of authority and conviction. As the clock struck midnight, Mengistu demanded a short break for everyone, and without goodbyes, he swiftly departed through the back door back to Addis Ababa, leaving behind a sense of anticipation and responsibility lingering in the room.

As the extended meeting inside the city hall dragged on, and the room gradually emptied of the weary officials, Colonel Hailu remained rooted in his seat, a portrait of stoic resolve. His eyes, sharp and perceptive, surveyed the dwindling group, silently absorbing the weight of the decisions made and the unspoken tensions that simmered beneath the surface.

Outside the city hall, after hearing the news of my father being driven to the heavily guarded city hall, as told secretly by the young familiar cadre who was my father's guardian, my mother and her friends sat outside all day and night, awaiting news of the meeting's outcome. Gunfire was heard from unknown directions, making my mother more anxious about my father's safety. Unaware of Mengistu's presence, they watched as the massive Soviet-made helicopter that carried Mengistu emerged from behind the walls, hovering above them at a low altitude, marking the end of the intense gathering.

With no clue about the shifts in my father's status, my mother returned home, her mind clouded with questions and uncertainty. Little did she know that my father had been promoted, ready to embark on a journey of transformation and responsibility under Mengistu's watchful eye.

As the city hall fell silent, the echoes of Mengistu's orders and promises lingered in the air, setting the stage for a new chapter in my father's life, filled with challenges, revelations, and unwavering loyalty.

Among those who knew my father well was Colonel Hailu, who had crossed paths with him, forming a bond built on mutual respect and shared values. It was this connection that led the Colonel to take my father under his wing, offering protection and guidance in a world fraught with danger and duplicity.

My father's admiration for Colonel Hailu ran deep. In a sea of corrupt and ruthless officials, the Colonel—despite rumours of his battlefield actions, which had seen some of the worst civilian casualties—stood out as a beacon of integrity and wisdom. Colonel Hailu helped my father gain access and protection when visiting the communities he was helping. He intervened on my father's behalf numerous times during his detention, shielding him from the merciless claws of the Red Terror that gripped the nation in fear. His words held sway over junior officials, and his decisions shaped the course of events with unwavering precision.

It was Colonel Hailu's keen insight and recommendation that influenced Mengistu's selection of new officials, elevating my father to the pinnacle of authority in Tigray—a position that carried the weight of civilian governance.

Despite the tumultuous landscape rife with betrayal and power struggles, Colonel Hailu remained a steadfast pillar of stability, his allegiance unwavering even in the face of adversity. It was this steadfastness that prompted him to recommend my father for the crucial position. His neutrality and proven track record marked him as a natural choice in turbulent times that required cool-headed intervention.

Colonel Hailu had visited our home on several occasions before my father's detention. Their closeness, due to their collaboration to reach the communities my father served, was remarkable. Colonel Hailu was a tall, stoic man with sharp eyes that held secrets untold. My mother's Italian meals seemed to captivate him, drawing him back to our table time and again. It seemed natural for an army officer, separated from his family by the vulnerabilities of his work, to enjoy a semblance of home life.

When visiting our home, Colonel Hailu was playful with children. We loved the energy and charisma that surrounded him. Little did we know, he was more than just an army colonel and connoisseur of fine cuisine. He was the guardian angel who silently watched over our family, unbeknownst to us.

It wasn't until much later that we learned the truth. During the dark days of my father's imprisonment, Colonel Hailu had been the one pulling strings behind the scenes, ensuring my father's safety and well-being. He bore the weight of silence, bound by duty and protocol, unable to reveal my father's whereabouts.

Colonel Hailu was responsible for maintaining civic and military order in Tigray and Eritrea, with his authority seemingly boundless. Yet amidst the sprawling dominion he held, there lurked a faction beyond his control—the enigmatic and volatile revolutionary cadres known as *yehizb derjit*. These merciless mobs, armed and cloaked in the guise of guardians of the revolution, operated with impunity under the veil of the government's Red Terror scheme.

Among the countless lives entangled in this web of power and chaos was my father, held captive by the erratic and deadly clutches of the *yehizb derjit*. Desperate to shield my father from the unpredictable wrath of these rogue enforcers, Colonel Hailu wrestled with the reality that even he had no sway over their actions, their autonomy a looming threat to all.

In a daring move, Colonel Hailu orchestrated the covert transfer of my father from the clutches of the *yehizb derjit* to the confines of the civilian prison Carcelli. This was masked under the guise of a falsified fraud case that required police investigation under the Department of Justice. The risk he undertook was monumental, knowing well the potential repercussions his interference could provoke from the unyielding cadres.

As the cloak-and-dagger operation unfolded, a delicate dance played out between power and rebellion, with the lives of many hanging in the balance. It was a precarious gambit—a bold act of defiance against the insurmountable forces that sought to plunge society into chaos. In the end, my father found sanctuary within the walls of Carcelli, shielded from the unforgiving grip of the *yehizb derjit*.

In this world of intertwined fates and unfathomable power dynamics, Colonel Hailu's courageous and clandestine intervention stood as the reason my father remained alive amidst the shadows of uncertainty—a testament to the enduring spirit of resistance against tyranny and oppression.

As the eventful meeting at Mekelle City Hall finally drew to a close, the last echoes of heated discussions faded into the night. Colonel Hailu, a figure of quiet authority in a world fraught with chaos and uncertainty, sat with my father alone in the empty auditorium. They shared personal stories, reflecting on my father's days in prison and their mutual admiration for each other's deeds.

One crisp, clear morning, as the first rays of sunlight filtered through the windows of our modest home, my brothers and I were getting ready for school. Suddenly, the unexpected sight of a white Fiat 124 saloon car, accompanied by two jeeps, coming to a halt outside our house caught our attention. The Fiat 124 was my mother's least favourite car—a wheeled messenger of despair. The memory of my father's arrest flashed briefly in her mind. The jeeps revived the dark days when soldiers ransacked our home. However, this time, the demeanour of the visitors seemed different—calm and non-threatening.

As three men in civilian clothes approached our metal gate, a sense of unease gripped my mother, her face a mixture of fear and uncertainty. Ever since my father's disappearance, every unexpected visitor in a white Fiat 124 brought with it a sense of impending doom.

The man at the forefront spoke in Tigrinya, reassuringly calling my mother *'embeitei'*—a term of royal respect meaning "my master." His warm smile dispelled the tense atmosphere. "Don't be afraid," he said, "we were hoping you'd invite us in for breakfast, as is our tradition. We're here to offer assistance, not cause harm."

Still wary, my mother defiantly asked if he was the one who had arrested my father. The man denied it, saying he had never met my father but hoped to do so in the future.

My mother's expression softened from fear to cautious hope as she led the men inside, grateful for their unexpected kindness. The soldiers in the jeeps stayed stationed outside, watching the unfolding scene with neutral gazes, giving off an air of quiet vigilance.

As we all gathered around the sofa, waiting to hear what they had to say about our father, the men introduced themselves. They belonged to a unit in the national security structure tasked with safeguarding officials and their families—a stark contrast to the oppressive soldiers of before.

The men advised that the children should not go to school that morning and reiterated they would remain in the house until they received further orders from their superiors. My mother, a resolute woman unaccustomed to being shielded or following strict protocols, raised an eyebrow. She asked if we were under house arrest. One of the men replied, "You might call it that, but in a good way. No one is allowed to leave until further instructions from our office."

In the meantime, a large, empty truck approached our home, positioning itself strategically as if preparing for a significant task. It was a stark reminder of past traumas, but this time, there was no sense of fear lingering in the air. On the other hand, we thought the truck was there to take away the rest of the belongings they had left behind during their last raid some two years ago. Nevertheless, the atmosphere did not conform to our thoughts. Instead, there was a shared sense of anticipation, a feeling of unity among us that seemed to melt away the shadows of past hardships.

The day's clocks turned slowly, each passing moment bringing with it a renewed sense of hope and resilience. As cars and trucks surrounded our home, the old family spirit we knew before my father's detention enveloped us, filling the air with a palpable aura of ease and revival.

The smell of fresh-spiced tea floated through the air, comforting the men as they discussed the day's events. Among them, a man burst in from the veranda, clutching a leather-clad transistor radio above his shoulder and tightly holding a Kalashnikov gun with one of his hands. His face was a mix of excitement and trepidation as he raised the radio high and turned up the volume.

"Listen, listen... here it is," he exclaimed, his voice tinged with urgency. The others leaned in, their attention captured by the crackling voice emanating from the device. The infamous music played before all decrees filled the room, bringing a mix of anticipation and anxiety. The reader's voice was distinctively familiar and commanding; it was the same iconic voice that announced the removal of Emperor

Haile Selassie and all other major decrees since, evoking a sense of authority and power that sent shivers down the entire nation's spine.

As the words of the decree unfolded, a wave of emotions washed over our family—fear for the unknown and hope for a better future. Among other high-profile topics, the government announced a significant change in leadership involving one of our own—my father, of the home they sat in.

Upon hearing my father's name and his new title, we were left feeling confused, but the plain-clothed cadres rejoiced involuntarily, hugging each other as if they were our own, congratulating my mother, rubbing the children's heads and telling us we should be proud of our father and follow his footsteps to become great men. The radio's crackling voice faded away, leaving them in a moment of shared joy, pondering the implications of the decree. In that intimate setting, where tea and news mingled, the men braced themselves for the family's reaction to the news, knowing what it meant to us.

The announcement of my father's surprising appointment as the highest authority sparked joy and celebrations in the neighbourhood and beyond, not because of the position he was given but because it marked his freedom from endless detention.

Suddenly, one of the soldiers from the jeep approached my mother with a gentle request to allow a visitor into the house. My mother, puzzled by the notion of needing permission for guests, waved them in, citing the frequent visits of supportive friends. The soldiers, insistent yet respectful, urged her to inspect the visitors before granting entry.

Accompanied by the soldier, my mother reached the gate to find a neighbouring woman terrified, undergoing an invasive body search against the fence. Shocked, my mother demanded an explanation. The soldier, his voice calm but firm, explained that it was a necessary precaution for the family's safety. Upon seeing my mother, the woman screeched in joy, pushing away the soldier who was searching her and hugging my mother. The soldier attempted to reach for his gun to take action, not knowing she was just an ordinary woman, a close neighbour and well-wisher who had come to congratulate my mother after hearing the decree. The tense atmosphere melted into a mix of understanding and discomfort, leaving my mother to grapple with a newfound realization of the protective measures surrounding her family.

The neighbour's house phone, which my mother had used and which had been quiet and lonely for as long as my father's detention, began ringing every minute with calls from well-wishing friends. My mother was escorted to the phone every time. No one could believe what they heard on the morning decree; most called not to congratulate us but to ask my mother to find out if it was true. We were filled with overjoyed excitement and kept asking the men where our father was and when he would be coming home. Clueless, the men answered vaguely, saying he was somewhere and would be home soon. Theirs was a logical answer, but they had no idea where he was.

My mother called Colonel Hailu's office. He wasn't in, but his secretary said she would tell him to ring back. Colonel Hailu had spent the night at the city hall talking to my father. It was strict protocol that officials did not announce new decrees and nominations before they were released on the official radio and in the newspaper, hence Colonel Hailu's silence.

It was a night of transformation and revelation, one that would forever alter the course of our family life. The city hall auditorium had been buzzing with tension and excitement as the decisive meeting unfolded; the fate of many changed instantly.

As the guests dispersed, my father found himself walking alongside Colonel Hailu with no questions asked about where they were heading. My father only wished to go home. Colonel Hailu, a man of power and influence, led my father through the dimly lit tunnels that connected the city hall to the royal palace. The guards trailed behind them, their footsteps echoing in the cold, dark passageways.

Upon reaching the opulent halls of the palace, my father's eyes widened in awe at the grandeur that surrounded him. Colonel Hailu turned to him with a knowing smile, indicating that this was to be his new abode. Exhausted by the dramas of that night, the Colonel insisted that my father take the master bedroom, a room fit for his new position, while he settled into one of the guest chambers.

My father stood in the lavish room, feeling like an imposter in such luxury. His mind flashed back to just a day before, when he was confined to a filthy cell, surrounded by darkness and despair. The contrast was staggering as he gazed at the gilded frames and intricate furnishings that adorned the master bedroom.

Exhausted from the events of the day, my father collapsed onto the plush bedding, still fully clothed. The softness of the sheets was a stark contrast to the harsh reality he had known for so long. As sleep beckoned him, he whispered a silent gratitude for this unexpected turn of events.

The following morning, my father awoke to the sound of birds chirping in the palace gardens. The sun streamed through the windows, casting a golden glow over the room. He marvelled at his surroundings once more, still unable to fully grasp the magnitude of the changes in his life.

Descending the short staircase, my father joined Colonel Hailu for breakfast in the ornate dining hall. Surrounded by royal house staff, the table was laden with delicacies, a feast fit for kings. It was a far cry from the meagre rations he had grown accustomed to in the prison.

Colonel Hailu watched my father with keen interest, his eyes betraying a hint of satisfaction. It was clear that the Colonel had orchestrated this entire turn of events, pulling strings behind the scenes to secure my father's newfound freedom and comfort.

As they dined, Colonel Hailu spoke of the responsibilities and priorities that awaited my father in his new role, reassuring him his bad days were over. He outlined the tasks and duties that lay ahead, offering guidance and support every step of the way. My father listened intently, grateful for the opportunity to make a difference in this new chapter of his life.

Still in his old sweater and faded khaki trousers, my father anxiously awaited to share the joy and news that could change our lives. As per the stringent government guidelines, absolute secrecy had to be upheld until the official announcement via a grand decree on mass media. The weight of this restriction gnawed at him, for it meant he couldn't inform his wife, my mother, immediately.

As the clock ticked on relentlessly, my father's mind wandered back to the humble home my mother and his children had adopted in his absence. The image of my mother's warm smile and unwavering support flickered in his mind, igniting a genuine desire to share the good news. Yet, he remained bound by the ironclad protocols that governed his new world.

At our family home, as lunchtime approached, an order came from another group of higher-ranking men in the same unit. They arrived in a larger Toyota Land Cruiser SUV, ready to transform our lives forever. The new men sounded firm as they told off the former cadres for still being there, stating that the family was no longer meant to stay in that house – it was too risky. They ordered us to act quickly and evacuate everyone.

We were rushed out of the house immediately, with the children put in the Land Cruiser first. My mother was left behind to negotiate a more orderly transfer, as she wasn't prepared to leave the house we had lived in for years in such a rushed manner. Our belongings, our lives, our memories of joy and sorrow, and our loving neighbours were all embedded in that house. It wasn't easy to abandon it just like that.

Without any mention of the destination, the men hurried everyone out, reassuring my mother that they would continue to guard the house and that she would be given a chance to return and take what she wanted safely. They also reminded her that a truck was on standby in case she wanted to take anything with her now.

In a city torn apart by violence, where the shadows of fear loomed over every street, relentless drive-by assassinations and kidnappings of officials and families were daily occurrences, every step the men took was laced with caution. Every decision was weighed carefully, and every move was calculated to perfection. The weight of responsibility bore down on their shoulders to keep us safe, each man carrying the burden of protecting not only themselves but also the families of their new boss – the governor, my father.

In a city where danger lurked at every corner, from unexpected perpetrators, the security men knew they couldn't let their guard down, not even for a moment. Before sunset, we were driven to the Royal Palace, called Emperor Yohannes Palace, named after one of the most outspoken emperors of Ethiopia from the past century. The ancient castle, with an extended modern residential palace built by the British for the Emperor, was the official residence of Ras Mengesha Seyoum, the last prince of Tigray under the monarch's reign.

Located in the heart of downtown Mekelle, this architectural masterpiece was crafted by British architects – a grand palace nestled atop high ground neighbouring the historic city hall, where the fateful meeting took place the night before. Upon reaching the city hall on the way to the palace, my mother told the men that she had spent the previous night sitting outside, waiting for news of my father. One of the men joked, "Yes, ma'am, we were watching you from afar. It would have been better if you came in; you might have been appointed to some important position, just like your husband."

The historic spot where my mother had been sitting on the night that changed our lives is the same square where the Red Terror was staged every week. It's striking how that same square became an undeclared shrine of our death and hope at different times.

Surrounded by towering walls, both the prestigious city hall and the palace buildings stood side by side, exuding an air of grandeur that demanded respect. Acres of meticulously manicured gardens enveloped the palace, creating an enchanting barrier that kept curious eyes at bay.

As we approached the gates at the rear of the palace, we were greeted by heavily armed uniformed guards and military salutes. A soldier, stern yet respectful, approached our vehicle, granting us passage with a solemn nod. The two jeeps still followed us; our journey through the winding path leading to the main palace building felt like a journey through paradise itself, each step bringing us closer to the unknown. In stark contrast to life outside the walls, the palace grounds were paved with clean white marble stones, reminiscent of a fairy-tale movie.

The anticipation bubbled within us as we realised we were being taken to see our father, but little did we know that this visit would mark the beginning of a new chapter in our lives.

Upon reaching the entrance to the central residential structure, my father emerged with Colonel Hailu, both smiling. His presence was a beacon of solace and familiarity. We rushed towards him with uncontainable joy, while my mother stood a few paces behind, her gaze fixed skyward as if seeking divine guidance.

Time seemed to slow as tears cascaded down my mother's cheeks, each drop a testament to the months and years of anguish and separation she had endured. My father's voice, laced with sarcasm but filled with affection, beckoned my mother forward, banishing her fears and uncertainties with a single gesture. Their embrace was a fusion of love and longing, a reunion that transcended the trials and tribulations they had faced.

The echoes of our past reverberated through the opulent halls of the palace, reminding us of the stark contrast between our former life as a humble civil servant's family and the unforeseen twist of fate that led us to the threshold of privilege. My mother, the unsung hero of our saga, had weathered the storm of adversity with a grace and resilience that remained unseen by her children.

As our weary minds crossed the threshold, we were met with a display of formality and grace – the palace's royal staff, adorned in regal uniforms reminiscent of their role under their previous monarch masters, lined up to welcome us. Their faces were etched with strict discipline, a testament to their royal training. It seemed the palace was immune from the revolution.

It was evident how Colonel Hailu orchestrated this transformation, as well as commanded the operations of our careful transfer from our old house, using military radio transmitters at every step of this reunion. His smile symbolised accomplishment and relief. Colonel Hailu told my mother not to waste time and to come in and prepare a good pasta al forno for his deeds. He added that they had been up all night trying to get this done. My mother replied that she would do anything, but God alone had the ultimate means to repay him as he deserved.

With courteous nods, they ushered us, the children, through the ornate halls, each step echoing a sense of grandeur that contrasted sharply with the humble lodgings we had known. My brothers and I couldn't contain our excitement, bounding from room to room, claiming our neatly made separate bedrooms with glee. The vastness of the palace seemed to swallow us whole, a world away from the cramped spaces we had called home for so long.

Amidst our jubilant exploration, I noticed a stark contrast in my parents' demeanour. My mother, usually drawn to beauty and elegance, appeared preoccupied. Her gentle touches lingered on my father's arm, and her words were a constant stream of reassurance, as if she feared he would vanish into thin air. It was clear that the weight of our past struggles still clung to her, casting a shadow over the lavish surroundings.

My father had lost significant weight and glamour. His smile and laughter, a rarity in recent times, filled the air as he strolled through the corridors with a newfound lightness. His eyes sparkled with a childlike joy, erasing the lines of worry that had etched themselves on his face. It was as if the walls of the palace held a magic that banished all traces of our former hardships.

As the day waned and the sun dipped below the horizon, we gathered in the opulent dining hall for a sumptuous feast already prepared by the palace kitchen staff. It was a traditional injera and lamb stew, served in different flavours. The table groaned under the weight of delicacies, milk, yoghurt, and fruits – a feast fit for the occasion. Servants moved with practised grace, attending to our every whim with silent efficiency. We ate like we hadn't eaten for months, and so did my father, a reminder of how not only our minds had been starving for good nurturing but also our bodies.

As the evening settled in after the sumptuous feast, Colonel Hailu raised his glass amidst the laughter and clinking of cutlery. "I won't take this meal for the payback you owe me," he said. With a dramatic flourish, he vowed, "I shall return soon for a good feast of pasta al forno, mark my words!"

He jokingly reminded my mother, "You know I don't get to eat good food. I live on those Soviet rations... You know well what I mean," a reminder of the secretly delivered rations we used to eat. Little did we know Colonel Hailu was behind those dark green boxes, delivered by his guards after dark to help with the poverty we were facing.

Amidst the clink of fine china and the murmur of contented conversation, I remember the moment my family rejoiced. My mother's eyes, softened by the warm glow of the chandeliers, found solace in my father's presence. My father's smile, radiant in the flickering light, held a promise of brighter days ahead – a silent reassurance that we had finally found our place in this palace of dreams.

On that first evening in our new lives at the grand palace, a sense of awe enveloped every corner as we stepped foot into a realm of opulence and luxury. The intricate architecture, the elegant furniture, and the majestic aura of the palace left everyone breathless, our eyes wandering in wonder. However, amidst the mesmerising surroundings, my mother stood out for her unassuming nature, her focus unwaveringly fixed on my father and her children, ensuring our comfort and happiness in this unforgettable moment.

As we settled into our newfound abode, the familiarity of our old life clashed with the luxury that now surrounded us. The palace, with its blend of historic charm and modern amenities, became our sanctuary, a place where our family could heal and grow together. Amidst the grandeur and splendour, it was the love and strength of my parents that truly transformed the palace into a home, a refuge from the tumultuous world outside.

As the lavish dinner concluded, we settled on the expansive sofa in the grand living room. My father engaged in casual conversation with Colonel Hailu while my mother found herself encircled by her children, much like a queen surrounded by her devoted subjects. Her presence exuded warmth and comfort, drawing us closer to her side like small kittens reluctant to leave their mother's embrace.

The attentive maids glided gracefully into the room, bearing trays of steaming tea and coffee for the adults and cups of warm milk for us, the children. With each delicate set of porcelain and silverware they placed before us, my mother's eyes sparkled with admiration. She marvelled at the beauty and quality of each piece, her words flowing in appreciation as she admired the intricate details of the chinaware that adorned the table.

While the rest of us revelled in the luxury of being served, my mother's humility shone through as she struggled to adjust to being pampered by others. Her innate sense of independence propelled her to her feet each time she desired something, determined to fetch it herself. With a gentle but firm insistence, the maids, already charmed by her humble demeanour, urged her to remain seated, assuring her that they were there to cater to her every need.

In a brief moment of respite, my mother's gaze wandered beyond the splendour of the palace to the faces of her loved ones, her eyes soft and full of affection. Despite the grandeur surrounding her, it was in the simple moments like these, surrounded by her family, that she found her true contentment and joy. The gentle hum of conversation, the clinking of silverware, and the laughter of her children filled the air, infusing the room with a sense of peace and belonging.

As the night drifted on, the palace walls echoed with the laughter and chatter of our newfound camaraderie. My mother, a pillar of strength and love, sat nestled in the heart of our family, her presence a beacon of warmth and solace in the midst of luxury and grandeur. And at that moment, amidst the splendour of the palace, we found that the true essence of happiness lay not in material wealth but in the bonds of love and togetherness that bound us together as a family.

As the night drew to a close and we retired to our luxurious chambers, a sense of gratitude washed over us. In this palace of splendour, amidst the trappings of royalty, we had found more than just a home – we had discovered a sanctuary where our past faded into insignificance, and our future shone with endless possibilities.

In the embrace of that iconic architectural marvel, we found not just a shelter but also a sanctuary of love, forgiveness, and resilience – a testament to the enduring power of family bonds and the spirit of those who weather life's storms with unwavering grace. As we gazed upon the towering walls that guarded our newfound haven, we knew that within those walls, our family's story would continue to unfold, rich with the echoes of our past and the promises of our future.

Days turned into weeks, and my father settled into his role with ease, making the palace his family's new residence. He proved himself to be a diligent and dedicated member of the civic leadership, earning the respect and admiration of his colleagues. The whispers of his past faded into obscurity as he embraced his new identity with grace and humility.

And so, the once-forgotten man found his place among the elite, his past hardships a distant memory. As he looked out over the palace grounds, basking in the warmth of the sun, my father knew that he was exactly where he was meant to be – a testament to the power of second chances and the resilience of the human spirit.

Kings At Heart

Stand By Me

In the midst of the chaos and uncertainty that gripped the cities and towns of Tigray, the palace seemed untouched by the political and ideological storms. As the rest of the region plunged into turmoil with fighting, assassinations, and lawlessness, the palace stood as a bastion of old-world charm and tradition.

The palace staff, comprising cooking staff, ushers, servants, babysitters, drivers, and even mechanics who had served the previous imperial residents, maintained their roles with unwavering dedication. Their daily routines, protocols, and titles remained intact, a stark contrast to the changing world outside, where communism and equality among citizens were preached on every level of society. The disciplined staff operated as if they were guarding a time capsule of the past, a relic of a bygone era.

Amidst this backdrop of stability, a new chapter began for our family, as we found ourselves thrust into the heart of this regal enclave. My father's new role as regional governor attracted a mix of admirers and adversaries. The heightened security measures surrounding our lives brought a sense of unease as the family adjusted to the peculiarities of palace living.

Daily life within the palace was a surreal experience, akin to residing within a military fortress. Soldiers patrolled the grounds, armoured vehicles lined the perimeter, and the air was punctuated with the sounds of military exercises. My brothers and I, all very young children at the time, navigated this new reality with a sense of trepidation and curiosity. We joined the soldiers every weekend, running around the palace perimeters just for fun.

School routines were transformed under the watchful eye of armed guards, who accompanied us, ensuring our safety in a volatile environment. The presence of soldiers in and around the school became the norm, offering a stark reminder of the danger that loomed just beyond the palace walls.

As our family delved deeper into this new world of privilege and peril, we began to uncover the intricacies of palace life. The corridors echoed with whispers of past glories and present uncertainties, a juxtaposition of grandeur and apprehension. The luxury of the surroundings clashed with the palpable tension that hung in the air, creating a sense of unease that lingered in every corner.

Through my father's new occupation, we were transported into a world where tradition clashed with modernity, where the secure walls of the palace offered protection while also trapping its inhabitants in a gilded cage.

Our family grappled with the complexities of this new reality – the thrill of living in a palace tempered by the constant shadow of danger. The risks to all members of our family came against the backdrop of a tumultuous political landscape filled with kidnapping and assassination, each one of us navigating our struggles and triumphs within the confines of the regal estate.

In the new golden era of palace living, our family found itself amidst a whirlwind of change. Though we were grateful for the renewed life with our father, it quickly became evident that this newfound luxury came with its own set of risks and constraints that tainted the fairy-tale facade we had imagined.

Big dinners adorned with crystal chandeliers and lavish centerpieces became the norm, setting the stage for the elaborate dance of power and diplomacy that unfolded within the palace walls. My father, an unaffiliated government official revered for his mediating prowess, donned the role of peacemaker and negotiator, welcoming a myriad of guests with varying energies and intentions into our opulent home.

Representatives of rebel groups, their eyes fraught with wariness and suspicion, often arrived at our doorstep demanding to keep their guns close and their bodyguards even closer. Aiming to maintain the continuation of the negotiations, despite the unease that lingered in the air, my father, ever the trusting soul, permitted these armed rebels to enter the palace, where negotiations would take place under the watchful gaze of their armed entourage, their firearms gleaming ominously in the dimly lit corridors.

Amidst this tumultuous backdrop, my mother, the epitome of grace and hospitality, would preside over these unusual guests, offering them steaming cups of fragrant tea and delicacies fit for royalty. The rebel bodyguards, displaying a curious mix of obedience and respect, would graciously partake in these offerings, their hardened facades momentarily softening in the presence of my mother's gentle warmth.

The tension within the palace walls sometimes reached a crescendo during meetings that brought together government army generals and representatives of disparate rebel factions, some of whom had never laid eyes on each other before. Accusations flew like sharpened arrows, plunging the grand halls into a fevered debate teetering on the brink of open conflict. The air hummed with a palpable sense of impending chaos as the looming presence of security personnel became pronounced, their stern faces mirroring the gravity of the situation unfolding within.

As we, the children, nestled in this captivating yet dangerous world, my brothers and I found ourselves confined to the safety of our bedrooms, shielded from the tumultuous affairs of the palace. Our days were punctuated by hours of diligent study under the watchful eye of the palace staff, our innocent laughter mingling with the whispered warnings that echoed through the corridors, cautioning us against venturing into the heart of the storm brewing in the main hall.

Each passing day brought with it a heightened sense of unease; the once-gleaming palace was now shrouded in an aura of uncertainty and tension. The routine of grand dinners and high-stakes negotiations became a delicate dance on the edge of a precipice, where one wrong move could plunge us headlong into the abyss of conflict and armed fighting.

As the days turned into weeks and the weeks into months, the palace walls bore witness to a tapestry of intrigue and power play, each thread woven with the intricacies of politics and the fragility of peace. And though our father's noble efforts as a mediator continued to cast a faint flicker of hope amidst the encroaching darkness, the reality of life in the palace, far from the fairy tales of our dreams, taught us that even the most glittering façade could crumble beneath the weight of ambition and strife.

In the opulent walls of the palace, my mother, adorned with grace and elegance, navigated through her days surrounded by a dedicated household staff. Their unwavering presence was like a symphony, each member playing their part seamlessly. While my mother had a penchant for the culinary arts and took joy in preparing meals for her family, the kitchen staff, with their precision and expertise, insisted on carrying out the culinary duties themselves.

Despite her initial resistance, my mother soon relinquished control in the kitchen as she saw the enthusiasm and dedication of the staff. They approached each task with a meticulousness that mirrored her own, quickly mastering the intricate recipes that once belonged solely to my mother. The fragrant aromas that wafted through the corridors of the palace were a testament to their skill and passion.

In contrast to her culinary endeavours, my mother found herself at odds with the domestic staff when it came to the simple act of making her bed. Each morning, she would attempt to straighten the sheets and fluff the pillows, only to be gently intercepted by the attentive attendants who insisted on tending to the task themselves. Despite her protests, they saw to it that every corner of the bed was perfectly arranged, leaving my mother with idle moments that she hadn't experienced in years. My mother joked with the staff about how she made five beds, washed piles of children's dirty clothes and bedsheets with bare hands, and completed several other tasks on her own every morning.

With the constant presence of a special prayer room inside the palace, filled with several Biblical and religious books and a caring staff around her, my mother's struggle with epilepsy showed remarkable improvement in the relative peace of mind she embarked upon in the palace. The once debilitating seizures had become less frequent, allowing her to find a sense of stability, both physically and mentally. The prayers and blessings from the divine power seemed to have a calming effect on her, soothing the storm within. And in that sacred space, where prayers mingled with holy water and even priests came regularly to pray with her and for her, my mother found a semblance of peace, a respite from the tumult of her illness. The palace became a beacon of light in her journey, illuminating a path towards healing and hope.

It was during these stolen moments of leisure that my mother rediscovered her love for knitting and sewing. The gentle click-clack of knitting needles filled the air as she worked tirelessly on crafting sweaters for each member of our family. Her hands moved with practised ease, creating intricate patterns and designs that spoke of her creativity and devotion. With each completed garment, she would inquire about our preferences for the next, ensuring that each sweater was tailor-made to our tastes.

As the days passed in a tranquil rhythm within the palace walls, a new dawn broke with the arrival of a significant change. My father's prestigious position afforded our family access to communication lines that extended all the way to Asmara, a city teeming with stories of war and killings, as well as memories from our past. It was Colonel Hailu, attuned to my mother's yearning to reconnect with her roots, who orchestrated the intricate arrangements that would allow her to communicate with her family in a far-off land.

The military communication apparatus became the conduit through which my mother's voice reached across borders and mountains. The palace phone, now linked to the secure military network under the authorisation of Colonel Hailu, served as a lifeline to her loved ones in Asmara. Every call was a meticulously planned affair, requiring advanced notice and a series of intermediaries to connect my mother to her distant family members.

The process was convoluted, reminiscent of wartime communications, with my mother having to relay her wishes through a chain of operators until her voice finally reached its intended destination. The crackling static and occasional interference from military transmissions added an air of urgency and intrigue to each conversation, as if the weight of history and conflict hung in the air alongside the words spoken between family members. My mother extended her privilege to others by connecting many Eritrean families in similar situations, allowing them to make calls whenever they wished. This humanitarian service brought lives together and bridged long-lost families once more.

Despite the challenges and obstacles that came with this newfound mode of communication, my mother's voice remained a beacon of love and resilience, bridging the physical distance between us and our kin in Asmara. Through the unpredictable connections and the din of soldiers and rebels on the line, her unwavering spirit shone through, reminding us of the strength and bonds that transcended borders and time.

My mother would regularly sit by the rotary landline, waiting for the familiar ring that brought news from her homeland. Each phone call brought a mix of emotions, a rollercoaster of highs and lows that had defined the past five to six years of her life.

The crackling voice on the other end would relay stories of tragedies and developments, painting a vivid picture of the turmoil that had engulfed her family and friends. Some had fallen victim to the violence; others had fled their homes, seeking safety in distant lands. And then there were those who had passed away from the relentless grip of natural causes, leaving a void that could never be filled.

However, amidst the sorrow, there were glimmers of hope. The news of marriages and births brought joy and warmth to her heart, reminding her that life, despite its challenges, continued to flourish and renew itself.

As she listened to each tale, my mother held onto the memories of her life as a young girl, reconnecting with her past, weaving them together with the present to create a tapestry of resilience and love that bound her to her roots, no matter how distant they may seem. Each phone call ended with a bittersweet melody, a reminder of the fragility and beauty of life's delicate balance.

As the days turned into weeks and the weeks into months, the palace transformed into a tapestry of memories, woven together by the threads of family, tradition, and the enduring resilience of a mother's love. And in the heart of it all, my mother, with her needles clacking and her voice echoing across the miles, remained the steadfast pillar around which our lives revolved, a living testament to the power of connection and the enduring legacy of home.

My father continued to juggle his new responsibilities, using every opportunity to compensate for his family's emotional and material loss suffered in his absence. Despite his busy schedule, filled with office work and frequent travel to the capital, Addis Ababa, he always found time to play games and wrestle with us, tell us funny and humbling stories from his prison days, and, of course, the classic tales of how he met our mother. On weekends, he played football with us on the grounds of the palace, sometimes with members of the guarding soldiers in our team, kicking us and the ball with their army boots.

In the heart of a grand palace, hidden behind towering walls of stone and ivy, we existed in a world of our own. While the lush gardens and sprawling courtyards stretched around us, we were not privileged to play beyond the palace gates. Restrictions loomed over us like shadows cast by safety and the unspoken rules of class and hierarchy. Our only neighbours were the sons and daughters of the palace staff, who sometimes accompanied the servants. Their lives intertwined within the confines of the royal estate, just like ours.

Within the palace walls, a bustling community of dedicated staff members worked tirelessly to ensure the smooth running of the 'royal' household. My mother observed with a keen eye how most of the palace staff, from the cooks to the cleaners, travelled long and arduous journeys to come to work each day. Many of them came from nearby villages, leaving behind their families to embark on dangerous roads in the early hours of the morning. The weight of this knowledge settled heavily upon my parents' hearts, prompting them to take action.

With a determination fueled by empathy and a desire for change, my mother approached the palace estate managers. Together, they devised a plan to repurpose some of the disused servant rooms within the palace grounds to accommodate the families of the staff. This significant gesture meant that the hardworking individuals could now live in the safety of the palace, close to their workplace.

Not stopping there, my parents went above and beyond to ensure a brighter future for the staff's children. They spearheaded the allocation of schools for the youngsters, granting them access to education within the palace's proximity, some of them attending the public schools we went to. Furthermore, my parents worked tirelessly to provide learning and employment opportunities for the staff and their spouses in their free time, within and outside the palace walls. The transformative impact of these initiatives was profound, elevating the quality of life and opening doors to new opportunities for the dedicated workers and their families.

Armed with a compassionate heart and unwavering resolve, my mother took it upon herself to educate the staff about the responsibilities that came with these newfound privileges. To her surprise, the staff seemed to already possess a deep sense of awareness regarding their duties, their gratitude shining through in their every action.

As the days passed, the palace grounds witnessed a remarkable change in demography. New civilian faces and the laughter of children echoed through the previously quiet corridors. The servants' quarters, located about two hundred metres away from the main palace building, served as self-contained living spaces, separated by a gated wall that delineated the boundary between luxury and humble abodes.

Over time, the gates to the servants' quarters began to stay permanently ajar as the once distinct worlds started to merge. Curiosity bloomed within our young minds, drawing us closer to the welcoming environment of the staff's living quarters. We found ourselves venturing into the yards, playing joyfully with the children of the dedicated workers.

While my parents welcomed this newfound integration with open arms, the staff remained cautious, as if unsure of the moral implications of this unexpected mingling. At times, they would gently steer us back towards the main building, hesitant to fully embrace the newfound proximity between worlds.

The palace staff, wary of their children mingling too freely with the young children of their 'masters', kept a close eye on their interactions. There were whispered warnings of the dangers of crossing social ranks, of the consequences that could befall those who dared to mix with the 'masters'. Some parents forbade their children from playing with us, erecting invisible barriers that divided the children even further.

Despite the restrictions imposed upon them, we found solace in our shared experiences and forged bonds that transcended social boundaries, seeking out hidden nooks and secret passageways where we could escape the watchful eyes of their parents to play with us. In these moments, they were free and liberated from the constraints of their birth and social standing. The staff were reluctant to break the traditions they learned from their previous masters, who maintained strict boundaries in fear of blame and repercussions if anything went wrong.

Undeterred by these initial reservations, my mother extended gestures of kindness and inclusivity towards the staff and their families. She would often gift the children sweets and fruits, encouraging a sense of camaraderie and shared joy. But even in these simple acts of generosity, there lingered a respectful acknowledgment of boundaries, as the children were always instructed to seek permission from their parents before partaking in the offerings.

In the palace, amid the expanse of elegance and privilege, a bridge was being built between two worlds. Through her compassion and dedication, my mother sparked a transformation that transcended social barriers, ushering in a new era of unity and understanding within the palace walls. As the laughter of children echoed across the gardens, it became clear that the true wealth of the kingdom lay not in gold and gems, but in the bonds of compassion and shared humanity that now flourished within its very heart.

In a realm where the boundaries between mystic relics and societal classes were blurred, the palace grounds were a hub of intrigue and wonder. The staff children, privileged to interact closely with the formidable palace guards, often found solace in exploring the mysterious barracks that housed the protectors of the realm.

Among these inquisitive souls was my older brother, Simon, whose insatiable curiosity often led him to unearth hidden treasures within the barracks. One fateful day, Simon ventured with his peers to the heart of the soldiers' abode and stumbled upon a peculiar sight—a weathered frame hanging above a soldier's bunk, depicting the majestic "flying rooster."

To Simon's astonishment, he recognised the image instantly, exclaiming, "That is our rooster... I found our rooster, it is here!" In a repeat of the similar reaction our mother had some years ago when the flying rooster disappeared, a soldier, bemused by Simon's claim of being the rooster's secret guardian, questioned whether he referred to the rooster itself or the framed picture, puzzled by the significance Simon attached to the aged photographic work.

Simon's audacious forays into the barracks were a testament to his thirst for knowledge, risking the consequences of trespassing into forbidden areas.

Running back with excitement and urgency, he relayed his discovery to our mother, who, sensing the importance of the message, dispatched the estate manager to investigate further. Oblivious to the artifact's history, the estate keeper, accompanied by Simon, retrieved the frame and presented it to our mother.

As my mother's eyes lit up with joy and recognition at the sight of the rooster, she clutched the frame tightly, reminiscing about its lost significance. The estate manager, witnessing this emotional reunion, vowed to uncover the origins of the treasured relic. Through the soldiers' accounts, it was revealed that the frame had been pilfered as collateral from a comrade who had defaulted on a mere two cigarettes borrowed from the current possessor. On one corner of the frame was a wrinkled black-and-white picture of the soldier and his young girlfriend posted on the outer side of the glass, which our family still holds as treasured memorabilia of the rediscovery of the flying rooster from its brief captivity.

In a realm where past and future intertwined, the discovery of the flying rooster symbolised not just a forgotten heirloom but a connection between various times of upheaval, bridging the gap between our harsh past and a delightful present. And as the story of the rooster's reclamation spread, it became a testament to the benefits of some children's brave and defiant attitude to explore beyond the rules set by their guardians, signalling the slow return of our family's happier days.

The soldiers who raided our house after my father's arrest some three years ago had acted without orders, driven by greed for anything they deemed valuable. Among the stolen possessions was the flying rooster, one that held deep sentimental value to our family.

Simon, undeterred by the consequences of his trespassing act into the barracks, had made a priceless discovery that brought one of our father's prized treasures back to its glorious place—our family's possession, where it belonged.

Encouraged by the discovery of the flying rooster, my father navigated various avenues trying to trace and retrieve our stolen belongings. Unrecognisable by name or division, these soldiers were like ghosts in the turmoil of the conflict, consumed by their own inner battles. Some bore the weight of regret in their haunted eyes, hinting at the senseless violence they had witnessed and partaken in.

Among them, my father noticed a young soldier among the palace guards, his gaze a mix of guilt and fear. Intrigued by his presence, he approached him tentatively, seeking answers. To his surprise, the soldier opened up, revealing the chaos that had led to the raid on our home. He spoke of a bleak reality where young soldiers like him were pawns in a larger game, lost in the senseless brutality of politics and war.

With newfound understanding, my father realised that the soldiers, too, were victims of a war that devoured everything in its path. My father had forgiven the soldiers, a bond forged by compassion—a fragile beacon of humanity amidst the chaos of conflict—promising himself not to pursue his complex and fruitless mission of recovering our belongings.

After the school days ended, we retreated into the vast halls and chambers of the palace. Here, we found solace in each other's company, forming a tight-knit circle that transcended the boundaries of our respective family positions.

With little homework to occupy our time and restrictions on the other children, we turned to games to pass the long hours within the palace walls. My father introduced us to the world of board games. Scrabble became our favourite pastime, the intricate dance of words filling the air with excitement and competition. Chess followed, with its intricate moves and strategic manoeuvres, challenging our minds and sharpening our intellects. Card games became a staple, the flick of a wrist and the turn of a card bringing moments of triumph and defeat.

The Scrabble and chess boards we played on were daily reminders of my father's life behind prison walls. They were all beautifully crafted by him in his prison carpentry club and gifted to us when we visited him on Sundays. These beautiful masterpieces weren't used until he came home and showed us how to play.

As we immersed ourselves in these games, sometimes with my father when he was free, we discovered a new world of possibilities. The intricate rules and strategies of Scrabble taught us the power of words, the beauty of language, and the importance of thinking ahead. Chess honed our strategic thinking, teaching us to plan our moves carefully and anticipate our opponent's next move. Card games fostered quick thinking and adaptability as we learned to navigate the twists and turns of luck and chance.

Through these games, our minds expanded, our skills sharpened, and our bonds deepened. We grew closer, united by the shared joy of competition and camaraderie. In the hushed corridors of the palace, our laughter rang out like music, echoed through the ancient halls and chambers. We revelled in our newfound activities. Our days were filled with laughter and learning as we honed our skills and forged lifelong friendships. And though we were confined within the walls of the palace, we found freedom in the world of games and imagination we had created for ourselves.

And so, within the walls of the palace, a new chapter in our lives began. Our love of games united us, forever connecting us by the unbreakable bonds of friendship that had blossomed within the gilded confines of our world. And though the outside world may have looked down upon us, within the palace walls, we were kings of our own realm, where imagination knew no limits and friendship knew no bounds.

In the heart of the grand palace grounds, my father decided to instil a love for nurturing the land in us, his children and the offspring of the palace staff. Each of us was allocated a plot of fertile land, where we were tasked with cultivating a bounty of vegetables—from the slender elegance of carrots to the leafy emerald of spinach and the comforting solidity of potatoes.

Under the watchful eye of my father, who seemed to possess a sixth sense of the needs of plants, we embarked on a journey of growth and discovery. The gleaming array of agricultural tools that adorned the palace shed became our trusted companions, helping us to till the soil, plant the seeds, and tend to our little green kingdoms with care.

As the spirit of friendly competition infused our daily routine, the promise of rewards for the best growers hung in the air like a sweet fragrance, driving us to water our plots with diligence and shield them from pests.

Every evening, my father would make his rounds; he would inspect each plot, offering gentle advice and sharing the wisdom of generations past. His words nourished our budding skills and fostered a sense of camaraderie among us. Though we competed for the title of the best grower, in my father's eyes, we were all winners—each a testament to the power of patience, dedication, and love for the land.

And when the time came to harvest the fruits of our labour, we gathered the vibrant produce from our plots. The bounty was divided between our family and the palace staff, a gesture of generosity that mirrored the spirit of unity that flourished among us.

My father's journey was one of resilience and determination, from humble beginnings to a position of influence. As fate would have it, he found himself in a highly privileged role, not for personal gain but to serve a greater purpose.

Behind the towering walls of the palace, life persisted with a deceptive veil of tranquillity that shielded us children from the chaotic world outside. Despite the tumultuous political climate that had plagued the country for years, within those opulent walls, our days were a sanctuary of play, joy, and laughter.

As the dust of family hardship settled and the echoes of past struggles began to fade, a semblance of normalcy seeped back into our lives. Our family was fortunate enough to be among the privileged few nestled in the safety and stability of the palace. However, we found ourselves trapped in a web of power struggles and conflicting allegiances.

My father, a civilian figure caught in the crossfire of political machinations, faced relentless pressure from native Tigrayans, pretentiously aligned with the Derg, seeking to shift the tides of power within their region. Despite his impartial role, suspicions clung to him like shadows, fuelled by insidious rumours orchestrated by those ethnocentric individuals coveting his position for their hidden political agenda.

As my father executed his duties, making his humanitarian work a priority, he ensured that all political prisoners in Tigray were freed following a reinvestigation of their individual cases. Most prisoners, detained and tortured for months or years without any substantial evidence of their alleged crimes of dissent or anti-government activities, were reunited with their families and returned to their livelihoods. This was a risk my father took in the face of uncertainty and lawlessness in a land ruled by ruthless gangs such as the Yehizb Dirijit.

The air within the palace was heavy with tension, whispers of assassination plots weaving their way through the corridors like evil spirits. While the rebels were painted as the orchestrators of these sinister schemes, the truth unfurled a different tale – one woven by traitorous hands seeking to usurp my father's authority for their selfish gains. Some were familiar figures who visited our home regularly as private guests or came to meet my father during out-of-hours urgent meetings.

Among these opportunistic individuals lurked charismatic figures adept at manipulating the hearts and minds of their people. Leveraging historical grievances between Eritreans and Tigrayans, they painted a narrative of oppression and discrimination, rallying support from extremist pro-Tigray groups with dreams of independence.

As the dangers loomed larger, security measures tightened around us like a suffocating shroud, restricting our movements and confining us within the gilded confines of the palace. Even my mother, socially active in her circles of friendship, found herself a captive of circumstance, unable to step beyond the palace gates. No one was allowed in or out of the palace, and even some members of the palace guards were implicated in the conspiracies for financial gains and promised promotions after my father's removal. Some were detained; others relocated, leaving no one to trust.

With prolonged restrictions on re-joining school for our safety, a retired teacher turned private tutor was brought in to ensure that we did not fall behind in our studies. Armed with textbooks and a heart full of patience, he guided each child individually through our lessons, instilling in us a thirst for knowledge that matched the intensity of my passion for art.

The staff children, who continued to attend school, became the bearers of tales from the outside world, regaling their classmates with stories of adventures and mischief, of mysteries unravelled and lessons learned. Each whispered anecdote was met with a mixture of curiosity and wistfulness as we clung to these fragments of normalcy in a world that seemed increasingly distant.

As the days turned into weeks, we found ourselves forming a tight-knit community within the confines of our home, cut off from the rest of the world. Playful laughter and spirited debates filled the air. Hungry for knowledge and reading, with no access to other books, we resorted to reading communist magazines and indoctrination books we found around our home and the guards' accommodations. Despite the warmth of our companionship with the staff children who were still allowed to attend school, a sense of longing began to seep into our hearts – a yearning for the familiar rhythms of school life and the comforting presence of our friends.

Whenever we returned to school for a short period, until we were restricted again, unbeknownst to my teachers, I had delved into the depths of communist literature in a desperate quest to satisfy my hunger for reading in a world of little or no choices for children's books. Having read most of the books at home, mostly chosen by their covers rather than their content, one stood out among the sea of books I devoured – Karl Marx's *Capital*, a profound exploration of the tenets of socialism.

At the mere age of ten, I had immersed myself in the Amharic-translated three volumes of *Capital*, each page a revelation, each idea a spark igniting my young imagination into the utopian world it introduced. The words of Karl Marx painted a vivid picture of a world where communal spirit reigned supreme, where wealth was shared, and equality was worshipped. The privilege that the likes of the palace staff and children didn't have was not just a dream but a tangible reality.

With each passing chapter, I found myself drawn deeper into the intricate web of communist philosophy. The idea of a society built on cooperation and solidarity resonated with me in ways I could not fully articulate. It was as if I had discovered a new bible through which to view the world, a lens that brought clarity to the chaos and confusion that had clouded my young mind.

As I delved into the depths of *Capital*, I found myself questioning the very fabric of society, challenging the norms and conventions that had shaped my worldview. The book became my bible, my guiding light illuminating a path toward a future where the barriers of class and privilege would crumble, and a new dawn of equality would rise.

For a child who had pondered the mysteries of creation and evolution, *Capital* offered a different kind of truth, a truth rooted in the principles of social justice and collective progress, with little or no worries about how we were created. It spoke to my heart in a language I instinctively understood, drawing me into a world where every voice was heard, and every individual mattered.

Therefore, with a newfound sense of purpose and determination, I took the wisdom of *Capital* and the fire of youthful idealism burning in my heart. I set out to challenge the status quo, to question the foundations of a society that had long overlooked the voices of the marginalised and the oppressed.

As the final pages of *Capital* turned beneath my fingertips, I knew that I had found not just a new religion but also a calling – a purpose that would shape my destiny and define my legacy for generations to come. In the quiet depths of my soul, the seeds of revolution had been planted, waiting to bloom into a future where the dreams of a young boy could become the reality of a new world. As I crossed that invisible boundary, I knew that the creativity and skills honed in moments of desperation would be my guiding light in the ever-unfolding journey that lay ahead.

In the backdrop of this journey of knowledge and enlightenment, my journey of self-discovery intertwined with my exploration of communism, creating a tapestry of growth and transformation.

My love for art and literature became intertwined with no inspiration or admiration for the subjects in the portraits I was drawing. In my young mind, individuals didn't matter. Humanity and worldwide social justice, forming a singular vision of a world where creativity and equality walked hand in hand, became my motto.

I found myself captivated by the words that filled the dense pages of books that my father, a diligent civil servant in the process of being converted to communism involuntarily, would bring home after his meetings in Addis Ababa. The topics that my father delved into were foreign yet familiar, echoing the essence of his daily toils – the importance of basic knowledge, the notion of abolishing private land ownership, and the advantages of collective farming. It was as if the author had peered into my father's daily struggles and penned them with precision, leading me on a path of inspiration and enlightenment.

As I grew more curious about my father's work and the principles embedded in those pages, a newfound bond formed between us. The discussions we shared delved deep into the realms of societal structures and economic systems, with probing questions often met with my father's patient explanations. It was during these moments of serious debates and recitals of chapters from *Capital* and *The Red Book* that my father and his friends humorously referred to me as a 'young cadre' in the making.

While my thirst for knowledge seemed insatiable, my father, while supportive, cautiously guided me towards age-appropriate readings, steering me away from texts that delved too deeply into ideologies beyond my years. Yet, recognising his son's burgeoning passion for learning, my father would return from his ventures to the city bearing an assortment of books that catered to my budding interests. This gesture warmed my heart and shaped my intellectual curiosity.

Through the shared experiences of bonding over literature and learning, my father and I forged a lasting connection that transcended the mere exchange of words on a page. We wove a tapestry of understanding and respect, where the seeds of knowledge sown in my youthful mind would one day blossom into a legacy of wisdom and unity, nurtured by the gentle guidance of a father who recognised the power of education and the beauty of his own journey as a young enthusiast who forged his future. The echoes of our conversations lingered in the air, a testament to the transformative power of familial love and the enduring influence of a father's unwavering dedication to his son's growth and enlightenment.

Despite my initial fascination with the radical ideas presented in the books, as I resumed school and immersed myself in academic pursuits, I found myself slowly drifting away from the allure of revolutionary ideologies like socialism and communism. Instead, I began to focus on the practical applications of knowledge, blending the theoretical teachings of the books with the pragmatic wisdom passed down by my father, setting my sights on a future where education and hard work became my guiding lights.

The walls of the prestigious palace became our world, both a playground and a classroom where we were home-schooled. The whispered rumours of a return to school, of a resumption of normalcy, started to come and go. Our hearts swelled with a mixture of joy and trepidation as we prepared to step out of our sheltered cocoon and rejoin the world we had temporarily left behind. Among them was me, a boy with a keen eye for detail and a passionate love for art. From a young age, I found solace in sketching intricate portraits that captured the essence of those around me.

In the midst of this atmosphere of longing and isolation, my art flourished like never before. With each passing day, my portraits grew more intricate, each line and shading a testament to the depth of my ability. Through my art, I found a sense of connection to the world beyond the secluded haven, a way to express the longing that weighed heavy on my young heart.

In the quiet days of confinement, I also found solace in art, which I was deeply interested in. From the moment my parents placed a crayon and paper in my hands, I knew that creating beauty with colours and strokes was my calling. Encouraged by my parents' unwavering support, I honed my skills, evolving from doodles on scrap paper to intricate designs adorning any surface I could find.

The hauntingly beautiful depiction of family portraits filled the palace. It was a place where curiosity was nurtured, and dreams were woven into the fabric of the future.

As time passed, my passion for art only grew stronger. Having finished with family portraits, I began to replicate magazine covers, transforming them into mesmerizing freehand artworks. It was during this period of exploration that I met Joseph, the son of one of the household staff who lived on his own outside the palace. Melaku, a talented teenager with a natural gift for drawing, introduced me to the technique of scaling up portraits using square grids.

Under Melaku's guidance, I delved into the world of scaled-up portraits, meticulously adding layers of detailed shading to bring my creations to life. Each stroke of the pencil was a testament to my dedication and love for art. The walls of our home soon became adorned with my masterpieces, each one a testament to the passion that had blossomed within me during those days of confinement.

As I found myself running short of creative inspiration, I turned to the pages of magazines and newspapers in search of new images to copy. Among the sea of photographs, it was the full-page portraits of communist dictators that caught my eye. From the stern gaze of Kim Il-sung to the commanding presence of Joseph Stalin, Brezhnev, and Mao Zedong, their images exuded power and authority. Mengistu, in his military uniform, solely occupied the front pages of the weekly propaganda magazines my father brought home.

These images, gracing the front pages of countless communist publications, became my source of artistic solace. The clarity and grandeur of these portraits made them perfect subjects for replication, even without the aid of a grid. With meticulous care and attention to detail, I set to work scaling up these iconic faces onto large drawing papers.

As I immersed myself in the intricate process of recreating these powerful figures, I found a newfound sense of purpose and satisfaction. Each stroke of my pencil brought me closer to capturing the essence of these larger-than-life personalities. And to my delight, my parents watched in awe as my creations took shape before their eyes.

My parents' admiration and genuine appreciation fueled my passion, driving me to push the boundaries of my artistic abilities. In those moments, surrounded by the images of dictators past and present, I found a sense of fulfilment in my craft that I had never experienced before.

As the days passed and we returned to school, whispers of my talent spread like wildfire through the school corridors. My teachers took note of my advancement not only in art but also in my knowledge of communist ideology, a subject that seemed to have captured my interest like a flame consuming dry kindling.

With a confident stride, I presented my artwork to my classmates and teachers, a gesture meant to showcase my artistic prowess. However, there was a subtle indifference in my eyes, as if the subjects of my portraits were mere vessels for my creativity rather than individuals with their own stories to tell. I carried a collection of portraits, meticulously crafted with strokes of passion and creativity. Each portrait was a masterpiece in its own right, capturing the essence of communist subjects with stunning accuracy.

Moving Pictures

Tunnel of Love

In the gardens of the grand palace, where architecture entwined with the history of old, and new family stories echoed off the ancient stones, we remained increasingly inquisitive minds, fuelled by the promise of unknown secrets waiting to be unravelled within the palace's vast grounds.

On a luminous morning, a group of young explorers, bound by the palace's confines but unrestricted in imagination, embarked on a journey to uncover hidden realms within the palace's expanse. As though drawn by an invisible force, we ventured towards the recently abandoned barracks, once inhabited by the vigilant palace guards before being deserted due to a restructuring of security protocols.

The barracks, cloaked in a shroud of mystery and dust, beckoned us deeper into the secluded enclave, enticing us with remnants of a bygone era. Among the discarded relics of the soldiers, glinting with untold stories, lay bullets and dormant military hardware, waiting to be cleared—a lingering testament to the palace's militaristic nature.

There also lay a scene that had become all too common: a sea of green, Soviet-made military food ration boxes scattered haphazardly across the courtyard. These boxes, once the lifeline of our family during times of scarcity, were now being devoured by the palace guards as their daily sustenance.

Among the intrepid explorers was Simon, my older brother, a peculiarly curious soul with a fascination for all things military. In a daring move that sent shivers down our spines, he picked up a bullet—a heavy piece of bronzy capsule with the weight of history. Yet another unexpected sign of the dangers and vulnerabilities of living in a heavily fortified institution, unfit for the lives of innocent children. Gasps and urgent pleas rang out, prompting the swift intervention of our concerned father, whom we accidentally informed, and the immediate enforcement of new boundaries for our playtime.

Adhering to the stern directives, our world took on a new aspect of caution and restraint. Yet, fate had more discoveries in store for us as we defied instructions and continued wandering into the old barracks, taking one more step every day until we found a long-forgotten footpath concealed behind the barracks, amidst the remnants of disused, bullet-ridden Mercedes and Ford cars at the palace's periphery.

As childhood burgeoned in the palace's gardens, entwined with the tendrils of history and draped in the allure of the unknown, we, the young explorers, unearthed a tapestry of secrets and whispered legends. Each discovery breathed new life into our cherished memories of a world where adventure awaited around every corner.

In one of the far corners of the grounds, nestled beneath the grandeur of a palace that bore witness to centuries of history and secrets, lay a hidden passage that held the weight of a nation's past. This underground tunnel, stretching for around one hundred steps, was a conduit for stories, ambitions, and betrayals that shaped the destiny of those who walked its shadowed corridors.

The footpath, hidden from plain sight, led us—the adventurers—through an underground tunnel, a secret passage connecting the regal majesty of the palace to the stately elegance of the city hall. It whispered of secret rendezvous and clandestine escapades, revealing a past where the previous royal family had stealthily traversed its shadowed corridors to attend functions and gatherings at the city hall's auditorium, a place of festivity and wonder.

For generations, the old royals had used the tunnel as a means to connect with their heritage, hosting plays and theatre within its echoing depths to entertain their court and subjects. It was a place where grand meetings were convened to address the social and political messages of the time, and where decisions that would echo through history were made.

This purpose-built tunnel, a direct link between the palace and the secret backdoors of the grand auditorium, had witnessed both grandeur and tragedy. It had been a haven for the old royals when the shadow of revolution darkened their doorsteps. In the chaos of revolutionary soldiers storming the palace, the tunnel had become a refuge for those who had nowhere else to turn.

The memories ingrained in the stones of the tunnel bore witness to the bloodiest moments of history when the clash between revolutionary armies and royal guards reverberated through its walls. The bullet scars on the once-gleaming royal Mercedes and Ford limousines that had sought shelter within its confines were a sombre testament to the violent upheavals that had shattered lives and futures. As time marched on and the echoes of the past faded into whispers, the tunnel remained a silent witness to the ghosts of history that haunted its passages. It bore the weight of secrets, of promises broken and dreams unfulfilled—a silent testament to the enduring legacy of a nation torn asunder by the tides of change.

Pondering the passage later in time, within the shadows of this tunnel, beyond the glittering veneer of royal revelry, lay a brighter truth. It was here that my father, one day a political prisoner shackled by the chains of oppression, found his path to redemption in the next phase of his life. The tunnel was his gateway to freedom—a passage that led him from the confines of injustice to the high grounds of leadership on the night he was appointed to his new role while still a prisoner.

I often pondered later what thoughts raced through my father's mind as he walked that fateful journey through the tunnel, leaving behind a family confined to a dim two-bedroom dwelling that had become our prison. The uncertainty of his fate, the weight of his responsibilities, and the burden of his newfound purpose must have weighed heavily on his shoulders as he emerged into the light of a world transformed.

For in the heart of that tunnel lies a tale of resilience, courage, and the indomitable human spirit that refuses to be cowed by the weight of history. As I trace my father's footsteps through that hallowed passage, I am reminded that even in the darkest of times and places, there is always hope and "light at the end of the tunnel."

As we stood at the entrance of that secret underground tunnel, feeling the weight of its history pressing down upon us, we wondered about the stories it holds within its dark embrace. The whispers of the past, the echoes of lost lives, the dreams that never came to be—all lie buried deep within its depths, waiting to be uncovered and remembered.

Emboldened by the newfound location, we made the tunnel, a secluded part of the palace away from the sights of soldiers and military hardware, our secret hideaway—a place of solace and shelter from the outside world. One day, fuelled by insatiable curiosity, we decided to push further. We followed the tunnel to another set of doors that beckoned us with a faint glow of dim lights and a chorus of muffled laughter.

Hidden beneath the grand façade of the palace and the austere walls of city hall lay a secret that would change the lives of a group of adventurous children forever. Unbeknownst to us, the doors at the end of the underground tunnel, which once welcomed dignitaries and officials to high-stakes meetings and conferences, were to become our gateways to a newfound world of wonder and discovery. A reverse journey, the one my father took to his new kingdom, opened our version of flight into the unknown and unexpected.

It all began when our group—four children, the son of a cook in the palace kitchen, myself, and two of my brothers—stumbled upon a hidden passageway behind a set of heavy doors at the end of the wall-clad secret passage. After days and weeks of playing in the tunnel, we had traversed its labyrinth; we came upon a recently cleared passageway we didn't know existed.

Curiosity piqued, a spirited group of children spent our days playing in the shadow of the palace walls. Together, we ventured into the depths of the tunnel, guided by the dim rays of natural sunlight and the thrill of the unknown.

As we followed the new passage, to our surprise, we found a large double door that was latched with metal rods. When we pressed down the latches, the doors opened outwards. Not knowing what we would find, we took small steps to pass freely into a dark, small alley with a lowered ceiling before it opened to the grand chamber with its high vaulted ceilings and ornate tapestries.

Following the alley, there was another empty, dark space with flickering lights that seemed to beckon us toward the unknown. As we stepped past its narrow entrance, a heavy blanket of silence enveloped us, suffocating us as if we were venturing into a deep, dark cave.

As we crept through the dimly lit alley, the air heavy with anticipation, suddenly, the silence broke with unexpected sounds: deafening roars of machine guns rattling mercilessly, loud explosives, and the chaos and destruction of a war zone. Flashes of explosions lit up the room in a hellish glow, with women and children screaming frantically from gunshot wounds. Their cries of terror blended with the cacophony of destruction.

In that split second, all thoughts vanished, replaced by a primal instinct for survival.

We clung to each other, eyes wide with disbelief and terror, as we navigated the chaos, dodging those who fell in panic and desperate souls fleeing for our lives. The ground trembled beneath our feet with each explosion, threatening to swallow us whole. We ran through the dimly lit alley that spilled out into a larger space, hiding the source of the chaotic scene that felt like death brought to life. Our hearts pounded in our chests as we were met with the most gruesome sounds—gunshots we had heard during the red terror rounds. Bullets whooshed through the air with menacing whistles. The air felt thick with the acrid scent of smoke and fear; we expected to see dead bodies all around.

We ran back the way we had come, but as we reached the exit, the sturdy door designed to open only from the outside wouldn't let us out—a measure to protect the sanctity of the palace from unwanted intruders from the city hall. The realisation that our adventure had taken a dangerous turn hit us like a ton of bricks crushing our heads. We sat trapped in the battle zone, crying and panicking, our hands over our ears. The shooting, which lasted around ten minutes, finally came to an end.

Trapped between the exit door and the grand hall, we were engulfed in eerie silence, broken only by distant whispers and a sudden cheer that pierced the air. Lost in the darkness veiling the alley, uncertainty clung to us like a shroud. The once thunderous chaos was now replaced by an unsettling calmness, as if the world had paused to catch its breath.

As the voices grew louder and the alley began to pulsate with an ethereal glow, we exchanged puzzled glances, our hearts pounding with a mix of relief and apprehension. Were we approaching salvation, or stepping closer to an unforeseen danger?

Following the trail of whispers and cheers, drawn like moths to a flame, we emerged from the oppressive shadows and found ourselves at the edge of a surreal scene. Before us, a group of people sat transfixed, their eyes fixed on a flickering screen that illuminated their faces with an otherworldly glow.

On the screen played a mesmerizing spectacle, a Chinese revolutionary propaganda film depicting heroes battling against a backdrop of gunfire and chaos. The cheers and chants we had heard were emanating from the captivated audience, enraptured by the on-screen heroes' bravery.

One of the most viewed films in Mekelle City Hall cinema was a Chinese revolutionary battle film titled *From Victory to Victory*. The city hall was buzzing with anticipation as the screen flickered to life, casting a warm glow over the gathered audience. It was an ordinary afternoon turned extraordinary by the promise of cinematic history. The propaganda film unfolded on the screen, drawing the viewers into a tale of revolution and courage.

At that moment, amidst the surreal fusion of reality and fiction, we found ourselves embraced by a newfound hope, inspired by the resilience of those on-screen heroes and the unexpected camaraderie of the spectators. As we lingered in the glowing alley, a glimmer of courage lit up within us, guiding us toward the uncertain future that awaited within the confines of the grand hall.

As we delved deeper into the mysterious void, chasing ethereal lights and haunting sounds, our senses were bombarded by a cacophony of sights and sounds unlike anything we had ever experienced. The darkness was vast and all-encompassing, swallowing us whole as we ventured further, unsure of what we would find at the end of this surreal journey.

Suddenly, as if emerging from the depths of a cosmic black hole, we stumbled upon a colossal screen pulsating with vibrant images that reverberated through our very beings. It was like standing at the edge of a bottomless abyss, the display stretching infinitely into the unknown.

Unable to tear our eyes away, we found ourselves drawn into the mesmerizing scenes unfolding before us. Strange landscapes and multi-coloured smoke danced across the screen, each frame more bizarre and captivating than the last. It was as if we had been transported to a distant realm beyond the reaches of our understanding.

The last victorious scenes of the revolutionary propaganda film depicted the Chinese revolutionary army draped in their uniforms with their trademark red and gold hats, standing poised for their final battle against the imperialist forces that sought to crush their spirit of freedom. The narration, delivered in a voice both solemn and proud, painted a vivid picture of the soldiers' daring plan.

The Chinese soldiers, brimming with resolve, had stealthily infiltrated the enemy camps under the cover of darkness. Their breath fogged in the chill night air; they moved like phantoms through the shadows, their spears gleaming in the moonlight as they struck down the unsuspecting guards.

The tension in the room was palpable as the audience followed the soldiers on their treacherous journey. They dug in close to the enemy lines, their hands steady as they planted mines with precision, creating a deadly trap that would soon spring shut on their foes. Each moment was tinged with urgency, each action a step closer to the final, decisive attack that would determine their fate.

And then, as the signal echoed through the night, the soldiers sprang into action. The sound of gunfire shattered the stillness, catching their enemies and us unawares. The air reverberated with the thunder of cannons and the roar of tanks as the Chinese forces surged forward, their determination unyielding.

It was during this scene inside the city hall that we emerged from the other side of the doors on the historic journey of the tunnel. Panic had gripped us as we thought we had stumbled into the midst of a war zone. But as the sudden sounds of clapping and chanting followed, we were confused, not realising the presence of a full house audience in the dark auditorium.

As we crept deeper into the auditorium, we watched the last part of the victory in awe as it played out, the intensity of the imagery washing over us like a tidal wave. And then, in a moment that seemed to stretch for eternity, the dust settled, and victory was won. The Chinese revolutionary army stood triumphant, their spirits unbroken, their freedom secured.

The screen was a canvas of chaos and courage, each frame a testament to the resilience of a people fighting for their liberty. The city hall was a cauldron of emotions; the audience was held captive by the unfolding drama, their hearts pounding in unison with the soldiers on screen. The battle raged on, the clatter of steel and the cries of victory blending into a symphony of defiance. Their final battle to victory, with heavy gunfire and chaotic marches, were the scenes being played when we accidentally entered the hall, not knowing where the sounds were coming from.

As the final scenes played out and the credits began to roll, a sense of disbelief washed over us. The images on the screen defied all logic and comprehension, pushing the boundaries of our reality to its very limits. We were left speechless, grappling with the impossible truth of what we had just witnessed.

At that moment, amidst the swirling chaos of lights and sounds, we realised that we had stumbled upon something greater than ourselves—a glimpse into a world beyond our wildest imagination. And though we may never fully understand the mysteries of the cinematic display, we knew that our journey into the unknown had changed us forever. By mere coincidence, with no sight of what was playing on the screen behind the wall, we were met with a vivid depiction of the final act of a long silent ambush that flared into explosions and gunfire in a historic battle film, where the Chinese revolutionary army had triumphed over their imperialist foes.

We were caught in the crossfire of this cinematic warfare; the intensity of the propaganda film ambushed us. The sounds of warfare reverberated in our ears, the flashes of gunfire searing our vision.

As the viewing came to an end and the screen faded to black, the spectators rose to their feet, applauding the display of bravery and sacrifice. We stood there, blinking in disbelief at the strange twist of fate that had led us to this unexpected sanctuary in the midst of turmoil. Among the sea of panic and chaos, we heard sounds of hands clapping and cheering "well done, hero, well done" in Tigrinya. Upon returning to the hall in silence, we caught glimpses of individuals sitting and enjoying what they had just finished watching.

We had stumbled upon a cinema, a place of magic and mystery where stories came to life on the silver screen. For in that darkened auditorium of City Hall, we had experienced the might of propaganda, the allure of revolution, and the power of cinema.

Unsure of how to process our first experience with cinema, we exchanged bewildered glances, our minds reeling from the onslaught of emotions. We had entered the tunnel seeking adventure, but we had stumbled upon something far greater—a glimpse into history and a new beginning in our own lives.

With no previous exposure to moving pictures and mesmerised by the spectacle before us, we stood in awe, our eyes wide with wonder at this marvel of technology we had never encountered before.

The images of that fateful moment marked the beginning of our lifetime relationship with cinema.

Before we could fully comprehend the magnitude of our discovery, a figure emerged from the dark: an old man who worked as an usher in the cinema. He greeted us with a mixture of curiosity and suspicion. Sensing our innocence, he inquired about our origins and how we had found our way into the secret enclave of the cinema and the restricted viewing, which was only for adults.

Unprepared and filled with a mixture of trepidation and excitement, we recounted our journey from the palace tunnels to the hidden world of the cinema, unaware of the consequences our escapade might entail. When we showed the usher the door, the long-serving usher, who knew some details about the building's layouts, realised our identity and offered us to use the main door accompanied by adults next time. Recognising our innocence, the usher insisted on taking us to the reception for further inquiry. A sense of unease gripped us, the fear of the unknown and the certainty that our parents would not approve of our forbidden adventure.

Our hearts raced as we dashed through the dimly lit corridors of the cinema; soon, we forgot about the magic we had found there. Fear and excitement still echoed in our ears from the magical film we had just experienced. But now, with the looming reality of repercussions, panic began to set in.

Tears streaming down our cheeks, we poured out our misadventures, begging for forgiveness and for help to return home safely. With a heavy heart and the first breaking of our security covenant, we revealed our full identities and addresses, hoping the usher would show us mercy and help us go home.

Moved by our genuine plea and shocked at knowing our identities, the usher led us to the reception, where a kind cinema staff member agreed to accompany us back to the palace. The journey back was long and arduous, the path meandering almost a kilometre around the outer parameters of the imposing walls of the city hall and the palace. With each step, the weight of our mistake bore down on us. We, the children who were constantly guarded from danger, were now walking on the street without any safety measures.

When we finally reached the palace gates, a soldier stationed there spotted us, his hand instinctively reaching for his gun. Alarmed by the children's worried faces, he barked a command to stop, his voice laced with urgency and concern. We froze, our hearts pounding in unison.

The cinema staff member swiftly intervened, calming the soldier and explaining the situation. The soldier, amidst his relief that we were unharmed, couldn't fathom how we had managed to escape his watchful eyes and find ourselves within the confines of the cinema hall.

Curiosity gnawed at him as he asked us how we had escaped. With a mixture of fear and honesty, we recounted our ordeal, detailing our journey through the hidden tunnel that had led us astray. The soldier's expression softened, a hint of guilt creeping in at the thought of the breach that had endangered our lives.

With a sense of responsibility weighing heavily on his shoulders, the soldier arranged for another of his comrades to escort us back to the main building to reunite us with our parents, who didn't know we had travelled to the moon and back. As we reached and were handed to one of the staff, the once blossoming friendship between the children from both sides seemed to wither away, replaced by a sombre understanding of the consequences of our actions.

And so, we returned to our safety, our minds filled with the images of Chinese soldiers in battle and the flickering lights of the secret cinema. We had tasted the forbidden fruit and glimpsed a world beyond our wildest dreams. In that fleeting moment of discovery, we had become the masters of our destinies, bound by a secret that would forever link us to the hidden wonders of cinema.

And so, as the day settled down and, while we were sanctioned to our bedrooms on our mother's order, our father came to hear our dangerous story that had witnessed our escapade. We and our friends learned a valuable lesson in the importance of trust, responsibility, and the true meaning of home.

Amidst the hushed grandeur of the palace, my father came into a quiet home. He was briefed about the day's events by my mother, his stern expression softening slightly as he listened to our adventurous tale unfold. Soon, we crawled out of our bedrooms with our little eyes squeezed shut and our mood withdrawn. His eyes held a mix of amusement and concern as we recounted the daring escapades that had led us through the labyrinthine corridors and hidden passageways of the palace building, and the horror we had faced at the end of the tunnel.

As we described how we had stumbled upon a secret tunnel concealed behind a tapestry, my father's brow furrowed with disapproval. He scolded us gently for venturing into forbidden areas, emphasising the importance of respecting boundaries and rules. However, his initial reprimand gave way to a chuckle when we recounted the comical incident involving a Chinese film that had startled us to near hysteria.

Despite his strict demeanour, my father was a man of understanding and compassion. He recognised the innocence and curiosity that had driven us to explore the palace's hidden depths and promised to look into ways to make the premises safer for future escapades.

It was during a subsequent discussion with Tariku, the estate worker, that a solution presented itself. Tariku offered to accompany us on our future endeavours, ensuring our safety and providing valuable insight into the palace's intricate layout. He suggested a safer route that led to the upper levels, where the executive seats reserved for royalty were situated. This exclusive area had been off-limits to the public since the cinema had opened its doors to the masses.

As my father pondered the suggestion, a look of contemplation crossed his features. He was torn between allowing us to continue our adventurous pursuits and ensuring our well-being. Ultimately, his paternal instincts won out, and he agreed to Tariku's proposal, permitting us to explore the upper echelons of the palace under his watchful eye. After assessing the safety of the cinema, which had a strict search protocol for its audiences, assured by Tariku and the guards, my father allowed for a supervised and well-planned use of the executive lounge for our cinematic adventures.

On the day of our next escapade, Tariku met with the cinema staff and advised them on adhering to the already strict search procedures for cinemagoers. He also briefed the staff on the newly established route and the strict conditions that children should not access the lounge without his accompaniment or prior authorization.

That same week, we found ourselves once again standing at the entrance to the hidden tunnel, excitement bubbling in our veins. With Tariku leading the way, we navigated the dimly lit passageways, the air thick with the scent of age and history. The journey to the upper levels was fraught with steep steps, twists, and turns, but we felt safe and reassured in the knowledgeable presence of our guide.

As we emerged into the opulent surroundings of the executive lounge, we were greeted by a sight that took our breath away. Plush velvet seats, gilded chandeliers, and intricate tapestries adorned the space, creating an atmosphere of regal elegance.

We marvelled at the luxury surrounding us, imagining the distinguished guests who had once occupied these seats.

The dusty executive lounge echoed with the sounds of the Chinese war film again, enveloping us in a whirlwind of action-packed battles and intense drama. For two and a half captivating hours, we were entranced by the screen, witnessing heroism and sacrifice play out in vivid colour.

As the final scenes flickered across the massive screen, a wave of exhilaration washed over us. The sense of accomplishment in completing the full film for the first time was palpable, sparking an idea that would become our obsession. With fervour and excitement, we began re-enacting our favourite scenes in the vast palace garden behind the main building.

Each child donned a role, embodying the characters with unwavering dedication. Hiding behind trees and crawling on the grass, we breathed life into the epic battles, our voices providing the soundtrack. The garden transformed into a stage for our spirited performances as we relived the glory and left the tragedies out of the film.

Amidst the grandeur and elegance of the palace gardens, I stepped into the shoes of Jun, a brave, short soldier from the Chinese film. With each enactment, I breathed life into his character, embodying his unwavering courage and valour on the battlefield. The lush greenery and delicate cherry blossoms provided the perfect backdrop for our scenes, enhancing the enchanting allure of our performances.

As the story unfolded, Jun's heroic deeds captivated the audience, transporting us into a world of battles and noble sacrifices. Together, we painted a vivid picture of honour and sacrifice, each movement choreographed to perfection and each line delivered with our own adaptation of the Chinese dialogue, filled with passion and conviction.

The Chinese film became our weekly entertainment. However, amidst the applause and admiration, a subtle unease began to take root as we became familiar with the film after tens of repeated viewings. We noticed during one fateful scene that a directorial error came to light. In a heart-wrenching moment, Jun was swallowed by a blaze of explosives, his body evaporating into the air in pieces of flesh, his noble sacrifice etched into the hearts of the viewers. Yet, to our bewilderment, Jun reappeared towards the end of the film as an extra, marching forward with a big Chinese flag held high. The error was glaring, a misstep in the narrative that threatened to disrupt the delicate balance we had strived to achieve. Despite the confusion, Jun's presence radiated a sense of resolute determination, a symbol of resilience and strength in the face of adversity.

Watching us in our acts, my father's laughter rang out, filling the air with warmth and joy. His eyes sparkled with pride and amusement as he watched us take in the splendours of our surroundings, realising that our adventurous spirit had led us to a place of wonder and a new hobby.

Our enthusiasm spilled over as we shared our adventures with school friends, though our animated retellings were met with confused expressions.

The Chinese war film, which seemed to have an eternity on the screen, mesmerised us each time with its gripping storyline and action-filled scenes. We could practically recite every scene, often mimicking the actors and even attempting to sing along with the Chinese revolutionary songs. The cinema also showcased various propaganda films after *From Victory to Victory*, our favoured action film. This film brought us into the world of cinema, yet it was replaced by a dull Russian propaganda film about a youth campaign to grow and harvest potatoes in remote villages of Soviet Russia, expanding our cinematic adventures. Just for the record, we did not attempt to enact the Russian potato harvest film, but we used some of its teachings on the science behind successfully growing some of the world's biggest potatoes.

Therefore, under the watchful gaze of my father and Tariku, we embarked on a new chapter of exploration and discovery, guided by the wisdom of those who cared for our safety and nurtured our thirst for adventure. As we navigated the intricate corridors and hidden chambers of the palace, we knew that our days of daring escapades were far from over and that, with each new discovery, we would continue to evoke the laughter and pride of a father who recognised the boundless joy of his adventurous children.

Cinema became a cherished routine, especially with my mother's permission and under the watchful eye of Tariku, the kind-hearted caretaker.

Our film escapades took a thrilling turn when we excitedly informed our mother about an upcoming film we saw in preview – *Mother India*, a timeless classic that held a special place in her heart. It was the Bollywood film my parents saw on their first date but never got the chance to finish. The story my mother narrated to us as a bedtime tale transported us to a world where emotions ran deep in the backdrop of a story about an Indian peasant woman who is idealised as a bride, mother, guardian of sons, long-suffering, stoically loving, redemptive, and conservatively wedded to the maintenance of the social status quo. The songs of *Mother India* were the soundtracks of our growing years, always played to my mother's delight. *Mother India*, one of the most acclaimed films in the world, is a true story that touched everyone in my mother's generation.

The day arrived, and with Tariku by our side, we embarked on the adventurous journey to the cinema hall. Even our mother, who once sanctioned us for trespassing into the hall, was now a party to the 'crime'. Such is the power of cinema.

With safety concerns preventing my mother from using the public entrance, she surprised us all by suggesting that we use the tunnel she had once forbade us from entering.

As we navigated the dark and damp passageway, the walls whispered stories of clandestine adventures and forbidden thrills. Emerging on the other side, we found ourselves in the back alley behind the cinema. My mother's eyes shone with a mix of guilt and determination as Tariku led us to the upper-level executive lounge.

Settling into our seats, the movie began, but the real show was the unity we felt as a family, breaking the rules and venturing into the past together. At that moment, the tunnel was not just a passageway but a symbol of history that carried transformative moments in our resilience and the bond that held us together.

The presence of an armed soldier as an added security measure only increased the anticipation. As the film commenced, my mother's eyes brimmed with tears even before the first scene unfolded. Clutching our hands tightly, she immersed herself in the poignant narrative that seemed to echo her own life's trials and tribulations.

Surrounded by loved ones and lost in the waves of nostalgia, my mother wept openly, her emotions intertwining with the unfolding drama on the screen. What we hadn't expected was the burly soldier, who stood stoically at attention, visibly moved to tears by the raw emotions depicted in *Mother India*. It was a testament to the film's power to evoke profound emotions in anyone who witnessed its tale of love, loss, and resilience.

The experience of watching *Mother India* with my mother transcended mere entertainment. It was a journey through her past, a poignant reminder of her youth in Asmara, and a precious memory shared with her mother. The film's haunting melodies resonated with a generation, each note carrying echoes of bygone days and cherished memories. And so, my mother had the chance to finish her favourite film after fifteen years, despite several interruptions due to power cuts and reels breaking.

In the backdrop of *Mother India*, my mother's life unfolded like a tapestry woven with threads of tradition and struggle. Born into a society where arranged marriages were the norm, she navigated the highs and lows of raising children in a society that demanded perfection from women. Her days were a delicate balance of nurturing love and disciplinarian authority, her strength tested by the challenges that came with motherhood.

Through it all, *Mother India* cast a shadow over my mother's life, shaping her experiences in ways both profound and heartbreaking. There were moments of abundance when the sun shone brightly on her family, and they basked in the glow of prosperity. But there were also times of darkness when poverty swept in like a relentless storm, stripping them of their dignity and security.

Just like in the film, in a world where men held the reins of power, my mother witnessed her mother walk a tightrope of emotions, her heart torn between duty and desire. My grandmother weathered the emotional rollercoasters that came with being a woman in a traditionally male-dominated society, finding solace in the unbreakable bond she shared with her children.

Through it all, *Mother India* stood as a silent witness to the unfolding drama of my mother's life, her presence a constant reminder of the strength and resilience that defined the women of the generation before her. And though her journey was marked by hardship and sacrifice, my mother emerged as a beacon of hope, a testament to the enduring spirit of *Mother India* that lives on in the hearts of women everywhere.

In the weeks to come, my mother arranged for all the palace staff to experience their first cinema viewing of *Mother India*. With Tariku's arranged escort for each group, the staff was drawn into the story of *Mother India*, though they were equally confused by how the whole cinema thing worked. Nevertheless, they were happy to know their experience was a privileged one, a reward for their hard work.

Following this emotional cinematic odyssey, we yearned for the luxury of reliving the experience. Encouraged by the profound impact of *Mother India*, we implored our father to join us for a second viewing. With heightened security measures in the hall and a sombre mood pervading the theatre, we embarked on another emotional rollercoaster.

The sight of soldiers, deeply moved by the film's portrayal of familial bonds and sacrifices, transformed the viewing experience into a collective introspection. As the credits rolled for the second time, the lounge echoed with hushed whispers and tearful reflections from the soldiers. For many, it was a newfound appreciation for the art of cinema, a medium capable of stirring the deepest recesses of the human soul. The soldiers who experienced cinema for the first time entered into a big debate on how cinema worked. While some said live men were acting behind the screen, others said it was beyond their capacity to discuss technology at that level and left it for God to sort out.

In the end, our cinematic escapades with our parents, and the presence of Tariku, the ever-watchful guardian, created a tapestry of memories that would forever be etched in our hearts. The collective sobbing, the shared emotional journey, and the unbridled joy of experiencing timeless classics together formed the foundation of our family's cinematic legacy. As we stepped out of the theatre, our souls enriched by the profound stories we had witnessed on the silver screen, we knew that these moments would stay with us forever, a testament to the power of storytelling and the enduring bonds of family.

Every now and then, we would gather in the cosy lounge, dimly lit by the flickering light of an old projector, to immerse ourselves in more Indian films. The timeless tunes of Indian films seemed to transport us to a different era, eliciting a range of emotions that only music with such depth and soul could provoke.

The songs of *Mother India* remained the soundtrack of our lives, weaving through our memories and intertwining with our experiences, creating a tapestry of emotions that resonated deep within our hearts.

With each passing day, we became more discerning in our selection of films to watch during our lounging sessions. Yet, amidst the enchantment of the melodies, there was a whimsical interruption that never failed to break the spell.

During most of our movie marathons, as we were engrossed in the dramatic scenes unfolding on the screen, a voice would suddenly pierce through the darkness of the lounge. It was the voice of the palace maid, who, hesitant to enter the dimly lit cinema hall, would stand at the door and call out the names of the children one by one, summoning us for afternoon tea.

With a loud sound that covered the entire depth of the quiet cinema hall, she would call, "Kaleb, Simon, Theo, Biruk, Alazar, 'Embeitei' is calling you, come immediately for afternoon tea," the maid would announce, her voice echoing through the room, creating a moment of humorous disruption in the midst of the cinematic reverie. We would exchange knowing smiles, acknowledging the familiar interruption that had become part of our cherished routine. The whole audience would laugh, not knowing where we were or who would call their children for tea in the middle of a viewing. Little did they know there was a group of non-paying, next-door children seated in the upper lounge.

The mysterious occurrence of the maid's call during our movie sessions became a delightful quirk of our shared experiences, adding a touch of whimsy to our otherwise ordinary afternoons. It was a scene that repeated itself every Saturday afternoon, like clockwork, and had become a source of amusement and fond memories for the group.

'Embeitei' is a title given to those high in the feudal system of the past, meaning "My Master," and was declared a political taboo in the new government. For the other audience members, hearing the forbidden word being used so openly and loudly was a mystery they couldn't solve. The ghostly names and phrases calling for afternoon tea became the legendary talk of the town, everybody knew about it. My mother would hear about it from her friends who knew through their young children.

After hastily finishing our tea and biscuits at home, we would rush back to the lounge, eager not to miss a single moment of the film we had seen countless times before. Despite the interruption, we continued to enjoy the films as much as the other paying audiences.

And so, in the heart of Mekelle, amidst the chaos and political unrest, the enchanting songs of *Mother India* and the heroic scenes of *From Victory to Victory* served as a thread that connected us to the past, evoking a sense of joy and nostalgia of the present that would never fade away from our hearts and minds in the future.

Flights Of Horror

Come Fly With Me

In northern Ethiopia, the air was thick with tension and sorrow. The political and military landscape was in constant flux, with territorial controls changing hands within mere days, leaving a trail of young lives sacrificed in the name of war. The military government, desperate to secure victory, resorted to brutal tactics, including indiscriminate mass murders in cities and villages, carpet bombings of suspected rebel hideout towns, and ruthless extra-judicial political assassinations that had become an everyday occurrence in cities and towns around Tigray and Eritrea.

With communication and transport severed between Eritrea and the rest of the world, the only movement northward came in the form of military aircraft, tanks, armoured vehicles, and trucks carrying soldiers. As the rebels had destroyed most bridges and roads to impede the government's advances and logistical capabilities, costly air transport remained the main route of supply for the government's war efforts. This affected the government's ability to fight the war effectively. Asmara was sealed, with no one allowed in or out.

The fortified airports of Mekelle and Asmara, though operational, served solely military purposes, witnessing a continuous influx of Ethiopian Airlines commercial aircraft carrying men and military hardware through unscheduled flights. However, some of these flights, which carried fuel and explosives in one cargo and were poorly managed from a ground operational viewpoint, met tragic ends, crashing and erupting into massive explosions on the outskirts of Asmara, claiming the lives of many innocent residents. Others were shot down with simple rockets launched from the rebels' shoulders just outside the airport.

Eritrean freedom fighters shelled the city from its outskirts to attack the army, which had camped in different parts of the city. Many of the shells landed on private homes, killing and injuring innocent people.

Asmara airport, a frequent target for attacks, stood as a testament to the brutality of the conflict. Amidst the chaos, the Eritrean Liberation Front executed a daring mission, destroying a significant portion of the government's air force fleet and crippling the government's aerial capabilities. The military leader, Mengistu, arrived at Asmara airport the next day and executed most of the top officers for incompetence and conspiring with the rebels.

While the government garnered support from the Soviets and other friendly Eastern powers, the Eritrean Liberation Front found unwavering backing from citizens and wealthy Middle Eastern countries, escalating the intensity of the war. Military flights landing in Asmara ferried weapons and soldiers for the ongoing battle, sometimes making pit stops at Mekelle airport for refuelling, strategically positioned midway between Addis Ababa and Asmara.

Soviet helicopters and Antonov cargo planes navigated the skies, shuttling between Mekelle, Asmara, and the rest of Ethiopia, carrying supplies northwards and wounded soldiers to the south. Families of officers and military personnel, relocating between the war-torn regions, were transported in the same flights.

In the vast and war-torn lands of Tigray and Eritrea, where families were torn apart by conflicts and borders, there existed a story of resilience and love that transcended all boundaries. My parents, like many Eritreans, had been separated from their loved ones for years, with the ache of distance carving a deep hole in their hearts.

Despite the cruel twists of fate, my mother held onto a glimmer of hope through the faint connection of secret military phone lines. It was through these lines that she would speak to her parents, a lifeline tethering her to her roots. The ache of not being able to see them weighed heavily on her soul, knowing that her siblings had scattered like seeds in the wind—some joining the resistance fight, while others sought refuge across distant borders.

Amidst these familial and national upheavals, a figure always saved the day from the chaos: Colonel Hailu, a man of significant power and authority in the heart of the conflict. Despite the enmity brewing in Tigray and Eritrea, Colonel Hailu, chief commander of the northern division in charge of military operations, harboured a deep respect for my parents and extended a helping hand, arranging flights on military aeroplanes for my mother to travel to Asmara and back, bridging the chasm that separated her from her parents.

The first flight to Asmara was a mix of nerves and anticipation for my mother, stepping onto the military aircraft that would carry her across the divide. Colonel Hailu had ensured every detail was meticulously organised, from a reserved seat for my mother to informing officers at both airports of her presence, ensuring her safe passage from our home to her parents' abode in Asmara.

The joy that radiated from my mother upon reuniting with her parents was indescribable, a balm to the wounds of separation. Every two to three months, she embarked on these emotional journeys, carrying gifts and photos that brought smiles to her family's faces, lighting up their humble household with the warmth of her presence.

But amidst the routine of these visits, there was a secret cargo that my mother carried—a cargo that held a deeper significance. My portraits, rolled and concealed from prying eyes, were among the personal items she brought to Asmara. These were no ordinary portraits; they depicted communist leaders, including Mengistu, the military leader who was hated by Eritreans for his leading role in this dark history. My mother, unaware of the contents of these portraits, carried them with a sense of duty and love, unaware of the impact they held in the hearts of her people. As a child, I was unaware of the messages I was sending in those portraits. My main aim was to share my artistic products, with no knowledge that I was sending a killer's glorified portraits to its victims.

And so, the flights continued, each journey a testament to the resilience of the human spirit, each portrait a silent witness to a story that transcended time and space, weaving a tapestry of love for art, hate for the subject, and longing that spanned the distance between past and present, heart and homeland.

Months had passed, and the shifting seasons had painted their vibrant hues across the landscape. Each change brought a new energy and a fresh perspective on the world around us. It was amidst this ever-evolving backdrop that the seeds of adventure were sown, waiting to blossom into an experience beyond our wildest dreams.

The news came to us like a whisper in the wind, carried by our mother's gentle voice. She spoke of Asmara, a name we knew only in passing, a distant land filled with stories and mysteries waiting to be unravelled. The mere thought of embarking on a journey to this unknown destination sent ripples of excitement through our hearts.

As the unknown day of departure drew near, anticipation hung in the air like a thick fog, enveloping us in a shroud of eager expectation. We gathered our belongings, our hearts brimming with a mixture of curiosity and apprehension. The time had come to leave behind the familiar comforts of the palace and venture into the great unknown.

The moment arrived, and we found ourselves standing before the Soviet-made SU-18 helicopter, a formidable machine with a commanding presence. The roar of its engines filled the air, drowning out any other sound as we climbed aboard, taking our places on the foldable canvas seats. The helicopter trembled beneath us, eager to take flight and carry us away to distant lands.

As we soared above the rugged lands of northern Ethiopia, a patchwork of earth and sky stretched out before us, a breathtaking collage of colours and shapes. We pressed our faces against the windows, eyes wide with wonder, pointing and guessing the names of every visible object on the ground, drinking in the sights below. The landscape unfolded like a living painting, each brushstroke a testament to the beauty and cruelty of the natural world.

The hours passed in a blur of excitement and awe, the noise of the helicopter's engine fading into the background as we lost ourselves in the majesty of the world below. We did not speak, for we could not produce voices loud enough to surpass the helicopter's engine noise. We only dreamt of the promised adventure that lay ahead. The Russian pilots, sipping vodka from bottles during the flight, sometimes came to the cabin and spoke in their language with a grin on one of the pilots' faces. All the passengers stared, misunderstood, but one middle-aged gentleman looked both amused and angry.

The passenger, who later explained he was one of the thousands of young officers who completed a military science course in Russia, translated the pilot's announcement. What we thought was a decent flight drill was actually a distasteful joke by the pale, silver-toothed pilot in a green coverall military uniform, buttoned only up to his big belly, contemptuously telling passengers, "Welcome to the military version of Aeroflot. Sorry, we don't have in-flight snacks and drinks for you, but we are happy to offer vodka to anyone who wishes to have it—children and adults, all welcome." He continued his indecent announcement: "By the way, if we crash and you die—and I think you will, because I have a parachute—of course, you will not be compensated for your losses, because you didn't pay for this flight… ha… ha."

After hearing the full translation, my mother angrily commented, "Our God, the one you don't know but knows you, will keep us safe, you fat-bellied idiot."

Finally, after hours of flight, the distant silhouette of Asmara came into view— a city steeped in history and tradition, its ancient streets winding like a maze through time. The pilots expertly guided the helicopter towards the airport, descending gracefully amidst the hustle and bustle of the afternoon.

As we stepped onto the solid ground of Asmara, a sense of wonder washed over us, mingling with the nervous excitement of the unknown. We were greeted by a civilian driver, a friendly face amidst the crowds of strangers, who whisked us away to our grandparents' home—a haven of familiarity in a sea of new experiences.

The day that followed our first meeting with our grandparents was a whirlwind of discovery and adventure, each moment etched into our memories like a precious gem. We roamed the neighbourhood streets of Asmara, soaking in the sights and sounds of the city and immersing ourselves in its rich tapestry of architecture and history.

In the heart of Asmara, a city of architectural marvels filled with historic cathedrals, mosques, and beautiful houses, we saw roads unlike anything we had seen before. This city, which lives in history and remnants of past conflicts, unfolded a winter like no other for us. Our opulent palace life was momentarily set aside as we embarked on an unforgettable journey to stay with our grandparents in a modest villa. Despite the visible scars of war and hardship that painted the city's exterior, within the tight-knit community, warmth and generosity flourished.

Our days were filled with laughter and play as we forged connections with children in the neighbourhood, our young hearts relishing the simplicity and authenticity of these new friendships. Every doorstep we crossed welcomed us with open arms, offering food, fruit, and sweets shared willingly—even in times of economic struggle.

Strolls to the suburbs of Asmara revealed echoes of the city's turbulent reality, remnants of military hardware serving as sombre reminders of the fierce battles that once raged nearby. Yet, amidst these stark reminders, we found solace in the familiar sights and sounds of the Catholic school near our grandparents' abode, its grounds becoming a playground of blissful innocence.

Evenings brought gatherings of all ages into the vast compound once owned by our grandfather, but now taken by military rule. The smaller houses inside the massive compound, once part of our grandparents' estate, were rented to other tenants.

Our play continued into the evening inside the big gates of our grandparents' estate, past the government-imposed 7 pm curfew. All members of the neighbourhood gathered, grouped by age and gender, to make the best of their forced confinement. Mothers cooked corn and other small bites, while fathers socialised, listening to various radio broadcasts to get news and updates on the ongoing war. Children played around them, while the more mature ones studied under candlelight as electricity and water were cut. My grandfather always made sure we were not harmed or bullied; he treated us preciously, so the other children were more caring towards us than they were to each other.

During the day, we were transported into worlds of cinematic wonder in the myriad cinemas that dotted Asmara. From Indian epics to old western classics, the silver screen became a continuation of our old hobby and a portal to boundless imagination and shared joy. We told our new mates about our 'private' cinema back home and bragged about how we had seen most of the films that were currently playing in Asmara's cinemas.

However, it was the simple pleasures that resonated deeply with us. The freedom of carrying pocket money and venturing to local shops, the thrill of selecting sweets and toys with autonomy we had never experienced in our gilded upbringing in Mekelle. In these moments, we embraced newfound independence, a taste of self-reliance that bloomed like a winter flower in our hearts.

Our grandfather gave us change every morning. I remember that, while all my brothers and uncles spent theirs before midday, I would have change remaining in my pocket. When my grandfather understood my special financial efficiency, he called me 'the economist,' entrusting me to hold everyone's pocket money and control their spending.

That didn't make me very popular among my siblings, but my grandfather, 'Goitapa,' had also noticed my ability to articulate, read, and understand Amharic, the national language. He needed help with his official correspondence. I read and translated important letters for him. He must have silently promised himself that the boy by his side was his trusted aide. Goitapa also became more informed about the news as he enjoyed my line-by-line translation of the news and articles on the radio, which he found exciting, especially considering the need to update himself with political developments in the region. Amharic, which was dubbed the language of the 'enemy' due to its speakers being considered the aggressors in the ongoing war, wasn't popular even in Emperor Haile Selassie's time. Eritreans always viewed it as a tool of oppression, spoken only by the occupiers. In many cases, listening to Amharic songs and reading books was considered punishable treachery in rebel-held territories.

Despite the government's efforts to nationalise schools and make Amharic compulsory in the school curriculum, young Eritreans were defiant in learning and understanding it. They showed their reluctance in various ways, including showing disrespect to Amharic teachers and missing classes continuously.

Walking to town with our grandfather became a cherished ritual. The tantalising aroma of freshly baked cakes from Asmara's renowned bakeries beckoned like sweet melodies, creating memories that transcended time and place. Venturing into European cafes and restaurants owned by Goitapa's Italian friends was a unique experience that introduced us to new culinary adventures. Scoops of ice cream, paninis filled with cheese and mortadella slices were all part of our newfound world.

Yet, it was the unwavering love and care of our grandparents that painted the most vivid hues on our winter canvas. Spoiled with attention and affection, we discovered more of a familial bond and comfort that surpassed the grandeur of our palace life. In the warmth of our grandparents' embrace, we found a haven of unconditional love and security.

As the winter drew to a close, we carried within us a treasure trove of memories, each moment etched in our hearts like precious gems. The lessons learned in the simplicity and humanity of our time spent in Asmara would forever alter our perspective. For in the small villa among welcoming neighbours and loving grandparents, we discovered the true essence of family and the beauty of life's simplest joys.

And as we prepared to bid farewell to Asmara and return to the familiar comforts of home in Mekelle, we carried with us a piece of this magical city in our hearts, vowing to return—a reminder of the boundless possibilities that await those brave enough to embark on a journey into the unknown. Our adventure had only just begun, with each new horizon promising new stories, new experiences, and new dreams waiting to unfold.

The case for more frequent flights for familial and cultural connections was established after our first successful trip. We made the best of every opportunity available to us.

Our mother, with the responsibility of caring for my much younger brothers—Biruk and Alazar—found the journey on military planes most uncomfortable as she was also battling epilepsy and gallbladder illnesses. These bore the weight of caring for her youngest on those difficult flights. The arduous military aircraft journeys had taken a toll on our mother's health.

Our parents agreed to use the lulls between school semesters as opportunities for us to take bi-annual flights to Asmara. They decided it was best for my mother to abstain from travelling until commercial flights became available. Thus, it was left to the children to embark on the flights, accompanied by a designated guardian during our journeys.

One fateful morning, as the school term drew to a close, we were caught off guard by the sudden announcement of our impending flight to Asmara. The process of securing seats on the military aircraft was shrouded in unpredictability, with Colonel Hailu's men determining the availability of space on the cargo planes and helicopters.

Our home was a bustling hub of anticipation and preparation whenever the call came from the airport, signalling the time for us to make our way to embark on the unscheduled military flights to Asmara. Many times, we would spend all day at the airport and then be brought back home when they couldn't find seats for us. Each journey was a mix of excitement and apprehension, a blend of the unknown and the familiar that awaited us at our destination.

Our carefree morning was abruptly interrupted when a maid's urgent voice rang out, breaking the tranquillity of the scene. In the same way she had called us from the city hall auditorium, she now cried, "Children, come quickly! 'Embeitei' says the driver is waiting to take you to the airport," her tone laced with urgency. We exchanged a puzzled glance, our innocent faces creased with confusion at the unexpected turn of events. With a shared look of curiosity and the continuation of the excitement from the previous day, we dashed towards the maid, our feet dancing lightly on the soft grass.

As we hurried back to our houses, our laughter filled the air, mingling with the distant hum of cicadas. Our joy was untainted by the impending departure, our innocence shielding us from the gravity of the situation.

Inside the house, our mother greeted us with a mixture of surprise and concern, her hands moving swiftly to clean our dirty faces and hands. "No time for a proper wash, children; they said your flight is taking off in two hours," she said, seizing the opportunity that might not come again soon. Her eyes were filled with both apprehension and affection. The driver, an imposing figure with a stern face, stood waiting outside, a sense of impatience emanating from him.

"We must hurry," he announced, his voice brooking no argument. "I have another family to collect, and time is of the essence." Without further delay, we were whisked away from the familiarity of our home, the remnants of grass and mud clinging to our clothes like souvenirs of our playful morning.

The drive to the airport was a blur of motion, the car cutting through the landscape with a sense of urgency. We watched the passing scenery with wide-eyed wonder, the world outside our windows a kaleidoscope of colours and shapes. As we approached the airport, the sight of small aircraft resembling fighter jets caught our attention, igniting a spark of excitement within us.

Upon reaching the airport terminal, we found ourselves amidst a flurry of activity, the air alive with the sounds of engines and voices. Contrary to the strict schedule that had seen us rushing out of our home in our football shorts and shirts, we waited with anticipation for the right aeroplane to arrive. The minutes stretched into hours as the sun dipped lower in the sky.

The airport terminal looked like a battlefield with military activities of all kinds. We were surrounded by a diverse array of people, including freshly wounded soldiers and foreign faces from East European medics to Soviet and Cuban military personnel with briefcases. It felt as though an entire town had been evacuated into the airport. The airport's population grew by the hour, suffocating the space we played in. Soon, we would lose our dignitary status and be told to sit quietly by some of the older people around us. Boredom began to creep in. With no activity and less food, the day stretched into night, and the anticipated flight that was supposed to arrive "in an hour" never seemed to come. My parents had agreed to our prolonged stay, as there might be night flights. The person entrusted with looking after us was himself busy helping to clean the bloodied floors of the terminal and making space for the injured soldiers arriving in truckloads.

Among the inhabitants of the airport terminal were hundreds of severely wounded soldiers, their faces etched with pain and exhaustion. They were being carried or helped from one corner to another with a sense of urgency. Our innocent eyes widened at the sight; our hearts filled with compassion for the suffering we witnessed.

We had witnessed the horrors of war firsthand, the scenes of carnage and blood etched into our minds like a scar that never faded. We saw broken skulls of soldiers, their arms and legs ripped asunder, their screams of agony echoing in our ears like a haunting melody.

The scenes of carnage and blood from the Chinese war film we saw daily at the city hall played out before us like a macabre dance of death. As each frame unfolded, it carried with it the weight of human suffering, the brutal face of war laid bare for all to see.

The young soldiers, barely out of their teens, their faces contorted in agony, their eyes filled with fear as they faced the horrors of the battlefield. The sound of agony and despair echoed through the vast terminal hall, mingling with the stifled sobs of those watching.

In one particularly harrowing moment, a large group of wounded soldiers arrived, their bodies torn apart by shrapnel. Limbs were ripped from bodies, blood spattering the ground in a gruesome display of violence. Their eyes lingered on our faces, pleading for mercy as they gasped for breath, their screams of pain echoing in search of help from the overstretched medics.

As the scene played out in front of our eyes, a hush fell over the occupants of the terminal, the horror of the war seeping into our very souls. Each sight etched itself into our minds, a stark reminder of the everyday operations of the terminal. The faces of the soldiers haunted us, their silent cries for help echoing long after the screen had gone dark.

The world outside seemed to spin on, oblivious to the horrors that had unfolded in the airport terminal. The scenes of carnage and blood had left their mark, a stark reminder of the true cost of conflict and the real suffering of humanity.

Little did our parents know the horror we were witnessing as they waited for news of our safe arrival on the other side. Our parents made several calls to their contact person at the airport, who spoke about unexpected delays. They were reassured that the flight to Asmara hadn't yet arrived and that we would be put on the first available flight.

The scenes of carnage and blood that once haunted our eyes and ears were now replaced with the promise of a new calm after we were moved to an empty warehouse-like office at one end of the terminal, where peace and calm reigned once more.

The adults among us spoke in hushed tones and whispered prayers, a beacon of hope in a world ravaged by war.

Amidst the chaos of the airport warehouse, we found solace in the company of other children. We played and shared snacks; our bond grew stronger with each passing moment, playing hide and seek until we slept on the chairs and old sofas in the office, tired from what we had been through all day and night. What started in the morning as a rushed journey to catch a plane ready to fly had now dipped into an uncertain territory of endless waiting.

The next morning, we boarded the Antonov, a massive Soviet military cargo plane that had arrived while we slept, with a mix of trepidation and excitement.

The huge Antonov loomed in front of us, its sheer size casting a shadow over the worn-out tarmac. My two brothers and I stood in awe amongst the nervous chatter of the few selected passengers who were to board this cargo plane. As we made our way towards the tail of the aircraft, the anticipation in our hearts slowly melded into a nervous knot as we were met with a scene we had not expected.

Wounded men lay strewn across the entire cargo hold floor, their pale faces illuminated by the flickering lights above. Intravenous drips hung from hooks, the smell of disinfectant mingled with the metallic tang of blood, creating an unsettling atmosphere that clung to the air like a heavy fog. At the far end of the plane, amidst the wounded soldiers, were rows of green army boxes, their contents unknown but their presence foreboding.

We were ushered to a corner of the cargo hold, where the few folded canvas seats awaited us. Some of our fellow passengers, lightly wounded soldiers themselves, perched precariously atop the boxes of ammunition, offering us their seats as a gesture of camaraderie. The canvas seats felt flimsy beneath us, a stark contrast to the weight of the situation that surrounded us.

With no seatbelts in sight, we were instructed to hold onto the ropes that lined the walls of the Antonov, their coarse texture a stark reminder of the gravity of our situation. The engines roared to life, drowning out the sounds of the wounded men's quiet moans as the plane taxied down the runway, ready to take flight.

As the Antonov ascended into the sky, the world outside faded into oblivion, leaving behind a sense of unease that settled deep within our hearts. The hum of the engines became a steady drone, lulling us into a state of uneasy rest as we clung to the ropes, our knuckles white with tension.

Time passed in a blur of noise and motion, the rhythmic pulse of the engines a constant backdrop to our thoughts. The wounded soldiers slept fitfully, their bodies wracked with pain even in their dreams. My brothers and I sat in silence, the weight of our situation heavy upon us, each passing minute dragging like an eternity.

The cargo plane filled with an air of tension and unease as the wounded soldiers lay scattered across the canvas seats, a sea of worn-out faces and bodies ravaged by the brutality of war. There was no nurse or medical personnel on board, only us— a group of unfamiliar passengers turned reluctant caregivers in this unlikely scenario.

As the engines roared and the plane cut through the sky, the soldiers groaned in discomfort, their faces a mosaic of blood and sweat. They whispered requests for water, for a kind hand to wipe their brow—words barely audible over the hum of the plane. We were not trained for this, but there was an unspoken understanding among us that we couldn't turn a blind eye to their suffering.

Against the instructions given to us, we slowly rose from our seats, navigating through the maze of wounded bodies with a sense of purpose. Hands outstretched, we offered small comforts—a sip of water, a gentle touch to wipe away the traces of battle from their weary faces. In those moments, we became more than mere passengers; we became angels in the air, providing solace in the face of chaos.

Some soldiers slept, their bodies still and peaceful, while others lay awake, their eyes haunted by the memories of war, calling for their mothers. It was difficult to differentiate between those who slumbered and those who teetered on the edge of the unknown. The plane was a medley of hushed whispers and silent prayers, a sanctuary for the wounded who bore their burdens with quiet dignity.

As we made our rounds, moving back and forth between the canvas seats, our hearts heavy with the weight of their suffering, we scanned the floor for any signs of distress. Every gasp, every trembling hand raised in silent supplication, sent one of us rushing to their side—a beacon of hope in a sea of uncertainty.

In the dim light of the cargo plane, we were bound by a shared humanity, our disparate lives converging in this moment of compassion and kindness. The soldiers, once strangers to us, now bore the imprint of our empathy, their stories etched in the lines of their faces, in the quiet resilience of their spirits.

As the flight continued onwards, each passing minute a testament to our collective strength and resilience, we found solace in the knowledge that we had done what we could in the small ways that mattered most. And though the journey was far from over, we took comfort in the knowledge that, for a brief moment in time, we had been angels in the air—guardians of the wounded souls who soared with us through the night.

Finally, as the first sight of the ground beneath the sky crept through the tiny windows of the cargo hold, the Antonov began its descent. The wheels touched down with a jolt, the sudden impact reverberating through the plane. As we slowly disembarked, the wounded soldiers were carried off to receive medical attention, their faces etched with a mix of relief and pain.

We stepped onto the unfamiliar-looking tarmac, the cold air hitting us like a physical force, the breezy air casting long shadows behind us.

In the late morning's cloudy day, a Soviet-made Latvijia mini-van trundled along the tarmac, carrying us bewildered passengers toward an unfamiliar airport terminal. The airfield was a hive of activity, with scores of old military aircraft scattered across the landscape. Some lay in disrepair, while others roared to life, preparing for take-off. Helicopters whirred overhead, their blades slicing through the air as they zipped around the field.

Inside the van, there was an unspoken unease among the passengers. The terrain and climate were unlike anything we had experienced before, adding to the sense of disorientation. As we neared the terminal, it became clear that this was no ordinary airport. The building appeared to be a hybrid of a terminal and a military camp, its exterior blending seamlessly with the surrounding green and brown hues of the landscape.

The van came to a stop by the side of the terminal camp structure, and we disembarked, our small bags heavy with exhaustion. We trudged wearily behind a man who led us toward the entrance, our eyes darting nervously around the militarised environment. With no clear idea of our whereabouts and hesitant to question our situation, we followed in silence.

Inside the terminal office, confusion reigned as we took our seats, unsure of what was to come. Soon, the other passengers departed, leaving us three very young individuals stranded inside the terminal, waiting to be attended to. Minutes turned into hours as we sat on metal seats, our anxiety growing with each passing moment.

Finally, a lady who had been going up and down all afternoon noticed our loneliness and approached us, her expression a mix of curiosity and concern. She inquired about our presence and our intended destination, prompting us to reveal our identities. We told her about our intended journey to Asmara to visit our grandparents. The lady's shock was palpable as she realised the mix-up that had occurred. She became more confused when she learned we had departed from Mekelle airport.

Upon further investigation, it became apparent that a communication error at Mekelle airport had led to us being placed on the wrong flight to Debre Zeit—over a thousand kilometres south of our intended destination. The lady sought out an officer for assistance, relaying our plight and true destination.

The tall officer's demeanour shifted from curiosity to surprise as he listened to the details of our predicament. He instructed us to wait while he delved into the matter further, determined to unravel the mystery of how young, unaccompanied children had ended up in a military airport far from their intended destination.

After a brief absence, the officer returned, his expression grave yet determined. He questioned us more extensively, piecing together the timeline of events that had led us to the current situation. With no flight number to provide and no boarding pass to show, we recounted the time of our arrival, aiding the officer in identifying the flight that had originated from Mekelle without a passenger list or flight manifesto, as would normally be the case with the unscheduled military flights run by the disconnected, unprofessional team.

With newfound clarity, the officer instructed the lady to assist us while he investigated the series of errors that had brought us to Debre Zeit. It soon emerged that our accompanying adult, who was chosen randomly from among the passengers to Asmara, had been inadvertently left behind in the chaos at Mekelle airport as he helped in the sorting of the wounded soldiers. This oversight had resulted in our misplacement. It also seemed that, as the unbearable scenes at the Mekelle airport terminal were deemed unsuitable for children's eyes, some of the ground staff had decided to move children and mothers to a more secluded side, and we may have been mistaken for being children of one of the mothers.

Amidst the chaos and uncertainty, as we anxiously awaited our fate in an unfamiliar territory, a sense of relief slowly enveloped us like a comforting embrace. The officer, a beacon of hope in the midst of confusion, worked tirelessly to rectify the situation and ensure our safe return home.

With determination etched on his face, the officer established communication with Mekelle Airport, his voice carrying the weight of our collective worries. His reassuring words echoed through the air, promising a safe passage back to familiar grounds. We held onto his every update—a lifeline in a sea of uncertainty.

As the hours ticked by, my father received updates through Colonel Hailu's men, who kept him informed about our unexpected exploration of new territories, offering a glimmer of hope that soon we would find ourselves reunited with our loved ones. However, a veil of protection shielded my mother from the unfolding crisis—her delicate heart shielded from the harsh reality of my father's comforting lies. My father and Colonel Hailu told my mother that we had landed safely in Asmara, but the military phone lines were not available due to the usual technical interruptions of that service.

The officer's unwavering resolve instilled in us a newfound courage, a belief that no matter the challenges ahead, we would weather the storm together.

It was an unusual situation—stranded at Debre Zeit military airport for two days, waiting for a flight home. The bustling atmosphere of the airfield was a stark contrast to the chaos of Mekelle, with cargo being loaded onto aircraft, men in military uniform scurrying about, and fighter jets roaring above in training exercises. Helicopters swooped in and out on an hourly basis, adding to the constant hum of activity.

After being ushered into a small office before sunset, we were greeted with two canvas military beds, complete with scratchy army blankets. The accommodations were basic but serviceable, and the toilets were surprisingly clean, given the industrial nature of the surroundings. Our meals consisted of army rations, similar to those secretly supplied to my mother by Colonel Hailu, a familiar sight from our difficult days in Mekelle. Our family had faced financial hardship when my father remained captive. We smiled at the sight of the rations, which we never thought we would eat again. They took us back to the days when we were more accepting of that meal. We had no choice.

Having not eaten a decent meal for two days, we felt hungry and weak. Our energy was low, and we missed the outside world. As we examined the contents of our ration packages before eating, the dry crackers and apricot jam were our old favourites. We also found the small tablets, which had no labels or instructions. These tiny tablets, sometimes found in the olive-green packages among various components, had never caught our attention at home. Alongside the mysterious tablets, the package also contained needles, pins, and threads, which we always disposed of.

To unlock an old puzzle, my brother Simon, again the curious little man with militaristic interests, inquired about the tiny pills to a nearby soldier. His response was chilling. He hesitated, then shared a grim explanation: some soldiers carried suicide pills or vials of poison in their rations to avoid capture by the enemy. The thought sent shivers down our spines as we realised we might have unknowingly ingested these lethal substances. The idle soldier continued with a disturbing anecdote about the belief that it was more honourable to take one's own life than to be captured and reveal sensitive information to the enemy. His words evoked a scene from a Chinese film we had watched, where a wounded soldier had chosen to end his life by taking the potion attached to his necklace rather than face capture. The tales stirred a sense of unease among us, lingering like a dark cloud over our stay at Debre Zeit.

Our eldest brother, Kaleb, started crying bitterly, remembering he had swallowed many of the pills at our old home. We mocked him for thinking he was dying years after he had ingested the pills.

However, as the days passed, we decided to seek clarification from a higher-ranking officer at the palace. To our relief, the officer dispelled the soldier's unsettling stories, explaining that the tablets were merely painkillers provided to soldiers for self-medication in case of minor ailments. The soldier's fanciful tales were mere products of imagination, perhaps fuelled by the intense environment of a military airfield, or he may have watched too many Chinese revolutionary films.

As we absorbed the truth behind the mysterious tablets, a sense of calm settled over us. The fears that had gripped us for months dissipated, replaced by a newfound appreciation for those who treated us humanely.

In the end, our stay at Debre Zeit military airport became a curious memory, a blend of uncertainty and reassurance. The experience taught us to question the stories we heard, to seek the truth behind the rumours that swirled in the air like wisps of smoke. As we finally boarded our flight home, leaving behind the tarmac and the echoes of military life, we carried with us a newfound sense of resilience, born from the strange circumstances of our unexpected stay in the heart of an airfield.

We observed the comings and goings of aircraft, the chaotic and disorganised work of the ground staff, and the distant thunder of jets taking off and landing. The constant hum of activity became a symphony of efficiency, a testament to the discipline of the military personnel managing the airfield.

The sun hung low in the sky as we prepared to board the helicopter back to Mekelle. After days of waiting in Debre Zeit, the promise of finally returning home was a beacon of hope amidst the uncertainty that surrounded us. The soldiers who looked after us, with their guns and stories of distant battlefields, had painted a picture of a world far removed from the comforts of home.

As we approached the white helicopter with a red cross emblazoned on its body, a sense of unease settled over us. The officer's sarcastic remark about the helicopter being big enough to play football when we asked him how big it was inside did little to alleviate our growing apprehension. Could this really be a flying ambulance or a football field in the air, as we had hoped? Or was there something more ominous lurking beneath the surface?

With each personality manifesting our fears and strengths, my elder brother Simon, always curious and eager for adventure, was drawn to the mysteries of the helicopter, narrating its might and complex body. We clung to each other in a mixture of excitement and trepidation.

In the end, the journey that had begun with uncertainty and miscommunication culminated in a tale of resilience and determination as we navigated the challenges thrown our way. Through collaboration and perseverance, we overcame the obstacles that had temporarily derailed our plans, emerging stronger and more united than before. As we boarded the correct flight back home, a newfound sense of gratitude and camaraderie filled our hearts, binding us together in an unforgettable journey of unexpected twists and turns.

Stepping inside the helicopter, along with a family with two small children, the sight that greeted us was both mesmerising and chilling. Green boxes filled with weapons lined the interior, a stark reminder of the harsh realities of the world we were about to soar over. Boxes of Chinese grenades and land mines were stacked with precision, creating an unsettling presence that sent shivers down our spines. Although not visible, the presence of those explosives inside the boxes could be felt from outside, sending chills down our spines and fear into our hearts.

The space between the deadly cargo seemed vast, emphasising the weight and danger that they carried. With only two pilots for the company, one of them Ethiopian with a warm and reassuring presence, we couldn't help but feel like small islands adrift in a sea of uncertainty.

The Ethiopian pilot, with his kind demeanour and easy smile, tried to ease our fears with conversation and safety instructions. His offer to knock on the cockpit door if we needed anything was a small comfort in the face of the unknown.

As the helicopter lifted off the ground, the roar of the engines drowning out all other sounds, my brother Simon did not waste time sneaking around the cockpit door. After giving a gentle knock, he soon disappeared into the cockpit with the Ethiopian pilot's permission.

Soon, we took out a small light ball from our rucksack and started bouncing and volleying it between our opposite-facing seats. We then began fetching the ball when it veered astray between the green boxes. What started as a simple, meaningless game of ball passing morphed into a full-scale competitive shoot-out game, counting scores at 10,000 feet above earth. We used the boundaries made from ammunition boxes as goalposts, kicking the ball as hard as we could, as if we were afield. The vast space of the helicopter's almost empty cargo allowed for a fierce game of penalty shootouts, realising the overheard depiction of the helicopter's capacity, equating it to a football pitch.

Looking back at this adventurous journey now, I still wonder if anyone else in this world had the thrilling experience of playing football in space, or what I would call it, 'Sky Football.'

Simon, ever the curious one, stayed in the main pilot's cabin asking about the countless buttons that controlled the helicopter, watching the landscape below with a mix of wonder and worry, while the Ethiopian and his co-pilot spoke in Russian and laughed.

As the journey unfolded, the contrasts of the experience became more pronounced. The endless expanse of the Ethiopian landscape, with its rugged beauty and hidden dangers, stretched out below us like a tapestry of light and shadow. The helicopter, a fragile metal bird in a vast and unforgiving sky, carried us towards our destination with a sense of urgency and inevitability.

In the cargo hold, the remaining of us, grappling with our fears and hopes, found solace in the shared experience of the flight. The uncertainty of the future loomed large, but in that moment, high above the earth and surrounded by the echoes of distant conflicts, we found a bond that transcended our fears.

As the helicopter descended towards Mekelle, the lights of the city twinkling in the distance like a promise of safety and home, we knew that this journey, with all its twists and turns, would be etched in our memories forever as a tale of suspense, contrast, and the enduring power of family amidst chaos.

The sun was setting over the vast horizon as our flight touched down at Mekelle Airport. The dry heat on the ground greeted us as we disembarked, weary from our unexpected journey to the south. We exchanged confused glances as we searched the crowd for any sign of our father's driver, who usually picks us up and takes us home.

As we walked towards the terminal, a familiar face emerged from the bustling crowd. It was our father's loyal driver, Biru, standing tall and stoic against the backdrop of chaos. His strong presence gave us a sense of comfort, knowing that we were finally in safe hands.

With a nod of his head, Biru guided us towards the waiting car, the dust swirling around our feet as we made our way through the empty parking lot. The drive back home was quiet, the tension palpable in the air as my brothers and I sat in the backseat, replaying the events of the past three days in our minds.

Our father had only hinted to my mother minutes ago about the mysterious circumstances that led us on this unexpected journey south, leaving us to piece together the fragments of a story that seemed almost too surreal to be true. Telling our mother how we ended up on that mistaken flight, she could not believe it. The twists and turns of our adventure and the harrowing moments that tested our resilience and courage, it all felt like a distant dream from which we were slowly waking up.

As we finally arrived home, the familiar sight of our parents waiting on the doorstep brought a wave of relief that washed over us. My mother's eyes brimmed with tears as she ran towards us, enveloping us in a tight embrace that spoke volumes of her imagination about what she had heard regarding our flights to hell and back.

She held us close, whispering prayers of thanks to her God, her trembling hands betraying her efforts to stay strong for our sake. I could see the guilt etched in her eyes, blaming herself for letting us out of her sight, even for a moment. And in that moment, she made a silent vow—to never let us out of her protective embrace again.

As the evening unfolded, we sat with our parents, recounting the details of our misadventure with a mixture of amusement and relief. My mother's tears flowed freely at every twist and turn of our saga, her disbelief slowly giving way to overwhelming gratitude that we were back home, safe and sound.

The plan to spend our holidays in Asmara, Eritrea, was put on hold until my father could arrange for a reliable escort to ensure our safety. Two weeks later, with all precautions in place, we set off on another journey, this time to a destination that held the promise of cherished memories.

As we journeyed back home from Asmara a few weeks later, our hearts were full of gratitude for the experiences we had shared, the bonds we had forged, and the adventures that had shaped us into the resilient souls we had become.

We did this again several times until we left Mekelle behind on our final flight; a sense of bittersweet nostalgia settled over us, knowing that our days of hardship and poverty, of life in the palace, the cinema experience, and tales of horror flights and unexpected detours were behind us. And yet, in the quiet depths of our hearts, we knew that the memories of those turbulent days would always linger, a testament to the strength of our family bond and the enduring power of love we found in the truly historical city of Mekelle.

The Greatest Gift

Another Brick On The Wall

In 1983, a year after our family had moved to Asmara with my mother, my father bid farewell to his beloved Tigray, leaving behind a legacy of humanitarianism, environmental stewardship, and civic service. Despite the challenges and adversities he had faced, his dedication to the communities he loved had never wavered. As he set out on this new chapter of his life, he carried with him the indomitable spirit of a man who had dedicated his life to serving others.

My father, a man of unwavering determination and unyielding commitment to the people and communities of Tigray, found himself entangled in a web of political intrigue and ethnic animosities. As a respected leader in the region, he had dedicated his life to fostering prosperity and peace among the diverse communities that called Tigray their home. However, his noble intentions had unwittingly attracted near-fatal adversaries who sought to disrupt his efforts and undermine his authority.

The turning point came when a powerful group of native Tigrayans organised a clandestine assembly, where my father was warned of dire consequences should he continue his work. Threatened and outnumbered, he realised that it had become nearly impossible for him, an Eritrean by birth, to lead the people of Tigray towards a brighter future. With a heavy heart but a steadfast resolve, my father made the difficult decision to request a transfer from his position of leadership. He requested the central government to relieve him of his responsibilities, citing his inability to continue working among some native officials who were close to the leadership.

My father's request was granted as the government seemed to win the hearts of Tigrayans through propaganda and war, controlling most areas of the region, resulting in relative stability.

Soon, my father found himself at the helm of a resettlement project in the remote reaches of Western Ethiopia. Here, amidst the vast expanse of fertile land and thick forests, new towns were being established to accommodate famine-stricken farmers from the northern villages who were in desperate need of a fresh start. This was a task unlike any he had faced before, requiring not only special knowledge and skills but also a profound empathy for the struggles of the displaced families.

The farmers from the north, wary of abandoning their ancestral lands, were reluctant to accept the proposal of resettlement. Their defiance was fuelled by fear and uncertainty, as their once fertile fields had been ravaged by conflict and nature. The government and international organisations worked tirelessly to provide aid and devise a sustainable solution, but progress was slow and fraught with challenges due to the continuous war.

Amidst this tumultuous backdrop, my father laboured dutifully, utilising his knowledge and experience with the plights of those communities, bridging the gap between the reluctant farmers and the officials tasked with their resettlement. His tireless efforts to implement the government's unpopular plans and unwavering compassion did not sow the seeds of trust and understanding among the host communities.

And so, in the vast expanse of western Ethiopia, amidst the dense forests and golden plains, my father continued his journey of service and selflessness with other demographic missions. Though the road ahead was long and arduous, my father faced it with the same unwavering resolve that had guided him through the trials of Tigray, his family some 1,500 km away in Asmara, Eritrea.

The sun hung low in the sky as our last flight out of Tigray descended towards Asmara, the capital city of Eritrea, a familiar place that would become our new home. For my brothers and me, this move marked a significant change in our lives. It was a decision made by our parents with a mixture of hope and apprehension, a sacrifice for our education and safety amidst the political turmoil that had gripped our previous home in Tigray.

As the wheels of the aircraft touched the runway, a sense of uncertainty flooded our minds. I glanced at my brothers, their faces reflecting the same mix of emotions. We had been through so much with our father – the good, the bad, and everything in between. The thought of not having him by our side was both daunting and heartbreaking.

Stepping outside the terminal, we were greeted by the warm embrace of our grandparents, who had eagerly awaited our arrival. The air was filled with the scent of blooming flowers and the distant hum of city life, a stark contrast to the bustling streets of Mekelle.

Our grandparents had prepared accommodation for us within the large compound, a cosy space that would be our sanctuary in this new and unfamiliar land. They showered us with love and reassurance, easing the ache of missing our father, if only for a moment.

As the school term started, we were enrolled in Geza Kenisha, one of the few remaining private schools in Asmara known for its rigorous academic curriculum and strict behavioural codes. As I walked through the gates of the school, a sense of determination filled my chest. I was here to learn, to grow, to make my parents proud.

In Geza Kenisha, I was placed in the 7th-grade class, surrounded by classmates eager to welcome the new arrivals. The teachers were firm but fair, pushing us to excel in our studies and conduct. My brothers, too, found their places in their respective year groups, each forging their path in this new chapter of our lives.

Days turned into weeks, weeks into months, and before we knew it, we had settled into a routine in Asmara. The city, with its pastel-coloured buildings and bustling markets, became our home. We explored its winding alleyways and immersed ourselves in its rich culture.

Despite the distance from our father, we found solace in the hope that one day, we would be reunited and that he would find a more settled appointment in Addis Ababa, a city far removed from the chaos that had driven us away. Our parents' sacrifice had given us a chance at a brighter future, and we were determined to make the most of it.

We had completed our first year of high school in a more peaceful environment, away from the upheaval and conspiracies that had once threatened to consume us in our own home. Though our father's absence still weighed heavily on our hearts, we knew that his love and guidance would always be with us, guiding us through the challenges that lay ahead.

Asmara may not have been an easy change, but it had given us the opportunity to grow, to learn, and to thrive in the face of adversity. And for that, we would always be thankful.

During the three years I attended Geza Kenisha, a previously private school managed by The Evangelical Lutheran Church, later renamed Issak Tewoldemedhin School, my journey through learning was not just about textbooks and exams; it was a tapestry woven with unique experiences that shaped my relationships with teachers and peers.

In Eritrean schools, a shadow loomed over the dreams of young students who grew up learning in different curriculums, including Italian and other private institutions. They had never learned Amharic, the official national language. The language they hated and labelled as 'the occupier's language' had been weaponised by the regime as a tool of oppression. It was now mandated, alongside maths and English, that students had to earn a passing mark or face repeating the year. It became a mark of academic prowess and loyalty to the ruling elite.

Many bright students with a hunger for knowledge found themselves caught in this web of balancing their ideology with their academic future. Their Italian schools were closed when they reached secondary levels and were forced to join our school. They had to learn Amharic embarrassingly at foundation levels, alongside grade four and five children. The language tasted even more bitter on their tongues as it had diminished their dignity. The language was being used as a psychological weapon to defeat young students' minds. Resisting to learn Amharic was an expression of ideological reluctance, not a choice of academic subject. Amharic was spoken only by those who upheld the regime, by those whose hands were stained with the blood of dissenters.

Despite using the same Geez alphabets as Tigrinya, the local dialect in Eritrea, every lesson was a battle, every word a struggle. To excel in the language seemed like aligning with the oppressors, a betrayal of the students' own beliefs and values. Yet to falter meant risking their future; their chance to advance academically was in question.

In the heart of this storm, young Eritrean students stood tall with resistance in a sea of conformity. With each passing day, they walked the tightrope between success and rebellion, their academic balance a testament to their unwavering spirit. And though the path was fraught with obstacles, they refused to let the darkness consume them, holding onto the light of knowledge that burned within.

Here, I found myself in a pivotal role, bridging the gap between the teachers imported from mainland Ethiopia, who were not familiar with the local language, Tigrinya, and students who considered anyone and anything from Ethiopia as the enemy.

In Tigray, I grew up surrounded by Amharic-speaking house staff and guards. In this land, where tensions ran deep between regions, Amharic was not just a language for me but a lifeline to navigate through the complexities of the various communities who lived and worked there. From a tender age, I absorbed the lyrical sounds of the language like a sponge, weaving its intricate words into my everyday life. I also developed an understanding of its literature through my early education at school.

Living and growing up in an institution—a melting pot of Ethiopian cultures and languages—communicating in Amharic was the natural and only option. From the housekeeping staff, who shared stories of their Amhara heritage, to the security guards, stern yet gentle in their Oromo roots, and the palace guards, proud descendants of the noble Gurage people, each interaction enriched my understanding of the language.

As I grew up reading many books written in Amharic, my proficiency blossomed—a testament to the diverse tapestry of my upbringing in Tigray, where the language was spoken in every corner of my world. It became a legacy of cultural exchange and understanding that would shape my future endeavours and define my path forward.

My days as a junior high school student at Geza Kenisha in Asmara were often filled with the rhythmic clacking of the Amharic typewriter as I meticulously typed exam papers, helping the school due to a shortage of staff with good knowledge of the language—a skill that made me stand out.

The newly graduated teachers, sent from mainland Ethiopia to help with the transformation of the school system, were unfamiliar with the nuances of the local culture and language. They relied on me for many tasks that required translation, such as preparing Amharic study materials and handouts, translating during school assemblies and parent-teacher meetings, and even interpreting during disciplinary proceedings to ensure their messages were delivered accurately.

Through these tasks, I became not just a student but a crucial link in the school's communication chain. I was popular for my ability to mediate between defiant students and the unwelcome teachers, translating, suggesting solutions, and influencing narratives as well as decisions. Despite the weight of responsibility on my shoulders, I found joy in being able to help build bonds with both teachers and students along the way.

These tasks brought me closer to teachers in a personal sphere. I spent some of my free time with the Amharic-speaking teachers, going to restaurants and cinemas and helping with their visits to the city centre for shopping and socialising. My teachers felt more comfortable and safer with me than on their own. This relationship, and their confidence in my commendable academic status, led to their trust in me to help with preparing and marking exam papers for my fellow students. They even trusted me to take exam papers home for marking and comments. I was doing an honest job despite the opportunities to boost some of my fellow students' and brothers' grades, who were struggling with their Amharic exams.

My journey of self-discovery and linguistic mastery had another advantage. My grandfather, Goitapa, a respected rights advocate and community leader, recognised the importance of my proficiency in Amharic for his legal and administrative work.

Goitapa, whose admiration for linguistic skills found a usable talent in a young person in his own yard—me—quickly recognised my linguistic and clerical abilities and chose me as his personal assistant. Together, we became a formidable duo, with me acting as a valuable partner in his work advocating for communities through letters and applications.

To enhance my skills further and get my other siblings to adopt similar skills, Goitapa enrolled me and some of my uncles in a summer Amharic and English typing school, where I honed my typing efficiency. As a clever business decision and investment, he bought a typewriter—an essential tool that would soon become an extension of my capabilities. Goitapa saved significantly by not having to pay professionals. Our days were filled with meticulous sessions of typing official letters under his dictation in Tigrinya, with endless cycles of editing and deleting until perfection was achieved. I simultaneously translated Goitapa's dictation and typed it instantly in Amharic.

In Asmara, where residents had many legal cases that required a skilled approach—whether recovering properties or saving imprisoned family members—Goitapa was always there to help, using his influence to the best of his ability. That also meant I had to prepare several letters and applications. As every letter and application had to be notarised with a stamp and signed by the applicant, I also had the task of shuttling between houses and government offices.

The sound of typewriters clacking in our home resembled that of a legitimate office. When not in school, I, a small teenager with determination etched on my face, carried a full metal typewriter that seemed to weigh half my body, enclosed in a sturdy leather box. This typewriter was not just a cumbersome burden; it was a potent tool I used with the eloquent dictation from Goitapa, my mentor and partner, in navigating the bureaucratic maze that engulfed us.

Our mission was clear—to tackle problems, submit applications, and craft letters with precision and speed. Whenever Goitapa and I ventured out to handle affairs in municipal offices, courts, or other governmental departments, the typewriter was our trusty companion. Its metallic sheen reflected the intensity of our purpose as we wove through the crowded streets, attracting curious glances from passers-by. With Goitapa's habit of walking to all destinations, the burden was heavy on me as I followed, carrying the typewriter, half my body size and weight. The need to carry the heavy metal typewriter everywhere was due to the daily chances of having to type letters instantly or amend those I typed at home.

On numerous occasions, we found ourselves in urgent situations where a quick letter or application needed to be typed on the spot. Whether we perched on a weather-worn rock under the shade of a sprawling tree or sought refuge in a nearby café bustling with chatter, the typewriter hummed under my nimble fingers. Goitapa, with his commanding presence and eloquence in Tigrinya, would dictate the words that I meticulously translated into Amharic, each keystroke resonating with determination.

During my urgent typing sessions inside cafés, Goitapa, the enigmatic man with an air of authority, demanded silence from other patrons. Whenever he sensed the noise escalating, he would unleash his sharp tongue, reprimanding them for disrupting my focus. He would tell them to have respect for the young man, half their age, doing more important work. People would agree and fall silent. As his words cut through the air like a sharp blade, the café fell into a hushed reverence. Even the clinking of cups ceased as I watched in awe at the power he wielded over the bustling crowd. With his mere presence, Goitapa commanded a silence that was both eerie and awe-inspiring.

Under his watchful gaze and immense pressure on me to produce strong letters, I continued to type, the rhythmic clicking of the keys punctuating the stillness. The apologies from the patrons hung in the air, a token of their acknowledgement of Goitapa's authority. At that moment, I realised that amid chaos, Goitapa was the quiet force that allowed me to find peace. His actions were a testament to his unwavering dedication to my craft. As I typed away, enveloped in the cocoon of silence he had created, I knew that in the chaos of the city, I had found my sanctuary in the unlikeliest of places.

As I focused on the task at hand, oblivious to the whispers and gazes of those around us, the rhythmic tapping of the typewriter became a melody of efficiency and purpose. The clatter of keys echoed the urgency of our mission, each letter imprinting a piece of our determination on the blank paper. People's curiosity turned into admiration as they watched a small teenager handling a typewriter with such proficiency and seriousness, breaking the mould of conventional expectations.

Through the haze of cigarette smoke from patrons and the aroma of freshly brewed coffee from the café, our partnership thrived in the midst of chaos. Goitapa, the wise and seasoned guide, led the way with his unwavering resolve, while I, the young apprentice, embraced the challenges with unwavering dedication. The typewriter, with its metallic gleam, symbolised not just a tool of communication but a beacon of hope and change in a world governed by paperwork and protocol.

With each letter typed and each application submitted, we left an indelible mark on the bureaucratic landscape, a testament to our unwavering commitment to making a difference. The typewriter, though burdensome, carried the weight of our aspirations and dreams, travelling with us through the labyrinth of red tape and formalities.

In the heart of Asmara, amidst the flurry of activity and the symphony of typewriters, a small teenager and his mentor forged a path of resilience and determination, armed with nothing but perseverance, a trusty typewriter in a leather suitcase, and a shared vision of a better tomorrow. As we navigated the challenges that came our way, one clack of the keys at a time, our story unfolded—a narrative of courage, grit, and the transformative power of words and problem-solving.

Despite the arduous hours spent crafting documents, Goitapa's appreciation was evident. He rewarded my dedication with small coins and thoughtful gifts. Together, we ventured into town, where my translation skills proved invaluable in navigating courthouses and government offices.

As the days passed, Goitapa's motivational words spurred me on, instilling in me a sense of purpose and determination. Together, we navigated the convoluted government offices, where printed Amharic documents were a prerequisite for advancing cases. The weight of responsibility pressed down on my shoulders, but Goitapa's unwavering faith in my abilities gave me the strength to persevere.

Through our collaboration, a bond of mutual respect and camaraderie blossomed, bridging the gap between mentor and apprentice and forging a partnership that went beyond mere words on pages. Under my patient tutelage, the intricate curves and loops of the Amharic script slowly became familiar strokes on my mechanical keyboard.

Through tireless practice and unwavering dedication, I honed my typing skills to precision, effortlessly transcribing the complexities of typewriting in Amharic. There are no vowels and consonants in the Amharic script. The consonant letters are often combined with the vowel letters to form an ancient syllable known as "Fidel" or Geez letters. There are a total of 231 possible Fidel combinations woven into the 37 keypads of the typing machine, using the half and full shift buttons to type each letter, excluding punctuation marks, numbers, and symbols. Before the age of computers, typing in Amharic was a laborious task of pressing two or three keys to form one letter.

With each of Goitapa's documents submitted, I felt a swell of pride, knowing that I was contributing to my grandfather's tireless efforts in upholding justice for the marginalized communities and tribes of Eritrea. At that moment, amidst the click-clack of keys, I realised that our intertwined journey was not just about mastering a language but about boldly championing a cause greater than ourselves.

Despite my academic pursuits and artistic endeavours, I found time to assist teachers at school, eager to learn and give back the knowledge and guidance they had provided me. But perhaps the most special role I played was that of my grandfather's secretary. Sitting by his side, I soaked in his wisdom and knowledge, typing away his words of wisdom on the clunky mechanical typewriter.

Looking back now, I marvel at how I managed to juggle these diverse roles with such grace and dedication. Each task enriched me in its own way, shaping me into the multifaceted individual I am today. As I reflect on those busy, successful days in Asmara, I can't help but feel grateful for the opportunities that shaped me into the person I am today.

Under Goitapa's guidance, I learned the delicate dance of leadership, and my intelligence and intuition were nurtured by his mentoring. The intricacies of diplomacy, power, and the art of negotiation revealed themselves to me, shaping me into a confident and poised young individual. My once timid voice found strength within the hallowed walls of our home, where discussions swirled like gentle breezes, each word laden with respect and consideration.

Goitapa's discerning eyes, honed by years of wisdom, had singled me out among my siblings for special favour. It was a privilege that felt weighty yet exhilarating, as I was ushered into the inner circle of decision-makers alongside my grandmother and mother.

As the seasons turned, I watched my brothers and siblings with a mix of empathy and pride, knowing that Goitapa's favour had bestowed upon me a unique responsibility. Together with my esteemed household members, we steered our family through the political and social hardships of those difficult times. As the flickering firelight danced across our faces each evening, I felt a deep sense of gratitude for the blessing of Goitapa's favour, a mantle I wore with both humility and grace.

United in Hardship

Glory Days

Life in the war-stricken Eritrea was a stark contrast to the opulent life we once lived in the palace in Tigray. Gone were the days of lavish comfort and household staff catering to our every need. In Asmara, we were thrust into a harsh reality where necessities were a luxury, and survival was the top priority. Despite the hardships, there was a sense of resilience and camaraderie among the residents that made life bearable, even at its toughest.

As children, my siblings and I quickly adapted to our new surroundings as residents. We embraced the simplicity of our new life, finding joy in the little things that brought us together with the other children in the neighbourhood. Our days were filled with simple pleasures, like playing marbles on the streets or sharing stories under the shade of a lone tree. The laughter of children echoed through the war-torn city, a testament to our ability to find happiness amidst chaos.

Our grandparents, who had known of our life of luxury in Tigray, tried their best to shield us from the harsh realities of our new home. They attempted to recreate the comfort and luxury we once knew, but the constraints of war and scarcity made it an impossible feat. Still, their love and efforts were evident in the small gestures of kindness and warmth that they bestowed upon us.

Despite the lack of material wealth, we found richness in the friendships we forged with the locals. The community welcomed us with open arms, their resilience and spirit inspiring us to embrace the challenges of our new life. We learned the value of perseverance and adaptability, traits that would serve us well in the years to come.

In the midst of uncertainty and turmoil, there were moments of pure joy and fun that we treasured dearly. We organised impromptu soccer matches in the dusty fields, the shouts and cheers cutting through the tense air of the neighbourhoods.

The simple act of coming together to play and laugh helped us forget, if only for a moment, the harsh realities that surrounded us.

As time passed, we grew accustomed to the rhythm of life in Asmara. The once unfamiliar streets we visited as tourists became our playground, and the faces of our neighbours became familiar and comforting. We found solace in the shared experiences of struggle and survival, knowing that we were not alone in facing the challenges of war.

Looking back, I realise that the hardship we endured in Asmara taught us valuable lessons about resilience, empathy, and the true meaning of happiness. It was not found in material wealth or comfort but in the strength of community, the bonds of friendship, and the unwavering spirit of hope that carried us through the darkest of times. In the end, it was these intangible riches that shaped us into the resilient individuals we would become, forever grateful for the lessons learned in the poverty-stricken city of Asmara.

In war-stricken Eritrea, people were tested for their resilience and strength in the face of unforgiving living conditions. The scarcity of basic necessities like water and electricity had woven itself into the fabric of everyday life for the families residing in the region.

During weekends, we were told to sit outside and spot the arrival of the tanker trucks, which came with a limited amount of potable water. When we spotted them from afar, we would call our mothers to come and fight for the limited supply. The tanker truck would come to distribute water for families, a few buckets for each household. Families gathered around a central point where these private tanker truck owners distributed rationed water in large buckets. As young boys, we helped our mothers with our small hands gripping tightly onto the handles of these heavy vessels and dutifully carried them back to our homes. The weight of the precious liquid was a physical manifestation of the daily struggles faced by our families.

Our mothers, the pillars of strength in our household, controlled the economical usage of water with great attention to ensure every drop was utilised efficiently. Water, the elixir of life in this parched land, was not to be wasted. It served multiple purposes in our home—from quenching thirst to washing dishes and bathing.

The meticulous management of this scarce resource extended to other aspects of daily life. Water used for washing clothes and kitchen utensils was never discarded recklessly; it was carefully saved to be repurposed for flushing toilets, a practice that had become the norm among the inhabitants of Asmara. Gutters were improvised to accumulate rainwater in large barrels to be used for washing and flushing. This water, a symbol of abundance in a land plagued by scarcity, was cherished and utilised wisely. Despite the challenges posed by the limited water supply, the families in this community maintained a remarkably clean and hygienic lifestyle, a testament to the resourcefulness and determination ingrained in their culture.

The struggles did not end with water; electricity was another luxury that eluded the residents of Asmara. Rationed to specific areas for a few hours in the evening on selected days of the week, the arrival of electricity was a moment to be cherished. When the soft glow of light illuminated their humble abode, mothers wasted no time in utilising this precious resource to its fullest potential. From preparing meals to completing household chores, every minute of electricity was maximised before darkness enveloped their world once again.

Amidst the bleakness of their circumstances, the resilience of the people shone brightly. Our mothers' unwavering determination to navigate through the challenges of restricted resources with grace and fortitude inspired those around them. They were not just mothers but guardians of hope and stability in a world where uncertainty loomed large.

Through shared grief, the essence of a community is bound by shared struggles and unity in resilience. The harsh living conditions, though challenging, had forged a spirit of camaraderie and strength among the inhabitants of Asmara. Amid adversity, they found solace in each other's company and determination to overcome every obstacle thrown their way.

Many Eritrean families received financial help from worried, hardworking members in the diaspora that helped Asmara to continue the indomitable spirit of its people and illuminated the poverty like a beacon of hope. And in the serenity of the candle-lit nights, the sound of laughter and whispered conversations echoed through the alleyways, a testament to the unwavering bond that held this community together in the face of adversity. Despite the harsh living conditions, the people of Asmara had learned to thrive in the midst of scarcity, their resilience a testament to the human spirit's ability to persevere against all odds.

Having recently moved from the less developed region of Tigray, we found ourselves enveloped in the novelty of urban life in Asmara. Back in Tigray, television was nothing but a distant idea, something we had only glimpsed in grainy films or heard whispered tales about. The arrival in Asmara opened up a new world for us—a world filled with endless possibilities and the enchanting allure of the small screen. It wasn't long after we settled in our modest abode that a wave of excitement swept through the neighbourhood: the national TV broadcast was set to resume after years of silence, not as the government's token of generosity, but as a media tool to flush reluctant minds with propaganda.

As the news spread like wildfire, anticipation brimmed in the hearts of the residents. Stories of bygone days when Asmara boasted multiple TV stations, including one owned by Americans, floated through conversations like cherished memories. The void left by the absence of television broadcasting for so many years was about to be filled once again. And for our family, this resurgence brought an unexpected gift from across the seas—a black-and-white 20-inch Grundig television sent by our uncle from Italy.

The moment the TV crackled to life in our modest living room, it was as if a portal to another dimension had been opened. The neighbourhood gathered around the screen, their eyes wide with wonder, as the Ethiopian National Television Broadcast flickered to life, illuminating their faces with its ghostly black-and-white glow. The initial programmes were mostly news and propaganda, but to us, it was a treasure trove of knowledge and entertainment unlike anything we had experienced before.

In those early days, our family devoured every programme from start to end, regardless of the content. The novelty of television was so intoxicating that even the most mundane shows held a magical charm. As the weeks passed, the TV programmes began to evolve, offering a diverse range of entertainment—from music programmes that stirred the soul to short dramas that tugged at heartstrings. It felt like we had free cinema delivered to our home once more, on a much smaller screen.

The real revelation, however, came in the form of Soviet films dubbed in Amharic. Many young members of the neighbourhood had never encountered such cinematic marvels at home; we found ourselves captivated by the gripping narratives and haunting visuals that unfolded on the screen. Each viewing was like a journey to a distant land, a glimpse into a world beyond our wildest dreams.

But what made the TV experience truly extraordinary for us was not just the content itself, but the communal spirit it fostered. Whenever there was electricity, our home became a sanctuary for the entire neighbourhood—a place where families from all around would gather every evening to partake in the marvels of television. As the clock struck six, the streets would empty, and a procession of eager faces would converge at our household, all eager for another night of shared entertainment.

For most Eritrean families, having a TV in their homes was a luxury they couldn't afford, especially the low-income families who lived in my grandparents' housing complex. To be more precise, there weren't even TVs for sale in the market, as they were deemed unaffordable.

The air inside the small living room buzzed with anticipation as the crowd settled in, with children nestled on the floor and adults perched on chairs and makeshift cushions. Laughter, gasps, and whispers filled the room as the TV illuminated the faces of the audience, turning their once mundane existence into a spectacle of wonder and delight.

For our family, those evenings spent in the warm glow of the television were more than just a form of entertainment; they were a bridge to a new world of possibilities and connections. The flickering images on the screen sparked conversations, fostered friendships, and created lasting memories that would be cherished for years to come.

As the national TV broadcast continued to mesmerize and captivate the viewers, we realised that our move to Asmara had brought us not just a new home but a newfound sense of belonging and unity. And it all began with the simple joy of discovering the magic of television in a place where it had been absent for far too long. Just like we had friends watching with us on the big screen in Mekelle City Hall, we found other little company on the small screen. We were never alone in front of the screen.

It was a cosy home nestled in the heart of a quiet neighbourhood, where the sounds of laughter and the pitter-patter of little feet once brought joy and warmth. As time went by, the number of children attending the daily TV shows at my grandparents' house seemed to multiply magically. What was once a manageable gathering had grown into a bustling hub of activity that our home could barely accommodate.

My grandmother, a gracious hostess, found herself facing a new challenge each day as she tried to manage the logistical and home management issues that accompanied the influx of little guests. After every TV show, she would diligently clean up the remnants of snacks and spilled drinks, the marks of little hands and feet on the furniture and floors a testament to the joyful chaos that ensued.

Children, oblivious to the mess they sometimes left behind, would scamper indoors after hours of playing in the mud, their innocence shining through their dirt-streaked faces. The white marble floors, once pristine and gleaming, now bore the marks of countless little adventures and impromptu games, a silent witness to the boundless energy and laughter that filled the house.

As the number of attendees increased, the once-private sanctity of our family space was gradually eroded. Both children and adults would linger long after the TV shows ended, turning evening visits into extended stays that tested the limits of our hospitality. It was a tradition to share meals with guests, but the scarcity of resources and the sheer volume of people in the room posed a challenge.

Dinners were now consumed hastily, either before six in the evening or after eleven at night, a departure from the usual family routine. The hustle and bustle of so many guests disrupted the peace and rhythm of our daily lives as we adapted to accommodate the expanding crowd within our humble abode.

The joy and innocence of the young children, though endearing, sometimes clashed with the desire for quiet conversations among the adults. Cheering and excited screams would punctuate the air, interrupting the flow of conversations and prompting exasperated sighs from the grown-ups, who sought solace in hushed tones.

Facing the mounting challenges of maintaining order and peace within the household, it was eventually decided that a change was necessary. With a heavy heart, it was decreed that children were to be banned from the sitting room during TV shows—a decision made in an attempt to restore a semblance of calm and order to the gathering space.

The decision to curb the presence of children in the sitting room marked a turning point in our household dynamics. The atmosphere shifted, the once-vibrant and chaotic gatherings now tinged with a hint of solemnity and restraint. The lust for watching TV was put on hold as the rhythms of our family life were recalibrated to accommodate this new arrangement.

As days turned into weeks and weeks into months, the echoes of children's laughter gradually faded, replaced by a sense of tranquillity and order that had long been absent. The white marble floors regained their lustre, the furniture no longer bore the marks of youthful exuberance, and a sense of calm settled over our home once more.

And so, as the days passed and the number of audiences dwindled, a sense of serenity and peace returned to our humble abode—a testament to the enduring bonds of family and the ever-evolving tapestry of life.

The absence of children in the sitting room marked a turning point in our household dynamics. The atmosphere shifted, the once-vibrant and chaotic gatherings now tinged with a hint of solemnity and restraint. The lust for watching TV was put on hold as the rhythms of our family life were recalibrated to accommodate this new arrangement.

In Asmara, under the tight grip of a communist regime, where television was a treasured possession that delivered only state-controlled programming, one of the rare glimmers of freedom came in the form of a single Western song played on Saturday nights. This snippet of musical rebellion was carefully crafted by the government to be a departure from the usual cultural programming—a calculated move to modernise the viewing experience for citizens who yearned to get their hands on Western culture through illegal means.

The show's producers, under strict surveillance and censorship, handpicked a modest Western song to air, ensuring it had no flashy visuals or provocative lyrics that could incite dissent among the young minds watching. The chosen tune was often a country ballad sung by seasoned artists with an undeniable charm that transcended borders. And among the limited selection of Western songs that made it past the Iron Curtain, one particular track stood out like a beacon of hope amidst the bleakness—"Islands in the Stream" by Kenny Rogers and Dolly Parton.

For the viewers, this weekly single dose of Western music was a lifeline to a world beyond their constrained reality. The forbidden allure of these foreign melodies sparked a quiet revolution within the hearts of the viewers, especially the younger generation hungry for a taste of the forbidden fruit. Despite the government's efforts to shield them from outside influences, the mesmerizing notes of Rogers and Parton found a way to weave into the fabric of their existence, becoming a source of solace and unity in a society rife with restrictions.

And so, as the strains of "Islands in the Stream" filled our humble abode on those Saturday nights, the family found solace in the shared experience of defiance—a silent rebellion that bound us together in a clandestine celebration of freedom. Each note carried a weight of resistance, a testament to the indomitable spirit that refused to be silenced by the shackles of tyranny.

But for one particular family, as would be for few others, the allure of Western music was not a novelty in our modest home filled with remnants of a bygone era. Old vinyl records lay scattered like forgotten treasures—remnants of a time when music flowed freely and hearts sang without fear. These relics of rebellion belonged to the older uncles who had fled their homeland seeking freedom, leaving behind a legacy of resistance in the form of Rolling Stones, Beatles, CCR, and Bee Gees records.

The younger members of the family, inspired by the stories stored in storage rooms around the house, delved into the world of Motown records with eager curiosity. We pored over the worn-out album covers, deciphered the cryptic lyrics, and sang along in hushed tones—a secret bond that transcended generations and borders. Despite the risks involved in possessing such contraband, we found solace in the melodies that echoed through the dimly lit rooms—a reminder of a world that existed beyond the confines of our reality.

As the years passed, the family's collection of vinyl records dwindled from mishandling and age; others were hidden away from prying eyes—a silent testament to their defiance against oppression. The forbidden music became our sanctuary, a refuge from the harsh realities of our everyday lives, a reminder that freedom was not just a distant dream, but a tangible heartbeat pulsating through the grooves of each record.

In the heart of Eritrea, where traditions ran deep and pride held strong, the sounds of old vinyl records resonated through the homes. With the Eritreans' disdain for the Amharic language and music, and the limited existence or absence of their musical heritage, the dusty vinyl became cherished treasures. And as the world outside remained cloaked in shadow, we held onto the music in our hearts, a beacon of light that guided us through the darkest of times. For in the harmony of our voices and the melodies that transcended borders, we found a glimmer of hope — a promise of a brighter tomorrow, where freedom would reign supreme and music would be the universal language of defiance.

Years passed, and Asmara began to witness a transformation. The city that had once been a hub of fashion and elegance saw a resurgence of its people, embracing their identity with a renewed sense of pride and purpose. The youth, who had once dreamt of fleeing the country, now found themselves drawn back to their roots, inspired by the resilience and determination of their diaspora siblings.

As the first generation of Eritrean diasporas settled in their new homes, they faced countless challenges, yet their unwavering determination and resilience paved the way for a brighter future. Working tirelessly to support their families back home, they also became the guiding light for their younger siblings, facilitating their escape from the oppressive regime and helping them start anew in foreign lands.

Despite the physical distance that separated them, the Eritrean diaspora remained connected to their roots and their homeland's struggle for independence.

They actively contributed to the fight for liberty by organising awareness campaigns, fundraising events, and cultural festivals around the world. Their dedication and unwavering support echoed across the globe, igniting a sense of solidarity and hope among Eritreans for the cause of independence.

With more youngsters reaching Europe and North America after long and difficult journeys through Sudan and the Sahara desert, the streets of Asmara once again became a colourful tapestry of fashion and style as the people rediscovered the beauty of their heritage and culture. The sense of visual attraction and competition that had once defined the city now took on a new meaning — a celebration of individuality and unity in diversity.

Through the struggles and triumphs, the people of Asmara learned that true beauty lies not just in what meets the eye but in the strength of the human spirit and the resilience of a community united in purpose. As the echoes of the past mingled with the promises of the future, Asmara stood as a testament to the enduring power of hope, love, and the unwavering spirit of its people. Innovation and the youth understood that true cultural evolution lay in the harmonious coexistence of old and new.

And so, the streets of Asmara continued to buzz with the vibrant energy of change as Eritreans in the diaspora and at home navigated the delicate dance between tradition and transformation. The clash of cultures gave birth to a new era of creativity and self-discovery in art and sports, where the boundaries of identity blurred, and a sense of unity emerged from diversity. In the ever-evolving tapestry of Eritrean society, the threads of tradition and modernity intertwined, weaving a narrative of resilience, adaptation, and growth.

As for our family, the journey of embarking on fashion and pop music that had taken the city of Asmara by storm was no different. Our family was enveloped in a flurry of fashion and lifestyle changes. Our uncles and aunts from both parents in distant lands sent their blessings in the form of gifts and treasures, each parcel a testament to their unwavering love and support. From Germany came sleek electronics and gadgets that sparkled with modernity. Those in Italy sent exquisite fabrics and designer clothing, a tapestry of colours and textures that reflected the country's rich heritage. Canada contributed books and educational materials, a tribute to the land of knowledge and innovation. Norway, known for its pristine landscapes and artistic sensibilities, gifted musical instruments and artwork that spoke of creativity and expression.

Asmara became a land of excitement as humble households were filled with joy, especially as parents and grandparents were allowed to travel abroad for treatments and visits. They returned from their trips to the far-off lands of the West renewed, revived, and full of hope after seeing their beloved children after a long time since they had left home. It was a time when the iron grip of the government's restrictions seemed to loosen, especially for the elderly.

Each time our grandparents returned from their European adventures, they carried with them a treasure trove of forbidden goods. Tens of bags overflowing with old and new clothes, music tapes, video cassette players, and the coveted cassettes themselves spilled into the living room, transforming the once-modest home into a haven of Western indulgence.

As teenagers living in a society where the government tightly controlled the influx of Western culture, we revelled in the newfound luxuries that adorned our homes. The colourful fabrics, vibrant music, and exotic gadgets became symbols of rebellion against the suffocating norms imposed upon us.

With joyful defiance, we embraced the cultural transformation that arrived in those bulging suitcases, savouring each moment of freedom that came with it. Our grandparents unknowingly became our allies, our cargo deliveries in a silent battle against the oppressive restrictions of the regime, infusing our lives with a taste of the forbidden fruits of the West.

In our grandparents' home in Asmara, where simplicity reigned and time seemed to move in a slower rhythm, we found ourselves on the cusp of a transformation. It was a time of adolescence when the pull of self-awareness and the allure of fashion started to weave their way into the fabric of our humble lives.

With eager hands, I unpacked my art supplies, each brush and tube of paint a promise of creativity waiting to be unleashed. The colours beckoned, eager to capture the vibrant energy of the football world that now consumed my thoughts after our first TV viewing of the World Cup experience in 1982. Hanging on the walls were posters of my favourite teams and players — Rossi, Socrates, and others — vividly depicting the stars that lit up the pitch with their skill and charisma.

Dressed in the authentic jerseys of my beloved teams, I delved into a realm where passion met artistry, where every stroke of the brush mirrored the precision of a well-executed goal. Hours melted away as I immersed myself in a world where colours and emotions intertwined, where the spirit of football breathed life into my creations.

In that moment, surrounded by my treasures from Europe, I found a sanctuary where art and football intertwined seamlessly, feeding my appetite for creativity and sport in equal measure.

My world was further coloured by the posters of English Premier League footballers adorning my walls, their vibrant jerseys and iconic poses a stark contrast to the earthy tones of my surroundings. For me, the arrival of football uniforms and art supplies became a lifeline to a world beyond the boundaries of my imagination.

It was when the government softly introduced another new television programme, *The Big League Soccer*, that the winds of change began to swirl in our childhood. Every Saturday evening, from 6 pm to 7 pm, we would gather around our flickering television set, drawn into the world of football with an enthusiasm that bordered on obsession.

The presenter, Brian Moore, became a familiar voice weaving tales of the week's matches in short, flashing summaries that ignited a fire within our teenage hearts. The thrill of watching our favourite players in action, the adrenaline of the game coursing through their veins, created a new kind of magic that transcended the simplicity of our daily lives.

As we sat anchored to the floor from 5 pm, eagerly awaiting the start of the programme, we found ourselves drawn into a world where fashion and football intertwined in a dance of self-expression. The uniforms of our beloved teams became more than just clothing; they became symbols of identity and aspiration.

In those fleeting hours of televised magic, we discovered a new sense of sport and the realisation that one day, we could become football stars. The once-muted teenagers of Asmara began to blend with the vibrant hues of fashion, music, and football, creating a tapestry of individuality and style.

As the sun dipped low, casting a warm golden hue over the neighbourhood, we gathered on our street for the daily game of football. What was once a casual kick-about had evolved into something more structured and organised since the arrival of football on TV.

Excitement buzzed through the air as we, now clad in jerseys emblazoned with the names of our favourite players, took to the makeshift pitch. Each one adopted the persona of a footballing icon, strutting around with the confidence and swagger of their idols.

The rules became more defined, mimicking those we saw on the screen. Passing became precise, shots were executed with finesse, and celebrations were extravagant. The love for the beautiful game was reignited, fuelled by the passion of youth and the inspiration drawn from those larger-than-life figures we saw on TV.

European leather balls, impeccably stitched and shiny, replaced our makeshift products made from thick clothes and disused socks. Our skills and safety improved as we started to play with the smooth orbs in our possession, replacing our raggedy creations.

With the introduction of these fine balls came a new sense of discipline. The elders, recognising the potential for unity and fair play, organised matches with rules to ensure no physical abuse marred the games. Teams were formed by age, each representing a different area of the neighbourhood, all vying for the coveted trophy – a homemade cup fashioned from steel wires and covered in shiny aluminium foil stripped from cigarette packaging.

The matches became events of great excitement and camaraderie, drawing spectators from far and wide to witness the exhilarating games. The once-simple football matches had evolved into a display of skill, teamwork, and mutual respect, all centred around the gleaming trophy that symbolised not just victory but the spirit of unity that bound the village together.

As the game progressed, friendships strengthened, and bonds were forged through shared victories and defeats. The once-humble street matches had transformed into vibrant spectacles, drawing spectators from the surrounding houses who cheered on the young talents with gusto.

Under the watchful eye of parents and adults, we not only honed our athletic prowess but also imbibed important life skills. From teamwork and perseverance to discipline and resilience, the lessons learned on the sports fields were invaluable.

As the days passed, the impact of these neighbourhood physical exercises became evident. Taking these skills to our schools, we not only excelled in sports but also grew healthier and stronger. Our academic performance improved, and there was a newfound zest for life that permeated the air amidst the hopelessness and despair that had gripped everyone in the near past.

In those moments of unity and excitement, the teenagers of Asmara transcended their humble beginnings, stepping into a world where fashion and self-awareness intertwined, transforming our lives in ways we could never have imagined. As the final whistle blew, marking the end of another exhilarating match, we knew that this newfound sense of identity and style was just the beginning of our journey towards self-discovery and empowerment.

Through The Big League Soccer, a programme sponsored by Gillette, 'the best a man can get'… as the intro music would say, I found myself drawn to the world of football news and the allure of fan clubs that united enthusiasts around the globe.

It all began on a typical Sunday morning after I had finished another weekly football programme hosted by the renowned presenter Brian Moore the day before. Moore, with his charismatic personality, encouraged viewers to send in their comments and messages, promising to connect them with their favourite football clubs and stars. As the programme drew to a close, Moore would display the postal address for eager fans to reach out. During that call, the TV displayed rewards of memorabilia and football artefacts for new club fan members, without a price tag.

Fascinated by the opportunity to engage with the football world on a deeper level, I shared my idea with my brothers and friends. Excitement filled my voice as I expressed my desire to write to Brian Moore and enrol as a fan club member for Manchester United, my beloved team. However, my companions scoffed at the notion, doubting my chances as a young man from Africa to be acknowledged in the vast world of soccer fanatics.

Undeterred by the scepticism of my peers, I decided to put pen to paper and composed a heartfelt letter to Brian Moore. In my message, I expressed my joy in watching his programme every Saturday and shared my immense passion for Manchester United. I humbly requested to become a fan club member, hoping to receive match memorabilia to indulge in my favourite team's victories. Even though I knew I wasn't allowed to leave the country under the military regime, I didn't want to decide on my fate, so I asked for the season ticket without even understanding how it worked or what it meant. I only requested the season tickets because Brian had mentioned them. Why not, if not?

Days turned into weeks, and a sense of anticipation lingered in my heart as I awaited a response. To my astonishment, one fateful Saturday, Brian Moore read my letter on air with genuine appreciation. My eyes widened in disbelief as Moore acknowledged me as the first person from Ethiopia to reach out, struggling slightly with the pronunciation of my full name. Everyone around me thought I was daydreaming as no one noticed how my name was read, quickly continuing with the content of my letter.

The news spread like wildfire through the city of Asmara, by those who heard my name aired. With confirmation from some adults, my friends and brothers started to believe I was actually on TV, or at least my name was. I made history by becoming the pioneer fan club member from Ethiopia, a feat that many thought impossible. Emotions of pride and accomplishment surged through me as I listened to Brian's words of praise on the television screen. The once-sceptical voices of my friends and family now echoed with admiration and respect.

From that day onward, my name echoed across the streets of Asmara as the young man who dared to dream big and reach out to the world of football. My story inspired many, proving that geographical boundaries could not limit the power of a shared love for the beautiful game.

In the following weeks, I received a parcel collection note from the post office and found a package bearing a flag and jersey with the emblem of Manchester United, along with several posters and forms. With my trembling hands, I unwrapped the contents to reveal my official fan club membership card, a symbol of my unwavering dedication to the sport I loved. As I held the card in my hands, a sense of fulfilment washed over me, knowing that my passion and perseverance had led me to this moment.

I returned home from the post office, which was located in downtown Asmara. I proudly displayed my fan club membership card, knowing that my journey had only just begun. The world of football awaited me with open arms, ready to embrace my enthusiasm and connect me with fellow fans from every corner of the globe. And so, with each match and every victory, my heart beat in rhythm with the pulse of the beautiful game, a testament to the power of passion and perseverance in the world of sports.

Soon, my delight at being the only Ethiopian fan club member in the English Premiership turned into a great disappointment. It was when I reopened the package and started studying my gift in the large red box more closely.

The sleek membership card I had been displaying for the last two days and put back in the box, embossed with the club's emblem and the name 'Mr. Smith' printed boldly across the front. As I turned it over to see who Mr. Smith was, my excitement turned to confusion. Stamped in bold letters on the back was the phrase 'sample only', a stark reminder that this was not meant for me to keep as a prized possession. It was a fake card sent only to show how the original card would look when received. It didn't have any value except that it was printed to look like the real thing.

Next, I discovered a stack of forms detailing the fan club membership application process, complete with terms and conditions that seemed to go on for pages. My eyes widened as I realised the gravity of what was being asked of me – a commitment to become a full member of the prestigious club, with all the privileges and responsibilities that entailed. It even said I needed a guarantor if I was under 18 years of age. Everything pushed me further away from the proud membership I had declared to the world. I felt embarrassed and ashamed.

As I read through the paperwork, I became more determined to restore my dignity and pride by fulfilling the required criteria and becoming a real Manchester United fan club member. "I won't let this happen to me," I told myself with anger and disappointment.

It was only when I sifted through the paperwork further that a sinking feeling began to gnaw at my stomach. The request for an initial payment of £120 loomed large, a steep sum that was beyond the means of my family. The options for payment – postal order or bank transfer – might as well have been impossible, for they felt as distant and inaccessible as the moon.

But it wasn't just the financial burden that weighed heavily on my heart. It was the realisation that I was being treated just like another applicant, a faceless name in a sea of hopeful fans vying for a coveted spot in the club's inner circle. The illusion of being a special kid from Ethiopia singled out for recognition and appreciation shattered like glass at my feet.

My disappointment was palpable as I laid out more of the contents of the package before me. The glossy brochures showcasing the upcoming season's fixtures, the tantalising promise of discounted season tickets, the glossy photographs of the team's star players—all of it now felt like a cruel joke, a reminder of my place on the outside looking in.

But as I sat in the room, the fading light of the day casting long shadows across the walls, a spark of defiance ignited within my heart. I may not have the means to travel to England, pay the entrance fee, or enjoy the luxury of attending matches at Old Trafford, but I had something far more precious—my dreams.

My heart raced in anticipation as I pulled out the last gift from the package, a red-and-white Manchester United jersey. However, as soon as I unfolded it, my excitement turned to disappointment. The jersey was not the right size; it was an XXL, comically large as if it were made for a giant, or perhaps intended for the wall. It looked like it could fit my grandfather with room to spare.

Sighing heavily, I held up the oversized jersey against my smaller frame, feeling dwarfed by its sheer size. Despite my disappointment, I couldn't help but chuckle at the absurdity of the situation. It was clear that this jersey was never going to be worn by me during any of my football games.

Reflecting on the jersey in my hands, I remembered the numerous Manchester United uniforms my uncles had sent me in the past. They were always the perfect size, tailored for a budding football enthusiast like myself. But this XXL jersey felt like a stark reminder that I was no longer seen as a child by the very team I idolised.

As I slipped the jersey over my head, the fabric engulfed me, billowing around me like a parachute. Standing in front of the mirror, the oversized jersey hanging off my shoulders, I couldn't help but feel a pang of sadness. The realisation that Manchester United, the team I loved and admired, saw me as an adult rather than the special kid I once thought of myself as, hit me hard.

Despite the disappointment, I tried to look at the situation with a sense of acceptance. Perhaps the mix-up with the jersey size was just a simple mistake, an oversight in the grand scheme of things. My age was not included in my letter, making the confusion understandable.

But deep down, I knew that the issue went beyond a simple sizing error. It was a reflection of how I was perceived by those around me. The fact that Manchester United's players and managers now saw me as just another fan rather than a lone, young, passionate supporter from Africa—the reasons that made me feel unique—began to question my own value and identity.

Lost in my thoughts, I finally made peace with the oversized jersey hanging off me like a flag. It was a physical symbol of my transition from a child to an adult, a bittersweet reminder of how perceptions change as we grow older. As I folded the jersey and placed it back in its package, I knew that, while the disappointment stung, it was also a sign of a new chapter in my life, where I would navigate the world of football fandom as a young adult with a different perspective and understanding.

And so, with a quiet determination, I carefully repackaged the items from Manchester United Football Club and tucked them away in the corner of my room. I knew that, one day, I would find a way to make those dreams a reality, to step onto the hallowed grounds of a stadium half a world away and feel the roar of the crowd wash over me like a wave.

For now, the package remained a bittersweet reminder of the distance between where I stood and where I longed to be. But I refused to be defined by my circumstances or limited by the boundaries of my small community. I was a boy with a heart full of hope and a spirit that soared higher than the African sky, ready to chase his dreams with unwavering determination and faith.

And as the stars twinkled in the night sky above Asmara, casting a silver glow over the sleeping town, I closed my eyes and whispered a promise to myself—one day, I would make it to Manchester United, not as a member or fan by heart and soul, but as a player with feet and body.

In our neighbourhood in Asmara, a towering figure named Rezene stood as a respected and feared presence. Rezene, the alpha male who carried the weight of hard work on his broad shoulders, was known for his prowess in the art of splitting logs and slaughtering sheep and chickens during festive seasons. He commanded respect not just for his physical strength but also for his meticulous skill with a blade.

It was on a hot, sunny afternoon that Rezene's routine visit to our compound for another slaughtering task took an unexpected turn. Clad in a full Manchester United jersey, the fiery red colour contrasted sharply against the dusty backdrop, catching me off guard. My eyes widened in disbelief as Rezene emerged from the shadows, his towering form intimidating, holding a gleaming knife in his hand, ready to carry out his duty.

The Manchester United jersey, adorned with my favourite player's name and number, was a treasured possession that seemed to have found an unlikely new owner in Rezene. Confusion clouded my mind as I confronted my mother about the sudden disappearance of my cherished jersey. With a hint of regret in her eyes, she explained how she thought I had abandoned it and decided to pass it on to someone who could fit into it.

Feeling a sense of powerlessness, I held my tongue and bit back the words that threatened to spill out. My mother's apology hung in the air, offering to have one of her brothers send a new one if it meant that much to me. But the damage had been done, and the jersey had found a new purpose on Rezene's body, much to my dismay.

As days turned into weeks and weeks into months, the haunting image of Rezene in that vivid Manchester United jersey lingered in my mind like a ghost. Every time I spotted him traversing the neighbourhood with his machete or axe in hand, the jersey acting as a shield against the splatters of blood, I couldn't shake off the unnerving sight.

Rezene, oblivious to the turmoil his wardrobe choice had stirred within me, took pride in the jersey's practicality. In his eyes, it was not just a piece of clothing but a symbol of appreciation for the wise folks in England who had gifted me with such a useful item. The crimson hue of the jersey masked any tell-tale signs of his grim task, allowing him to go about his slaughtering duties with efficiency and precision. Every time I crossed paths with Rezene in his red slaughtering attire, he would proudly ask me to tell my English friends to send more red jerseys.

The memory of that fateful encounter continued to haunt me, casting a shadow over my days in Asmara. I watched as Rezene carried out his gruesome tasks with a stoic demeanour, the jersey becoming a permanent fixture in his attire during every slaughter, a reminder of a lost possession that had taken on a macabre significance.

As the seasons changed and the years passed by, the image of Rezene in that Manchester United jersey became etched in my memory, a symbol of unexpected connections and strange twists of fate. The jersey, which had once held no immediate significance for me, had turned into a haunting nightmare, a constant reminder of the strange and unexplainable events that unfolded in the bustling streets of Asmara.

And so, as I bid farewell to the neighbourhood that had been both my home and my torment, the image of Rezene in that crimson jersey remained embedded in my mind, a poignant reminder of a story that defied logic and reason, leaving a lingering sense of unease in its wake.

Talking Hands

Painter Man

Throughout my life, art has been my constant companion, weaving its way through the fabric of my existence like a colourful thread that changes hues with every passing season. As a child, I found solace in sketching in the margins of my textbooks, lost in a world of my own creation while the humdrum of the classroom faded into the background.

Despite this ever-changing artistic landscape, one thing remained constant—my unwavering love for creative expression. Despite the lack of formal education in art, I knew that my soul resonated with the act of creation. Therefore, I continued to explore new mediums and styles, never settling on one path but revelling in the freedom to wander where my imagination led.

Today, as I stand surrounded by memories, I realise that my journey through the world of art has been a kaleidoscope of experiences, each one shaping me into the person I am meant to be. Though I may not have pursued art as a career, I know that the fire of creativity burns bright within me, lighting the path for my next artistic evolution.

My journey into the world of art, particularly through the lens of calligraphy and graffiti, is a vibrant testament to the constant shift in my creative exploration. The change in the form of expression—from portrait art and graffiti's bold, colourful statements to the disciplined elegance of calligraphy—might seem like a leap to some, but in reality, both forms share a foundational appreciation for the beauty of letterforms. This journey is not just about changing mediums but about exploring the vast possibilities of visual communication and personal expression.

The encouragement I received from friends and family was a crucial part of this narrative. It underscored the importance of support in the creative process. Art, in many ways, is about connection—connecting with oneself through the act of creation and connecting with others through the act of sharing. My choice, as a primary school student, to decorate my friend's exercise book covers and to embellish letters with decorative love titles was a beautiful reflection of this. It was a gesture that extended my artistic exploration into the realm of personal relationships, making my art a bridge between my inner world and the people around me, allowing recognition and appreciation.

This evolution of my artistic expression—from drawing portraits to graffiti and calligraphy—through the ways I chose to share it highlights a journey of growth and exploration. It is a reminder that art is not just a solitary act but also a communal one, enriched by the feedback and encouragement of our community. Even my art teachers in school repeatedly warned me to scale down my artworks and make them appropriate for the level they were teaching. My art appeared too professional compared to my peers' scribbly, amateurish work. I worked on my art assignments with heart and hand, and the result was always beyond everyone's expectations. Drawings of anatomy in my science class and other visuals in my geography exercise books were done meticulously with colouring and clear labelling. It was as if I didn't know any other way of completing drawing assignments. In the absence of books for individual students, we were given daily drawing tasks in our science and geography exercise books—a passionate homework I spent hours decorating and colouring, sometimes in 3D. I quenched my thirst for art through my academic duties—a win-win task.

The inspiration I received by budding with artists everywhere encouraged me to experiment, embrace my evolving interests, and recognise the value of the support around me. Whether it's through the bold strokes of graffiti or the meticulous lines of calligraphy, I was crafting messages that resonate, connect, and beautify, turning everyday objects into canvases that speak of my journey and passion.

Asmara, a city known for its diverse cultures and artistic heritage compared to Mekelle, had been a catalyst for my change in the direction art was taking me, steering me away from drawing and towards the vibrant world of calligraphy and graffiti art. It's fascinating how such a shift in surroundings can lead to the discovery of new passions or the reimagining of existing ones.

Calligraphy, with its disciplined beauty, and graffiti art, with its bold and unrestrained nature, might seem like contrasting interests, but both require a deep understanding of form, space, and colour, bridging an artistic journey from one medium to another seamlessly.

Graffiti, the vibrant language of the streets, has long been a dynamic form of expression, especially in the West, where it symbolises rebellion, creativity, and the raw energy of young artists. It's a world where urban canvases are brought to life with bold colours and powerful messages. Inspired by this movement, yet geographically and culturally removed from its epicentre, I embarked on a personal journey to not only master this art form but also to infuse it with my unique perspective and the essence of my environment.

At the young age of 13, lacking direct access to Western media and magazines—which are treasure troves of inspiration and technique for aspiring graffiti artists—I turned to my family network across Europe, who sent me material and posters to study and emulate. This bridging of worlds through art and family underscores the universal appeal of graffiti; it transcends boundaries, connecting disparate individuals through the shared language of creativity.

My mastery of graffiti and sign writing did not go unnoticed. What started as a personal endeavour to capture and convey my thoughts and observations through large, expressive formats soon captivated a wider audience, including my teachers. It's not just about the aesthetics; it's about making a statement, telling a story, and, perhaps most importantly, creating a dialogue with the viewer. My journey from an admirer of graffiti to becoming a self-taught artist in my own right highlighted the transformative potential of art to bridge cultures and inspire individuals.

In the isolated ambience of the communist era, where conformity often overshadowed individual expression, the art of graffiti was a rare sight in Eritrea. A revolutionary expression of protest and creative art exploded into the mainstream in the mid-80s. Here, amidst the uniformity and controlled expressions of the time, my graffiti on paper became not just a form of artistic expression but also a bold statement of individuality in the choice of subjects. It is not an overstatement to say I was among the pioneers of this art form in my area, practising graffiti when it was far from being widely accepted. My contributions added colour and voice to a landscape that was, perhaps, in dire need of it.

In an undeliberate act of using graffiti for a more noble purpose than it was originally created to, I decorated spaces around my school and neighbourhood, youth clubs, prayer halls, and small local cafés in Asmara. These ordinary spaces were transformed into meaningful and educating canvases that narrated stories, dreams, and boldly declared the presence of creativity in an environment where many disillusioned young people sought help and inspiration. This act of artistic expression was not just about the beautification of interior spaces but about inspiring others to see beyond the grey hues of their immediate reality, offering fascinations and showing how these visuals could instantly capture the admiration of onlookers. It gave them a glimpse into a world where the young proved to be contributing members of society.

My unique journey as a young artist underscores the power of art to challenge norms, connect people, and spark conversations in even the most unlikely places. Through my graffiti, I offered a beacon of hope and beauty in a setting that might have otherwise been devoid of such expressions. It served as a poignant reminder of the resilience of the human spirit and the enduring desire to express oneself, no matter the circumstances. My story is not just about the art of graffiti; it is a testament to the indomitable will to create and communicate in ways that transcend barriers, physical or ideological.

The encouragement I received from friends and family was a testament to the universal language of art. It connects people, communicates emotions, and beautifies spaces. My initiative to decorate exercise book covers with personalised calligraphy, carrying pop art and sometimes individual political statements, and creating decorative love titles for love letters, showcased how art can be a personal and intimate gift—transforming everyday items into objects of affection and tokens of friendship. It's more than just aesthetic appeal; it's about the personal touch and the joy derived from creating something unique for someone special.

My own life experience underscores the importance of environment and community support in nurturing artistic talent. It also highlights the adaptive nature of creativity—how it can evolve to find expression through different mediums and in response to changing circumstances. As I continued to explore and expand my artistic abilities, each phase of my journey contributed to my growth as an artist. Whether through the precise lines of calligraphy, the vibrant hues of graffiti, or perhaps another form of art that I explored, my creativity was a reflection of my own life experiences, my environment, and the connections I forged with those around me.

My unexpected journey into the world of sign-making, sparked by a simple act of decorating exercise books, unfolds as a testament to the serendipitous nature of discovering one's talents and passions.

Berhane, a brother of one of my closest friends, was in his mid-twenties, earning a living from shop sign-making. With his keen eye for potential and generous heart, he didn't just see a decorated space I created on his younger brother's book; he saw a budding artist with the promise to flourish in the realm of creative sign-making. This twist of fate not only highlights the importance of being open to opportunities, no matter how small or unexpected, but also the value of mentorship in the creative fields.

Working alongside Berhane, I embarked on a transformative journey from assistant to skilled sign maker, mastering the intricate dance of designing on paper, cutting a stencil, and bringing those visions to life on a grand scale. This hands-on experience, under Berhane's guidance, allowed me to not only hone my technical skills but also to understand the business aspects of this creative gift. The satisfaction derived from seeing my creations come to life and being appreciated by others served as a powerful affirmation of my burgeoning talent and the pivotal role of creativity in connecting and communicating with the community. Our colourful shop signs filled Asmara's city centre, and I was able to see myself in my own art every day.

It also underscores the unexpected ways in which opportunities can present themselves and the importance of seizing them. As I continued to leave my mark on the beautiful city of Asmara through sign-making, my journey from decorating exercise books to creating large-scale signs served as an inspiring reminder of where curiosity and openness to learning can lead.

On the national front, the slow transition in Eritrea to align with changes in political ethos, specifically the shift towards socialism, catalysed a unique economic and cultural metamorphosis within its urban landscape, particularly in Asmara. The government's mandate to eliminate foreign names from public signs and businesses, which were predominantly Italian, in favour of revolutionary names reflective of the new ideology, initiated a sweeping change across various sectors. This directive affected a wide array of establishments, from cinemas and supermarkets to schools and bakeries, all of which were integral to the daily life and identity of Asmara's streets. The urgency imbued by the threat of heavy penalties for non-compliance spurred a citywide rebranding effort, painting a vivid picture of transformation driven by political change.

This sweeping rebranding effort and the shortage of sign-makers created an unexpected economic niche—sign painting. The scarcity of skilled sign painters, in the face of overwhelming demand for services, turned this craft into a lucrative profession, especially for enterprising individuals willing to seize the opportunity. The anecdote of personal growth and entrepreneurial spirit within this unique historical context highlights the adaptability and resilience of individuals amid significant societal shifts. Being allowed to take on a complete project under the supervision of Berhane, a presumably experienced sign painter, marked a significant milestone in my journey from apprentice to a more confident practitioner of the trade.

In Eritrea, the impact of such upheaval was acutely felt in the labour market across various sectors, not least in the realm of sign painting. The exodus of professionals fleeing the fear of persecution and violence under the military regime had left a noticeable void, exacerbating the challenge of meeting the demand for shop signage. Businesses, now more than ever, needed to attract customers, yet the scarcity of artists capable of producing hand-painted signs meant that many were left wanting. This shortage was not just a logistical issue but represented a deeper loss of cultural craftsmanship and identity, as the skills and traditions of sign painting were at risk of being lost to a generation.

Before the advent of large-format vinyl printing, hand-painted signage was the norm—a craft that required not just skill but a considerable amount of time and patience. This method of creating signs was not only labour-intensive but also an art form, allowing for unique and personalized touches that modern techniques often lack. However, the reliance on skilled artists to produce such signage presented significant challenges, particularly in times of social and political upheaval.

This period highlights the resilience of communities and the importance of artistry in everyday life. As Eritrea and similar regions faced these challenges, the value of amateur skills became even more pronounced, underscoring the need for preserving such craftsmanship against the tide of modernisation and the adversities wrought by political strife. The story of hand-painted signage, in my context, is a testament to the enduring spirit of creativity and the critical role of artisans in both the economic and cultural tapestry of society.

My story touches on the personal sacrifices and changes that came with this unexpected career path. My disregard for the permanent stains of paint on my clothes, much to my mother's chagrin, symbolised the deep immersion in my work and the personal as well as financial transformations that accompany such pivotal moments in life. This disregard for the tangible remnants of my labour on clothing underscores a broader narrative of change, adaptation, and the pursuit of opportunity amidst the upheavals brought about by political changes. It is a reflection of the broader socio-economic shifts in Eritrea, encapsulated in the microcosm of a young sign painter's journey.

Balancing academics with part-time work was a commendable feat that required dedication, time management, and a strong work ethic. My journey as a young entrepreneur and a top student exemplifies the essence of hard work and determination. While my peers enjoyed leisure activities, I chose to immerse myself in the craft of sign-making—a skill not only artistic in nature but also demanding precision and creativity. This decision to utilise my time productively not only set me on a path of financial independence but also instilled in me a sense of responsibility and discipline.

Achieving academic excellence alongside the growing demand for sign-making speaks volumes about my ability to prioritise, focus, and excel in multiple facets of life. My success in academics, despite the time and energy invested in my sign-making business, demonstrates an exceptional level of intelligence and commitment. When I sat for the National Junior High School Certificate exams at the age of thirteen, I scored the second highest in our school, with 98%. My uncle Johon, who was transferred from an Italian school, was the highest with 99%.

My parents' trust in my decision-making was well-placed, especially with my mother playing a crucial role in guiding me through the financial aspects of my business. This partnership likely served as a learning platform for me, not just in finances but also in life management skills.

Navigating work relationships turned sour when my incredibly challenging experience with Berhane, especially with his increasing exertion of power, control, and exploitation, came into play. The exploitation of my innocence and labour for minimal compensation, under the shadow of an age gap and authoritative behaviour, highlighted the beginning of the end of our business partnership.

I recognised that no job should entail the sacrifice of my dignity or self-respect. Berhane's behaviour, including neglecting his professional responsibilities to pursue personal interests at the cost of my workload, was not only unprofessional but also unethical.

Berhane, a man of romance, followed young girls stopping to see our work outside city shops. He was very quick to communicate and secure an instant date. He left me to work alone, giving strict instructions to finish and go to the next job while he enjoyed himself in nearby cinemas and cafés with his new catches.

Over time, my work relationship with Berhane deteriorated as, with age and wisdom, I realised I didn't have to continue working with or under him. Although I am still fully and unconditionally grateful for Berhane's invaluable opportunities and experience, I decided to become independent, contemplating my next move to maintain my passion for art and continue to earn from it.

Navigating the complex dynamics of personal and professional relationships within a small community can be challenging, especially when learning to become independent in a trade clashes with existing monopolies and expectations.

The unexpected offer from a well-established shop owner to paint uniform signage across his many branches was a golden opportunity for me to break free and showcase my talent independently. However, this opportunity was not without its conflicts.

Berhane, a figure of authority and a mentor in my artistic life, perceived this new venture as a direct threat to his business interests. Berhane's reaction, though extreme, underscored the delicate balance between nurturing young talent and protecting one's economic turf. The confrontation with Berhane was the intricate dance between loyalty, ambition, and personal growth.

My predicament sheds light on a universal truth: progress often requires navigating through a web of relationships and expectations. The encounter with Berhane also presented a valuable lesson in trust and integrity. Moving forward, the challenge for me lay in finding a path that honours both my personal ambitions and the relationships that shaped my journey. As I navigated this complex landscape, my story is a reminder of the resilience and creativity required to forge one's path while remaining mindful of the community and connections that sustain us.

A sad end to my business partnership with Berhane followed the acceptance of the contract offer from my new client, who also knew my family. The conditions of the offer included that the business owner would seek my mother's permission and pay her directly. I agreed and completed painting name signs on all his seven shops in 3D letters, a skill I developed from magazines behind Berhane's back. My work exceeded everyone's expectations, including Berhane's.

As my reputation grew, so did my portfolio, with each piece of work bearing my distinct signature—a testament to my skill and a beacon of my burgeoning legacy. This practice, while customary, served as a bridge, connecting me to the people and businesses I served and subtly etching my mark onto the fabric of the city.

Berhane and I used to cross paths, as was common for residents of Asmara. We often met accidentally, working on the same street and even on the windows of next-door shops. We would then exchange ideas, share tools, and even walk home together, as we lived in the same direction.

Despite the labour- and time-intensive nature of my work, Berhane and I found common ground. Our rivalry gave way to a mutual respect and understanding that transcended our business interests, and we collaborated on some projects in the months that followed. Money wasn't a motivation for my continued work. I didn't have the skills to negotiate or give a monetary estimate of the work I was doing, but I was earning more than I could spend.

Our newly established friendship, founded on mutual respect forged in the fires of competition, evolved into a supportive bond. We shared meals, enjoyed leisurely weekends at the cinema, and lent a hand in times of need. We navigated our professional lives with a sense of camaraderie that respected each other's boundaries. I taught Berhane new creative fonts and graffiti writing techniques he had never known. Berhane mostly used plain shapes, but he was now exploring more ways of making his art attractive to compete with mine.

Berhane, recognising the fleeting nature of my academic commitments, saw beyond friendship and viewed me as a source of more business. He understood I wasn't capable of taking all the job offers I was getting through my personal and familial connections. Together, we exemplified how shared passions and mutual respect can transform competitors into allies, enriching lives beyond the boundaries of their work.

My story of embarking on such an intense passion for sign painting, working, and even managing a small business at such a young age has given me many invaluable skills and experiences that I still treasure and apply in my daily life. Stepping into the limelight at such a young age, not by mere chance but through a twist of fate sealed by hard work, hopes, and a stranger's generosity, was a turning point. My first contract as a solo sign-maker not only paved the way for my independence but also ignited a rivalry that soon blossomed into a profound camaraderie with Berhane, an established sign-maker in the trade.

The experience of sometimes being compensated in kind, rather than with cash, for my creations as an underage artist was both unique and heart-warming. It highlighted a sense of community and mutual appreciation between me and the local shop owners. This scenario brought to life the age-old tradition of bartering, where goods and services were exchanged directly. This method of payment, while unconventional in today's digital and cash-driven society, offered a deeply personal touch to the transaction. It speaks volumes about the value placed on creativity and the personal connections fostered through such exchanges.

Receiving items like a pair of shoes, watches, trainers, and even slices of cake—depending on the amount of work—or baskets of meat and bread as payment was not just a testament to the appreciation of my art, but also a reflection of the community's support for my young talents through familial routes. Many of my employers knew me because of my family, so they paid me with bags of groceries, loaves of meat, and poultry for my family. I would then tell my parents who paid me, and they would send their gratitude for supporting me. These tangible items, used in daily life, serve as constant reminders of the impact my work has had on local businesses and my family's relations with the community. It is a unique form of compensation that carries with it an emotional value money cannot buy. This method of exchange also underscored the importance of supporting local economies and the symbiotic relationships that can exist between artists, families, and businesses.

Moreover, the joy I derive from seeing my colourful works adorning Asmara's city centre's iconic shops—restaurants and bars, pharmacies and supermarkets, and many more—for years to come is a reward in itself. It's a legacy of beauty and creativity left for the community to enjoy, enhancing the urban landscape and bringing smiles to those who pass by. This form of satisfaction, coupled with the unconventional method of compensation, highlights the profound impact of community engagement and support. It's a beautiful reminder that the value of art transcends monetary worth, residing instead in the connections it fosters and the happiness it brings to both the creator and the viewers.

City Of Opportunities

I Can See Clearly Now

A new chapter unfolded for our family when our parents decided to reunite after three years of living apart. Our family's reunion in the heart of Ethiopia's capital marked the beginning of a tumultuous journey that would test their bonds and convictions in ways they never imagined.

I was at the tender age of fifteen when my father had been working tirelessly on various projects across Ethiopia, showcasing his expertise and commitment to environmental and humanitarian causes. However, his life took an unexpected turn when he was approached with a proposition that would change the course of his career and our family's future.

The Workers' Party of Ethiopia (WPE), a newly formed entity through which the military government sought to rebrand itself under the guise of civilian socialist-led governance, extended an offer to my father that he couldn't refuse. As an Eritrean in a politically charged environment, rejecting the party's offer would have been seen as an act of rebellion or insult with severe consequences. Reluctantly, my father accepted the conditions set forth by the party, knowing it meant sacrificing his autonomy for the sake of advancement.

In 1984, my father became a full-fledged member of the central committee of the WPE, paving the way for potential diplomatic placements in other countries. Despite the promises of esteemed positions, my father found himself in limbo, working on sporadic projects and providing occasional consultations with the Ministry of Agriculture, without a permanent title or role for nearly two years.

During this uncertain period, we settled in Addis Ababa, while my father was stationed in the western region of Ethiopia, Gambella, leading a challenging settlement program fraught with obstacles and setbacks. Whispers of my father's imminent candidacy for a diplomatic post lingered in the air, adding a layer of complexity to our already tumultuous circumstances. Even though we had moved a thousand kilometres closer, we still did not live with our father except for his sporadic work visits that brought him to the capital for a few days. Even on those days, he was occupied in long meetings from morning till evening, so we hardly saw him.

In the bustling streets of Addis Ababa, the vibrant energy of the city pulsated through every corner. The people, warm and hospitable, welcomed visitors with open arms, embracing diversity and unity. Yet, amidst this atmosphere of camaraderie, there lingered an unspoken tension when it came to Eritrea and its people.

Though the younger generation were less affected, Eritreans were viewed with suspicion, seen as outsiders—secessionists who harboured a desire for separation from Ethiopia, supposedly fuelled by hate. This perception cast a shadow over the otherwise harmonious coexistence in Addis Ababa. The air, usually filled with the aroma of spices and sounds of laughter, carried a weight of unease for Eritrean families.

Despite efforts to bridge the divide, the historical wounds seemed too deep to heal completely. Animosity and reservation simmered beneath the surface, creating a subtle barrier between the two communities. While most Ethiopians were welcoming, some openly expressed their hostility, especially those who had embraced the government's narrative that painted all Eritreans as agents of the rebels. The military leader Mengistu and his cadres repeatedly claimed that Eritrean independence rebels could not survive without the support of those living among Ethiopians, which was true.

Yet, hope still flickered in the eyes of some—those who believed in reconciliation and solidarity beyond borders. In the heart of this complex city, the struggle for understanding and unity continued, a delicate dance between humanity and politics, between prejudice and acceptance. And amidst it all, the spirit of Addis Ababa persevered, a beacon of hope for a brighter, more inclusive future.

As I navigated my adolescent years in the vibrant yet politically and ethnically charged city of Addis Ababa, I witnessed the ebbs and flows of my father's career within the Party. The ideological underpinnings of the Party's formation, aimed at localising authority and implementing customised policies under the communist manifesto, cast a shadow over our parents' aspirations and the family's stability.

Amidst the backdrop of political intrigue and personal sacrifices, I grappled with my own sense of identity and belonging in a land rife with complexities and contradictions. The dichotomy of my Eritrean heritage and Ethiopian reality created a tapestry of conflicting emotions and allegiances that shaped my worldview and interactions with the world around me.

Life in 1980s Ethiopia was one where political allegiance could make or break one's future, where family ties were tested by external forces, and where the pursuit of personal ambitions intertwined with the complexities of a nation in flux.

My journey mirrors the trajectory of my family's destiny, navigating the tides of uncertainty, loyalty, and resilience in a world defined by shifting allegiances and unforeseen challenges. The tapestry of my family's lives, woven with threads of ambition, sacrifice, and love, unfolds against the backdrop of a nation on the brink of transformation.

In the end, my story serves as a testament to the enduring power of family bonds, resilience in the face of adversity, and the indomitable spirit that propels individuals to navigate uncharted territories with courage and conviction. And as I look back on the past, I carry with me the lessons learned from my family's journey, etched in the fabric of our shared experiences and unwavering unity.

In the heart of Addis Ababa, the capital of Ethiopia, stood a newly built low-rent sustainable housing complex unlike any other in the area. It was a government initiative aimed at providing affordable homes to those in immediate housing need, primarily party members facing difficulties with private property rentals. My family was fortunate enough to secure one of these social houses, a modest two-bedroom dwelling that became our sanctuary amidst the vibrant chaos of city life.

The complex itself was a marvel of modern design for its time. It was a community within a community, designed to foster a sense of togetherness among its diverse residents. Playgrounds and football pitches dotted the landscape, inviting children to laughter and play. Nearby, a school stood as a beacon of knowledge, offering education to the young minds that called the complex home. It was a self-sustaining microcosm, complete with shared facilities that encouraged a communal way of life.

Despite its forward-thinking design, the houses within the complex were simple structures, built economically to accommodate as many families as possible. Our own house was a testament to this efficiency, with shared storage areas and entrances that blurred the lines of privacy between neighbours. While the intention was to bring people together, it often led to clashes of individuality and cultural differences within the close-knit community.

Our home was a cozy haven, with one master bedroom for my parents and another shared by my two brothers. To accommodate our growing family, my resourceful mother ingeniously converted the large sitting room into a split bedroom, where three more siblings found a place to rest their heads. In Ethiopia, the idea of children having their own bedrooms was a luxury reserved for the elite; most families shared living spaces until their offspring reached their late teens.

Life in the social housing complex was a mixed bag of emotions. On the one hand, the sense of camaraderie among neighbours was heartwarming, with impromptu gatherings and shared meals under the communal gazebo. On the other hand, the lack of individual gates and detached houses meant boundaries were often crossed, both physically and culturally, leading to occasional tensions among the residents.

As we settled into our new abode, the allure of the modern complex beckoned to many, with its fresh paint and well-maintained surroundings. Families vied for a chance to experience the sense of community that the government-designed housing promised, eager to escape the rising costs of private property rentals that burdened so many in the city.

Through the lens of our family, the complexities of life in the housing complex unfolded. We navigated the delicate balance between shared spaces and personal boundaries, learning to adapt and compromise amidst the cultural diversity. Our humble abode became a melting pot of traditions and values, a microcosm of Ethiopian society encapsulated within the walls of our two-bedroom temporary refuge.

In the end, the social housing complex was more than just a shelter; it was a testament to resilience and unity in the face of adversity. It was a tangible symbol of hope for those struggling to find their place in a rapidly evolving cityscape. And for my family, it was the backdrop against which our shared experiences and cherished memories were forged, a chapter in our lives that would forever be etched in time.

With a fair amount of Amharic learned from our time spent in Mekelle, the transition to a new community became unexpectedly smooth for us.

As we arrived in our new neighbourhood, we felt both excited and nervous about fitting in. I remembered the days spent in Mekelle, where we practised speaking Amharic with others. Little did we know that those language skills would soon become our golden ticket to assimilation.

From the very beginning, we noticed how our ability to communicate in Amharic set us apart. While there were moments of teasing and mimicking from curious peers, we adapted quickly and effortlessly. Soon enough, we were engaging with our fellow classmates and making friends at an impressive pace.

Our mother was a beacon of light in this new environment. With her warm smile and excellent social skills, she effortlessly found her place among the diverse communities in our new housing complex. My mother's ability to connect with people from all walks of life opened doors to meaningful friendships and connections that enriched our lives.

What made our integration even smoother was the presence of other Eritrean families and friends who had lived in Addis Ababa for years. They shared their experiences, offered guidance, and provided a sense of familiarity that was comforting in this new setting. Their stories and advice became a valuable resource for navigating the challenges of settling into a new city.

As time passed, our family flourished in the new surroundings. The children excelled in school, finding joy in their newfound friendships and experiences. With our good upbringing, we became a cornerstone in the community, known for our kindness and willingness to support those around us.

Together, we embraced the vibrant culture of our new home, from the colourful shops to the rich traditions that filled the streets of Addis Ababa. Each day brought new adventures and discoveries, and we felt grateful for the seamless transition made possible by our language skills and the support of our loved ones.

As the dust of relocation settled, our family found itself immersed in the vibrant tapestry of our new environment. The initial thrill of change gave way to a gradual realisation that our cultural and familial rules were distinct from those of our newfound friends.

In the heart of our new community, where laughter and chit-chat filled the air, we felt a subtle sense of disconnection. Our family gatherings were marked by solemn traditions and heartfelt conversations, starkly different from the casual camaraderie we observed in our neighbours.

In Mekelle and Asmara, we had lived under the shadow of strict rules and cultural traditions. Economic hardships shaped our behaviours and lives, and every member of the community adhered to a rigid code of conduct. This was the only way we knew how to survive in a harsh world.

Despite the limitations imposed by our upbringing, we longed for freedom and adventure beyond the confines of the cities and families we grew up in. However, the level of freedom we found here in Addis Ababa exceeded anything we had ever experienced.

As we entered this new world, filled with bright lights, running water, and endless possibilities, a wave of anxiety washed over us. The easy-going attitudes and lack of strict regulations among our new friends left us feeling like aliens, unsure of how to navigate this unfamiliar territory.

Slowly, we began to adapt to the carefree society, finding moments of joy and self-discovery amidst the chaos. But deep within us, a part of the past still lingered, reminding us of the struggles and resilience that defined our upbringing. As we forged our path in this new world, we carried with us the lessons of our past, a constant reminder of where we came from.

It wasn't long before the invisible threads that bound us to our past began tugging at our hearts, reminding us of the precious traditions and values we held dear. Though our differences with our new friends were stark, they served as a poignant reminder of the rich tapestry that makes up the world, woven with threads of diversity and unity.

In Mekelle, we grew up surrounded by guards and house staff. Our childhood was as much a world of seclusion and constraint as it was filled with discipline and good manners. Our days were marked by the quiet hum of daily life, with the distant laughter of neighbouring children a rare occurrence. We were raised under the watchful eyes of our parents, shielded from the harsh reality of the social and political turmoil that plagued our region.

In Asmara, we lived under the protective gaze of our grandparents, especially Goitapa, our no-nonsense grandfather. We navigated the intricate web of social and house rules that governed life there. Permissions were required for every venture outside our block, and curfews were strictly enforced both by our parents and the government for our safety. We ate food cooked by our mothers daily, and our movements were always closely monitored, with our parents knowing exactly where to find us if needed.

Our parents were deeply involved in our education. It was not uncommon for them to visit our schools unannounced, eager to observe firsthand how we were progressing. Their involvement extended beyond surprise visits; they met with teachers privately, discussing our strengths and weaknesses, always looking for ways to support our academic growth. These conversations weren't intrusive but came from a genuine desire to see us succeed.

But despite the structured nature of life in Asmara, we found safety in the sense of family that surrounded us. We played mostly with our family members, our laughter and camaraderie making us feel inseparable, as if we could not live without each other. We shared our meals, secrets, and dreams, forging bonds that would last a lifetime.

Yet, as we settled into our new life in the vast city of Addis Ababa, restlessness began to stir within us. The freedoms we witnessed in the bustling hearts of the children of Addis Ababa beckoned to us—a siren song that could not be ignored. The children of Addis Ababa moved with carefree abandon, unchecked by the rigid hand of government curfews or family rules. Their parents, who worked full-time, seemed more liberal in their ways, granting them the freedom to explore and discover the world on their own terms. It was a stark departure from the structured upbringing we had known in patriarchal Asmara, where mostly men worked and mothers stayed at home—a society where every step was guided by the watchful eyes of our parents and elders.

When we ventured out with our new friends, we felt the weight of our past lives bearing down on us. The need for permissions and the curfew looming on the horizon were shackles we could not easily discard. Our friends would laugh, teasing us for our perceived childishness, but beneath the embarrassment, we felt a sense of pride in the values that had shaped us.

As we navigated the complexities of friendship and freedom, we came to realise that our upbringing in Mekelle and Asmara had instilled in us a sense of resilience and discipline that set us apart. While the children of Addis Ababa roamed freely, we carried with us the lessons of our past, rooted in tradition and respect for authority.

In the end, as we stood at the crossroads of our two worlds, we understood that the path we chose would define us. And so, with a bittersweet farewell to the innocence of youth, we embraced the challenges that lay ahead, secure in the knowledge that our past would always guide us home.

Some of the issues associated with the compromised quality of life in the social housing complex were the absence of shared values. The housing complex, a symphony of concrete structures, was where children from different parts of the country settled due to their parents' work relocations. Each child carried with them a distinct essence of their origins—a blend of traditions, dialects, and beliefs that set them apart from one another.

As days turned into years, the children of the social housing complex found themselves trapped in a cycle of isolation and misunderstanding. The lack of a common culture further widened the chasm between them, making it difficult to find shared values. While some children struggled to string together a sentence in English, others found solace in their native tongues, creating pockets of exclusion within the community. The children and their parents were entangled in webs of ethnic discrimination among small ethnic groups. Here, children from various backgrounds and regions of Ethiopia found themselves entwined in a tapestry of unfamiliarity and disconnection.

The children in the social housing complex navigated a world where the echoes of their diverse origins clashed and converged, shaping their identities and paths in unforeseen ways. In this melting pot of experiences and struggles, the tale of the children in the social housing complex unfolded the complexities of human connection and the resilience of the human spirit in the face of adversity.

Among these children, a sense of camaraderie seemed elusive, like a distant dream hovering just beyond their grasp. They struggled to find common ground, their interactions devoid of the warmth and unity that often bonds young people together. The absence of brotherhood or friendship left a palpable void in the community—a silent rift that widened with each passing day.

One prominent reason for this disconnect was their diverse upbringing. The differences extended even to personal hygiene and presentation. The children who grew up in more privileged environments exhibited a keen sense of grooming and aesthetics, their attire reflecting a touch of fashion consciousness. In stark contrast, their counterparts from less affluent backgrounds appeared unkempt and neglected, their personal appearance lacking the finesse and care that the former were accustomed to.

Language also served as a dividing line among the children. While some were proficient in Amharic, able to articulate their thoughts with ease and grace, others struggled with even the simplest words in the language. Their poor command of Amharic further isolated them, making it challenging to bridge the gap and foster meaningful communication with their peers.

Amidst the sea of issues that left the children in the housing complex disadvantaged, most had single working mothers. Others had two working parents, leaving housemaids to do the parenting while the parents socialised after work. Most children came home from school to an empty house, with no one to check their homework assignments. Instead of finding solace in constructive activities, they resorted to idle pastimes and questionable pursuits. They indulged in wasteful distractions, seeking refuge in fleeting moments of camaraderie that lacked depth and substance.

As we eagerly registered for school, embarking on a journey of learning and self-discovery, we found friends with whom we gravitated towards each other, drawn together by our shared experiences and upbringing.

As the school days passed, we made new friends who seemed to have backgrounds similar to ours. We quickly realised that the challenges faced by the children and parents in our social housing were unique to that environment.

Soon, in search of new friendships, we stumbled upon a group of students from a more affluent neighbourhood in Addis Ababa. To our surprise, we discovered that these students, born and raised in the city, were incredibly organised in both their personal lives and academics. Intrigued, we decided to expand our circle of friends and learn from our newfound companions.

As we got to know the students from different parts of the city, we found ourselves in awe of the diversity and richness of Addis Ababa. We realised that beyond the boundaries of social housing, there existed a vibrant tapestry of personalities and experiences waiting to be explored.

Despite making new friends from various areas, we cherished the bond we had formed with some boys in our neighbourhood. Our connection with them was forged by our shared interests in sport, music, and art. Together, we navigated challenges, supporting each other through thick and thin.

Over time, we learned valuable lessons from a diverse group of friends. We embraced the differences in their upbringings and celebrated the unique qualities that each individual brought to our circle. Through our interactions with boys and girls from all walks of life, we grew not only academically but also personally.

Back in the social housing complex, our family found solace in the company of a few chosen friends. Among them stood out the Samuel family, consisting of four boys: Nebiyu, Negede, Neamin, and Abraham, who were raised solely by their devoted father. The boys' mother had ventured abroad after a bitter divorce, yet she showered her children with unwavering support, providing them with private schooling and material comforts. This family, though faced with hardships, exuded resilience and strength that drew us to them like a magnet. Of the four, Nebiyu was my age, and I spent more time playing and exploring with him, while my brothers became friends with his other siblings.

Alongside the Samuel brothers, we formed a bond with another household, the Negash family—a family of two boys and a girl: Abel, Emrias, and Feven—a vibrant mix of Ethiopian, Italian, and Eritrean heritage. The father, an esteemed marine communications engineer working on a foreign ship, brought the luxuries and lifestyle of distant lands, while the mother, with her Eritrean roots, infused warmth and hospitality into their home. Together, these families created a tapestry of cultural richness that filled our days with laughter and companionship. Abel was my age, and we clicked, forming a good friendship along with Nebiyu from the Samuel family.

The three of us—myself, Abel, and Nebiyu—became close friends, discovering many common interests that strengthened our bond. In the vibrant tapestry of adolescence, where friendships intertwined like threads of vivid hues, a new friendship was formed by the trio of exceptional individuals: me, Abel, and Nebiyu.

Abel possessed an unyielding intellect; his mind was a labyrinth of electronics inherited from his father, an accomplished electronics engineer. He revelled in the intricacies of gadgets and electronics, weaving intricate tapestries of understanding. Abel also fed our thirst for quality stereo sound and Western music with the modern hi-fi systems his father imported from the Far East.

As for Nebiyu, his spirit soared like an eagle, driven by his knowledge of auto mechanics and everything about driving. His infectious enthusiasm for cars stemmed from the many utility vehicles his father, an architect and contractor, had abandoned in their backyard. With his understanding of auto mechanics, Nebiyu could start a faulty car and take us on fun drives now and then. He inspired us with adventures of speed and dreams of becoming future drivers by sometimes letting us take the wheel.

I was more academic and a creative wizard, my hands dancing across canvases and boards like celestial bodies in a cosmic expanse. My art creations ignited souls with their ethereal beauty and profound depth. I inspired the group by creating platforms for engaging in creative artwork and sculpting, which they found interesting and eventually picked up to some level. Being academically stronger, I helped them with their studies, providing guidance and preparing for exams, simplifying educational tasks they found challenging.

My curiosity for electronics and mechanics kicked in after I met Abel, who had access to tools and instruments from his father, with a small workshop in their house. We were filled with enthusiasm and a willingness to tackle repairs, achieving some successes along the way. We weren't discouraged by the times we couldn't fix something; every attempt was a learning opportunity. We always believed that even experienced technicians encounter challenges they can't always solve on the first try.

I was more interested in improving my skills than Abel was and even considered studying electronics more formally through courses in the future to understand the principles behind how things work, which is just as important as the practical experience I was gaining. I kept nurturing my passion, and with time and practice, I found that I was able to fix even more complex issues.

I saved money to buy books and resources on basic electronics and circuit design, showing how different components function together. This provided me with a more structured approach to my experiments and led to even more successful repairs and innovations.

Fueled by my new obsession with electronics, the knowledge and experience came at a high cost, as I had to dismantle devices that were working and used daily by my family. I became addicted to opening devices without knowing how to put them back together. I damaged several devices in this way and would tell my family they were already broken when confronted. It was clear that my curiosity and passion for understanding electronics led me to explore and experiment, even though it sometimes resulted in damaged gadgets. It's a common phase many enthusiasts go through when learning about electronics. The important thing is that I recognised the need to learn more structured methods for repairing and reassembling devices.

If I failed to reassemble devices to their original form, I would ask a local repairman named Seifu for help, and he would do me a favour by reassembling the devices for a small fee before any of my family knew. Working with Seifu was a helpful step; I learned more from him than from my own practice. Additionally, being honest about my learning process may have benefited me. My family would have been more supportive from the beginning if they had known I was earnestly trying to learn and improve.

As a member of the British Council Library, I had access to valuable books, which allowed me to continue learning in this field through more formal education. This provided me with a solid foundation in theoretical electronics, diagnostics, and repair solutions effectively.

My short-lived experience in electronics is a testament to the value of lifelong learning and the practical application of knowledge. Whether for personal satisfaction or necessity, my skills are a resource you can always rely on.

Abel, Nebiyu, and I formed an unbreakable bond rooted in friendship, modernity, style, and leadership. We navigated the labyrinthine halls of our neighbourhood with an air of confidence and purpose, leaving an indelible mark on the hearts and minds of our peers. Our parents found solace in our companionship, knowing that their children were engaged in meaningful and enriching pursuits that fostered our growth and well-being.

Together, Abel, Nebiyu, and I became a dynamic trio admired by our parents and friends for our exemplary leadership. We served as role models for our younger siblings, and our parents found peace in our companionship, knowing we were always engaged in useful and innovative activities, both individually and as a group.

As our families intertwined, we found ourselves sharing more than just casual conversations. We, the children, played in the shared courtyard or engaged in creative activities together in one of our homes, our laughter echoing through the corridors of the social housing. We opened our doors to each other, inviting one another into our humble abodes to share meals and watch films. In these moments, the barriers of race, nationality, and social status melted away, leaving behind a bond forged in camaraderie and understanding.

There was a sense of secluded unity in our little community, a shared feeling of navigating this journey called life together. The parents exchanged tips on raising children single-handedly, finding solace in each other's struggles and triumphs. They leaned on one another for support, bridging the gap between cultures through their shared experiences in parenthood. Within the trio's sanctuary, a shared passion for knowledge and creativity flourished. Beyond our academic pursuits, we ventured into community service, leaving our mark with innovative projects and unwavering dedication. We organised gardening and deep cleaning for the homes of elderly members of our community.

As the friendship between Abel, Nebiyu, and I grew, our passion for community service blossomed. We became active volunteers in the neighbourhood. Inspired by my parents' example, I initiated a cleanup programme, rallying my peers to beautify our surroundings and foster a sense of pride in our community by taking actionable steps to restore the complex, which had already started to fade.

My artistic creations inspired the trio to embrace their own creativity, while Abel's love for music created festive moods everywhere. Nebiyu's mechanical curiosity awakened a thirst for knowledge about auto mechanics even in the younger boys.

As we approached the twilight of our high school years, preparing to embark on new chapters in our lives, our friendship remained an unbreakable thread connecting us through time and space. We knew that wherever our paths might lead, the memories we shared and the lessons we had learned together would forever be etched in our hearts.

Earlier, in the labyrinthine corridors of the social housing complex, resentment from other groups began to develop. These groups, who envied us for our achievements and more affluent upbringings, saw our families as weak and an opportunity for exploitation. They puffed their cigarettes on street corners and would demand money to feed their little addictions. Taunts and threats escalated into physical intimidation, turning our once-safe haven into a battleground.

Among the band of young thugs were the sons of fallen soldiers and officers, left fatherless and consumed by a thirst for revenge. Their lives were defined by the absence of their fathers, who had perished in the bloody conflicts that had ravaged the region. These boys had no time for school or childish pursuits; their only dream was to follow in their fathers' footsteps and become soldiers themselves. With no resources or organised plans to support them, the government had given their orphaned families free housing within the same social complex we lived in.

These boys also harboured a deep hatred for Eritreans, whom they blamed for their fathers' deaths. The Eritrean War of Independence had left countless lives lost on both sides, and the boys' fathers were among the fallen. Their loss had left an unfillable void in their hearts. They were enraged by our presence, seeing our families as symbols of their enemy.

They confronted my siblings and me openly, taunting us with insults and threats, and taking away our shopping bags and bottles of fresh milk we were carrying home from shops. One of them, driven by hatred, spat in my face and vowed to make my life a living hell. Although frightened, I refused to be cowed by my tormentors. I stood my ground, my eyes blazing with defiance.

As the days turned into weeks, the boys' harassment escalated. They followed us to school, threw rocks at our windows, and threatened us with violence. Despite my fear, we refused to give in. We knew that we had to stand up for ourselves and our younger siblings.

Determined to protect ourselves, we devised a plan. We enlisted the support of other like-minded youth, forming a united front against the bullying. Together, we confronted them, intercepting the thugs' attempts to harass and extort money from the vulnerable.

One evening, as we intervened in a confrontation, violence erupted. The thugs, outnumbered but emboldened by their reputation, fought back fiercely. Despite our smaller stature, we fought with unwavering determination. In the chaos, Abel sustained a deep cut to his face.

As the sirens of our younger siblings' screams wailed and our parents arrived, the thugs scattered. Abel's injury, which left a lifelong scar on his face, served as a grim reminder of the consequences of our defiance. However, it also ignited a fire within the community.

Parents, neighbours, and even some former members of the bullying groups rallied around Abel and our group. Together, we organised community watch programmes and sought support from local authorities. The once-feared thugs were gradually driven out, their reign of terror broken.

In the aftermath, our friendship became a symbol of hope and safety. Our unwavering courage had not only protected us but had also transformed the community into a safer place for everyone. The social housing complex became a sanctuary for all, where the bonds of friendship and the power of collective action prevailed over fear and intimidation.

One afternoon, as we were walking home from school, we were ambushed by the thugs and beaten mercilessly, leaving me bloody and bruised. As they prepared to finish me off, Abel and Nebiyu, along with others, intervened, driving the thugs away. I was taken to the hospital, where I was treated for my injuries. Later that day, as I lay in my bed, I realised that my tormentors were not just heartless bullies but also victims of a cruel and senseless war. I resolved to forgive them—not out of weakness, but out of compassion. I knew that the cycle of violence would never end if people continued to hate each other based on their ethnicity.

This group of unruly teenagers, sons of soldiers who were fighting in the north known as 'nebelbal', meaning flame, was named after a military unit known for their horrendous atrocities and mercilessness as protectors of the revolution. They continued to terrorise the neighbourhood, mainly targeting Eritreans and leaving a trail of shattered windows and stolen properties in their wake.

Driven by desperation, my mother and other concerned parents approached the families of the thugs, hoping to reason with them. However, their pleas fell on deaf ears. The boys' mothers, consumed by their own struggles, admitted that their sons were beyond their control. They confessed that the boys stole from them to feed their insatiable addictions to cigarettes and gambling.

Undeterred, my mother resolved to confront the thugs herself. With unwavering determination, she approached their hangout. As she stepped closer, she was met with a thick cloud of smoke and the pungent smell of alcohol.

The thugs sat around a pile of rocks and building blocks, their eyes glazed, and their voices slurred. My mother's presence startled them, but their initial shock quickly turned to defiance. They sneered at her, threatening to harm her sons if she interfered.

Undeterred, my mother stood her ground. With a voice trembling with both fear and determination, she declared, "I will not let you bully my sons. I will protect them with everything I have."

One of the thugs replied, "You can take your children back to where they came from." My mother threatened to inform the police and the local council, known as kebele, if they continued their unruly behaviours. And so she did. The thugs were arrested and warned about their actions. The council office also promised severe punishment if they continued with their antisocial behaviours.

As a result, the social housing complex was once again a place of peace and tranquillity. Our protective mothers had not only restored calm to our neighbourhood but had also shown that even the most troubled souls can find redemption.

We young boys, with our innocent but curious hearts and boundless energy, found common ground in our shared sense of belonging. From impromptu football matches to imaginative artworks, music, and driving, we painted the canvas of friendship with hues of laughter and acceptance.

As the seasons changed and the years rolled by, our bond deepened, weaving a tapestry of memories that would forever remain etched in our hearts. The challenges we faced as individuals and as families only served to strengthen our connection, solidifying the belief that true friendship knows no boundaries.

The stories of the Samuel and Negash families unfolded in ways that no one could have predicted. As time ticked by, the challenges and adversities that befell these families changed the course of their children's destinies, leading them down dark and tumultuous paths.

The Samuel family, once a picture of happiness and stability, was shattered when their patriarch succumbed to a sudden illness, leaving behind his four children in the clutches of a cunning stepmother. With greed in her eyes, the stepmother seized control of the family's wealth, earned through years of hard work by their father, a renowned civil engineer. Neglecting the children, she squandered the resources on her own lavish lifestyle, leaving the siblings to fend for themselves.

Despite their mother's attempts to support them from afar, the children, deprived of love and guidance, found themselves on a downward spiral. Neglected and abandoned, they lost interest in their studies, ultimately failing to complete high school. Without purpose or direction, they grew idle, their potential wasting away in the shadows of a broken family.

On the other side of our neighbourhood, the Negash family was torn apart by the bitter flames of divorce. The children, caught in the crossfire of their parents' discord, were left in the care of their despondent mother, while their father moved on to start a new life with someone else. Struggling with depression, the mother was unable to provide the stability and nurturing environment the children desperately needed. With no father figure to guide them and a mother lost in her own despair, the Negash children found solace in the wrong places. Their striking looks attracted attention from older men and women who exploited their vulnerability for their own gain. This exploitation led the family into disarray, with no one stepping in to bring order or discipline.

As the years passed and the children of both families approached the age of completing high school, the once-bright futures that lay ahead seemed dim and uncertain. The Samuel siblings and Negash children were adrift in a sea of neglect and misfortune, their potential stifled by the harsh realities of their circumstances.

In a city where dreams were meant to thrive and opportunities abound, the Samuel and Negash families stood as testaments to the fragility of familial bonds and the devastating impact of adversity. As they navigated the treacherous waters of adolescence, their paths diverged, with each family facing its own set of challenges and hardships that threatened to derail their hopes and dreams of a brighter tomorrow.

Abel and I shared a fascination for the intersection of electronics and music, which began when we started mastering the art of repairing simple domestic electrical devices, from irons to stoves. Our curiosity led us to delve deeper into the world of DJing, and soon we found ourselves venturing into organising house and community parties. Abel, with his family's hi-fi stereos and big speakers, and I, armed with cassettes and CDs of Western pop music sent by my relatives in Europe, provided the rarely available soundtrack for these gatherings. Together, we formed a formidable musical team, introducing DJing and pop culture to our neighbourhood and beyond.

As we delved further into our newfound passion, our collection of music grew, spanning from the iconic beats of Michael Jackson to the rebellious energy of Madonna and the soulful melodies of George Michael and Kool & The Gang. We had all the music needed for any occasion, and our DJing skills became the talk of the town. Our peers were drawn to our electrifying performances, mastering the art of breakdancing. Girls were attracted to us as we played their favourite tunes, always eager to share in our extensive collection of music. It was as if we had unlocked a new world, where the power of music and technology intertwined to create an atmosphere of pure excitement and joy.

We created playlists on 90-minute cassettes to avoid delays in transitions between songs when using the hi-fi, which was not made for DJing. We would use a Walkman with headphones to select the next tape. We mastered DJing like no other.

Our journey into the world of DJing was not just about playing music; it was about creating an experience that resonated with everyone who crossed our path. We became known for our ability to read the crowd, seamlessly transitioning from one track to another and infusing each party with an infectious energy that left people craving more. It was in these moments, surrounded by the thumping bass, that I felt most alive, as if the very essence of adventure coursed through my veins.

As we continued to hone our skills, our popularity soared, and we found ourselves in high demand, not just within our immediate circle but also in the wider community. Our passion for music and technology had not only brought us closer as friends but also opened doors to a world of endless possibilities. With each party we hosted, each beat we dropped, and each soul we moved, the undefined tone of our journey resonated with the hearts of those who joined us in our electrifying adventure.

My uncles in Europe efficiently sent newly released songs, and we would have them before anyone else. Introducing these tracks at the parties gave us a sense of triumph and excellence in the industry, with excitement and fame delivered to us each week.

Despite the risks of being questioned by the local council or kebele and the revolutionary guards, who despised anything Western, we continued to organise these small gatherings, knowing they brought joy and a sense of freedom to our friends. Abel and I were determined to keep the spirit of music and celebration alive, even in the face of the strict anti-Western government regulations, where parties featuring Western music and dance were totally banned and punishable by detention and community service.

As time went on, the pressure from the authorities increased. Abel's defiance and lack of cooperation with the council office led to harsher penalties for him, including short jail time and community service. It was a difficult time for both of us as we faced the consequences of our passion for music and bringing people together.

When our parties were raided by the local council's revolutionary guards, I continued to use my influence in the community to remain unpunished. My involvement in volunteering and creating political art for the council office provided me with some protection, but it was a constant struggle to balance my passion for music with the oppressive restrictions of the government.

As the tension between the authorities and our small group of music enthusiasts escalated, we knew that our defiance could only last for so long before the consequences became too severe. But for now, we were determined to keep the music playing and the spirit of celebration alive, no matter the cost.

During high school graduations and birthday celebrations, young boys and girls loved to have daytime home parties and enjoy life to the fullest. They would often throw parties in their homes, dancing to the latest pop music and wearing trendy clothes that were considered too provocative by the conservative revolutionary guards.

On several of these fateful days, as the parties were in full swing, the sound of boots stomping on the ground interrupted the music. The armed revolutionary guards, known as kebele, arrived, ready to raid the party and arrest anyone who dared to defy their strict rules. Panic ensued as the partygoers scrambled to find ways to escape the impending arrests. Some tried to jump over fences, only to be caught by guards waiting on the other side. Others hid in attics and gardens, hoping to evade capture, but the guards were thorough in their search and eventually found nearly everyone trying to hide.

The young partygoers were rounded up and taken to the council or kebele office, where we were locked up for days. During our time in captivity, we were subjected to endless communist indoctrination sessions, where we were lectured on the evils of Western influence and the importance of toeing the line set by the government.

During these raids, our devices, such as music players and tapes, were confiscated, leaving us feeling disconnected from the outside world. Our crimes were judged by the amount of Western clothing we wore and our level of skill in our dancing. A special committee was formed to pass judgment on us. The court and jury were all staunch supporters of the communist government, leaving little hope for a fair trial. We were accused and found guilty of crimes ranging from wearing inappropriate clothing to listening to forbidden music.

As if things couldn't get any worse, our parents were called in to receive warnings about the clothes and devices they had provided for their children. They signed bail papers to take us home. It was a humiliating experience for both us youngsters and our families, who never imagined that a simple party could lead to such dire consequences.

Each time, after what felt like an eternity, we were finally bailed out with a stern warning and a promise not to engage in similar activities in the future. Each time, we emerged from our ordeals with a newfound appreciation for our freedom and a determination never to take it for granted again. Despite the hardships we faced, we managed to find humour in our situation. We joked about our failed attempts to escape the guards and poked fun at the ridiculousness of being arrested for simply having a good time.

At one of the parties we attended, in a dimly lit room, the music was blaring, and the smell of alcohol hung heavy in the air. The party was in full swing, with young guests dancing and laughing without a care in the world. But little did they know, our joy would be short-lived.

The revolutionary guards stormed into the house, their guns raised and expressions cold. The partygoers scattered, some trying to flee, while others simply froze in fear. Among them was a young girl, only sixteen years old, who was in the toilet when they arrived. She knew she had to think fast if she was to survive.

As panic gripped the house, the girl's mind raced. She had seen an infant in one of the back rooms earlier that hour, and she knew that was her only chance at escape. Without hesitation, she bolted towards the room, the guards hot on her heels. She reached the door just in time, slamming it shut behind her.

With trembling hands, she picked up the sleeping baby, wrapping him in a flannel. She held him close, pretending to breastfeed him as she prayed for mercy from the guards. One of them, a shrewd man with a piercing gaze, approached her slowly.

The guard's brow furrowed in suspicion as he glanced around the room. He knew this was no ordinary scene, and he suspected there was more to this girl's story than she let on. He motioned for the rest of the guards to search the house, and they soon discovered the truth.

He reached out and pulled the flannel, revealing the baby's face. His eyes narrowed as he studied the child, then turned to the girl with a questioning look. She held her breath, willing herself to stay calm.

"What are you doing here with this baby?" the guard asked, his voice low and dangerous. Without missing a beat, the girl looked up at him with wide, innocent eyes. "I am looking after him; he's mine," she said simply, her voice barely above a whisper. "Who is the father?" the guard asked. The girl replied that he was out of town. The guard then asked, "How old is your baby?" The girl replied, "One year." The guard continued his interrogation: "When was he/she born?" The girl, both scared and confused, replied, "I don't remember the date; it was about six months ago." That did it for the guard.

The owners of the house confirmed that the baby was not hers, and the girl's lie was exposed. She was dragged out of the room, handcuffed, and forced to join the others who had been caught trying to escape. The party was over, and the consequences were harsh. As she was led away, the girl caught her captor's eye for a fleeting moment. There was a spark of defiance in her gaze, a silent challenge that spoke of her unbroken spirit. Despite the odds stacked against her, she refused to go down without a fight, paying the heavy price of having fun.

To her embarrassment, her story was told in front of a full audience of young adults during the indoctrination session we and our parents received days after our arrests.

But even in the face of danger, the girl's quick thinking had not gone unnoticed. The guard who had uncovered her deception couldn't help but admire her courage and resourcefulness. In a different time and place, he mused, she could have been a great asset to their cause.

And so, the raid came to an end, with some partygoers scattered and others apprehended. But the memory of the girl who had dared to defy the guards lingered in the air, a testament to the lengths people would go to for their freedom. In a world filled with chaos and oppression, her act of bravery shone brightly—a beacon of hope in the darkness.

In the end, we learned an important lesson about the power of unity and resilience in the face of adversity. Although we never forgot the harrowing experience of being raided by the revolutionary guards, we chose to look back on it with a sense of humour, knowing that we had survived one of the most bizarre events in our lives.

At another party we attended as DJs, away from our neighbourhood, a young lad was hosting a farewell gathering for his friends when the revolutionary guards raided the house after being tipped off by residents. The day party was a lavish affair, with the host's family leaving the house for the young people to enjoy freely in their absence.

One of these young men, a reckless and impulsive lad, had been causing quite a stir with his bold behaviour throughout the evening. It was rumoured that he had a penchant for mischief and a taste for danger.

As the afternoon wore on and the alcohol flowed freely, he found himself in the company of a young girl who had caught his eye. Their flirtations turned into a passionate encounter, and before long, they had retreated to one of the bedrooms for privacy. Little did they know, the house was about to be raided.

The commander of the revolutionary guards was the first to observe the illicit activities taking place in the bedroom and swiftly mobilised his guards to raid the room. Bursting in with authority, they caught the lad in a compromising position, his trousers down and his bare bottom exposed as he hovered over the girl.

Shocked and embarrassed, the lad and the young woman were quickly apprehended by the guards and taken into custody. The commander was incensed by the disrespectful behaviour displayed by the young couple and vowed to teach them a lesson they would not soon forget.

The following day, as the rest of us gathered for roll call and counting at the local council office, the commander addressed the assembled crowd. "There is a young man among us who disgraced himself and the host family with his lewd actions," he announced gravely. "I did not witness his face, for I was taken aback by the scene before me. But I will not rest until he is identified and punished accordingly."

With a steely gaze, the commander made a bold request. He demanded that all the young men present line up with their bottoms exposed so he could identify the culprit by this unique mark of shame. We murmured in astonishment at the bizarre spectacle unfolding before us, but the commander was resolute in his determination to uphold the honour of his society's traditions. He was doing this with the sole purpose of humiliating and psychologically punishing us, assaulting our dignity in the process.

The commander stood stern and resolute, his eyes scanning the line of exposed bottoms before him. Two rounds had passed, but still, the guilty bottom remained elusive.

With a heavy sigh, the commander spoke, his voice echoing across the clearing. "I don't think I can find this person in this way. I will give this person a chance to identify himself, or face even harsher punishment if I have to find him with the help of my comrades."

The lad, fearing the consequences of remaining silent, slowly raised his hand. The commander's gaze fell upon him, and with a sense of disappointment, he singled the lad out. "How embarrassing," the commander began. "Your actions have brought shame not only upon yourself, but upon the girl and the host family as well."

The lad hung his head in shame, knowing that he had failed to uphold the traditions of respect and honour. But the commander was not finished. "If you dare to commit such an act, then you must also have the courage to face the consequences. Bring forth the girl who was caught in the act; let her share in your embarrassment."

As the girl stepped forward, a sense of unease settled over the crowd. The commander's words struck a chord, highlighting the importance of humility and accountability in their community.

And so, the commander's actions served as a reminder to all that honour and respect were not to be taken lightly. With shame exposed and heads held low, the indoctrination continued, and lessons were learned, strengthened by the events of that fateful night.

In the end, the lad was subjected to severe punishment for his transgressions, serving as a cautionary tale for all those present. The lesson was clear: in the rarefied world of the elite, even the smallest lapse in judgment could lead to dire consequences. As the partygoers dispersed, the host family was summoned and told the whole story.

In communist Ethiopia, where traditional values and strict moral standards held sway, even the simplest acts of joy could be met with harsh consequences. Such was the case for a humble DJ, whose only wish was to bring a bit of happiness to the weary souls of my friends.

In those difficult ideological times, even a DJ faced bans and prosecutions for carrying a sound device. But through the power of our songs, we brought a bit of light to a darkened world, proving that sometimes, it is the simplest acts of joy that can spark a revolution.

Party Of One

Winds Of Change

My father was still working in the Gambella region when he made rare visits to see us in Addis Ababa. He frequently contacted us by phone, patiently hoping to reunite with us once more. He was bestowed with a rare honour—an invitation to attend the grand inauguration of the Workers' Party of Ethiopia in Addis Ababa, which would be followed by his ascension to full membership of the central committee.

The anticipation of this monumental event swept across the country like a tidal wave, engulfing the nation in a frenzy of preparations and jubilation. The government spared no expense in creating a spectacle, constructing a colossal headquarters resembling a modern-day Colosseum, which boasted one of Africa's largest conference halls.

That summer, our father extended a special invitation for us to visit the projects he was leading in the western Ethiopian region of Illubabor. He was eager for us to experience the natural beauty of the tropical forests and immerse ourselves in the unique culture of the Agnwak people. It was to be a farewell trip of sorts, as he was preparing for a permanent relocation following the inauguration, promising better working conditions. As we embarked on our journey, the lush greenery and vibrant atmosphere of the region filled us with a sense of wonder and excitement.

Our father had meticulously planned various sightseeing trips and adventurous drives through the wetlands, ensuring that we made the most of our time there. It was a time of togetherness and joy, a rare opportunity for our family to bond amidst the stunning backdrop of nature's splendour.

Amidst the exploration and family bonding, a significant event unfolded during our visit. My mother, who had been plagued by various health conditions attributed to the evil eye for decades, finally found relief. She embarked on a significant journey to meet a renowned healer, whose cure brought about a profound change in her life. This experience was transformative, instilling a renewed sense of hope and optimism within our family. It was a momentous occasion that left an indelible mark on our hearts, shaping our outlook on life and the future.

As our time in Illubabor drew to a close, we returned to Addis Ababa one week before my father's final departure. The impending separation weighed heavily on our hearts, casting a shadow of melancholy over what had otherwise been a joyous and fulfilling trip. The bittersweet nature of our experiences in the region mirrored the uncertainty that lay ahead.

The journey back to Addis Ababa was marked by a sense of impending change, as my father and his colleagues prepared to embark on a bus arranged by the government for their grand conference. The atmosphere was tinged with a palpable sense of optimism as we grappled with the impending farewell and the unknown future that awaited us.

As we navigated through the dramatic landscapes and emotional complexities of our journey, vivid descriptions and strong character development brought our experiences to life. The undefined tone of our story encapsulated the myriad emotions that accompanied our time in Illubabor and Gambella, leaving an indelible impression on our family's collective memory.

Upon our arrival in Addis Ababa, the days drew closer to the eagerly awaited inauguration of the Workers' Party of Ethiopia, and the nation buzzed with excitement. Festivals filled the air with music, colour, and the scent of exotic foods. Street parties dotted every corner, while local communities organised activities to celebrate this historic occasion. Yet, amidst the grandeur and festivity, a shadow of criticism loomed over the government's extravagant spending.

The international community raised eyebrows at the millions of dollars poured into the construction of the party headquarters and the lavish decorations adorning the streets. While dignitaries indulged in opulent parties, the harsh reality was that the country grappled with multiple internal conflicts and a devastating famine that had left thousands dead and millions starving. The stark contrast between the grandeur of the inauguration and the nation's grim realities sparked debates and outcry both locally and abroad. The discord between the extravagant celebrations and the pressing issues plaguing the country became increasingly apparent, casting doubt on the legitimacy and priorities of the ruling elite.

Meanwhile, within the corridors of power, promises of reshuffling and the allure of new opportunities stirred intrigue and anticipation. The list of the party's central committee, to be unveiled with great fanfare, revealed an unexpected inclusion—my father. Among the names that graced this prestigious roster, his stood out, signalling a potential shift in his professional trajectory.

With bated breath, my family awaited the promised change in my father's role, which was speculated to elevate him to one of the highest posts in the diplomatic sector. The prospect of embarking on a new chapter, one that held the promise of international exposure and enriching experiences, ignited dreams of a life as the children of a diplomat living abroad.

As inauguration day dawned, a palpable buzz reverberated through the air, carrying with it a sense of anticipation and uncertainty. The towering edifice of the party headquarters loomed in the city centre, a symbol of power and authority that overshadowed the reality of the nation's struggles. Dignitaries from far and wide descended upon the grand hall, their opulent attire and ostentatious displays of wealth contrasting sharply with the sombre backdrop of societal unrest and suffering.

As we pondered the uncertain path that lay ahead, the whispers of change and opportunity intertwined with the harsh realities of a nation in turmoil. In the wake of the grand inauguration, as the echoes of celebration faded into the night, the true test of leadership and integrity awaited—a test that would define not only my father's future but also the fate of a nation at a crossroads.

In the bustling city of Addis Ababa, preparations were underway for the grand inauguration. It was a week filled with meetings and colourful festivals that culminated in the much-anticipated event. Families eagerly awaited the arrival of their loved ones, including one particular individual—a man whose journey from Gambella to the heart of Addis Ababa was not just a physical one, but a symbolic transition into a new era.

My father's destination was a designated accommodation where he would prepare for the official photographs in the new party uniform. This uniform, inspired by North Korean style, was a bold statement of camaraderie and solidarity of the regime with the global communist camp. It marked a departure from the conventional Western attire typically seen in high offices, signalling a shift towards a more unified and disciplined approach to governance.

The unveiling of the uniforms on national television sparked a wave of curiosity and intrigue among the populace. It was not just a change in clothing; it was a visual representation of a new beginning—a fresh start for the nation, a transition from military to one partly led by civilian administration. The government's plan to gradually implement the uniforms across all levels of society, with colour-coded attire to signify different statuses, was met with a mix of enthusiasm and apprehension.

Ordinary citizens would don brown khaki colours, a humble yet dignified choice reflecting their role in society. Government officials would wear authoritative blue, a colour that commanded respect and authority. At the pinnacle of the party hierarchy, those adorned in dark blue would embody the essence of power and leadership.

Amidst the sea of changes sweeping through the country, we found ourselves at the heart of it all, our father, a future diplomat in his blue uniform, a badge of honour and duty.

The final day dawned with a sense of anticipation and excitement as dignitaries and officials gathered to witness the historic event. National television dedicated 24 hours to broadcasting propaganda, showcasing communist leaders arriving at the airport to attend the inauguration, with the military leader Mengistu welcoming each dignitary in his new dark blue uniform, honing a new wardrobe away from the full combat green military attire he wore every day.

In every small and large city and town across Ethiopia, the air was charged with excitement. Within our family and friends' circles, news spread like wildfire that our beloved father, a respected figure in the community, was finally returning home for good.

Meanwhile, at home, my mother—a woman of grace and strength—was a flurry of activity. Her heart brimmed with cautious excitement at the thought of her husband's imminent arrival. She had spent countless nights praying for his safe return, weaving dreams of a united family once again. With her lifelong illness cured by the miraculous healer, my mother was looking forward to a new beginning with her beloved husband.

As the sun began to set, my mother found herself unable to sit still. She moved around the house with purpose, ensuring that everything was perfect for my father's homecoming. The smell of traditional Ethiopian spices wafted through the air, mingling with the sounds of laughter and chatter from neighbours who had gathered to celebrate the promotion and the long-awaited reunion.

My mother and her friends had prepared a feast fit for royalty, with platters of injera, spicy doro wot, and fragrant alicha waiting to delight the senses. The table was adorned with colourful flowers, symbols of joy and new beginnings. Every corner of their modest home shimmered with the promise of a brighter tomorrow.

My mother, a beacon of cautious excitement, exuded a blend of nerves and hope as she awaited the call from my father, heralding his long-awaited return. The news of his impending arrival had transformed our humble abode into a festival venue, bursting with the scent of delicacies prepared in abundance—each dish a labour of love and celebration.

As evening descended like a velvety curtain, casting shadows that danced along the walls, my mother fussed over each detail with meticulous care. The table groaned under the weight of savoury dishes and sweet desserts—a feast fit for a king. Neighbours and friends flowed into our home, their laughter and chatter blending with the joyous air of reunion. It felt as if a mini inauguration was underway, a prelude to the grand ceremony that would mark our family's unity once more.

In the corner of our sitting room, the flickering light, struggling against the over-illuminated national grid, highlighted the creases of my mother's weary face, softened by the radiance of hope and anticipation. Her eyes sparkled with unshed tears, a silent testament to the love that bound our family together through distances and hardships. In my father's absence, she had been both mother and father, holding our household steadfast with her unwavering strength and grace.

As the hour grew late, a hushed expectancy settled over the gathering of friends and family. The distant sounds of drums beating and voices raised in song drifted through the night, adding to the ambiance of festivity that enveloped our home. My mother, her hands clasped in silent prayer, willed the phone to ring, each passing moment stretching out like taut strings of anticipation.

Then, like a sudden burst of light in the darkness, the phone trilled its melodious chime, breaking the spell of silence that had descended. With trembling hands, my mother reached for the receiver, her heart pounding in her chest with the force of a thousand drums. The familiar voice of my father filled the room—warm and comforting, promising a future of togetherness and love.

Tears of joy streamed down my mother's cheeks as she listened to my father's words, his voice a balm to her weary soul. He spoke of new beginnings and opportunities, of promises fulfilled and dreams realised. In that moment, surrounded by the warmth of loved ones and the promise of a bright tomorrow, my mother basked in the glow of a reunited family, her heart full to bursting with gratitude and love.

My father told her that he would be staying at the government accommodation until the day after the inauguration but would make as much contact as he could until he came home. He spoke to everyone in the house, thanking them for their kindness and promising to see them in two days' time.

The homecoming celebration continued well into the evening, a testament to the enduring bond of family and the resilience of love.

As the sun set, the city came alive in a way it hadn't in years. The anticipation that buzzed through the streets of Addis Ababa on the night before the grand inauguration was palpable, especially as the night curfew was lifted for the first time. The residents of the city had been waiting for this moment—the chance to break free from the shackles of restrictions that had bound them for so long.

The night sky erupted with bursts of colourful fireworks, painting vibrant streaks across the darkness. The air resonated with the lively beats of music festivals and the joyful chatter of people enjoying their newfound freedom. It felt as though all the rules that had governed their lives had been cast to the wind, replaced by an infectious sense of liberation.

Amidst the revelry, the presence of military personnel and hardware on every corner served as a stark reminder of the turbulent times the country had endured. Yet, instead of instilling fear, it fostered a sense of unity among the people. Residents greeted the soldiers patrolling the streets with smiles, offering them drinks and food as gestures of goodwill—a promising sign of reconciliation between the citizens and the guardians of the regime.

Families, friends, and strangers alike flooded the streets, drawn out by the irresistible allure of the fireworks and the promise of a carefree night. Children ran ahead, their laughter echoing through the night, while adults strolled leisurely, taking in the sights and sounds of the city they had missed so dearly.

I was among the throngs of people making my way to the city centre, accompanied by friends and family. Revolution Square was awash with light, the grandeur of the fireworks mirrored in the wide-eyed wonder of the onlookers. For the first time in years, Addis Ababa felt alive, pulsating with the energy of a city reborn.

As we stood amidst the crowd, I couldn't help but feel a surge of gratitude for this moment—the chance to witness history in the making, both for the country and for my own family. I felt as though this was a celebration for my father and our family. The night was a kaleidoscope of colours and emotions, a celebration of resilience and unity that brought tears to my eyes.

Groups of teenagers found themselves caught in the throes of youthful exuberance. The air was thick with the scent of adventure and mischief as young people roamed the vibrant streets in search of thrills and fun. Among them was I, a charismatic boy with a mischievous grin, along with my friends Abel and Nebiyu, eager to break free from the constraints of our everyday lives.

As we strolled through the bustling city, our eyes were drawn to a group of girls gathered in front of the colossal newly built Workers' Statue in the city centre. Like a vision, they exuded a sense of allure and mystery, their laughter floating through the air like a melody. Addis Ababa girls, known for their shy and reserved demeanour, seemed liberated for one night, adorned with a newfound sense of freedom, their eyes sparkling with a hint of mischief.

The atmosphere was charged with an exhilarating sense of liberation, a mood unlike anything we had experienced before. Emboldened by the spirit of love and freedom that hung in the air, Abel nudged us with a mischievous twinkle in his eye. "Let's go over there and talk to them," he whispered, his voice brimming with excitement. Nebiyu and I exchanged hesitant glances, unsure of what would happen, but the allure of adventure was too strong to resist.

Approaching the girls with nervous smiles, we were welcomed with open arms. Their cheeks flushed with excitement; the girls seemed delighted by our unexpected company. In a simple attempt to break the ice, we offered a round of soft drinks and snacks, which brought smiles to their faces.

As the night began to dip into the early morning hours, a cold breeze swept over the city. We moved to a cleared space in the grassy park behind the new statue. Music filled the air; the mix of live traditional melodies compelled us to sway and move in time with the beat. Laughter and joy mingled with the music, forming a symphony of happiness that echoed through the night.

Emboldened by the lively atmosphere, we danced—a fleeting moment of shared joy and excitement that bound us together in that ephemeral dance.

In the heart of the bustling night, the neon lights illuminated the streets as we ventured out further. Excitement buzzed in the air amidst the chaos.

As the night progressed, the girls mentioned that they lived a bit further away and were hesitant to walk home alone in the chaotic city filled with drunken revellers. Without a second thought, we, the kind-hearted souls and fresh daters, offered to walk them home for their safety. The girls, grateful for the gesture, accepted with smiles.

As we set off along the city's twisting streets, we found ourselves relying on the girls to lead the way, walking in pairs rather than as a group. Laughter filled the air, and occasional touches of camaraderie cemented the bond formed in that fleeting moment. Time seemed to slip away, with two hours passing in what felt like mere minutes.

Finally, the girls announced their arrival in their neighbourhood, expressing gratitude and bidding farewell. Just as the last goodbyes were exchanged, a sudden voice pierced the night air from a shadowy corner. "Hey, hey you! What do you think you're doing with my sister?" a rough, angry voice bellowed.

Panic ensued as the girls, recognising the voice, scampered off in fear of their brother's wrath. Left behind, we attempted to explain our humble intentions and consensual companionship, but our pleas fell on deaf ears. The enraged brother, fueled by a protective instinct over his sibling, called upon his friends, who were lurking nearby, their drunken slurs echoing through the night.

Before we knew it, the group of boys descended upon us, fists flying in a blur of anger and confusion. Accusations of flirting and ill intentions filled the air, drowning out any attempts at reasoning. In a city where loyalty and familial bonds ran deep, the boys viewed us as potential threats to their sister's dignity.

Caught in a whirlwind of chaos, we found ourselves outnumbered and overpowered by the older boys' drunken rage. With no other choice, we broke free from the attackers and ran for our lives, the sounds of angry shouts echoing behind us.

As we sprinted through the dark streets, our hearts pounded with fear and adrenaline. The city that had once felt inviting had transformed into a maze of dangers and shadows. Eventually, we outpaced our pursuers, escaping into the safety of the night, cloaked by darkness, our bodies bruised but our spirits unbroken. It was the price we paid for spending a romantic night with girls.

In a city where the line between friend and foe blurred in the darkness, we learned a valuable lesson about the unpredictable nature of human emotions and the thin veil separating camaraderie from conflict.

In the late hours of the night, we found ourselves meandering through an unfamiliar neighbourhood, the darkness conspiring against us. Laughter and youthful banter filled the air as we strolled along, our eyes twinkling under the faint glow of the scattered streetlights.

As we ventured further from the unfamiliar streets, the surroundings grew increasingly desolate, the once lively bustle of the urban landscape fading into a hushed stillness. None of us had ever wandered this far before, and the looming uncertainty began to cast a shadow over our carefree night.

Lost amidst the labyrinthine roads, we found ourselves trapped in a maze of unfamiliar alleys, fields, and dead ends. With each wrong turn, our desperation grew, and the sense of foreboding crept into our hearts like a sinister whisper in the night. We sought guidance from the rare passersby, only to be met with drunken slurs and misguided directions that led us astray.

Despite our best efforts to retrace our steps, the night seemed determined to keep us captive in its dark embrace. Hours bled into eternity as we wandered aimlessly, our exhaustion mounting with each futile attempt to find our way home. The girls' flirtatious banter had given way to weary silence, our once bright eyes now dulled by fatigue and frustration.

Finally, as the first faint hues of dawn painted the sky in soft pastels, we stumbled upon the city centre—a sight of familiarity in the uncharted territory. Relief washed over us like a cool breeze, momentarily lifting our spirits at the sight of well-known landmarks marking our way home after a four-hour walk. From the city centre, our neighbourhood was still an hour away, making our total journey a gruelling eight hours on foot in just one night.

Yet, even as we set out on the final leg of our journey, a sense of discord hung in the air. Bruised egos clashed, tempers flared, and accusations flew between us like arrows in the stillness of the early morning. We blamed each other for the series of misfortunes that had befallen us—from agreeing to walk the girls home to running in the wrong direction to escape the attack by the brother and his gang. Our camaraderie wavered under the weight of fatigue and frustration.

And so, with the first rays of sunrise casting long shadows behind us, we trudged wearily towards the familiar comfort of our neighbourhood, each step a painful reminder of the night's misadventures. As the city slowly began to stir from its slumber, we finally reached the sanctuary of our homes, our bodies aching and spirits bruised, but our bond tested and tempered by the trials of the night that had not yet released its grip.

As we made our way back home, weaving through the throngs of people still out on the streets, I couldn't help but smile. Tonight, Addis Ababa had come alive in a way that transcended the mere lifting of a curfew. It had reminded us all of the power of community, of the strength that lay in unity, and of the resilience that defined us as a city.

Under the watchful gaze of the morning sun, we returned home, our hearts lighter and our spirits lifted by the magic of that fleeting encounter. In the heart of Addis Ababa, amidst the bustling streets and colourful lights, a bond had been forged—a connection that transcended boundaries and brought a sense of joy and unity to all who had been a part of that magical night.

As the last echoes of the celebrations faded into inauguration day, I knew this was a night that would be etched in our memories for years to come. The lifting of the curfew had not only marked the beginning of a new era for Addis Ababa but had also reignited a spirit of hope and camaraderie that had been dormant for far too long.

As I looked up at the morning sky one last time, I knew that this was just the beginning of a new chapter for Addis Ababa—a chapter filled with promise, possibility, and the unwavering spirit of its people, especially my family.

The inauguration day of the Ethiopian Workers' Party marked a significant moment in Ethiopian history, symbolising a transition to semi-civilian rule under the auspices of a single political entity. The streets of Addis Ababa erupted in vibrant celebrations, the air filled with nonstop martial music, and the city adorned with banners proclaiming a hopeful future. Large portraits of Mengistu Haile Mariam, now modelling in his dark blue suit instead of his military uniform—a symbol of change not only in his mind but also in style—underscored the shift towards a new chapter in governance. This public display of festivity aimed to foster a sense of unity and progress among the populace.

However, the grandeur of the inauguration was starkly contrasted by the escalating conflicts in the northern regions of Ethiopia. Rebels, resistant to the central government's authority and sceptical of the promised reforms, intensified their military actions. They captured small towns and villages, making significant advances while the government's focus seemed diverted towards the celebrations in the capital. This surge in rebel activity served as a stark reminder that not all parts of the country were ready to embrace the changes or the leadership of the Workers' Party of Ethiopia.

Amidst these internal conflicts, the government faced a delicate balance during the inauguration. High-ranking military commanders were summoned to Addis Ababa, leaving some areas potentially vulnerable to further rebel attacks.

The government chose to maintain a façade of peace and stability, especially in front of international visitors, by downplaying the ongoing strife. This strategy highlighted the challenges of transitioning to civilian rule in a country marked by deep-seated regional and political divisions. As the country stood on the brink of a new era, the juxtaposition of celebration in the capital and conflict in the north underscored the complex and arduous path ahead in achieving true national unity and peace.

As I woke up from my sleep around midday on Inauguration Day, our home was filled with a mix of excitement and tension about the upcoming inauguration speech that all citizens eagerly anticipated. For our family, this was a significant turning point. My mother and her friends anxiously awaited the moment, preparing fresh coffee as they gathered around the TV, which streamed live colour images for the first time, eager for the broadcast of the proceedings from the new Workers' Party conference hall.

This day held immense importance not just for our family but for countless others across the nation, as the government continued to announce its manifesto, promising changes that would transform the country into a liberal system of governance. The air seemed to buzz with a collective sense of hope and uncertainty as people from all walks of life looked forward to the new leadership's vision and promises. The television, which usually played a few hours of daily news and popular revolutionary dramas, was now broadcasting live shows in broad daylight for the first time. People were excited to stay indoors and watch TV. Programs that were not known to exist during those odd hours transformed into a portal of national engagement, drawing everyone into its excited glow.

As the clock struck the designated hour, the room hushed, and the broadcast began. The camera panned across the grand conference hall, capturing the faces of dignitaries and delegates gathered for this historic moment. My mother clasped her hands tightly, her eyes fixed on the screen as she waited to see my father among the crowded sea of blue uniforms. Groups of people everywhere gathered in front of screens, reflecting the dreams and aspirations of many Ethiopians who yearned for change and progress. This inauguration was more than just a political ceremony; it was a beacon of hope, signalling the dawn of a new era for Ethiopia.

As the names of the central committee members were read—sometimes interrupted by music and short announcements—a sense of anticipation and anxiety filled our home, much like in many others gathered around their television screens, eager to hear the fate of their loved ones and acquaintances.

I woke up to the sound of my mother and her friends discussing the latest developments in the political landscape. I joined them in the living room, pouring myself a cup of tea while answering questions about my whereabouts the night before as we listened intently to the names and titles being announced. It felt like a game of musical chairs, with some members being promoted to more important positions while others were dismissed from the party altogether.

As the list of names continued to be read, tension filled the air. We heard familiar names called out, their titles indicating new power and responsibility within the government. My heart skipped a beat when I heard my father's name mentioned, but the reader paused before announcing his new title.

For what felt like an eternity, we waited in silence, anxious to hear what role my father had been assigned. Would he be an official based in Addis Ababa, or was his long-hushed diplomatic career about to take off? The news anchor, known for his unwavering professionalism, hesitated before continuing with the list of names. A brief instrumental piece interrupted his reading, heightening the moment's significance and leaving us on edge.

Finally, the reader apologised for the interruption and proceeded without revealing the new title bestowed upon my father. He moved on to call other names. We breathed a collective sigh of relief, grateful that he had not been among those dismissed from the party. It was a bittersweet moment, knowing he would now bear even more responsibility and scrutiny.

The room filled with heavy and mixed feelings. The announcement had been made, and while most of us expressed delight in hearing my father's name, the absence of a new title left us concerned. We exchanged forced smiles and half-hearted congratulations, trying to push away the unease that lingered in the air.

As the celebrations continued, my mother's suspicion only grew. She had seen enough of the government's unpredictable actions throughout her lifetime to know that nothing was ever certain. While the rest of us basked in the momentary relief of my father being named a party member, her worry deepened.

After a long silence, she finally spoke up. "I can't shake this feeling," she said, her voice filled with concern. "Why wasn't your father's title omitted, and why wasn't he shown on screen, even from afar? They covered every angle, every participant, but not him. It doesn't make sense—there must be something wrong."

Her words hung heavy in the air, casting a shadow over the room. We all knew she was right. The government was known for its secretive and manipulative ways, and my father's name being mentioned without a title among the thousands of others—and the fact that we hadn't seen his face on the screen—was deeply worrying.

Phone calls began to flood in, familiar voices on the other end from friends and family around the world; from Los Angeles to Rome, and Riyadh to Oslo. They expressed their happiness, concerns, and confusion about the events surrounding my father. The mysterious absence of a new title and the involuntary pause had sparked worry among everyone.

News had spread like wildfire, reaching even our relatives abroad who dialled in to ask my mother about the title and the forced pause. The phone didn't stop ringing throughout the day, with friends and well-wishers offering their support and prayers, but also bombarding my mother with questions she had no answers for. Why was there a pause? Why wasn't my father's title mentioned? Had she spoken to him?

My mother's replies were always the same—asking them to pray for my father. She tried to remain strong, but the uncertainty and constant stream of calls took a toll on her. Some callers claimed to have seen my father, dressed in his blue uniform, while others believed they had caught a glimpse of him on a screen during the conference. Their well-intentioned words only heightened her anxiety and left her longing for any form of communication from him.

As the day wore on and the conference came to a close, my mother became increasingly withdrawn, lost in her own thoughts and fears. She would sit by the phone, hoping for it to ring, her eyes filled with a mixture of hope and dread. The uncertainty of not knowing my father's whereabouts or well-being felt like torture for her, and she struggled to find peace amidst the chaos. She was familiar with this feeling; she had been there many times before.

Amid all this turmoil, I grappled with my own emotions. It was hard to see my mother so devastated, and my inability to provide any answers or reassurance only added to my helplessness. I tried to distract myself by focusing on chores and everyday tasks, but the weight of the situation hung heavily over our household.

As the sun began to set, casting long shadows across the living room, a sense of unease settled over us. The house was eerily quiet, interrupted only by the occasional sound of a phone ringing in the distance. Each ring felt like a jolt, sending waves of anxiety through us. Yet, no matter how many times we answered, there was no news, no update, no indication of my father's whereabouts.

In that moment of silence and uncertainty, I realised the true power of communication. The absence of words, of information, of connection left us feeling isolated and vulnerable. We were left to grapple with our fears and doubts, unable to reach out and bridge the gap that separated us from my father.

As darkness enveloped us, we clung to each other, seeking solace in the warmth of our shared presence. The phone calls may have come and gone, filled with questions and concerns, but in that moment, all that mattered was our bond as a family, our love for each other, and our unwavering hope that we would hear from my father soon.

That night, as I drifted off to sleep, I said a silent prayer to a God I had never known, asking for my father's safety and for strength for my mother—challenging him to prove His true existence. In that moment of quiet reflection, I found a sliver of peace amidst the storm, knowing that no matter what challenges lay ahead, we would face them together, united in love and resilience.

As the next day wore on, my mother's worry morphed into fear. She couldn't shake the feeling that something was wrong, that a storm was brewing on the horizon. I tried to reassure her, telling her everything would be okay, but even I couldn't deny the sinking feeling in the pit of my stomach. Finally, as the sun began to set and the week-long celebrations drew to a close, my mother pulled me aside.

Her eyes were filled with a mixture of fear and determination. "We need to find out what's really going on," she said, her voice steady despite the turmoil inside her.

Together, we set out to uncover the truth. We spoke to my father's friends in government, party members, anyone who might offer insight into his sudden disappearance. It soon became clear that my father's new title as a party member was nothing more than a façade, a means to silence him and keep him under control. The government had no intention of granting him any real power or influence; he was merely a pawn in their twisted game of politics.

As the truth unravelled before us, my mother's fear transformed into anger. She refused to let them get away with their deceit and manipulation. Together, we devised a plan to confront the government, to demand justice for my father and for all those who had been silenced and exploited for their own gain.

In the end, we stood united, a family torn apart by the cruel machinations of those in power. But we refused to be broken. We would fight for the truth and for justice, no matter the cost. As the shadows of uncertainty loomed over us, we stood firm, ready to face whatever may come our way.

Our home, filled with heavy and mixed feelings, could not diminish our resolve. As we stepped into an uncertain future, we knew we would confront whatever lay ahead, together.

As new days unfolded, we watched the political landscape shift and change before our eyes. Excitement buzzed among some party members who had been promoted, while others grappled with the disappointment of being demoted or ousted. This volatility served as a reminder of the unpredictable nature of politics and its myriad twists and turns.

Weeks passed without news of my father's whereabouts, deepening our worry and etching lines of concern into my mother's face. She spent countless hours on the phone, reaching out to anyone who might have information. Yet each call ended in disappointment, leaving us with no new leads or clues. The uncertainty of my father's fate weighed heavily on our family, casting a pall over our once-happy home.

Meanwhile, the nation celebrated the new government system, filled with promises of a brighter future and improved living conditions. But for us, those promises felt hollow and distant, overshadowed by my father's absence. It was as if our family inhabited a different world, one marked by fear and unanswered questions.

Despite the darkness that loomed over us, my mother remained determined to find my father. She refused to give up hope, tirelessly pursuing every possible avenue for information. With each passing day, we clung to the belief that someday, somehow, we would be reunited with my father, and our home would once again be filled with light.

I remember the day when news spread like wildfire through the Eritrean community in Addis Ababa. During some of the phone calls my mother made, she heard unconfirmed reports of prominent Eritreans disappearing from their workplaces and homes. Some were released immediately, but others remained in detention, their whereabouts unknown. It marked the first time that so many high-profile Eritreans had been detained in a mass arrest. Businessmen, university lecturers, and CEOs of major companies were swept up in a secretive operation hidden from public view. The government's actions following the conference brought the bustling city to a standstill, as Eritrean businesses were seized, paralyzing Addis Ababa's business networks.

The atmosphere in the Eritrean community was one of fear and uncertainty. The sudden disappearance of prominent figures had sent shockwaves through our tight-knit community. Once vibrant Eritrean businesses had been confiscated, and the commercial transport trucks belonging to some of the wealthiest Eritreans were now in the hands of the military. Bank accounts and valuable possessions had been seized, leaving many Eritreans feeling helpless and vulnerable. A sense of pessimism hung heavy in the air as we grappled with the harsh reality of a new war being waged against Eritreans in the city.

As the days turned into weeks, anxiety and despair deepened. Families were torn apart, and the once-thriving Eritrean community in Addis Ababa was now shrouded in fear and uncertainty. The government's actions had left a void in the lives of many, and the future seemed bleak. The once-bustling streets felt desolate, and lively conversations were replaced by hushed whispers of concern and apprehension. It was a time of great turmoil, and the resilience of the Eritrean community was put to the test as we struggled to make sense of the grim turn of events.

In the midst of the chaos, a sense of solidarity began to emerge. Despite the overwhelming pessimism, the Eritrean community banded together in secrecy, hiding from the rumored phone tapping, offering support and comfort to those affected by the government's crackdown. It was in these moments of adversity that the true strength of our community shone through. As we navigated the uncertain path ahead, we held on to the hope that one day the darkness that had descended upon us would lift, and we would emerge stronger than ever.

As the news of high-profile Eritreans being rounded up intensified, our family was gripped with fear and uncertainty. My father, a respected civil servant with ties to the government, had gone missing, and we were almost certain he had been detained for questioning. We clung to the hope that it would be a temporary ordeal, but the days stretched into weeks, and the lack of information about his whereabouts gnawed at our hearts. Each passing moment felt like an eternity as we grappled with the ominous silence surrounding his disappearance.

Then, one morning, a glimmer of hope emerged. A close relative of my father, whose husband held a high-ranking position as the governor of the Ethiopian Commercial Bank, came to us with news. She had learned from her sources within the government that my father had been detained under what was referred to as 'sostegna', meaning 'the third', for questioning. According to her, he was to be released after a short due process. It was a small comfort to know that he was alive and that there was a possibility of his release, but the uncertainty of the situation still loomed over us.

As the days passed, the situation for Eritreans in Addis Ababa and other parts of Ethiopia grew increasingly dire. More high-profile individuals were being detained, and it seemed that anyone with business or influence was a target. The government's actions appeared erratic, as the country was embroiled in a chaotic war. The rebels' advancements on the frontlines made the government more nervous and unsettled, forcing it to employ blanket arrest measures against Eritreans. It was a time of great upheaval, and the cycle of fear in our lives had been reignited after many years of calm. We struggled to make sense of this new reality, clinging to the hope that my father would soon be returned to us.

In the midst of this turmoil, our family's resilience was tested. We had to navigate shifting alliances and allegiances while holding on to the belief that there was still hope for a brighter future. The uncertainty of my father's fate weighed heavily on us, but we found strength in each other as we faced the challenges ahead. Our story became intertwined with the larger narrative of a country in turmoil, and as we fought for my father's freedom, we also fought to maintain our optimism in the face of overwhelming pessimism.

Days turned into weeks, and weeks into months, with no sign of my father's release. Our once-bustling home now felt desolate, and the laughter that used to fill our souls was replaced by a heavy silence once more. I watched as my mother's hopeful façade crumbled, and my own optimism waned. The world around us seemed to be closing in, suffocating us with its uncertainty. In this environment of dramatic twists and turns, we were forced to confront our deepest fears and darkest thoughts, as the unknown fate of my father became a haunting presence in our lives.

As the fading celebrations for the formation of the new party brought no substantive changes to people's daily lives, a sense of unease settled over the city once again. The intensifying wars in various parts of the country cast a shadow over the once joyous atmosphere. It was amidst this uncertainty and military defeat that the government made an unexpected announcement: compulsory national military service for anyone above the age of 18 was declared, sending ripples of shock and fear through the population.

The new decree outlined the conditions and terms of the service, linking it to privileges such as access to higher education and work opportunities. However, it also made it clear that families must voluntarily submit a family member for service, or the local councils, known as 'kebele', would enforce the call-up of young men and women.

I vividly remember the day the announcement was made. The air crackled with tension as people gathered in hushed groups, exchanging worried glances and murmuring anxiously about the implications of the new decree. As a family with five boys, some of us close to the threshold age, the news hit us like a sledgehammer. As we approached the completion of my high school education, our dreams of pursuing further studies and carving out a future for ourselves suddenly seemed uncertain, overshadowed by the looming spectre of mandatory military service. The once vibrant city now felt suffocating, filled with a palpable sense of pessimism as people grappled with the harsh reality of the situation.

In the midst of this turmoil, I found solace in the company of my friends and fellow students, each of us wrestling with our own fears and uncertainties. The once-carefree laughter that filled our schools now carried an undercurrent of anxiety as we navigated the uncharted waters of an uncertain future. The looming prospect of compulsory military service cast a pall over our lives, and as the days turned into weeks, the daily sight of fleets of trucks loaded with conscripted young men and women became a horrifying reality unfolding before our eyes. The city transformed into a battleground, with revolutionary guards rounding up young men and women and taking them forcibly at gunpoint to military training centres, while the fading celebrations served as a stark reminder of the uncertain times we faced.

As the days passed, the impact of the new law became increasingly evident. Families faced the agonising decision of which member would be enlisted, while young adults grappled with the abrupt disruption of their plans for the future. The local councils, or kebele, assumed newfound authority as they enforced the law with unwavering determination, leaving little room for dissent or negotiation.

As weeks turned into months, with little and fluctuating news about my father's whereabouts and wellbeing, the tension within the Eritrean community in Addis Ababa grew palpable. Rumours began to circulate about the arrest of a controversial Eritrean figure, Woldu, who held significant influence in both business and political circles.

Woldu's notoriety stemmed from his ambiguous wealth accumulation and his disdainful attitude towards Eritreans, particularly his public condemnation of the Eritrean independence struggle. Whispers suggested that he had been collaborating with the government, aiding in the identification and persecution of rebel supporters. Despite his perceived protection from the authorities, Woldu had always feared retribution from sympathisers of the rebel group in Addis Ababa.

The community's apprehension reached a fever pitch when news broke of a major crackdown on a clandestine cell operating in the heart of Addis Ababa. This cell, led by Woldu, a double agent, had been orchestrating complex financial and political support for the Eritrean rebels, amassing and channeling vast sums of money to further their cause. Shockingly, the cell had deep connections with high-ranking government officials and army officers, who had been divulging crucial secrets to the rebels, significantly bolstering their operations. The revelation of this intricate web of betrayal and subterfuge sent shockwaves through the Eritrean community and the political landscape of Addis Ababa.

Amidst the turmoil, Woldu's once enigmatic figure was cast in a starkly different light, with his actions laying bare the depths of his treachery. The community grappled with the disheartening reality of betrayal from within their own ranks, as the connections between the rebels and influential figures in the government came to light. The pervasive sense of pessimism that had settled over our community was now suffused with profound disillusionment, as the once-unshakeable trust in certain figures was shattered. The events that unfolded served as a stark reminder of the complexities and betrayals that can lurk beneath the surface of even the most tightly-knit communities, leaving us to navigate a world fraught with uncertainty and mistrust.

In an apparent revelation regarding the circumstances that led to my father's arrest, it became clear that Woldu, well connected to many businessmen and officials, had attempted to recruit my father several times in the past. He had approached my father through mutual friends to discuss his moral duty to join the Eritrean rebels. Woldu was known for his persuasive nature, and he had tried to sway my father through friends and direct meetings. He painted a picture of imminent danger, warning my father that the rebels were closing in and that neutrality would only lead to regret and accountability for historic mistakes.

It was later revealed that Woldu had preyed on my father for a long time, working diligently to convince him to join the secret cell. Despite Woldu's relentless efforts, my father remained steadfast in his neutrality, refusing to tread the treacherous path of becoming a double agent. My father had witnessed enough persecution and detainment to know that such a life was not for him.

Then came the shocking news of an investigation into Woldu's secret operations. A search of his hidden office uncovered a diary detailing many of his activities, including numerous meetings with important figures, my father among them. However, it offered no insight into the outcomes of those encounters. My father's biggest risk lay in the undeniable fact that he hadn't informed the authorities about his meetings with Woldu, which could have led to Woldu's arrest much earlier.

Amidst the investigations into Woldu's complex operations, my father, along with many others, found himself subject to arrest because his name was implicated in various ways. The government, overwhelmed by the sheer size and complexity of Woldu's operation, resorted to a rapid blanket arrest, immediate executions of some, and a slow, painstaking investigation for those who were spared from the sword.

In these mysterious circumstances of loyalty and betrayals, Woldu was released to continue his lavish life and take care of his businesses around the capital, while all prominent Eritreans were either executed or still languishing in prisons.

As the days turned into weeks, my father languished in a notorious prison known for the disappearance of political prisoners. The air was heavy with the weight of uncertainty and fear, and the walls seemed to close in on those who dared to defy the status quo.

As we continued our search for his whereabouts, news of more disappearing Eritreans became a crucible of despair, testing our limits of endurance as we grappled with the grim uncertainty of our fate. It was in those moments of darkness that I truly understood the cost of standing firm in the face of adversity.

After months of relentless searching, and with the help of some of my father's friends in high places, my mother was granted one-time access to see him.

As she entered the bleak visiting area of the notorious 'sostegna' detention centre, sometimes referred to as 'makelawi', meaning central, my mother's eyes immediately sought out my father under the watchful gaze of two security officers.

What she saw shattered her heart into a million pieces. My father had deteriorated significantly from weight loss since she had seen him months ago. His once robust frame had shrunk, and his eyes held a glint of hopelessness. It was evident that the weight of his incarceration had taken a heavy toll on him. He looked confused and unable to speak, consumed by anger and disappointment. The strict conditions of their meeting prohibited them from discussing the details of his case, leaving their conversation filled with cries and a sense of despair. Meeting my father created a new wave of emotional distress for my mother.

A few weeks after that brief and heart-breaking meeting, the investigations seemed to slow down. Most of the convicted prisoners had either been eliminated or transferred to other detention centres, leaving my father and a few others behind. They were given limited access to receive food from their families, with no visual contact allowed.

With the same unwavering determination she had shown many years ago in Mekelle, my mother embarked on a new journey. She took it upon herself to bring food to the prison for my father and the other helpless inmates. This journey was filled with the theme of pessimism, as she navigated the challenges and obstacles that stood in her way. The circle of life had become a reality; my mother, who had seen herself transformed through various stages of life, was once more the wife of a prisoner, with no clue about when it would end.

As the days turned into weeks, my mother's visits to the prison became routine. She faced numerous hurdles, from bureaucratic red tape to the emotional toll of seeing my father in such a desolate state. Yet she persevered, driven by an unyielding love and determination to provide some semblance of comfort to my father and the other inmates. The prison walls could not contain her unwavering spirit, and her actions spoke volumes about the strength of her character. Each visit was a testament to her resilience and unwavering love, serving as a stark reminder of the harsh realities many faced behind bars.

Haunting rumours swirled outside the prison walls—whispers of families bringing food for their loved ones, only to discover that those they sought to nourish had long been eliminated months ago. It was said that the guards took the food for themselves, leaving the families in the dark about the fate of their kin. My mother, consumed by worry for my father's existence, clung to the hope that delivering food would confirm he was still alive. But it never did. The government's announcements of political prisoners' releases only added to our anticipation, yet each time, my father's name was not among those set free. Two long years slipped by without a glimpse of our father or any sign of his existence.

Despite the lack of confirmation that my father was receiving the food we sent, we continued to send it every day. The containers always returned empty, leaving my mother to ponder whether she was unknowingly feeding the ruthless, hungry guards with her nutritious, homemade meals. The thought gnawed at her as she questioned the fate of the food she had so carefully prepared to ensure my father's health and well-being. Was it possible that she had been unwittingly sustaining those who held my father captive?

As we delved into the stories of other mothers who had brought food for loved ones who were not even within the prison walls, we couldn't help but wonder if my mother's efforts were similarly in vain. The theme of pessimism loomed large as we grappled with the uncertainty of my father's fate and the possibility that our gestures of love and care were being misdirected. The world around us seemed shrouded in ambiguity, and the weight of unanswered questions pressed heavily upon us.

In this drama-filled world, the undefined tone of our existence mirrored the uncertainty that enveloped us. We were left to navigate the murky waters of doubt, clinging to hope while grappling with the harsh reality that our efforts might be in vain. As I reflect on those tumultuous years, I am reminded of the strength and resilience my mother displayed in the face of such adversity and the indomitable spirit that sustained us through the darkest of times.

Amidst the vicious circle of freedom and despair that haunted our family for decades, my mother's resilience and unwavering love kept us together despite the relentless challenges we faced. For most of our lives, she juggled the roles of both parents, providing us with the guidance and support we needed while shouldering the burden of caring for my father. Her strength was a beacon of hope in the midst of our tumultuous circumstances.

As I grew older, I witnessed the toll that the government's oppressive policies took on my family. My father's absence, both physically and emotionally, left a void that my mother valiantly tried to fill. She worked tirelessly to provide for us, often sacrificing her own well-being for the sake of our family. Her determination and sacrifice were a testament to the unbreakable bond that held us together.

Despite the hardships we endured, my mother's love and resilience instilled in us a sense of perseverance and determination. We learned to navigate the complexities of life with courage and fortitude, drawing strength from the example set by our mother. Her unwavering commitment to our family became the cornerstone of our unity, and her sacrifices taught us the true meaning of love and selflessness.

As we faced the challenges imposed by the government, my mother's steadfast devotion and unyielding spirit became our guiding light, illuminating the path forward in the midst of adversity. Our family story, though marked by hardship, was also a testament to the power of love and resilience.

My father's days in prison seemed to stretch on endlessly, each one blending into the next in a monotonous blur. Every day, we were confined to our small bedrooms, with only the occasional visit from our mother breaking the suffocating silence. She would come to us with a brave smile, but her eyes betrayed the fear and uncertainty that gripped her heart.

As teenagers, we struggled to comprehend the gravity of the situation. Our once carefree existence had been shattered, replaced by the harsh reality of our father's imprisonment. The endless wait for life in the promised land turned into a slow, grinding cycle of despair. We longed for the familiar embrace of our father, for his comforting words and unwavering strength. But now, all we had were memories and the ache of his absence.

Amidst our despair, a flicker of determination began to kindle within us. We refused to accept this unjust fate without a fight. We sought solace in each other's company, finding strength in our shared resolve to seek justice for our parents. We delved deep into our hearts, searching for the courage to face the unknown future that loomed before us.

For us, the children, it felt as if the last dice had been thrown, and we had been deceived one final time with no hope of a better future. The journey we had travelled—from an ordinary life to poverty, to living like royals—flashed before us, reminding us of the unpredictability and complexity of life, over which we had no control. We had prepared ourselves for a future reunited with our father, never to leave us again, but the reality of life behind bars was not something we had expected. It was heartbreaking, leaving us struggling to make sense of it all. The harshness that had intruded upon our carefree youth now felt real, affecting our emotions and filling us with anger that we could not contribute to our parents' freedom.

Questions haunted our consciences: What had we done? Why was our family subjected to such repeated cycles of peril? Which God would do such a thing to decent parents who always did good for others? Who was in charge of our fates? Whoever it was, they were not doing what they preached. These questions filled our minds, but no one had the answers. It seemed fundamentally wrong, by all definitions, principles, and religions, that good people like my father should be tested in this way.

As we sat in our confined space, memories of our time at Mekelle Palace flooded back. The laughter, love, and sense of security we once had felt like a distant dream. As time passed, our father's absence became palpable, and the weight of our mother's worry hung heavy in the air. We were just children, trying to make sense of a world that seemed determined to crush our spirits. The uncertainty of our future loomed over us like a dark cloud, and the once vibrant colours of our lives had faded into shades of grey.

In the midst of our despair, a flicker of determination ignited within us. We may have been young, but we were not powerless. We vowed to fight for our family, to seek the truth, and to bring justice to those who had wronged us. Our journey had taken an unexpected turn, but we refused to let it define us. With newfound resolve, we set out to unravel the mysteries that had shattered our world, determined to reclaim the hope that had been stolen from us.

Personally, my father's recent imprisonment changed my perspective on life. It felt as though the solid ground I had always stood on had crumbled beneath me, leaving me adrift in a sea of uncertainty. My once hesitant belief in justice and fairness was replaced by a gnawing sense of emptiness. It seemed that doing good and being fair in life brought no rewards; instead, the world felt like an unpredictable chaos that decided our destinies without reason.

At seventeen, in the quiet moments, I found myself grappling with the idea of joining the rebels as a possible way to save my father. The thought of taking such a drastic step weighed heavily on my mind, but the image of my mother's grief loomed large in my thoughts. I couldn't bear the idea of causing her more pain, and the potential repercussions for our family and my younger brothers were unfathomable. As I contemplated the ideology behind the independence war, I realised that my sole motivation could implicate my father, increasing the risks to his life—a decision fraught with its own dangers.

Despite the turmoil within me, I knew that the only way to honour my parents' love and sacrifice was to stay strong and excel in my education. It was the one thing I could do to make them proud and show them that happiness could still exist within our family, even in the face of such tragedy. I poured myself into my studies, seeking solace and purpose in the pursuit of knowledge and achievement.

As the days turned into weeks and the weeks into months, I felt a sense of resilience growing within me. I refused to let the darkness of my father's imprisonment consume me entirely. Instead, I channelled my energy into my studies, determined to carve out a future that would make my parents proud. The weight of the world felt heavy on my shoulders, but I carried it with quiet determination, knowing that my perseverance was a testament to the strength and love that bound our family together.

Behind the prison walls, my father's situation remained unchanged. Yet, the fact that he still drew breath, amidst the countless souls eliminated by the government, kindled a flicker of hope within our hearts. Every New Year, we clung to the promise of mercy that the government extended to hundreds of prisoners. We waited with bated breath, yearning for that glimmer of hope, but each passing year brought only disappointment. With no semblance of a fair court or justice system, my father languished in captivity for what felt like an eternity. His captors, however, seemed to recognise his non-threatening nature, and in a small act of compassion, they allowed us weekly family visits—albeit from a distance, without the luxury of conversation.

The mere sight of him, alive and breathing, lifted our spirits from the depths of despair. Interestingly, we later learned that this privilege was granted to him because he had been appointed the 'Chairman of The WPE for inmates.' He was given the responsibility to lead the newly formed party inside the prison, sharing his involuntarily induced ideology with fellow prisoners and addressing issues using the party's ethos. He had a small makeshift office inside the prison cell where he checked in for two hours daily, allowing inmates to consult him on any ideological concerns, as if that was a concern to them. Officially called 'Chairman,' no inmate was permitted to refer to him by his name. He received circulars and weekly party magazines to better understand his role, which included leading meetings to provide progress updates and gather feedback on the party's performance.

Every Sunday, we made the solemn pilgrimage to the prison, where we would catch a glimpse of our father through a minuscule hole in the wall, barely 20 cm in diameter. He would stand approximately 10 metres away, straining to see through that tiny aperture. As we huddled near the hole, we could make out his form and wave our hands, taking turns during the precious 10 minutes we were allotted. He would wave back, a faint smile gracing his lips, but we knew that from that distance, he couldn't truly see us.

Months passed, and then a glimmer of change emerged when my father was transferred to another section of the prison, allowing our Sunday meetings to become slightly less distant. The inmates were corralled on one side, while we, the visitors, stood on the other, separated by a distance of approximately three metres, with guards vigilantly monitoring our interactions. In this cramped space, about 20 prisoners faced an average of 100 visitors, all raising their voices to the maximum in an attempt to converse. The cacophony enveloped us, rendering our conversations indecipherable, but at least we could see each other's full faces and bodies.

My father, a man of few words, would stand there with a faint smile, saying very little during our brief 10 minutes together. Then, as abruptly as it began, the visit would end, and the prisoners would be herded back to their cells without a proper goodbye. In those fleeting moments, the tragic reality of our circumstances was laid bare—the cruel separation, the stifled communication, the unspoken longing for freedom. Yet, amidst the despair, there was an unspoken bond that transcended the barriers, a silent understanding that connected us in our shared tragedy.

As time passed, the prison conditions for all inmates slowly improved. Using his influence as party chairman, my father negotiated with the prison authorities to introduce activities aimed at enhancing the inmates' minds. With material and logistical support provided by families through contributions to a learning club managed by my father, various educational activities were established as new inmates came and went. Those who were released contributed financially and brought additional books and materials to support the club they had benefited from. Gradually, the club gained formal recognition, earning accreditation to conduct national school-leaving exams for distant learners and issue completion certificates. Many professionals volunteered their time to share knowledge in small makeshift classrooms, where some learned English, others explored art, and many pursued various subjects.

My father, adept at turning downtime into useful opportunities, learned Italian and Spanish from a foreign inmate named Mario, who had been imprisoned under suspicion of being a CIA agent many years ago. Mario, a Spanish citizen, was multilingual—a skill typically mastered by spies. He had been in prison since the early days of the revolution after being caught under mysterious circumstances involving an intrusion into the country via a small helicopter. Having never been tried, he had no prospects of release. My father clung to him as a mentor, gaining enough knowledge to read, write, and speak almost perfectly in both Italian and Spanish.

As the days turned into weeks and months, the prison transformed into a place of learning and growth for many inmates. The learning club flourished, and the once desolate walls echoed with the sounds of languages being spoken, art being created, and knowledge being shared. Mario, with his enigmatic past and multilingual abilities, became a beacon of hope for those seeking to expand their horizons within the confines of the prison. My father, once confined by physical walls, found freedom in the realms of language and culture, thanks to Mario's unlikely mentorship.

However, the language department was abruptly shut down. It felt as though a shadow had fallen over the prison, casting a pall of fear and uncertainty. The guards grew increasingly paranoid, complaining about inmates practicing Western languages they couldn't understand. They perceived it as a threat to the prison's security and an indulgence in Western language and culture, as if even the act of speaking a foreign language was an act of rebellion. It was absurd, really, but their fear was infectious, spreading through the prison like a virus. They sought to erase these languages from their minds, to silence the playful chatter that had brought a glimmer of joy to our bleak existence. But they couldn't, and that was what frightened them the most.

The inmates had always been drawn to studying languages, finding solace in the rhythms and melodies of words from distant lands. They sometimes used their knowledge sarcastically: "Buenos días, ¿cómo estás hoy?… ¿puedo invitarte a un café en la tienda?" It was a form of escape, a way to transport themselves beyond the confines of the prison walls, but to the guards, it sounded as though they were planning their escape. The laughter that once echoed through the corridors had been replaced by a stifling stillness, and the playful banter that had provided comfort had been snuffed out. It felt as if the very essence of our humanity was being stripped away, leaving behind a hollow shell of existence. As the guards patrolled the halls with watchful eyes, my father and his friends couldn't shake a growing sense of unease, as if they were all teetering on the edge of something dark and unknown.

My father was summoned for his part in promoting Western 'cultures' within the prison walls. He was handed papers detailing the party's disciplinary rules, which he was asked to read aloud to ensure he understood the consequences of his actions. Before that, the officer clarified that this wasn't just a piece of paper—these lines were well-thought-out guidelines written by our wise party leaders to streamline members' behaviours.

My father, unsure of what awaited him in punishment, read the whole document, which clearly outlined the consequences of such acts of traitorship and corruption of citizens' minds by party members. The guidelines stated that the ultimate punishment was indefinite imprisonment and expulsion from party membership. The prison officer, who obviously hadn't read the papers, froze in awe and asked my father to repeat the last line. So, my father did, only for the officer to regret his instinctual reaction when he said, "What does that mean? Which stupid person wrote that? You are already in prison." The officer, shaken by his own insulting remarks about the authorities, warned my father not to share his last comments with anyone.

Uncertain about how the disciplinary measures would be enforced on a person who was already imprisoned, my father promised to comply with the orders given to him: to erase the languages from the inmates' minds through indoctrination and brainwashing, cleansing them of the 'toxic' knowledge they had gained.

The prison, once a symbol of despair, transformed into a place where minds were liberated, and souls found solace in the pursuit of knowledge. The tragic circumstances that had brought these men together were overshadowed by the resilience and determination blossoming within the prison walls. Amidst this unlikely camaraderie, my father and Mario forged a bond that transcended the boundaries of their confinement, proving that even in the darkest places, the human spirit could find light and purpose.

In return for his service, my father helped Mario establish contact with his friends and family in different countries. Mario's contacts in Europe sent letters and books to our home address, which we then passed on to him through my father. In this delicate humanitarian act of support, we had to carefully censor the packages for appropriateness to keep ourselves and Mario safe.

My father, a man of quiet strength, had always been a source of inspiration for my art, especially during my younger years. I had noticed his ability to sketch simple freehand drawings with ease, though he never indulged in art seriously. He often told me how he loved art as a young man but never pursued it beyond his school days. When I visited him, he beckoned me closer, his voice barely above a whisper as he shared the tale of an inmate who had captured his attention. This inmate, a renowned artist, had mastered the ancient Ethiopian Orthodox art, depicting angels and biblical scriptures with a skill that seemed almost otherworldly. As my father recounted the inmate's mesmerizing work, I felt a shiver run down my spine, a sense of unease settling in the air.

My father became captivated by the artist's mastery of ancient art. Although he had no particular interest in religion, he found himself drawn to the colorful, mysterious drawings that exuded a sense of antiquity and beauty. Despite the constraints of their environment, the artist's work seemed to transport my father to a different world. Each stroke of the brush held a story of its own, a tale of hope and resilience in the face of adversity.

As the artist shared his skills with my father through daily practice, they worked tirelessly, day and night, honing their craft. While my father learned the art, my family supplied them with the necessary materials. To make their venture even more intriguing, the artist provided us with a list of professional drawing supplies, which we promptly sourced from our relatives in Europe, who were happy to help. This collaboration transformed into a partnership, and soon they were producing postcards for religious holidays, birthdays, and well-wishing cards for inmates to purchase and send to their loved ones outside the prison walls. The demand for these meticulously crafted cards was overwhelming, with each inmate eager to buy dozens to share with their families and friends. Their art evolved into a full-time production operation, requiring my father and the artist to prepare in advance to meet the rising demand for each upcoming holiday.

The cards they created were of such exceptional quality that they were virtually indistinguishable from those available outside the prison. By selling these cards to fellow inmates, my father managed to gather enough money to support our household financially and purchase more materials without imposing any extra burden on my mother and their suppliers in Europe. The profit they made was significant; my father could send enough money to cover our family's expenses for months during the holiday season, along with additional pocket money for us, his children. He often joked, albeit with a hint of truth, that he was making more money in prison than he ever did on the outside. The sight of these cards exchanging hands during cultural and religious holidays became a symbol of the inmates' resilience and determination to maintain connections with their loved ones despite their circumstances.

Additionally, they produced a few extra cards to be sold in the visitors' waiting area, raising funds for those who did not have close relatives or visitors. The cards made by my father found their way out of the prison each month, serving as a bridge between the incarcerated and the world beyond the prison walls. After the artist left, my father continued to pursue his art, generating more income and sending it to my mother.

My father, a man of unwavering compassion and selflessness, possessed a nature that transcended his own personal hardships. Through his fundraising idea and friendly demeanour, he sowed seeds of hope in the lives of others. In a world where optimism was a rare and precious commodity, my father's innate desire to help those in need shone like a beacon of light in the darkness. Despite facing his own struggles, he dedicated himself to assisting those around him, offering a glimmer of hope to those who had lost all faith in the world.

It was during one of the most challenging periods of our lives that my father's true character emerged. Even as we faced adversity, he continued to extend a helping hand to others, including inmates who had crossed paths with him. His empathy and kindness resonated deeply with these individuals, and they, in turn, became our closest family friends after their release. Former prisoners, who had experienced the depths of despair, came bearing gifts and money on various occasions, expressing their gratitude for the hope my father had instilled in them during their darkest hours.

The impact of my father's actions was profound. These ex-inmates shared stories of how he had saved them from depression and planted seeds of hope in their hearts. Their tales painted a vivid picture of my father's unwavering commitment to uplifting others, even amid his own struggles. As I listened to their accounts, I gained a deeper understanding of the extraordinary impact one individual's selfless acts of kindness could have on the lives of others. My father's legacy of hope and compassion left an indelible mark on those he had touched, and his influence continued to resonate long after his passing.

In a world where hope was a scarce commodity, my father's altruism and unwavering dedication to helping others stood as a testament to the power of compassion. His actions transcended the boundaries of personal hardship, leaving an enduring legacy of hope and kindness that would inspire generations to come.

Derailed By Success

Highway To Hell

Growing up as teenagers without a father was a heavy burden that weighed on my siblings and me. Our mother, already overwhelmed with the responsibilities of raising us five teen boys, was often stretched thin. As adolescents in a bustling city, the lack of guidance left us vulnerable to the influence of our peers.

I remember those tumultuous years vividly, when the world seemed to spin out of control and chaos reigned supreme. In our housing complex, where the lines between right and wrong blurred, my brothers Kaleb, Simon, and I found ourselves navigating a treacherous path. The allure of rebellion and the influence of unhelpful acquaintances led us astray, and our once-innocent ages gave way to the temptations of indecent practices. Despite our initial resistance, the pressure to conform to these unholy activities became too great to bear. Small-time backstreet gambling and other ill-fated pursuits became our pastimes, and our previously unyielding resistance to drinking and smoking slowly crumbled under the weight of peer pressure.

The weight of our mental suffering bore down heavily on our shoulders, and the previously undefined tone of our lives became tinged with rebellion and self-destruction. It was in those uncertain years, amidst the chaos and confusion, that we grappled with the consequences of our actions, with no father to guide us out of the darkness.

As the days turned into nights filled with reckless abandon, we stumbled further into the clutches of habits that stained our souls and clouded our judgment. The once-clear path of academic pursuit became obscured by the fog of our misdeeds, and the tarnish of our manners became apparent to those who once held us in high regard. The hopeful dreams we envisioned for ourselves seemed to fade into the background, overshadowed by the grim reality of our choices.

In the historical backdrop of our tumultuous youth, the boundaries between good and evil blurred, and the allure of rebellion cast a shadow over our once-bright spirits. The housing complex, which had once been a haven of innocence, became a breeding ground for temptation and moral derailment. As the third eldest of my brothers, I witnessed the transformation of Kaleb and Simon alongside my own descent into the abyss of unholy practices.

Earlier, my friends Abel and Nebiyu, both grappling with their own family struggles, succumbed deeply to the allure of alcohol and tobacco. Nebiyu, living with a cruel stepmother, found solace in these vices. After their father had passed away, his mother sent him money directly, often in excess, as the stepmother was known to be exploitative. Nebiyu encountered money at a vulnerable age, allowing himself to spend freely on gambling and drinks.

Abel, on the other hand, had a mother who stocked boxes of wine and tobacco, readily providing us access to these substances. In my own vulnerable state, I easily fell into the trap, indulging in these unholy habits and gradually drifting away from healthier pursuits. Our DJing hobby flourished, taking us to weekly extravagant parties where life seemed transformed.

As our habits deepened, we found ourselves drawn to the company of like-minded individuals, leading us to experiment with marijuana. Our once-cherished hobbies in art, cars, and electronics faded into obscurity. With my friends having abandoned their education, I too found little motivation to excel academically. The culmination of these choices resulted in poor academic performance, closing the door to my dreams of attending university. With a shattered spirit and no clear path ahead, I languished for a year until a concerned relative offered to pay for my university tuition to save my future.

Meanwhile, my elder brother Simon had also abandoned his studies due to behavioural issues, while our eldest brother Kaleb struggled with similar habits and temptations. Despite our potential, the path to a brighter future seemed elusive.

Even the prospect of pursuing a privately paid medical degree, which I began with the support of a distant wealthy aunt's financial intervention, felt like a futile endeavour. The allure of quick fixes and instant gratification provided by our vices overshadowed the long-term benefits of a doctor's salary. Empty dreams of going abroad like many others surfaced, defining our plans for a meaningful future.

The spectre of national military service loomed over our family, with the local council, or kebele, incessantly pressuring my mother to sacrifice one of her sons. The kebele revolutionary guards, responsible for conscriptions, demanded more than one child from our family, citing a supposed payback order for our father's 'transgressions'. To protect us, my mother resorted to bribing these corrupt officials, who extorted her for regular payments, threatening to take us away if she didn't comply. The fear and uncertainty that gripped our family were palpable. While many of our friends were conscripted and never returned, our mother kept us safe with her hard-earned money, some of which came from my father's art sales. The tragic cycle of despair seemed unending, casting a shadow over our once hopeful lives.

I remember my brother Simon as a fearless soul, always yearning for militaristic adventures despite the harsh realities we faced. The guards would come regularly to collect money in exchange for our freedom, and Simon, with his dreams of becoming an air force jet pilot or an army commander, felt the weight of these circumstances deeply. His academic struggles didn't conform with his ambitions, and he sought ways to make his dreams come true. He even registered to become an army cadet, which didn't require any credentials, unaware of the conflict his personal and ethical beliefs would bring. My mother and relatives had to intervene, discouraging him from pursuing this path, but Simon's determination remained unyielding. In his wildest dreams, Simon always said, "When I graduate as a fighter pilot and given my first mission, I would turn around and bomb all the presidential offices and start a government change that will see my father's freedom." He always seemed to be seriously working on these plans as he continued improvising his theory.

Simon's situation took a dark turn when a man named Shume, who led the revolutionary guards in our district, held a grudge against him. Despite the bribery scam Shume was involved in, taking money from our mother in exchange for our freedom, Simon persistently asked to be registered for military service, unaware of the danger he was putting himself in. Again, his 'plan-b' theory for joining the army at any rank was to train and get hold of a gun to secretly assassinate Shume, leader of the revolutionary guards for our local council.

Shume, who would lose his regular bribe money if one of us joined, told our mother that Simon was seeking conscription in the national military service. Simon's immediate goal was to stop Shume extorting our mother with his freedom-for-money trade.

My mother quarrelled with Simon, expressing her disapproval of him joining the army, especially when it meant fighting against his own people. In a desperate act, Simon and his friends ambushed Shume as he emerged drunk from a local bar, where he spent our bribed money, beating him badly and leaving him injured and hospitalised as a warning to leave our family alone. However, this act of vengeance led to Simon's arrest and subsequent forced enlistment in the military. The military service was often used as a means to cleanse neighbourhoods of anti-social youths.

During Simon's ten-day detention at the local council office, my brothers and I visited him, and his words weighed heavily on us. He spoke of sacrificing his life for our sake, urging us to focus on our studies and make our parents proud. He warned our mother to stop paying Shume, as it was no longer relevant. Despite her compliance, she continued to pay small amounts to keep Shume at bay, knowing he had the power to take another child from her. Simon's sacrifice and the turmoil it brought upon our family left us in a state of despair, grappling with the tragic consequences of his actions.

As the days passed, we saw Simon and many young souls loaded onto a fleet of AMCE trucks being sent to a military training camp, leaving us with a sense of helplessness and uncertainty. His attempts to expose Shume's illegal deeds fell on deaf ears, as Shume was perceived to be a loyal revolutionist by the authorities. Simon's fate seemed sealed, and as we watched him being taken away in one of the AMCE trucks, his words echoed in our minds—a haunting reminder of the sacrifice he had made for us. The tragic events that unfolded left an indelible mark on our lives, shaping our understanding of sacrifice, loyalty, and the harsh realities of the world we lived in.

Simon, a clever, streetwise, and sociable young man, had completed his military training just as the war was reaching its peak. Despite his best efforts to avoid being sent to the front lines, he found himself serving as an assistant to a corrupt training officer who shamelessly extorted money from him to avoid being sent to the war fronts.

In a remote part of Ethiopia, near Simon's military camp, where law enforcement was a distant memory, Simon found himself in a precarious position. With no police presence around the training camp, some 600 km away from home, he and two soldiers were dispatched to raid an illegal gold pit operated by village miners. As they ventured into the depths of the pit, they expected to find a group of lawless gang members, probably armed, extracting their hard-earned gold. However, what they stumbled upon were just two weak men toiling away in the darkness with simple tools.

Simon, a man of conscience, couldn't bring himself to arrest these miners who were simply trying to make a living in a world where survival was a constant struggle. Instead, after noticing the men had extracted a sizable amount of gold, he and his colleagues conspired against their orders. In a bold move, Simon decided to let the miners go in exchange for payment. They reported to their commanders that it had been a false alarm and suggested that no further action was necessary.

From that day on, Simon found himself caught in a web of deceit and compromise. He continued to wear his uniform and visit the miners, demanding payment to keep them safe from the authorities. Each time, he would collect the bribe and ensure that the miners were left unharmed. This became his way of life—a means to finance the bribes he paid to his superior to keep himself inside the camp, away from the horrors of the front lines, where so many others left never to return. As he navigated this treacherous path, Simon grappled with the weight of his actions, knowing that he was perpetuating a cycle of corruption and injustice. Yet, in this unforgiving world, he saw no other way to survive in a society that had his family in captivity.

Shume, the camp officer, and Simon were engaged in a vicious circle of corruption at different levels—a world where the powerful feasted on the weak without remorse. Simon described this world perfectly: "dog-eat-dog," as he would mockingly call it.

With his quick wit and charm, Simon managed to keep himself safe, but the constant fear and uncertainty weighed heavily on his spirit. Determined to find a better life, he made the difficult decision to flee to neighbouring Kenya in search of new prospects further in Europe. When Simon came home for his break, he consulted my friend Nebiyu to join him, knowing that he too was interested in fleeing. With another friend who had good driving skills, as Simon and Nebiyu did, they stole their boss's military jeep as a gateway car and fled to the border, where they abandoned it and crossed into Kenya. After a few months in Nairobi, Simon seized an opportunity to be smuggled on a Commonwealth cargo flight, eventually seeking asylum in the UK. He financed his own smuggling using money he saved from his illicit earnings from the dodgy gold pit.

After a successful asylum application in the UK, Simon's life took a new turn. He found work and built a family, but the scars of his past experiences lingered. The trauma of fleeing his homeland and the constant fear of being discovered haunted him, casting a shadow over his newfound stability. Despite his efforts to integrate into his new surroundings, the memories of war and the hardships he endured continued to shape his perspective. The tragic weight of his past experiences coloured his interactions and relationships, leaving him with a sense of detachment and longing for the life he had lost. Yet, through it all, Simon remained resilient, finding solace in the love of his family and hope for a brighter future. Nebiyu, later joined by his two brothers in Kenya, went to the United States on a family reunion visa arranged by their mother.

Our family had endured more than its share of hardships, with our father in detention, our oldest brother Kaleb lacking motivation for self-improvement, and Simon in the army barracks and later fleeing the country. I found myself thrust into the role of the man of the house, a fatherly figure to my two younger brothers. However, luck seemed to smile upon us when Simon's enlistment allowed Kaleb the freedom to explore life outside the country. With the financial support of our uncle living abroad, Kaleb was able to pursue his studies at a UK university, opening doors for him to venture beyond our homeland.

Meanwhile, I took on the responsibility of caring for my younger brothers, guiding them through their junior high school years. Despite our father's absence, our family was fortunate to receive generous support from relatives abroad, both material and moral.

Our father's transfer to a more civil prison brought a glimmer of relief. The improved facilities and visitation arrangements allowed us to spend quality time with him and exchange letters and gifts every Sunday, providing a sense of normalcy amidst the turmoil. Despite the uncertainty of his release, our father remained optimistic, finding solace in the fact that he was spared from the fate that befell many of his fellow detainees.

My father appeared better; he had access to wash and iron his own clothes, shaved regularly, and tried his best to maintain a good appearance for my mother.

With no trial or hope of release, he remained there indefinitely, continuing to work on his art, which allowed him to benefit from a larger customer base among the larger prison population.

Amidst the challenges, my father found a way to make a positive impact on our learning from behind prison walls. He dedicated himself to teaching us English through the exchange of lengthy, meticulously crafted letters. Each week, he would write ten to fifteen pages to each of us, underlining new vocabulary in red and providing an index for their meanings to expand our knowledge of the English language. In turn, we would respond with our own letters, filled with exciting vocabulary and chosen topics, eagerly awaiting his corrections and guidance. This method of learning not only strengthened our command of the English language but also fostered a deep connection with our father, despite the physical distance between us. During visits, we brought our exercise books for him to check and make comments. He would encourage us in our strong areas and discuss those needing improvements.

As the years passed, my father's letters became a source of joy and inspiration, offering glimpses of his resilience and unwavering spirit. His dedication to our education and his optimism in the face of adversity left an indelible mark on our lives, shaping us into individuals capable of navigating the complexities of the world with strength and grace. Through his letters, he imparted wisdom, love, and a sense of hope that transcended the confines of his prison cell, weaving a tapestry of resilience and familial bonds that sustained us through the darkest of times.

Over time, living in the housing complex became more community-oriented, with families bonding over shared interests and supporting one another through thick and thin. As new families arrived and old ones departed, the sense of camaraderie remained strong. The residents took great pride in maintaining the facilities, as most were allowed to buy the properties they lived in. Due to the location, the value of individual properties increased exponentially, attracting wealthier buyers looking to redevelop them. The complex transformed into a welcoming environment, free from the antisocial elements that had plagued the area in the past. However, amidst this sense of unity, an undercurrent of unease lingered, stemming from the unchanging presence of the local authorities—specifically, the kebele revolutionary guards, who were familiar with every family's inner stories.

The local council office, also known as the kebele, alongside the revolutionary guards who enforced its laws, stood just a few blocks from the complex. They wielded a strict and unwavering authority that the residents found difficult to navigate. For my family, being Eritreans, this strictness often manifested as discrimination and baseless accusations. Our adherence to Western culture, evident in our clothing and shoes provided by our relatives abroad, made us easy targets for the guards' harassment. Our father's imprisonment was cited at every opportunity to label us as 'children of a traitor,' with comments suggesting we had to pay for our father's crimes. It hurt deeply to hear illiterate guards call our father a traitor and a harmful person.

They would arrest us without cause, citing our attire as a reason, and demand that my mother forbid us from wearing Western clothes. At times, she had to resort to bribery to secure our release, while other times, she stood her ground, refusing to yield to their unjust demands.

The guards' interference extended beyond our clothing; they took it upon themselves to police our entertainment as well. The mere act of using a Walkman and headphones in the neighbourhood was enough to warrant arrest, followed by thorough interrogation about the source of the gadgets and the contents of the tapes we carried, as well as a disdainful critique of the music we listened to.

Shume, the most notorious guard, took particular pleasure in targeting our family. He would confiscate our electronic gadgets and subject us to physical punishment. His disdain for Western influences was palpable, and he made it his mission to stamp out any semblance of it within the community. Even our attempts at emulating Michael Jackson's dances—a trend at the time—were met with ridicule and condemnation, as Shume viewed them as a corrupting influence on our traditional values. He, our guardian evil, could not comprehend our fascination with music, the universal language.

I remember the day my brother Biruk decided to try the hip hop dance, snake dancing, he had seen in a music video. As he attempted the dance, Shume scoffed, saying he looked like he was having a seizure. He would often grill us, questioning how we could find Western music and dance more appealing than our traditional ones or those of Soviet Russia. Shume's disapproval was palpable, and his disdain for anything remotely Western was evident in every word and action.

One sunny afternoon, as we played music from a small Sony stereo cassette player outside our bedroom window facing the street, Shume stormed over and smashed the player to pieces, calling it a "devil's machine" that was corrupting our minds. His arrogance knew no bounds, and his misguided addiction to communism, which he barely understood, coloured every interaction he had with us. Shume was illiterate, devoid of any reading or writing skills, yet he held strong opinions about everything, particularly regarding our choices and preferences. His narrow-mindedness was tragic, casting a shadow over our otherwise vibrant world.

Shume took it upon himself to fight Western culture in our household. When he occasionally came to collect his bribe, he would insist on searching our home for music videos and cassettes. On one occasion, he tore down my Guns N' Roses poster from my bedroom wall, calling Axl Rose, the lead singer, a "white devil." Shume proudly announced his findings in our bedroom to groups of youth he summoned for indoctrination. He told the audience how our household was the most possessed of all the houses he searched. He continued with his claim that our home was haunted by powerful Western evils and that he was working on curing us from the ghosts who gripped our minds. As a first measure of his cure from our 'demonic illness,' Shume imposed a curfew just for our family, warning us of severe consequences if we were found outside our home after 7 pm. He regularly referred to us as the "little reactionaries."

Shume's presence was a constant reminder of the clash between revolutionary ideology and modernity, and his inability to appreciate anything beyond his narrow worldview only deepened the divide. His disdain for Western influence and fervent belief in communism created a tension that permeated our interactions, forcing us to navigate the delicate balance between embracing change and honouring our roots.

Despite the oppressive atmosphere created by Shume and his ilk, my brothers and I refused to relinquish our natural love for pop music and Hollywood films. We found solace in the melodies and rhythms that transported us beyond the confines of the housing complex, offering a glimpse of a world that Shume could never comprehend. Shume's relentless crusade against our cultural inclinations only strengthened our resolve, as we clung to our passions in defiance of his narrow-mindedness. In the face of adversity, we found unity within our family, drawing strength from each other to withstand the oppressive forces that sought to stifle our individuality.

In the labyrinthine tapestry of life, where destiny's threads intertwine and unravel with capricious grace, I found myself ensnared in a web of societal adversity and familial strife. The allure of oblivion and influence beckoned me, and I succumbed to the intoxicating embrace of illicit substances, seeking solace in a world of fleeting pleasures, joining my friends Abel and Nebiyu.

As days blurred into nights and nights dissolved into an endless cycle of indulgence, I retreated further into my self-imposed exile, oblivious to the world beyond my hazy perception. My family became my sole refuge, their struggles overshadowing any aspirations I may have once harboured.

The future stretched before me like uncharted territory, fraught with uncertainty and trepidation. I clung to the familiar, eschewing any opportunity for growth or change, lest it disrupt the fragile equilibrium I had constructed. Like a ship lost at sea, I allowed the currents of life to carry me aimlessly, surrendering control to fate.

Opportunities arose, beckoning me to distant shores, but I remained anchored by a misguided sense of duty to my mother, who had endured countless hardships alone. In the twilight of my youth, as friends embarked on new chapters in faraway lands, I found myself adrift, tethered to a past that held me captive. The weight of unfulfilled dreams pressed upon me, yet I remained paralysed, unable to break free from the chains of sabotage imposed on me by society.

Years turned into a monotonous blur, marked by the constant hum of harmful habits and the absence of purpose. My mother's unwavering love and concern were met with my indifference and denial. In the depths of my despair, I stumbled upon an unexpected lifeline.

After Nebiyu fled to Kenya, Abel, my only companion and a product of a broken family, became ensnared in a toxic web of dependence. Together, we embarked on a perilous journey, confronting our demons head-on. It was a path fraught with setbacks and false starts, but the flickering flame of hope within us refused to be extinguished.

The days when the streets echoed with the laughter of friends were now gone, scattered across the globe. All except Abel, who found himself tangled in a futile citizenship process to become Italian through his mother's ancestral connections. He was ensnared in a web woven by bureaucracy and a lack of documentation, leading to a lonely existence, with hardly anyone left from our carefree youth. Abel, once a charming and attractive young man, became dependent on wealthy older women for financial support, adding to the sense of desolation.

A group of extremely wealthy women used him as a gigolo to satisfy their desires, and in return, he was showered with large sums of money, which they readily provided. Sometimes, he would even visit their business outlets, commanding the workers to hand over money as if it were his birthright.

Abel had left home at a tender age, with no hope of returning or forging his own path to financial independence. Instead, he squandered the wealth he received, indulging in an opulent lifestyle reserved for the elite. The wealthy ladies who travelled to Arab countries to import goods brought Abel clothing and expensive ornaments.

As I watched Abel immerse himself in this world of extravagance, I felt a pang of nostalgia for the days when our dreams were unburdened by the weight of wealth. The adventures we had embarked on, the innocent thrill of exploring the world with nothing but youthful exuberance, seemed like a distant memory. Abel, once a spirited companion, had become a mere shadow of his former self, lost in the trappings of luxury and materialism.

Sponsored and accompanied by the wealthy women, we spent our evenings in grand hotels and luxurious resorts, frequented by foreigners and government officials, reveling in the excesses that only money could afford. It was a stark contrast to the humble beginnings we had shared—a world away from the simplicity of our childhood.

As local teenagers amidst the grand hotels teeming with foreign diplomats, NGO workers, and African Union representatives, Abel and I found ourselves under government surveillance. Despite the watchful eyes, we formed unlikely connections with a diverse array of individuals—from Nigerian drug dealers and Arab tourists to diplomats and businessmen who frequented the only five-star hotel at the time, the Hilton Addis Ababa, seeking local knowledge and a free supply of marijuana. In exchange, we borrowed uncensored Western movies, music CDs, and magazines like *Time* and *Newsweek*, which were strictly banned outside diplomatic compounds. Our constant presence in the hotel and clubs grew our popularity among foreigners, leading to invitations to national day celebrations at various embassies. Dressed in tuxedos and chauffeured to these events, we mingled with diplomats and their families, entering every embassy in Addis Ababa—from the

British to the French, American, and Libyan. We also forged close friendships with African Union representatives from countries like South Africa, Morocco, and Nigeria, gaining free access to the heavily protected African Union offices.

I never imagined that our diplomatic ventures would lead to unexpected sources of income. As foreigners sought to benefit from the black-market foreign exchange rates—the parallel market, as they would call them—which were four times the official rates, Abel and I found ourselves in a lucrative position. People from various embassies and NGOs approached us to exchange large sums of money in the parallel market, as they couldn't do it themselves due to the heavy surveillance imposed on all foreigners. This allowed us to profit massively at double-digit percentage commissions.

Our business ventures didn't stop there; we also began asking our travelling foreign friends to buy large quantities of Western tobacco, spirits, and perfumes from airport duty-free shops. They generously gifted these to us, despite our offers to pay. Due to their diplomatic status, there was no limit on the quantities they could bring in. Soon, we became suppliers of these sought-after goods in the night entertainment industry, frequented by foreigners. These high-end clubs struggled with the supply of genuine spirits such as Johnny Walker, Gordon's Gin, and Courvoisier due to the government's reluctance to allow them foreign currency to import legally. Buyers were willing to pay extravagantly.

We often joked about the unusual supply chain and how those drinks were consumed by the same people (foreigners) who brought them to the country. Vodka was available in plenty, thanks to Russian military officers who smuggled it in their Antonov cargo planes, concealed among weapons.

As we continued to immerse ourselves in the world of the diplomatic and business community, we experienced a life of luxury and exclusivity previously unknown to us. Attending ceremonies, celebrations, and exclusive nightclubs reserved for foreigners, we relished the opulence and privilege that surrounded us.

Embraced by this elite environment, we became members of a world that seemed like a dream—a stark contrast to our everyday lives.

We received clothing and gadgets as gifts from our foreign friends when they returned from their travels. Aware of how difficult it was to buy a pair of Levi's jeans or T-shirts in communist Ethiopia, they brought us plenty. Some even extended their gifts in the form of food, treating us to McDonald's burgers and boxes of Pizza Hut takeaways, flown with passengers just for us, giving us a little taste of the Europe we lived in but longed to see.

To satisfy the growing demand and supply of free marijuana, we sometimes travelled to Shahshemene, a remote town inhabited by Caribbean Rastafarian settlers who cultivated the herbs for their own use but would also give us some in exchange for other favours. We would be driven in luxurious embassy cars, with drivers oblivious to our missions. Sometimes, when we didn't have enough supply, we resorted to placebo dry plants, packed and presented as the genuine herb. No one knew or complained, as if everything was okay. We sometimes joked freely about the replacement supplies, and our foreign friends would laugh at our tricks.

In this new world, I assumed the role of a diplomat and businessman, adeptly navigating conversations, making new friends, and upholding the facade we had constructed. Abel, less fluent in language skills but truly an attractive young man, often observed from the sidelines, focusing on playing the field with beautiful women from various nations. Abel was content to partake in the revelry while I took on the responsibility of doing business. Our dynamic was one of complementarity, with me shouldering the diplomatic duties and Abel embracing the hedonistic pleasures that came with our newfound lifestyle.

Amidst the glamour and extravagance, a sense of nostalgia began to permeate our experiences. We were living a life that felt surreal, a far cry from our humble origins, but more like the hottest scenes from DiCaprio's film *The Wolf of Wall Street*. The dichotomy between our real identities and the personas we had adopted created a bittersweet undercurrent, evoking a longing for the simplicity of our former lives. As we navigated this world of opulence and deception, the allure of the foreign and the pull of our roots intertwined, shaping our journey in unexpected ways.

The adventurous world we had once inhabited had transformed into a gilded cage, trapping us in a cycle of illegal transactions and uncontrolled spending. The vivid descriptions of our escapades now seemed like faded echoes of a bygone era, overshadowed by the hollow pursuit of opulence. As I observed Abel's descent into this world of excess, I couldn't help but wonder if he, too, longed for the simplicity and authenticity of our past. The undefined tone of our present existence mirrored the uncertainty that had crept into our lives as we navigated the complexities of adulthood in a world that seemed to value wealth above all else.

Despite our financial success, I struggled to keep the amount of money I was receiving a secret from my family, especially my mother. I discreetly supported my family by purchasing a big colour TV set and other essential household items, claiming they were gifts from my departing foreign friends. The thrill of the adventure and the allure of the income blinded me to the potential consequences of my actions.

Abel and I were lost in this comfortable but finite world of luxury and easily made wealth, to the extent that we forgot our true identities. Life felt so good that it didn't matter what was coming for us in the future. While families in the country struggled to make ends meet, feeding their children by buying rationed, discounted supplies from government outlets, my family was living comfortably—at least on the material and financial side. We did not have to queue at government stores for discounted supplies of sugar and flour. I carried all the necessary shopping home, purchasing from upmarket stores which supplied only European-imported products for diplomats.

Estranged by our presence in those high places, the foreigners were curious about our backgrounds and occupations. In response, we spun elaborate lies, adapting to fit into their world. I portrayed myself as the son of a diplomat, weaving a fictitious narrative around my father's supposed diplomatic career. To others, we claimed to be part of the diaspora, blurring the lines between reality and fantasy. In these interactions, the truth seemed inconsequential, as we effortlessly slipped into the roles of sophisticated diplomats, engaging in casual conversations and maintaining our newfound status with ease.

In this adventurous world, I often found myself reminiscing about the days when life was simpler, when the value of a meal wasn't measured by its cost but by the love and effort put into preparing it. The nostalgia for those days filled my heart with a bittersweet longing for a time when we didn't have the luxury of forgetting about the future. As I navigated through the bustling streets of the city, I couldn't help but feel a pang of longing for the sense of community and togetherness that seemed to have faded into the background of our comfortable but detached existence.

Despite the opulence that surrounded us, I yearned for the simplicity of life, where happiness wasn't defined by material possessions but by the warmth of family and the genuine connections we made with others. The adventure of navigating through this world of excess and abundance often left me feeling adrift, searching for a sense of purpose beyond the superficial trappings of wealth. As I gazed at the glittering skyline, I couldn't help but wonder if there was more to life than the pursuit of comfort and luxury. The nostalgia for a time when our priorities were clearer and our hearts were fuller tugged at my soul, urging me to seek a deeper meaning in this comfortable yet finite world we called home.

As time passed, the nostalgia of our early diplomatic ventures began to fade, replaced by the weight of the secrets I carried and the moral ambiguity of our business dealings. The once vibrant and exciting world of adventure now felt suffocating as I grappled with the guilt of deceiving my loved ones and the fear of being discovered. The line between right and wrong blurred, and I found myself questioning the true cost of the wealth I had amassed. Despite the material comfort, I longed for the simplicity and honesty of family life, where the thrill of sharing a simple joke over a meal was the true source of happiness.

In the midst of this lavish facade, I found myself yearning for the genuine connections and unbridled adventures of our youth—a longing that echoed through the corridors of my heart. As I witnessed Abel's entrapment in this futile pursuit of wealth and status, I couldn't help but hope that someday he would break free from the shackles of materialism and rediscover the joy of genuine human connection. His future worried me more than my own, as he had no family to turn to and no skills to trade. Every night, he slept in different places, such as hotels and short-term rentals, while I returned home daily regardless of the late hour, except on weekends.

My mother started to worry about my frequent nights away and my sometimes dizzy, battered appearance when I returned home with a hangover. I often vomited at home and exhibited signs of an unhealthy lifestyle, but she refrained from scolding me for fear of rebellion and worsening my situation.

All hobbies forgotten, Abel and I resorted to constant drinking and smoking. As the days passed, I could feel the weight of my choices bearing down on me, suffocating me with regret and despair. The once vibrant and hopeful spirit within me had been dimmed by the darkness of my circumstances. I longed for a way out, a glimmer of hope to guide me back to the light, but it seemed so distant, almost unattainable. The tragic reality of my existence had become an inescapable burden, dragging me deeper into the abyss of despair.

One night, after a fun-filled evening out, we were leaving a members-only nightclub located in the city centre. The club, called Four Corners, was an upper-class establishment with diplomatic immunity status akin to that of a diplomatic mission. Law enforcement and security agents were not permitted to enter the building. Owned by a Greek Ethiopian businessman, it was one of the few places where licensed prostitutes operated. The prostitutes were all foreigners, comprising Africans, Europeans, and Asians. Patrons were required to present a diplomatic ID, known as 'CD' for Corps Diplomatique, to gain entry, adding an air of exclusivity to the venue. Additionally, a responsible foreigner could sponsor a local person for a single visit, a rare opportunity in our city.

As we exited the club, which we had frequented for a few months, we were suddenly surrounded and forcibly loaded into a waiting car. In a swift and unsettling move reminiscent of a mafia operation, we were driven off to 'sostegna', a familiar place I visited weekly to see my father.

Unaware of the dangers surrounding us, we had found ourselves arrested by a group known as 'diplomatic security', an entity responsible for keeping diplomats safe but also notorious for spying on foreigners. They had been tailing us due to our interactions with foreign diplomats and tourists. In the interrogation room, my friend Abel and I were grilled about the nature of our friendships with foreigners. They presented detailed accounts of our interactions, making it clear that they had been shadowing us closely. We had little room to deny their accusations, especially when they found foreign money, cigarettes, and contact details of numerous foreign friends in our possession.

As they warned us of the potential consequences of carrying foreign currency, including the possibility of imprisonment, I felt a sense of dread. Being Eritrean, with a father who was a political prisoner, and sitting on the same bench where he had been questioned, I knew the stakes were high. Abel, however, had papers from the Italian Embassy, as he was in the process of obtaining Italian citizenship through a reintegration scheme. This led to him being separated from me for further questioning, while I faced a barrage of inquiries about my ethnicity, parents, and any involvement in financial transactions or exchanges of information with foreign journalists. I had to navigate the interrogation carefully, knowing that telling the truth could lead to dire consequences. I used my knowledge of Tigrinya, with a Tigrayan accent that is distinctly different from that of Eritreans, to conceal my ethnicity. I was still able to speak in that accent, thanks to my days living in Tigray.

As I sat in the brightly lit interrogation room, the weight of my detainment settled heavily on my shoulders. The possibility of years of imprisonment loomed before me, and I couldn't shake the image of my parents' faces when they heard the news. My mind raced, and at that moment, my whole life flashed before my eyes like a fast-changing slideshow. I saw myself, my family, and the tumultuous journey we had endured. I saw my mother, a pillar of strength, navigating the hardships of raising us in difficult circumstances. Her resilience and unwavering love for us were etched into every frame of my memory.

The images flickered, showcasing both the good and the bad—the moments of joy and the trials we had faced. I relived the years spent in a country at war, where uncertainty and fear had become constant companions. Then, the scenes shifted, transporting me back to the lavish diplomatic life I had once led, a stark contrast to the hardships of my earlier years. It felt as though I was revisiting my entire life, each moment playing out before me in vivid detail, as if this were the last time I would do so before facing an uncertain fate.

In the midst of this terrifying sixty-second journey through my imagination, I felt as though I was on the brink of a complete mental breakdown. The weight of my situation, combined with a mix of drinks and the marijuana that had been plentiful earlier, fractured my state of mind beyond belief. I teetered on the edge of despair, unsure if I would survive the ordeal that lay ahead.

The Bruckheimer-style flash slideshow of my life reduced to slow-moving, blurry images—a future scenario of being in the same prison cell as my father. That thought pierced me deeply; it was a form of mental torture.

However, amidst the chaos of my thoughts, a glimmer of relief emerged. The poorly equipped government security lacked the means to test for narcotics, and as long as I didn't have any in my possession, I wouldn't have to answer for any drug-related questions. The knowledge that we wouldn't be held accountable for narcotics and that my false Tigrayan identity seemed to be accepted provided a fleeting sense of peace and fear of being prosecuted for the crime of being Eritrean. It was a small reprieve in the face of impending uncertainty, but in that moment, it felt like a lifeline. As the images of my life continued to flicker in my mind, I clung to the hope that my parents wouldn't have to bear the burden of knowing that their child, sitting on the same bench as his father when he was first brought in, was facing imprisonment. The nostalgic reel of memories, both poignant and bittersweet, offered a temporary respite from the harsh reality of my detainment.

After a night of intense scrutiny, we were both released due to the absence of any tangible evidence, after the small change in foreign money was confiscated, thanks to having spent a lot of it at the nightclub. Had we been caught before entering the nightclub, we could have been convicted for possessing currency beyond the permissible threshold for locals. We were freed with a stern warning that we would be under close surveillance. The threat of severe punishment if we were arrested again loomed over us, leaving us with a sense of unease and uncertainty about our future.

As we left the intimidating presence of the diplomatic security, the weight of their warning lingered in the air, casting a shadow over our once carefree existence. The experience had left an indelible mark on us, shaping our perceptions of friendship, trust, and the precarious nature of our world.

As Abel and I scaled back on our diplomatic ventures, we began contemplating the next phases of our lives. We still managed to engage in business without making close contacts or being seen in the nightlife around clubs and large hotels. Money continued to flow in, but our leisure activities took a back seat as we became more involved in less affluent areas.

It was during one of these ventures that I found myself in a small downtown hotel called the Ras Hotel, where my girlfriend Mekdi worked as a folklore singer and dancer in a small pub within, frequented by foreigners and tourists. Avoiding the familiar foreigners I used to mingle with, my girlfriend accused me of not seeing her on stage for a long time, especially after they had introduced a new show. This young, beautiful soul, whom I had met some months ago, came from a wealthy family who did not approve of her occupation as a dancer. After an attempt by her sister to control her life, Mekdi had decided to leave the family home at a young age, making her vulnerable. Desperate for love and support, I provided her with companionship aplenty and gently. As she was also a renowned sculptor, we shared moments of appreciating art in exhibitions, while I helped her sell some of her sculptures to my interested foreigner friends for valuable money. We were a good match, and our purposeful relationship was complimented as such by several of our friends.

That night, I had a casual interaction with an Ethiopian woman named Roman, who was sitting at the table next to me. As we engaged in light conversation, which later developed into buying each other drinks, she found my ears receptive to her unique story, one that seemed to have congested her chest and was eager to be let out.

As she poured shots of French cognac for both of us from her small flask, Roman, who lived in France, shared that she had come home to see her family after many years. Married to a French man, they had flown in to introduce him to her family. However, she continued her story with a troubling revelation: she had been arrested by diplomatic security when she left their hotel room. The notorious diplomatic security, who usually lurked around big hotels frequented by tourists, had spotted her going in and out of the hotel with a foreigner—her husband.

The government had imposed a law prohibiting Ethiopian women from dating foreigners outside marriage and forbidding them from approaching foreigners for financial gain through prostitution. Violating these laws would result in severe punishments, ranging from military service to time in one of the many labour camps or imprisonment.

As Roman narrated her ordeal from a fateful morning just a few days prior, she reflected on how she had never imagined that a simple stroll through the streets of Addis Ababa would lead to such a nightmare. As the sun began to rise above the horizon, she suddenly found herself surrounded by a group of stern-faced men, their faded diplomatic security badges glinting in the light. Without a word, she was whisked away, her protests falling on deaf ears.

Meanwhile, her husband stood on the balcony of their hotel, overlooking the bustling streets of Addis Ababa. His mind raced with thoughts of the woman he loved being kidnapped. The drama unfolding below captivated his attention, but his thoughts were consumed by the efficiency of the Ethiopian intelligence apparatus. He couldn't help but admire how they had organised her arrest, seemingly for a crime she had committed long before leaving her homeland. It dawned on him that he had underestimated the country's establishments; they had kept the case active for many years, waiting for her return a decade later. The French man acknowledged the meticulous planning behind her arrest.

Descending to the lobby, he sought help to find her. The weight of uncertainty pressed heavily on his heart as he navigated the unfamiliar surroundings. He knew that Roman, his beloved, had crafted a carefully constructed narrative to secure asylum in France, claiming she was sought by the government for her political activities. The hope that she would emerge unscathed from this ordeal was the only thing keeping her husband going.

Roman, on the other hand, was taken to a detention centre filled with despair. The air was heavy with the collective fear of the women huddled together. Her heart sank as she realised the gravity of her situation. Stripped of her European clothes and belongings, she was handed a rough coverall, a stark symbol of her newfound status. The women around her bore the same haunted look in their eyes, their spirits broken by the uncertainty of their fate. It was then that Roman learned of the infamous Humera cotton farm, a place where hope seemed like a distant memory.

In the smelly confines of the prison cell, Roman faced a barrage of accusatory glances from her fellow inmates. One woman, with a hardened look in her eyes, leaned in and asked Roman where she had been caught 'working,' her tone insinuating that Roman had been found red-handed, involved in prostitution. The other asked if it was her first arrest, suggesting she was a serial offender and would share with her some of the survival skills at the labour camp. Taken aback by the woman's certainty and the harsh reality of her situation, Roman felt a surge of shock and disbelief. She recoiled, her mind racing with a mix of fear and indignation. She knew she was innocent, yet the weight of the accusation hung heavy in the air, suffocating her with its implications.

Shaken by the encounter, Roman retreated to the far end of the cell, seeking solace in the darkness that enveloped her. She vowed to herself not to engage with anyone, to shield herself from the judgment and suspicion that seemed to lurk around every corner. As she sat in solitude, the flickering overhead light cast eerie shadows across the walls, and Roman grappled with a surge of conflicting emotions. Despite the bleakness of her surroundings, a glimmer of hope flickered within her. She clung to it fiercely, determined to believe that justice would prevail and that the truth would ultimately come to light. In the midst of the harsh reality of her confinement, Roman found herself grasping at the fragile thread of hope—a beacon of light in the darkness that threatened to consume her.

An announcement was made, allocating bus numbers that would take them to the Humera cotton farm, a notorious labour camp the government used to punish female offenders. Roman screamed constantly for attention, but no one listened.

The other women bullied her, telling her to shut up, reminding her that they too had lives, and that hers was no more important than theirs.

The journey to the cotton farm felt like a descent into the depths of hell. As the miles stretched on, Roman couldn't shake the feeling of impending doom. The cotton farm loomed in the distance, a sprawling expanse of fields and barracks that promised backbreaking labour and unimaginable suffering. She was informed by reoffenders on the bus that it was a place where the very essence of womanhood was stripped away, where dignity was a luxury, and survival was a daily battle. Roman braced herself for the trials that lay ahead, her spirit warring against the crushing weight of her circumstances. In the midst of such darkness, she clung to a sliver of hope—a flickering flame that refused to be extinguished.

Little did she know that a kiosk owner outside the hotel had witnessed the entire ordeal and wasted no time in informing the hotel staff. Her French husband, deeply troubled by the incident, immediately contacted his embassy, prompting an urgent inquiry.

As the truth began to surface, it was revealed that Roman had been wrongly apprehended—a victim of mistaken identity. The security agent's error had led to her being transferred to the cotton farm 400 kilometres away, a fate she shuddered to contemplate. As she recounted her harrowing experience to a sympathetic listener, she couldn't help but reflect on the fragility of freedom.

Roman's fateful journey was traced in a massive operation that involved the French embassy, the Ministry of Foreign Affairs, and the diplomatic security office. She was sent one of the embassy drivers who brought her back to Addis Ababa. The couple, shaken by the ordeal, decided to leave the country on the earliest available flight, vowing never to return. Amidst their shared trauma, Roman found solace in the unexpected bond she had formed with the kiosk owner, who had gone above and beyond to help her.

As she told me her shocking story, I reflected on my own recent experiences and realised how even those leading decent lives can be so vulnerable under a government that mismanages everything and everyone. The couple left the country the next day, determined never to return. I reciprocated with my story, and in that shared experience, we forged a good friendship. She introduced me to her husband, Dominic.

Roman's husband, Dominic, was a man of few words; his steely gaze revealed nothing of the turmoil that lay beneath the surface. In the dimly lit corners of the smoky bar, we formed an unlikely bond, united by our shared experiences and the unspoken understanding of the dangers that surrounded us.

My encounter with Roman and Dominic left an indelible mark on my soul, prompting me to re-evaluate my own priorities and values. The adventurous world I had been navigating suddenly seemed more treacherous, and I felt a newfound determination to change my ways in this lawless society where individuals could profoundly impact others' lives for the worse.

That evening, Roman and Dominic invited me to join them for dinner, and we made our way to the bustling restaurant. I felt a sense of security in Roman's presence, a comforting shield against the uncertainties that had recently clouded my life. As we settled in and began to dine, our conversation was interrupted by the arrival of a distinguished black man who introduced himself as Ramzi, head of citizens' affairs at the French embassy. It seemed Ramzi, an ex-military man who had organised Roman's rescue, had come to offer reassurance in the wake of the tragic events that had shaken the couple. He extended his hand in greeting, and I found myself drawn into his aura of calm authority.

Roman, fluent in French, conveyed my story to Ramzi, who had Cameroonian roots, recounting how I had been unjustly apprehended simply for associating with foreigners. As we dined and conversed over a few more drinks, they expressed genuine interest in my background. With no reason to conceal the truth, I shared my experiences openly, and they offered their sympathy regarding my father's detention, wishing me and my family well. Before departing, Ramzi handed me his business card and urged me to reach out if I ever required assistance. Once Roman and Dominic bid their farewells, I seized the opportunity to contact him, expressing my desire to secure a job in any capacity I could fit into.

To my surprise, he responded promptly, acknowledging the limited vacancies at the embassy but assuring me that he knew individuals within NGOs who might have a suitable position for me, as they needed educated local employees. I provided Ramzi with our home phone number, and in the days that followed, I received a call from a Frenchman named Pierre, who invited me for a meeting to learn more about my background.

Upon meeting Pierre, I found him warm and welcoming. There was a sense of duty in him; he felt he had to help me in any way possible. He mentioned that Ramzi had spoken highly of me, praising my command of English and interpersonal skills. Pierre expressed his willingness to hire me based on these qualities alone, but he also inquired about my academic credentials to see where I might best fit.

I confessed to Pierre that I had left university to support my family but assured him of my dedication to adapting to new environments and my quick learning abilities. He then introduced me to the work they were doing, explaining that they ran a UN-sponsored educational radio programme focused on HIV awareness in various Ethiopian languages. Pierre offered me the freedom to explore where I could fit in, and as he guided me around the office building, I caught sight of a woman amidst the intricate studio recording equipment, preparing to record the day's transmission in Tigrinya. Intrigued, I asked Pierre if I could observe the studio's operations, eager to immerse myself in this new world of possibility. He informed the lady to assist with anything I wanted to know.

As the recording technician, who happened to be from the Tigray region, asked me to pull up a chair and sit, I found myself intrigued by the prospect of hearing her experiences. We settled in front of a large window, the sunlight casting a warm glow over the room. Inside the recording room, a man sat poised and ready to begin his casting. The technician gave him the green light, and he started, but it was immediately clear that he was struggling. The woman had to ask him to start over multiple times, and what was supposed to be a thirty-minute reading stretched into more than two hours. The frustrated man took several breaks, and the constant re-recording made the technician visibly nervous, as it meant she had a lot of editing and stitching to do after the recording.

Curious about her daily work, I asked if this was a common occurrence. She explained that while they had many readers come and go, Tigrinya was particularly challenging, and people often became nervous for some reason. I glanced at the script on her table and asked if I could take a look. As I quietly read through it, I couldn't discern any reason for the man's struggle. In fact, I noticed numerous grammatical mistakes and poor word choices that may have contributed to his difficulties. In that moment, I envisioned myself running the entire show and inquired about the scriptwriting and casting process.

The technician, a very kind and disciplined person, seemed surprised and asked if I was interested and capable of reading Tigrinya. Eager to demonstrate, I read a passage from the script, and to her astonishment, she remarked on my eloquence and confidence. She offered me another script to read, and to her full satisfaction, I delivered the lines with ease.

She described me as God-sent and assured me that she would do everything in her power to get me hired. The prospect of working for WHO a United Nations health organisation was enticing. She explained that they paid at European labour rates, equivalent to $5 an hour or its equivalent in other currencies of my choice. As an employee of the UN, I would have access to health and learning facilities reserved for foreign and diplomatic workers. She also mentioned that, as a UN employee, I would not be restricted from mingling with foreigners, a solution to my biggest problem. She also said I would be paid at increased rates for part-time and out-of-hours work and could have transport allowances or a driver to pick me up, if that was my wish. It felt like the world was turning its face back to me once again, offering hope and opportunity, this time legitimately. This was unheard of!

We returned to Pierre, the director of the programme representing Radio France International (RFI). As we entered his office, he inquired about my experience, but before I could respond, the technician interjected, insisting that they must hire me. She praised my Tigrinya reading skills, my confidence, and fluency, declaring that I was precisely the kind of person they needed. The air in the room seemed to crackle with anticipation as the possibility of a new beginning unfolded before me.

I was elated when Pierre offered me the opportunity to work with his team on the highest salary scale for my grade. He somehow felt obliged to help as he sensed confidence in my ability. The prospect of contributing to a radio programme that would be broadcast in Tigrinya was both thrilling and daunting. As I was ushered to another office for the formalities, the weight of the responsibility settled on my shoulders. The ID, with my name and a congratulatory message, felt like a badge of honour. The contract, though just a piece of paper, signified a new chapter in my life. I was ready to embrace the purpose that Pierre had entrusted to me.

On my first day, I was handed a script to be aired that evening. As I read through it, my medical school background and general knowledge prompted me to suggest some changes to the woman in charge. With her permission, I made the alterations, which enhanced the story. When I listened to my recording, I felt a surge of pride. Pierre was called in to listen, and the woman praised my ability to deliver the script flawlessly and dramatically. I seized the opportunity to explain the nuances of Tigrinya to Pierre, who was intrigued by the language's complexities. This led to the decision to create separate editions for Eritrean and Tigray audiences, a solution that showcased my insight and understanding.

As the days passed, the workload of editing the translated scripts became overwhelming. I approached Pierre to inquire about the scriptwriting process, only to discover that all scripts originated from the head office in Geneva and were then translated at Addis Ababa University. Learning about the university's struggles with translation, I offered to assist for free. Pierre, however, emphasised the value of fair compensation and encouraged me to include the additional work in my timesheet. This exchange highlighted the integrity of the team and the importance of respecting one's expertise.

My journey with Pierre's team was not just about work; it was a journey of self-discovery. I found purpose in contributing to a programme that bridged language barriers and celebrated cultural diversity. The experience taught me the value of collaboration, the power of communication, and the significance of embracing challenges. As I reflect on those days, I realise that my time with Pierre and his team was not just a job; it was a transformative experience that shaped my understanding of hope and possibility.

As one opportunity opened the door to another, I found myself immersed in a whirlwind of unexpected success. The technician had offered me the chance to work on an Amharic version, both in translating and reading, and before I knew it, this endeavour had become a full-time job. My days were filled with paperwork and casting, but the satisfaction of receiving compliments from Pierre and his visiting bosses from Paris and Geneva made it all worthwhile. They praised how I had transformed their work, making it flawless and independent of the bureaucratic university officials. I was working between 40 and 60 hours a week, translating and reading in three languages, and earning up to $800 per week, including transport and out-of-hours pay. At the age of only 19, I was making more than the salary of an average diplomat.

This financial success, coupled with income from my exchange and merchandise business, which now includes money exchange services to my UN colleagues—intensified by my growing network of foreigners at the radio station and their friends—meant I was earning a lucrative $2,000 to $3,000 every single week. Before starting with my new placement, I already had cash savings of more than $250,000 at home, unable to deposit it in the bank due to strict government rules. By the end of that year, my savings grew to a whopping $400,000, equivalent to Four million in today's value, in raw cash. I had a constant battle with managing hideouts for the money that grew exponentially, both physically and numerically. With the fear of our house being searched for western films and music tapes by Shume and his comrades, replicating episodes from several heist films I had watched over the years, in the absence of my own family, I dug massive holes in the garden to stash it all, wrapped in plastic bags and locked in metal cages, buried underground concealed beneath flower pots. I only kept small amounts at home to share freely with my mother, enabling further improvements in our living situation.

My parallel foreign exchange business blossomed organically and effortlessly, with plenty of cash available in both currencies in hand, which enabled me to trade within my own 'bank,' instantly making hundreds in a single transaction—several transactions a day. In this risky business, many foreigners required me to provide local cash to pay their domestic workers and drivers, as well as to spend in local amenities. To put the scale of my financial operations in numbers, I was exchanging hard currency to the tune of between $100,000 and $150,000 a month, earning a profit of around $13,000 on profits alone. Add to that my salary from the UN work, and I was getting anything between $20,000 and $30,000 monthly, making me an unidentified young millionaire among the few elites in the country at the time.

However, amidst this apparent prosperity, my father's continued indefinite detention remained an unresolved issue, impervious to the influence of money.

The historical world in which I found myself was one of contrasts and contradictions. On one hand, there was the heady rush of financial success and the freedom it brought; on the other, the heavy weight of my father's unjust imprisonment. It was a world where hope and despair coexisted, where the promise of a better future clashed with the harsh reality of the present. The setting was a tapestry of complexities, layered with societal and political dynamics that shaped the lives of those within it. In this environment, the pursuit of success and the yearning for justice intersected, creating a narrative that was both compelling and challenging.

Amidst this backdrop, my character underwent a profound evolution. The relentless pursuit of success transformed me into a determined and resourceful individual, capable of navigating the intricacies of a world that often seemed unfathomable. Yet, beneath the veneer of confidence and accomplishment lay a vulnerability born from the unresolved anguish over my father's plight. This internal conflict added depth to my character, painting a portrait of resilience tinged with a poignant sense of longing for justice and closure.

As I reflected on my journey, I grappled with the theme of hopefulness. The success I had achieved was a testament to the power of perseverance and the unwavering belief in a better tomorrow. It served as a beacon of hope, illuminating the path forward and offering solace in the face of adversity. Yet, the shadows of injustice loomed large, casting a pall over the otherwise bright tapestry of my life. It was in this juxtaposition of triumph and tribulation that the true essence of hopefulness revealed itself—a force that propelled me forward even in the darkest of times. The main justice that was missing was that of my father. Not even the wealth I accumulated needlessly could buy his freedom.

In this world of complex phenomena, where the echoes of the past reverberated through the present, I found myself at the crossroads of ambition and compassion, success and struggle. It was a realm where the pursuit of excellence coexisted with the yearning for justice, and where the promise of a better future was tempered by the harsh realities of the present. As I navigated this intricate landscape, I discovered that hope was not merely a fleeting emotion, but a steadfast companion that sustained me through the trials and triumphs of my journey.

As I toiled away in my work day in and day out, I found myself immersed in a routine that demanded discipline and focus. The demands of my occupation left me with little time to indulge in the vices that had once consumed my life. I noticed a significant shift in my lifestyle: I gradually began to drink less and smoke less, leading to a healthier and more balanced existence. The rigours of my work inadvertently instilled in me a sense of organisation and purpose, transforming my habits and ultimately contributing to an improvement in both my mental and physical well-being.

Amidst the demands of my job, I found solace in the company of Abel, a friend whose life seemed to be in constant flux due to his unstable income. I took it upon myself to offer him financial support, hoping to steer him toward a more meaningful occupation. However, Abel remained fixated on the endless pursuit of obtaining Italian citizenship, believing it to be his ticket to a better future abroad. As his obsession with this goal grew, our paths began to diverge, and I sensed a growing distance between us. In my absence, he sought out new friendships, but these connections lacked the depth and stability that our bond had once held. His decline became palpable, marked by a noticeable shift in his choice of companions and how he spent his time.

As Abel's life took a downward turn, mine seemed to be on an upward trajectory, filled with hopeful prospects. The contrast between our paths was stark, and it became increasingly evident that our lives were moving in different directions. Despite the challenges I faced at work, I embraced the positive changes unfolding around me, while Abel struggled to find his footing amidst his own uncertainties. Our foreign friends, initially drawn to the vibrancy of our shared experiences, began to distance themselves from Abel due to language barriers and his lack of consistency. It was a bittersweet realization to witness the diverging courses of our lives; yet it underscored the transformative impact that my dedication to work had brought about. I tried to support him financially to have stable accommodation and a structured lifestyle, but Abel chose to spend the money on drinks and girls, corrupting his soul by pretending to be a businessman masking his true self. On several occasions, afraid to ask for money, he withdrew from prepaid accommodation contracts, taking a refund for the remaining term to spend on drinks. After I found out he had no address, I reinstated his tenancy with strong advice to manage his life, but he didn't take my words wisely. Rather, he called me snobbish and opportunistic on some drunken sessions. I also linked him to various businessmen for potential partnership start-ups, but Abel didn't care to present himself even at first appointments.

As I continued to praise my father for his unwavering dedication and hard work in teaching us English and the discipline of work—the most powerful tools that helped me transform my life, even from the most unlikely places of his prison cell—I couldn't help but feel a profound sense of gratitude for the values and lessons instilled in me by my family.

The discipline and manners I learned from my mother, the work ethic and the importance of structure instilled in me by my grandfather Goitapa—these were the foundations upon which I built my life. I praised them every day, realising that I was not merely a product of my own self, but rather a reflection of those who had shaped me. The only things I felt I had taught myself were the harmful habits I had immersed myself in over the past few years. All the good qualities were gifts from my parents and family members who supported us through both the good and the bad times. I navigated the twisted paths of life with their guidance, forever grateful and exploring the theme of hopefulness.

My thoughts often drifted back to my father, a man of resilience and determination, who had defied the confines of his circumstances to impart the gift of language to his children. His voice echoed in my mind, urging me to embrace the power of words and education, even in the face of adversity.

My mother, with her gentle yet unwavering presence, embodied grace and strength. Her teachings on etiquette and compassion had shaped me into the person I was becoming. I could still hear her soothing voice guiding me through life's trials and tribulations, leaving an indelible mark on my soul. Then there was my grandfather, a man of unwavering principles and an unyielding work ethic. His lessons on the importance of structure and diligence had become the cornerstone of my approach to life, guiding me through the labyrinth of challenges that lay ahead. The typewriting course he made me partake in, the countless letters I wrote in Tigrinya and Amharic under his dictation, and all the trust and confidence he instilled in me are part of who I am now.

As I sat amidst the echoes of the past, a surge of determination coursed through my veins. The weight of my family's sacrifices and unwavering support fuelled my resolve to overcome the shadows that threatened to engulf me. I vowed to honour their legacy by rising above the darkness that sought to define me, carving a path toward a future illuminated by hope and possibility. With each breath, I embraced the profound truth that I was not alone on this journey; I carried within me the strength and wisdom of those who had shaped my existence.

Every night, in the hushed embrace of quietness, I made a silent vow to weave a narrative of triumph and resilience—one that would honour the enduring spirit of my family. With each word penned and each page turned, I sought to etch a testament to the enduring power of hope and the unyielding strength of the human spirit. As the ink flowed across the parchment, I embraced the boundless possibilities that lay ahead, fortified by the indomitable legacy of those who had walked this path before me.

In the historical world that enveloped us, the ebb and flow of our lives mirrored the shifting tides of fate and circumstance. The vivid tapestry of our experiences was woven with threads of hope and resilience, each of us navigating the complexities of existence in our own unique way. As I reflected on the changes that had unfolded, I felt a deep sense of gratitude for the positive influence that my work had exerted on my lifestyle. It was a testament to the transformative power of dedication and discipline, shaping not only my own journey but also the lives of those around me.

As I reconciled my past with my present, I realised that the key takeaway was not self-glorification based on carving success out of challenging circumstances, but rather the profound impact of family on one's trajectory. In the midst of chaos, I found solace in the unwavering presence of my parents, flawed though they were. Their commitment to weathering the storms together and their unyielding resolve to provide security for their children left an indelible mark on my soul. It was this complex fabric of family that became the cornerstone of my existence, shaping my values and aspirations in ways I would not fully comprehend until much later in life.

Navigating the labyrinth of adolescence, I witnessed the divergent paths of my friends, Abel and Nebiyu. They were left to navigate the turbulent waters of life without the stabilising force of parental guidance. Their struggles underscored the significance of having someone to look up to—an authority figure within the confines of one's home. It became increasingly evident that our parents' toil and unwavering commitment were the bedrock upon which we could build our own lives.

With the passage of time, I found myself at the helm of my own family, entrusted with the profound responsibility of nurturing the next generation. It was then that I realised the weight of the legacy I had inherited and the imperative to pass on the values of stability and resilience. I made it my mission to ensure that my children experienced the security of a two-parent household, unwavering in my conviction that there could be no excuse for parents to unravel the very foundation upon which their children's lives were built.

In the tapestry of my personal story, the threads of hope and resilience are interwoven with the complexities of family dynamics. It is a narrative that transcends time, resonating with the echoes of generations past and the aspirations of those yet to come. As I gaze upon the faces of my own children a generation later, I am reminded that the true measure of success lies not in individual achievements, but in the enduring legacy of a stable and nurturing family.

Freedom At Last

Jail Break

The massive prison camp in Addis Ababa became my father's home. It had been three years since he was transferred there. The government had segregated the prison system into categories based on the severity of crimes, yet my father, who had never been charged or tried, seemed to have been forgotten by the very system that had imprisoned him. It was as though nature itself had to intervene to rescue him from the clutches of injustice.

During his time in prison, my father forged deep connections with his fellow inmates, often extending a helping hand to those who had no families or who hailed from distant regions. He learned to navigate the treacherous waters of confinement, finding solace in small victories and moments of joy. His resilience and unwavering commitment to social causes earned him the respect and admiration of many within the prison walls, even from his captors.

For our family, the absence of my father was a heavy burden to bear, but we managed to weather the storm without succumbing to despair. My father's steadfast belief that the country was spiralling down a dark and unforgiving path had become a guiding principle for him. He had grown convinced that the outside world was nothing more than a larger prison, fraught with even greater dangers. In his eyes, the chances of survival were better within the confines of the prison walls than in the chaotic streets of Addis Ababa, ruled by a government that showed no regard for the safety and well-being of its citizens, especially Eritreans.

Despite the overwhelming sense of foreboding that hung in the air, my father remained resolute, determined to carve out a semblance of normalcy for his family in this nightmarish world. His eyes, once dulled by the weight of his incarceration, now held a glimmer of fierce determination. He would not allow the horrors of this world to extinguish the flame of hope that burned within him. And so, with each step he took, he sought to reclaim a sense of purpose, refusing to be cowed by the shadows that threatened to engulf him.

The years passed, and my father's reputation within the prison only grew. He became a beacon of hope and kindness in a place where darkness often reigned. His advocacy for the less privileged inmates and his unwavering smile endeared him to many, and even the guards and administrative officials couldn't help but respect him. It was as if he had found a purpose within the prison walls, despite never having committed any crime.

As time went on, my father's status as a civic prisoner became a topic of intrigue and mystery within the prison. He was a symbol of resilience and compassion, and his presence brought a sense of humanity to an otherwise bleak environment. The prison officials, while unable to openly advocate for him, granted him privileges that were unheard of for a prisoner in his position. His hospital visits and home visits on special occasions were a testament to the respect he had garnered.

I remember the day of my high school graduation, when my father was escorted home by two guards. The joy and warmth that filled our home during his visit is something I will never forget. The feasts prepared by my mother and our neighbours, the laughter and conversations that filled the air – those were the moments that made us forget, even if just for a while, the reality of my father's confinement. As we surrounded him, not wanting to let him go, it was clear that his presence brought light into our lives, no matter the circumstances.

It was a strange and surreal situation, but it became our new normal. My father's periodic visits brought joy and a sense of stability to our otherwise tumultuous lives. We cherished those stolen moments, savouring every second of his presence. It was during those brief respites that we could forget the harsh reality of his imprisonment. The bond between my father and the prison administrators grew stronger with each passing visit. They would invite him to their offices and engage in deep conversations, discussing everything from politics to philosophy. It was as if they were forming a brotherhood, united by their shared experiences and understanding of the world. The administrators' kindness and compassion towards my father were beyond what anyone could have expected in such a place.

As time went on, the administrators went to great lengths to ensure my father received the medical care he needed. They arranged visits to specialists to check his eyes and change his reading glasses. It was clear that they genuinely cared for him, and their actions spoke volumes about the depth of their friendship. They even faked medical visits, and he would spend the day with us before returning to the prison compound. His guards were informed by their superiors, and they happily escorted him straight to our house rather than to the supposed specialist medical centre.

Meanwhile, my mother, the master of bribery, continued to use her resourcefulness to keep the guards at bay, ensuring that the family's short reunion remained undisturbed. She became adept at navigating the delicate dance of bribery, always finding ways to ensure that our time with my father remained uninterrupted and peaceful.

Despite the challenges and the harsh reality that my father was still in captivity, our family found solace in these clandestine visits. They were a lifeline, a glimmer of hope in the darkness of my father's incarceration. Through it all, the unlikely friendships that blossomed between my father and the prison administrators remained a beacon of light in our otherwise bleak existence. The adventure of navigating the treacherous landscape of the prison, the emotional rollercoaster of hope and despair, and the unwavering determination of our family to defy the odds created a tapestry of excitement and resilience that defined our world.

As my father's constant worry about my discontinuation of my education became a weekly topic of our conversations, I found myself torn between his expectations and my own desires. He advised me to pursue a university education and would settle for nothing less. Despite my financial success, he saw it as nothing more than a temporary stroke of luck, not a viable profession. He insisted that I use my earnings to buy education, believing it to be the best investment for my future. With no other aim than to satisfy my father's dreams, I registered at Addis Ababa University for a privately paid degree programme in science. This would allow me to work during the day and study in the evening.

As I embarked on my learning journey once again, I found it difficult to balance my studies with all the other daily responsibilities I had. The need to engage in higher learning was also to shield myself from military conscription, which exempted university students. The struggle persisted for two years until an opportunity presented itself in the form of an advertisement from the Ethiopian Ministry of Defence. They were offering a study programme abroad in nuclear therapy, a technology that had just been introduced to the country for the first time. It was a two-year course in an undisclosed foreign country to learn the techniques of diagnosing and treating illnesses using radioactive material and doppler machines. This advanced technology had been imported by the General Army Hospital in Addis Ababa, the highest medical facility in the country, where high-ranking army officers and government officials were treated.

I easily met all the criteria required for the scholarship, and it fit well with my current situation. The criteria stated that candidates must have at least a year or two of science-related university education, and the selected individuals would first shadow or assist with the machine's operations for one year. This would allow me to continue my work in radio broadcasting and other duties I was engaged in, so I decided to apply. I passed the exams and was allocated shifts in the army hospital to work as an assistant radiotherapist. It felt like another adventure into the world of technology as I explored more about the use and operation of various machines in the department, which was run by Bulgarian army doctors and technicians.

I couldn't contain my excitement when I received the news that I had been accepted into the elite team of medical professionals. It was a chance to explore the uncharted territories of medical technology. However, my elation was almost cut short when some members of the recruitment team raised concerns about my Eritrean background, citing potential security risks. I felt a pang of disappointment and frustration, knowing that my heritage was being used against me. Just when it seemed like my adventure was slipping away, the decision maker intervened and took a closer look at my references.

To my relief, the decision maker thoroughly reviewed my background and discovered that I had a spotless record, with glowing references from the local council office. The reference letter not only vouched for my impeccable character but also confirmed the unique circumstances of my background, including the fact that my brother was serving in national military service. This revelation proved pivotal, clearing any doubts about my commitment and loyalty. With the decision maker's support, the objections from the recruitment team were overlooked, and I was granted the opportunity to embark on this new journey.

The army hospital was a vast building, equipped with various facilities and modern medical equipment, housing the best doctors in the country. The government had moved the top practitioners to this hospital to serve its own interests. Some of the surgeons and specialists were internationally recognised professionals, granted army ranks, privileges, and substantial salaries. The senior doctors, fully enrolled army personnel, were highly respected and enjoyed the same protection and status as government ministers. Other specialists in the hospital hailed from Russia, Bulgaria, Cuba, and other Eastern European countries. Due to the nature of its clientele, the hospital had stringent security measures and confidentiality rules. During my induction, I was firmly warned about the consequences of sharing information, especially with foreigners.

The main army hospital was connected to another medical facility for low-ranking army officers and their families. The two sections offered a stark contrast in the quality of service they provided. The lower-level hospital, referred to as

Section B, consisted of wards and offices made from prefabricated buildings constructed from shipping containers. The facilities were substandard, and no specialists were assigned there. Some lucky officers with rare conditions were referred to the main hospital, which had the appearance of a state building, complete with manicured gardens, cafés, and even a helipad. The hospital was also attached to a military airport where small and large aircraft took off and landed every minute. The airport, previously a civilian facility, had been converted for military use, primarily to transport officials to war fronts and to bring wounded officers to the hospital in small aircraft.

Section B of the hospital, a sprawling expanse of makeshift tents and unstable housing, was a grim testament to the escalating casualties from the northern war fronts. The air was thick with the acrid scent of blood and despair, and the grounds seemed to stretch endlessly, as if the hospital had grown haphazardly over the years in a desperate attempt to accommodate the increasing influx of wounded soldiers. The outpatient section was a sea of ghostly figures, shuffled aimlessly, their gaunt faces etched with the ravages of tuberculosis, pneumonia, and HIV. It was a place where suffering had become the norm, and hope was a distant memory.

The military police, charged with maintaining order amid the chaos, treated the poor outpatients with a harshness that bordered on cruelty. Those who did not speak Amharic were met with disdain and suspicion, their pleas for help falling on deaf ears. In stark contrast, the main hospital exuded an air of discipline and reverence, where each patient was greeted with salutes and praised by highly disciplined military officers. But in Section B, the patients arrived in overcrowded trucks, dumped unceremoniously onto the open fields to be sorted and treated. Many of them lacked army numbers or even a coherent sense of self, their memories lost in the fog of war. Among them were irregular soldiers, militias, conscripts from national military service, and those who had been conscripted against their will.

As the war in the north intensified and the rebels gained ground, the government teetered on the brink of collapse. Frantic orders and decrees were issued daily, each one more desperate than the last. The military ruler, facing a coup attempt from within, resorted to drastic measures, executing high-ranking officers with his own hands. The army's morale plummeted, and a new decree was introduced, demanding that everything and everyone be directed to the war fronts. Men and women were forcibly conscripted from the streets and sent into battle with only days of training, while resources from across the country were funnelled into the war effort. Private vehicles were confiscated, factories churned out weapons and supplies, and the entire nation was consumed by the relentless march of war.

The seizure of Massawa port by the Eritrean freedom fighters marked a turning point—a devastating blow that signalled the government's imminent downfall. The rebel fighters gained control of the Red Sea ports, cutting off the government's crucial sea-based military and economic imports, trapping the Ethiopian army with no escape, while the Tigray front intensified its advances. The Ethiopian forces had no choice but to fight to the death or flee into the unforgiving sea. The once-proud Ethiopian navy lay in ruins, its machines and men sacrificed in a futile bid to hold back the tide of war. As the horrors of battle closed in around the government, I found myself engulfed in a world where hope had all but vanished, and the only certainty was the relentless march of death and destruction.

Everything in the country felt hopeless. The economy was in tatters, with the government diverting every penny towards purchasing weapons and maintaining army camps. Frantic decrees and laws were issued, further narrowing people's opportunities for decent business. As the economy struggled, the foreign exchange rate soared, exacerbating the hardships faced by ordinary citizens. New, stricter laws were introduced to combat the booming illegal exchange market and contraband trade. The government's crackdown on those involved in parallel money exchange, coupled with harsh punishments, signalled the start of a new era, forcing me to reconsider my choices.

Being of Eritrean heritage, working in an army hospital and for a foreign organisation made me a prime target in the eyes of the government. The risks associated with continuing the money exchange business were no longer worth it. I decided to cease my involvement in the illegal trade and instead relied on my income from the radio station with reduced weekly hours. Unable to deposit my earnings in government-controlled banks, I kept enough cash at home, adapting to a more subtle lifestyle in order to blend into the current political climate.

Navigating my daily life became a delicate dance, as the spectre of conscription loomed over everyone. The military police showed no mercy, rounding up people from the streets to be taken to training camps without a second thought. I had to be cautious, self-imposing curfews and carefully planning my outings. Even my evening studies at the university had to be halted to minimise the risk of being forcibly conscripted by the army, which patrolled the city streets, particularly in the evenings.

The air felt thick with despair, and hope seemed like a distant memory. Daily news of the rebels gaining ground and the government losing control of its apparatus only added to the sense of impending doom. Ministers and diplomats fled, and more young people in the north joined the rebels, further destabilising the already precarious situation. The once vibrant and bustling streets now felt desolate, with fear and uncertainty casting a long shadow over the country.

As the darkness of this war-torn world enveloped us, I found myself constantly on edge, my senses heightened to the slightest hint of danger. The undefined tone of the world mirrored the uncertainty that plagued my every waking moment. It was a world where survival meant adapting to ever-changing rules and regulations, where one wrong move could have dire consequences. In this nightmarish reality, my character evolved, shedding the naivety of the past and embracing a newfound resilience born out of necessity. The horrors of the world had transformed me, forcing me to confront the depths of my own strength and resourcefulness in the face of overwhelming adversity.

As I continued to work at the army hospital—a place frequented by high-level officials and their families—I seized every opportunity to speak to these influential individuals about my father's unjust detention. I sought their help in getting his case reviewed and securing his freedom.

I now found myself in a world where the lines between good and evil were blurred, and the high-ranking men and women who once seemed untouchable were now surprisingly approachable. As I walked through the dimly lit corridors of the hospital, I witnessed scenes that defied all expectations. The hard-looking generals, whose stern faces had graced daily TV programmes, now stood before me, speaking softly and seeking my assistance. Their eyes, once filled with the weight of war, now held a glimmer of compassion and understanding. It was as if the medical conditions they were suffering from had softened their hearts, transforming them from feared figures into humble human beings. The contrast between their public personas and private interactions was both jarring and intriguing.

As I continued to observe, I came across some officials who were once believed to have committed unspeakable acts during the country's controversial revolution. Yet, here they were, engaging in ordinary conversations and sharing genuine smiles with those around them. The air crackled with a sense of disbelief and curiosity as I witnessed these individuals—once portrayed as ruthless enemies—now exuding an unexpected warmth and humanity. It was a theme that both excited and unsettled me, as the boundaries of perception and reality began to blur in this horror-filled world.

In this undefined atmosphere, I found myself grappling with the complexities of these characters, each one defying the stereotypes and expectations ingrained in my mind. The setting itself took on an eerie quality, as the familiar faces of those in power revealed layers of vulnerability and compassion that I had never thought possible. I formed close relationships with some of them, using my position in the team to help save their lives from serious illnesses they suffered from. At every opportunity, I pushed my father's case.

During my conversations with the officials, I recounted my father's innocence and his significant contributions to the country and society. Many sympathised and vowed to help, but their promises often faded into the background, leaving me with a sense of frustration and helplessness.

Meanwhile, my work in the hospital's radiotherapy department became predictably routine. Having mastered the operation of the new machines within a few weeks, I realised there was limited scope for growth in the sector. My daily routines became monotonous, and the prospect of a stagnant career loomed. The Bulgarian specialist who led the unit left everything for me and my Ethiopian colleagues to run, and it was soon decided that the planned scholarship abroad was no longer necessary. Instead, we were assimilated into the department as permanent staff with unattractive, fixed monthly salaries.

Feeling disheartened by the lack of progress in my father's case and disillusioned with my career prospects at the hospital, I found solace in my involvement with the radio station. Balancing a full-time job at the hospital with my commitments at the radio station became a delicate juggling act. I used the free time I had in the hospital to translate and type my scripts, concealing my involvement by telling my curious colleagues that I was writing a book. However, as the hospital administrators struggled to fill gaps in the workforce, our roles became increasingly undefined. We were pulled into different sections of the hospital to help with the overwhelming demand for medical care and logistical operations.

As all civilian hospitals were transformed into military medical facilities, the ethical and physical boundaries of the army hospital's different sections also blurred to meet the growing demands for space and services. Soon, with Section B's grounds filled with tents and makeshift wards occupying every inch of space, the authorities decided to open the once-exclusive main Section A to treat ordinary soldiers.

Under the decree, "Everything and everyone to the war fronts," I found myself engaged in operations, taking on various non-medical duties to support the influx of wounded soldiers and civilians. The haunting memories of my childhood duties during our harrowing flight from Mekelle resurfaced, reminding me of the cycle of suffering and imprisonment that seemed to plague my life. The hospital work felt like a relentless echo of the past, with no sign of reprieve in sight. Life in Ethiopia seemed like a never-ending nightmare, and I wondered if the cycle of suffering and horror would ever come to an end.

As I contemplated resigning from the hospital work, the weight of guilt and fear pressed heavily on my shoulders. It was an impossible and risky question to raise, especially at such a desperate time for the government. We continued to work day and night, sometimes not going home for days. The endless number of wounded soldiers coming in, their anguished cries echoing through the corridors, served as a haunting reminder that the war was only a few kilometres away from the city. Fresh wounds, still oozing with blood, told the grim tale of a conflict that refused to relent.

On the global stage, the sudden end of the Cold War at the end of that decade sent palpable political tremors, changing the face of conflicts in many countries. With most wars fought in proxy allegiances between the superpowers, the fall of the Soviet Union and its global communist network, through which it provided weaponry and ideological support to countries like Ethiopia, was marked by confusion and uncertainties about shifting allegiances, impacting the outcome of the war. This situation had contributed to the sudden deterioration and lack of governance, as well as vision, in the corridors of Ethiopian leadership, pushing the already fragmented government to the brink of its imminent downfall, with a number of its leaders, including high-ranked ministers, not returning from negotiation meetings in Europe, and several army generals fleeing to neighbouring countries in military planes and helicopters.

The government denied its losses, claiming victory on every front, but it wasn't clear where the war fronts truly lay. Eritrean rebels were closing in, their presence casting a shadow of dread over the already beleaguered city. The hopeless government increased its efforts to save Tigray, but the odds seemed insurmountable.

Amidst the chaos and despair, I found myself questioning the very essence of hope. Several peace negotiations at the international level had failed, with the rebels holding a dominant position that seemed to guarantee their imminent victory. Their rapid advancements in a few short months had eclipsed the decades of war they had waged. The city was gripped by a sense of impending doom, and the once-bustling streets now lay eerily silent, haunted by the spectre of impending destruction. As I walked through the desolate city, the air thick with the stench of fear and despair, I couldn't help but wonder if there was any glimmer of hope left in this world.

The darkness seemed to seep into every crevice, suffocating any semblance of light. The horrors of a fast-approaching war had transformed the city into a nightmarish landscape, where every shadow held the promise of unspeakable terror. As news filtered in about the war spreading to the outskirts of Addis Ababa, the tension grew more palpable. Wounded soldiers brought with them the grim reality of the conflict, their haunted eyes telling stories of unspeakable horrors. The air was thick with fear and uncertainty, exacerbated by repeated reports that peace negotiations in London had failed.

On the 22nd of May 1991, at 1 p.m., the national radio announced the shocking news that military leader Mengistu Hailemariam, the man who had vowed to fight to the last man and bullet, had fled the country. The mysteries surrounding his disorganised escape were shrouded in speculation and conspiracy theories, leaving the nation in a state of disarray.

With Mengistu's abrupt departure, a new state of chaos descended upon the country. The sudden vacuum of power left by the former leader's departure plunged Ethiopia into a lawless state, where confusion reigned supreme.

Meanwhile, Eritrea fell fully into the hands of the Liberation Front, marking the end of decades of devastating war. The remaining Ethiopian soldiers, already weakened and disorganised, attempted to defend against the rapid advances of the Tigrayan rebels. However, their efforts proved futile as their commanders fled in all directions, leaving the soldiers to fend for themselves. The once-proud defenders of the nation now found themselves scattered: some fleeing to neighbouring countries, others surrendering to the enemy, and many simply returning home in defeat.

Amidst this chaos, the army hospital and all other medical facilities were overwhelmed by the sheer number of wounded soldiers. The capacity was exceeded to a point where providing medical assistance became impossible. The scenes within the hospital were harrowing, with soldiers left unattended on the driveways, without food or medical aid. Even the army staff working in the hospital fled, fearing the imminent arrival of the rebels, leaving only a handful of civilian workers to bear witness to the overwhelming tragedy. The shortage of equipment and supplies, combined with the sheer volume of casualties, meant that many lives were lost before our eyes. The hospital's gardens and driveways became haunting reminders of the horrors of war. The desperation and helplessness that engulfed us were indescribable, as we struggled to save as many lives as we could amidst the overwhelming tide of death.

The city of Addis Ababa had descended into chaos, a lawless wasteland where the line between rebel and soldier had blurred beyond recognition. The returning soldiers, some wounded and others fully armed, marched through the streets, their uniforms a mismatched array of colours and insignias. It was impossible to differentiate between friend and foe, and the sporadic sounds of gunfire echoed through the once-bustling city. Armoured vehicles and tanks rumbled through the streets in an uncoordinated manner, adding to the sense of impending doom. The state media churned out rapidly changing news and propaganda, leaving the city's residents in a state of constant worry and uncertainty.

As the situation deteriorated, the people of Addis Ababa took matters into their own hands. Self-imposed curfews became the norm, and the streets emptied as everyone sought refuge within the confines of their homes. Desperation led to a surge in the black market for guns and ammunition, with even the hungry and destitute soldiers selling their weapons for coins. In a city preparing for war, the agonising dilemma of whether to remain unarmed or to arm oneself consumed many.

For two days and two nights, the city remained on edge, with the populace unable to find respite in sleep. In the midst of this chaos, I found myself confined to the hospital, the outskirts of the compound being fortified as a last line of defence. The constant sound of gunfire and the distant rumble of armoured vehicles served as a grim reminder of the horror unfolding outside. Every spare moment was spent on the phone, reassuring my mother and advising her to stay safe. She had taken my two younger brothers to a neighbour's house, seeking safety in numbers and the protection of armed men who patrolled the neighbourhood to safeguard their families.

The once-formidable council office, known as the kebele, now lay abandoned. Its members had scattered, leaving behind only confusion and an air of disarray. Shume, who had long pretended to be the revolution's protector, was nowhere to be found. The office stood open, its files and equipment strewn haphazardly—an eerie symbol of the city's descent into anarchy. The gun storage room, once a secure stronghold, had been looted by desperate citizens seeking to arm themselves in the face of growing uncertainty. Addis Ababa had become a place where survival was no longer certain, and the once vibrant streets were now cloaked in fear and dread.

When we searched the revolutionary guards' deserted barracks at the council office, we found most of our belongings, which had been confiscated from our streets and houses over the years. Some of our celebrity posters had been used as decorating wallpaper, glued to the clay walls in full glory. We also recovered some tapes and videos from the kebele office's storage rooms, just as we had found our looted flying rooster in the palace barracks many years ago.

Behind the prison walls, my father and the other inmates were left in a state of confusion and isolation. The usual trickle of news from the outside had turned into a drought, leaving them cut off from the seismic shifts taking place beyond their confines. They had only heard vague whispers of Mengistu's departure, but they remained unaware that their own freedom was now only hours away, as the government system crumbled under the weight of the final phase of the long war.

The armed captors and prison staff had fled, much like the uniformed men and women across the country. It soon became apparent that the prisoners, locked inside for fear of rebellion, were unaware that no one was guarding the prison. They sat in large groups, deprived of food, water, and access to toilets. The guards had locked them in and absconded, taking the keys with them or discarding them in some unknown location.

As the hours stretched into an agonising eternity, the atmosphere within the prison walls became increasingly charged with tension and desperation. The once stoic and hardened inmates now appeared as mere shadows of their former selves, their faces etched with fear and uncertainty. The absence of any news or communication from the outside world had plunged them into a state of profound disorientation, as they grappled with the surreal reality of being left to their own devices within the confines of the prison. The air was thick with nostalgia, as memories of freedom and normalcy taunted them from the recesses of their minds.

In the absence of external authority, a peculiar transformation began to unfold within the prison. The hierarchical structures that had once governed the inmates' interactions began to erode, giving way to a raw and unfiltered display of human nature. Some banded together in a bid for survival, while others retreated into the recesses of their own minds, grappling with the overwhelming sense of abandonment. Amidst this tumult, my father emerged as a figure of quiet resilience, offering words of solace and wisdom to those who sought refuge in his presence. His unwavering composure and quiet strength became a source of comfort in the midst of chaos. He navigated the shifting dynamics within the prison with a grace and dignity that seemed to transcend the confines of their bleak reality.

As the minutes turned into hours, the once-impenetrable walls of the prison began to feel less like a fortress and more like a fragile façade. The inmates, once resigned to their fate, now found themselves on the cusp of an unforeseen liberation, as the tides of change swept through the country, dismantling the very structures that had held them captive. In the midst of this upheaval, my father and his fellow inmates stood on the threshold of a new beginning. Their hearts were heavy with the weight of the past, yet brimming with the tentative hope of a future yet to unfold.

As my father stood at the edge of the prison yard, watching the chaos unfold in the city beyond, a wave of nostalgia washed over him. The Tigray Liberation Front rebels, backed by the Eritreans, had finally broken through the city limits and were marching towards the parliament building to seize the nerve centres of the nation. The sound of gunfire echoed in the distance, mingling with the shouts and cries of the people.

Amidst the chaos, a group of people living in the prison area noticed that all the guards on the tower posts and outside the gates were nowhere to be seen. It was as if they had vanished into thin air, leaving the prison unguarded. Without a second thought, they stormed into the prison and opened the metal doors of the rooms where the inmates were locked. "Flee for your safety," they urged, their voices urgent and filled with a sense of responsibility.

Some of the prisoners hesitated, their eyes reflecting confusion and disbelief. It was as though they had grown accustomed to the confines of their cells, finding a strange comfort in the familiar walls that held them captive. Or perhaps they didn't have homes or families to go to—not every inmate was from the capital. Others, however, seized the opportunity and ran towards the open gates, their freedom within reach.

As my father watched the inmates make their choices, he couldn't help but wonder about his own. Nostalgia gripped his heart as he longed for the days when the city had been a place of peace and unity. But amidst the turmoil, a glimmer of hope emerged as he realised that perhaps, just perhaps, the chaos could pave the way for a new beginning. Without a second thought, my father made his way straight to the prison office building, with only one aim in mind. He entered the familiar offices of the administrator and picked up a phone to call my mother about his safety and imminent return home. After speaking with her, my father passed the phone to other inmates before leaving the building.

In the heart of the chaotic city, where the air was heavy with the scent of fear and desperation, the Tigrayan rebels, backed by their Eritrean comrades, made their way through the prison gates. The clanging of metal against metal echoed through the corridors as they swiftly took control, their determined expressions offering a glimmer of hope to the weary inmates. With measured words, they reassured the prisoners to stay calm, promising to separate the innocent from the guilty before allowing them to return home. The air crackled with tension as the rebels meticulously sorted through the sea of faces, their eyes searching for signs of allegiance and defiance.

Amidst the chaos, the rebels methodically separated the political prisoners from the other criminals, their movements purposeful and unwavering. Some faces were already familiar to them, recognised as their active supporters who had stood by their cause through the darkest of times. These loyal allies were met with nods of acknowledgment, their unwavering spirit serving as a beacon of resilience in the midst of turmoil. As the hours passed, the prison walls bore witness to the unfolding of a delicate dance between captors and captives, each moment laden with the weight of uncertainty and the promise of redemption. The air hummed with anticipation as the rebels navigated the labyrinth of allegiances, their actions shaping the fate of those held within the prison's confines.

In the hushed moments that followed, the prisoners held their breath, their fates hanging in the balance as the rebels deliberated. Through the dimly lit corridors, the echoes of whispered conversations and muffled sobs intertwined, painting a poignant portrait of humanity's unyielding resilience in the face of adversity. As the rebels made their final decisions, the air seemed to still, the weight of their choices settling upon the weary shoulders of the prisoners. With measured resolve, they began to release those deemed innocent, offering a glimmer of hope to those who had weathered the storm of uncertainty. The prison gates creaked open, ushering in a new chapter for my father and the others who had long yearned for freedom. Their faces, etched with a mixture of relief and trepidation, reflected the weight of years spent in captivity as they stepped into the uncertain embrace of the world beyond.

As my father sat inside his cell for the last hour, the memories of those fateful years flooded his mind like a torrential river. The rebels had stormed into every room of the prison, their determination palpable in the air. My father recalled the fear that gripped his heart as they searched for the traitors, their eyes ablaze with a fierce sense of justice. Among them, a name echoed with chilling finality—Woldu. The mere mention of his name sent shivers down my father's spine, for Woldu was the man whose betrayal had led to his detention all those years ago. It was said that he had fled from another prison, only to meet his end at the hands of the rebels, without a chance to utter a single plea. The memory of his lifeless body lying in the dust still haunts my father's dreams, a stark reminder of the unforgiving consequences of mistrust and greed in times of war.

As the inmates were led to safety, my father and the other prisoners could hardly believe that their ordeal was finally coming to an end. They had endured years of uncertainty, deprivation, and fear, but now, at last, they were being given a chance to start anew. The rebels, though stern and determined, treated them with a surprising level of compassion, understanding the suffering they had endured at the hands of the previous regime.

Amidst the chaos, my father and the others were offered transport by the rebels—a glimmer of hope in the midst of despair. As my father journeyed through the rugged roads of the capital, the weight of seven years of senseless imprisonment hung heavy in the air. The journey home was fraught with tension and uncertainty, but my father clung to the hope of being reunited with his family. As they travelled through the tense city, he couldn't help but feel a sense of disbelief that he was finally on his way to freedom.

The anticipation of reuniting with his family after so long filled the air with a bittersweet nostalgia, a longing for the warmth of home and the embrace of loved ones. The landscape blurred past, each passing mile bringing him closer to the familiar sights and sounds of his home. The journey was a poignant mix of relief and trepidation, for the scars of the past had etched themselves deeply into his soul, shaping him into a mosaic of resilience and longing.

Finally, as the sun dipped below the horizon, the silhouette of the city emerged in the distance—a beacon of hope amidst the desolation of war. The air was thick with the scent of home, and the familiar melodies of laughter and conversation wove a tapestry of nostalgia that tugged at their weary hearts. When he reached his destination, my father was overwhelmed with emotion as he embraced his family. The years of separation, the anguish of not knowing whether he would ever see them again, all melted away in that moment. There were tears, laughter, and a profound sense of gratitude for the rebels who had facilitated their release.

My father stepped out of the small car, a white Fiat 124—the seemingly workhorse of the government's security apparatus, a wheeled messenger that had transported my father to despair—now ceased by the rebels, bringing him back home. He carried with him a single piece of luggage, a white plastic shopping bag in hand, his eyes brimming with unshed tears and his heart overwhelmed by the reunion. The Italian-made machine on wheels had been the transporter of our family's joys and fears for many years.

As my mother saw the car approach our street, flashbacks of her past feud with the Fiat 124 seemed to vanish. It was now the messenger and deliverer of her beloved husband to his home, where he belonged.

In that moment, time seemed to stand still, and the weight of the years melted away in the embrace of his family. The echoes of the past mingled with the present, creating a symphony of emotions that resonated through the very fabric of our being—a testament to the enduring power of love and the unyielding spirit of those who had endured the trials of war.

That afternoon, I was reunited with my family after a brief detention of my own. The hospital walls had become my temporary refuge, a place where the scent of antiseptic mingled with the cries of the wounded. As an Eritrean, my presence in the hospital had raised suspicion among the rebel commanders who controlled the area. However, it was also this very identity that led to my unexpected release. I found myself standing before one of the rebel commanders, my voice steady as I recounted the tale of my father's disappearance and my subsequent role in the hospital. The commander, a man with weathered features and piercing eyes, listened intently, his expression softening as my words unfolded. In that moment, my Eritrean heritage became a bridge rather than a barrier, and he swiftly ordered his comrades to drive me home to reunite with my father.

The journey back was a blur of dusty roads and distant gunfire, the weight of uncertainty lifting from my shoulders with each passing mile. I had already spoken to my father, who was reunited with the rest of our family.

As we approached the familiar streets of our neighbourhood, a surge of nostalgia washed over me, bringing to mind the laughter of childhood and the warmth of family gatherings. The car came to a halt outside our modest home, and I stepped out into the golden light of the setting sun. The door swung open, and there, framed in the doorway, stood my father. His eyes, once clouded with worry, now sparkled with unshed tears as he enveloped me in a tight embrace. The years of separation melted away in that embrace, and for a moment, we were simply a father and son, bound by love and the unbreakable ties of family. The rebel driver lingered in the background, a silent witness to this poignant reunion, his gaze holding a depth of understanding that transcended the boundaries of conflict. In that fleeting moment, amidst the echoes of a war-torn world, the power of nostalgia and the enduring strength of family prevailed.

As I sat across from my father, the weight of the last 48 hours hung heavy in the air between us. We had exchanged our experiences—the highs and the lows, the moments of fear and hope. It was in that charged atmosphere that I finally mustered the courage to ask him about the suspicious-looking, wrinkled shopping bag he had brought with him. His eyes met mine, and for a moment, I saw a flicker of hesitation before he reached into the bag and pulled out a bundle of weathered, yellowing pages. It was then that I realised what he had chosen to bring with him from his years in prison: the hundreds of pages of handwritten letters we had exchanged as part of our English learning journey. Each page was a testament to our shared struggle, our triumphs, and the unbreakable bond that had sustained us through the darkest of times.

As he carefully unfolded one of the letters, the memories came flooding back—the late nights huddled under dim prison lights, pouring our hearts and souls into those letters, the ink smudged with tears of longing and nostalgia. In those letters, we had woven a tapestry of our dreams, fears, and the relentless yearning for freedom. Each word was a testament to our unwavering determination to hold onto hope, to cling to the promise of a better tomorrow. And now, as I traced the faded lines of his handwriting, I realised that those letters were not just a record of our journey to master a new language, but a testament to the enduring power of love and resilience in the face of adversity.

In that moment, as the weight of those letters settled in my hands, I understood the depth of my father's sacrifice and the magnitude of his love. It was in those pages that our shared narrative was etched—a narrative that transcended the confines of prison walls and spoke of the unbreakable bond between a father and his child. And as I looked into his eyes, I knew that those letters held within them the essence of our shared journey—a journey marked by nostalgia, longing, and the unyielding hope for a brighter future.

As the city came to terms with the new changes and the rebels began their formal administrative tasks, little did they know that their struggle to liberate a small region in the north would thrust them into the daunting responsibility of ruling an entire country, left in chaos by the previous regime.

The Tigray Liberation Front, along with their Eritrean comrades, found themselves facing the monumental task of stabilising the country and instilling the rule of law. The city's residents, confused and weary, had mixed feelings of both triumph and defeat. On the one hand, they were relieved to be liberated from a murderous regime, but on the other, the prospect of being ruled by a rebel ethnic group did not settle easily in the minds of many. For the time being, stability and peace were paramount, so the city's residents had little choice but to cooperate with the rebels for their own safety.

Through harsh measures, the rebels managed to normalise the city, preventing further looting and lawlessness. Slowly, they began to gain the trust of the people.

The city, once a place of fear and oppression, now found itself in a state of cautious optimism. The rebels, once seen as outsiders, were now the ones tasked with rebuilding and restoring order. The streets, once filled with the sounds of gunfire and screams, now echoed with the sounds of reconstruction and hope. The rebels, who had once fought in the shadows, were now thrust into the spotlight, their every decision scrutinised and their every move watched.

Amidst this newfound responsibility, the rebels found themselves grappling with the weight of their duties. They had fought for freedom and justice, but now they had to navigate the complexities of governance. The once-clear lines between right and wrong had blurred, and the rebels were forced to make decisions that would impact the lives of countless individuals. As they delved deeper into the intricacies of administration, they were met with challenges that tested their resolve and unity. The burden of leadership weighed heavily on their shoulders, and they were acutely aware of the eyes upon them, waiting to see if they would falter or rise to the occasion.

The city, once a place of division and fear, now stood at a crossroads, with the rebels at the helm. The residents, though cautious, began to see glimmers of hope amidst the uncertainty. The rebels, in turn, grappled with the complexities of their newfound roles, navigating the delicate balance between power and responsibility while trying to unite a country fragmented into more than 80 tribes. As they forged ahead, they were driven by the memory of their initial struggle and the desire to create a future defined not by the scars of the past but by the promise of a new beginning.

As my father sat with his family, recounting the harrowing events of his imprisonment and the miraculous turn of events that had led to his release, he couldn't help but feel a sense of awe at the resilience of the human spirit. Despite the darkness of his past, he had emerged into the light, ready to embrace the future with hope and determination.

As history repeated itself, I found myself standing at the threshold of uncertainty, watching the familiar figure of my father return home once again. It was a sight that brought back memories of his release from his long detention in Tigray, when he had been held captive for what felt like an eternity. The air was thick with anticipation, and as he adjusted to his real home—the place where he truly belonged—I couldn't help but wonder what this new chapter in our family's story would bring. Would it mark the end of our trials and tribulations, or were there more challenges waiting for us on the horizon? These questions lingered in the back of my mind, overshadowed by the overwhelming happiness and euphoria that enveloped us, painting the scene with a nostalgic hue.

As my father navigated the small corridors of our home, the lines etched on his face told a story of their own—a tale of resilience and unwavering determination. His eyes, once clouded with uncertainty, now held a glimmer of hope that seemed to pierce through the veil of our collective apprehension. It was as if his very presence breathed new life into our weary souls, infusing the air with a sense of possibility that we had long forgotten. The weight of his absence lifted from our shoulders, replaced by a renewed sense of purpose and determination.

In the days that followed, our family found itself navigating uncharted waters once again, grappling with the unfamiliar terrain of this second chance. The world seemed to hold its breath, waiting to see what fate had in store for us. Each day brought a blend of excitement and trepidation as we ventured into unknown territory, unsure of what lay ahead in this new governmental system—one that, in some ways, excluded Eritreans, though no one had anticipated it would take shape in this way. The echoes of our past ordeals reverberated through our thoughts, serving as a constant reminder of the trials we had overcome and the scars we carried as a testament to our resilience.

Amidst the uncertainty, our family began to weave a new tapestry of memories, each thread interwoven with the lessons of our past. We found ourselves embracing the gifts that this second chance had bestowed upon us, cherishing the moments of joy and laughter that punctuated our days. The journey was far from smooth, marked by twists and turns that tested our resolve, but through it all, we clung to the hope that had been rekindled within us.

As the days turned into weeks, and the weeks into months, our family found itself standing at the precipice of a new beginning. The trials of our past had sculpted us into resilient individuals, and the gifts of this second chance had breathed new life into our weary souls. With each step forward, we carried with us the echoes of our history—a reminder of the ordeals we had overcome and the gifts that illuminated our path. And as we looked toward the horizon, we did so with a newfound sense of purpose, ready to embrace whatever the world had in store for us.

Eritrean families, long separated by war and struggle, were now reunited, their spirits unbroken by the years of hardship. The rebels, once labelled 'terrorists' by Ethiopians, had assumed control with surprising grace, weaving a tapestry of order and hope across the nation. As I pondered their journey to freedom through the rugged Eritrean landscapes, I witnessed a sea of faces filled with both the weight of the past and the promise of the future.

The Eritrean Liberation Front, once at odds with the Tigrayan rebels, now stood side by side, their shared goal of independence forging an unlikely alliance. The scars of their bitter rivalry seemed to fade in the wake of their mutual victory, replaced by a determination to stabilise the country they had fought so hard to free. The restoration of phone lines and air travel with Eritrea and beyond brought families together, reuniting loved ones who had long been separated by the turmoil of war. It was a time of joy and sorrow, as we paid homage to the fallen and embraced the living, our hearts heavy with the memories of those we had lost.

The air crackled with a sense of unity and purpose, as if the very land itself exhaled a sigh of relief. For my family, the resumption of communication and transport meant a reunion with relatives and friends—a joyous celebration that seemed to stretch on for weeks.

Returning to Eritrea after seventeen years felt like stepping into a dream. My father, his eyes filled with both sorrow and pride, had returned to the land that had shared his pain. His thoughts turned to the brothers and friends who had given their lives in the struggle for independence. The resilience of those who had endured hardships at home, as well as those who had supported their families from afar, was a testament to the unbreakable spirit of the Eritrean people.

During one of the frequent, fun-filled trips we took to Eritrea, there was also a touch of tragedy in the clash of cultures. As we flew in to visit some cousins we had never met before—born abroad but part of the wider family—a reunion of unexpected proportions was about to unfold. My family and I were on a journey to meet our long-lost cousins from around the world, a connection we had known existed, yet had never experienced. The prospect of expanding our family tree and bridging the gap between different worlds filled us with a sense of excitement and curiosity.

The meetings, however, turned out to be testimonies to the differences in upbringing and culture, and the encounters with our cousins were nothing short of a revelation. Among the visiting 'European' cousins were Selam and Zemen, two young children aged four and five, who had grown up in the affluent surroundings of Germany. Despite their tender age, the girls exuded a sense of grace and innocence that immediately drew us to them. They had a unique bond with animals, particularly the chickens in our grandparents' compound, where we were staying. Selam and Zemen had named the chickens, fed them diligently, and spent hours playing and caring for them, forming a special friendship that was heart-warming to witness.

However, a cultural clash was imminent—one we were unaware of at the time. In Asmara, it was a tradition for families to purchase live chickens for food, with the male family members responsible for slaughtering them. On one fateful day, my grandmother requested that a chicken be prepared for dinner, and I was tasked with carrying out the sacrificial act by selecting one from the few chickens we had. Oblivious to the emotional connection Selam and Zemen had formed with one of the chickens, I proceeded with the task under the watchful eyes of my family.

The moment Selam and Zemen returned to witness the traumatic scene unfolding before them, their world crushed. The sight of their beloved pet chicken being slaughtered, with blood gushing from its neck, sent the young girls into a state of shock and despair. Their screams pierced the air, tears streamed down their faces as they struggled to comprehend the abrupt loss of their feathered friend. The trauma they experienced in that moment was etched deep into their innocent hearts, leaving a lasting scar that would shape their view of the world.

From that day on, Selam and Zemen could not bring themselves to eat chicken meat. What had once been their favourite food was now a painful reminder of the trauma they had endured. Their relationship with me, tainted by the unfathomable event, turned sour as they harboured resentment and aversion towards me. The bond we had hoped to forge during our time in Asmara was shattered, replaced by a rift that seemed insurmountable.

Years passed, and the memory of that unforgettable incident lingered, casting a shadow over our family ties. When I eventually travelled to Germany to visit Selam and Zemen some thirty years later, the wounds of the past remained raw and unhealed. The horror they had witnessed in Asmara continued to haunt them, a poignant reminder of the day their innocence was shattered by the harsh reality of life and death.

In the tapestry of our shared history, the story of Selam and Zemen became a poignant chapter that taught us the profound impact of cultural differences and the fragility of human relationships. As we reflected on the events that had unfolded, we were reminded of the complexities that lie beneath the surface of our connections. It became clear that empathy and understanding are the pillars that support the bridges we build between hearts and souls. Amidst the turmoil and regrets, there remained a glimmer of hope—a hope that one day, forgiveness and healing would pave the way for a new chapter of reconciliation and renewed kinship.

As the initial euphoria of liberation began to settle, a sense of nostalgia crept in, blending with the hope for a brighter future. The scars of war ran deep, etched into the very fabric of our nation, and the road to true healing seemed daunting. Every Eritrean home bore the weight of conflict, and the collective longing for relief from years of turmoil hung heavily in the air. Yet, as we navigated this new chapter in our history, the true colours of our reality began to unfold, revealing the complexities and challenges that lay ahead. The echoes of our past would continue to shape our present, and the questions that had long lingered in our minds would demand answers as we ventured into an uncertain future.

THE LAST MILE

One Way Ticket

As our family grappled with the complexities of starting anew, the weight of our individual aspirations and the collective burden of our shared future loomed over us in a rapidly changing world. With two of my siblings, Kaleb and Simon, pursuing their education in the UK, the rest of us were left to navigate the intricate web of choices and obligations that lay before us. My father, still acclimating to a world that had evolved in his absence, carried the heavy burden of regret for not being there during our formative, most vulnerable years. His haunted past cast a shadow over our present, as he struggled with the belief that he could have shielded us from the hardships we endured. His obsession with higher education, coupled with the fact that none of his sons had earned a university degree, made him feel personally responsible for our perceived failures. Meanwhile, my mother yearned for a respite, a moment to break free from the long years of constraint that had defined her existence.

Amidst this tumultuous backdrop, I found myself caught between conflicting paths. The allure of finite wealth and the trappings of a career I was reluctant to abandon filled my days with uncertainty. My father, disapproving of my past involvement in illicit activities and my lack of formal education, sought to impress upon me the importance of values that transcended material success. He longed for me to seek fulfilment beyond the confines of monetary gain, to find something that would nourish my soul and endure long after the fleeting riches had vanished. My mother, ever the cautious supporter, pressed me to chart a clearer path forward, urging me to discern my next steps with purpose and clarity. Meanwhile, my younger siblings, Biruk and Alazar, poised to complete their high school education, awaited guidance for their next move, their futures hanging in the balance.

In the midst of our personal struggles, the political landscape of Eritrea was undergoing seismic shifts. The new government, fervently pushing for a referendum to declare independence, sought to assert its authority both within the region and on the global stage. The People's Front for Democracy and Justice (PFDJ), a rebranded iteration of the liberation front, now wielded an iron-fisted grip over civil and military institutions, having absorbed businesses and properties previously held by private citizens. The national mood was one of anticipation, but also anxiety, as Eritrea faced an uncertain future amid the promise of newfound sovereignty.

As the threads of our individual lives intertwined with the tumultuous political backdrop, we found ourselves at a crossroads, grappling with the weight of our past and the uncertainty of our future. Each member of our family carried their own burdens, their own hopes and fears, as we sought to navigate the complex maze of choices and obligations before us. Our journey toward a renewed beginning was fraught with challenges, as we endeavoured to piece together the fractured fabric of our family, while the spectre of political and geographical allegiances loomed large over our aspirations. In the midst of it all, we were confronted with the daunting task of reconciling our individual ambitions with the collective quest for a shared future, as we sought to honour our commitments to each other and the lives we hoped to build.

As my father and I stood in silent face-off, the weight of our family's future hung heavy in the air. The delicate fabric of our family was being tested by the history of distant connections, and finding a balance between individual aspirations and the need to forge a better future for all seemed an insurmountable challenge. My father, a man of quiet strength and unwavering determination, respected my wishes but also sought to guide me towards a path that would lead to stability and personal growth, away from the allure of material wealth.

Our roots in Ethiopia, as Eritreans, presented a complex web of choices and expectations. While my family was expected to embrace the newly liberated Eritrea, I found myself torn, knowing that the fledgling nation might not provide the opportunities I sought. The prospect of uprooting my life and starting anew in Eritrea felt like a compromise on my dreams, a sacrifice I was not yet ready to make. With a sense of confidence built on the earnings from my work, I felt prepared to face the world beyond the familiar confines of my parents' home. However, when my father hinted at plans to build a new house on land gifted to us long ago by our grandfather, Goitapa, in Eritrea, I grappled with conflicting emotions. While I understood the significance of this gesture, I also felt the pull of my own ambitions and the desire to secure a stable future for myself.

Amidst the uncertainty, I made a heartfelt offer to contribute to the construction of the house, recognising that my parents' savings might not suffice for such a significant undertaking. Although my father hesitated at first, he eventually acquiesced, acknowledging the practicality of redirecting my resources towards a tangible investment in our family's future. As the plans for the house began to take shape, I found myself struggling with the juxtaposition of my personal aspirations and the responsibilities that came with being part of a family navigating uncharted territory.

The political landscape of the region, which had been shaping our lives and controlling our fates thus far, added another layer of complexity to our family's story. The post-war era in Ethiopia brought about sweeping changes, with the government striving to establish democratic structures based on the principles of ethnic federation and to rebuild an economy ravaged by years of conflict. The Tigrayan liberation front, which had included other ethnic parties, rebranded itself as the EPRDF (Ethiopian People's Revolutionary Democratic Front) and was entrusted with the monumental task of reconstruction. At a crossroads, the EPRDF had to navigate the complexities of international alliances and the influx of support from Western nations eager to restore their ties with Ethiopia. Meanwhile, the Eritrean liberation movement remained steadfast in its resistance to external influence, seeking to carve out a self-reliant path for the newly independent nation.

Amid these seismic shifts, our family found itself entwined in the fabric of history, grappling with the implications of political realignments and the uncertain future they heralded. As the world around us underwent profound transformations, I couldn't help but feel a sense of nostalgia for the familiar rhythms of the past, even as the winds of change swept through our lives, shaping our destinies in ways we had yet to comprehend.

Reflecting on the stark contrast between the new governments of Ethiopia and Eritrea, I was struck by the profound impact their ideologies had on the lives of their citizens. Ethiopia, with its embrace of economic and political liberalism, was undergoing a transformation marked by national dialogues and a commitment to inclusivity. The leaders, seasoned in the politics of national and international coexistence, were navigating the complexities of a diverse population, seeking to forge a path towards democracy and respect for fundamental human rights. The promise of free speech and fair representation was enshrined in the constitutional consultations, offering hope for a brighter future. The slow but steady progress towards a more open society was a testament to the resilience and moderation of the Ethiopian people.

In stark contrast, Eritrea's new government seemed consumed by a fixation on preserving newfound freedom through militaristic means. The hard-won liberty, achieved at great cost with the blood of countless martyrs, was swiftly overshadowed by the spectre of authoritarian rule. The ruling elite of the PFDJ appeared to be driving economic and political changes without meaningful consultation, leaving the populace yearning for a return to normalcy. With less than two years in power and a year following the declaration of independence after a referendum, their governance style, steeped in militaristic overtones, imposed compulsory national service on Eritrean adults under the guise of safeguarding freedom, evoking a sense of nostalgia for a bygone era. The imposition of national military service, the lack of clarity surrounding the return of the diaspora, delays in addressing property rights, and the allocation of resources all pointed to a government adrift, seemingly devoid of a coherent vision for the nation and its people. In one of his first widely publicised interviews, the president ruled out any prospects for a multi-party system or elections. When asked about human rights, he simply said, "Humans do not have rights."

My father, a man of unwavering optimism and a deep love for his homeland, found himself caught in the midst of these divergent paths. His desire to contribute to the reconstruction of Eritrea led him to engage with officials and influential figures, hoping to offer his expertise and experience. Despite his earnest intentions, his lack of affiliation with the liberation front seemed to relegate him to the periphery of consideration. The government's dismissive attitude left him clinging to the hope that, in time, his commitment to building a modern nation would be recognised and embraced.

As I listened to my father recount his encounters and frustrations, I couldn't help but feel a sense of nostalgia for the Eritrea of yesteryear – a place of hope and unity that now seemed distant and elusive. The stark dichotomy between the two neighbouring nations, one forging ahead with cautious optimism and the other mired in uncertainty, painted a poignant picture of the complexities of governance and the enduring resilience of the human spirit.

After his return from a three-month stay in Eritrea, where my father had reconnected with his roots, visited his childhood village, and met families and friends he hadn't seen in decades, he felt like a new man. The time spent with his brothers, who had come to visit from Europe, was incredibly special, binding them together as a family once more. It was a rejuvenating experience, and he vowed to start living again, determined to make this last chance a good one.

Upon his return to Addis Ababa, he continued to meet with other friends and families, including members of the new Ethiopian government, some of whom had been involved in the struggle for many years, and others from his circles as inmates. As the Tigray Liberation Front, now known as the EPRDF, extended an invitation for my father to contribute his knowledge to the reforms taking place in the Ministry of Agriculture, he was both honoured and excited. The Tigrayan-led government even offered him a short-term external contract to work for the ministry at the headquarters in Addis Ababa, focusing on restructuring staffing and rejuvenating the agricultural and farming industries, primarily in the Tigray region.

With a chance to revisit his old projects in Tigray, my father accepted the offer and led a group of experts in this temporary role. The offer was complemented by an opportunity to go abroad for further postgraduate studies to update his skills. Other benefits accompanying his new role were generous, including a brand-new car and access to facilities at a deputy ministerial level. He couldn't resist this offer, using it as a means to transition from his old life to a new one, while his plans to serve in Eritrea were taking shape in his mind.

The generous salary he received from the Ethiopian government allowed my parents to upscale the house they were building and purchase furniture and other essentials, as well as a private car in Asmara for their eventual settlement. The dozens of meetings and workshops at various international conferences helped him modernise his administrative skills, including learning to use a computer and enhancing other personal skills for the modern office environment.

After a year of hard work, making good friends, and gaining invaluable experience, a high-level party was thrown in my father's honour. He was rewarded financially and presented with a certificate that finally acknowledged his contributions to the community and the wider nation. Following that, he was ready to head to the UK to study a management postgraduate programme at Reading University, all expenses paid by the Ethiopian government, including accommodation and daily allowances. His choice of the UK, among a worldwide sea of options, was primarily to reconnect with his two sons, Kaleb and Simon, who had made the UK their home for several years. The prospect of furthering his education and reuniting with his children filled him with a sense of nostalgic anticipation.

My father completed his studies at Reading University, during which he visited London and reunited with my brothers, Kaleb and Simon, for a joyous family gathering. The warmth of that reunion lingered in the air, a stark contrast to the uncertainty that had enveloped our family for years.

In 1993, while my father was in the UK, my mother and the youngest members of our family had relocated to Asmara, eagerly awaiting his return. Our newly built house stood as a symbol of hope and new beginnings – a place where we could build our future together. The plan was for my father to secure employment in Eritrea in his field, while my brothers, Alazar and Biruk, would pursue their studies at the only university in the capital, Asmara University. It was a time of anticipation and optimism, when our dreams seemed within reach.

However, fate had other plans in store for us. As my father sought to catch up with the family's academic pursuits, a new challenge emerged. The government had implemented new entry rules for students waiting to pursue higher education, and my brothers had to navigate the complexities of university entrance exams. Alazar, the youngest, achieved high marks and secured a place in the law department, his eyes shining with determination and ambition. But Biruk, my other brother, fell short of the required marks and found himself facing a daunting reality: a future without education.

Biruk wasn't much of an academic person. He always had a knack for entrepreneurship and dreamed of starting a small business of his own. Despite his lack of interest in traditional education, our father, like many others, was adamant that Biruk should pursue a university degree. "University way, or no way," our father would say, blind to Biruk's true passions. Biruk's lack of preparation for university was evident, and his subsequent failure to gain admission did not come as a surprise. Our father's relentless push towards academia left Biruk feeling nostalgic for his dreams of building something of his own.

With no other choice, our father reluctantly conceded to Biruk's wishes, but deep down, he knew that his heart wasn't in it.

As the days passed, Biruk drifted further away from the academic world. His mind was consumed with thoughts of the small business he had always wanted to start. The nostalgia for his entrepreneurial dreams grew stronger with each passing day, and he couldn't shake the feeling of longing for something more meaningful to him. He knew that his future lay in following his entrepreneurial spirit, and he could no longer ignore the pull.

In Eritrea, compulsory conscription awaited all able-bodied adults, including my younger brother Biruk. This peacetime service was intended to instil military skills and discipline, without the imminent threat of combat. Many, including Biruk and our uncle Belay, volunteered for the national service, which was mandated for two years. For Biruk and Belay, this was not just about military training; it was a necessary step towards realising their dream of starting a clothing shop business. They embraced the obligation with the hope that it would lead them towards a future beyond the confines of military service.

When my father returned from his time in the UK, a deep sense of nostalgia enveloped him. He spoke fondly of the lush green landscapes of Reading, the bustling streets of London, and the warmth of family gatherings. Yet, amidst the nostalgia, a new reality awaited him in Asmara—a reality shaped by his own aspirations and challenges, as well as those of his sons. It was a reality marked by the resilience of our family and the unwavering hope that filled our new home.

As I made several trips from Addis Ababa to Asmara while my family completed their move, I couldn't help but be enchanted by the city's charm.

Asmara, a modern city built by the Italians, radiated an atmosphere of tranquillity and hope in the post-war era. Families would gather and stroll along the famous high streets, lined with tall palm trees, sharing meals and drinks in the many Italian restaurants with outdoor seating. The city's nightlife had a festive quality, with people filling restaurants and cafés after work, creating a vibrant, communal atmosphere. It was said that in Asmara, an evening out with one or two people would inevitably lead to joining a larger group of ten. The sense of community and camaraderie was palpable, and I found myself drawn to the genuine warmth of the city.

Diasporas flocked to Asmara, adorning the city with Western attire and modern styles, turning it into a lively rendezvous for the young. Many found their future partners here, while others returned to rebuild their neglected homes and properties, improving the lives of those who had stayed behind. It felt as though Eritrea, and its people, were being reborn.

During my visits to Eritrea to help my family settle, I reconnected with numerous friends from my school years. We revelled in the genuine family spirit that permeated the city, and I found myself falling in love with Asmara's new, free, and easy-going way of life, where laughter and banter were the only languages spoken.

Despite the happiness and sense of community, I couldn't envision a future for myself in Asmara. The government's slow or non-existent progress in promoting the private sector was disheartening. Local and diaspora entrepreneurs faced stringent regulations when attempting to establish businesses, and those who submitted business plans were met with disappointment. The high documentation requirements and bureaucratic red tape made it nearly impossible to import even the simplest goods. The government appeared more focused on taxing existing businesses than fostering new growth. It became clear that the government was not prepared to allow the country to flourish through business and construction, shattering the hopes of many Eritrean diasporas who dreamed of returning home to invest and build their lives.

The unexpected and unprovoked behaviour of the government before and after the referendum dealt a heavy blow to Eritreans. Some who had returned never came back, and rumours spread about the mistreatment of prominent Eritreans by officials when they sought permits to contribute to the economy. It seemed that the government was consolidating its power through harsh policies, led by ex-rebel members who lacked the qualifications to make such decisions. Officials and decision-makers appeared to be selected based on their ideology and military contributions to the fight for independence, rather than their academic qualifications or experience. Business opportunities seemed to be reserved for those who had contributed to the armed struggle, while the government continued to nationalise more businesses and properties, failing to return those confiscated by the previous military regime.

The titles and nicknames of the ministers and officials in high places bore the hallmarks of their bravery and militaristic ability. Some ministers had risen through the ranks by leading victorious battlefield operations during the fight for independence. Others were appointed as ambassadors or representatives to international organisations like the UN, honoured for their heroic acts of planning and executing decisive battles. Every official's credentials were war-related, and no civilian was considered fit for such positions.

Eritrean scholars, too, were sidelined by the government when they returned to our homeland with hopes of supporting the difficult reconstruction tasks. It soon became clear that the government had no intention of entertaining ideas of governance derived from the West, delivered by the diaspora.

As a scholar who had gained knowledge and experience from living and working in the West for many years, my uncles and others like them were seen as a threat to the positions of the government officials. The ex-rebels, it seemed, were determined to lead the country regardless of what the people or the outside world said. It was as if they had retired from their military duties and found governing the country to be their new post-retirement hobby. It was disheartening to witness the sidelining of individuals who had the potential to contribute positively to the nation's development. The atmosphere was suffocating, and a pervasive sense of pessimism hung over us like a dark cloud. We were silenced, our voices drowned out by the militaristic regime that had taken hold of our beloved homeland.

Despite the government's efforts to suppress the people, we continued to hold onto our ideals and aspirations for a better Eritrea.

In the midst of this oppressive environment, I found solace in the memories of my time in Addis Ababa. The endless business opportunities, the freedom to express ideas, and the sense of hope for a brighter future were stark contrasts to the grim reality I now faced in Eritrea. I longed for the day when our nation would embrace a diversity of thought and welcome the contributions of its scholars and intellectuals. The pessimism that had settled over the country weighed heavily on my heart.

As I observed these developments, I came to the realisation that Asmara was not the place for me. The city's potential was overshadowed by the government's policies, and I knew I needed to seek my future elsewhere, despite the fond memories and strong sense of community that Asmara held.

In the heart of Eritrea, tension hung thick in the air like a suffocating fog. Soon after the referendum and the demarcation of its borders, the Eritrean government found itself entangled in armed conflicts with its neighbours—Sudan, Yemen, and Djibouti—leaving the nation isolated and embroiled in a web of violence. The once serene landscapes were now marred by the echoes of gunfire and the cries of young conscripts thrust into the throes of war. What had been presented as a national service, initially touted as a reconstruction mission, had morphed into a harrowing ordeal for the youth, who were mercilessly caught in the crossfire of border and political agendas.

Amidst the chaos, the government's frustration manifested in a state of emergency, shrouding the country in an eerie aura of militaristic vigilance. Former fighters donned their uniforms once more, evoking a chilling reminder of the nation's readiness for further conflict. The government-controlled media became a mouthpiece for incendiary rhetoric, ceaselessly exhorting the populace to brace themselves for a prolonged war. The national service, once a finite commitment, now extended indefinitely for both young boys and girls, consigning them to poorly facilitated military camps as the government continued its relentless recruitment drives every six months.

As the border issues with neighbouring countries were tentatively resolved and agreements were signed, the Eritrean government remained ensnared in a perpetual state of high alert. It used the lingering spectre of conflict to manipulate and subdue its people. Panic became a tool wielded by the government, exploiting the residual fear from the recent skirmishes to enforce compliance with its draconian policies. The once-vibrant streets now bore witness to a populace shackled by apprehension, their freedoms curtailed by the government's insidious machinations.

Amidst this turmoil, disparate perspectives emerged, each a testament to the toll exacted by the government's cynical grip on power. There were those who defiantly clung to the flickering embers of hope, their spirits unyielding in the face of adversity. Others, however, found themselves ensnared in the suffocating web of fear, their once-bold aspirations eclipsed by the oppressive shadow cast by the government. The people, each bearing the weight of their own struggles, navigated the treacherous landscape of Eritrea. Their fates intertwined in a tapestry of resilience and despair. The undefined tone of the country echoed the dissonance that permeated, mirroring the conflicting emotions that reverberated through the hearts of its people.

I continued working at the WHO-run radio station in Addis Ababa, relishing the independence of having our family home all to myself. As I learned to manage life without my parents, I found myself mostly eating out, lacking the skills to cook for myself. It was a mix of loneliness and newfound freedom, where I could invite friends over for drinks and enjoy the space as my own. I matured quickly, learning new survival tricks and adapting to the responsibilities that came with living alone.

My mother, concerned about my solitary lifestyle, would call me every evening to ensure I was home early, had eaten, and completed all the tasks I would have done if I were still living with her. I proved to her, and to myself, that I could manage well, even in her absence.

Meanwhile, my father returned from the UK, and we both lived in the house before he went to Asmara for the last time, with no plans of permanently returning to Addis Ababa. During our evening discussions, we talked about my brothers, Kaleb and Simon, who were in the UK. My father would show me pictures taken with them, along with other friends and family. We also discussed my experiences during my short trips to Asmara, and how pessimistic I was about the country's future.

In most instances, my father thought I was trying to find excuses to justify my decision not to settle in Eritrea. On the other hand, he was aware of the current affairs in Eritrea and how the government was slowly slipping into dictatorship. My father, ever the optimist, would say, "The country will need time to settle down after nearly forty years of war. Everything will be okay." We agreed that Asmara may not be the place for me, but it would be perfect for the rest of our family, especially if Biruk completed his national service and started his business as planned.

As I navigated this period of transition, I also grappled with the shifting dynamics of my relationship with my father. His departure for Eritrea marked a significant turning point, one that underscored the divergent paths we were each destined to follow. Our conversations, once filled with spirited shared dreams, now carried an undercurrent of unspoken tension. I struggled to reconcile my father's unwavering faith in the future of Eritrea with my own apprehensions, rooted in the stark realities I had witnessed during my visits.

With that agreement, it was time for my father to bid farewell to Addis Ababa and embark on a new beginning in Eritrea, a journey which explored the theme of cynicism.

As my father departed for Eritrea, I found myself reflecting on the complexities of our family dynamics. His unwavering optimism clashed with my more cautious and skeptical outlook. Living alone in our family home, I grappled with the solitude and the newfound responsibilities that came with it. I yearned for the warmth of family gatherings and the comforting aroma of my mother's cooking, yet I also relished the freedom to invite friends over and create my own space. The dichotomy of emotions tugged at my heart, leaving me with a sense of both longing and liberation.

In the midst of this internal struggle, I found solace in my work at the radio station. The vibrant energy of the studio and the diverse stories I encountered provided a welcome distraction from the solitude of my home. With the HIV awareness programs long concluded, I was doing admin work for the organisation. Although most of the colleagues who had been there when I started had already left, replaced by new employees, I had become the most senior in my grade. I threw myself into my work, honing my skills as a department administrator with a moderate pay, much less than what I earned as a multi-tasked broadcaster in the past. Each day brought new challenges and triumphs, and I felt a sense of purpose in amplifying the voices of those whose stories often went unheard. It was in these moments that I found a sense of belonging, a purpose that transcended the confines of my family home and the uncertainties of the future.

Amidst these conflicting emotions, I found myself grappling with the complexities of identity and belonging. As an individual straddling the worlds of Ethiopia and Eritrea, I carried within me the echoes of history and the weight of familial legacies. The shifting tides of politics and ideology cast a shadow over my sense of self, leaving me adrift in a sea of uncertainty. Yet, within this tumultuous landscape, I sought to carve out my own path—one that honoured the rich tapestry of my heritage while embracing the complexities of my own truth. In the quiet moments of solitude, I found the courage to confront the shadows of doubt and forge a sense of resilience that would carry me through the trials ahead.

In the heart of Eritrea, a tale of ambition, friendship, and disillusionment unfolded within the corridors of the Ministry of Agriculture. My father, a man of wisdom and experience, was appointed as deputy minister in charge of the Environment and Sustainable Agriculture Division. His arrival brought hope for positive change, but it also stirred the waters of power within the ministry. His boss, the minister, was an ex-fighter with no prior experience in agricultural matters, and the clash of their expertise was palpable from the start. The dynamics of the ministry were further complicated by the presence of Dr Zerai, a scholarly Eritrean researcher from Oklahoma University in the United States, who served as their technical adviser at the Minister de Etat level.

As fate would have it, my father and Dr Zerai, two intellectuals who had never crossed paths before, found an unexpected camaraderie. Their shared passion for tennis became a Sunday morning ritual, a brief respite from the tumultuous world of government and politics. Together, they toiled tirelessly, striving to reorganise the ministry and make it more effective. Dr Zerai, in his advisory role, brought forth valuable ideas based on proven practices, seeking to guide the ex-rebel minister in implementing policies that could benefit the country. However, the ex-rebel minister was suspicious of Dr Zerai's counsel, dismissing it as the work of a 'western puppet' and irrelevant to Eritrea's needs, refusing to entertain the notion of adopting his ideas.

In the face of the minister's resistance, my father and Dr Zerai persevered, drawing upon their collective knowledge and experience to propose innovative solutions for the complex agricultural and climate-related issues that plagued Eritrean farmers. Despite their efforts, the ex-fighter minister remained obstinate, implementing policies without consulting them and disregarding their expertise. Frustration mounted, and the once-promising environment within the ministry soured. My father and Dr Zerai found themselves at odds with the very system they had hoped to improve.

As the rift between the scholars and the minister deepened, Dr Zerai, an American citizen of Eritrean descent, made the difficult decision to resign, citing irreconcilable differences with the minister and the futility of his blocked projects. His departure cast a shadow over the ministry, leaving my father to navigate the increasingly hostile terrain alone. With each passing day, the weight of disillusionment settled upon him, and the once-vibrant vision of transformation began to fade. The government's rigid governance further compounded his discomfort, denying him the privileges he had been accustomed to, such as a car or driver.

The absence of Dr Zerai and the growing isolation within the ministry gnawed at my father, eroding his sense of purpose. The once-promising collaboration had unravelled, leaving my father adrift in a sea of cynicism, where his expertise and dedication were no longer valued. As the days stretched on, the shadow of disillusionment loomed large, casting a pall over the very fabric of the ministry and its governance.

My father had harboured a vision of hope and renewal for the heart of the newborn nation, Eritrea. He had dedicated his life to the service of various communities, believing in the promise of a better future for everyone. However, as the years passed, the dream seemed to fade like a mirage in the desert. My father's unwavering commitment to his job as a civil servant was overshadowed by a growing sense of disillusionment. The administration seemed mired in ineptitude and power struggles. The weight of disappointment lay heavy on his shoulders, a burden shared by many Eritreans. My father's frequent travel to attend international meetings and conferences only deepened his cynicism, as he found that he could not bring international organisations to work with him on issues requiring global efforts. Meanwhile, the Eritrean government blocked all avenues of aid and cooperation. The leaders at the top appeared inexperienced and disconnected, leaving him with a bitter sense of apathy toward his work.

Amidst this disillusionment, my father, who had grown up witnessing the unwavering dedication of others to their country, found himself torn between his own idealism and the harsh realities unfolding around him. His vision and determination remained intact, but as he ventured into the world, he encountered the same cynicism that had taken root in society. The once-vibrant streets of Asmara now echoed with whispers of discontent, and the people's faces bore the weight of unmet expectations. My father grappled with the conflicting emotions of pride in his heritage and frustration with the current state of affairs. As he navigated through the labyrinth of disillusionment, he sought to understand the complexities of his own perspective and the changing landscape of our beloved nation.

In the heart of Addis Ababa, the vibrant capital of Ethiopia, a new chapter was being written. The sun rose over the bustling city, casting its golden glow over streets alive with the energy of progress. Under the leadership of the EPRDF government, a sense of optimism filled the air as the country embarked on a new journey towards a promising future, with full-steam support from the West and other international financial institutions. New mega-projects and financial agreements were struck daily, creating jobs for thousands.

Construction boomed as the government issued new licences and distributed land. Businesses flourished, supported by improved banking and finance facilities, creating even more jobs for the people. New universities were built, and the once-government-controlled financial system was opened for privatisation.

People from all walks of life moved through the city, their faces reflecting a newfound sense of hope and determination. The once-struggling economy now showed signs of growth, with promising economic plans paving the way for a brighter tomorrow. Despite occasional political unrest and civil rights concerns, Ethiopia was reclaiming its glory and restoring its place as an important partner in the region and beyond. With the African Union and many other international organisations based in Addis Ababa, the city became a magnet for diplomacy, tourism, and investment.

Unlike in Eritrea, the Ethiopian diaspora were actively encouraged to return home and invest in the country. Incentives were offered to support their entrepreneurial endeavours, whether in starting new businesses or revitalising old ones. The government recognised the invaluable contributions of its expatriate communities and sought to harness their skills and resources for the nation's benefit.

The city's administrative buildings, new roads, and railways stood as a testament to the progress underway. The civil and court systems were being reshaped, with a renewed focus on fairness and justice for all. Freedom of speech had been realised, and new private media outlets flourished through press and TV. A new constitution had been crafted with the full participation of the people, reflecting their hopes and aspirations for a democratic Ethiopia. Amid this transformation, Addis Ababa shone as Africa's diplomatic capital, a hub of international engagement and cooperation. The government seized every opportunity to strengthen ties with foreign partners, making the city more welcoming to workers and investors from around the world. The streets buzzed with excitement as cultures and ideas intersected in a harmonious blend.

The government in Addis Ababa seemed to be following the correct path for the country's future. The EPRDF-led government had formed an inclusive parliamentary system with the help of the West and international financial institutions, and the economy had already begun to show signs of progress.

Amid the chaos of contrasting economies and lifestyles, I found myself grappling with decisions that would shape my future. As I toiled away, trying to carve a path toward financial independence through a business venture, my friend Abel lurched deeper into a downward spiral of dependence and reckless behaviour.

Abel had always been a charismatic figure – a whirlwind of charm and looks that drew people towards him. However, his magnetic personality was overshadowed by his vices: drinking, smoking, and late-night revelry that seemed to consume his every waking moment. His longtime girlfriend, Hannah, a patient and understanding soul, had tried in vain to steer him toward a more responsible path. But Abel's heart was set on a self-destructive course, leaving his relationship with Hannah strained.

I found myself caught in the crossfire of Abel's unravelling life. His girlfriend confided in me about his infidelities, his blatant disregard for her feelings, and his reckless spending of her hard-earned money on younger women. I tried to reason with Abel, to shake him out of his stupor, but he denied any wrongdoing, lashing out with anger and defensiveness whenever confronted.

Our interactions grew strained, limited to fleeting moments on weekends when we would meet briefly. Each encounter was marred by Abel's volatile behaviour, turning every conversation into a battleground of words and accusations. Despite our friendship, I watched helplessly as Abel spiralled further into self-destruction, his once-vibrant spirit dimming with each passing day.

As the cracks in Abel's façade deepened, his long-time girlfriend made the difficult decision to end their tumultuous relationship. She offered him support and assistance for a fresh start, but Abel, consumed by pride and stubbornness, refused her help. Left adrift, Abel found himself with no place to call home. He turned to me as his lifeline, seeking refuge in my home as he grappled with his uncertain future. Facing financial struggles and nowhere else to turn, he sought solace in the humble abode of a friend — me. I welcomed him with open arms, eager to provide him with a safe haven amidst the chaos of his unstable circumstances.

I did my best to make Abel feel comfortable, offering him a warm place to stay and a space to call his own. However, it quickly became evident that his reckless behaviour and dependency on me to maintain a livable environment posed a challenge. Despite my efforts to uphold the pride and sanctity of our family home — just as my mother would have done — Abel seemed oblivious to the rules and boundaries that had always been in place.

As days turned into weeks, Abel's behaviour took a destructive turn. He disregarded the house rules, brazenly smoking indoors and indulging in alcohol that stained the once-pristine walls. His careless actions extended to the abuse of our belongings, undermining the sanctity of the home that had been a safe haven for generations.

Frustration simmered within me as I confronted Abel, attempting to assert my authority and instil a sense of respect for our shared space. Yet, despite my efforts to guide him towards a path of decency and responsibility, Abel remained resistant to change. The once harmonious atmosphere of our home now echoed with tension, as our conflicting lifestyles clashed in a battle for dominance.

In the end, Abel's inability to conform to the values and principles that had defined our household left me with a heavy heart. The realisation dawned upon me that some souls are destined to wander, seeking solace in chaos rather than embracing the tranquillity of a loving home. And so, with a heavy heart, I bid farewell to Abel, knowing that his journey towards redemption would be a solitary one, far removed from the warmth and comfort he had once found within our humble abode.

We decided that Abel would find a small apartment, for which I would pay the rent while he tried to secure his own source of income. I paid all his expenses, but Abel continued to use some of the money I gave him to buy drinks and tobacco. Despite my best efforts, he remained stubborn and resistant to change, his pride blinding him to the reality of his situation.

Meanwhile, the city of Addis Ababa hummed with a sense of change — change as palpable as the rising sun that bathed its streets in golden light each morning. The new government, led by the EPRDF, had sparked a wave of transformation that touched every corner of the bustling metropolis. But amidst the hopeful whispers of progress and renewal, there lingered a stark reminder of the past: the dismissed soldiers of the old regime.

Determined to help Abel find his footing again, I rallied our friends in the business world to seek out opportunities. And, as fate would have it, we stumbled upon the perfect chance not only to breathe new life into an old restaurant but also into Abel's weary soul.

Amidst this tumultuous backdrop stood a quaint Italian restaurant, a haven of warmth and laughter in a busy district of the city, caught between yesterday and tomorrow. Owned by an elderly lady whose smile was as comforting as her cooking, the restaurant had long been a gathering place for the rich and famous. But fate, it seemed, had other plans for the old lady and her beloved establishment. The contract with an Italian investor had run its course, leaving the restaurant up for sale — a silent witness to the ebb and flow of time.

The potential in the restaurant was undeniable. With its spacious service area, a bustling kitchen hidden in the basement, and two apartments sitting atop, waiting to be filled with purpose, it was a canvas waiting to be painted anew — a stage set for revival.

Propelled by a mix of hope and determination, I envisioned Abel taking residence in one of the apartments, immersing himself in the vibrant world of the restaurant. The older staff, seasoned in their craft, were eager to pass on their knowledge, paving the way for Abel to learn the ropes of running a bustling eatery.

Beneath the layers of the restaurant's long history — which had been frequented by famous customers — the place whispered tales of bustling nights and laughter-filled evenings. Abel and I had been regular patrons of this restaurant for a long time, enjoying its excellent Italian cuisine and serene atmosphere. As we walked through its hallowed halls, surveying it for a potential buyout, a spark ignited in Abel's eyes — a glimmer of a future reborn.

It was in this moment of uncertainty that a chance encounter changed the course of destiny. One balmy evening, as Abel and I struck up a conversation with the manager, a weathered man with a twinkle in his eye, we were told of a golden opportunity hidden within the shadows of adversity.

As Abel, the manager, and I shared our musings, a seed of possibility took root in our minds. We researched, deliberated, and finally decided to breathe new life into the fading glory of the restaurant. Encouraged by friends who pledged their loyalty, we embarked on a journey of revival and reinvention.

After we acquired the business, the restaurant began to come alive once more. With each passing day, it was infused with the warmth of fresh beginnings and the energy of newfound purpose. As Abel slowly found his place in this world of sizzling pans and clinking glasses, he discovered that sometimes, in the quiet corners of forgotten dreams, miracles wait to be rediscovered.

The restaurant was reborn. Its walls echoed with the laughter of a new beginning. Imported furniture graced its floors, casting a sheen of elegance upon the familiar setting. On the day of the grand opening, the city of Addis Ababa bore witness to a spectacle of jubilation and hope. Famous personalities graced the event with their presence, their smiles a beacon of light in a world still shrouded in shadows. A full weekend inauguration, complete with a live band, filled the air with melodies of promise, serenading the guests as they partook in the feast of renewal.

In the wake of the new government's swift ascent to power, the city had teetered on the edge of uncertainty. Among the most disheartened were the ex-soldiers, cast aside by the new regime without a second thought. Once revered defenders of the nation, they now roamed the streets, shadows of their former selves.

A bitter chill settled over the city as winter descended, mirroring the coldness in the hearts of those who turned a blind eye to the ex-soldiers' plight. Shunned by society, their once-proud uniforms now tattered, their eyes haunted by the memories of battles fought in the name of a nation that had forsaken them.

These young men, still clad in their worn uniforms, haunted the city like spectres of a bygone era. They slept outside shops, their empty gazes fixed on a world that had moved on without them. Their once-proud ranks now reduced to tattered insignias, they wandered the streets, their hands outstretched in a silent plea for mercy.

Many in Addis Ababa averted their eyes, their hearts heavy with the weight of history. It was a difficult time — a time when compassion warred with fear, when the scars of the past threatened to reopen with every glimpse of a soldier in need.

Weeks passed, and with each one, the number of customers at Romina, the revitalised Italian restaurant, steadily increased. Yet, amidst the clinking of glasses and the hum of cheerful conversation, a storm began to brew on the horizon.

A few months into the restaurant's successful run, where patrons sought solace in the delicious aroma of freshly prepared meals and the gentle ambiance that enveloped them, the manager — known for his unwavering dedication to providing a peaceful dining experience — faced an unexpected challenge.

On a sunny Saturday afternoon, the restaurant was buzzing with life, its tables overflowing with laughter and camaraderie. Then, like a dark cloud descending upon a clear sky, two ex-soldiers in civilian garb stumbled into the midst of the revelry.

Their faces bore the scars of countless battles, and their eyes were haunted by the memories of a past they could not forget. They moved from table to table, hands outstretched in silent supplication, their voices desperate as they begged for sustenance.

The manager, ever vigilant in his duty to safeguard the sanctity of the restaurant, approached the soldiers with firm resolve. He urged them to leave, to seek their solace elsewhere, away from the fragile tranquillity of the diners.

But the soldiers, their spirits broken and their pride wounded, refused to yield. They spoke of hunger, of despair — their words a symphony of anguish in a world that had long ceased to hear their cries. The manager, his patience growing thin, gently but firmly pushed them towards the door, his actions a silent decree of departure.

Then, in a moment of desperation, one of the soldiers lashed out, grabbing a lady's handbag in a futile attempt to claim restitution. Chaos erupted, the air thick with tension as confrontations flared and tempers rose.

The manager, a bastion of order amidst the storm, stood his ground. His voice rang out, authoritative and commanding, as he pushed the ex-soldiers out, his hands firm, his resolve unyielding. His only allegiance was to the safety and well-being of his patrons.

As the soldiers were finally expelled from the restaurant, their curses lingered in the air like a dark shroud. They wished death and misery upon those who had turned them away, their words a bitter reminder of a past that refused to be forgotten.

The group of disgruntled ex-soldiers re-entered the restaurant, their faces etched with anger, their eyes ablaze with resentment. In an instant, the tranquillity was shattered. One of the ex-soldiers, a man with a twisted scar on his cheek, stood up abruptly and reached into his pocket, pulling out a hand grenade. Panic gripped the diners as they scrambled to find cover, their voices blending with the clatter of overturned chairs and shattering glass.

The manager, usually a pillar of strength in times of adversity, was nowhere to be found. The ex-soldiers, their faces contorted with rage, demanded his presence, threatening to unleash chaos upon everyone present.

Amidst the chaos, a lone figure emerged from the crowd. An elderly man, his silver hair catching the dim light, stepped forward with calm resolve in his eyes. He spoke softly, but with an authority that demanded attention.

"Please, gentlemen, let us find a way to resolve this peacefully. Violence will only beget more violence," he implored, his words cutting through the tension like a blade. He addressed the ex-soldiers, showing his solidarity and familiarity with their situation. The ex-soldiers turned their attention to the man, their expressions shifting from fury to curiosity. The elderly man revealed himself to be a retired high-ranking police officer who had once walked a similar path of anger and disillusionment.

With a sincerity that touched even the hardened hearts of the ex-soldiers, he offered them a chance at redemption. He proposed that they join him in starting anew, finding purpose in work that would not only sustain them but also uplift their spirits.

Slowly, the tension began to ebb away as the ex-soldiers considered the elderly man's words. They laid down their weapons, their faces weary but hopeful for the first time in a long while.

As the day wore on, the restaurant, once a scene of terror, transformed into a place of reconciliation and understanding. But business was never quite the same after the harrowing experience. Rumours of the incident spread throughout the city, making customers question the safety of the restaurant.

Reflecting on the challenges of running a business in such a volatile part of the city, I made the difficult decision to lease the restaurant for far less than its true value. The weight of ensuring the safety and well-being of both customers and staff proved to be a burden too heavy to bear alone.

As I watched the restaurant change hands, a new chapter began. It became not just a place for food and drink, but a space for healing and second chances—a beacon of hope in a world often overshadowed by darkness.

Meanwhile, Abel's mother, a woman of both Italian and Eritrean heritage, was battling her own demons with alcohol. In an effort to escape her past, she made drastic decisions. She sold their family home, left by her ex-husband, and moved with her other two children to a modest abode in Asmara, a city steeped in history and nostalgia, which held the key to her fractured past.

In a bid to salvage what was left of Abel's future, I reached out to his family in Asmara, offering my assistance and support. Whenever I travelled there, I would visit Abel's family and share my concerns about his downward spiral with his mother and siblings, hoping we could find a solution to his mounting troubles.

I decided to take Abel to Asmara, hoping that a change of scenery might shake him out of his self-destructive stupor. It was his first time there, and Abel, for the most part, enjoyed the life in Asmara. I showed him around, taking him to various places, balancing both leisure and work. We met important people to explore opportunities for Abel to establish himself in Asmara, perhaps with a small business to support himself and his family. Abel and I agreed that he would start afresh in Asmara and leave his troubled past behind. I encouraged him, saying that this was an opportunity to change his future in a new environment, and also to revitalise the process of his Italian citizenship. Abel agreed wholeheartedly, stating that he no longer wanted to return to Addis Ababa and that he would make Asmara his new home. I insisted, however, that we return to Addis Ababa first and make an organised move.

Upon our return to Addis Ababa, the rift between us deepened, fuelled by Abel's indecisiveness, frustration, and resentment towards his own shortcomings. The slow progress of his citizenship application, a potential lifeline towards a better future, remained stagnant. Abel and his mother failed to pursue the process diligently, lost in a haze of irresponsibility and apathy. This obsession with the unrealistic hope of obtaining Italian citizenship under his long-gone great-grandparents, a process that had been held up for several years, pending the submission of forensic evidence such as DNA he could never produce.

In the end, I realised that I couldn't save Abel from himself. His pride and stubbornness were barriers too high for me to scale, and his dependence on me had become a crutch that only enabled his destructive behaviours. As I stood at a crossroads, torn between loyalty to a friend and the need to prioritise my own well-being, I knew that the ultimate decision rested with Abel himself. He had to decide whether to rise from the ashes of his past mistakes and forge a new path towards redemption, or to remain shackled by his own demons, forever trapped in a cycle of self-destruction.

As the reality of the situation dawned on me, I knew I could no longer shoulder the burden of Abel's lifestyle and expenses. It was a tough decision, but it was time for him to leave Addis Ababa and join his family in Asmara. I hoped that the change in environment would prompt a fresh start, making him realise that he couldn't rely on others to support his habits. The more structured governance and less relaxed lifestyle in Asmara would compel Abel to slow down and learn to live within his means, earning his keep.

With a heavy heart, I informed Abel that I could no longer finance his lifestyle, and it was time for him to move on. Reluctantly, he accepted his fate and packed his bags for Asmara. After consulting with his mother, they decided that applying for Italian citizenship in Eritrea would be a strategic move. The Italian embassy in Asmara was reputed to process citizenship applications faster for individuals in their circumstances, increasing their chances of approval due to the country's colonial connections, which resulted in several ancestral ties between the two peoples.

As Abel embarked on this journey, I couldn't help but feel a sense of relief, mixed with a tinge of sadness. It was a necessary step for him to learn self-sufficiency and responsibility, away from the enabling environment of Addis Ababa. To kickstart the process, they needed to obtain Eritrean citizenship—a significant step towards securing a stable future in their new home.

The bustling streets of Asmara welcomed Abel with a mix of hope and uncertainty, marking the beginning of a new chapter in his life—one where he would have to navigate challenges and embrace change in order to carve out a better tomorrow for himself.

In the heart of both cities, Asmara and Addis Ababa, the former freedom fighters turned government officials were struggling to navigate the transition from rebels to rulers. It had not been easy, and differences in ideology and cracks in border issues were beginning to surface, threatening to tear apart the fragile unity that had brought them independence. The Declaration of Independence had set off a chain of events that nobody could have predicted. Disputes over the use of ports, currency, and the demarcation of borders soon became hot topics.

Meanwhile, across the border in Ethiopia, whispers of discontent were growing louder. Eritreans were being met with suspicion and hostility, particularly those with roots in the Tigray region. The Ethiopian government, once open to its neighbours, was now passing new regulations that subtly pressured Eritreans to choose their citizenship. Checkpoints were erected on land borders, and the taxation of goods on both sides began without any formal agreement on its execution.

At Addis Ababa airport, Ethiopian security and immigration officers scrutinised the passports of Eritreans, questioning their loyalty and origins. They gently urged them to switch to Eritrean documents, citing the changing political landscape as the reason behind the shift. But underlying this seemingly reasonable request was an undeniably ominous tone, hinting at deeper tensions simmering beneath the surface.

For Eritreans like myself, caught in the middle, the choice was not a simple one. Decades of shared history and intertwined lives as citizen Amiche, along with a future still in the balance, made the decision to renounce our Ethiopian identity a painful one. And for those Eritreans who had not supported independence, the ultimatum from Ethiopia to switch allegiances brought a wave of uncertainty and fear.

As days turned into weeks, the atmosphere in the region grew increasingly tense. Old rivalries between the two rebel groups, once forgotten due to their shared goal of defeating the central government, flared up again, fuelled now by political manoeuvring and economic power plays. The once seamless flow of goods and people between the two countries was now choked with restrictions and barriers, a stark reminder of the deepening divide.

In the midst of this turmoil, ordinary citizens like myself found themselves grappling with an impossible choice—whether to forsake their past or risk an uncertain future. Families were torn apart, friendships strained, and loyalties questioned in a world where borders were no longer just lines on a map but barriers to belonging.

As the situation escalated, it became clear that the decisions made in quiet rooms behind closed doors in the powerhouses of both cities would have far-reaching consequences for generations to come. The path towards reconciliation seemed fraught with obstacles, and the shadow of conflict loomed large over the once hopeful promise of independence.

And so, in the twilight of a new era, the people of Eritrea and Ethiopia stood at a crossroads, their destinies entwined in a complex dance of politics and power. The choices they made in the coming months would shape the future of an entire region, testing the limits of loyalty, identity, and the enduring bonds of humanity.

In the midst of a hot afternoon in Asmara, the sun beat down relentlessly on the worn streets, casting long shadows as my father and I sat on the sun-bleached veranda of an old Italian restaurant. We were deep in a discussion that weighed heavily on our hearts. The air was thick with tension, mirroring the political climate that gripped our country, Eritrea. We gazed out at the cityscape—a jumble of ancient buildings and bustling market stalls, each with its own story to tell.

As we sipped our strong, bitter coffee, my father's voice was tinged with concern as he brought up the increasing political discomfort in Eritrea. The once-promising future of our beloved nation, built on the sacrifices of thousands of our brothers and sisters, seemed to be fading into a haze of uncertainty and fear. The government's grip on its citizens was tightening, stifling dissent and creativity in its suffocating grasp.

The very fabric of society seemed to be unraveling before the eyes of its own citizens. The national service, once a source of pride, had morphed into a suffocating web of control and oppression. Businesses that had once thrived now lay empty, casualties of an economy in freefall. Restrictions on the movement of citizens and the prohibition of free speech became bitter reminders of past oppressive regimes, leaving Eritreans to wonder: Is this what we fought for?

As time passed, reality unveiled a stark truth. The national service, once seen as a duty to the nation, had transformed into a relentless military mission. With the clouds of war gathering on the horizon, the once hopeful returnees found themselves trapped in a cycle of fear and despair as the government decreed a recall of all trained citizens, including my brother Biruk.

Amidst the turmoil engulfing Eritrea, only five years into its independence, government employees found themselves walking on eggshells. Their every move was scrutinised, their voices muzzled. The streets, once alive with chatter and laughter, now echoed with the heavy silence of fear and uncertainty. Movements were restricted, and free speech had become a relic of the past. The once bright vision for the future had dimmed into a bleak haze of hopelessness. The prospect of a democratic multi-party government system was a distant dream—a dream the government had openly announced would never exist. The Eritrean president and its government lacked transparency about the state of the nation, rejecting interviews by international news agencies, raising speculation about its domestic and international plans. The only rehearsed interviews they gave were to government-controlled media.

In a rare and highly anticipated chilling interview with Al Jazeera news network's Anna Dutton, the president responded to questions about his timeline for transitioning to democratic elections. He said he never said Eritrea was going to have elections. To quote him more accurately, he renounced the journalist for fabricating stories and interfering in his country's affairs, hammering the final nail on the dying hopes for free and modern governance.

And so it was that the people of Eritrea found themselves faced with a choice they never imagined they would have to make: to leave their homeland behind. The exodus began, mirroring the events of two decades before. Families packed what little they could carry, their hearts heavy with the weight of leaving behind everything they had ever known.

Among them were the diasporas who had returned, hoping to rebuild their lives in the land of their ancestors, only to find themselves once again uprooted. Relinquishing their foreign passports, they crossed borders in search of a new beginning, a fresh start in a place where freedom still reigned. And so, Eritreans began to flee their own homes, seeking refuge in foreign lands much like their predecessors had done two decades ago. The diaspora, who had once eagerly settled back in their homeland, now found themselves fleeing through the borders, desperate for another chance at a life free from oppression and control.

It was a scene no one had foreseen—a mass exodus of a proud people who were forced to abandon their roots in search of a better tomorrow. Eritrea, once a beacon of hope, was now a shadow of its former self, a place its own citizens could no longer recognise as home. And as the exodus continued, it left behind a bitter taste of farewell—the memory of what once was and what could have been.

Asmara, once a beacon of hope and prosperity, now stood as a shadow of its former self. The streets that had once echoed with laughter and song were now hushed, the vibrant market stalls replaced by boarded-up shops and empty storefronts. As the days turned into weeks, the city seemed to shrink in on itself, echoing with the hollow sounds of empty streets and deserted alleyways. The once vibrant heart of Eritrea was now a ghost town, haunted by the memories of a time long gone.

Both my father and I knew that the prospect of a life without problems was nothing but a distant dream in the current state of affairs. The thought of relinquishing my Eritrean citizenship to become Ethiopian, as some had suggested, seemed like a desperate grasp at fleeting stability. My father shook his head solemnly, his weathered face etched with lines of worry.

"It's not a guarantee of a lifetime of peace, my child," my father mused, his eyes reflecting the flickering rays of the setting sun. "We need to look beyond our borders for a chance at a brighter future." I assured my father of my capacity to make the right decision based on my own interests and circumstances, not those of the country.

My father shared with me his honest early conviction that Eritrea was spiralling down a path of no return. As we set out on our individual paths, leaving behind the shadows of a troubled past, we knew the road ahead would be long and arduous.

But we faced it with heads held high and hearts full of hope. For in the darkest of times, it is our dreams that light the way forward.

And so, we both agreed that maintaining my Eritrean citizenship and seeking a life elsewhere was the wisest and safest choice, rather than remaining in Ethiopia amidst the political climate where hostilities towards Eritreans were a daily phenomenon, set to intensify.

Still holding the more widely accepted Ethiopian passport, in the spring of 1998, I decided to seek life abroad. On the advice of a close friend, I went to Dubai to explore business opportunities. In that dusty city, under the scorching Dubai sun, I found myself standing at a crossroads, facing a pivotal decision that would shape the course of my life. With a heavy heart and a sense of urgency, I made the bold choice to partner with an Ethiopian woman I barely knew, but whose reputation as a successful businesswoman preceded her.

She was a prominent figure in the shoe import industry, known for her sharp business acumen and impeccable negotiation skills. Introduced to me through mutual friends, she was seeking a business partner to help manage her business in Dubai, as she could no longer commit full-time due to other familial obligations. Driven by a mix of desperation and determination, I offered to purchase shares in her established business and vowed to make a mark in this foreign land.

As life in Dubai began to unfold before me, I soon found myself drawn towards a different avenue: the lucrative world of shipping as a side business. With Ethiopia and Eritrea's imports primarily passing through Dubai at the time, I saw a golden opportunity to establish a strong client base and conduct business dealings spanning both nations. Making frequent trips to Addis Ababa and Asmara for work and visits, I marvelled at the bustling trade and the intricate network of connections that intertwined the Ethiopian and Eritrean communities in Dubai.

Despite the growing tensions between their respective governments, business relationships between Ethiopian and Eritrean merchants thrived, bridging gaps and forging alliances amidst political turmoil. With no viable alternatives, Ethiopians continued to use Eritrean ports—Massawa and Assab—as their primary gateways. Many Eritreans engaged in the shipping industry, some even owning large cargo vessels, maintaining robust business ties with their Ethiopian counterparts. However, this reliance on Eritrean ports gradually diminished as Ethiopia began to shift its focus to other ports, seeking alternatives amid the changing political landscape.

With a glimmer of hope in my heart, I longed for the return of my younger brother, Biruk, who was serving in the national service and whom I believed would bring a touch of home to my endeavours. Still stationed in Asmara after nearly four years of deployment in one of the harshest landscapes in the world, Biruk was now assigned lighter duties. Together, recognising a gap in the market, we ventured into a new business in the music and video industry, opening the first fully digital audiovisual production centre. Entrusting the daily operations to Biruk and a team of young Eritreans, I divided my time between Dubai, Addis Ababa, and Asmara, expanding the business and investing in state-of-the-art equipment to elevate our services.

The success of the business not only brought me a sense of accomplishment but also filled my family with pride as they witnessed the transformation of a humble idea into a thriving enterprise. The bond between my brother and me grew stronger as we navigated the challenges of entrepreneurship together. Eventually, Biruk took the reins and steered the business towards becoming one of the most recognised establishments in Asmara.

With no meaningful banking system and limited funding streams, our expansion plans progressed one step at a time. We bought new equipment and acquired additional spaces across the city to broaden our services, which included video rentals and sales. From modern recording studios to a film production centre, we spared no effort to elevate our business, reinvesting every penny earned to further propel our dream forward.

Through the whirlwind of challenges and triumphs, the journey of building a business from scratch in an uncertain political environment was not just a testament to our steadfastness, but also to the unwavering bond of family, the resilience of the human spirit, and the enduring power of determination and hard work in shaping our destinies.

In Asmara, the capital of Eritrea, my father, a dedicated civil servant, toiled away in a high-level but low-profile position at the Ministry of Agriculture. Despite his dissatisfaction with the lack of recognition for his efforts, he remained steadfast in his commitment to contribute to the nation-building process. With a keen eye for opportunities and a network of international contacts, my father managed to secure a free scholarship programme for ministry employees to pursue specialised studies in agriculture.

Eritrea, a country with only one university at the time, faced a shortage of postgraduate programmes specialising in agricultural fields. Undeterred by the challenges, my father reached out to a university in Cape Town, South Africa, to arrange for a select group of students to undergo a one-year postgraduate education funded by the Australian government. This initiative was crucial in addressing the expertise gap in the agricultural sector, a vital component of Eritrea's development goals.

Despite his best intentions, my father faced obstacles from within the government. The authorities, mainly the ex-rebel ministers, hesitated to allow individuals below the age of forty to participate in the programme, citing mandatory national service requirements for younger citizens. My father advocated for investing in the youth, believing it would be more beneficial in the long run, but he had to navigate the bureaucracy cautiously to avoid potential repercussions.

Accompanying the first group of thirty students to Cape Town, my father witnessed their successful enrolment and eventual completion of the courses. He returned home with newfound knowledge and skills. However, when the second batch of students went, complications arose. This group became embroiled in disputes with the government over withheld salaries during their education, at a time of severely fractured national sentiment, leading them to consider seeking asylum in other countries rather than returning to Eritrea.

Despite his best efforts to mediate and resolve the escalating tensions—making multiple trips to Cape Town and conferring with the defiant students—my father found himself at an impasse. During each visit, the students offered my father their heartfelt respect and gratitude, but they demanded a solid commitment and resolve from the government. Frustrated and disheartened by the situation, he watched as the students grew more determined to defy the government's expectations and forge their own paths abroad. The rift between the authorities and the students deepened, casting a shadow over what had once been a promising scholarship programme.

As the standoff between the government and the students reached a critical juncture, an unexpected twist unfolded. The former fighter turned minister, known for his brash demeanour, decided to fly to Cape Town personally to intervene and persuade the students to return home. In a tense and heated meeting, the minister faced a barrage of politically charged questions and grievances from the disillusioned students, each one expressing their concerns and fears for their future.

After hours of high tension and accusations, the minister, who felt hopeless of achieving his goals, abruptly declared that he would entertain only one more question before concluding the gathering. As the students vied for his attention, a young man stood up, his eyes blazing with defiance. True to his nature, the minister pointed towards him dismissively, likening his fervour to that of a 'barking dog', and invited him to speak his mind.

Unfazed by the minister's condescension, the student retorted with a piercing clarity that left the room stunned. "You call me a dog, that's fair enough. But remember, a dog only barks when a thief enters his home."

The room erupted into chaos, with all the students throwing tantrums and insults at the minister, a potent reminder of the deep-seated discontent and desire for change simmering within the hearts of the youth. The situation escalated quickly, requiring the minister's police escort to usher him out of the room safely before he was physically attacked.

Embarrassed by the incident, the minister returned home without achieving any success in his mission to convince the students to come back to Eritrea. With that, the scholarship programme was suspended.

In the heart of Eritrea, a land marred by political and social turmoil, my father stood at a crossroads. His rugged features bore the wisdom of years spent navigating the treacherous waters of a nation in flux. When news of the incident reached him, a shadow of concern crossed his weathered face. He knew all too well the signs of impending trouble.

As a man who had dedicated his life to doing good in the face of adversity, my father was no stranger to challenges. Yet the gravity of the situation now unfolding before him was unlike anything he had encountered before. The stakes were high, and the spectre of past injustices loomed in the background, threatening to engulf all who dared to oppose the powers that be.

The ex-rebel minister, a figure shrouded in mystery and tainted by a dark past, stood as a formidable adversary. Surprisingly, when confronted with the implications of the incident in Cape Town, the minister chose silence over confrontation. It was a decision that sent a shiver down my father's spine. In a land where words held power and silence spoke volumes, this hesitant gesture was a harbinger of troubles to come.

In Eritrea, where dissent was met with imprisonment, men and women who opposed the system vanished into the night, their voices silenced by fear and oppression. The minister's reluctance to address the issue at hand hinted at a deeper conspiracy, one that threatened to upend the fragile peace my father had fought so hard to preserve.

Rather than scheduling a formal meeting to discuss the incident in Cape Town, the minister approached my father informally. He said, "I am sure you've heard how your boys in Cape Town have humiliated the country and themselves. We will get them all, one by one." More than anything that had happened thus far, my father was struck by the two words, 'your boys', as if the minister was implying my father's ownership of the incident.

As the days turned into weeks, the tension in the air grew palpable, like a storm gathering on the horizon. The minister, true to form, escalated the matter to higher decision-makers, including the elusive president, whose word was law in the land. My father, who had braced himself for a confrontation that never came, found himself on the sidelines, a mere spectator in a dangerous game of power and politics.

The imprisonment of civil servants, the kidnapping of dissenters, and the disappearances of those who dared to speak out against the government — these were not isolated incidents but part of a broader pattern of oppression that mirrored the darkest days of Eritrea's recent history. The spectre of a military regime, long thought vanquished, loomed large, casting a long shadow over the present.

In the end, my father's resolve remained unshaken, his determination to uphold righteousness unwavering in the face of adversity. As the storm clouds gathered overhead and the winds of change swept through the land, surrounded by tyrannies, my father stood tall, a solitary figure against the backdrop of a nation in distress. His unwavering spirit was a testament to the resilience of the human soul in the face of dictatorship and oppression.

Fast forward to 1994, in the heart of Asmara University, amidst the ancient architecture and weathered buildings, the Law department stood as a beacon of hope for the burgeoning nation of Eritrea. Led by a distinguished professor who had returned from the USA to lend his expertise to the nation-building efforts, the department faced monumental challenges as it endeavoured to lay the groundwork for the country's legal system.

The professor, a close friend of my father, had brought with him a wealth of resources and volunteers to establish the University's Law department from scratch. The task at hand was monumental: to create the foundation upon which the new Eritrea would be governed. However, the ideals of the Western experts clashed fiercely with the ex-rebel lawmakers, who held vastly different views on governance and democracy.

As the professor and his team navigated the murky waters of bureaucracy, attempting to sway the hardened minds of ex-rebel ministers and lawmakers, they also undertook the crucial task of educating the first batch of students who would lead the country through the turbulent times ahead. Among these promising young minds was our brother, Alazar, the youngest in the family. He was a bright and eager student, studying under the mentorship of the professor and his team.

Alazar's exceptional capabilities did not go unnoticed, and he was selected to be part of the student group tasked with drafting the first Eritrean constitution. This prestigious opportunity led him to various countries for knowledge exchange workshops and an annual conference organised by the US government, where he gained invaluable insights into different legal systems and the structures of both established and newly formed governments.

Meanwhile, in Eritrea, the government grew increasingly discontented with the Western-influenced education being imparted at Asmara University. The law team began publishing papers outlining their vision for a constitution tailored to Eritrea's unique circumstances. These publications were circulated among the populace for feedback, and interviews on state-controlled media further fuelled the government's anger. Officials grew extremely nervous about the idea of sharing power and the possibility of Eritrea becoming a democracy.

The government's unease soon turned into open hostility towards the professor and his team at the University's Law Department. Threats of expulsion and closure loomed large, casting a shadow of uncertainty over the future of the fledgling department. Despite the mounting pressure, the professor remained steadfast in his commitment to imparting knowledge and fostering critical thinking among his students, while attempting to balance the government's political views and opinions. Ex-fighters and agents of the ruling regime, disguised as students and administrative workers, were embedded within the faculty to spy and report to the state security apparatus.

As tensions reached a boiling point, a series of clandestine meetings were held between the professor, his team, and a select few students — including Alazar — to devise a plan to safeguard the department's independence from government forces and ensure its mission could continue. Together, they formulated a strategy to engage with the government and the public in a constructive dialogue, emphasising the importance of diversity in legal education and the benefits of a broad-minded approach to governance.

The professor, the American teachers, and my brother Alazar became intricately woven into the complex tapestry of Eritrea's struggle to create a legal system that would resonate with the global shift in political alignments. Their courage in the face of oppression, their resilience in adversity, and their commitment to the ideals of justice and equality left an indelible mark on the history of a nation striving to find its place in the world. As the winds of change continued to blow through the streets of Asmara, the spirit of defiance and hope embodied by the professor and his allies created a bitter taste in the mouths of those with no clear ideology or alternative plans for the nation.

In a climactic meeting at Asmara University, where minds clashed and ideas collided, no consensus could ultimately be reached. The government refused to allow the Law department to continue its work, accusing it of being a Western puppet, with a renewed focus on killing the constitution before it could be born.

In the heart of Eritrea, a country now scarred by a tumultuous past of struggle and resilience, the professor was known for his dedication to both his homeland and education. A towering figure in legal and academic circles, he was revered not only for his intellect but also for his unwavering commitment to the cause of independence.

During the war for Eritrean independence, the professor had been a passionate advocate for the rebel group on the international stage, representing their interests with eloquence and conviction. His voice resonated far beyond Eritrea's borders, garnering widespread support and sympathy for the struggle of the Eritrean people. When independence was finally won, the professor turned his attention to the monumental task of building the legal framework that would define the new nation.

As an American citizen, the professor was shielded from the immediate dangers that befell those who challenged the Eritrean government. This allowed him to confront officials and authorities who stood in the way of his vision for Eritrea without fear for his safety. His stature among the ex-rebels and the general population was such that his words carried weight and his actions commanded respect.

However, the professor's bold stance soon drew the ire of the Eritrean government, which, on the international stage, was staunchly opposed to Western influence. Allegations of espionage were fabricated to tarnish his reputation and those associated with him. The American teachers and professionals the professor had brought to Eritrea were expelled under the false pretense of espionage, their voices silenced, and their expertise replaced by imported individuals who were willing to bow to the government's whims.

My brother Alazar, a bright young man with a quick wit and a passion for human rights and justice, found himself caught in the crosshairs of suspicion. Having completed his law degree under the watchful eye of the government security apparatus, Alazar received hushed warnings to tread carefully. He was advised to keep a low profile, refrain from speaking about the failed draft constitution, and protect the secrets of the clandestine activities that had taken place within the university's law department.

The government officials were well aware of Alazar's close association with the professor and the American teachers, leading them to cast a shadow of doubt and suspicion over him. Despite the looming threat, Alazar remained steadfast in his convictions, refusing to be cowed by the oppressive regime. His popularity among the people of Asmara, fuelled by his charisma and kindness, only served to deepen the authorities' suspicion of his alleged involvement in espionage. Alazar had given numerous interviews advocating for a democratic parliamentary system to be instilled in the new nation of Eritrea.

As tensions in Eritrea simmered and the process of drafting the constitution was halted, Alazar continued to fight for the legal framework he believed would pave the way for a just and democratic Eritrea. His unwavering determination and his willingness to challenge the status quo inspired a new generation of Eritreans to dream of a better future, even in the face of adversity. However, the government's grip was tightening, and the risks to his life became ever greater, compelling him to consider giving up and leaving the country, like many of his compatriots.

In the fractured and tumultuous political and social landscape of Eritrea, our family found itself entangled in a web of chaos that threatened to tear us apart once again. At the helm stood my father, a man weathered by the relentless storms of bureaucracy and power struggles within the ministry. He bore the weight of a nation's failed promises, the echoes of fallen martyrs, and the looming shadow of uncertainty that gripped him every waking moment. Meanwhile, my brother Alazar faced the ever-present danger of being accused of dissent, a charge that could lead to indefinite detention without trial.

With heavy hearts, both of them navigated the treacherous waters of the government, where alliances shifted like sand dunes in a desert storm. Their once steadfast resolve now wavered as they witnessed the unravelling of the very fabric they had once sworn to protect. The sacrifices of my father's two brothers, along with countless friends, were etched into the fabric of a permanently depressing scene that haunted them at every turn.

Meanwhile, the once bright star of our family, Alazar, found himself at the centre of a colossal scandal that sent shockwaves through the government. His name was plastered across headlines, every move scrutinised under the harsh gaze of a nation on the brink. The government fought tooth and nail to contain the fallout, but the tendrils of the scandal had already seeped into the very foundation of the nation's existence.

Tensions simmered beneath the surface of our family, a grand and unique tapestry woven with threads of ambition, sacrifice, and betrayal. My mother, ever the vigilant guardian, maintained her role as the voice of reason amid the chaos that threatened to consume us. Her steady guidance served as a north star in the storm, a beacon of hope in a sea of uncertainty.

The unexpected imprisonment of fifteen Eritrean government ministers and officials, some of whom were my father's closest friends, struck a devastating blow that reverberated through the nation's very core. As I write this, twenty-five years later, the whereabouts of those officials remain unknown. The looming threat of my father's own capture hung heavy in the air, a spectre of dread that could not be ignored.

In the midst of upheaval and uncertainty, the threads that bound us began to fray at the edges, threatening to unravel the delicate tapestry of our existence. As the shadows of distrust and fear closed in around us, my father stood at a crossroads, torn between loyalty to his nation and the primal instinct to protect his own.

In a land haunted by the ghosts of the past and the uncertain whispers of the future, our family found itself teetering on the edge of a precipice. The lines between right and wrong blurred, and the boundaries of family and nation were stretched to their limits.

In that moment of fear and suspicion, it was not the trials and tribulations that defined us, but the unyielding bond that held us together—a testament to the strength of family in the darkest of times. And as we stood on the precipice of an uncertain future, we knew that no matter what trials lay ahead, we would face them as one, bound by love, loyalty, and the unwavering spirit that had always kept us together as a family.

In the heart of Eritrea, a land once filled with the promise of unity and prosperity, an increasingly dark cloud of militarism loomed over the country, making way for an imminent war with Ethiopia. The government's relentless obsession with armed conflict had transformed the national military service into an interminable mission for the young boys and girls of the nation. As the call for conscription echoed through the valleys and mountains, a wave of despair swept over the youth, driving many to flee their homeland in search of refuge in distant lands.

Among those who remained behind, steadfast and resolute in their duty, was my brother Biruk. Called up for duty and away from his business, he stood tall as a soldier—a beacon of loyalty in a sea of uncertainty. As our family grappled with the disheartening descent of his homeland, my brother Biruk languished in the unforgiving jaws of national military service. Bound indefinitely to the call of duty, he was thrust into perilous missions along the Sudan border, where danger lurked at every turn. The weight of fear and uncertainty bore down on our family, a constant reminder of the fragile threads that held us together.

We had built our enterprise with dreams of growth and prosperity, but as the government's insatiable hunger for war devoured our workforce, the very foundation of our business crumbled. Biruk donned his uniform and marched off to serve, while the business we had once nurtured together began to wither and fade, like wilting petals in the harsh desert sun. Those we had entrusted to carry on our vision succumbed to the call of duty, leaving us stranded in a sea of corruption and deceit.

The once-bustling halls of our establishment now lay empty and silent, echoing with the ghosts of lost opportunities. With each passing day, the weight of dwindling manpower, resources, and vanishing prospects pressed down upon us like a heavy yoke. We struggled in vain to keep the doors open, but the winds of change blew cold and unyielding, forcing us to face a harsh reality.

In a last, desperate bid to salvage what little remained, we made the agonising decision to sell our business at a meagre price, a bitter pill we swallowed with clenched jaws and heavy hearts. Before we could even bid farewell to our life's work, whispers of impending accusations reached our ears, weaving a tangled web of deceit and betrayal around us.

Unprovoked accusations began to surface, casting a dark cloud over our family. It seemed as though someone was determined to tarnish our reputation, to paint us as criminals in the eyes of the law. Shadows whispered about our family and the audio-visual business that had attracted the attention of the authorities. With my father and Alazar already under the scrutiny of the security apparatus, their every move being monitored closely, pressure mounted on us. We knew we had to tread carefully, for the wolves were at our door.

Soon, the government's security services began collaborating with the city licensing office, digging into our business activities with relentless fervour. They pored over our records, inspected our equipment, and secretly questioned our clients, trying to find any hint of wrongdoing.

Amidst the chaos, my father remained stoic, his eyes reflecting a steely determination to protect his family at all costs. Alazar, on the other hand, was visibly shaken by the accusations, his usual jovial demeanour replaced by a grim resolve to clear our name.

The city licensing office, a shadowy institution in the background of our crumbling world, levelled allegations of illegal activities against us, accusing us of involvement in importing and distributing 'forbidden' Western media productions and the sale of uncensored films. As the walls closed in around us, the echoes of past injustices reverberated through our minds—a cruel reminder of the oppressive regime that had once held sway over our neighbouring lands. The accusations sounded like a familiar place from our confrontations with kebele and Shume back in the days of our lives in Addis Ababa.

Fear gripped my heart like icy tendrils as I contemplated the dire consequences of these accusations. I would not let my mother visit another member of this family in jail again. The spectre of imprisonment loomed large, casting a shadow over any semblance of normalcy in our lives. With uncertainty as my only companion, I made the painful decision to distance myself from Asmara, the heart of the storm, seeking sanctuary in the safety of the shadows.

In the absence of a response to the government's allegations and court summons, the city licensing office quickly obtained a warrant to confiscate the business from the new owners just a few weeks into their acquisition. I made a logical and humanitarian decision to refund the new owners, as I thought it would be unfair for them to be implicated in a scandal they did not expect. In a closed, small society like Eritrea, I did not want my family's name to be tarnished in this complex business and political affair filled with deceit and betrayal, instigated by our own government—an institution that was supposed to protect us.

With courage as my shield and determination as my sword, I stood firm in the face of adversity, resisting the tide of oppression and tyranny. Though the road ahead was fraught with peril and uncertainty, I moved forward with steady resolve, determined to carve out a path of my own in a world torn asunder by conflict and chaos.

As the sun dipped below the horizon, casting long shadows across the land, we embraced the uncertainty of the future with open arms, standing tall amidst the wreckage of a fractured world. In the silence of the night, as the stars whispered tales of hope and resilience, we set forth on a journey into the unknown—a journey filled with danger, uncertainty, and impossibility.

For in the heart of darkness, where shadows lurked and fears loomed large, my family discovered the true measure of my strength and resilience. We became a beacon of light in a world consumed by darkness. And as we ventured forth into the unknown, we carried with us the echoes of the past, the whispers of the present, and the hopes of a brighter future yet to come.

Still based and working in Dubai, the bustling cityscape of Addis Ababa—its ever-growing high-rise buildings piercing the sky like modern monuments to progress—became home once again, after I had abandoned my country out of fear of apprehension for crimes I did not commit. The vibrant streets of Addis Ababa buzzed with energy, a stark contrast to the stagnant city of Asmara I had left behind.

The decision to make Addis Ababa my home again was not an easy one. Leaving behind the familiar streets of my childhood in Asmara—once known as 'Piccola Roma' (Little Rome)—was like leaving a piece of my heart behind. The city we had once enjoyed in our youth, and later in its early years of independence, had now descended into neglect. Stray dogs roamed freely, and the once-beautiful streets had fallen into disrepair. This left me with no choice but to seek a brighter home elsewhere.

As I made frequent trips to Addis Ababa from Dubai, I marvelled at the transformation the city had undergone. The government's policies had borne fruit in the form of improved public services, a new airport that gleamed like a jewel, and a skyline dotted with shiny new buildings reaching for the heavens. It was a city on the rise, embracing the winds of change with open arms. The nightlife was now comparable to cities like Bangkok, Nairobi, and Johannesburg.

As my brother Alazar settled into his new life after graduating with a law degree and working as a judge overseeing civil cases in the government law offices, he began to feel a sense of fear and unease that he hadn't experienced in years.

Two years into his new role as a district judge, Alazar received a life-changing invitation from one of his former university professors. The invitation was to pursue postgraduate studies at St. Louis University in the USA—an opportunity that would open doors to a world of possibilities. With the financial help of a family member to cover his tuition and travel expenses, as well as a hefty bond to assure the government of his return, Alazar was granted permission to leave the country. His departure was supported by a family friend who held a position in the Justice Ministry, allowing him to embark on this new chapter of his life with a promise to return home.

In the pulsating heart of the USA, Alazar immersed himself in his studies, driven by a determination to excel and make a difference in the world. He completed his postgraduate studies and passed the bar exams in four states, honing his legal skills to a razor-sharp edge. Yet, as he looked toward the horizon, he knew that his journey was far from over.

As the years passed, Alazar's hard work and determination bore fruit. Together with his wife, he carved a niche for themselves in the property business, leveraging their skills and seizing opportunities to create a prosperous life for their children. His wife and their twin children flourished in the vibrant state of Virginia, surrounded by the warmth of a community that recognised and appreciated them.

Alazar's story was one of courage, perseverance, and the enduring power of hope. From the dusty streets of Asmara to the gleaming skyscrapers of Alexandria, Virginia, his journey was a testament to the transformative power of determination and the unwavering spirit of a man who refused to be bound by the constraints of his past.

In the heart of a chaotic world, my younger brother Biruk stood—a soldier devoted to fighting in endless wars propagated by the government's insatiable hunger for power. Exhausted by the violence and turmoil, Biruk took a courageous leap of faith, abandoning the military and embarking on a treacherous journey by foot to Sudan, seeking solace in the searing heat and vast expanse of the desert.

As Biruk recounted his harrowing odyssey, his eyes reflected the pain of loss as he spoke of comrades fallen in the scorching embrace of the Sudanese desert, their dreams swallowed by the unforgiving landscape. His survival seemed nothing short of miraculous, a testament to his indomitable spirit and unwavering determination to forge a new path.

Finally reaching the shimmering metropolis of Dubai, Biruk found refuge by my side, breathing in the promise of a new beginning. His presence brought a sense of hope and renewal, a beacon of light amidst the shadows of our troubled past.

However, the Eritrean government's ever-watchful eye did not falter. Upon learning of Biruk's disappearance, they enforced their ruthless decree, imposing a hefty penalty on our unsuspecting parents. The weight of their decision bore heavily on our family, threatening to tear us apart.

With the looming threat of our parents' detainment hanging over us, a sense of urgency gripped our hearts. We were forced to pay the government's unjust demand of fifteen thousand US dollars as a penalty for Biruk's desertion. As Biruk started a new life in Dubai, together we stood strong—united in our resolve to protect our loved ones and defy the oppressive forces that sought to break us.

In the face of adversity, Biruk's courage shone brightly, a symbol of defiance against tyranny and a beacon of hope for a brighter tomorrow. And as we stood together, facing the storm that raged around us, a sense of unity and strength enveloped us, binding us together in unbreakable bonds of love and resilience.

In the heart of the Horn of Africa, where the lands of Ethiopia and Eritrea meet, lies a tale of resilience and unity within a family torn apart by the tumultuous tides of political strife. At the core of this narrative is our mother, a strong-willed woman whose unwavering determination served as a guiding light for her loved ones in the face of uncertainty.

Amidst the faded tapestries of conflict and division, our family struggled uphill, each member bearing the weight of their own experiences, shaped by the relentless forces of external influence. As the political landscape shifted, casting shadows of doubt and fear over our once familiar world, our parents stood tall—a beacon of strength and resilience in the storm. Their resolve was unwavering, a testament to the power of love and family amidst chaos.

Through trials and tribulations, each member of our family embarked on a unique path, braving the highs and lows of a life uprooted by the winds of change. Some found solace in the bonds of community, while others sought refuge in distant lands, our hearts forever tied to the memories of the home we had left behind.

Despite the challenges we faced, one thing remained constant—the unbreakable bond of family love that transcended all boundaries. In the darkest of times, we leaned on each other for support, drawing strength from the shared experiences that bound us together as one.

As the chapters of our lives unfolded, our family's story mirrored the larger tapestry of the forgotten war that ravaged our homeland, leaving a trail of devastation in its wake. Millions suffered, lives were lost, and countless others were forced to flee in search of safety and peace.

Yet, amidst the turmoil and chaos, our family's tale stood as a poignant reminder of the enduring power of love and resilience. Our journey may have been marked by hardship and sorrow, but it was also illuminated by moments of joy and unity that transcended the confines of time and place.

In the end, our family stood together—weathered by distance but unbroken—a testament to the indomitable spirit of the human heart in the face of adversity. And though our story may be just one among many in the vast tapestry of existence, its echoes reverberated through the annals of time as a tribute to the enduring power of love and family in a world plagued by uncertainty and strife.

Recycled Conflict

War Pigs

Living for several years in the bustling city of Dubai, I had found a sense of purpose and fulfilment through my work and the life I had built for myself. Living in this modern metropolis opened up opportunities beyond my wildest dreams, allowing me to support my family back in Asmara while also enjoying the company of friends and exploring the vibrant cultures of both cities.

Having embarked on a life of financial independence from an early age, it had always been my responsibility to take care of my parents, especially during times of hardship and uncertainty. With determination and hard work, I managed to secure a stable business in Dubai, enabling me to provide for my loved ones both emotionally and financially. Knowing that my family deserved a comfortable and modern home to call their own, I suggested selling the old villa and contributed to building a second home—more lavish, purpose-built, and better suited to their needs—a modern space where they could find solace and joy.

The process, which started in 1995, was not without its challenges, but with each brick laid and every detail carefully planned, I saw the vision of a better life for my family taking shape. The sale of our previous house in Asmara provided the necessary funds to supplement the construction of a larger and more luxurious home, complete with all the comforts and facilities my parents deserved.

The old family house stood proudly at the end of the winding road, nestled among tall trees and blooming flowers that seemed to embrace its weathered walls. From the outside, it exuded a sense of history and warmth, as though it held the whispers of both good and bad times within its very core. It was a house that was not just a home, but a monument to the family that had resided there for so many years—a living testament to their struggles and triumphs, their joys and sorrows.

Built with love and foresight, the new house was intended to be a gathering place for the entire family, a space where memories would be made and cherished for years to come. Each brick, each beam, had been carefully laid with the intention of creating a place that would witness the laughter of grandchildren and the wisdom of elders—a space where traditions could be passed down from one generation to the next.

Inside, the walls were adorned with photographs capturing moments frozen in time—birthdays, weddings, holidays—each telling a story of love and togetherness. The furniture had been chosen with care, each piece holding a memory or sentiment that added to the tapestry of the family's history. The aroma of home-cooked meals lingered in the air, mingling with the sounds of laughter and chatter that once filled the rooms.

But as time passed, and the government resorted to authoritarian rule, keeping citizens isolated, the house seemed to hold a sadness within its walls—a melancholy that whispered of unfulfilled dreams and broken promises. The family that was meant to fill its rooms with life had scattered to the winds, torn apart by governmental failures and accusations that festered like an open wound. The vision of children and grandchildren coming together under one roof, held in the embrace of loving parents and grandparents, remained just that: a vision, a dream left unfulfilled.

Instead of echoing with the joyous glamour of a reunited family, the house stood silent and empty, its rooms filled with a tangible sense of absence. Each child had fled, with no prospect of returning. The house that was meant to be a beacon of love and unity had become a monument to lost opportunities and shattered bonds. The family's history, written behind its walls in faded memories and untold stories, remained a silent witness to what could have been—a reminder of the fragility of relationships and the cost of pride.

As the sun set behind the family house, casting long shadows across its familiar façade, the ghosts of the past seemed to whisper through its empty halls, lamenting the love that was lost and the dreams left unfulfilled. And as night fell, the house stood alone—a silent sentinel to a family torn asunder, waiting in vain for the day when its halls would once again resound with the laughter and love of those who had once called it home.

Despite the physical distance separating us, the frequent visits my parents made to Dubai allowed us to cherish precious moments together as a family. The fact that they could come at any time, without the hassle of visas under my sponsorship, made our reunions even more special. The laughter, shared meals, and conversations we had served as reminders of the love and bond that held us together, despite the challenges we faced.

However, even amidst the joy of family gatherings and the comfort of our new home, there were shadows of worry that lingered in the background. My father's dissatisfaction with his work in Asmara, and my brother Biruk's prolonged stay in the military, cast a cloud of concern over our happiness. The aggressive policies of the government towards neighbouring countries, and its tight grip on the political system, were sources of unease and tension within our community.

In the bustling city of Addis Ababa, the air was always filled with the vibrant energy of a fast-growing metropolis, where new opportunities seemed to bloom on every corner. For my parents, these journeys to the city were not just about reuniting with old friends and neighbours, but also a refreshing escape from the turmoil back home in Eritrea.

As the plane touched down at Bole International Airport, my mother's eyes sparkled with anticipation. She couldn't wait to see the familiar faces of our old neighbours whom she had left behind. It had been years since they had last met, and the memories of the difficult times they had all endured together still lingered in their hearts.

The reunion was a bittersweet affair, filled with laughter and tears as they reminisced about the challenges they had faced and the strength they had found in each other during those trying times. The bond they shared transcended borders and time, a testament to the resilience of the human spirit.

Meanwhile, my father eagerly caught up with his old friends from his time behind prison walls, who still called him "chairman" from his days as the inmates' chairman of the Workers' Party. The stories they shared ranged from the absurd to the profound, each anecdote a reminder of the shared experiences that had shaped them into the men they were today. Despite the hardships they had endured, there was a sense of camaraderie that kept them all connected, even as their lives took different paths.

As they navigated the vibrant streets of Addis Ababa, my parents couldn't help but marvel at the city's rapid growth and development. The towering buildings and modern infrastructure stood in stark contrast to the struggles faced by their homeland, where the shadow of a government in self-destruction loomed large. It wasn't just the physical landscape that highlighted the disparity between the two nations, but also the personal and professional progress of their friends in Ethiopia.

Some of their friends had climbed the ranks of their careers, landing significant opportunities in peaceful environments where personal and professional growth seemed limitless. My father couldn't help but feel a pang of sadness as he compared their success to the grim reality back home, where arrogance and dictatorship were tearing the nation apart, consuming its people in the process.

The juxtaposition of the two worlds weighed heavily on my father's heart as he walked the streets of Addis Ababa, a city pulsating with life and progress. The contrast between the hope and promise of Ethiopia and the despair and destruction of Eritrea was a painful reminder of the choices and challenges that defined their destinies.

Each time their stay in Addis Ababa drew to a close, my parents carried with them a mix of emotions—gratitude for the joy of reuniting with old friends, sadness for the struggles of their homeland, and a sense of hope for a brighter future. The city had offered them a temporary respite from the harsh realities of their everyday lives, a brief moment of solace in a world plagued by uncertainty.

As they boarded the plane back to Eritrea, my parents knew they would always carry a piece of Addis Ababa with them—a beacon of possibility and potential in a world fraught with conflict and division. And as the plane took off, carrying them back to their homeland, they held on to the memories of their time in the vibrant city, a reminder that in the darkest of times, friendship and hope could light the way forward.

Elsewhere in the world, Eritreans found themselves divided between those who supported the government's approach and those who longed for change and progress. Through discussions with friends and family, we pondered the reasons behind the government's decisions and the impact they had on our lives. While we understood the need for resistance to foreign influences, we also recognised the importance of staying connected to the global community and making concessions for the greater good.

The bold and uncompromising stance of the Eritrean government towards its people and outsiders puzzled us. The reluctance to promote trade, freedom of speech, and engagement with the international community seemed unnecessary and counterproductive. We could see the social and economic fabric of our country unravelling as other nations in Africa and beyond reaped the benefits of economic cooperation in the post-communist world order.

The winding streets of Dubai hummed with life as bustling crowds moved through the city's gleaming skyscrapers and luxurious shopping districts. Amid the opulence and extravagance of this affluent metropolis, I was one individual whose heartbeat was not just for personal success, but for the upliftment of those less fortunate. I had amassed a considerable amount of wealth through my successful business ventures in Dubai, and with this financial prosperity, I found a purpose beyond the mere accumulation of riches.

Guided by a deep sense of compassion instilled in me by my mother, I sought out opportunities to support families in need. Some had found themselves in dire straits due to their own mistakes, while others were simply victims of life's cruel twists and turns. Regardless of the reasons behind their hardships, I was determined to make a positive difference in their lives.

With my mother's wisdom and discernment as a guiding light, we carefully selected families who were in desperate need of assistance. Among them was the family of my friend Abel, who lived just a short distance from our home. Abel's plight was particularly heart-wrenching, as he struggled to make ends meet with no meaningful source of income.

I remembered Abel vividly from our teenage years, a time when the world seemed full of endless possibilities. Together, we roamed the streets with hearts brimming with dreams, navigating the choppy waters of adolescence and clinging to each other as we braved the storms of youth. Abel was a beacon of light, his infectious smile lighting up the darkest corners of our shared adventures.

But the years had not been kind. His eyes, once bright with hope and ambition, were now clouded with the weight of the world. Abel, a product of a modern upbringing that had instilled in him seeds of ambition and hope, had transformed into a shadow of his former self.

Fate, with its cruel sense of irony, had a different plan for Abel. His once idyllic world was shattered by the callous decision of his parents to destroy the very foundation upon which their family had been built. The fabric of their household was torn asunder, leaving gaping wounds that festered with each passing day. The pain of abandonment etched deep into Abel's soul, a wound that refused to heal.

As time passed, I followed our familial affairs from a distance and watched helplessly as Abel's spirit waned. His once steady gaze, full of promise, was now haunted by demons that lurked in the shadows. His descent into darkness was slow but relentless—a downward spiral fueled by the absence of familial warmth and guidance. The void left by his fractured family was a chasm too deep to fill, pushing Abel into the waiting arms of vices that promised fleeting solace.

The jovial boy I once knew was now a mere spectre of his former self, his laughter replaced by the hollow echo of emptiness. Abel sought refuge in the bottom of a bottle, drowning his sorrows in a haze of alcohol that dulled the sharp edges of his pain. Each sip was a desperate attempt to forget, to numb the ache that gnawed at his soul.

I tried to reach out, to pull him back from the precipice that threatened to consume him whole, but Abel was adrift in a sea of self-destructive tendencies, too far gone to be saved by mere words or gestures. The light that had once shone brightly within him flickered feebly, a mere glimmer in the darkness that engulfed him.

And so, I stood by helplessly, a silent witness to Abel's descent into the abyss of his own making. The echoes of our past adventures were now drowned out by the deafening silence that enveloped him. Abel, once a beacon of hope, was now lost in the labyrinth of his own pain, a casualty of a family torn asunder. As I watched him fade into the shadows, I couldn't help but wonder what might have been if the threads of his life had not been so cruelly unravelled.

Through my mother's eyes, I witnessed the gradual deterioration of Abel's physical and emotional well-being. Despite repeated efforts to support him practically and financially, Abel seemed trapped in a cycle of self-destructive behaviours. Instead of using the money provided for his well-being, he chose to indulge in drinking and smoking, numbing his pain with vices that only served to exacerbate his troubles.

Despite the unwavering care and concern showered upon him by my compassionate mother and me, Abel appeared to be on a path of no return, consumed by disappointment and devoid of hope for a better future. Even offers of employment from my kind-hearted father and his friends failed to spark any interest in Abel, who seemed resigned to his fate.

The complexities of Abel's Italian citizenship process further complicated his already tumultuous existence, as the looming spectre of national military service hovered over him like a dark cloud. Abel and his brother found themselves entangled in a web of deceit and evasion, playing a dangerous game of cat and mouse with the government that only served to compound their troubles.

The scenes of Abel's downward spiral painted a bleak picture of a life spiralling out of control. His future was now reduced to a mere shadow of what it could have been. As my mother recounted the heart-breaking sight of Abel, intoxicated and desolate on the streets, tears welled up in my eyes. They were filled with a sense of helplessness, knowing I couldn't rescue Abel from the self-inflicted disaster that awaited him.

In a time before the convenience of mobile phones, the barrier of communication stood as an insurmountable obstacle between Abel and me. Despite the desire to reach out and offer a guiding hand, I was painfully aware of my inability to influence his decisions or alter the course of his life.

Abel was a mysterious figure, whose journey into the lavish world of the elite began with a chance encounter with a wealthy woman who offered him a taste of opulence in exchange for his companionship. Little did he know that this fateful love affair would pave the way for a life of opportunities and success, not just for himself, but for those around him.

I can't forget how Abel and I embarked on our 'diplomatic' venture in the heart of the city, with money provided by his girlfriend. His effortless charm and charisma drew people to him like moths to a flame, and it wasn't long before we forged a bond that transcended mere acquaintanceship. As we delved deeper into the world of the diplomatic community, navigating the intricate web of international relations and financial intrigue, I realised the profound impact Abel had on my own journey toward success.

The connections he had cultivated through our dalliance with the elite circles opened doors I had never dreamed possible. Opportunities bloomed like flowers in spring, and the seeds of ambition that Abel had planted within me flourished. As I stood on the precipice of achievement, basking in the glow of accomplishment, I couldn't help but feel indebted to Abel.

Abel's part in my journey had been the catalyst that propelled me toward success, and the moral debt I owed him transcended mere social responsibility. It was a debt of gratitude, of loyalty, and of acknowledging the pivotal role he had played in shaping my destiny. As I looked back on the winding path that had led me to where I stood, I knew that Abel's early love affair with the rich woman had been the cornerstone of my success, forever intertwining our fates in a symphony of ambition and opportunity.

As the days passed and the sun set over the glittering skyline of Dubai, I found myself grappling with a profound sense of responsibility. The blessings and gratitude of those I had helped served as a source of strength, propelling me to seek out new ways to make a difference in the lives of others.

As I reflected on Abel's plight and the challenges that lay ahead, I vowed to continue my mission of spreading hope and warmth to those in need, despite the obstacles that stood in my path.

In the vast cultural landscape of Dubai, where wealth and prosperity intermingled with tales of hardship and resilience, I stood as a beacon of light, illuminating the way for those lost in the darkness of despair. And though the road ahead may be fraught with challenges and uncertainties, my unwavering commitment to making a difference continued to burn bright—a flame of hope in a world that often seemed devoid of light.

As I juggled the complexities of my life in Dubai, the care for my family, and the contemplation of the political landscape back home, I realised that my journey was far from over. Building a better future for my loved ones meant navigating through challenges and uncertainties while holding onto the hope of a brighter tomorrow. In the heart of bustling Dubai, amidst the glittering skyscrapers and busy streets, I found solace in the love of my family and the support of friends, creating a haven of warmth and belonging in a world of fleeting uncertainties.

In the rugged, sun-scorched lands of Ethiopia and Eritrea, a simmering rivalry that had festered for years between the Tigrayan Liberation Front, now EPRDF, and the Eritrean Liberation Front, re-baptised as PJDF, finally erupted into a full-scale war in 1998. Both factions, once allies in the fight against a repressive military government, had now turned against each other, driven by deep-rooted disagreements in ideology, ethnic discrimination, border disputes, and ill-planned economic partnerships.

The release of the new Eritrean currency, Nakfa, marking Eritrea's independence from the Ethiopian monetary system, ignited the already escalating tensions, as small border skirmishes morphed into full-blown conflict. Long-forgotten border disputes became mainstream agendas for war. Behind closed doors, attempts at reconciliation faltered. Discussions regarding questions of reparations to Eritrea, changes in the use of ports by landlocked Ethiopia, and disagreements over how to settle future trade and transactions only fuelled the flames of animosity. The blood of villagers and soldiers spilled freely on both sides of the border, opening wounds that seemed impossible to heal.

The two former rebel leaders, once accustomed to resolving conflicts through the barrel of a gun, now found themselves at the helm of a war that would claim the lives of nearly a million people on both sides. Ethiopia, with its vast economic resources and massive population, threw its men and war machines into the fray, determined to crush the Eritrean resistance. Meanwhile, Eritrea, with its limited resources and a population brimming with nationalism and patriotism, rallied its people under the banner of defending their hard-won freedom, mustering every ounce of strength and determination.

As the war raged on, grinding the people's hopes of a better future into dust, the once vibrant lands of Ethiopia and Eritrea became stained with the blood of their own citizens once more. The Eritrean government, facing an existential threat, decreed the enrolment of all able-bodied individuals under sixty into the war effort, while mobilising millions of dollars from its diaspora population to sustain their defence. The world watched in horror as the two nations tore each other apart, driven by arrogance and personal grudges between their leaders.

In the midst of this chaos, amid the deafening roar of gunfire and the acrid scent of smoke, individuals on both sides found themselves caught in a maelstrom of devastation and despair. Families were torn apart, dreams shattered, and lives lost in the name of misguided leaders' pride and stubborn defiance. The endless cycle of violence, deportations, and destruction seemed to consume everything in its path, leaving behind a trail of broken spirits and shattered souls.

In the heart of bustling Dubai, amidst the gleaming skyscrapers and crowded streets, I found myself entangled in a web of intrigue and betrayal—all stemming from the tragic expulsion of Eritrean families at the hands of the Ethiopian government. It was a period of turmoil and uncertainty, a time when the bonds of friendship and loyalty were tested, and the consequences of war reverberated through every interaction.

The once vibrant Eritrean community in Ethiopia was torn apart as families were uprooted and forced to flee their homes and businesses, seeking refuge in foreign lands with uncertain futures. The Ethiopian government's sudden and draconian decision to expel all Eritreans triggered a wave of panic and despair.

Flights were suspended, and communication between the two nations was severed, plunging both countries into a state of isolation and hostility reminiscent of darker times.

As the Eritrean exodus unfolded, we witnessed harrowing scenes of families being loaded onto buses and dumped at the borders, their lives irreversibly altered by the whims of political powers beyond their control. Those who had the means fled to various countries, with Dubai emerging as an easy gateway and a beacon of hope for many seeking sanctuary and a chance to start anew. It was a bittersweet sight: seeing my fellow Eritreans arrive in a land of opportunity, but with the knowledge that their homeland was no longer a viable option for return.

Amidst this chaos, I found myself at a crossroads, grappling with the personal and professional consequences of the conflict. As someone involved in the shipping business, which had previously thrived on trade with Ethiopia, I saw my clientele dwindle as relationships fractured along political lines. Former clients abandoned me in favour of other compatriot shippers, driven by long-held resentments and animosities that had simmered beneath the surface for years.

Left with a handful of Eritrean clients, my business took a nosedive, plummeting to less than fifty percent of its former size, as trade and imports from both countries dwindled in the wake of war.

In the small city of Asmara, Eritrea, the effects of the senseless war were deeply ingrained in the fabric of every family. The once vibrant streets were now filled with sorrow and despair, as news of fallen soldiers and devastated homes spread like wildfire. Among those entangled in the web of destruction was Biruk, my brother—a young man whose life had taken a drastic turn since he joined the national military service.

Biruk, a spirited soul with dreams of entrepreneurship, had never been free since he was drafted into the military at a young age, like many of his peers. Now in his sixth year in the army, little did he know that his path would lead him to witness horrors that no one should ever have to endure. Assigned to various fronts of the brutal war, Biruk was exposed to the grim realities of combat, where men and women fell victim to the merciless bullets and explosives that ravaged the land.

Despite the chaos surrounding him, Biruk found solace in his role within the logistics division of the military. Driving heavy trucks to replenish ammunition and supplies, he managed to avoid direct engagement in the bloody battles that raged on. His proficiency behind the wheel, honed by his passion for driving since a young age, kept him away from the frontline, but it did not shield him from the haunting images of his fallen comrades that lingered in his mind.

As the war dragged on, the toll it took on the nation became increasingly evident. Comparisons were drawn to previous conflicts, highlighting the staggering number of lives lost in just two years. The once proud forty-year struggle for independence now felt overshadowed by the devastation wrought by this new war, with casualties reaching a grim milestone of a million lives.

Amidst the turmoil and tragedy, the resilience of the Eritrean people was broken. Families gathered in hushed tones, mourning the loss of their loved ones and grappling with the uncertainty that the war brought. In every home, there was an empty chair, a missing voice, a void that could never be filled.

For my brother Biruk, my uncle Belay, and many other young Eritreans, the war had stripped away their youthful optimism, leaving behind a hollow shell of the boys who once dreamed of a brighter future. The sights and sounds of battle had etched themselves into their memories, a constant reminder of the price paid for the folly of arrogant political leaders who played with the lives of their people as if they were mere pawns on a chessboard.

As the days turned into weeks, and the weeks into months, Biruk found himself at a crossroads. The war had taken its toll on his spirit, leaving him adrift in a sea of pain and sorrow. The once clear path to his dreams was now obscured by the fog of war that clouded his mind.

In the midst of this turmoil, a glimmer of hope emerged. A chance encounter with a fellow soldier, who had returned from the frontlines with a message of peace, sparked a tiny flame of possibility in Biruk's heart. Could it be that, amidst the chaos and destruction, there was still a chance for redemption? Was there a way to reclaim the dreams that had slipped through his fingers like grains of sand?

With renewed determination, Biruk set out on a journey of self-discovery, seeking to make sense of the senseless war that had torn apart both his homeland and his soul. Along the way, he encountered stories of resilience and courage—of families torn apart and rebuilt, of hope rising from the ashes of despair.

As he traversed the war-torn landscapes of Eritrea, Biruk bore witness to the scars left by conflict, both physical and emotional. The once vibrant towns now lay in ruins, their buildings battered and broken, a stark reminder of the futility of war. Yet, amidst the rubble, he found signs of life—laughter and tears intermingling in a symphony of humanity.

The once bustling market towns now lay in ruins, their streets echoing with the cries of the wounded and the dying. The verdant countryside, once teeming with life, now bore the scars of war—its fields trampled, its rivers stained crimson. Amidst this wasteland of despair, stories of courage and resilience emerged. Ordinary individuals rose above the chaos to help their fellow countrymen, offering a glimmer of hope in the darkness.

And so, the war dragged on for another two long, excruciating years, grinding the people of Ethiopia and Eritrea into submission, testing their resolve and their humanity. As the world looked on, aghast at the senseless violence and destruction unfolding before their eyes, one could only wonder how two nations, once united in the fight for freedom, had descended into such a pit of despair and bloodshed. Phone and transport lines were cut off once more, as were trade and businesses, separating the two peoples in a more devastating way than it had been under the previous regime.

As the divisive political storm swelled between the neighbouring nations of Ethiopia and Eritrea in the heart of the Horn of Africa, the global political landscape and alliances were also shifting, largely due to the war on terror. With a cunning display of global influence, the Ethiopian government falsely linked Eritrea to international terrorist groups in Somalia and the Middle East, tarnishing its reputation on the world stage.

Swiftly, the West, already at odds with Eritrea, imposed harsh sanctions, severing its international relations with organisations like the UN, EU, IMF, and the World Bank. The once-vibrant streets of Eritrea now echoed with the cries of a people plunged into poverty and hardship, their livelihoods stripped away by the weight of the embargo.

As the sun set over the barren landscape of Eritrea, a sense of defiance and anger simmered within the government halls. Fueled by a deep-seated resentment towards the West, they stood tall with arrogance, their diplomatic skills worn thin by the relentless onslaught of isolation and injustice.

In the shadows of despair, the Eritrean diaspora emerged as a symbol of resistance. With unwavering determination, we rallied fellow citizens, inspiring them to resist the suffocating grip of international condemnation. Together, we formed a grassroots movement, united in our defiance against the unjust sanctions imposed on our homeland.

Against all odds, the people of Eritrea found solace in their unity—a flicker of hope amidst the darkness of their plight. As the world watched with bated breath, the stage was set for a battle of wills between a government fuelled by anger and a resilient populace yearning for justice and redemption.

In the end, as the war dust settled, followed by 20 years of a 'no war, no peace' status, a fragile agreement was reached to defuse the situation. New international borders were demarcated, and a buffer zone was established, managed by a UN peacekeeping mission. A 50km buffer zone was formed between the two countries, and the once-proud lands of Ethiopia and Eritrea stood scarred and battered, their people forever changed by the horrors of war.

As the two nations began the arduous task of rebuilding their shattered lives and fractured communities, one could only hope that the lessons learned from this dark chapter in their history would serve as a beacon of light, guiding them toward a future of peace and reconciliation.

As I attempt to capture the essence of the thirty-third Eritrean Independence Day in my memoir this week in May 2024, I am overwhelmed by the profound sorrow and despair that have clouded the nation over the past three decades. Eritrea, once a beacon of hope and promise under the leadership of the ex-rebel dictator Isaias Afwerki, now stands as a grim reminder of shattered dreams and lost potential.

In the early days of independence, Afwerki had grand ambitions of transforming Eritrea into the 'Singapore of Africa'—a vision of prosperity and progress that captured the imaginations of many. However, as time passed, this lofty goal gave way to a stark reality of economic ruin and political repression. Instead of flourishing like Singapore, Eritrea found itself dubbed the 'North Korea of Africa,' a nation trapped in a cycle of tyranny and isolation.

The ageing ex-rebel leadership, still in power and now in their twilight years, continue to rule with a heavy hand, their grip on power fuelled by ignorance and a blatant disregard for the well-being of their people. The promises of a brighter future have faded into oblivion, leaving behind a population burdened by a multitude of hardships.

State-sanctioned kidnappings, arbitrary arrests of journalists and intellectuals, and the forced conscription of young men and women into indefinite national military service have characterised the last three decades of the 'free' Eritrea. The spiralling cost of living has driven people to the brink, reminiscent of the harsh rationing measures of the past. The tyrannical government penalises families of absconding children with heavy payments, leading some citizens into a lifetime of debt to pay the government or face imprisonment. Those who cannot pay have been imprisoned indefinitely—a brutality that has never been seen, even in the worst days of the military regime that the rebels claimed to have liberated the people from.

As Eritreans around the world wove through their lives, the conversation among the people increasingly turned to the state of their beloved Eritrea. It was a topic that weighed heavily on everyone's hearts. They knew all too well that the challenges facing their nation went beyond just the government's shortcomings. Whispers of Western interference and the influence of puppet regimes in Africa added a layer of complexity to their struggles.

Despite the external pressures, my fellow peace-loving patriots and I believed in the power of diplomacy. We were convinced that with careful planning and strategic dialogue, Eritrea could navigate the treacherous waters of international politics and carve out a path towards coexistence with the world.

However, as the day turned to dusk and internal political opinions shifted, a sense of frustration lingered in the air. The failure of the Eritrean government to engage in meaningful consultations with its own people had left a gaping void in the nation's quest for progress. Their defiant stance, combined with limited resources and a lack of diplomatic finesse, had created a recipe for disaster.

As we gazed up at the starry sky, our hearts heavy with concern for our homeland, we knew that the road ahead would be challenging. But we also clung to the glimmer of hope that, with unity, resilience, and a renewed commitment to dialogue, Eritrea could rise above the obstacles that threatened to tear it apart.

Eritreans continued to whisper silent prayers for their country—a beacon of strength and resilience in the face of adversity, a land where peace-loving patriots like my family dared to dream of a brighter future.

With each passing Independence Day, the façade of celebration masks the deep-seated anguish and despair that permeate every corner of the nation. The diaspora, longing to return to their homeland, is met with silent bans and insurmountable barriers, further deepening the rift between the nation and its exiled sons and daughters.

Against this bleak backdrop, the stories of the people of Eritrea unfold—those who dared to speak out against the regime, only to vanish without a trace, leaving behind grieving families and silenced voices. My brother Biruk, a conscripted soldier forced to leave his family behind and endure the brutality of military service, saw his dreams of a peaceful future shattered by the harsh realities of war. Now, he lives in Dubai, running a small logistics business to support his family of three children.

Today, in the dusty streets of the capital city of Asmara, a palpable sense of fear and resignation hangs heavy in the air. The once vibrant markets now stand deserted, the laughter and chatter of the people a distant memory. The colourful buildings, remnants of a bygone era, serve as a stark contrast to the sombre mood that grips the city.

As the sun sets on another 'Independence Day' in Eritrea, a sense of futility and despair lingers in the hearts of its people. The hopes and aspirations of a nation once filled with promise have been crushed under the weight of tyranny and oppression. And yet, amidst the darkness, a flicker of resilience remains—a glimmer of hope that one day, the shadows of despair will give way to the light of freedom and renewal.

But for now, Eritrea stands as a testament to the enduring spirit of its people: a nation scarred by the horrors of war and political self-destruction, yet its people resilient in the face of adversity. And as I pen down these words, I can only pray for a brighter tomorrow, where the echoes of suffering and sorrow will be replaced by the promise of a new dawn.

Desperate for a lifeline in the wartime economy, I turned to an unexpected source of income: bidding on tenders for Eritrean government ration and clothing supplies and becoming an informal purchasing agent for the Eritrean Defence Forces, tasked with supplying essential provisions, such as food and blankets, to support their troops in the conflict.

But the murky waters of war proved treacherous. I soon found myself entangled in a web of clandestine dealings and questionable practices orchestrated by the highest echelons of power. Tasked with coordinating funds from Eritrean embassies and business units worldwide, I was thrust into a world of covert transactions and shadowy alliances, all under the watchful eye of the president's office.

As the conflict escalated, through my office in Dubai, I was drawn deeper into the heart of darkness, tasked with facilitating the transfer of Ukrainian commanders and experts contracted by the Eritrean government to install specialised air defence systems at exorbitant prices. Despite my reservations, I complied with their demands, fearing the repercussions on my family if I dared to refuse.

In a twist of fate, my linguistic skills and negotiation prowess were put to the test when I found myself embroiled in the negotiations for the purchase of a small helicopter from Chechen rebels in the breakaway region, who were locked in their own conflict with the Russian government. A German arms broker named Mark, whom I had met in the ports of Dubai while brokering marine spare parts, entered the scene, offering a transport helicopter and pilots for sale at an undisclosed location in Chechnya. The deal was shrouded in secrecy and uncertainty.

The Russian-made cargo helicopter, captured intact by Chechen fighters under mysterious circumstances, was sold for a fraction of its market value in dollars. The transaction was facilitated through my company, using falsified documents and forged papers. As the helicopter embarked on a convoluted journey from the mountains of Chechnya to Syria and later Iran, destined for a mysterious port to be shipped to Eritrea, the deal went awry when the aircraft was intercepted by another group of Iraqi rebels. Mark, the elusive broker, vanished without a trace.

Caught in the aftermath of a failed arms deal, I found myself tasked with chasing down Mark—a task fraught with danger and uncertainty. The hard-earned million dollars I had made vanished in a haze of deception and betrayal, a stark reminder of the high stakes and dire consequences of operating in the shadows of war and conflict.

As the dust settled on the failed deal and the echoes of the conflict began to fade, I was left to grapple with the weight of my actions I couldn't avoid, the involuntary risks I had taken, and the toll it had taken on my conscience. In a world where loyalty and betrayal often walk hand in hand, I found myself at a crossroads, unsure of where my allegiances truly lay and what price I was willing to pay for survival in a landscape full of shifting loyalties and hidden agendas.

Sweat beaded on my forehead as I typed furiously on my laptop in my dimly lit office. The weight of the dangerous game pressed down on my shoulders as I grappled with the web of deceit I had found myself entangled in. What had started as a simple brokerage and translation role in an army helicopter deal had spiralled into a nefarious conspiracy with no way out.

Every forged invoice, every falsified travel document, painted a damning picture of my unwitting involvement in a shadowy affair. The Eritrean government, desperate to resolve the mystery of the missing helicopter and Mark's disappearance, had turned their scrutinising gaze towards me. I could feel their suspicions closing in, tightening like a noose around my neck.

With my company's name used in the transactions and its bank accounts involved, I had unwittingly become a legitimate target for investigation. The stakes were high—my very life, and the safety of my family, were on the line. The weight of guilt and fear bore down on me as I realised that the only way out was to delve even deeper into the darkness that threatened to consume me.

Despite the Eritrean government's silence, with no one asking me directly to act, I believed they thought I had conned them, colluding with Mark in a treacherous scheme. But the truth was far more sinister and convoluted than they could imagine. As I embarked on a perilous mission to unearth the real culprits behind the disappearance, I understood that the path ahead was fraught with danger and uncertainty.

The clock ticked ominously in the silence of the night, each passing second a reminder of the perilous tightrope I now walked. With steely resolve and a heart weighed down by the burden of my actions, I braced myself for the treacherous journey ahead, determined to save not just my own soul, but the lives of those I held dear.

In the heart of Dubai, where luxury and ambition intertwined in a dance of shimmering lights and towering structures, Mark—the retired German marine officer turned arms dealer—was a shadow that moved with the whispered currents of the underworld. His presence was felt, yet unseen by many. It was in the lavish surroundings of the Hyatt Regency Hotel, on the Deira side of Dubai, that I finally laid eyes on him after many months of searching and luring him with fake crude oil deals.

The air inside the hotel was thick with the scent of opulence—a heady mix of perfumes and expensive colognes that masked the darker intentions lurking beneath the surface. As I made my way through the marble-floored lobby, headed toward a meeting with another contact, my eyes scanned the faces of the well-heeled guests, searching for the one familiar figure among the strangers. And there, sitting at a corner table in the plush lounge, was Mark.

His weathered face bore the lines of a life lived on the edge; the sharp angles softened by a pair of piercing blue eyes that seemed to hold the weight of a thousand secrets. Dressed in a simple, old suit that betrayed nothing of wealth or power, Mark exuded an aura of danger that drew me in, even as it sent a shiver down my spine.

I approached his table with caution, my heart pounding in my chest as I prepared to face the man who held the key to my future—with a glimmer of hope to retrieve some of the funds I could return to the Eritrean buyers. With a forced smile, I took a seat across from him, my hands clenched tightly in my lap as I braced myself for the conversation ahead.

"Mark," I began, my voice steady despite the nerves threatening to betray me, "I have a business proposition for you. A lucrative opportunity to supply black market crude oil from a Middle Eastern source. But first, we need to clear up the misunderstanding surrounding the previous transactions. The Eritrean government has tasked me with investigating the matter, or I'll face criminal charges at the state level."

Mark's eyes flickered with interest, a knowing smile tugging at the corners of his lips. He leaned back in his chair, steepling his fingers beneath his chin, his gaze cool and detached, sending a chill down my spine.

"Ah, a bold move, my friend," he murmured, his voice like silk over steel. "But I'm afraid I'm not interested in discussing your helicopter deal. The officials in the Eritrean embassy in Riyadh already messed that up themselves. They went behind my back, making their own shipping arrangements and routes with a shipping agent known for concealing illicit cargo from the prying western forces in the Persian Gulf, instead of following my recommended plan. Why did they do that? I had already arranged a false cargo manifesto for the shipment to avoid detection," Mark claimed.

My heart sank at his words, the weight of disappointment crashing down on me like a ton of bricks. I'd pinned my hopes on this meeting, on the promise of a new beginning. But now, it seemed as if everything was slipping through my fingers, like sand running out of my grasp. The revelation—the breach of protocol, the state secret—it could have serious implications for the officials involved in the shipping arrangements. Should I confront them with this new knowledge? Or should I conceal what I had learned and leave the president's office unaware?

Mark continued, bitterness edging his tone as he recounted the chain of events that had led to the deal's failure. Some Eritrean diplomatic officials based in the Saudi capital, with the help of Ukrainian dealers, had cut him out of the loop. They made their own arrangements, leaving him without his rightful commission on the shipping deal—a commission of which I was also owed a part. The Chechens, too, had denied any involvement in the group that had seized the cargo under mysterious circumstances, leaving Mark with nothing to show for his efforts. The helicopter was transferred to another cargo ship at an undisclosed location in the mid-Persian Gulf. The newly appointed shipping agents had ransomed the shipment, demanding payment the Eritrean government owed for several expensive, hurried air and sea shipments of Ukrainian arms. To add misery to the already complex story, the shipping agents had held a grudge against the Eritrean government for not assisting with insurance claims for a civilian cargo plane that crashed on the outskirts of Asmara, fully loaded with explosives imported from Ukraine. They were not willing to release the helicopter unless the Eritrean government compensated them with funds more valuable than the price of this precious cargo.

As he spoke, a surge of anger and frustration rose within me, a burning need to hold someone accountable for the money that had slipped through our fingers. But as I looked into Mark's steely gaze, I knew that there would be no recourse. In this world of deceit and greed, there was no justice, no way to make things right.

With a heavy heart, I rose from my seat, the weight of resignation settling over me like a dark cloud. I knew then that there was nothing more to be done, no way to undo the mistakes that had led us to this point of no return.

As I walked away from the table, Mark's words echoed in my mind—a haunting reminder of the high-stakes game we'd played and lost. After cutting short another meeting, distracted and disillusioned, I stepped out into the glittering streets of Dubai, surrounded by the whispers of wealth and power. But as the lights of the city shimmered around me, I couldn't shake the thought of how the Eritrean government had implicated me in this mess—a naïve, inexperienced player caught in a dangerous web of secrets and lies.

In the end, as my business in Dubai returned to a feasible level—though still far from where it once stood, casting long shadows across the city—I was left with lingering questions and a deep sense of unease. The scars of the arms deal, in which I had only tried to help without getting too deeply involved, remained. The war ran deep, and the choices made in the heat of conflict would haunt me for a lifetime. Beneath the glittering façade of a city built on ambition and opportunity, I was constantly reminded that hidden below the surface was a world of darkness and deceit, where the lines between friend and foe blurred, and the stakes were high.

In the heart of Dubai, amidst the lavish skyscrapers and opulent malls, a different kind of story unfolded. It was a tale of unexpected connections, hidden alliances, and a sense of duty that transcended borders and ideologies.

I found myself at the centre of this clandestine world, where an essential part of the Eritrean government's war effort took shape behind the closed doors of my small office in Dubai. It all began with encounters with a high-ranking Eritrean official, who had come to the city for secret meetings and dealings related to the ongoing conflict. His main objective was to secure supplies of basic commodities for the Eritrean army. Many officials in his position were inexperienced in international diplomacy and trade, relying heavily on the assistance of ordinary Eritreans living abroad.

Dubai, being the ideal market for such supplies, quickly became their go-to hub for handling the intricate web of business transactions that helped keep the Eritrean government afloat during these turbulent times. My office became a nerve centre for arranging bank transactions, organising shipments, and producing official documents. Despite the high stakes involved, the officials I worked with exuded a sense of humility and guilt over their government's actions, which made me empathise with their plight.

As my role in this underground network deepened, I forged close relationships with officials not only in Dubai but also in Asmara, the capital of Eritrea. They entrusted me with crucial tasks: from shipping vital equipment to arranging urgent financial transactions. There were moments when I received direct phone calls from the highest offices in Eritrea, instructing me to recover funds from embassies around the world and send USD cash to Asmara to pay their East European contractors, mainly Ukrainians. At times, I was required to make swift decisions, including flying to Asmara with a briefcase of cash, assisted by Eritrean Airlines staff at the Dubai airport, in order to maintain secrecy facilitated by the Dubai government, which helped avoid questioning the contents of my hand luggage by authorities at the airport. It was a high-pressure environment where every decision I made impacted the war effort in some way.

Despite the risks, I found myself drawn deeper into this world of clandestine operations and high-stakes diplomacy. The sense of nationalism and patriotism that permeated the air, following the Ethiopian government's actions against Eritreans, fuelled my dedication to the cause. Though there were no significant monetary benefits from these high-risk tasks, my intention was not to support the government itself, but to support my people and my country. The spectre of losing our hard-won independence loomed large, and it was a time of uncertainty and fear.

I threw myself into the war effort with unwavering determination, doing whatever was necessary to support the Eritrean people in their time of need. Whether it was arranging shipments of vital supplies or facilitating financial transactions, I became a crucial link in the chain that kept the war machine running. The demands were relentless, the deadlines tight, but I never wavered in my commitment to the cause.

In the streets of Asmara, the once-vibrant capital that bore the scars of past conflicts, my journey continued to unfold—a tale of unexpected friendships, loyalty, and redemption in a world shaped by war, politics, and the price of survival.

As an individual with vast experience of the past and unwavering support for the war effort, I cultivated relationships with officials and influential figures, which paved the way for my entry into the inner circle of power. With a blend of competence and charisma, I navigated the corridors of authority with ease, earning the respect and admiration of those in high positions. These relationships went beyond mere professional alliances, blossoming into enduring friendships that transcended boundaries.

Among this eclectic mix of companions were former rebels-turned-statesmen, individuals who had bravely fought in the tumultuous conflicts that had defined Eritrea's recent history. Bearing both physical and emotional scars from their past battles, these seasoned warriors carried the weight of their sacrifices with dignity. Some still bore the remnants of bullets lodged in their bodies for years, while others struggled with health and financial challenges stemming from their war wounds and insufficient salaries.

Moved by compassion and gratitude, I selflessly embarked on a mission to alleviate the suffering of these comrades. I provided support for medical treatments, including laser eye surgeries, false dentures, and minor surgeries, easing the burdens that had plagued them for years. Furthermore, I extended gestures of kindness by footing the bill for gifts they bought for their loved ones, showcasing a generosity that transcended mere financial transactions.

In return for these acts of kindness and unwavering loyalty, I received invaluable support from those in high places. Allegations related to my past audio-visual production business were swiftly dispelled, clearing my name of any lingering doubts or suspicions. The officials went a step further, offering assurances and guarantees of safety, paving the way for my safe return to Eritrea after a prolonged absence of four years.

However, the weight of the doomed helicopter deal still hung heavy in the air, casting a shadow over my reputation within the core of the government. With a determined expression, I began to present the new findings revealed by Mark, hoping to shed light on the mystery that had tarnished my name.

As I carefully explained the details in every meeting with officials, one official who had visited Dubai had eyes filled with anger at the revelation of what might have led to the disappearance of the precious cargo. His tone cut through the tension as he revealed that he knew the individuals responsible for rerouting the shipment in an effort to evade detection and save on shipping costs. The gravity of the situation hit me like a ton of bricks as I realised the extent of the deceit that had unfolded, including the ongoing efforts by the government to recover the helicopter or its value. He gave me a clue that the Eritrean president's office knew which foreign groups were involved and what exactly had happened.

With a sense of urgency, the official promised to escalate the information to the highest levels of the Ministry of Defence in order to clear my name. I seized the opportunity to emphasise that my actions had been driven by a genuine desire to support the war effort through my company, even if it meant bending the rules.

In that crucial moment, I made it clear that there had been no personal gain in the dealings—only a deep-rooted commitment to assisting the government using the resources at my disposal. My integrity and unwavering dedication to the cause shone through, painting a picture of a man driven by altruism rather than a personal agenda.

As the discussion unfolded, my underlying good intentions and selfless acts of assistance to the government emerged as powerful testimonies in my quest to redeem my name. With the support of the officials and the newfound clarity on the situation, a glimmer of hope flickered in the room, signalling the beginning of a path toward redemption and exoneration.

Unconfirmed rumours about the missing helicopter started to surface slowly. Apparently, some Eritrean officials had dealt with an Iraq-based business group they had known through previous links involving shipments of cheaply sourced oil and arms from the parallel market to Eritrea. It was that group that must take full responsibility, as there was an unresolved, controversial transaction from their previous dealings. The helicopter, it seemed, had been held hostage for their demands.

As I set foot once again on Eritrean soil, a wave of nostalgia and emotion washed over me. Despite the changes that had occurred in the once vibrant city of Asmara, the sense of familiarity and belonging enveloped me like a warm embrace. The officials who had stood by my side welcomed me with open arms in recognition of my service, facilitating my reintegration into the fabric of Eritrean society.

Navigating the bureaucratic mazes of government offices became a seamless endeavour, thanks to the unwavering assistance and guidance provided by my esteemed new friends. Through their collective efforts, obstacles were overcome, and challenges were met with resilience and determination. My return to Eritrea symbolised a homecoming of sorts—a reconciliation with a land that held both memories of strife and dreams of renewal.

As the days unfolded, I found solace in the simple joys of camaraderie and shared experiences. The laughter and conversations shared with my parents, my newfound and old friends echoed through the narrow alleyways of Asmara, bridging the gaps of time and distance. Together, we forged a bond that transcended politics and power, a bond built on mutual respect, trust, and solidarity.

In the midst of this intricate tapestry of relationships and alliances, I discovered a profound sense of freedom and acceptance. The past suspicions and doubts that had haunted me for years melted away in the warmth of friendship and understanding. As the sun set over the ancient city of Asmara, casting a golden glow over its weathered buildings and cobbled streets, I realised that true wealth lay not in riches or accolades, but in the intangible treasure of genuine connections and shared experiences—especially with family.

And so, my journey in the presidential circle of Eritrea came full circle, a tale of redemption and reconciliation set against the backdrop of a nation rebuilding itself from the ashes of conflict. In the embrace of my new friends and allies, I found a sense of purpose and belonging that transcended borders and boundaries—a testament to the enduring power of friendship and forgiveness in a world marked by turmoil and uncertainty.

In the heart of Asmara, amidst the rugged landscape and vibrant streets, a quiet revolution brewed within the walls of restaurants and cafes. As a passionate advocate for change, I found myself entwined in conversations that shaped the destiny of my nation.

Open and frank discussions had become the norm in my interactions with officials. They acknowledged the flaws in governance and the areas in dire need of rectification. Yet, a prevailing sentiment lingered: a deep-rooted belief that alternative solutions were synonymous with Western ideologies, threatening the very existence of Eritrea unless it submitted to Ethiopia.

As I drove with some officials around Asmara for business and pleasure, heated debates ignited between passengers inside our cars, adorned with traditional artefacts—a clash of ideals echoing through the corridors of power. We delved into the complexities of Eritrea's future, visions of progress pitted against fears of compromise. Each argument, each exchange, fueled by passion and conviction, failed to permeate the stalwart minds at the top.

Amidst the fervour of discourse, a sense of disillusionment settled upon me. Despite the fervent discussions and unwavering dedication, the winds of change seemed hesitant to sweep through the halls of authority. The walls echoed with voices yearning for transformation, for a brighter tomorrow, yet the shadows of resistance loomed large.

As the sun dipped below the horizon, casting a golden hue over the city, I reflected on the complexities of governance and the uphill battle for reform. The work was far from over, the journey fraught with obstacles, but a glimmer of hope remained—a flickering flame that refused to be extinguished in the face of adversity.

And so, the discussions continued, the voices of dissent growing louder, reverberating through the heart of Eritrea—a testament to the resilience and unwavering determination to shape a future free from the shackles of the past.

In the end, as the conflict slowly reached its conclusion, I looked back on my time in the shadows with a mix of pride and weariness. I had played a small but significant role in supporting the Eritrean government during its time of need, and that was a legacy I would carry with me forever. The bonds forged, the challenges overcome, and the sacrifices made were all part of a chapter in my life that I would never forget. And as I conducted my business from Dubai, I knew that I had done my part in a story that was much larger than myself.

As the dust settled and the echoes of battle faded, I looked back on the path I had tread—a path that intertwined my fate with that of a nation embroiled in turmoil. Through trials and tribulations, I had emerged not just as a facilitator of transactions, but as a steadfast ally, committed to upholding the values of courage and sacrifice that defined the Eritrean spirit. And in that realisation, I found solace, knowing that in the crucible of war, bonds forged in the fire of adversity burn brightest.

As the streets of Asmara greeted me once again, I couldn't shake the heavy feeling that settled in the pit of my stomach. With each visit, it became more apparent that my father's fire was slowly dwindling, his once-bright ambitions fading into the background. He was a man who had always dreamt of making a significant contribution to society, but circumstances beyond his control had hindered his journey.

I would often find him sitting in the dimly lit living room, staring into the distance with a sense of resignation in his eyes. His days were now filled with idle moments, the weight of unfulfilled aspirations pressing down on him like a heavy burden. Despite my best efforts to encourage him, nothing seemed to reignite the spark that once drove him forward.

Beside my father, my mother stood as a pillar of strength, her weary eyes silently pleading for a break from the hardships that life had thrown her way. I took it upon myself to be their companion, providing the emotional and material support they needed to navigate through the rough waters. While my father seemed to have resigned himself to his fate, my mother's resilience never failed to inspire me.

But it wasn't just my parents who occupied my thoughts during my visits to Asmara. My dear friend Abel, once a vibrant and energetic young man, was now a shadow of his former self. The signs of a serious illness had begun to manifest themselves, with his constant coughing serving as a grim reminder of the battle he was fighting.

I took Abel to countless medical appointments, watching helplessly as his condition deteriorated with each passing day. The diagnoses ranged from tuberculosis to typhoid, each revelation sending a wave of despair through his fragile frame. I made sure he had all the medications he needed, but in my absence, he would neglect his health, his once lively spirit fading into a haze of hopelessness.

Every time I returned to Asmara, I found Abel in a more precarious state, his hollow eyes reflecting a deep sense of resignation. He would dismiss my concern with a weak smile, urging me to focus on my own life instead of worrying about his dwindling existence. His days were spent confined to his bed, the outside world a distant memory he could no longer afford to engage with.

It was heart-breaking to witness the transformation of Abel, a young man full of charm and skills, descend into a mere shadow of his former self. The vibrancy that once defined him had now been replaced by a haunting stillness, a stark reminder of the fragility of life.

As I bid farewell to Asmara once again, the weight of the stories I carried with me lingered in the air. My father's fading ambitions, my mother's unspoken sacrifices, and Abel's battle against an unseen foe were etched in my memory, reminding me of the delicate balance between hope and despair that defined the human experience.

The two brotherly Horn of Africa nations, Ethiopia and Eritrea—once united in a common struggle for freedom and prosperity—had now become embroiled in a bitter conflict over disputed borderlands and personal egos. The war between the two countries had raged on for two years, with neither side able to gain a decisive advantage. Countless lives had been lost, villages razed to the ground, and families torn apart. The international community, weary of the bloodshed and suffering, stepped in to broker a peace agreement.

And so, in the hushed halls of diplomacy, the infamous Algiers Agreement was born. Signed under the watchful eyes of the International Court of Justice, it awarded most of the contested borderlands to Eritrea. A binding agreement, it was meant to bring an end to the hostilities and pave the way for reconciliation between the two nations.

But peace proved elusive. Ethiopia, smarting from what they saw as a defeat, rejected the agreement, plunging the region into a state of stalemate for the next two decades. The Ethiopian government, backed by its powerful allies in the West, launched a relentless campaign to discredit and isolate the Eritrean regime.

Accusations flew on the global stage, with Ethiopia making it central to its foreign policy to claim that Eritrea was a terrorist state. These allegations, whether true or not, gave the wary West the pretext they needed to impose full sanctions on Eritrea. The already diminished nation found itself more isolated and ostracised, its economy in ruins and its people suffering under the weight of internal and external political chaos.

In the streets of Asmara, the Eritrean capital, the impact of the sanctions was keenly felt. The once bustling markets now stood empty, their shelves bare. Families struggled to put food on the table, and the spectre of poverty loomed large over the city. This dire situation continues to worsen, as the government, three decades after claiming to have freed Eritreans from oppressive regimes, remains increasingly reluctant to make changes to its policies. The suffering of the people persists, and Eritreans, who gave their lives for freedom and peace, are still waiting for the dignity and rights they were promised.

Third Time Unlucky

Every time You Go Away

In post-war Eritrea, a false pride of victory and the shadow of fear of another war engulfed the nation. It was a time when the political winds blew harshly, carrying with them the cries of the oppressed and the whispers of the silenced. Scholars and ordinary citizens alike found themselves trapped in a web of injustice, imprisoned without reason or reprieve.

The government, desperately grasping for control amid growing unrest, resorted to ever-harsher administrative rules to quell dissent and opposition. The echoes of war still haunted the land, and the support lent by neighbouring Ethiopia only fuelled the flames of instability. As the dust settled after the conflict, Eritrea found itself isolated, shunned by the international community and subject to crippling economic sanctions. The once-bustling streets now lay desolate, the once-welcoming borders now sealed shut, turning the country into a pariah state where hope seemed a distant memory.

Western embassies stood shuttered, their flags no longer fluttering in the breeze. NGOs and humanitarian organisations, once beacons of light in times of darkness, had vanished, leaving behind a void of aid and support. The government's erratic behaviours bred uncertainty, turning day to night and back again in unpredictable rhythms that kept the populace on edge.

Amidst this turmoil, a poignant tragedy unfolded. Young souls, seeking a chance at a better life, embarked on perilous journeys across the unforgiving expanse of the Saharan desert, their dreams carried on winds of desperation. Mothers wept for their children, lost to the ravages of war or swallowed by the merciless sands of the desert. News of Eritrean youth perishing in the desolate wastes of the Sahara and the treacherous waters of the Mediterranean Sea reverberated across the globe, each heart-breaking tale etched into the annals of tragic history.

Eritrea, once a proud nation with a rich cultural heritage, now stood on the brink of a population decline unparalleled in modern times. Low birth rates, a consequence of young men trapped in endless military service, combined with the exodus of dissenters fleeing the tightening grip of oppression, saw the country bleeding its youth at an alarming rate. Every day, thousands fled across the borders, seeking sanctuary in foreign lands, leaving behind a homeland steeped in sorrow and uncertainty.

With no foreign investments to bolster its shattered economy and no local initiatives to offer a glimmer of hope, Eritrea plunged deeper into the abyss of poverty. Jobs vanished like whispers in the wind, leaving the populace bereft of livelihoods and prospects for the future. Families found themselves adrift, caught in a maelstrom of despair, their once-vibrant communities reduced to shadows of their former selves.

And yet, amidst the darkness, a flicker of resilience burned in the hearts of the Eritrean people. In the face of adversity, they clung to their traditions, their stories, and their shared history, which bound them together as one. Despite the trials and tribulations that beset them, they stood united — a beacon of hope amidst the storm.

Though the road ahead was fraught with challenges, the spirit of Eritrea endured, a testament to the indomitable will of a people who refused to be extinguished. And as the world looked on, witnessing the hardships that befell this once-proud nation, Eritreans around the globe fought their own battles, confronting personal challenges in a world of economic uncertainty, while also striving to alleviate the lives of those they left behind — a tradition inherited from their fathers, who had supported their loved ones even before independence.

The air in all government offices was thick with tension and uncertainty, as whispers of a major reshuffle among those at the top of departments spread like wildfire. Civilian workers anxiously eyed each other, wondering who the next victim of the sudden changes would be, sweeping through the departments. The once-familiar faces now seemed masked with apprehension, knowing their jobs were at stake.

In the midst of this chaotic atmosphere, my father, a dedicated and experienced employee, found himself caught in the crosshairs of this uncalculated upheaval. As the ageing ex-rebels, who had long complained about feeling neglected, were ushered in to replace the civilian workers, my father's fate was sealed. He was abruptly summoned to his office one fateful afternoon, unaware of the storm that was about to hit his life.

A woman, accompanied by two imposing men, approached my father with a resignation letter in hand. His disbelief was palpable as the reality of the situation began to sink in. Despite the dishonourable manner in which he was being removed, a small part of him felt a strange sense of relief. Deep down, he had wished for a way out of the suffocating environment that had become his workplace. However, the abruptness of it all left him reeling, unable to process the whirlwind of emotions crashing over him.

Complying with the orders, my father rose from his chair and made his way to the cabinet in his office to collect his personal belongings. His camera, laptop, and other mementoes of a career dedicated to serving his country awaited him within the confines of his desk. But as he reached out to gather his possessions, the woman's stern voice halted him in his tracks. He was forbidden from touching anything, barred from entering his own office, as though he were a criminal on trial.

Confusion and humiliation mingled in my father's eyes as he tried to explain his intentions, only to be met with a dismissive statement from the lady. The threat of an investigation loomed overhead as she warned him that they would inspect his belongings and call him if any personal items were deemed unfit to belong to the state. With a heavy heart and wounded pride, my father was escorted out of his workplace, his head hanging low as he was sent home — a shadow of his former self.

Upon returning home, the weight of the day's events bore down on my father, and he recounted the ordeal to my mother. Her expression mirrored a mix of fear and despair as she witnessed the mental and emotional toll this unjust removal had taken on her husband. In a country where discrimination and mistreatment by successive governments had become the norm, this latest blow struck deeper than any before.

The timing couldn't have been worse. How many heartbreaks could one man endure, especially at such a mature stage in his career? Despite his love for his work and unwavering ethics, the unexpected plunge into early retirement left my father grappling with feelings of loss and disorientation.

Days turned into weeks, and weeks into months, as the ministry's calls served as a stark reminder of the surveillance that loomed over him. The subtle threat embedded in their messages — warning him against seeking employment elsewhere — left him feeling like a marked man. The silence surrounding his personal belongings only added to the sense of abandonment and betrayal he felt.

Without a sense of purpose or direction, my father began aimlessly wandering the city, seeking solace in fleeting encounters and idle conversations with old friends. He visited his tennis club, where he had once played competitively with many of his friends, most of whom now no longer existed. Their shock at his sudden downfall was met with an unspoken understanding that delving into the reasons behind his dismissal was a taboo subject, best left untouched.

As my mother and I tried to lift his spirits with trips abroad and distractions, the shadow of uncertainty and injustice continued to haunt my father's every step. The suggestion of seeking asylum in a foreign land, where he could start anew, was met with a resolute refusal. His pride refused to accept handouts or seek refuge elsewhere; he was determined to face whatever lay ahead in his own land.

With each passing day, my father's routine became a monotonous cycle of reading books, travelling aimlessly, and grappling with the scars left by systems that had failed him. The once-vibrant man who had dedicated his life to serving his country now found himself adrift in a sea of uncertainty — a casualty of forces beyond his control.

And as the months turned into years, the echoes of his forced departure lingered like a ghost in our lives, a testament to the unforgiving reality faced by many good citizens who had fallen victim to the ever-changing tides of politics and power. My father's resilience and unwavering spirit in the face of adversity served as a beacon of strength, a reminder that true dignity and honour could never be stripped away, even in the darkest of times.

In the bustling streets of Dubai, where the sun glinted off the towering skyscrapers, I was going about my usual business when a surprising call from my mother interrupted the flow of the day. Confusion washed over me as I had just spoken to both my parents the night before, leaving me wondering what urgent matter she had forgotten to tell me.

Normally, when my mother calls me, she starts her conversation with banter and jokes, but this time her tone was different. She inquired about my well-being and morning routine, which struck me as unusual since she often kept conversations short due to the expensive cost of calls from her location in Asmara. Sensing something was amiss, I cut straight to the point and asked her if everything was alright.

Her trembling voice conveyed a sense of urgency as she divulged the shocking news: our father had been taken for questioning. Despite assurances that he would return by the end of the day, my mind was clouded with disbelief. It felt like a surreal nightmare, and I bombarded my mother with questions she couldn't fully answer.

The news of my father's detainment shattered the fragile peace of my existence once more. Memories of his previous incarcerations flooded my thoughts, each time leaving a deep scar on my family's heart. As I sat in my car outside the warehouse I had come to visit, a whirlwind of emotions engulfed me. The fear and uncertainty of my father's future, and the overwhelming sadness of his plight, weighed heavily on my shoulders. I wished I could shield my beloved father from the harsh realities of his world, but I was just a mere spectator in the cruel drama of our lives.

I thought about our father, locked up in a cold, sterile cell, his spirit slowly crumbling under the weight of his circumstances. I imagined the despair in his eyes, the heaviness in his heart, and the longing for freedom that must have consumed him. The thought of him enduring this injustice once again broke something inside me.

In that moment, a haunting thought crept into my mind. The overwhelming sense of hopelessness and despair made me question the purpose of my own existence. The pain of witnessing my father's suffering, coupled with the crushing weight of our reality, made me feel as if the only way to escape this never-ending cycle of misery was to selfishly end my own life.

But as the tears silently streamed down my cheeks, a small glimmer of resolve ignited within me. Despite the darkness that threatened to consume me, I found strength in my love for our family. I vowed to fight against the shadows that loomed over us with the same strength as before, to hold onto the flickering flame of hope that refused to be extinguished.

In the midst of despair, I relied on a newfound determination to keep our family together, to weather the storm that threatened to tear us apart. With this resolve, I silently vowed to be the beacon of light that would guide them through the darkness, no matter how dim the flame might burn.

As tears welled in my eyes, I voiced my fear and anxiety, murmuring words of regret and guilt. It pained me to hear my own anguish as my mother spoke of our supposed punishment for their sins. In that moment, a surge of determination rose within me—to do whatever it took to support my family.

Promising my mother that I would fly in the next day if necessary, I reassured her that we would navigate this crisis together. Despite the distance between us, the bond of love and solidarity resonated strongly, anchoring us during this unforeseen storm. And as I hung up the call, the vibrant streets of Dubai blurred into the background, overshadowed by the weight of uncertainty that now loomed ahead.

With each passing hour, my anxiety mounted, fuelling a frantic flurry of calls to government contacts, pleading for information and reassurance about my father's safety. Promises of updates were made but never fulfilled, leaving my family in a state of limbo, grasping at straws for any semblance of truth or justice. Days turned into weeks, and weeks into months, with no sign of my father and no concrete explanation for his sudden disappearance.

Struggling to make sense of the inexplicable situation, I flew back and forth from Dubai to be with my mother, risking my own life as the files of allegations related to our business were not closed. With informal assurance from close friends in government who had work relations with me, I decided to return with determination, leaving no stone unturned in our quest for answers. The ambiguity surrounding my father's arrest gnawed at my sanity—a relentless anxiety that refused to abate, leaving us trapped in a state of perpetual uncertainty and fear. Desperation drove me to seek a direct audience with the president himself, but my plea for my father's release fell on deaf ears as the wheels of bureaucracy ground on, indifferent to the anguish of a family torn apart.

It wasn't until a faint glimmer of hope emerged in the form of Araya, a friend working in the national security office whom I had met through another official some months earlier, that I saw a chance. Araya had previously asked me to buy a video camera for his son, who aspired to be a wedding videographer. When I learned that his budget wouldn't cover the cost of a decent camera, I offered to pay the difference, and his order was fulfilled within days. Araya, deeply grateful, thanked me from the heart and vowed to return the favour.

After speaking to Araya in person, I could see the sorrow he felt. He had met my father when he came to our home to pay the money for the camera. My father had actually liked him, describing him as a very funny man with optimistic views. Araya, who had come to deliver the money, spent hours talking to my parents, praising me for my deeds.

Araya later returned with a sliver of insight into my father's whereabouts. He had been detained over issues related to his work at the Ministry of Agriculture, supposedly being held for questioning—an explanation that offered little solace amidst the lingering shadows of uncertainty.

Finally, some six months into my father's captivity, a ray of light pierced the darkness when Araya orchestrated a rare opportunity for me to visit my father. It was a chance laden with trepidation and heartache. Stepping into the compound of 'Edaga Hamus' prison camp, in the centre of Asmara, the air was heavy with foreboding. I was led to the investigator's office, where my father sat—a mere shadow of the man I once knew. His face, fully covered with hair, his eyes, nose, and mouth obscured by a bushy beard, was barely recognisable.

His once robust frame had diminished, his features obscured by an unkempt beard, and his hollow eyes revealed the toll his captivity had taken on him. My heart shattered at the sight of my father's physical and mental deterioration. The walls of the prison seemed to close in around us, suffocating the remnants of hope that clung to my soul.

My father, with a stony expression, uttered his first faint words: "Did you bring food for me?" He didn't say hello; he asked for food—a testimony that he hadn't eaten proper food in months. It was difficult for me to tell whether that question came as a result of mental or physical malfunction.

The investigator, a stern figure nicknamed "Kebaz," meaning 'hopeless' or 'desperate,' disrespectfully replied, "Why are you asking him for food? Does he look like a waiter to you? We give you good food every day, don't we?" He laughed. That was the cruellest treatment of a fellow human being I had ever witnessed. Kebaz then added, "You'd better talk about something else you may have, because your 30 minutes are running out quickly."

As the fleeting moments of our visit slipped away, words remained unspoken between us. A chasm of silence bridged the growing gulf of pain and separation that loomed large, while Kebaz admonished me for my tears, a harsh reminder of the constraints imposed by a system devoid of compassion or empathy.

With a heavy heart and a soul weighed down by grief, I watched as my father, barely ten minutes into our meeting, rose unsteadily. A ghostly figure in a land of shadows and despair, he chose to end the meeting and return to his cell. The investigator led him away, leaving me to grapple with the harsh reality of our fractured existence—a family torn apart by forces beyond our control.

As I was escorted out of the prison building, the echoing silence of that cold, desolate place reverberated in my ears—a haunting reminder of the injustices that lingered like a dark cloud over our lives. In that moment, I vowed to fight for my father's freedom, to defy the odds, and to reclaim the shattered pieces of our family's disrupted harmony.

With a heavy heart and a burdened conscience, I became a shadow in my own life, concealing the truth from the one person who held my heart—my mother. The weight of my father's mysterious captivity pressed down on me, threatening to shatter the fragile façade of normalcy I had carefully crafted for her.

As I navigated the maze of legal pathways, each corridor seemed to lead me deeper into the enigma surrounding my father's imprisonment. The Minister of Justice, a close family friend, her hands tied by the jurisdiction of a clandestine special court, revealed the complexity of the web of extra-judicial systems in which my father was ensnared.

Desperation drove me to seek out Kebaz, the enigmatic figure holding the strings of my father's fate. His cryptic responses and veiled accusations only added layers to the mystery that shrouded my father's predicament. The special court, cloaked in secrecy, held sway over high-profile cases, including the detention of fifteen former ministers and PFDJ central committee members in a remote, undisclosed location.

In our darkest hour, a glimmer of hope emerged in the form of Araya — a trusted ally with connections that would prove invaluable in our quest for justice. Together, we breached the walls of bureaucracy and came face to face with Kebaz, the elusive figure entrusted with my father's fate.

In a clandestine meeting arranged by Araya, the whispers surrounding my father's alleged crimes painted a damning portrait that clashed with the man I knew. Mismanagement of funds, covert dealings with foreign entities, aiding the escape of a supposed Israeli spy, orchestrating protests by scholarship students, and defying the government's principles — the accusations swirled around him like a dark storm. I was given a strict order not to discuss my father's case with anyone. I was warned of the dire consequences that would follow for both myself and my father if I breached this order.

My meeting with Kebaz was cloaked in veiled threats and false accusations, leaving me no closer to understanding the charges levelled against my father. With each revelation, a chilling realisation dawned upon me — my father's life was entangled in a sinister dance of shadows and deceit, orchestrated by unseen forces. The tendrils of conspiracy reached far and wide, threading through the very fabric of power and manipulation. One truth, however, seemed clear: this was the masterwork of the minister who despised my father. He had used his position to entrap my father at his most vulnerable and defenceless state, organising an investigation with the help of the woman who had replaced him in a degrading manner.

With each allegation laid bare, I felt the ground shift beneath my feet, the foundations of my belief in my father's innocence shaken to the core. The weight of betrayal and deceit threatened to suffocate me, but a steely resolve burned within me, driving me to uncover the truth, no matter the cost.

As I delved deeper into the intricacies of my father's downfall, the threads of truth and manipulation became entwined, blurring the lines between friend and foe. Betrayal lurked in the shadowed corners, whispering tales of treachery and deceit.

In a daring move to unravel the tangled web of lies, I attempted to venture into the heart of the Special Court, where the puppeteers of power pulled the strings that dictated the fate of many. The Special Court, which has no physical existence, is a virtual collection of officials at the top of the power hierarchy, conducting investigations through their handpicked investigators and making decisions on individuals' lives. This ghostly court system does not carry out trials. Suspects are not allowed to have lawyers, nor are they permitted to defend themselves. The process is simple: a suspect is apprehended indefinitely while the investigation is carried out. The final decision is based solely on the investigator's opinions, not on any actual findings, which leads to the person's fate being sealed.

Amidst the labyrinthine corridors and hidden chambers, I uncovered a truth more sinister than I could have imagined. The façade of justice crumbled, revealing a grim reality where innocence and guilt blurred into a murky haze of power and corruption.

Desperate to shield my mother from the harsh reality, I put on a brave face and assured her that all was well, though the weight of her husband's predicament bore down on me like a heavy burden. The whispered rumours of the special court, shrouded in secrecy, only fuelled her determination to unravel the truth behind my father's sudden disappearance.

In a final confrontation with Kebaz, the truth was laid bare in all its brutal clarity. The accusations against my father were myriad and damning — a mosaic of transgressions that painted a portrait of a man I barely recognised. The web of deceit and betrayal extended far beyond my father's actions, entangling him in a tapestry of personal vendetta and political intrigue that threatened to consume him.

And so, against all odds, and in the shadow of a system determined to silence justice and truth, I vowed to stand tall and unyielding — a force of nature in a world where secrets and shadows reigned supreme. In the heart of darkness, a light shone bright, illuminating the path towards justice and redemption for my father and all those who stood against the tyranny of power. It all started with the ex-rebel turned minister, a man whose eyes mirrored the flames of a forgotten war, seeking vengeance wherever he could.

The minister, his pride wounded by a clash with students demanding justice, seized upon my father as a scapegoat for his own failings. With fervour fuelled by old grudges and a thirst for power, he concocted a tale so twisted that even the shadows shivered in disbelief.

Accusations flew like arrows from the minister's lips, claiming my father had orchestrated the rebellion that threatened to tear his department apart once more. In a frenzy of paranoia and desperation, the minister raided my father's office, searching for evidence to veil his deceit.

Books and papers were torn asunder, their whispers of truth drowned out by the thunderous lies woven by the minister's skilled tongue. The scent of betrayal lingered in the air, choking the very essence of justice like a noxious cloud.

Yet, as the dust settled and the echoes of falsehoods faded into the ether, the truth emerged like a phoenix from the ashes. The students, with fiery passion in their eyes, stood by my father's side, their unwavering belief in his integrity shining brighter than any falsehood the minister could muster.

As things became clearer later, it emerged that the accusations made by the ex-rebel-turned-minister, highly embarrassed by his encounter with the South African students, were baseless. He had falsely accused my father of organising the rebellion, using everything found in my father's office to support further allegations.

Among the piles of files in the cabinet and his personal laptop, they selectively pulled a few documents and created their own narratives, without even asking my father to explain the circumstances of these dealings. My father had been contacting various donors for financial and technical assistance to alleviate his department's budgetary shortfalls. He had received funds through official channels and made decisions with full records of how they were used. He had rented warehouses from private landlords to store machinery for the projects, and he had adhered to the proper tendering processes.

The supposed friendship with an Israeli man named Elan was nothing more than a professional acquaintance. The so-called spy who later fled the country had no special connection with my father, apart from working as a part-time consultant for a friend who owned a farm. My father had attended a few meetings over dinner when the Israeli expert was introduced to the farm owner, but there was no deeper involvement. The Israeli, a specialist in irrigation, was privately contracted by the ministry and is said to have doubled as a spy. He had been previously accused of espionage and political meddling in Ethiopia before moving to Eritrea.

My father had opened the door for educational exchange with a more experienced South African and could not have had any ill-intended connection to the students. The riot in which the minister was humiliated was a response to his harsh approach. It later came to light that the Chancellor of Cape Town University, without realising the consequences to my father, had written directly to the minister, criticising his inappropriate behaviour at the prestigious institution and the instability it had caused among the students. He had concluded his letter by recommending my father, whom he respected greatly, to deal with the matter further. This became the catalyst for the minister's revenge, plotting his venomous, deadly attack on my father.

The weight of the false accusations hung heavy in the air, casting a shadow over every conversation and interaction.

The drama of the situation was palpable, like a thick fog that obscured reason and fairness. My father, once a respected figure in the department, now found himself isolated and vilified. The uncertainty of the future loomed over us like a storm cloud, casting a sense of fear and helplessness. The once vibrant and lively home now felt like a sanctuary under siege, the walls echoing with the whispers of betrayal and deceit.

My determination to clear my father's name and restore his reputation became a beacon of hope amid the turmoil. With each passing day, I tirelessly worked alongside friends to gather evidence and build a case to refute the baseless accusations, in the unlikely event of a future trial. I spoke to everyone implicated in the cases, including the Chancellor of Cape Town University, asking him to request that his government write a letter of support for my father on a state level.

I travelled across the country, investigating the alleged contraventions of the procurement process, even obtaining copies of contracts from the landlord of the warehouse. With no access to the official paper trail, I gathered as much evidence as I could. However, sharing this evidence with any officials was a forbidden task, as per Kebaz's warning.

The relentless pursuit of truth became a defining characteristic of my father's fate. Our unwavering commitment to justice and integrity inspired those around us, breathing life into the suffocating atmosphere of doubt and suspicion. As the days turned into weeks, the tide began to shift. The truth, like a beacon in the darkness, slowly emerged from the tangled web of lies and deceit. Gradually, the pieces of the puzzle fell into place, revealing the orchestrated nature of the accusations. The ex-rebel minister's vendetta against my father became glaringly evident, and the once murky waters of uncertainty began to clear.

It had been a year and a half since my father's captivity, and every day felt like a battle against an invisible enemy. My mother, once a pillar of strength, had become a shadow of her former self, worn down by the relentless uncertainty that hung over our family. With no progress made in our efforts for a fair trial or release, we felt as though we were swimming against an unyielding current. The weight of helplessness pressed down on us, and my mother's only solace was her prayers. I, on the other hand, had to continue working in Dubai, navigating the power corridors to secure my father's release. It seemed like an insurmountable task, but I couldn't give up.

As I sat in front of my computer in my apartment in Dubai, browsing the latest news on Eritrean affairs, my heart raced with a mix of hope and fear. Then, an unexpected opportunity presented itself. I stumbled upon an article about the Eritrean president's visit to the USA to meet the diaspora. The website announced a virtual Q&A session where citizens from around the world could present their questions about the nation's state in real-time that evening. It was a slim chance, but it felt like a lifeline in the vast ocean of despair. Should I take the risk and present my father's case, even though it could potentially worsen his situation as the public would become aware of the injustices taking place in Eritrea? The dilemma gnawed at me, but in the end, I decided to seize the opportunity.

I drafted and redrafted my question, carefully omitting names but pouring my heart into the plea for my father's release. It was a message that could either seal his fate or offer a glimmer of hope.

As the sixty-minute Q&A session commenced late that evening, I submitted my question with trembling fingers, hoping it would be selected from the multitude of inquiries flooding in. The president, known for his charismatic yet arrogant nature, answered questions with a careful balance of reassurance and pessimism.

Fifty-six minutes had passed, and my question remained unread, lost in the sea of submissions. As the session drew to a close, a sense of unease settled over me. Was it mere coincidence that my question had been overlooked, or was there a deliberate intention behind it? The uncertainty gnawed at me as I watched the screen, hoping for a chance to voice my concerns. Then, as if by some mysterious design, my question appeared as the final query to be addressed. A lady's voice, tinged with stern concern and unmistakable emotion, echoed through the computer's speakers as she read out my words. The president, whose image was not visible, began addressing my question, his expression unreadable.

As he began to respond, his words felt general rather than personal. He spoke of ensuring fair justice for all, acknowledging that some investigations may take longer than others. His voice held a hint of regret, but no apology, as he expressed that no citizen should endure such hardships. Yet his words felt empty, lacking the depth of understanding I longed for. I couldn't shake the feeling that my concerns had been brushed aside, lost in the grandeur of the event. The president's response left me disillusioned, longing for a time when justice was more than just a hollow promise.

But in the final moments of the session, the president asked if I minded sharing my father's name and messaging him directly to see if there was any further help he could provide. Without hesitation, racing against the seconds ticking away, I typed my father's name and his last position and clicked the send button. Just as the presenter made a closing statement, thanking the president and everyone for their participation, the screen closed automatically, leaving me unsure whether my message had gone through the live messaging system.

As I left the session, the air outside felt heavy with the weight of unspoken truths. The mystery of my unanswered question lingered in my mind, blending with a sense of nostalgia for a time when voices were heard, and justice was more than just a distant ideal. I found myself retracing the steps that had led me to this moment, delving into memories of a world where hope and determination had once thrived. The characters around me blurred into a backdrop as I immersed myself in thoughts, seeking solace in the echoes of a past that seemed to hold the key to understanding the present. In that moment, I realised that the mystery of my unanswered question was only a fragment of a much larger enigma—one that resonated with the echoes of a nostalgic yearning for a time when justice was not just a distant dream.

The aftermath was a whirlwind of conflicting emotions. Friends and relatives, who recognised me from the anonymous story that could only relate to me, congratulated me on crafting a powerful question without mentioning names—unaware that I had, in fact, shared my father's identity in full detail. The weight of my decision bore down on me, and I grappled with the fear that I might have endangered my father even further. It was a moment of reckoning—a gamble that could either bring about a breakthrough or deepen our family's plight.

The days that followed were shrouded in suspense as we waited for any sign of change, any glimmer of hope amidst the relentless storm of uncertainty.

I spoke with my brother, Alazar, the weight of my recent actions heavy on my mind. As a law professional with a solid understanding of the context, Alazar had a keen insight into the potential consequences of my actions, and I sought his analysis on what might happen next. To my surprise, he offered a congratulatory nod, affirming that it was a shot worth taking. His words brought a sense of reassurance, but the uncertainty of the future still loomed large in my thoughts.

In the following weeks, a significant turn of events unfolded. The Minister of Justice, a close family friend, returned home to share her elation with my mother. She had accompanied the president on his visit to the USA and had been following a pivotal interview from her hotel room. As she met with the president later that evening, she deliberately brought up the last question, making a strategic but careful move to advocate for my father's release. The president, acknowledging the injustice of my father's prolonged incarceration, expressed his willingness to intervene. His consideration for my father's two martyred brothers, and my brother Biruk's service to defend the country, prompted him to instruct the Minister of Justice to transfer my father's case to the civil court for a fair trial.

As my mother relayed this hopeful news to me over the phone, in the presence of the minister, a sense of relief washed over me. The minister, whom I had never met, extended her congratulations, acknowledging the bravery and quick thinking I had shown, adding that we were the true products of our caring parents. Her familiarity with Alazar, stemming from their connections during his studies at the Law Department at Asmara University, added a layer of personal connection to her compliments. She had always admired his intellect and foresaw his potential for high-ranking positions within her department. However, her admiration was tinged with the bittersweet memory of assisting in his departure from the country, recognising the danger he faced due to his bold approach and outspokenness while working on the national constitution. She assured us of her commitment to assist, now that the case had fallen under her department's purview.

The unfolding events brought a mix of emotions—hope, gratitude, and a renewed sense of determination. The uncertainty that had clouded my thoughts began to dissipate, replaced by a glimmer of optimism for my father's impending trial. As I reflected on the interconnectedness of my actions and the impact they had on the unfolding events, I couldn't help but marvel at the power of courage and strategic advocacy. The journey we had embarked on, driven by a sense of justice and familial love, had led us to this pivotal moment, where the possibility of a fair trial for my father seemed within reach.

As the Justice Minister continued her relentless pursuit of my father's case, I found myself caught in a whirlwind of frustration and hope. Her determination to navigate the ghostly corridors of the special court, under the president's instructions, was both admirable and disheartening. Despite her efforts, the elusive nature of the court and its lack of response to her queries only added to the mystery shrouding my father's situation. It became apparent that I needed to take matters into my own hands, urging the minister to contact the interrogator, Kebaz, directly. Reluctantly, he transferred my father's files to her, a process that dragged on for an additional six weeks, adding to the mounting tension.

As the minister delved into my father's case, she discovered that it was deemed a civil matter, not warranting the special court's attention due to its lack of threat to national security. Kebaz fiercely advocated for my father's case to remain under his jurisdiction, expressing disdain for external interference. Undeterred, the minister invoked the president's name, compelling Kebaz to relinquish the files to her. Her tenacity and resolve were truly remarkable, and I found myself clinging to the hope that justice might finally prevail.

Upon concluding her investigation, the minister determined that my father could be tried under her department, prompting her to issue a warrant for his transfer to a more humane prison. However, the revelation of my father's whereabouts sent shockwaves through our family. He had been secretly hospitalized for over a month, enduring multiple health crises, including strokes, falls, and a broken arm. The image of my father, secluded in a guarded room within a public hospital, left me reeling with a profound sense of helplessness and despair.

Despite the minister's efforts, Kebaz, filled with his unjustified excessive sense of revenge, remained reluctant to disclose my father's location or files, requesting additional time to facilitate the transfer. He reasoned that he hadn't finished his investigation, eighteen months after my father's detainment.

Meanwhile, in Dubai, I encountered an individual who had been detained in the same prison as my father. This man, involved in the construction business, had been unjustly accused of fraud after his business partner absconded with millions of dollars intended for purchasing building equipment for a government construction project. As he recounted my father's plight, his emotions overflowed, painting a harrowing picture of my father's deteriorating health and the suffering he had endured in solitary confinement. The man told me that my father had been moved from solitary confinement to a communal cell after he required constant care due to his frequent strokes and falls.

This man, with whom I had partnered in shipping his merchandise, shared many stories about my father's daily struggles during the time they shared the same cell. He revealed that my father had been so weak that he hadn't heard a single word from him during their shared confinement. Despite their own hardships, the inmates did their best to help my father. To the other inmates, my father didn't seem like someone who belonged there. The man described how all the other inmates, regardless of what they had done, appeared suspicious, but my father was like an angel sitting among devils. The man told me that my father had multiple fractures on both his arms following falls because of his physical and mental fragility. Yet, he was only bandaged without proper medical care to mend his broken bones, leaving him in constant pain and immobility. He was fed by inmates as he couldn't use his hands.

I had to conceal this information from my mother to protect her from an emotional breakdown at a time when she was already enduring so much.

The encounter with the businessman, who had been a witness to my father's suffering, left me shattered. I grappled with the injustice that had befallen my father, questioning why he had been subjected to such unimaginable torment, multiple times in his lifetime. The weight of his anguish, combined with the uncertainty of his future, weighed heavily on my heart, casting a shadow over the once cheerful world I had known.

The power struggle between the justice minister and the interrogator continued to escalate, creating an atmosphere of tension and uncertainty. I found myself caught in the middle of this political turmoil, desperately trying to navigate the complex web of deceit and manipulation surrounding my father's case. The exchange of documents and the relentless pressure from the security apparatus only served to further complicate an already convoluted situation. It was a constant battle to ensure that my father received a fair trial and that justice prevailed in the face of overwhelming opposition.

As I returned to Asmara with the shocking news of my father's condition, a glimmer of hope emerged. A compromise had been reached to separate the espionage cases from the civil ones, with the latter to be handled by the civic justice system. This agreement also promised to disclose my father's whereabouts, offering us a semblance of relief amid the turmoil. However, our hopes were quickly dashed when, unbeknownst to us and the minister, my father was abruptly returned from the hospital to the notorious prison, leaving us feeling helpless and betrayed.

Despite the setback, the minister pressed for my father's expedited trial in the civic court. It soon became apparent that his accusers were woefully unprepared, lacking the basic understanding of the legal process. With no charge sheet, no legal representation, and no substantial evidence, my father's lawyer skilfully navigated the proceedings. As a result, all charges were dismissed, and the cases were closed before they even reached trial. It was a small victory in the face of overwhelming adversity, but it reignited our hope and determination in the relentless pursuit of justice.

Far to the north, amidst the cold, unforgiving waves of the North Sea, stood an oil rig—a marvel of human engineering. This offshore platform was not only a testament to modern technology but also a place where skilled individuals like my uncle, my mother's brother, Johon, thrived.

Johon is a man of precision and intellect—a structural engineer whose expertise was highly regarded in Norway. His sharp mind and outspoken nature set him apart in the oil rig's bustling environment. Despite the harsh marine conditions, Johon excelled in his work, earning a reputation for his dedication and problem-solving abilities.

However, amidst the clang of metal pipes and the roar of the ocean, Johon received a message that would change the course of his life. It was a call from his family back home, informing him of the developments in my father's unjust incarceration. Determined to seek justice, Johon made a decision that would alter his comfortable life in Stavanger, Norway.

Leaving behind the comforts of his work and the allure of offshore life, Johon made several trips back to Eritrea to assist our family in the search for my father and, later, his release. As he followed my father's case closely, keeping in constant contact with me and my mother, his mission became clear: to work tirelessly to free my father from the shackles of false accusations.

With unwavering resolve, Johon combined his engineering expertise and sharp intellect to navigate the complexities of the legal system, worked with me tirelessly, sharing information, and meeting various officials. He stood by my father's side, offering steadfast support and guidance, as he embarked on a risky and tumultuous journey towards justice.

As my father's case was split into different courts, Johon and a dedicated lawyer, paid expensively by him, worked relentlessly to uncover the truth and present a compelling case. Through long nights of meticulous research and strategic planning, they leveraged every available tool within the legal framework to dismantle the false allegations against my father.

Their efforts eventually bore fruit. After a gruelling legal battle, the court ruled in my father's favour, dismissing the false charges and clearing his name of the stain of injustice. It was a moment of triumph, made possible by Johon's unwavering dedication and relentless, costly pursuit of justice.

With the weight of injustice lifted from his shoulders, my father embraced Johon, deeply grateful for his brother-in-law's selfless devotion. Together, they stood as a testament to the power of determination and the strength of family bonds.

As Johon returned to his life in Stavanger, the echoes of his actions reverberated through the oil platform. He was no longer just an engineer but a hero—a beacon of hope and justice for all who knew his story. In the heart of the North Sea, amidst the turbulent waters, Johon's legacy shone bright, a testament to the resilience and unwavering spirit of a man who dared to make a difference.

Meanwhile, on the front of the special courts, the interrogator Kebaz continued to manipulate and delay my father's case, despite the lack of any substantial evidence. His relentless efforts to fabricate a case, aided by the minister in my father's former office, only added to the mounting frustration and despair.

An unexpected turn of events occurred when a familiar face, Zewdi, who worked as a clerk for an official, reached out to us with urgent news about my father's bail and the immediate need for financial readiness. A special court session had already taken place in her boss's office, a district administration headquarters, unannounced. In a whirlwind of emotions, my mother and I hastily gathered the required bail money and rushed to the location where my father was being held.

Zewdi, the wife of my father's former colleague, who had been unfairly nicknamed 'Aba Hana'—meaning 'stingy' for his tight-fisted approach—stepped in as an unexpected source of hope in an otherwise bleak situation. Her determination to facilitate my father's release by retrieving money from her home, just a few meters away, provided a ray of light amidst the darkness that had engulfed us. Zewdi had to act swiftly, as Kebaz had ordered my father's return to prison until the 5,000 Nakfa, equivalent to USD150 bail money, was sorted. Zewdi, well aware that it could take another two weeks to secure his bail release after the payment, was furious. In a moment of raw emotion, she confronted Kebaz, saying, "I know this man well, and I also know he shouldn't be here, will never be again—never again."

The judge had listened to Zewdi's tearful plea to grant my father bail in the absence of a charge sheet. Zewdi even offered to pawn herself for detention to bail my father out. Moved by his own secretary's emotional encounter, the judge granted my father a short bail, with a return to court in thirty days.

When we finally arrived at the location, the sight of my father—weary, bandaged, and sitting on a bench—was a stark embodiment of the turmoil and uncertainty that had plagued us for so long. Zewdi, standing protectively in front of him, tried to engage him in conversation, as though to reassure both him and herself. The interrogator and his soldiers had left my father unattended, a callous oversight that underscored the disregard for justice that had defined our struggle. Amidst the chaos, a sense of determination and resilience took hold of me, propelling us forward in our relentless pursuit of truth and justice.

As I gazed upon my father's stony face, devoid of any visible emotion, my heart sank with deep concern for his mental health. His gaunt face, broken arms in bandages, and severed leg painted a picture of suffering that was almost unbearable to witness. With great effort, we supported him out of the building, tears streaming down our faces as we thanked Zewdi for her invaluable help. Her parting words—urging us to let him rest—echoed in my mind as we drove away in the blue Toyota Land Cruiser I had bought for him before his detention. The sight of my father slowly reconnecting with the outside world filled us with a mix of hope and despair.

Arriving at a private hospital straight from his release, my father underwent an immediate check-up and ECG tests, which revealed the devastating truth: multiple strokes had ravaged his brain, leaving permanent damage to his brain vessels. The doctor at Sembel Private Clinic delivered the grim news that my father needed immediate specialist attention, as he had suffered his most recent stroke only hours earlier. The crushing reality that my father had been attending his fraudulent trial while suffering strokes—defenceless and semi-conscious—was more painful than anything we had endured during his thirty years of ordeal.

As there were no facilities in Asmara capable of providing the necessary care at the level my father required, the doctor advised immediate action or we would lose him. My father had been enduring a daily barrage of strokes, triggered by his weakened body, hypertension, and the diabetes he had developed during his recent captivity. The only hope for his survival lay in seeking treatment abroad. With a heavy heart, I contacted Zewdi to inquire about my father's bail conditions, hoping there might be a possibility of taking him out of the country for the urgent medical care he desperately needed.

While my father was admitted to Sembel Hospital for close monitoring, the next day, Zewdi confirmed that we could pay an additional 50,000 Eritrean Nakfa or $1,500 in bail money to facilitate his departure. Without hesitation, I renewed his expired passport and urgently applied for a visa to Dubai, determined to get my father the help he desperately needed. The following day, as we departed for Dubai, my father, my mother, and I embarked on a journey filled with uncertainty and hope.

The prestigious American Hospital of Dubai became our sanctuary, where the doctors and staff treated my father with the utmost respect and care. As he began his treatment, the toll of the strokes became evident, leaving him with slurred speech, memory loss, and restricted movement in various parts of his body. The fractures and injuries sustained during his ordeal had left him half-alive, struggling to comprehend the world around him. His recollection of the past six months was shrouded in a fog of confusion, a result of the relentless onslaught of strokes leading up to the day of his bail.

Deprived of adequate food and water, he had developed hypertension and diabetes—ailments that were foreign to him before his detention. As I witnessed my father's battle for survival, a deep anger simmered within me, directed at the injustices he had endured and the toll it had taken on his once vibrant spirit.

In the surreal world we found ourselves in, the undefined tone of our journey mirrored the uncertainty that lay ahead. As my father fought to reclaim fragments of his former self, I grappled with the anger that threatened to consume me—a silent fury at the forces that had brought us to this harrowing juncture. The vivid descriptions of his suffering and the profound character development that unfolded within the walls of the hospital painted a portrait of resilience in the face of adversity as we navigated the uncharted territory of his recovery.

I couldn't believe how events had unfolded. My father, once strong and independent, now lay in a hospital bed, battling the aftermath of several strokes. The American Hospital had become our second home, a place where my mother refused to leave his side, sleeping there and doing everything in her power to provide the love and care my father needed. Meanwhile, I found myself juggling between the hospital and work, desperately trying to provide financial support for the mounting medical bills. The specialist care my father required was extensive—dieticians, cardiologists, speech therapists, and every other specialty the hospital offered. The costs were staggering, reaching hundreds of thousands of dollars as each day passed.

As if the medical challenges weren't enough, my father also had a looming court hearing, scheduled for a month after his bail release. The situation was dire, and despite my efforts to explain my father's condition through my contacts in Asmara, Kebaz, the person in charge, refused to agree to a proposed postponement of the hearing date. With no other options, we had to bring my father back in a wheelchair, unable to walk, for what felt like a final trial of his life.

I reached out to influential individuals in high offices, detailing my father's condition and the neglect he had suffered at the hands of Kebaz. I was assured that his imminent release would be confirmed, and the shocking state in which my father had been found had sent ripples through the corridors of power.

With my father's immediate medical needs under control and his body slowly regaining strength, we appeared at the court, my father in a new wheelchair we had purchased for him. The encounter with Kebaz at the court's reception was chilling. His callous remarks, expecting my father to arrive shackled and handcuffed from prison rather than from his home after a good breakfast, revealed the inhumanity that lurked within him. He remarked that we violated their strict rules that all bailed defendants should be brought to the prison and transported to court handcuffed and in an official vehicle.

The trial commenced behind closed doors in the same office, and within approximately three short minutes, Zewdi emerged behind my father's wheelchair, instructing for him to be taken away and never return. We were left inquiring, and we learned that the judge of the special court had scolded Kebaz for arriving unprepared again, without a charge sheet or case files, wasting everyone's time. The judge had ordered the cancellation of all cases altogether and declared that he didn't want to see my father in his office again. Kebaz's attempt to justify his lack of preparation and request for an extension fell on deaf ears, and the judge threatened to report him for his unethical practices, stating that he was tarnishing the government's name and damaging innocent people's lives. It was a moment of unexpected triumph in the face of adversity.

My father's unexpected turn of events at the court marked a new chapter for our family. Despite the lingering effects of the strokes on his arm and speech, there was a sense of relief and hope that had eluded us for so long. The ordeal had taken its toll, but it had also revealed the resilience and strength within us. As we left the court that day, I couldn't help but feel a surge of anger towards Kebaz and the system that had subjected my father to such suffering. Yet, amidst the anger, there was also a glimmer of justice, a reassurance that sometimes, against all odds, the truth prevails.

We returned to Dubai to continue his recovery, which included inpatient treatment, physiotherapy, and hundreds of other follow-up lab and ultrasound tests. The cost of my father's treatment at the prestigious American Hospital for multiple bone surgeries, inpatient physiotherapy, and specialist diagnostic tests became financially challenging, threatening my financial stability as I also had to take plenty of time off traveling back and forth since my father's detention. My mother also had to undergo several tests to ensure she was in optimal health after having suffered multiple emotional and biological illnesses, including unexplained rapid weight loss, goitre, and severe back pain, which she still has.

As I sat in my apartment in Dubai, my mind wandered back to the day I made the life-changing decision to leave Eritrea, despite my father's wishes. Little did I know then that this decision would ultimately become a lifeline for him. My father had endured years of imprisonment under various regimes, using his time in captivity to engage in productive activities and care for his fellow inmates. His resilience and strength were truly remarkable, but the final imprisonment under a brutal regime had left him physically and mentally shattered.

The doctors at the American hospital in Dubai were astounded by the increasing frequency of strokes my father was experiencing, even while under their care. These were direct results of the anger, disappointment, and flashbacks he continued to carry in his memory from the solitary confinement he had endured for over a year and a half, which had left his brain weakened and vulnerable. The conspiracy orchestrated by an ignorant ex-rebel minister, and the inhuman treatment my father suffered without any substantial accusations, highlighted the suffering of Eritreans under a system that rendered lives worthless and families broken. My father's mental and physical disablement was a poignant symbol of the collective suffering endured by millions in Eritrea.

As I reflected on my father's plight, I couldn't comprehend the need for such brutality. The fractures within the country, caused by the actions of individuals who made lives meaningless, weighed heavily on my mind. The anger and despair that permeated the air in Eritrea had reached a point where it threatened to consume everything in its path. My decision to move to Dubai, initially driven by a desire for a better life, had inadvertently become a crucial factor in my father's survival.

It was a reminder of how sometimes destiny aligns to make certain events the best decisions of our lives.

Amidst this turmoil, I found myself grappling with conflicting emotions. The anger and helplessness I felt towards the system that had caused my father's suffering were juxtaposed with a profound sense of gratitude for the opportunity to be by his side in Dubai. The uncertainty of the future loomed large, but in that moment, I was determined to be a source of strength and support for my parents, just as they had been for so many others during my father's years of captivity. As I gazed out at the glittering Dubai skyline, I knew our journey was far from over, and the shadows of the past would continue to shape our present and future.

Amidst the backdrop of a constantly shifting world, my father's journey to recovery unfolded with slow and arduous grace. The familiar sights of bustling cities like Dubai, the historic charm of Europe, and the vibrant energy of North America became fleeting markers on his path towards regaining his strength.

As he made his way through the clouds and the roads, he couldn't help but feel a mix of emotions. He had lived with the screams of inmates being tortured, the stench of infestation, and the suffocating air of fear. He had witnessed his friends and family torn apart and watched as his country lay in ruins. The memories of his homeland, with its war-torn streets and shattered buildings, haunted him as he walked through the bustling streets of New York and Hamburg. The contrast between the two worlds—the one he had sacrificed himself for and the one his friends had made their home—was stark and jarring.

He found joy in the encouragement and care from the people he met, the families he saw, and the lives he had touched. He had helped countless people escape to start new lives in free lands, giving them hope and a chance at a fresh start. But at what cost? He had given up his own life, his own freedom, for the sake of his people. The weight of his sacrifice pressed heavily on his shoulders, and he couldn't shake the feeling of doubt that gnawed at him. He thought about his own family—the one he had left behind to suffer with him. Had he made the right choice? Was his decision to stay and fight worth it?

Each trip, where he was received with a hero's welcome, served as a bittersweet reminder of the turbulent times he had left behind and the family and siblings who stood by his side with unwavering determination.

As the days passed, my father immersed himself in the rhythm of rehabilitation, embracing physiotherapy sessions and leisurely strolls that whispered promises of vitality. Yet, the shadows of his past lingered in the form of slurred speech and a fractured arm, which cast a pall over his once beloved game of tennis. Despite his relentless efforts to conquer his limitations and demonstrate his resilience, the road to recovery was fraught with obstacles that often overshadowed his progress. He had to stop driving, as it was deemed unsafe for him. His hobby of reading was altered by a lack of attention and comprehension. At times, he would ask others what a simple sentence meant, as though he was an illiterate person who had never been to school. He couldn't bear the sight of himself asking others to read for him. Despite all the support he was receiving, his healing efforts seemed fruitless, and every small setback made it harder for him to believe in his recovery.

In the depths of his despair, my father's spirit wavered, weighed down by the burden of his diminished faculties and the spectre of a future marred by uncertainty. Despite the urgings of those around him to seek asylum abroad so he could benefit from much more advanced medical treatment, he stood firm in his resolve, a solitary figure amidst a sea of doubts and fears. He bore his struggles with a heavy heart, his gaze fixed on a horizon tainted by shadows of doubt and sorrow.

As the days passed in a haze of unspoken sorrow, my father's silent struggle spoke volumes of a man grappling with his shattered self-image and a future that seemed dimmed by the shadows of his past. In a world that moved on, he stood still, his spirit adrift in a sea of regrets and unspoken dreams—a survivor in body, but a prisoner of his own broken hopes and fading memories.

As my father's condition worsened, the atmosphere at home became heavy with unspoken fears and unaddressed concerns. His once vibrant personality was now overshadowed by a cloud of frustration and helplessness. The house, once filled with laughter and warmth, now echoed with the weight of his silent suffering. Every day seemed like a battle—not just for him, but for all of us who watched him struggle. His eyes, once filled with determination, now held a glint of resignation, as if he had accepted defeat in the face of his debilitating condition. The air crackled with tension, and the walls seemed to absorb the heaviness of his unexpressed emotions.

Despite the efforts of the medical professionals and the unwavering support of his loved ones, my father's anger and frustration only seemed to intensify. His once agile movements were now replaced by slow, laboured steps, each one a reminder of his diminishing strength. The once lively conversations were now punctuated by long pauses and strained attempts at communication. It was as if a thick fog had descended upon our lives, shrouding everything in a veil of uncertainty and despair. The world outside continued to spin, but within the walls of our home, time seemed to stand still, frozen in the grip of my father's unspoken anguish.

As my father's recovery slowed significantly, he made less frequent trips abroad, seeking various medical treatments under the care of relatives and siblings who were equally devastated by his ordeal. Over time, he regained enough strength to engage in small activities. Determined to get his life back, he took part in different therapeutic and leisure activities, including daily walks. However, as he struggled to accomplish tasks he had once done easily, his speech became more slurred, and his fractured right arm restricted him from playing his favourite sport, tennis. Despite his efforts to show everyone that he was a survivor, with their support, he continued to struggle, eventually giving up even the smallest activities one by one.

His long travels abroad also became an immense burden. Due to the lack of direct flights from Asmara, he had to endure multiple layovers, which meant hours of sleepless waits in cold airport corridors while confined to a wheelchair. After each flight, he would arrive utterly exhausted, needing days to recover. His medical team advised against further long journeys, as the temperature inside the aircraft, the long waits at airports, and the altitude of the flights exacerbated the condition of his severed ligaments, which were still healing after years of complications caused by cramped positioning in the damp floors of the small solitary cell he had been confined to for over a year. Despite the constant support he received from everyone, he remained with permanent mental and physical impairments, as diagnosed by specialists everywhere.

As the days turned into weeks and then months, the weight of my father's unexpressed anger and frustration seemed to seep into every corner of our lives. It felt as though we were all caught in the grip of a relentless storm, unable to find shelter from his silent suffering. Each day became a battle—not just for him, but for all of us who watched helplessly as he struggled to reclaim the life that had been so cruelly taken from him. The weeks turned into months, and it became increasingly clear that the road to recovery was not only a physical one but a journey that would test the limits of his resilience and the strength of our family's love and support.

My father's anger was palpable, replacing the fixed smile he had once displayed, even during his captivity in Ethiopia. He looked permanently sad and disappointed, especially when he tried to speak but had to stop because of his impairment and memory loss.

In 2004, the year when life seemed like a tapestry of tangled moments, my family faced a poignant crossroads. My brother, Alazar, was getting married in quaint Virginia, USA—a celebration that called for unity and joy. However, a dark cloud loomed over this joyous occasion: my father's health had deteriorated to the point where long flights became a daunting challenge. Yet, determined to witness his son's union, my father made the brave decision to embark on one last journey to a foreign land.

With meticulous planning and all necessary arrangements made for his safe travel, our parents braved the skies to attend Alazar's much-anticipated wedding. The occasion promised to be a grand affair, a deservedly lavish celebration that not only marked the union of two souls but also served as a reunion for long-lost families and friends from all corners of the globe.

As the days rolled by, the air was thick with anticipation, a blend of excitement and apprehension. The photos and videos from the event would immortalise every moment of this family reunion and the beginning of a new one. Amidst the intricate tapestry of emotions, my father stood as a pillar of strength, his weathered face adorned with an uncontrolled and forced smile. Each gesture, each show of respect from the guests resonated deeply with him, for they too were aware of the perilous journey he had undertaken, which prevented him from fully partaking in the merriment.

On the day of the wedding, my father sat in his designated chair, a silent observer amidst the bustling celebration. The traditional rituals unfolded before him, each moment etching itself into his memory—a mosaic of joy and longing, interwoven with threads of sorrow and hope. As the guests swirled around him, offering congratulations and words of encouragement, my father maintained his steady smile, a façade that concealed a thousand untold stories of decades of both sorrow and happiness.

His eyes, though tired, sparkled with a rare fervour, reflecting the bittersweet reality of the moment. Watching his sons participate in the age-old customs of marriage, my father's heart swelled with pride—a profound sense of fulfilment mingled with a tinge of regret for the joys he could not wholly partake in. Yet, in that moment, surrounded by loved ones and well-wishers, he found solace in the simple act of being present, of witnessing the union of his flesh and blood.

Beside him, my mother, usually a vibrant woman who revelled in expressing joy at such functions, stood as a pillar of support. Her eyes mirrored a kaleidoscope of emotions, wavering between happiness and sorrow as she tended to my father—feeding him morsels of food, offering silent reassurances, and holding his hands without even realising it. Her tears, though unspoken, spoke volumes—an emotional expression of the intricate dance between love and sacrifice that defined their journey together.

In the heart of this new matrimonial story, amidst the harsh winds of life's challenges, there stood a family that had weathered many storms. Alazar, the youngest child, born into treacherous conditions, had blossomed into a beacon of hope and perseverance. Our parents gazed upon him with a mix of pride and disbelief—their once fragile infant now a successful man, a testament to their unwavering dedication.

Within the walls of the luxurious wedding hall, our mother offered prayers of gratitude for this day—a day that had once seemed like a distant dream in the face of past struggles. She prayed for joy and happiness to fill the lives of her son and his family, shielding them from the hardships she had known all too well. As the sun dipped below the horizon, casting a warm glow over the Hilton Hotel, our mother whispered a silent wish, hoping that the future would be kinder to her beloved Alazar and his new family.

Amidst the echoes of their shared past, a sense of contentment settled over the family, a quiet assurance that no matter what challenges lay ahead, they would face them together, bound by love, determination, and the unshakable faith that had guided them thus far. As the stars twinkled in the night sky, a new chapter began for Alazar and Rachel, as well as for their parents—a chapter filled with promise and the certainty that their bond would endure all that life had yet to offer.

As the night wore on, the festivities continued in full swing, a symphony of laughter and music that reverberated through the hearts of all present. And amidst the revelry, our parents stood as a testament to love's endurance, to the unspoken sacrifices made in the name of family and unity. In that fleeting moment, as the dance floor beckoned and the guests twirled in joyous abandon, my father's smile—though worn and weathered—held a depth of emotion that transcended mere words.

And so, as the night drew to a close and the stars twinkled overhead, casting a soft glow upon the gathering, our family stood united in a moment that would forever be etched in the annals of our shared history. For in the midst of joy and sorrow, celebration and sacrifice, we found a common thread that bound us together—the unyielding power of love, a force that defied all odds and illuminated even the darkest of nights with a glimmer of hope.

Alazar had carved his own path, rising above the adversities that once threatened to engulf our family. With a compassionate heart and a sharp mind, he not only excelled in his career but also became the pillar of support for our ill father. His wife, Rachel, who had been by his side since their university days, now his wife, stood as a steadfast companion in his journey through life's trials and triumphs.

In Asmara, where tradition blends with modernity, the air was filled with anticipation as eldest brother Kaleb's wedding quickly approached that summer. It was a time of mixed emotions for our family, as just weeks prior, we had celebrated my brother Alazar's union with his bride, followed by our parents urgently needing to be flown back for my father's much-needed respite before the next joyous occasion.

Kaleb's event was held in a quaint, medium-sized hall that reverberated with joy and laughter, showcasing Kaleb's quiet yet incredibly expressive demeanour. Everyone present enjoyed the celebration, marking the beginning of a journey filled with love and togetherness.

As fate would have it, that same year marked my own engagement to my now wife, Helen, though it was overshadowed by the urgent return of our parents to the USA for my father's kidney treatment. Despite the challenges, both our parents underwent various medical procedures while visiting friends and family, ensuring their presence at my wedding ceremonies a few months later.

Our parents, in a determined display of resilience, graced the lavish event with over a thousand guests in attendance at a grand hall in Asmara. The two-day affair was a tapestry of old friends, family, officials, and dignitaries, merging roots from villages, creating a harmonious blend of celebration and gratitude.

On the main wedding day, as I stood beside my father, my emotions ebbed and flowed, remembering his sacrifices and contributions to my life. Witnessing his physical decline from a once vibrant man to a mere shell, my heart swelled with a whirlwind of joy and sorrow. It was a night where love, gratitude, and bittersweet memories intertwined, creating a tapestry that encapsulated the essence of our lives in a single moment.

In a quaint hall nestled in the centre of Asmara, our wedding unfolded like no other. It was not just a union of two souls, but a celebration of survival, gratitude, and the binding ties of family history. As the light winter rains, marking the end of a season, finished pouring and the sun cast its golden hues over the gathering, the air was filled with a palpable sense of joy and grief—a mélange of emotions that wove through the tapestry of the day.

The bride, resplendent in a captivating cream designer wedding dress adorned with intricate flowers in vibrant colours, exuded a quiet strength that belied the turmoil she had endured. Her eyes shone with unshed tears of happiness as she glanced at her beloved groom, a man of quiet resolve and unwavering courage. He stood tall, his features etched with years of hardship and triumph, a testament to a life lived with purpose and resilience.

The guests, a diverse tapestry of faces from near and far, bore witness to the union of these two souls. Close family members mingled with strangers who had played pivotal roles in our journey—from the local villagers who had raised my father to the individuals who had fought tirelessly for his release from the inhumane prisons of Eritrea.

As the ceremony unfolded, there was a sense of unity and shared purpose that permeated the air. Zewdi, the special court clerk who had become a close friend after years of disconnection from our family, moved with grace and efficiency, ensuring that every detail of the wedding proceedings was executed flawlessly. Her presence was a reassuring anchor in a sea of emotions, a symbol of continuity and order amidst chaos.

The vows were exchanged amidst a backdrop of heartfelt speeches and joyous ululations, a symphony of voices rising in unison to celebrate the union of two souls destined to be together. My voice wavered with emotion as I professed my love and devotion to my bride, my words a testament to the trials we had overcome and the triumph of our love.

As the sun dipped below the horizon, casting a soft glow over the gathering, the festivities continued well into the night. Traditional dances and songs filled the air, a celebration of culture and heritage that spoke volumes of the community's resilience and spirit.

In that moment, surrounded by loved ones and well-wishers, we were not just two individuals coming together in matrimony. We were a symbol of hope, of love conquering all, of the enduring power of family and unity in the face of adversity.

And as the night drew to a close, and the last embers of the fire crackled into darkness, a sense of peace and contentment settled over the city. The wedding had been a testament to the strength of the human spirit, a reminder that, in the face of hardship and despair, love and unity could triumph.

As the new couple embarked on the journey of marriage, we carried with us the blessings and well-wishes of all those who had gathered to witness our union, a reminder that, in the tapestry of life, every thread—no matter how tangled or frayed—had its own place and significance.

And thus, the wedding of the whole family came to an end, a moment etched in time as a reflection of the past, a celebration of the present, and a promise of a future filled with love, hope, and enduring bonds that would stand the test of time.

In the revived family household, we stood as a testament to hard work and resilience. Three weddings, a trifecta of love and commitment, had taken place in the two years that had just passed. For our parents, this was not just a celebration of love but a triumph over the adversities they had faced.

In each moment, our parents felt a sense of accomplishment wash over them. They had weathered storms, endured hardships, and emerged stronger together. The weddings marked not only a new chapter for their children but also a victory over the struggles that had threatened to tear them apart. And as they looked towards the future, hope bloomed like wildflowers in their fields, promising new beginnings untainted by past sorrows.

The births of new grandchildren, following in the months and years after the weddings, were shared in a wave of joy that resonated through each household. With each child that came into the world, it was as if the essence of our parents was magnificently reflected in their tiny features, creating a beautiful circle of life that was constantly in motion.

Among the myriad of grandchildren born into the family, the story of Matthias stood out like a brilliant star in the night sky. His entrance into the world was not conventional, for he was the result of an instant love affair that took place when Alazar was just a young man of nineteen, indulging in the carefree days of his freshman year at Asmara University.

Matthias, born a mirror image of his father, was a gift that arrived unexpectedly but brought immense joy to his family. While he was the first grandchild, his upbringing was far from typical. Initially, Matthias was the sole grandchild and the centre of attention, showered with love and gifts as he accompanied his grandfather on his challenging journeys in Asmara, before finally reuniting with his father in the USA.

Raised by two sets of grandparents who adored him beyond measure, Matthias lived a life filled with abundance and privilege. He received an excellent education and had the freedom to explore his passions, excelling both on the football field and in the classroom. Despite the unconventional start to his life, Matthias grew up to be a fine young man, embodying the best qualities of both his parents.

As the years passed, the family continued to expand, welcoming more grandchildren who brought their unique gifts and personalities into the fold. Each birth was a celebration, a testament to the enduring bond of love and unity that held the family together. The grandchildren, like vibrant flowers in a garden, added colour and texture to the tapestry of the family, enriching the lives of all who knew them.

Through laughter and tears, triumphs and challenges, the family stood strong, united by the thread of love that intertwined their hearts. The births of the grandchildren symbolised hope and renewal, a reminder that life was a beautiful journey, filled with surprises and blessings waiting to be discovered.

And as Matthias stood tall among his cousins, a shining example of resilience and strength, the family rejoiced in the knowledge that the circle of life continued to spin, weaving together the past, present, and future in a tapestry of love that would endure for generations to come.

After a well-deserved two-month honeymoon, my wife and I returned to Dubai to plan our married future. My beloved wife, Helen, a British woman with Eritrean heritage, had been working as a skincare adviser for a global company at the prestigious Harrods in Knightsbridge, London. Her expertise in the field made Dubai, a burgeoning market for luxury brands at the time, the ideal place for us to relocate.

As we settled into our new life in Dubai, Helen found herself balancing her career aspirations with the news of her pregnancy. We decided to put her relocation on hold, allowing her to split her time between London and Dubai. It was a joyful yet challenging time as we awaited the arrival of our first child.

Meanwhile, back in Asmara, my father's health began to deteriorate rapidly. He required round-the-clock care at home, with a trained nurse attending to his needs and administering his medications. Singly incontinent and incapacitated to travel, my mother stayed by his side, unable to share in the joy of welcoming our first child into the world.

Despite the distance and the challenges we faced, my wife and I focused on the new chapter unfolding before us. In the bustling city of Dubai, where the scent of spices mingled with the salty breeze of the sea, we made plans for the future. The towering skyscrapers seemed to reach for the heavens, mirroring our ambitions and dreams.

As the months passed, my wife's pregnancy progressed smoothly, surrounded by her loving sisters in London. Their support was a comfort to us both, grounding us in the midst of our changing circumstances. The anticipation of welcoming our child into the world overshadowed the challenges that lay ahead.

Finally, on a warm summer day, our first child, Delia, was born at St. Mary's Hospital in Paddington, London. The joy and relief were palpable as we held our precious daughter in our arms, her arrival marking a new beginning for our family.

My mother, the pillar of our household, a tender soul who had raised five rambunctious boys with unwavering love and care, had always carried a deep longing beneath her tough exterior. A longing to cradle a daughter in her arms, to share the joys and sorrows of womanhood with a child of her own.

Years passed, marked by the boisterous laughter of her sons and the gentle whispers of unfulfilled dreams. And then, like a whisper in the wind, fate smiled upon our family. Delia, the first granddaughter, was born unto us. With her arrival, a delicate shift occurred in the fabric of our home. My mother's heart sparkled with unshed tears of joy as she held the precious bundle in her arms, feeling the weight of her dreams finally realised.

Delia was a beacon of light, a breath of fresh air in our midst. Her presence filled the house with a sense of peace and serenity, like a soothing balm for our weary souls. With each passing day, she grew and bloomed like a delicate flower, her laughter ringing through the halls and chasing away the shadows of the past.

As Delia flourished under my mother's distant yet loving gaze, she became not just a granddaughter but the cradle of the family. She bridged the gap between generations, weaving a tapestry of love and belonging that enveloped us all. And in the warmth of her presence, my mother found solace, her heart finally at peace knowing she had been blessed with a daughter in the form of her precious granddaughter, Delia.

While we celebrated this precious moment, my heart ached for my parents, unable to share in our happiness. My father's frailty served as a poignant reminder of the passage of time and the fragility of life. Despite the physical distance that separated us, their presence was felt in our hearts, guiding us through the highs and lows of parenthood.

In the midst of our joy, we made the difficult decision to put my wife's career on hold as we adjusted to our new roles as parents. The bright lights of Dubai seemed to dim in comparison to the radiant love we felt for our daughter, binding us together in the shared journey of parenthood.

As we navigated the complexities of our intertwined lives, the threads of our stories wove together, creating a tapestry of love, sacrifice, and resilience. Our paths may have diverged, but the bond that held us together remained unbreakable, bridging the gaps between London and Dubai, past and present, dreams and realities.

And so, in the heart of a bustling city, where dreams were born and futures forged, we embarked on the next chapter of our lives, anchored by love and fortified by the unbreakable ties of family.

Written In The Stars

Fast Love

When I lived in Addis Ababa as a young high school graduate between 1987 and 1991, I witnessed the constant influx of young Eritreans seeking a better life abroad. The government had relaxed movement restrictions in an attempt to curb the overwhelming number of young men and women joining the liberation front. This led to a surge of Eritreans relocating to other regions of Ethiopia. With schools closed and the war-torn region offering little hope for the future, many young people saw no option but to seek opportunities in the relatively peaceful capital, Addis Ababa, or to leave for overseas.

As Eritrean households with relatives abroad became more common, it was not unusual to see younger siblings receiving paid scholarship offers to pursue education in Europe and North America—seen by many as the way out. However, the stringent criteria set by the Ethiopian Commission for Higher Education posed a significant challenge for those seeking to leave the country. Many Eritreans lacked the necessary documentation, making it difficult for them to meet the strict conditions required for their departure and to sustain a meaningful life without the financial support of their relatives.

Observing the struggles faced by these young Eritreans, I felt compelled to step in and offer assistance. With my knowledge of the city and the scholarship process, I began helping them navigate the complex application procedures. I attended appointments in various offices, offering translation and support. I even resorted to unconventional means, such as bribing underpaid school principals and officials to obtain academic certificates, military service exemption documents, and forge necessary paperwork to facilitate the departure of many young Eritreans from the country.

My efforts did not go unnoticed, and I quickly became sought after by officials in various departments who were willing to collaborate for financial gain. I helped hundreds of Eritreans navigate the bureaucratic hurdles, earning respect and gratitude from both the young applicants and their relatives abroad. Despite the temporary connections formed through this process, I forged a lasting bond with Jonas, a young man who flew to Sweden and became a successful computer analyst. Our correspondence continued, and a deep friendship blossomed, laying the foundation for significant and life-changing connections that would follow.

Descending from a well-known wealthy family that had amassed its fortune through a successful bakery business, Jonas exuded a certain air of sophistication and ambition that set him apart. With a bright mind and a thirst for adventure, he was a beacon of promise in a city alive with possibilities.

Through our continued support for each other, our bond grew stronger, transcending the initial purpose of facilitating the departure of Eritrean youth. Our friendship became a source of strength, shaping our lives in ways we could never have imagined. As the years passed, the nostalgic memories of our journey together remained a testament to the enduring power of human connection and the impact of reaching out to help others in need.

It was through a mutual friend that I came to know Jonas, and from the moment we met, there was an instant connection. We quickly formed a camaraderie that led to many memorable moments spent together, exploring the vibrant nightlife of Addis Ababa. As Jonas juggled the responsibilities of running one of his grandfather's bakery branches, he also found time for leisure, often accompanied by his girlfriend and me as we indulged in the luxuries the city had to offer.

In 2003, Jonas arrived in Dubai with his fiancée for a pre-wedding shopping spree after accepting my invitation, where I promised the couple a memorable time.

It was during this visit that I had applied for a US visa in hopes of attending my brother Alazar's wedding in Virginia, only to have my application rejected due to the post-9/11 political climate. My Eritrean passport impeded the progression of my application, as the United States had designated Eritrea as a supporter of terrorism. Disheartened by the unexpected outcome, I confided in Jonas, who was taken aback by the rejection, considering my accomplishments and assets. It was then that he made it his mission to help me obtain European citizenship and a passport, affording me the freedom to travel without hindrance. Jonas couldn't believe that I was still holding an Eritrean passport after having helped hundreds of others obtain European and American citizenship. Despite my explanation that I didn't mind and was happy with my Eritrean passport, which allowed me to travel freely, especially in Asia—where most of my business connections were based—Jonas vowed to change my status.

As we navigated the complexities of bureaucracy and geopolitics, my other grand plans to attend Jonas's wedding in Sweden the following summer were thrown into uncertainty. The rejection of my visa application at the US consulate served as a stark reminder of the challenges faced by those from countries deemed risky in the eyes of the world. With the large red 'DENIED' stamp placed on my passport, it was very likely that I would be denied entry to other European countries as well, given the visible marker of my US visa rejection.

Amidst the chaos of visas and uncertainties, Jonas not only extended his hand in friendship but also offered brotherly advice. He encouraged me to look beyond my focus on my parents and consider my own happiness, particularly in matters of love and marriage. Despite my involvement in relationships, I had yet to find someone who resonated with me on a deeper level, leaving me adrift in a sea of fleeting connections. Citing my on-off romantic affairs mostly with Ethiopian women and the absence of a steady relationship, Jonas made it his mission to support me in starting a family.

Weeks before I met with Jonas in Dubai, I had found myself immersed in the soft company of Eritrea's most renowned singer, Bereket Mengistab. Bereket had come to Dubai to purchase musical instruments for the government's cultural department, of which he was an honorary member. Known as the Frank Sinatra of Eritrean culture and the freedom struggle, Bereket was a well-respected figure in our society for his artistic contributions. He was not only a renowned singer but also a close friend I had met through his nephew Yamane, a musician based in Canada. As we drove through the streets of Dubai, Bereket's deep, soulful voice resonated with each chord, filling the air with a sense of tranquillity.

After a quiet moment, Bereket, a man of unique life experience in arts and relationships, with whom I had shared many personal stories during our long conversations, turned to me. He was very grateful for the help I had offered him and appreciated my honest approach. With a warm smile and his wise eyes twinkling, he asked gently about my plans to start my own family. I hesitated before confessing that I was waiting for a break in family matters. His response was unexpected, yet profound.

With a touch of seriousness, Bereket shared his thoughtful insight. He emphasised the importance of not delaying life's plans while waiting for circumstances to be perfect. He explained that some things do not require all conditions to be fulfilled before moving forward, and that time waits for no one. Life, he said, would present challenges one after another, and you must learn to juggle them and harmonise your tasks for your own benefit. He pointed out that it was a foolish perception to believe that all problems would eventually disappear. "You must get along with life's challenges," he told me, "and do what you need to do." Referencing my support for my parents, he added, "Nothing you do now will ever be enough for them; they will always need more. So, does that mean you'll wait forever?" Bereket added, "You must remember, your decision to have your own family will only make them happier, so you will be doing it for them as well as yourself."

His words struck a chord within me, resonating deep in my heart. I realised the truth in his advice and the wisdom behind his simple yet profound words. As the bustling city outside carried on with its relentless pace, I felt a sense of clarity wash over me, urging me to embrace life's uncertainties and challenges rather than waiting for the perfect moment.

In that brief encounter, Bereket had imparted a valuable lesson that would stay with me for years to come. With gratitude in my heart, I bid him farewell, carrying his fatherly advice like a precious gem, guiding me toward a path of courage and determination. As the days passed with a newfound perspective, I was ready to face whatever challenges life might bring, knowing that time waits for no one.

Bereket, jokingly but with notable sincerity, promised that he would sing at my wedding if I found happiness. In Eritrean terms, to have Bereket sing at a wedding is akin to having Michael Jackson or Beyoncé perform at your private event.

His words wove around me like a comforting blanket, wrapping me in a sense of purpose and clarity I had never experienced before. It was as if the universe had conspired to bring me to this very moment, allowing me to receive the guidance I so desperately needed.

I bid farewell to Bereket and Jonas at different times at the end of their visit to Dubai that year, their words echoing in my heart. As I walked away, I knew that these chance encounters had changed me in ways I couldn't yet fully grasp, setting me on a path of self-discovery and enlightenment. The valuable advice from two wise people, whom I had met in such a short span of time, hit me with the force of a revelation, as if I had something important to confront.

My parents had also hinted on several occasions that I must look beyond my mission of helping them and that it was time for me to settle down. Careful not to appear as though they were interfering with my own life plans, they offered their parental advice in carefully worded suggestions. They also expressed their wishes for women from circles of family friends whom they thought would be a suitable match for me. My mother, known for her humorous expressions, always mentioned, after attending family and friends' weddings, how she longed to pay back those invitations with her own children's weddings.

As Jonas embarked on his career, travelling across Europe and settling into a privately rented flat in the affluent neighbourhood of St John's Wood, in the Westminster district of London, he remained steadfast in his determination to help me find a partner and secure a European passport through a genuine marriage. With his extensive network of acquaintances, Jonas set out to introduce me to potential matches, hoping to facilitate a consensual union with another Eritrean that would bring stability and joy into my life.

However, despite his best efforts, the path to finding a suitable match proved to be fraught with obstacles. The women he approached often had their own commitments or hesitations, leading to a series of declined proposals and dashed hopes. In some cases, the women he suggested were even my close relatives, resulting in rejections that we jokingly referred to as a "slap on the wrist."

In Eritrea's small population, there is always the risk of inadvertently discovering that you have formed a romantic connection with a close relative, only to uncover the relationship when delving deeper into ancestral histories.

Through all the ups and downs, Jonas remained a pillar of support, unwavering in his belief that a brighter future awaited me beyond the shadows of rejection and uncertainty. As his own life blossomed with success and love, he extended his hand to uplift me, reminding me of the importance of forging my own path and embracing the opportunities ahead.

And so, as the chapters of our lives continued to unfold, intertwined by bonds of friendship and shared dreams, Jonas and I stood united in our pursuit of happiness and fulfilment, guided by the unwavering light of hope and resilience. In a world plagued by barriers and divisions, it was the power of human connection and empathy that shone brightest, illuminating our paths with the promise of a brighter tomorrow.

In the bustling city of London, amidst the grey buildings and crowded streets, resided an extraordinary Eritrean lady in her twenties. She was both Jonas's landlady and close confidante. A business-minded and clever woman, she was always looking for opportunities to turn even the most mundane situations into profitable ventures.

While working on a short contract for a telecom company, Jonas had rented a flat from this single landlady. Jonas, a charismatic young man with a glint of mischief in his eye, found himself embarking on an unusual mission. Armed with a vision that intertwined familial bonds and destiny, he approached his astute landlady with a proposal that was as unconventional as it was intriguing.

Within Eritrean communities around the world, tradition was woven into the fabric of everyday life. It was customary for friends to play matchmaker, orchestrating introductions between potential soulmates. Jonas, with his strong belief in destiny, found himself at the centre of one such arrangement.

On a crisp autumn morning, Jonas stood before his landlady in her cosy parlour, the room enveloped in the warm glow of sunlight filtering through lace curtains. With a nervous yet determined demeanour, he unfolded his plan like a tapestry of possibilities, weaving together the fates of two human beings separated by miles yet connected by chance.

Jonas spoke passionately about a certain someone—a man of impeccable character and success, whose essence, he believed, resonated with the very soul of the landlady. He painted a vivid picture of this enigmatic figure, invoking images of charm, ambition, and a heart as vast as the English moors. In his persuasive words, he crafted a tale of a match preordained by the stars.

But Jonas's proposal was not just about the landlady and the mysterious man he described. It carried a twist of fate that stretched across continents, as he revealed his intention to pair the landlady's sister, living in Israel, with one of the man's brothers in the UK. A symphony of siblings coming together to orchestrate a harmony of love, family ties, and shared destinies.

Intrigued by the audacity of the plan and stirred by the potential for a new chapter in her family's story, the landlady delved into a world of research and intrigue. She reached out to sources in Dubai and Asmara to gather information about the prospective match for herself and her sister.

As days turned into weeks and the clock ticked on, the landlady found herself planning a trip to Dubai. Her heart fluttered with a mix of anticipation and apprehension. She imagined stepping onto the bustling streets of the city, feeling the surge of excitement at the prospect of meeting the enigmatic man who could hold the key to her—and her sister's—future. Her casual checks with sources in Asmara had told her that the man was well known for his success and manners, and that his family were close friends with one of her aunt's husbands.

The landlady first decided to speak on the phone with the man from Jonas's tales. The air seemed to crackle with a sense of destiny as Jonas made the call and handed the phone to her. In that moment, as the two conversed maturely, the landlady saw not just a potential match for herself, but also for her sister and his brother—a glimmer of hope for their journey. And in that instant, as fate wove its intricate threads around them, the landlady knew that this unconventional proposal had the power to shape not just one, but two intertwined destinies.

Meanwhile, Jonas had finished his work assignment in London and returned to Sweden. As a supportive friend, he took charge of coordinating the meeting between the landlady and her sister's potential match in London.

As rounds of discussions unfolded between the landlady and my London-based brother about his future with her sister, it became apparent that there were doubts surrounding his commitment. My brother Kaleb, who was in a long-distance relationship with an Eritrean girl in Italy, seemed hesitant to marry the landlady's sister in favour of his distant partner, whom he had never met. The girl, a university student, had promised to move to London once she completed her education in a couple of years' time. Kaleb's reluctance raised concerns about his long-term plans and half-heartedness. It was as if he only wanted to go through with it to help me, but he wasn't even ready to marry, having only just resumed his university education after a several-year break.

Despite the landlady's hopes for a successful double match, it soon became evident that the exchange was not going to proceed as planned. Her reservations about Kaleb's dedication to the union led to the termination of the whole arrangement. The landlady, who had previously met with Kaleb in London to discuss the plan and already sensed his indecisiveness, was deeply disappointed by the outcome, feeling frustrated by the wasted efforts and expenses incurred throughout the process.

Reflecting on the failed endeavour, the landlady vowed never to venture into such dealings again. She lamented the time, money, and emotional investment that had been poured into the ill-fated matchmaking attempt. Her relationship with Jonas became strained as a result, overshadowed by the dashed hopes and broken promises that lingered between them.

The sun was setting, casting a warm glow over Dubai, when Jonas called me. His frustration was palpable through the phone as he recounted the series of failed meetings and encounters the landlady had experienced.

On the other end of the line, I listened in disbelief, having only heard vague details of the obstacles from my brother. Jonas's voice was strained as he detailed the setbacks and disappointments they had faced, seeking solace and understanding in my response.

But as he poured out his grievances, my own resolve strengthened.

"Stop this nonsense," I interrupted, my tone firm and resolute. "I will not partake in such endeavours again. It's just unrealistic. We will find our destinies elsewhere."

Jonas fell silent at my words, the weight of my refusal heavy in the air between us. In that moment, I realised that my path was different, my aspirations unique. I spoke confidently:

"My future wife will come to me in destiny's own time. I have no interest in a European passport, nor do I yearn to visit Europe. I am content and happy with the life I have crafted for myself."

I also told Jonas that the emotional damage this would cause the women involved would be unforgivable, and I did not want his friendship with me or with the landlady to be strained by this. "You have to let go," I insisted.

There was a pause, a breath caught in hesitation, before Jonas, resigned to the reality of my stance, stopped his task. The distance between us felt tangible, our paths diverging as we stood on opposite sides of a divide in perspective and desire.

In the end, the tale of Jonas's next stop at his landlady's in London became a narrative intertwined with ambition, familial ties, cultural clashes, and the harsh realities of failed aspirations. It was a story marked by the complexities of human relationships, the uncertainties of marriage, and the unpredictable nature of life's twists and turns. Amidst it all, the landlady stood as a resilient figure—a business-minded woman who learned that even the most carefully laid plans could unravel in the face of unforeseen challenges.

The following summer, Asmara buzzed with vibrant energy as diasporas from all corners of the globe flocked to this cosmopolitan city, seeking friendship, connection, and shared experiences. Among the sea of diverse faces, Daniel stood out. With his tall frame and pop-style, African American appearance, he hinted at a mix of cultures and stories waiting to be unveiled.

I first met Daniel through a mutual friend, Fasil an Amiche, drawn together by a shared curiosity and a desire to explore the rich tapestry of Asmara's streets. Despite his Amiche status from his upbringing in Addis Ababa, and this being his first-ever visit to Eritrea, Daniel effortlessly blended into the eclectic mix of languages spoken in Asmara, gracefully shifting between Amharic, English, and the occasional Tigrinya phrase. His upbringing in a prominent business family had gifted him with a polished demeanour and a command of multiple languages. Connected by our individual stories of life in Addis Ababa, Daniel and I bonded in an instant friendship.

As the summer unfolded, Daniel and I, along with our newfound friends, immersed ourselves in the charm of Asmara. Evenings were spent traversing the lively streets, sampling local delicacies, and sharing tales of our respective lives abroad. However, it was our frequent trips to the picturesque beach town of Massawa that forged a special bond between us. Daniel, with his easy smile and infectious enthusiasm, quickly became an integral part of my summer adventures.

One particular aspect that set Daniel apart was his passion for driving. He took to the wheel of my car with gusto, relishing the role of designated driver as we navigated the hilly, winding roads between Asmara and Massawa. His expertise behind the wheel and unwavering reliability soon made him my go-to chauffeur for both business meetings and social gatherings. I found solace in his steady presence, knowing I could count on him to ferry me to my destinations with precision and care.

Despite his proficiency with vehicles, Daniel's true talent lay in his ability to make my 4x4 feel like his own. With a meticulous eye for detail, he treated my vehicle as if it were a prized possession, tending to it with the utmost care and attention. On several occasions, Daniel would politely request the keys for a special outing, a glint of excitement in his eyes as he planned his route.

For Daniel, who lived in London, this first visit to Asmara had been nothing short of transformative. He had fallen in love with the city—the vibrant life, the friendly residents, and the sense of community. He was well-liked by everyone, including my parents, as his sociable nature and broken Tigrinya always made people laugh. Though Daniel's familial connections in Asmara were limited, his immediate family scattered across distant lands after their expulsion from Ethiopia, he had found a temporary home with his aunt while spending his summer holiday in the city. Despite this geographical displacement, Daniel's presence in my life brought a sense of joy and companionship that transcended borders.

As the summer drew to a close, I reflected on the unexpected friendship that had blossomed between Daniel and me. His towering frame, always adorned with a hat and sunglasses, cut a striking figure against the backdrop of Asmara's rain-soaked streets. I couldn't help but marvel at the seamless way in which he had woven himself into the fabric of my summer memories. His warm laughter and genuine camaraderie left an indelible mark on my heart.

In Daniel, I had found not just a friend, but a kindred spirit who had navigated the complexities of diaspora life with grace and resilience. Our shared experiences, from lazy afternoons by the beach to adventurous road trips through the Eritrean countryside, had forged a bond that transcended language barriers and cultural divides.

Amidst the bustling city streets, our friend Fasil was navigating a tumultuous phase in his marriage. Fasil, a devoted father of two, had arrived from Europe with his wife and children. However, as the strains in his marriage grew, he sought solace in the company of a visiting Eritrean woman from France.

We often met with Fasil and his new lover in the evenings, and it was during one of these encounters that he confided in me about his newfound connection with the slim Franco-Eritrean girl, who also happened to be Daniel's first cousin. With reckless abandon and moonstruck by the lady, Fasil made the risky decision to abandon his family and immerse himself in this new relationship, seemingly blind to the consequences.

Fasil's wife, a woman I knew too well, approached me with a heartfelt plea, asking me to convince her husband to return home and reconsider his actions. Despite her emotional request, Fasil had already made up his mind to divorce his wife long before their summer vacation, and his new life with the French girl, a banker by profession, only sped up the process. Daniel and I found ourselves entangled in the unravelling drama of friendship and family as we tried to mend the fractured bond between Fasil and his wife.

As tensions escalated, the desperate wife turned her frustration towards us, blaming Daniel and me for the breakdown of her marriage. She accused us of being careless in our actions, oblivious to the repercussions of our involvement. She believed that Daniel's familial connections with the girl and our meddling had led Fasil down the path of estrangement from his family and into the arms of a new flame.

The accusations weighed heavily on us, straining our friendship with Fasil and casting a shadow of doubt over our intentions. Despite our best efforts to reconcile the couple, the rift between Fasil and his wife only widened, fuelled by mistrust and miscommunication.

In a twist of fate, Fasil found himself drawn into the turmoil, standing by our side and defending our actions. As the situation spiralled out of control, my car became the symbol of guilty association, dubbed the "crime gateway car," with Daniel assigned the title of the "gateway driver" by the incensed wife.

The wife's unwavering belief in our culpability painted a bleak picture of our involvement, casting a shadow over our intentions and tarnishing our reputations. Despite our genuine desire to help our friend and navigate the complexities of his failing marriage, we found ourselves entangled in a web of accusations and misunderstandings, unable to salvage what was lost. In this tight-knit community, social connections intertwined families and friends in a web of familiarity, where everyone knew everyone.

I found myself caught in the middle of a brewing storm when Fasil's wife's parents levied accusations against my own family. It wasn't long before whispers of scandal reached my parents' ears, and I was summoned for a serious consultation.

Fasil, a man who had once led a prominent tech company in Dubai, was well-known to my parents. His own parents, frequent visitors to Dubai, had spent countless months at their son's spacious villa, hosting lavish parties and family gatherings where my parents and I were daily guests, leaving us with memories that lingered in the salty sea breeze.

As I set out to bring Fasil back home for the anticipated discussion, the weight of the town's prying eyes bore down on him. It was a burden he hadn't expected to carry, yet in Asmara, where everyone's business was everyone's business, there was no escape.

Fasil's affairs had suddenly become my own, a knot that seemed impossible to unravel. I found myself thrust into the role of mediator, tasked with mending the frayed threads of Fasil's troubled marriage. It was a responsibility that weighed heavily on me, for the stakes were high, and failure was not an option in a town where judgment came swiftly and without mercy.

Arriving at Fasil's modest home, I was met with a tense atmosphere that clung to the air like a dense fog. Fasil, once a pillar of strength and success, now appeared worn down by the weight of his marital woes. His wife's accusations hung between them like a shadow, casting doubt on the once-solid foundation of their relationship.

As I sat down with Fasil and his wife, the air crackled with unspoken tension. Words were exchanged like arrows, each one leaving a mark on their already fragile bond. Despite my best efforts to mediate and mend, the rift between the couple seemed too deep to bridge.

Days turned into weeks, and I found myself engulfed in the suffocating embrace of Asmara's relentless gossip mill. Whispers followed me wherever I went, judging eyes casting their collective gaze upon me as if I were the one at fault.

Eventually, despite my earnest attempts to help, Fasil and his wife made the painful decision to go their separate ways. I watched helplessly as their marriage crumbled under the weight of age-old secrets and accusations—another casualty of the unforgiving small-town life that bound them all together.

In the aftermath of the failed reconciliation, I found solace in the knowledge that I had done all I could to help my friend. Asmara's streets continued to hum with the stories of its residents, each life intertwined in a complex dance of love, betrayal, and redemption.

Life in Asmara carried on, its residents bound by the unbreakable ties of community and connection, where the echoes of one's actions reverberated through the town like ripples on a pond, never truly fading away.

As the dust settled on the fractured relationships and shattered trust, we were left grappling with the consequences of our actions and the harsh realities of love and loyalty tested against the backdrop of betrayal and heartache. Fasil's marriage stood as a sombre reminder of the fragility of relationships and the irreversible consequences of choices made in moments of weakness and uncertainty.

We were left to ponder the weight of our decisions, the ripple effects of our involvement, and the enduring impact of a friendship tested by the turbulent waters of love and loss. The tale of Fasil's broken marriage served as a cautionary reminder—a poignant lesson about the delicate balance between loyalty and temptation, trust and betrayal, in the intricate dance of human relationships.

Daniel had more plans for his visit to Eritrea. He always held a special place in his heart for one of his uncles, a man he hadn't seen in years since he was forced to leave Addis Ababa at the start of the recent Ethio-Eritrean conflict and start a new life in a small ancestral farming village in Eritrea. The distance between them seemed insurmountable, with rugged terrain and treacherous roads painting a bleak picture. But Daniel's determination to reunite with his beloved uncle burned brightly, and with my help, we embarked on a journey that would not only test our resilience but also bring them closer together.

As we set out in my SUV, the warnings from Daniel's aunt in Asmara echoed in our minds. Tales of perilous roads twisting around hills, with rocks tumbling dangerously from the cliffs, only fuelled our resolve. The uncertainty of the journey loomed large, but I, accustomed to traversing Eritrea's rural landscapes, saw beyond the challenges. It was an opportunity for adventure and a chance for Daniel to reconnect with his country—and his uncle.

After some two hours on the tarmacked road, the landscape began to transform. With each passing kilometre, the familiar gravel road gave way to vast expanses of untamed wilderness. The road ahead was unforgiving, demanding every ounce of skill and patience from the driver. Despite the obstacles, we navigated the rough terrain, taking turns behind the wheel with determination and precision, inching closer to our destination.

With no GPS navigation facilities or road directions available, and communication scarce in these remote parts of Eritrea, our trusty mobile phones offered only intermittent connectivity. It was a true test of our navigation skills, relying on local knowledge and instinct to guide us through a maze of unmarked roads and winding paths. As the sun dipped below the horizon, casting long shadows over the rugged terrain, we finally arrived at our destination—Daniel's uncle's humble abode, nestled in a picturesque village teeming with life.

The reunion was a sight to behold, with joy and laughter reverberating through the air. Daniel's uncle welcomed us with open arms, his eyes shimmering with emotion at the sight of his long-lost nephew. The evening was filled with stories shared over a sumptuous feast, the aroma of traditional dishes filling the air. Daniel marvelled at the simplicity and beauty of village life, the bonds of family and tradition woven into every aspect of daily existence.

The following day, Daniel and his uncle explored the ancestral village, tracing their roots back to a time long forgotten. The lush greenery, dotted with yellow daffodils, the vibrant colours of nature, and the serenity of the countryside enveloped them in a sense of peace and belonging, while I played with the village children. As they walked through the fields, tended to the animals, and exchanged stories under the shade of ancient trees, a sense of contentment washed over them.

For Daniel and me, it was a well-deserved respite from the bustle of city life in Asmara, where we had been caught up in Fasil's unfortunate troubles. As evening descended once again, the glow of the setting sun painted the sky in hues of orange and pink, casting a magical light over the village. Daniel and his uncle sat under the starlit sky, reminiscing about the past, discussing their hopes for the future, and savouring the moments of connection that had eluded them for so long. It was a time of bonding, of rekindling ties that time and distance had strained.

As night fell, enveloping the village in a blanket of darkness, pierced only by the twinkling stars above, I watched from a distance—a silent witness to the reunion that had unfolded before my eyes. In that moment, I realised the power of family, the resilience of the human spirit, and the beauty of forging connections that transcended barriers of distance and time.

The journey to reunite Daniel with his uncle had been fraught with challenges, but in the end, it stood as a testament to the enduring bond between family members, the strength of friendship, and the joy of rediscovering lost connections. As we bade farewell to the farming village, our hearts full of memories and our spirits lifted by the shared experiences, I knew that this journey would forever hold a place of honour in our hearts—a tale of love, perseverance, and the unbreakable ties that bind us together.

As the sun began to rise behind the distant mountains, casting long shadows over the dusty road, Daniel and I reluctantly bade farewell to the small village that had been our temporary sanctuary. We had spent two nights there, but relentless rain had plagued our journey back to Asmara. The air was heavy with the scent of wet earth and the promise of more rain to come, but we knew we had to press on, despite the looming threat of treacherous driving conditions.

The rain had transformed the dusty road into a muddy obstacle course, with deep puddles and slippery patches that made for a perilous journey. Our tyres struggled to gain traction on the slick surface, causing us to slide and fishtail as we navigated the winding path back to the city. It was a constant battle against the elements, with each passing mile feeling like an eternity.

Daniel, usually confident behind the wheel in the bustling city streets, now looked visibly tense as he gripped the steering wheel tightly, his knuckles white with exertion. I could sense his frustration and anxiety, mirroring my own inner turmoil. The thought of being stranded in the remote countryside, at the mercy of the unforgiving weather, gnawed at the edges of our minds like a persistent whisper of doubt.

As we pressed on, our progress hindered by flat tyres and fading daylight, I couldn't help but recall the cautionary words of Daniel's aunt, who had warned us about the dangers of driving in such conditions. Her voice echoed in my mind, a spectral reminder of the perils that awaited us on this ill-fated journey.

But amidst the despair and uncertainty, a glimmer of hope emerged when we spotted a convoy of old, weather-beaten AMCE trucks and tankers, usually pronounced as *Amiche*, trudging along the same road we struggled to navigate. If those massive vehicles could forge ahead despite the obstacles in their path, why couldn't we? After all, we were called *Amiche* for a reason. This testament to the well-reputed expertise of Eritrean truck drivers was a reassuring sight, a reminder that resilience and determination could conquer even the most daunting challenges.

With renewed determination, we pushed forward, spurred on by the sight of our rough-and-tumble companions on the road. My hands steady on the wheel, I expertly manoeuvred our SUV through the obstacle course of mud and debris, my focus unwavering despite the mounting fatigue.

The hours passed in a blur of adrenaline and uncertainty, the landscape shifting from muddy clay soil to gravel roads and then tarmac as we neared Asmara. Our journey had become a test of endurance, a trial by fire that pushed us to our limits and beyond.

Finally, as the city lights twinkled in the distance, a sense of relief washed over us like a welcome wave. We had made it, against all odds, defying the harsh driving conditions and our own doubts. The journey had been arduous, but it had also been a testament to our strength and resilience in the face of adversity.

As we rolled into Asmara, weary but triumphant, I glanced over at Daniel and saw a glint of pride in his eyes. We had weathered the storm together, navigating the twists and turns of fate with unwavering perseverance. In that moment, I knew that no obstacle, no matter how daunting, could ever truly hinder our spirit of adventure and determination.

As the rain continued to pour, a gentle lullaby of renewal and rebirth, I realised that our journey was coming to an end—a tale of resilience and fortitude that would carry us through the challenges we faced, against the odds of nature.

The dark clouds loomed overhead as we finally arrived in Asmara after a perilous ten-hour drive. Our clothes were soaked in mud and rainwater, clinging uncomfortably to our tired bodies. All we craved was a fresh start to our city life, beginning with a hearty meal to quell the hunger that gnawed at us like guilt. As we navigated the bustling streets of Asmara city centre in our mud-covered dark blue Toyota 4x4, our minds were consumed with thoughts of food and which restaurant would rejuvenate our spirits.

After much deliberation between traditional Eritrean cuisine and European fare, we settled on Top5, a renowned restaurant known for its delicious traditional dishes. It was a beacon of hope in our weary state. With our stomachs growling in anticipation, we parked our mud-splattered SUV and made our way to the restaurant. Arriving around 8 p.m., we were met with a heartbreaking revelation: the kitchen was closed for the day.

Disappointment and hunger weighed heavily on us as Daniel, typically polite and composed, grew visibly irate at the news. He argued with the apologetic waiter, questioning why an exception couldn't be made for us, given our desperate need for a meal. However, the kitchen staff had already departed for the day, leaving us with no immediate solution to our hunger pangs.

Amidst our frustration, my gaze fell upon a trio of strikingly beautiful girls seated in a corner of the restaurant, engaged in lively conversation over coffee. Their exotic features hinted at Arabian and Central Asian origins, and I was intrigued to hear them conversing in Tigrinya, a telltale sign of their Eritrean heritage. What caught my attention even more than their beauty was the array of half-eaten traditional Eritrean dishes adorning their table, seemingly abandoned despite their freshness and inviting aroma.

Driven by desperation, I mustered the courage to approach the girls and tentatively inquire if it would be acceptable for me to partake in their untouched leftovers. Before a response could be given, Daniel unexpectedly joined me, exclaiming in surprise as he recognised the familiar faces of the girls, whom he knew from London. His presence added a layer of complexity to the situation, as the girls seemed puzzled by my audacious request to share their leftover meal, not to mention our unusual attire, splattered with mud from our long journey.

As I began to eat from their unattended tray, Daniel's apologetic tone resonated with the girls, recounting the trials and tribulations of our journey. To my discomfort, however, the girls, though unfamiliar with me, politely requested that I cease my impromptu feast and allow Daniel—whom they knew—to partake instead. Their subtle disapproval hung in the air, questioning the appropriateness of my actions and highlighting the breach of cultural norms surrounding the sharing of meals with strangers.

I could hear them asking Daniel several questions about me, and he struggled to explain that I was simply hungry and would be happy to answer all their questions after I finished eating. To my embarrassment, I realised I had been acting as though I hadn't eaten for months.

One of the girls voiced her confusion, wondering aloud about my motives and the disregard for social decorum displayed by my impulsive behaviour. It was a stark reminder that hospitality and etiquette held significant importance in Eritrean culture, and my actions had inadvertently crossed a boundary that I was unaware of. Despite my embarrassment, Daniel's charm and familiarity with the girls helped to bridge the gap. He initiated a conversation about their stay in Asmara and their recent journey from London.

Daniel's connections and shared experiences with the girls, which had begun on their flight from London to Asmara, formed a bond of friendship characterised by acts of kindness and generosity. Daniel, ever the kind-hearted man, had bought them expensive perfumes during their layover at Cairo airport, a gesture to congratulate their sister, who had arrived in Asmara earlier to wed her long-time friend. Their camaraderie blossomed from the confines of London to the bustling streets of Asmara, where they found themselves reunited unexpectedly.

The girls, seated in the cosy booth area of the restaurant, filled the air with excitement as they recounted their eventful flight to Asmara. Each one took turns sharing their mishaps and adventures surrounding their near-miss with the connecting flight to Asmara, but one particular girl seemed to have gathered a collection of unprovoked falls, bumps, and accidents throughout the journey. I found myself wincing at the thought of how one person could have faced so many incidents—from a fall on an escalator to being hit by a floor-cleaning machine.

As the sisterhood of the three girls became apparent, their appearances hinted at their relative ages: the eldest, the youngest, and the middle sister. The middle girl, a vivacious soul, pulled up her dress sleeve to reveal an injury from one of the airport accidents. My eyes, almost unconsciously, drifted to the bruised wound, which painted a vivid purple on her otherwise immaculate skin. Her legs, I noted with surprising clarity, were perhaps the most stunning I had ever laid eyes on.

Caught in a moment of admiration, I was abruptly interrupted by the middle girl's disapproving gaze and stern reprimand. She promptly scolded me for my impertinence, questioning my sanity for attempting to sneak a peek at a part of her leg that she deemed personal. Flustered and sheepish, I quickly realised my mistake and hastily diverted my attention elsewhere, though I could feel the tingle of embarrassment creeping up my cheeks.

The room fell into a brief, awkward silence before the girls burst into giggles, teasing me for my failed attempt at sneaking a glance. Despite the slight embarrassment, the light-heartedness of the moment soon enveloped us all, turning what could have been an uncomfortable situation into one filled with laughter and camaraderie.

As the sisters reminded Daniel of the upcoming wedding, they expressed their strong desire for him to attend the festivities. However, their warm invitation came with a playful caveat: they jokingly admonished him not to bring along his 'mannerless' companion—referring to me with a teasing tone.

What had begun as an evening of hunger and disappointment had now transformed into a tale of cultural nuances, friendship, and the enduring bonds forged through shared experiences.

In the quaint little restaurant, Top5, tucked away in the heart of the bustling city, the atmosphere buzzed with curiosity. The girls eagerly awaited the revelation of the identity of the mysterious figure who had caught their attention. Daniel, ever the gentleman, ordered a round of drinks for everyone, while the girls sat, their excitement palpable.

Among the three sisters, the middle girl stood out with a charm that belied a sharp tongue. Though she spoke less than her sisters, her words carried weight, and her gaze was intense as she observed the scene unfolding before her.

The mystery individual—me—who had dined on their leftover food without engaging with the girls, had piqued their interest. As they waited for me to finish my meal, they exchanged whispers, trying to decipher the enigma before them.

The aroma of the delicious leftovers filled the air as I savoured each bite, completely engrossed in my meal. The chatter and laughter of the girls created a pleasant background to my dining experience. However, as I continued to indulge, I sensed a sudden shift in the atmosphere—an unexpected quiet fell over the table.

In an instant, while Daniel was away for a moment of companionship with others in the bar area, the girls' attention shifted, their eyes flickering with mischief. They began speaking to each other in a new language—Hebrew—one I didn't understand. Their words flowed effortlessly, and their tones were animated yet secretive.

As they conversed in hushed tones, I couldn't help but feel a pang of curiosity. Were they discussing me? Their rapid-fire conversation seemed to centre around a common topic. With every glance in my direction and every barely contained giggle, the mystery deepened.

Despite not understanding a word of Hebrew, I could sense the change in the room. The language barrier seemed to heighten the intrigue, and their clandestine discussion added a layer of mystery to the moment. It was as if the very fact that I couldn't understand them made the scene feel even more enigmatic.

Their fluency in Hebrew was evident, each word rolling off their tongues with ease and familiarity. I found myself captivated by the melodic cadence of the language, even though its meaning eluded me.

As their conversation continued, I couldn't help but wonder what they were discussing. Were they sharing anecdotes, exchanging secrets, or perhaps even commenting on my presence? Regardless, their shared language formed a bond that excluded me, yet also intrigued me.

In that moment, surrounded by the unfamiliar sounds of Hebrew and the enigmatic gazes of the girls, I realised that language could serve as both a barrier and a bridge, shaping the dynamics of our interaction in ways I had never considered before. As I lingered over the last morsels of my meal, I couldn't shake the feeling that something profound was unfolding in that room—something beyond the confines of mere words.

As I took the final bite, I was startled when the mysterious figure—the individual who had been silent up until now—finally spoke, announcing my readiness to engage in conversation. However, before I could offer any response, the middle girl sharply interrupted, expressing disinterest in hearing my story. Despite her outward rudeness, there was an underlying intrigue in her demeanour, a hint of something she was carefully concealing.

I attempted to defuse the tension, explaining that I had only consumed the leftovers to avoid waste, not out of desperation. I even tried to lighten the mood by making a jest about attending their sister's wedding, though I made sure to mention my own conflicting obligations—my brother Kaleb's wedding, which was taking place a week before theirs.

The middle girl's response was unexpected. Her smile, though warm, contrasted sharply with her harsh words. "You won't be welcomed at our family event," she declared, her voice cool and measured. "And if you dare to show up, I'll have my brothers remove you." I was taken aback by her contradictory behaviour, unsure whether to interpret her actions as a form of intimidation or an enigma meant to provoke intrigue.

While she threw her tantrum and opposition towards me, I found it hard to tear my gaze from her unnatural beauty. Her every movement seemed deliberate, calculated, and despite the tension, I couldn't help but feel a growing discomfort as my own skin flushed with heat.

With a mixture of confusion and unease clouding my thoughts, I was left standing at a crossroads. Should I stay and unravel the enigma of the middle girl, or heed her warning and make a hasty retreat?

The soft glow of the restaurant's ambient lighting cast a warm hue over the cosy booth where we sat, and my attention was entirely absorbed by the mesmerising figure before me. She was a tapestry of contradictions—a delicate balance of beauty and mystery, wrapped in a shroud of unpredictability. As I gazed at her, entranced by the way her eyes sparkled with mischief, I couldn't help but feel a surge of affection, tempered with confusion. It was an odd mix of emotions that stirred within me, intensified by the enchanting presence of this enigmatic woman.

However, our intimate moment was soon interrupted by the insistent prodding of the waiter, his voice cutting through the air like a sharp blade. He urged us to move to the bar, citing the closing time and the end of his shift. In that instant, he seemed less like a mere employee and more like a threat—a looming force poised to shatter the delicate equilibrium of our budding connection.

Despite his persistent requests, I couldn't bear to let this fleeting moment slip away. It felt as though fate had brought us together, and I was determined to unravel the mystery that lay beneath the surface of this captivating woman. Her occasional tantrums and unwelcoming comments only fueled my curiosity, hinting at a deeper complexity that perhaps even she herself didn't fully comprehend.

With resolve firm in my heart, I turned to the waiter and, with a confident smile, assured him that I knew the owner and would compensate him generously for allowing us a few more precious moments. Reluctantly, he acquiesced, and I felt a surge of triumph. I had bought us more time to explore the connection that seemed to blossom between myself and the captivating middle girl across from me.

And so, in the dimly lit sanctuary of the restaurant, surrounded by the soft murmur of evening chatter, I embarked on a journey to uncover the true depths of the mysterious beauty who had so effortlessly captured my attention. The night was still young, and the possibilities that lay ahead seemed boundless, tinged with the promise of a love story waiting to unfold.

Amidst the clinking of glasses and the hum of conversation, a silent standoff persisted between the enigmatic individual and the captivating middle girl. Our paths were now intertwined in a web of mystery and uncertainty, both of us caught in the gravity of the moment.

Under the faint, slow background music, I found myself entangled in a peculiar situation with the three curious sisters. As they bombarded me with questions, I couldn't resist the urge to fabricate tales about my identity, veiling myself behind a false name and a shroud of mystique. With each whispered falsehood, their eyes sparkled with intrigue, unknowingly stepping deeper into the web of deception I was weaving.

Amidst the charade, I casually mentioned that I resided in Dubai. The middle girl, with a glint of wanderlust in her eyes, dared to dream aloud, "I would like to visit Dubai one day. Would you be my guide?" Her sisters exchanged a puzzled glance, suspicion lingering in their gaze as they probed deeper into my fabricated persona.

Before I could conjure a reply, the middle girl hastily corrected herself, stumbling over her words in an attempt to retract the unintended intimacy of her request. "I mean, all of us, for a short trip," she stuttered, her voice tinged with uncertainty. The unexpected prospect of a jaunt to Dubai unravelled before them, their itinerary now a chaotic mix of spontaneity and disbelief.

The oldest sister, with her piercing brown eyes and commanding presence, interrupted the animated chatter with a stern tone. "You know well that, as Israeli citizens, we are not allowed to travel to Dubai. What are you talking about, all three of us going to Dubai? And you're not going alone, trusting this man to be your guide?" Her words cut through the air with an authority that silenced the table.

The middle girl, her hazel eyes still filled with determination and a hint of mischief, responded with a playful smile. "Of course, I know. I was only joking." Despite her light-hearted words, there was a subtle longing in her voice, a genuine wish to visit Dubai, with or without my guidance.

It was clear that the two Israeli citizen sisters, apart from the middle girl—whose accents revealed they were not from London—had flown in to accompany her on her journey to Asmara. The middle girl, however, was fluent in the local dialect, a testament to her deep connection with her heritage.

The eldest sibling, sensing the growing tension, took charge with a firm command to leave immediately. A veil of discomfort settled over the trio as the enchantment of our whimsical banter shattered, revealing the fault lines in our fleeting connection. Their disappointed expressions betrayed a mixture of confusion and apprehension, signalling the end of our brief rendezvous.

As the girls prepared to leave, I stood in silent contemplation, haunted by the consequences of my playful mischief. The echoes of their departing footsteps carried with them a lament of what could have been—a fleeting encounter marred by the illusions we had woven and the truths left unspoken. And amidst the fading whispers of their departure, with Daniel already in the company of other friends at the bar, I was left alone in the restaurant, pondering the fragility of fabricated connections and the weight of unspoken truths. The waiter in front of me wore an expression of quiet relief, as though his forced stay had finally come to an end.

Of the three sisters, it was the middle one who had caught my eye from the moment we met. Her easy smile and lively spirit had captivated me in a way I couldn't quite explain. And as they turned to leave, a sudden surge of courage overtook me.

With my heart racing, I made the split-second decision to ask for her phone number—a simple request that felt like a monumental leap of faith. I hurried to catch up with them, my palms clammy with nerves.

"Excuse me," I called out, the words tumbling from my lips before I could second-guess myself. The girls turned around, their expressions a curious mix of surprise and amusement.

"I know this might seem sudden," I began, my voice trembling slightly, "but could I perhaps get your number? I'd love to continue our conversation sometime." Not really, those were words hard to come by, and I remained silent.

In the hazy realm of dreams, where reality wavers and bends to the will of the subconscious mind, I existed as nothing more than a fleeting, wishful thought—fragile and ephemeral, lacking the courage or energy to become something tangible, always teetering on the brink of dissolution. But then, like a bolt of lightning in the still night sky, she appeared.

She stood before me in all her ethereal glory, a vision of beauty that seemed to transcend the boundaries of the dream world. Her features were delicate yet striking, her eyes deep pools that seemed to draw me in, ensnaring my very soul. In that moment, I felt a surge of emotions unlike anything I had ever experienced before—love, pure and intoxicating.

As I gazed upon her, I felt myself paralysed by her presence, my very essence trembling in her radiance. It was as though I was losing my sense of self, dissolving into the overwhelming tide of emotions that washed over me. She was more than just a girl; she was a goddess incarnate; a being of divine perfection that left me breathless.

In that dreamlike state, a sudden wave of realisation hit me—this was love. A force so powerful and all-encompassing, it consumed me entirely. It was a feeling

I had never known in my waking life, a symphony of emotions that resonated deep within my soul.

And in that dream, where reality and fantasy intertwined, I knew that this encounter with the goddess before me was a gift—a glimpse of love that transcended time and space. As the dream began to fade, leaving only a lingering sense of yearning in its wake, I was filled with a profound longing for a love that was both real and unattainable.

I had never felt anything like this before. The closest I could remember was when I had a crush on Brooke Shields in her classic movie *Endless Love*. I was stung by her portrayal, watching it hundreds of times in my teenage years. But this—this was real, touchable, and different. I was older now, and my feelings were deeper, sensed through every fibre of my being.

The thunderstorm of love and affection hit me unexpectedly, leaving me in a daze as I tried to make sense of the whirlwind of emotions swirling inside me. As I slowly regained my composure, I found myself standing amidst the bustle of the restaurant, my gaze drawn again to the middle girl of the trio, who had captivated my attention.

She was a vision of beauty, her presence exuding grace and allure that left me speechless. As the trio began to make their way towards the door, the middle girl suddenly excused herself to go to the bathroom. In that moment, I found myself subconsciously torn between following her and staying behind with her sisters.

In a state of semi-consciousness, I almost turned to follow her, but something held me back, a strange force compelling me to stay with the sisters. As we engaged in idle conversation, my mind was blank, my thoughts consumed by the image of the enigmatic middle girl.

The older sister, with a playful smile on her lips, observed my distracted state and gently asked if I was alright, questioning my unusual behaviour of lingering with strangers while my eyes followed the lady as she walked to the bathroom.

With a chuckle, she added a teasing remark, asking if I had a habit of following unfamiliar women walking to the bathroom.

Just as I struggled to find the right words to respond, the middle girl returned, her presence commanding attention as she rejoined her sisters near the door. As we prepared to leave the restaurant, a wave of recognition washed over me as I was greeted by several patrons who extended invitations to join them in the lively bar area.

Top5, the restaurant owned by a close friend, was a favourite haunt for the elite and affluent businessmen of Asmara, many of whom I knew personally. Stepping into the bar, I felt a mix of familiarity and curiosity as we navigated through the crowd towards the exit.

The patrons erupted in cheers and greetings upon seeing me, their voices blending with the clinking of glasses and soft music that filled the air. Despite their warm welcome, I noticed a shift in their expressions as they took in my dishevelled appearance—a far cry from my usual polished demeanour.

Confusion and amusement flickered in my friends' eyes as they wondered about the change in my attire—from the usual sharp business wear to worn and muddy clothes. As I exchanged nods and waves with familiar faces in the crowd, I was struck by the surreal contrast of the moment.

The middle girl observed the interactions with a mix of amusement and bewilderment, her playful teasing hinting at the air of mystery that surrounded me in such an extravagant setting. With a light-hearted jest, she questioned whether I was a secret celebrity or a renowned singer, drawing laughter from her sisters and the surrounding patrons. It was clear she was confused by my identity—why the full-house bar greeted me as if I were the president's son. Some patrons called out from afar, asking me not to leave without speaking to them, as they had important matters to discuss. Others simply wanted me to join them for drinks, while many offered to drop the girls off in case I didn't have a car. It was a mix of respectful invitations, underpinned by the gratitude they felt for the help I had offered many of these businessmen, thanks to my privileged position in Dubai.

As the girls left without exchanging contact details, I was left contemplating whether I should have told them my real name. They walked away, leaving me with an unfamiliar sense of hope and possibility—perhaps a fleeting encounter, the beginning of something extraordinary. I was left relying on Daniel for another chance with the middle girl. As Daniel offered to drive them, they declined, saying they had their own car, and made their way out of the restaurant.

And as we remained behind, the evening unfolded in a whirl of laughter and shared drinks. I found myself caught in a surreal blend of reality and fantasy, where unexpected encounters and chance moments wove together to create a tapestry of memories that would linger long after the night had faded.

As the streetlights of Asmara flickered in the night, casting a warm glow over the bustling streets, Daniel and I headed home to refresh before joining our friends for a night out. As we drove away, Daniel, offering limited details about his connection to the girls, observed that I had embarked on a new chapter in city life, enriched by the unexpected connections and shared moments that had unfolded in the heart of Eritrea. Daniel commented on my obvious surrender to the middle girl, advising me to take it easy but reservedly promising that he would do all he could to create an opportunity for us to meet again.

Late that fateful evening, the air buzzed with a palpable tension, mirroring the turmoil within me. The memory of the middle girl lingered like a haunting melody, her enigmatic presence wrapping around my thoughts like a shroud. I was completely transformed by her mere existence, drawn to her mystery like a moth to a flame.

As I replayed the events of that day, the middle girl's reactions spun in a continuous loop in my mind. Her subtle rudeness, the occasional flashes of a captivating smile, and her witty comments had left me utterly perplexed. I couldn't decipher what lay beneath her charming façade. Was she single, married, divorced with two children, or engaged to a lucky person? The uncertainty gnawed at me, fueling a sense of urgency I had never felt for anyone before.

I found myself grappling with unfamiliar emotions, uncertain of how to navigate this uncharted territory. In my busy life, where priorities constantly shifted, I had never been one to chase after women, let alone try to decipher their thoughts and feelings. The lack of experience in this realm left me feeling vulnerable, a novice in the intricate dance of attraction and courtship.

When Daniel arrived to whisk me away for a night out, I welcomed the distraction, eager to escape the labyrinth of my own thoughts. We headed to Sunshine Hotel, a popular diaspora joint that promised live music and vibrant energy. The anticipation of meeting friends and immersing ourselves in the pulsating rhythm of the nightlife offered a temporary reprieve from the tumult raging within me.

Stepping into the hotel lobby, we were enveloped by a sea of familiar faces and welcoming gestures. In Asmara, the diaspora community thrived, forming tight-knit bonds forged through shared experiences and late-night escapades. It was a place where strangers quickly became friends, and every corner seemed to hold a story waiting to be told. Every day, the diasporas would meet to review their experiences from the night before, laughing and bantering about their alcohol-driven adventures. In addition to the daily new friendships we formed, my connections with many of the community members—thanks to my assistance during their hard-fought processes of leaving the country years ago—extended to Asmara's business community and government officials I knew through my work in Dubai. These various connections had made me something of a social magnet, a figure able to pull people from all walks of life to one table.

Among the crowd that evening was the first son, whom I was introduced to for the first time. Upon meeting the president's own son, who rarely appears in public, those around us were quick to comment about our resemblance in looks, querying on any possible blood relations. I freely joked, "I'm more handsome than him," making the president's son and his entourage laugh at my banter. I had heard from mutual friends that he was a very sociable and friendly person, shy of his father's feared image. However, I wasn't excited about that encounter. I would have much preferred to have met the middle girl instead.

As I navigated through the sea of voices and laughter in the hotel lobby, a sense of isolation crept over me. Despite the numerous acquaintances and connections that surrounded me, I felt like an outsider in my own world. The weight of my internal turmoil stood in stark contrast to the jovial atmosphere, highlighting the deep divide between my emotions and the external energy of the night.

In a town where everyone seemed to know each other, I stood adrift, a solitary figure amidst a sea of familiarity. The echoes of past interactions and chance encounters reverberated around me, serving as a stark reminder of the intricacies that defined relationships in this vibrant community.

As the night unfolded, I found myself consumed by a singular thought—the middle girl. Her enigmatic presence continued to linger; a tantalising mystery that begged to be unravelled. Should I summon the courage to seek her out, to present myself and lay bare my emotions? Or should I resign myself to the uncertainty and let fate decide our path?

In the midst of laughter and music, I grappled with the weight of indecision, the invisible echoes of her presence guiding my every move. As the night wore on and the music filled the air, I found myself standing at a crossroads, my heart torn between longing and hesitation. The middle girl remained a distant enigma, a tantalising puzzle that beckoned me closer even as it eluded my grasp.

As the evening faded into night, I was left with a lingering sense of longing and uncertainty. The transformative power of her presence had left an indelible mark on my soul, a reminder of the complexities that defined human connection and the enigmatic dance of fate and desire. And so, as I stepped into the new moment, the memory of the middle girl lingered like a whisper in the wind, a haunting melody that echoed through the depths of my being.

Among the lively chatter and laughter that filled the elegant hotel, I navigated through the bustling crowd, greeting familiar faces and exchanging pleasantries. Amidst the sea of people, a short, somewhat reserved acquaintance caught my eye. He greeted me with rare warmth, informing me that my dearest friend, Jonas, was secluded in one of the private lounges within the hotel lobby.

My heart leapt with joy at the unexpected news of Jonas's presence in town. Without hesitation, I made my way towards the lounge he had mentioned, the anticipation building with each step I took. As I rounded a corner, I unexpectedly collided with Jonas in the dimly lit alleyway. The reunion was nothing short of magical, as we embraced in a tight hug, the joy of our reunion palpable in the air.

Jonas revealed that he had arrived from Sweden that evening and had intended to reach out to me by phone but had been caught up attending a couple of significant meetings over some events taking place in the coming two weekends. He mentioned being in the company of some friends and extended a warm invitation for me to join them. However, I explained that I was already with a group of friends and suggested we catch up later at my table.

As the evening progressed, Jonas made his way to our table, his eyes sparkling with excitement as he recounted his whirlwind journey to Asmara to attend his best friend's sister's wedding. Every summer, Asmara is filled with weddings of both diaspora and local couples seeking new lives in matrimony. Despite the fatigue from his rushed flight, Jonas's infectious energy filled the room, drawing everyone into his vibrant storytelling.

After a series of heartfelt conversations and shared laughter, Jonas excused himself, promising to return shortly. He reappeared with a wide grin plastered on his face, reminiscent of a child in a candy store. His eyes gleamed with a newfound enthusiasm, as if something was bubbling beneath his skin.

It turned out that Jonas had decided to spend his first evening in Asmara with a group of girls who were in town for a special event. Curiosity piqued, he eagerly listened to their accounts of a strange encounter earlier in the evening with a mysterious figure known to the locals as Efraim—a name I had playfully coined. The girls described a peculiar individual with an enigmatic aura, seemingly familiar to everyone in town, yet shrouded in mystery.

Jonas expressed concern over the odd circumstances, particularly noting Efraim's unconventional dining habits—behaviours that seemed out of place culturally and hygienically. He cautioned the girls to exercise caution in the unfamiliar surroundings, hinting at potential dangers lurking in the shadows, particularly for diaspora girls. Jonas also insisted that they should have called the police immediately, but the girls told him the questionable figure was accompanied by a mutual friend, and while the guy was harmless, he had acted strangely throughout the evening.

In a show of solidarity, Jonas vowed to protect the girls during his stay in Asmara, ensuring their safety and well-being amidst the uncertainties of the night. His unwavering commitment to safeguarding those around him reflected the depth of his character and the sincerity of his friendship.

While Daniel and I chatted with a group, the youngest of the girls—catching sight of me with my friends at a table in the front section of the lobby—hurried to inform Jonas of my presence. She described me vividly, prompting Jonas to come to our table to seek me out for a private conversation. With a mixture of curiosity and apprehension, I followed Jonas to a secluded corner, unsure of what awaited me in the shadows of the dimly lit room.

Jonas's inquiry about the trio of sisters whose dinner I had shared immediately heightened the tension in the air. His question lingered in the silence, leaving a trail of uncertainty in its wake. With a knot forming in my stomach, I confirmed having encountered the sisters and partaken in their hospitality, the gravity of the situation slowly sinking in. He also quizzed me on why I had given a false name and appeared dressed like a madman. I reasoned with him comfortably, though I couldn't shake the feeling that the conversation was about to take an unexpected turn.

Perplexed by the unfolding drama and the mysterious figure of Efraim looming in the background, Jonas, his smile wide but uncontrolled, instructed me to return to my seat and await his return, warning that I might have just made the biggest mistake of my life. I shared the cryptic conversation with Daniel, my thoughts a whirlwind of conflicting emotions and unanswered questions. What was it about the girls that could endanger my life? Were they the undeclared children of the president? And what was behind the big smile on Jonas's face that didn't seem to match his words?

Restless with anticipation, I observed the commotion around me. The hushed whispers and furtive glances only added to the air of mystery that enveloped the room. Should I venture back to Jonas, potentially intruding on the delicate balance of the girls' night out, or should I remain a silent observer, allowing events to unfold naturally?

As the night wore on, the looming presence of the unknown force and the intricate connections between our intertwined fates left me on edge, caught in a web of intrigue and uncertainty. The promise of impending revelations hung in the air, casting a shadow of suspense over the unfolding drama.

In that moment, amidst the whispered secrets and hidden truths, I realised that the night held more than mere chance encounters and fleeting conversations. It was a tapestry of interconnected destinies, each thread weaving a tale of love, friendship, mystery, and the unspoken bonds that bound everyone together in the labyrinth of life.

As the night sky faded into the late hours, casting a sense of joy over the hotel's opulent interiors, I awaited Jonas's return, eager to unravel the enigma at the heart of our intertwining journeys. In the quiet moments of anticipation, the echoes of whispered confidences and shared laughter lingered, a testament to the profound connections that transcended time and space, binding us together in a tapestry of shared experiences and enduring friendships.

Under the dim glow of the chandeliers, the air within the prestigious restaurant buzzed with whispers of elegance and sophistication. It was a world where luxury mingled with opulence, and high society moved effortlessly among themselves. Amidst this refined atmosphere, Jonas, with a glint in his eye, beckoned me to follow him, his demeanour filled with the anticipation of unveiling a mystery.

As I trailed behind Jonas, my curiosity piqued, we soon arrived at a table where three figures sat, their presence commanding attention. The middle girl, adorned in a breathtaking dinner gown, exuded an aura of grace that illuminated the room. Her eyes sparkled with a mixture of mischief and allure, adding to the mystique that surrounded her.

Jonas, ever the instigator, grinned mischievously as he addressed the trio. "Is this the mannerless guy who rudely ate your dinner? We must punish him now. What is your verdict and sentence for his sins?" The youngest of the three girls, her eyes twinkling with playful defiance, swiftly responded, decreeing that I must be given a warning and foot the bill for their table.

Seating myself reluctantly, I attempted to reason with the trio, arguing that my actions were merely a form of not letting food go to waste, and there was no financial harm in what I had done to suggest I should pay for it. In that trivial courtroom, Jonas cleverly intervened, saying, "It's not about the food, it's about your manners. Did you forget your mother's lessons on not eating other people's food without permission?" My protestations fell on deaf ears, however, as they insisted on their verdict.

In a gesture of reconciliation, I proposed to replace their judgement with a bottle of the finest champagne in the establishment, hoping to atone for my alleged transgression. At the mention of champagne, the middle girl's eyes widened in surprise, and her lips curled into a smile. Encouraged, I suggested that the conditions be that I sit beside her, promising to conduct myself with the utmost decorum. Before I could even finish, the middle girl graciously shifted in her seat, creating space beside her—a silent invitation for me to join her.

Lost in the enchanting presence of these intriguing women, I found myself ensconced in their company, the cares of the outside world fading into the background. Forgotten were the friends I had initially intended to spend the evening with, as I became engrossed in the laughter and camaraderie shared with the trio and Jonas.

When Daniel, a familiar face, approached our table to check on me, he witnessed a scene that surprised even him. Gone was my usual reserved demeanour, replaced by a newfound energy and courage that seemed to have been awakened in me. As Daniel shared the champagne with us, after telling him it was a punishment for my behaviours, he casually mentioned that he had already paid the bill, admitting that it was his fault and not mine. He explained that the hunger that led me to eat the leftovers was due to our trip to his uncle's village earlier that day.

With a cheer, followed by Daniel's departure, I continued to engage with the trio, their infectious laughter filling the air.

Swiftly, I turned the situation to my advantage and said that this meant we would have to meet again, as I still needed to be punished. The girls laughed, their melodious voices blending with the soft music that rustled through the room. Despite the beautiful surroundings, their taunting giggles filled me with unease.

As they conversed in rapid Hebrew, my frustration mounted again at being excluded from their intimate jokes. I demanded a full translation of everything said in Hebrew since our first meeting, determined to unravel the mysteries hidden in their whispered conversations. Sensing my annoyance, the girls fumbled with nervous laughter as they scrambled to provide the translations.

Insisting that each girl whisper the translations into my ear, I sat poised, ready to discern the truth in their words. With amusement twinkling in their eyes, they spoke one by one, sharing their versions of the whispered phrases. But as I listened intently, it became apparent that their translations didn't align; each one offered a different interpretation of the cryptic Hebrew words.

The mismatched translations sent a chill down my spine, signalling that their words held a deeper meaning—perhaps veiled insults or hidden truths. The air grew tense with anticipation as I realised the gravity of their whispered conversations. What had begun as playful teasing now felt like a deliberate game, their camaraderie a façade concealing their true intentions.

In that moment, the innocence of the evening faded, replaced by an undertone of deception. I knew then that this encounter held more than just punishment; it held secrets waiting to be uncovered. As I gazed at the girls, I braced myself for the challenges that lay ahead, determined to navigate the web of deceit and banter they had woven around me.

As I convinced them that their translations didn't match, I took control of the foreign language situation. We agreed not to use Hebrew again, and my disappointment was palpable. The girls, sensing my frustration, genuinely apologised, assuring me there was nothing malicious behind their words.

The girls, who had appeared stoic and impassive at the beginning of the evening, revealed themselves to be sensitive souls. Their laughter rang out melodiously, and their tears flowed freely in moments of shared amusement. Their emotional outbursts, triggered by the simplest of jokes or remarks, left me in awe of their genuine spirits and innocence.

In the midst of this newfound camaraderie, I found myself swept up in the tide of mirth and emotion, laughing along with the trio and Jonas as we shared moments of unbridled joy. The barriers that had initially stood between us crumbled, revealing the true essence of our connection—a shared bond of laughter and friendship that transcended boundaries.

As the evening unfolded with its tapestry of laughter and camaraderie, I realised that sometimes, it takes a chance encounter with unexpected companions to rediscover parts of ourselves we had long forgotten. In the company of the enigmatic sisters, I discovered a sense of belonging and authenticity that rejuvenated my spirit, bringing a newfound lightness to my soul. And as the night wore on, enveloped in the warmth of newfound friendships, I revelled in the magic of the moment, grateful for the serendipitous turn of events that had led me to their table.

In the heart of a bustling hotel lobby, while I sat and enjoyed the company of the girls and Jonas, I was met with familiar faces who called out my real name with warmth and recognition. Jonas had been jokingly calling me Ephraim until, with a hint of frustration, the middle girl exclaimed, "Enough with the disguises and mysteries. It's time for transparency and honesty in this gathering. Who are you, what's your real name, and what do you do for a living?"

It soon became apparent that the girls had also given me false names, as we began to introduce ourselves as if meeting for the first time. At that moment, Jonas, his demeanour laced with a sly smile, interrupted our exchange.

"Wait," Jonas said, his words hanging in the air, causing a hush to fall over the group. "Do you all remember the marriage exchange plan we hatched some months ago?" Confusion rippled through the crowd, each face reflecting a blend of surprise and intrigue.

Little did I know that the middle girl was Jonas's landlady, a woman I had once planned to marry in a time long past. Our affair had crumbled under the weight of unexpected circumstances, leaving a trail of broken promises and dashed hopes in its wake. To add to the tangled web of fate, the younger sister beside her was the intended match for my brother Kaleb, who was on the brink of marriage to another woman that very weekend.

As Jonas continued his revelations, a sense of disbelief and awe settled over us, like actors on a vast stage of destiny. The clash of past decisions and future possibilities loomed large, casting a shadow of uncertainty over our once-simple gathering.

Yet, amidst the chaos of emotions swirling around us, Jonas's eyes shone with a newfound determination. The revival of our long-forgotten arrangements sparked a glimmer of hope in his gaze, a chance for redemption in the face of past regrets.

"What you want to do is up to you now," he declared, his voice steady with resolve. "God has plans for you from the beginning, but it was interrupted unexpectedly. Now He is offering you both another chance. Your fates are in your own hands. God doesn't give a third chance."

His words hung in the air, heavy with meaning, and he clearly believed in the intertwined destinies he spoke of.

Bewildered by the sequence of events that led to our chance encounter, I—an eternal dreamer with a penchant for romanticising the ordinary—and the middle girl/landlady, a free spirit with a sparkle in her eyes that could rival the stars above, stood frozen in time. We were enveloped by the surreal moment, as if the universe itself had paused to hold our destinies in its grasp. As the rain drummed a rhythmic melody on the glass roof of the lobby, we exchanged hesitant smiles, both of us feeling the inexplicable pull of fate weaving its intricate web around us.

Was it mere coincidence that brought us together, or was it something more profound, something beyond our comprehension? I pondered these questions, my heart whispering that this meeting was divinely orchestrated, and that it was a meeting that would alter the course of our lives forever.

In that fleeting moment, as the live music buzzed around us, I looked into the middle girl's eyes and saw a reflection of my own hopes and dreams—a mirror image of a future I longed to embrace. With a certainty as steadfast as the rising sun, I knew she was the missing piece to my puzzle, the one who would walk beside me through life's tumultuous journey.

In that moment, amidst the chaos of the lobby, we found solace in each other, knowing that we were no longer alone in the vast expanse of the world. For me, the sequence of events that led to our second meeting was not just a coincidence—it was a divine proclamation, a confirmation that she was indeed my future wife, my soul mate, my everything.

Helen, the middle girl—now revealed as both my former 'fiancé' and landlady—struggled to comprehend whether this was a carefully orchestrated plan or a mere twist of fate. Her older sister, unknowing of the tangled affairs of the past, urged us to move forward. It was getting late, she insisted, and they should return to their aunt's house in the city centre. It was as if the eldest sister felt responsible for the two younger ones, tasked with deciding when to leave.

Their aunt, a stern presence who lived in central Asmara, would surely reprimand them for staying out late, especially with the impending family wedding drawing near.

In the dimly lit corner of the vibrant reception hall, amidst the swirl of music and laughter, a moment unfolded that felt like a stroke of unexpected fate. As the night drew to a close and we bid farewell to the girls, I found myself alone with the middle girl, her eyes reflecting the soft glow of the evening lights.

The evening had been a whirlwind of interactions, yet in that moment, the crowd seemed to part intentionally, leaving us to exchange our goodbyes in private. With a mix of nerves and excitement, I mustered the courage to ask for her phone number, a smile tugging at the corner of my lips. I asked if she would be open to me reaching out after her family's upcoming wedding, wishing her joy for the celebration and offering my assistance if needed.

Then came the moment when I reached for my phone, a mischievous glint in my eyes. I began typing her name into my contacts, registering her as "wife." The middle girl's eyes widened in disbelief, unable to grasp the boldness of my actions.

"Are you serious? You are registering me as your wife?" she protested, her cheeks flushed with a mix of surprise and delight.

With a playful smirk, I calmly replied, "I may not be your husband yet, but you are already my wife." The gods spoke for me, I didn't know what I was doing or saying.

My words hung in the air, carrying a weight of certainty and determination that sparked a newfound curiosity within her. She couldn't ignore the flutter of emotions swirling in her chest as she gazed into my eyes, sensing a connection that went beyond mere words.

The bold gesture of registering her as "wife" on my phone ignited a spark of excitement and anticipation, leaving us both eager to see where this unexpected journey would lead. And there, in that hotel parking lot, amidst whispered promises and shared laughter, two souls dared to dream of a future intertwined, guided by the courage of a single act that changed everything.

Although she kindly extended an invitation to their family wedding, I regretfully explained that prior commitments would take me to Massawa with my newlywed brother, meaning I would miss their special day. However, I promised that I would remain by her side for the rest of our lives—a vow delivered with sincerity that elicited a sheepish smile from her.

As I returned to the hotel alongside my friend Jonas, the weight of the evening's events lingered between us. His words resonated in the quiet of the night as he encouraged me, affirming that the middle girl was an exceptional match for me, both in beauty and character. His earnest belief in our connection sparked a newfound determination within me, knowing that nothing would bring him greater happiness than to see us together.

Re-joining our oblivious friends in the lobby, the world seemed unchanged, unaware of the profound shift that had occurred in my heart in the space of just a few fleeting moments. As I relayed the unfolding events to Daniel, his eyes held a knowing twinkle. He expressed his conviction that this union was meant to be, and with unwavering confidence, he praised the middle girl's unmatched qualities, offering his wholehearted congratulations, as though our future had already been sealed in destiny.

Assuring both Daniel and Jonas of my genuine feelings and intentions, I emphasised my deepening connection with the middle girl. I promised to nurture and elevate our budding relationship with honesty and authenticity.

As the night drifted towards its end, a sense of purpose and anticipation bloomed within me, setting the stage for a journey intertwined with love, destiny, and the unwavering companionship of kindred spirits embarking on a shared path. And so, under the watchful gaze of the silent night, a tale of unexpected beginnings and promising futures unfolded, paving the way for a love story destined to be written in the stars.

Yet, on the opposite corner of my life, where darkness loomed, stealing away my happiness, I watched my father's health continue to deteriorate that summer. It felt as though the very foundation of our family was crumbling. His once strong and vibrant presence was now reduced to a mere shadow, requiring round-the-clock care and constant monitoring. My mother, ever devoted, stood by his side, her unwavering love and prayers the only solace she could offer in the face of his declining health. Visitors came and went, offering their support and well-wishes, but it was clear that the burden of my father's care was taking its toll on all of us.

The situation at home not only deterred me from enjoying my new feelings but also denied me the joy of sharing the new romantic adventures with my father, my best friend with whom I had shared every tale, all my life.

The simple act of leaving the house had become an arduous task. The lack of suitable, disability-friendly transport made even small outings nearly impossible. Long flights abroad, once a source of joy and adventure, were now a distant memory, postponed at the advice of my father's medical team. Still, he was determined to attend my brother Alazar's wedding in America later that summer. His frequent strokes and other complications necessitated regular hospital admissions, each one a stark reminder of the fragility of life.

As I grappled with the emotional turmoil of witnessing the slow dismantling of my family, a new love blossomed in my life, bringing with it a sense of hope and renewal. Amidst the chaos and heartbreak, this newfound love became a beacon—a reminder that there was still beauty and joy to be found, even in the face of pain and uncertainty.

In the midst of our burgeoning romance, we bore witness to the slow unravelling of our friend Fasil's marriage. His eyes held the weight of a thousand burdens, the lines etched on his face telling a story of heartache and disillusionment. The summer of family chaos had taken its toll, and Fasil had made the difficult decision to part ways with his wife. As we revelled in the intoxicating rush of new love, Fasil grappled with the painful reality of a love once cherished, now crumbling before his eyes.

Despite the joy that blossomed within us, the contrast of our happiness against Fasil's turmoil left a bittersweet taste in my mouth. Fasil, burdened by the need to conceal his own love affair, moved through the summer with a heavy heart and a low profile. The shadows of secrecy clung to him, a constant reminder of the impending divorce awaiting him back in Sweden. Our adventures, once filled with carefree abandon, now carried the weight of Fasil's unspoken struggles, casting a poignant shadow over our idyllic days.

On another front, within the circle of friendship, trust and values were in constant turmoil, weighed down by illness and despair. My friend Abel, once full of life and laughter, now battled a multitude of illnesses with no sign of recovery. His drinking habit had worsened, and hospital visits had become a daily ritual. I did what I could to help, but it felt like an insurmountable challenge. I found myself conferring with his mother regularly, desperately seeking a way to save him. But without his own participation, there wasn't much that could be done.

As I continued to support Abel's family—emotionally and financially—I longed to pull him back into the world of adventure and joy we had once shared. But it seemed impossible. His once vibrant spirit was now shrouded in a veil of suffering, and my attempts to reach him felt futile. I watched as he withdrew further into himself, his eyes losing their sparkle, and his laughter becoming a distant memory. It was a painful sight, one that tugged at my heartstrings and left me feeling helpless.

Despite the overwhelming challenges, I refused to give up on Abel. I clung to the memories of our friendship, to the moments of laughter and camaraderie that had defined our bond. I held onto the hope that, one day, he would emerge from the darkness that had consumed him. And so, I continued to stand by his side, offering whatever support I could, even as the world around us seemed to crumble. The journey was fraught with uncertainty, but I was determined to be there for Abel, to remind him that he was not alone in this battle.

Amidst this heady mix of love and loss, I found myself navigating a world of undefined emotions. The rain-drenched days and balmy nights became a backdrop for the complexities of human connection, where themes of sentimentality played out in the intricate dance of our intertwined lives. As we embraced the unknown, our hearts brimming with the promise of a new beginning, we couldn't help but be haunted by the poignant contrast of my father's worsening health, Fasil's shattered dreams, and Abel's silent suffering.

As the summer drew to a close and the diaspora began returning to their homes abroad, I found myself caught in a whirlwind of emotions and new beginnings.

Amidst the weddings and honeymoons, my heart had been drawn to a woman whose presence had ignited a spark within me. After the joyous affair of her sister's wedding had concluded, I was determined to see her again before I had to return to Dubai.

Despite the hectic schedule following both of our family weddings, I made every effort to arrange a meeting with her. Finally, with my departure looming, I insisted that we meet and get to know each other better. She was cautious, and rightfully so, not wanting to rush into anything before we truly understood each other. We agreed to meet at The Intercontinental Hotel in Asmara, and I eagerly awaited her arrival at the Green Restaurant, where we planned to have dinner and see where the evening would take us.

Sitting at our reserved table, sipping cognac and watching the familiar faces around me, I couldn't shake the feeling of anticipation mixed with a tinge of nervousness. Minutes turned into an hour, and despite my repeated attempts to reach her by phone, there was no response. My emotions began to spiral as I made frequent trips to the smoking area, desperately trying to distract myself. The waiters were sympathetic, but she was nowhere to be found, and her phone remained switched off. The one call that rang was abruptly cut off before it was answered. I imagined she had hung up when she saw my number appear on the screen.

Frustrated and disheartened, I found myself in the lobby of the grand hotel, contemplating the possibility that she had intentionally stood me up. Amid the opulence of the hotel lobby, where chandeliers cast a soft glow on the marble floors, I sat lost in my own world of heartbreak. The air was thick with the scent of luxury, a stark contrast to the heavy burden weighing on my chest.

It was then that my friend Alem, owner of a struggling travel agency and chairman of the Travel Agents Association of Eritrea, found me. His face reflected the distress from the tense meeting he had just endured. The travel industry was on the brink of collapse, plagued by a chronic shortage of hard currency and unpaid debts that had lingered for years. The looming threat of foreign airlines ceasing flights only added to the chaos. Yet, despite the turmoil in his own life, he saw me sitting there, lost in my personal anguish.

As he settled into the seat beside me, his eyes showed a mixture of concern and resignation. He spoke of the turmoil in the industry, the looming crisis that threatened to upend everything he had worked for. But my mind was elsewhere, trapped in the memories of a love that had never even had the chance to bloom.

The hotel lobby buzzed with activity, a world of movement and sound that felt distant and disconnected from the turmoil inside me. Alem's words faded into the background as my thoughts drifted to a time when love had held such promise, only to slip through my fingers like sand.

As I confided in Alem, I felt a surge of anger and betrayal. I was convinced she had played me, and my mind raced with thoughts of her potential motives. Had she discovered something about my past romantic entanglements in Dubai? Or was she simply toying with my emotions, enjoying the power she held over me? My heart was heavy with frustration, and the weight of unanswered questions pressed down on me.

As my friend Alem and I prepared to leave, two hours after our planned meeting time, I caught a glimpse of Helen, the middle girl, hurriedly entering the hotel, her face partially concealed by a scarf. In my half-drunk state, I lashed out at her, accusing her of deceit and infidelity. With my mood soured and drink-infused behaviour, I refused to entertain any of her explanations, convinced that she had only come to another appointment with someone else. In my anger and hurt, I hurled accusations at her, portraying her as a manipulative woman with ulterior motives.

As I stood there, watching her car disappear into the distance, a surge of anger and frustration swelled inside me. How could she just drive off like that? The magnitude of my love for her had completely blinded me, leaving me incapable of rational thought. I hadn't even considered for a moment that there might have been factors beyond her control, that perhaps she simply couldn't make it on time. Throughout the two-hour wait, I was consumed by anger and jealousy, imagining her somewhere in one of Asmara's restaurants, enjoying herself with another man without a care in the world.

Love, I realised, is such a powerful emotional force that it can distort the mind, making it impossible to entertain even the simplest rational thoughts. I was overwhelmed by a cocktail of regret and wounded pride. My love for her had blinded me, and my inability to consider any reasons for her lateness or absence led to a bitter confrontation. I had allowed my insecurities and past experiences to cloud my judgement, and in my anger, I had pushed her away.

The frustration I felt was all-consuming, clouding my judgement and distorting my perception of reality. I couldn't shake the feeling that she had intentionally snubbed me, that she was revelling in her newfound happiness while I was left behind, wallowing in misery. The thought of her with someone else, laughing and smiling, sent me spiralling into a pit of despair and rage. I couldn't fathom how she could move on so easily, as if my love meant nothing to her. It was as if my entire world had crumbled, leaving me adrift in a sea of tumultuous emotions.

In my mind, I conjured up scenarios where she was deliberately avoiding me. The one time her phone rang and was immediately hung up, I imagined her sitting there, conspiring against me. Why else would she avoid me deliberately? I had been calling her for two weeks, and each time she'd answered on the first ring. Now that she had found her man, she no longer wanted to speak to me. I was jealous, furious, and completely out of control.

Before driving away, I picked up my phone and changed her contact's name from 'wife' to something far less endearing.

As I drove aimlessly through the city streets, my mind raced with thoughts of betrayal and abandonment. The feeling of true love I had discovered just days ago had slipped out of my life, never to return. The once-familiar landmarks blurred into a haze as I grappled with the overwhelming sense of loss and rejection. I couldn't comprehend how everything had unravelled so quickly, how the woman I loved had become the source of my torment. Like they say, it felt too good to be true. The darkness of the night and the heavy rain seemed to mirror the turmoil within me, engulfing me in a maelstrom of conflicting emotions. The anger and hurt raged like a storm inside, threatening to consume everything in its path.

As I reflected on the events of that evening, I couldn't help but wonder if I had allowed my own fears and suspicions to dictate my actions, ultimately sabotaging a connection that had once held so much promise.

The feeling at that moment felt like a summary flashback of the heartbreak Hollywood films I watched all my life. It was the realisation of the fictitious love-inflicted scenes of joy and sorrow in films such as *Endless Love* and *Moonstruck*.

It was a balmy midnight when I found myself at the town centre, ready to make my way home. The weight of the day clung to me like a heavy shroud, urging me to drown my sorrows in the amber liquid of alcohol. As I drove through the familiar streets of our neighbourhood, memories from three decades ago flooded my mind, intertwining with the echoes of an epic love story that had once gripped my heart.

The image of Bar Picolla, a quaint Italian bar nestled in our neighbourhood, flickered in my mind like a nostalgic beacon. With only four seats adorning its veranda, the bar held a special place in my heart, reminiscent of the early days when my older uncles would indulge in drinks while my youthful self savoured gummy sweets. Despite its weathered appearance, Bar Picolla—meaning "The Little Bar"—exuded a timeless charm, a bastion of memories that had weathered the sands of time.

As I settled into a solitary seat at the bar, lost in contemplation, a figure emerged from the shadows. It was Abel, a familiar face I had encountered weeks ago during my brother's wedding festivities.

Abel, who lived only a few metres from Bar Picolla, was visibly intoxicated. He settled beside me, his demeanour a stark contrast to the jovial soul I had met before. With a familiarity born of years gone by, I shared my inner turmoil with him, seeking solace in his seasoned advice on navigating the tumultuous waters of relationships.

In the darkness of the night, sitting under the dim lights at Bar Picolla, Abel and I found ourselves reminiscing about our youthful adventures. Abel, with his infectious laughter and rare sense of humour, never failed to bring a smile to my face, even when recounting the many mishaps we had encountered in our romantic pursuits.

Relating my current situation to our history of failed romantic incidents, one particular memory stood out vividly in our minds as we sat on the worn wooden bench, surrounded by the gentle after-rain breeze of the quiet night.

We chuckled as we remembered the time we had mustered up the courage to walk strange girls we had met at a workers' party inauguration night festivity in Addis Ababa many years ago. Only to find ourselves in a precarious situation, surrounded by a gang of protective brothers, intent on safeguarding their sisters from the likes of us. We were quickly beaten and chased through the dark streets, our hearts pounding with a mix of fear and adrenaline.

Abel grinned at the recollection. "We were no match for the swift and determined brothers. We were left bruised, battered, and thoroughly embarrassed. That was worse than what you have now—at least no one's chasing you!"

We also talked about our old Hollywood romantic favourites—how I was living a real-life replica of David from *Endless Love*, and Abel's obsession with *Grease* and his imitation of John Travolta's features, which had stayed with him all these years.

As we sat at Bar Picolla—for the longest time in years—laughing at the memory, I couldn't help but feel grateful for the enduring friendship and the shared adventures that had shaped our lives. In that moment, I knew that no matter what challenges lay ahead, with Abel by my side, there would always be laughter and camaraderie to see us through. Time slipped away unnoticed, weaving a cocoon of reminiscence around us until the bar owner's gentle reminder signalled the end of our rendezvous.

Too inebriated to drive, I bid Abel farewell and embarked on the half-mile journey home, leaving my car outside Bar Picolla in the cloak of darkness. Having also left my mobile phone in the car, it wasn't until the first light of dawn crept over the horizon that I roused from my drunken stupor. I made my way to collect my car and retrieve my phone, only to be greeted by a flurry of missed calls from an unexpected source—the middle girl. She had been trying to reach me all night.

With a mix of trepidation and curiosity, I returned her call, bracing myself for a storm of retribution for my reckless actions the previous night. To my surprise, her voice carried a tinge of concern, overshadowing any remnants of anger as she expressed relief at my safety, despite my intoxicated state.

As she unravelled the events, she warned me that she wasn't seeking forgiveness and only wanted to clear herself from the perceived guilt surrounding yesterday's misunderstanding. She explained the circumstances that led to her tardiness—an untimely power outage at the hair salon, which also affected their home. She had been stuck in a cask with her phone out of battery power and no way to recharge. The only call that got through was when she returned home and swapped her SIM card into her aunt's phone, but even that quickly died, succumbing to a day-long outage that had affected all of Asmara.

She added that the only reason she showed up after two hours wasn't because she had another appointment, but because she thought I might still be at the club inside the hotel, or perhaps the familiar waiters at the Italian bar would know where I was.

She laughed and told me I was crazy to think she'd come to a date with another man, especially with her face and hair covered in a turban-like scarf. The series of unfortunate coincidences that had disrupted her plans made my initial indignation melt into understanding. It was a deliberate submission not to lose her again. Life, I realised, had a way of being unpredictable, with fragile threads binding us together in unexpected ways.

In a swift turn of events, buoyed by newfound opportunity and a surge of energy, I extended an invitation for another date at a different place in downtown. But, in a spontaneous retreat, I called her again and asked her to join me on a trip to Massawa, a historic Red Sea coastal town ninety kilometres east of Asmara—a two-day escapade infused with the promise of shared moments and untold possibilities.

In a display of decency and respect for boundaries, I worked to build her trust with my assurances that I wasn't planning any games. I confirmed to her that she could bring her sisters and that all the girls would have their own designated rooms, while I would get a room for myself. After conferring with her sisters, the answer came: YES. Three YESs! It felt like winning a golden buzzer on a talent audition.

In the heart of Asmara's central district, the afternoon sunbathed the lush, Italian-built villa of the middle girl's aunt in a warm golden hue. Surrounded by sprawling gardens and elegant architecture, the atmosphere inside was one of familial intimacy and relaxation. The family had gathered for what seemed to be an after-wedding celebration.

Suddenly, the main gate door echoed with a knock. An elderly lady, a longtime maid who had witnessed the growth of the family's girls, cautiously opened the gate to see a stranger standing outside. The man, exuding an air of respectful decency, inquired about Helen's presence. The old lady, taken aback by the sight of the massive rose bouquet in his hands, hesitated before promising to fetch someone to attend to him.

Meanwhile, the aunt, Zaitu, a stern and quick-speaking woman, emerged with a furrowed brow, launching into a barrage of questions aimed at me. "Who are you and what are you doing here? How do you know the girls? They are not cheap girls that you can come unannounced and ask for," she demanded, hitting me with accusations of indecency. Before I could respond, the aunt brusquely ordered my departure, citing the need to protect the girls from unwelcome visitors.

Unbeknownst to the family, I had learned of the aunt's address through a mutual acquaintance, Jonas, who frequented the villa. Despite the aunt's objections, I persisted, explaining that I was an old friend seeking to congratulate the family on their recent celebration. Reluctantly, the aunt agreed to accept the bouquet on behalf of the middle girl but refused to grant me entry.

Just as the situation seemed to reach an impasse, the middle girl herself emerged from the villa, asserting her desire to handle the visitor personally. With a mix of horror and uncertainty, she questioned my presence and how I had come to know their address. As we deliberated, the middle girl hesitated to take the bouquet from me, citing the presence of her mother, elder sister, and guests inside.

However, before a resolution could be reached, the eldest sister of the family, whom I had never met before, radiating authority and grace, intervened. Her welcoming demeanour contrasted sharply with the aunt's suspicion, as she encouraged me to enter and join the family gathering. Overwhelmed by the unexpected turn of events, I followed the eldest sister inside, still clutching the elaborate bouquet in my hands.

The tale of a mysterious man—one who had crashed a dinner and eaten leftovers—had already begun to circulate. This story later transformed me into a popular figure among the city's elites, even being seen with the president's son. I had become a subject of intrigue, a person of interest, and the topic of covert investigations by the brothers, all under the strict instruction of the eldest sister.

Their goal was simple: to protect the family's most precious gem, the middle girl, from a potential 'thief.'

Stepping into the opulent sitting room of the villa, my gaze swept over the older women seated within. Their curiosity was palpable, and the aunt's earlier suspicious description of the commotion outside still hung in the air. Among them, a familiar face caught my eye—Sophie, the Justice Minister. A figure of power and influence, Sophie and I shared a personal connection due to her unforgettable support that had secured my father's release from detention. Another familiar woman among them was the wife of Dr. Zerai, the Oklahoma University researcher who also worked with my father at the Ministry of Agriculture.

As I settled into the company of the women, I surprised them all by going around, hugging them, and distributing roses with a gentle smile. The bouquet of roses I brought for the middle girl was now being given to the women, and their hearts were touched by this gesture; receiving flowers from a man after many years, their faces radiated surprise and joy.

The middle girl, standing at the door, was shaken by the unexpected shift in control of the room and the display of affection, which added another layer of intrigue to my enigmatic presence. She watched as I effortlessly integrated myself into their family network, offering each woman a single rose—symbolic of beauty and grace—which captivated their hearts.

Surprised by my presence, the minister vouched for my character, praising my bravery and gentleness to the bemusement of the family members. The women inquired about my father's health and apologised for not having visited him in a long time due to their busy lives.

As the unexpected visit unfolded, the tensions that initially clouded the atmosphere began to dissipate, replaced by a sense of intrigue and potential connection. Amidst the opulent surroundings and complex family dynamics, a new narrative thread emerged, weaving together past relationships and present circumstances in a tapestry of unexpected encounters and unfolding revelations. As the afternoon light softened into dusk, the villa seemed to resonate with the echoes of a story just beginning to unfold.

Sophie, the minister, a woman of great wisdom and grace, sat at the head of the room, her eyes filled with stories of the past, tales of bravery and courage. She began recounting a story to the women: the girls' mother, the aunt, another relative, and Dr. Zerai's wife. The women listened intently as the minister spoke of my father, who had been unjustly detained, and how his sons—one in Dubai and the other in the US—had bravely come to his rescue.

As the minister's story unfolded, the women nodded in agreement, each one moved by the tale of familial love and sacrifice. It was then that one of the aunts spoke up, remembering when my father had visited their home for dinner, invited by Dr. Zerai, who had since left the country due to a disagreement with the ex-rebel minister, leaving behind a legacy of integrity and loyalty.

The women exchanged glances, sensing a connection to this mysterious newcomer. The aunt, with a sudden change of attitude, boldly declared, "Of course, he is our son. Welcome him; he is one of ours." The women's faces lit up with happiness, and they welcomed me into their fold.

In the quiet moments that followed, I found myself at the centre of their attention, my every word and action drawing the women closer to me. The sisters, drawn by the middle girl's account of the stranger's arrival, joined the group in the sitting room. Their eyes were wide with wonder and curiosity.

The banter and laughter gave way to a gentle conversation as the wise women sought to unravel the mystery of the young man in their midst. I spoke of my parents' situation, their courage and grace, painting a vivid picture of love and resilience that resonated deeply within our family.

The power dynamics shifted subtly in the room. The older women's acceptance and approval enveloped me in a warm embrace. They ushered me to sit comfortably, offering cake and coffee. Their eyes were fixed on me with a mix of admiration and fondness, and I spoke with confidence and poise, basking in the warmth of their newfound connection.

Soon, the tension softened, and the blue-and-white-themed sitting room was filled with laughter and shared stories. My presence wove effortlessly into the fabric of the wise women's lives, adding a new energy to the room. We jumped from one topic to another, and in that moment, the once-stranger me had become part of a tapestry of love and kinship, bound together by the threads of fate and the warmth of newfound family.

In the heart of the room, a woman of quiet grace sat on a dining chair, her eyes fixed on me, as if reflecting memories of a bygone era. She was the girls' granbdmother, and when a moment of silence came after the other women spoke over each other, she began to speak of my grandfather, Goitapa. She held him in high regard for his friendship with her father-in-law, Ra'esi Beraki, the governor of Eritrea under the Emperor's rule. With every word, the connection between our families grew stronger, weaving a tapestry of shared history and mutual respect. As the other women listened attentively, she also spoke of my grandfather's stern appearance in his white traditional attire and the power and integrity he embodied. The care free old woman broke thetension by saying 'I know you are after our most previous girl and I like you a lot already. On your wedding, I will sit on your family's side, that's how much respect I have for your family" She added, "you are a perfect match, you look like each other and you will produce beautiful children". It was a bombshell remark no one expected.

After a brief laugh, I glanced around the room, taking in the intricate details of the décor, the soft glow of the lamps casting a warm ambiance over the space. But as I searched for the middle girl, who had been sitting behind me, seemingly to avoid eye contact, I realised she was nowhere to be found. Her absence was conspicuous in the midst of our gathering.

The authoritative eldest sister, with her commanding voice, questioned the whereabouts of her sibling. Her tone was firm yet tinged with concern. "Why is she sitting alone in the bedroom while everyone is here?" she demanded. "It's not appropriate to stay away when a visitor is in the house. Call her now."

The middle girl, shy and embarrassed by the unfolding drama, offered various excuses for her seclusion, her discomfort from being the focus of this gathering palpable in the air. Despite her attempts to justify her absence, the weight of the eldest sister's words lingered, a silent reprimand that hung heavy in the room.

As the afternoon progressed, I bid farewell to the women, expressing my gratitude for their hospitality and the stories they had shared. They ushered me out with grace, each extending an invitation to return at any time, a polarised contrast to the reception I received when I first showed up. Yet, it was not the invitation itself that I sought, but the feeling of acceptance – the sense of belonging that enveloped me in their presence. The suspicious intruder, who had arrived unannounced, was now ushered out of the villa with pride and respect.

The middle girl, seemingly trapped in her own reticence, found no way to escape the expectations that loomed over her. Yet, as night settled in, she reached out to me. Her voice was tentative, yet earnest, as she sought to unravel the tension that had simmered between us.

In our conversation, she revealed the turmoil that had gripped her during the day's encounter, the unspoken emotions that had coursed beneath the surface. I reassured her that my intentions had been simple – to deliver flowers as a gesture of friendship. But the events had spiralled into a complexity neither of us could have foreseen.

Despite the unexpected turn of events, I found solace in her words, in the wisdom and familial care she extended to me. Before we parted ways, she offered her sympathy for the struggles my father had faced, a gesture of empathy that touched me deeply. Her kindness and compassion painted a portrait of familial warmth, drawing me closer to her, as if she were already a part of my own kin.

As I reflected on the day's events — the intricate dance of connections and emotions that had unfolded — I realised that, within the quiet confines of that house in Asmara, bonds were forged, bridges crossed, and, in the midst of it all, a sense of acceptance and belonging was found. And in the middle girl, with her quiet strength and unspoken vulnerability, I discovered a kindred spirit. It was a connection that transcended mere acquaintance, blooming into something deeper — something that whispered of shared histories and intertwined destinies.

The following day, with the newfound freedom to pick her up from her house, Daniel, our trusted driver, at the helm, we embarked on a scenic journey through winding roads to the coastal haven of Massawa. We made a pit stop at Nefasit to enjoy its famous roast baby goat meat, 'Capretto', and a shot of Uzo or 'Areqi' as it is known locally, a sweet alcoholic shot which tastes like Sambuca, fulfilling the age-old traditions of the small hilly town. Nefasit is precisely halfway between Asmara and Massawa, two cities with an altitude difference of 3400 meters. It is almost traditionally, and scientifically, mandatory to drink Uzo to counteract the acute health effects of the rapidly changing climate. The temperature shifts from a single-digit, rainy season in Asmara to a scorching 50°C heat in Massawa, just a two-hour drive away.

After Daniel, the middle girl, and I shared the adventurous drive through the narrow, twisty, downhill tarmac roads, with the tyres almost touching the edge of 200-metre-deep cliffs on our right, I couldn't help but admire the middle girl's driving skills. Her confidence on the road only added to her beauty. She was a commendable driver — one I could trust.

We arrived in Massawa late that afternoon and checked into the beachfront hotel we had booked.

As the golden hues of the setting sun painted the sky in shades of warm oranges and pinks, we eagerly shed our heavier clothes and embraced the lighter, more freeing attire of the beach. The sand beneath our feet was still warm from the day's sun, inviting us to stroll towards the rhythmic melody of the crashing waves.

Amidst the vast expanse of the Red Sea stood the three sisters, each exuding a unique aura of grace and beauty. Their beachwear reflected their individuality: one in a flowing bohemian dress, another in a chic two-piece swimsuit, and the third — the middle sister — in a strikingly vivid beach dress that seemed as if it had been plucked straight from the pages of a summer fashion magazine.

Already struck by their beauty, it was the middle sister who truly captured my attention. Her sleeveless dress, with a hip-high side cut, revealed just enough to mesmerise without showing too much. The vibrant reds and yellows of her attire seemed to echo the infinite expanse of the sun setting behind the sea, as though she were a part of the breathtaking landscape herself.

With a straw hat in her hand, she exuded a radiant beauty that seemed to transcend the ordinary. Her presence was magnetic, drawing gazes and admiration from all who had the privilege of witnessing her in that moment. Yet, despite her striking appearance, what truly captivated me was the playful innocence that sparkled in her eyes. Her smile was infectious and genuine, as if she were a child caught up in the joy of a seaside adventure. As we reached the sandy beach, she suddenly became agile, free, and liberated, as though a heavy burden had been lifted from her shoulders.

The three sisters made their way toward the water's edge, the middle sister leading the way with a carefree skip in her step. I found myself drawn to her like a moth to a flame. Her laughter rang out like music in the air, mingling with the sound of the waves and the calls of seagulls in a harmonious chorus of delight. Like a paparazzi, I followed her everywhere, clicking away with my camera from every angle and distance, eager to capture the beauty of nature's gift to the world — the middle girl, a photogenic woman deserving of the attention of a model.

With a sudden impulse, she tossed her straw hat playfully into the air. The golden strands caught the dying light of the sun as it arced gracefully before landing softly on the sand. In that moment, she transformed before my eyes, shedding the veneer of sophistication and revealing a carefree spirit that was as enchanting as it was disarming.

As the sisters waded into the shallows, the salty waters embracing their ankles, I couldn't help but feel a surge of gratitude for the serendipitous encounter that had brought me into the orbit of such beauty and joy. In the fading light of the day, with the sounds of laughter and waves as my companions, I knew I had stumbled upon a moment of pure magic on the shores of the Red Sea — a place that had seen some of the worst atrocities during the independence war. And in that moment, surrounded by the beauty of heaven's creation in the form of those three captivating sisters, I felt truly blessed. The rhythm of the sea, the laughter, the good company, and the soft caress of the sea breeze filled me with peace.

As Daniel and the other sisters retired to their rooms after dinner at a beachfront seafood restaurant, the middle girl and I lingered behind. The night unfurled its velvety embrace, casting a tapestry of shimmering stars above us. We found ourselves ensconced on the sandy shore, our souls laid bare and vulnerable in the quietude of the night. Alone amidst the whispers of the waves, the ethereal glow of bioluminescent creatures danced in the water. Surprised by the vibrant nightlife of the seas, we marvelled at the creatures, their neon-bright coloured fins swivelling fast around the beach before diving back into the depths. It was a rare sight we had never imagined seeing, and as we gazed at the spectacle, we felt as though the creatures were celebrating our love.

In that moment, surrounded by the magic of the sea and the beauty of the night, we forged a bond that transcended time. In the purest admiration of nature, we experienced a connection that would stay with us forever.

The next morning, when we asked the friendly beach maintenance crew, they explained with a twist of fairytale belief that the bioluminescent creatures were heavenly messengers delivering their wishes and positive energy through an invisible frequency, coming straight to the shore whenever they sensed true lovers. Although it sounded like a metaphorical depiction of nature at work, the fact that it reflected our own story made us believe it. It felt as if our union had been blessed by a divine force, and even the heavens themselves were approving of our love.

In that fleeting moment of intimacy, under the canopy of a starlit sky, we shared our vulnerabilities, dreams, and fears, weaving a tapestry of trust and affection that bound us together in a symphony of love. And in that quiet, sacred space, we shared our first kiss. The weight of past heartaches and cultural divides dissolved in the warmth of our shared connection, culminating in a tender kiss that sealed our unspoken vows of forever.

In the arms of the middle girl, amidst the whispers of the sea, I found a sanctuary — a place where love transcended all barriers, and the promise of a future filled with endless possibilities beckoned us into the light of a new day.

As the first light of dawn painted the horizon in hues of pink and gold, we parted ways and went to our separate rooms. Both of us, consumed by love like we had never known before, exchanged a second kiss that seemed to last for an eternity — an intimate moment suspended in time.

At that moment, I knew that what had started as a chance encounter in the posh St John's Wood neighbourhood of London, sparked by a failed marital exchange plan set in motion by Jonas, and later found in a coincidental meeting at Top5, had blossomed into a love story worthy of a romantic fiction novel.

As we bid farewell to the summer of 2005, I knew that the memories of Asmara, with Daniel by my side, would forever hold a special place in my heart. And as he drove me to the airport on the day of my departure, the familiar hum of the car's engine providing a comforting soundtrack to our final moments together before we meet again, I felt a profound sense of gratitude for the friendship that had bloomed in the vibrant streets of Asmara.

The middle girl had accepted my invitation to explore the beautiful city of Dubai, and I gladly became her guide, eager to show her every hidden gem and secret spot the city had to offer. For a week, we wandered through the winding streets of old and new Dubai, marvelling at the majestic buildings that pierced the sky, and getting lost in the mesmerizing beauty of the Jumeirah Fountain's graceful dance. From traditional souks brimming with colourful treasures to luxurious shopping malls where dreams came to life, we shared moments that formed a bond between us.

As her time in Dubai drew to a close, she bid farewell and flew back to Asmara, then London, leaving behind a piece of her heart in the desert city. I felt a longing in my soul and found myself drawn to visit her in London. They say 'absence makes the heart grow fonder', and for me and the middle girl, it certainly did. With each visit, our connection deepened, blossoming into a love that neither of us could deny.

Three months after our first meeting, I found myself standing before her in London, my heart trembling with nervous excitement. With shaking hands, I proposed to her, pouring out my love and devotion. Without a moment's hesitation, she said yes, sealing our fate as soulmates destined to walk through life together.

We set a date for our engagement on St. Valentine's Day of the incoming year, choosing a lavish hotel in Asmara as the setting for the celebration. In the bustling city of Dubai, amidst the whirlwind of busy days and work commitments, my mind was consumed with preparations for the engagement in Asmara. As invitations were sent out with the help of my parents and friends, I felt a deep sense of anticipation and excitement for the special day that lay ahead.

One particular person I couldn't imagine celebrating without was my dear friend Abel. Wanting to make sure he felt included in the joyous occasion, I decided to surprise him with a designer black suit, thinking he might not have one suitable for the event. However, my mother's response to the gesture was unexpectedly cold and hesitant, urging me to personally deliver the gift to Abel.

Setting out on the mission to bring the suit I bought in Dubai to Abel's doorstep, I had no idea that my world was about to come crashing down. Upon arriving at his house, the sight that greeted me was both shocking and heart-wrenching. Abel lay in bed, his once vibrant spirit now replaced by a frail, emaciated figure. His pitch-black skin contrasted sharply with his bulging, white eyes, struggling for each breath as his body fought a losing battle.

His mother, a picture of grief and resignation, informed me that Abel had recently been discharged from the hospital with no hope of recovery. She revealed a shocking truth: Abel had been battling HIV, a fact I had been completely unaware of until that moment, as discussing the illness is considered a taboo like other sexually transmitted illnesses. The toll of the harsh medication had ravaged his organs, causing his body to wither away. Excessive alcohol use had further destroyed his health, and now his body was on the verge of collapse — a grim countdown marking his final hours, medically isolated in a secluded room. His mother tearfully advised that she had been given strict responsibility that no one should enter the room except well-protected medical personnel.

Torn between the desire to stay and offer comfort and the fear of unknowingly endangering myself due to the contagious nature of the disease, I bade my dearest friend a tearful farewell. His fragile form, etched in my memory, haunted me as I left his house. I stood alone outside, crying, cursing the world for its cruel and unfair treatment. Why Abel, why now, on the eve of my happiest day?

As I grappled with the shock of the sudden tragedy that had befallen my friend, I knew I had to steel myself for the engagement that awaited. Despite the heavy weight of sorrow that now lingered in my heart, I was determined to ensure that the day remained a celebration of love and joy, especially for my beloved fiancée.

Stepping into the engagement ceremony with a heavy heart but brave resolve, I found myself navigating the festivities with a mixture of emotions. Memories of Abel — the countless adventures, the shared laughter — flooded my mind like a bittersweet film reel, a poignant reminder of the stark contrast between the sheer happiness of the occasion and the impending loss of a cherished companion.

The night sparkled with elegance as guests arrived in their finest black-tie attire. A three-piece live band filled the air with music, laughter, and joy. Around us, a hundred close family and friends gathered to witness our commitment to each other, our love shining bright in the dimly lit ballroom.

As I exchanged vows and promises with my beloved, a sense of gratitude mingled with sorrow, a reminder that life's journey was often fraught with unexpected twists and turns. And as the day drew to a close, I couldn't shake the feeling that, while our lives were moving forward in joyous union, a piece of my heart would forever be tethered to the memory of Abel, a friend whose light had flickered out too soon.

In the midst of celebration and joy, a shadow of loss loomed large, a poignant reminder of the fragility and preciousness of every moment we are granted in this intricate tapestry of life. And as the sun set on that eventful day, I carried within me the duality of love and grief, a testament to the enduring bond that transcends even the most heartbreaking farewells.

Still clad in my tuxedo from the previous night, I decided to go to Abel's house before heading home to rest. Abel's suit, still neatly covered in a large gift bag spread over the backseat of my car, was something I had promised to deliver. I picked it up and brought it to where it belonged. As the first rays of morning sun kissed the horizon, I found myself standing outside Abel's home. The crisp air carried a sombre aura, amplified by the sight of a tent erected in the front yard — a silent mourning, a visual and cultural sign of someone departing the world.

I hesitated to step inside, knowing that within those walls lay heartache and sorrow. But duty called, and with a heavy heart, I crossed the threshold into the sea of grief and despair. Abel's family welcomed me with silent nods and tear-stained faces, their pain palpable in the air. I joined them in their mourning, a solemn observer in a world that had been shattered by loss. I hung the black suit on the centre of a metal frame that had erected the tent, right above his portrait.

Instinctively, I decided to ask the family to bury Abel in the black tuxedo that matched mine, if cultural and religious norms allowed. His mother agreed to do exactly that and confirmed it with a tight hug of gratitude and appreciation for the journey I had taken with her to save Abel from the demons that surrounded him.

The weight of our collective sadness pressed down on me, a heavy burden to bear. And as the day unfolded, I found myself torn between two worlds. On one side, the grief and loss that surrounded me — a stark reminder of life's fragility. On the other, the knowledge that I had to shield my own emotions, lest they impact my new fiancée waiting elsewhere.

The juxtaposition of joy and sorrow was a complex tapestry that I struggled to navigate, the threads of each emotion pulling me in different directions. I tried to offer solace and support to Abel's family, all the while wrestling with my own inner turmoil.

The hours stretched into eternity, each moment a painful reminder of the unfairness of the world. And as dusk descended, casting long shadows over the mounting tent, I realised that some wounds could never fully heal.

I left Abel's home that evening, the weight of the day heavy on my shoulders. The image of the mourning tent lingered in my mind, a stark symbol of life's unpredictability. And so, I drove away with Abel's tuxedo at centre stage inside the tent, carrying with me the heavy knowledge that I would never see him again in this life.

The summer of that same year arrived in a whirlwind of anticipation and preparations, as my beloved and I exchanged vows in a fitting wedding ceremony at the Asmara Expo halls. Surrounded by our families and friends, who had stood by us through thick and thin, we pledged our eternal love in front of an altar adorned with blossoming flowers and flickering candles.

As we danced beneath the starlit banquet hall, surrounded by the warmth of our loved ones, we knew that our journey together was just beginning. Through the highs and lows that life would inevitably bring, we would stand side by side, hand in hand — a testament to the enduring power of love.

And so, in the quiet whispers of the night, as the moon cast its gentle glow upon us, we embraced our future with open hearts, ready to face whatever challenges lay ahead, knowing that our love would always guide us home.

Our first daughter, Delia, was born exactly nine months after our enchanting wedding day, in June of 2006, bringing with her a newfound sense of completeness and love that filled our home. Delia was a mesmerizing reflection of her mother, with the same sparkling brown eyes that seemed to hold the secrets of the universe, and a smile that could light up the darkest of nights. From the moment she entered our lives, she wrapped us around her tiny fingers, filling our days with laughter and warmth.

An Unexpected Encounter

What's Going On?

In the weeks that followed Delia's birth in London, unexpected events began to unfold as I juggled between London and Dubai. While returning to Dubai from a short trip to London, I found myself stopped at the airport for further checks of my residency permit.

Dubai Airport, known for its strict immigration protocols and frequent detentions of suspected illegal passengers, presented a daunting sight as I was directed to sit alongside other stranded travellers, predominantly from Asian and African backgrounds. My passport was still being scrutinised by the young immigration officer who sat in the small cubicle, along with a senior officer. Despite my inquiries, the immigration officers remained tight-lipped as they scrutinised my documents.

Confident in my legal status, I patiently awaited the completion of the passport and visa verification process. However, as time ticked by, the waiting area swelled with an increasing number of passengers requiring checks, causing chaos and frustration. Eventually, we were moved to a more secluded area, further intensifying the air of uncertainty and tension among the detained individuals.

We were then herded into a large hall, with no seats available. We were instructed to leave our belongings behind and were led by officers as if we were criminals. In my handbag was my wife's wedding gift ornaments, a staggering 300 grams of gold jewellery I had purchased in Dubai, which she had asked me to exchange for a different design she had chosen.

The lack of transparency and communication only fuelled my growing apprehension, especially considering my longstanding residence and business presence in Dubai. Having witnessed the unjust treatment of Asian and African foreigners in the past by the Dubai authorities, I understood the gravity of the situation unfolding before me. Despite my attempts to assert my credentials, I was escorted onto a bus with no explanation, destined for an immigration detention centre outside the city.

Upon arrival at the facility, we were assigned to cells in groups. The atmosphere was heavy with anxiety and despair. The interactions with fellow detainees — mostly destitute Asian labour workers who only spoke their native languages — painted a stark picture of the harsh reality within the confines of the detention centre.

As the days passed without any contact with the outside world, my family and friends grew increasingly distraught over my disappearance. Despite their best efforts, they struggled to uncover my whereabouts or the reasons behind my detainment, plunging them into a state of helplessness and confusion.

Rejected access to phones or any form of communication, I felt isolated and powerless within the confines of the detention centre. Each passing hour brought a growing sense of uncertainty and dread, exacerbated by the swift removal of detainees without explanation, leaving behind a revolving door of new faces.

With the help of a few Arabic-speaking friends, some information about my detention surfaced, revealing the harsh reality: I was being processed for deportation with a lifetime ban from entering the UAE. The enormity of the situation weighed heavily on me and my loved ones, who waged a relentless battle to secure my release and to get to the bottom of these unclear affairs, amidst mounting challenges and unanswered questions.

In the midst of this turmoil and injustice, the resilience of family, friends, and allies shone through, underscoring the relentless pursuit of truth and justice in the face of adversity. Despite the tribulations endured, the unwavering support and determination to unveil the mysteries surrounding my detainment symbolised the unyielding spirit of those fighting for my freedom and vindication.

My wife Helen, completely oblivious to my unexpected disappearance, made several distress calls to various people she thought might have a clue about my whereabouts. It was unimaginable to think that her beloved husband, who had so joyfully celebrated the birth of their newborn, could board a flight to Dubai and disappear into thin air without a trace. Helen made frequent contacts with Qatar Airways, who confirmed I had reached my destination at Dubai airport, but could not comment on what might have happened after I left the aircraft. To the best of the information they had, they also confirmed there were no reports of medical emergencies or other incidents that could have implicated me in an untidy entry to Dubai.

Meanwhile, the atmosphere around my family and business circle was heavy with worry and tension. My brother Biruk, my registered next of kin and the one responsible for running my business in my absence, found himself at the centre of the chaos. With me incarcerated behind bars in an undisclosed place for no apparent reason and no means of communication to discuss anything, the burden of his business-related responsibilities fell heavily on his shoulders.

Worried family members and friends gathered around Biruk, their anxious murmurs filling the air. Creditors, business associates, and suppliers all clamoured for answers, their patience wearing thin with each passing day. Shipments were stalled, payments overdue, and the once bustling warehouse and office now stood silent and forlorn.

The weight of the world seemed to rest upon Biruk as he tried to navigate the intricate web of problems besetting our business. His heart ached for his brother's predicament.

As the days turned into weeks, the pressure continued to mount on Biruk. He felt like a ship adrift in a stormy sea, unsure of which way to turn. Creditors and suppliers demanded immediate payments, unsure of my future. Consignments held at ports bound for Ethiopia and Eritrea were left with their owners screaming for schedules and confirmations.

Rumours of my possible deportation and the eventual closure of my company began to circulate, followed by a series of dreadful events, each more catastrophic than the last. First, I was mysteriously detained. Then, my office was raided, my commercial licence revoked, and all personal and business bank accounts were closed. Suppliers filed charges against me, demanding untimely payments before I was deported.

A scandal involving one of our suppliers rocked the business world around my company, tarnishing our reputation in the industry. And finally, a sudden economic downturn hit me hard, causing the company to haemorrhage money at an alarming rate.

My business thrived on a delicate balance, with funds flowing in and out seamlessly. Hundreds of thousands in local and hard currency exchanged hands weekly, a dance of transactions crucial to maintaining my impeccable credit history. Never had I defaulted on a payment; my reputation was pristine in the business realm of Dubai.

However, amidst my unexpected predicaments, a shadow began to loom over my operations. My brother Biruk was helpless, as I was the sole director and signatory for all financial transactions, contractual matters, banking, payments, and port passes. The government's strict stance on bounced cheques sent a shudder through my acquaintances. Under Dubai's financial crime laws, a single default above the value of AED5,000 ($1,200) could trigger swift civil prosecution, with warrants issued immediately, demanding payment or risking closure and indefinite remand.

With my whereabouts unknown and uncertainties about the continuity of my business looming, cheques bounced one after the other. My creditors wasted no time in securing warrants, intent on recovering their funds before my rumoured deportation could be carried out. It was common in Dubai to see businessmen take bank loans and disappear through deportation and other planned ways. With my company's bank accounts drained by the first few large cheque payments and assets dwindling, I found myself transferred to a civic police detention centre, facing allegations of non-payment and fraud. Bounced cheques from Dubai Port and Customs authorities, office and residential landlords, and suppliers began to flood in, adding to my misery. There was no chance to address or speak to my creditors.

Unpaid cheques to government offices carried additional weight and required an immediate response. Failure to act quickly would result in stricter state-level prosecutions.

Desperate to fight the mounting accusations, I pleaded with the officers, but my words fell on deaf ears. The only escape from indefinite remand was to settle my debts promptly or face an uncertain fate in court.

Standing at the precipice of unjust and unexplained deportation, my fate was intertwined with the complexities of Dubai's immigration and business systems, where a single misstep could unravel years of hard work and legitimacy. In a land of glittering opportunities and unforgiving regulations, my journey in Dubai took an unexpected turn, navigating the treacherous waters of business, deception, and immigration laws.

The Eritrean consulates in Dubai and Abu Dhabi, nestled among modest buildings overshadowed by their grand neighbours, represented the citizens of our country residing in the United Arab Emirates. Yet, for my brother Biruk and my friends, the consulates had become symbols of disappointment and frustration. Biruk had hoped the consulate would be a source of support and assistance during such a difficult time. However, as he and others soon discovered, the reality was far bleaker. The services offered were minimal, the staff unresponsive, and the representation lacklustre. It seemed that being a citizen of a country with such a low international profile had its consequences — and I was paying the price for my country's weak links, unable to protect its citizens.

Born into a land plagued by constant instability and suffering, my existence seemed predetermined by the misfortunes and humiliation handed down through generations. The echoes of turmoil followed me like a shadow, even when I sought refuge far from the chaos of my homeland.

The importance of having stable roots and proper documentation became glaringly evident as I navigated a world that demanded conformity to stringent requirements. Cursed by my origins, I harboured a deep-seated resentment towards those responsible for our perpetual suffering. All I had yearned for in my childhood was the simplicity of staying close to my parents, being their helping hand in times of need.

Yet, fate had other plans. My father's deteriorating health added to my mother's never-ending burden of care. The weight of responsibility bore down heavily on our family, leaving us vulnerable and fractured. And just when it seemed our struggles had reached a breaking point, news of another son's unexplained detention in a faraway land shattered whatever semblance of peace remained.

The intensity of emotions that surged within me was overwhelming—a turbulent whirlwind of anger, despair, and helplessness. Each trial, each tragedy seemed to compound upon the last, threatening to engulf us in a never-ending cycle of suffering, all stemming from the lands of our origin.

As I stood amidst the wreckage of our shattered dreams, I grappled with the harsh reality that our past would forever shape our present and dictate our uncertain future. With a heavy heart and a burdened soul, I felt hopeless, unable to rise above the chaos or forge a path toward a stable homeland I could call my own—a place where the shadows of misfortune would no longer cast their long, oppressive reach.

Dubai had been a haven for me and my family, a sanctuary from the turmoil and hardships of the homeland I had left behind. It was a world of uncertainty and fear, and I sought a brighter future in this gleaming metropolis. But now, as I sat confined in the police jail, the familiar sights and sounds of the city felt suffocating. Dubai, once a place of hope and joy, now seemed like hell on earth to me.

Amidst the glitzy skyscrapers of Dubai, my business had once thrived, with hundreds of thousands in local and hard currencies flowing through my company accounts. The flow of money was like a well-oiled machine, ensuring seamless transactions and upholding my impeccable creditworthiness. Never had I defaulted on a payment in my entire business life in Dubai—a testament to my commitment to integrity and financial responsibility.

However, beneath the bustling business culture of Dubai lurked a shadow of vulnerability and deceit. The government followed strict rules regarding dishonoured cheques, swiftly penalising those who faltered in their financial dealings. A bounced cheque meant immediate consequences. The beneficiary could quickly obtain a warrant through a quick civil prosecution system, forcing the issuer to either pay up or face remand and the potential closure of their company. The mantra was simple: no pay, no going out.

As fate would have it, a string of unfortunate events unfolded, leading to a cascade of bounced cheques and mounting warrants against me. My creditors, sensing an opportunity to recover their funds, wasted no time in taking swift legal action. The first few cheques that bounced resulted in the closure of my bank accounts, depleting the funds within. Each passing day saw more cheques bouncing, triggering a chain reaction that led to my transfer to a civic police detention centre, where I faced allegations of non-payment and fraud.

I was taken to court for each bounced cheque, with no trial or representation. The verdict was passed immediately—pay up or remain in jail indefinitely. When I asked the civil court to allow me the chance to go out and settle my debts, their answer was one that explained they had no jurisdiction over immigration-related cases and wouldn't order my release, temporary or permanent. It was a grim reminder of the unfair justice system and the special court my father had attended during his own ordeal years ago.

Desperate to rectify the situation, I pleaded with the authorities to allow me the opportunity to resolve both the business and immigration-related issues. Yet, my pleas fell on deaf ears. The officers reiterated that the only means of avoiding indefinite remand was to settle all debts or face a prolonged stay awaiting court judgment and the potential seizure of assets.

While confined in police custody, a glimmer of hope emerged in the form of my brother, who managed to uncover the underlying reason for my sudden detention and deportation order. It appeared that a misstep by my lawyer during the transfer of my residency visa had inadvertently flagged me in the system.

As a result of the war between Eritrea and Ethiopia, which was ignited in 1998, my Ethiopian passport—one I had relinquished due to the segregation that followed the conflict—was still associated with a residency visa marked as absconding. It appeared that my lawyer hadn't cancelled my residency permit on the Ethiopian passport before issuing a new permit on my new Eritrean passport. This situation created a void which indicated I was an absconding offender overstaying in Dubai with an invalid permit. This oversight portrayed me as either living with expired documents or possessing dual identities with similar passports, a red flag for immigration authorities.

The revelation shed light on my predicament, outlining how a simple administrative error had snowballed into a case of suspected immigration fraud. The Dubai government, accustomed to scrutinising cases involving African and Asian residents, had swiftly labelled me as a potential offender without due process. The consequence for such suspicion was clear-cut deportation and a ban, with little room for recourse or appeal. The lawyer, who had closed his office and left the country years ago, was nowhere to address my case. Applications by other lawyers to represent me were rejected in the absence of a case number, as I wasn't prosecuted formally.

Caught in the web of bureaucracy and misunderstanding, I found myself entangled in a system that lacked the mechanisms to differentiate between genuine oversights and deliberate fraud. The blind eyes of justice in Dubai left no room for leniency, especially for those deemed to have breached immigration laws. The narrative of my business success was now overshadowed by legal woes and bureaucratic entanglements, threatening my life at its core.

As the days turned into weeks within the confines of the detention centre, I grappled with the harsh reality of my situation. The prospect of losing everything I had worked so hard to build loomed ominously, a stark reminder of the unforgiving nature of Dubai's legal system. Every passing moment was a testament to the unyielding grip of fate, shaping my destiny in ways I could never have foreseen.

In the end, as I awaited my fate in a foreign land that had once promised prosperity and opportunity, I reflected on the precarious balance between success and downfall. The intricate dance of business dealings and legal intricacies had unravelled a life I once thought secure, leaving me at the mercy of forces beyond my control. Dubai, with its glimmering façade and hidden perils, had become a battleground where fortunes were made and lost in the blink of an eye.

And so, my tale in Dubai seemed to come to a tumultuous end—a cautionary reminder of the fine line between triumph and tribulation in a city where dreams could either soar to new heights or crumble beneath the weight of unforeseen circumstances.

Once burdened by the weight of fraud cases and the looming threat of deportation, I found myself at a crossroads, unsure of what the future held. With the invaluable help of friends and the sale of assets, the darkness that had shadowed my life began to lift. As the last cheques were paid and my debts settled, I felt a glimmer of hope amidst the chaos.

While I grappled with the daunting task of normalising my personal, familial, and business life, my wife emerged as a pillar of strength, a source of unwavering encouragement and hope in the face of adversity. Her resilience in the face of overwhelming odds served as a guiding light, a reminder of the unbreakable bond that held us together.

Through the trying journey, the unexpected incidents, and unforeseen challenges, we found solace in each other's unwavering support and love. And as we weathered the storm that threatened to tear us apart, I vowed to never let anything come between us, to stand by her side through thick and thin, come what may.

Facing the harsh reality of being sent back to my homeland with no meaningful business plan, I made a bold decision to go to Uganda—a land of promise and opportunity, where whispers of good business prospects beckoned. With a heart heavy but determined, I set foot on Ugandan soil, ready to rebuild what once seemed lost forever.

With my Eritrean passport tarnished by the Dubai government and no supporting status to accompany the required documents, the chances of obtaining another visiting visa to the UK seemed unimaginable. We soon started the process for me to acquire citizenship through our marriage.

End Of The Road

Dance with My Father Again

Meanwhile, in Asmara, unaware of my recent unfortunate encounters, my father—due to deteriorating cognitive abilities and declining health—was reaching the final chapter of his life, one that none of us had been prepared for.

As the days passed, it became evident that my father's body was no longer responding to medications, and the inevitability of his passing loomed over our family like a dark cloud. I could do nothing but watch from a distance, helpless and overwhelmed by the impending loss.

In February 2008, my father took his last breath, ending a long, perilous life, marking a profound milestone in our family's history. I knew I had to travel to Asmara to attend his funeral and be there for our mother during these trying times. The journey was long and arduous, each mile bringing me closer to the painful realisation that I was about to bid farewell to the man who had shaped my life in ways I could never fully express.

Upon arriving in Asmara, I was greeted by a sombre atmosphere, as family and friends gathered to pay their respects. The funeral procession made its way to Kakbda, his birthplace, where he would be laid to rest among the rocky hills that had once been his playground.

Surrounded by loved ones, I felt a sense of closure as my father's body was slowly carried along the winding village road—a reverse journey to where he came from and walked miles as a child to attend school to escape poverty. Memories flooded my mind of the tales he had shared, of the hardships he had endured, and of the boundless love he had always shown.

As we reached the burial site, a sense of peace washed over me. The sun cast a warm glow over the rugged landscape, creating a serene light on the scene before me. The mournful wails of grief mixed with the gentle rustling of the wind, forming a melancholy melody of sorrow and acceptance.

I knelt beside my father's grave, the earth cool beneath my fingertips. I whispered my final goodbyes, tears streaming down my cheeks and mixing with the dust of the land that had cradled my father in life and now in death.

In that moment, I felt a deep connection to his roots—the land of Eritrea that had shaped his family's history—and to the legacy my father had left behind. I knew that this was not just an ending, but a new beginning, a chance to carry on his spirit and honour his memory in everything I did.

As the sun began to set, casting long shadows over the village, I stood up, my heart heavy but my spirit light. I took one last look at the place where my father now rested, feeling a sense of peace wash over me.

With a heavy heart and a renewed sense of purpose, I bid farewell to my father and to Eritrea, knowing that our stories would forever be intertwined, woven into the fabric of time and memory. As I turned to leave, I carried with me the lessons my father had taught me, the love that had sustained me, and the hope that would guide me on my journey forward.

The journey ahead, after my father's death, was a lonely one. My mother faced a new chapter in her life, and I had to rebuild myself from the ashes. It was not an easy path. It required patience, hard work, and trust to regain the confidence of my family and friends. Yet, amidst the challenges and setbacks, my priorities remained clear—my wife, my daughter, my mother, and the dream of rebuilding our lives from the ground up. This would require all my resolve and strength.

With unwavering determination, I entered the world of entrepreneurship once more, using the small capital I had managed to recover from services and goods I provided to clients while still in business. I started modestly, with a humble restaurant equipment sales and haulage business in Kampala, Uganda. The welcoming embrace of Uganda's business-friendly environment, coupled with the unwavering support of friends, paved the way for my resurgence in a land that had now become my new home.

It was not long before my wife, Helen, and our child, Delia, joined me, their presence infusing new hope and determination into our shared dreams of a brighter future. We began to enjoy life as a family, watching Delia grow and blossom. Delia became the centre of our lives, loved by everyone for her cheeky, playful nature and the pretty face that resembled her mother's. She became a source of renewed energy, making me forget all the misfortunes and trials of recent times.

My wife, Helen, ever the supportive and shrewd businesswoman, quickly recognised a gap in the property market. With funds mobilised from London, she embarked on a new venture, partnering with local businesses to make her mark.

Amidst the flurry of business activities, joyous news arrived—we were expecting our second child. It filled our hearts with anticipation and excitement. However, the path to welcoming our newest family member was fraught with challenges. Complications arose, requiring specialised medical care and constant monitoring that was unavailable in Uganda but available in London. To make matters worse, my wife battled frequent malaria attacks, which left us attending medical facilities almost daily. The weight of it all pressed heavily on my heart.

As my wife journeyed back to London for the sake of her health and the well-being of our growing family, I remained in Uganda, balancing the demands of financial stability to support us with the longing for my loved ones across the sea.

With each passing day, the toll of travelling between London and Kampala, managing family and businesses in two distant lands, and the lack of adequate funding facilities in Uganda prompted us to make a difficult decision. It was time to make London our permanent home, a place of stability and security. London was already home to my wife, who had always lived among her brothers and sister, a retreat where she could find comfort when the world didn't function well for her.

Through the unexpected path life had led us on, we discovered a newfound sense of belonging. With the realisation of my British citizenship through marriage, we bid farewell to our businesses in Kampala, collected what little we had left from the sale of the companies I had established, and built a new life in London, with no intention of leaving again.

I stayed behind in Kampala for a while to conclude the transfer of assets from the business I sold. Helen and Delia took the earliest flight to London to attend medical appointments.

Before moving to London for good, I had a quiet and lonely time, for the first time in my life. With not much to do, every evening, I recounted my journey, sitting in the quiet corner of my empty apartment in Kampala. The soft glow of the lamp illuminated the room as I listened to my collection of songs I call my life's soundtracks. I immersed myself in mixed memories of my childhood and time with my brothers, and how scattered we are now. I found myself in every lyric of every song. It felt as though they were all sung for me. I found myself lost in a sea of memories. It was a time of reflection, a time to delve deep into the journey my family and I had taken over the years. The highs and lows, the joys and sorrows—they all seemed to blend together in a whirlwind of emotions that I couldn't quite shake off.

The weight of my past decisions hung heavy in the air, tugging at the corners of my mind. I had always been a restless soul, constantly seeking the next thrill, the next adrenaline rush. But as I looked back at this time of closure, following our beloved father's final chapter in heaven, I realised that there had been no letting go, no moment of respite from the constant changes brought upon us.

As I leapt from memory lane to the present and pondered my future, a sense of unease settled in my chest. The world outside was a chaotic mess, plagued by injustice and the suffering of countless souls.

From a young age, I had absorbed more than I should have. My own intelligence had worked against me. I shouldered burdens that were never meant for me. I had sacrificed my childhood in pursuit of excellence, in the hope of making my parents proud.

I subconsciously chased after wealth and fame, making bold moves along the way. I have achieved where others failed, helped many in need, and lifted up desperate souls. I had tasted the fruit of success and the joy that comes with it. Knowing that I have completed my obligations to the world, I decided to step back, slow down, and watch the world pass by. The constant cycle of adventure and excitement had consumed me, taken its toll on my livelihood. Now, with a wife and children of my own, I knew that my actions could no longer be reckless. I needed to take the slow lane of life's highway to see the world through a different lens.

I dedicated myself to stepping back from the risky world of business and resorted to helping others, holding my father's torch high. I would use my skills and knowledge for the greater good, but this time I would do so with an awareness of the risks involved. I needed to find a balance, to master the art of giving without sacrificing myself in the process.

The changes I experienced in this one lifetime were too much to carry; they were too heavy to bear on my own. It was time to unpack my life, to sift through the baggage and focus on what truly mattered—my own family. And so, I turned my priorities to my wife and children, to the young souls who looked up to me for guidance and protection from the cruel world that was unfair to my family and many other human beings. I promised not to let myself be affected by what happened in Eritrea and Ethiopia. I had had enough of the careless politicians who did not care for our souls. We had been used as their bullets and shields for far too long. The UK would provide me with a neutral life, without having to worry about what might happen tomorrow to me or my children.

Surrounded by remnants of a life lived fast and hard, I made a promise to myself. I would be there for my children as my parents were for me. The misfortunes of my friends Abel and Nebiyu were the biggest lessons for me about maintaining a good family structure.

And as the playlist of my favourite songs came to an end towards the stretch of that night, a sense of peace settled over me. The tumultuous storm that had raged within me for so long began to calm, the motion came to a still, and the grinding echoes of my past tragedies faded into the background. I closed a chapter in my life, promising myself to start a new path with a low profile, slow and easy.

PAYING IT FORWARD

I'll be there

In the heart of the bustling city, amidst the promise of a fresh start, we found solace in the embrace of familyhood. The memories of our past struggles faded into the background as we looked towards a future filled with hope and possibilities. Our journey, once marred by uncertainty and upheaval, had brought us to a place of stability and newfound purpose, where we could finally call London our home.

In the small flat in St John's Wood, Westminster, London, where our connection started with Jonas's matchmaking plan that did not take off, our family flourished under the loving care of devoted family members. With no immediate need to engage in business, I found myself immersed in the world of caregiving, tending to my pregnant wife, Helen's medical needs with unwavering dedication, and watching Delia grow. Alongside us stood Helen's supportive sisters and brothers, forming a close-knit circle of love and support.

It was amidst this backdrop of familial harmony that our second child, Rakieb, entered our lives – a beacon of joy and jubilation. With her rosy cheeks and bright eyes, Rakieb brought a new level of happiness to the family, her presence filling our home with warmth and laughter. As a full-time parent, I embraced the role with grace and determination, watching over our children's every step as they navigated the world of growth and discovery.

As the children grew stronger and ventured into the realm of school, I began to shift my focus towards reinvigorating my life skills. With a heart full of compassion and a desire to make a difference, I slowly integrated back into the working world after two years of quiet and slow life, dedicating my time to humanitarian volunteer work. I started volunteering in various charities and projects, finally settling in supporting disadvantaged ethnic children with learning difficulties and their families, offering them solace and guidance in a world that often seemed daunting.

In a society known for its diversity and acceptance, I dedicated my time to helping young people from minorities find services to meet their needs. With a heart full of compassion and a mind brimming with knowledge, I tirelessly worked to uplift those in need.

With a kind soul, a gentle smile, and a passion for aiding others based on my own life experiences, I understood the struggles and challenges that families face. Determined to make a difference, I volunteered my time to advise and support families of asylum seekers with various disabilities, guiding them through the complex web of rights and responsibilities in their new homeland.

Often, I could be found helping others either by phone or face-to-face, patiently assisting individuals eager to learn and grow. I guided them through the intricacies of applying for social care support, seeking assistance from the Home Office, and accessing essential services such as special needs schools and care services. With a calm demeanour and infinite patience, I made sure no question went unanswered, and no concern went unheard.

Beyond practical assistance, I also served as a bridge for those struggling with language barriers. With my knowledge of multiple languages, I facilitated communication between service users and the various institutions they needed to engage with. I ensured that information about integration processes, rights, and responsibilities was clear and accessible to all, fostering a sense of empowerment and independence among my mentees.

Moreover, I shared valuable advice with families of disabled individuals, reminding them to balance their personal aspirations with the well-being of their loved ones back home. I emphasised the importance of prioritising one's own future while also considering the impact of their actions on those they left behind. My words resonated deeply with those I guided, instilling in them a sense of belonging and mindfulness.

For some families, whose journeys had been marked by turbulent pasts under various institutions, there are moments of both despair and hope—a constant battle between fear and determination. As these young men and women navigate the complexities of their lives in society, they find solace in the kindness of strangers—people who understood their pain, their struggles, and their dreams for a better future. It was through these acts of compassion that they began to heal, slowly but surely, finding a sense of belonging in a world that had once seemed so foreign. I helped these families connect to services that provided a safe space for them to share their stories, confront their demons, and forge a path toward a more fulfilled life.

Through it all, these families discovered a resilience within themselves that they had never known existed—a strength that came not from bravado or stubbornness, but from a quiet determination to forge a new path forward, to create a future filled with promise and possibility.

As time passed, my small acts of kindness and guidance had a ripple effect, transforming the lives of those I touched. Through my selfless devotion and unwavering commitment to humanitarianism—values passed down to me from my parents—I not only helped them integrate into society but also empowered them to strive for a better tomorrow.

In the heart of UK society, amidst the hustle and bustle of daily life, I stood dedicated to providing hope and support, a silent force of good in a world filled with challenges. My story, though quietly woven into the fabric of society, spoke volumes about the power of empathy, understanding, and courage in the face of adversity. And as I continued my work, one person at a time, my legacy of compassion and guidance shone brightly, illuminating the path for those in need of a guiding light.

Despite my newfound involvement in informal humanitarian work, I also kept an eye out for potential business opportunities, with the wheels of entrepreneurship ever turning in the back of my mind. I navigated the bustling streets of London, assessing the atmosphere for avenues that aligned with my values and goals, all the while basking in the security and freedom that the UK afforded me.

Meanwhile, Helen, my wife, found her passion in running a successful hospitality business that I helped manage. With an innate talent for creating culinary delights and a knack for business savvy, Helen poured her heart and soul into her venture, delighting patrons with her delectable creations and finding immense joy in the art of culinary craftsmanship.

Together, Helen and I carved out a life that blended caregiving, entrepreneurship, and humanitarianism. Our home became a sanctuary of love and laughter, a place where our children thrived under the watchful eyes of their devoted parents. Each day brought new challenges and triumphs, weaving a tapestry of experiences that enriched our lives and strengthened our bonds.

As the years passed, we moved to a larger house in leafy Buckinghamshire to accommodate our children's growing needs. I found fulfilment in my dual roles as a parent and a humanitarian, taking solace in the knowledge that I was making a difference in the lives of others. Helen's restaurant flourished, becoming a beloved establishment in the community—both a product of her skills and charm and a testament to her dedication and talent.

With love as our guiding light and compassion as our compass, Helen and I continue to journey through life hand in hand, our hearts full, our spirits buoyed by the beauty of our shared endeavours. In the embrace of our now-teenage children and loved ones, we found the true essence of joy and fulfilment—a testament to the power of love and unity in the face of all challenges.

Our children, Delia and Rakieb, have been a source of joy and inspiration for us. With their fulfilled upbringing, the excellence they attained in their education is a testament to their hard work and dedication. As a result, they have carved a life path for themselves based on the principles and morals we instilled in them. They already have clear visions at such an early age, understanding the world around them. As they watch the suffering of children in the Middle East and other parts of the world, they can't help but relate our childhood to the scenes they see on today's TV screens, shaping their views and beliefs that no child should be harmed because of decisions made by greedy and arrogant politicians.

The moments we shared—telling them bedtime stories, pushing them on swings, teaching them how to cycle as small children, and later preparing them for real life, helping them to drive cars and sharing the dos and don'ts in work life—have taught them valuable skills based on the principles and morals we instilled in them.

The Big Message

We Are Family

My family, like many others in the Horn of Africa and other fragile areas, is woven together by threads of culture, resilience, and unwavering love. Our story is a tapestry of trials and triumphs, of moments that tested the very fabric of our beings.

Our father was a man of quiet strength, his piercing gaze reflecting a depth of wisdom earned through years of hardship. Our mother was his steadfast companion, her gentle touch a balm to the wounds of their struggles. Together, they raised us—five boys, each bearing the mark of our parents' fortitude. Life in the heart of East Africa, where humanity itself began millions of years ago, was a patchwork of innocence and adversity, carrying the weight of its ancient past. Our lives, too, bore the scars of the region's natural and man-made wounds, akin to the rugged and harsh landscapes of the arid northern mountains.

Through it all, my family remained united. Our laughter echoed through the halls of both the cramped two-bedroom home and the palace abode. We had weathered the storms of change, embracing both the luxuries and the challenges that came our way.

In this juxtaposition of opulence and hardship, we discovered the true meaning of family—a bond that transcended both luxury and adversity, grounding us in love and laughter. The children—Kaleb, Simon, Theo, Biruk, and Alazar—lived unpredictable childhoods in stark contrast to the shadows looming on the horizon. As we grew, political shifts swept through the region like a dark cloud, casting fear and uncertainty in its wake. But as the winds of change grew fiercer, our family stood resolute, a beacon of hope in the midst of chaos.

Our home became a sanctuary, a fortress of love and solidarity in a world torn apart by division. The threats against our lives only served to strengthen our bond, reminding us of the unbreakable ties that bound us together. Through storms of adversity and valleys of despair, we marched on—our spirits unbroken, our hearts filled with a fierce determination to survive and thrive.

And in the end, as the world continued to change, we stood together—a testament to the power of family and unity in the face of adversity. We had weathered the tempest, emerged from the darkness, and found solace in each other's arms. As we looked toward the future—a future filled with both uncertainty and promise—we knew one thing for certain: with strong parents like ours by our side, we could overcome any obstacle, navigate any storm, and always see the light at the end of the tunnel.

Through the tests of time, we withstood the currents of life with unwavering love and care, a bond that transcended even the walls of a prison cell. At the heart of our family was our mother, whose spirit radiated warmth and determination. Despite the many challenges life threw her way, she stood tall—a pillar of strength for her five children and her husband, shining through even in the darkest of times.

Our family was shattered multiple times, but never broken. Each time, we rose again, stronger than before. Our world was turned upside down and then right side up. But our mother refused to let adversity break us. She shielded us from the jaws of ruthless governments, holding us close, her love a shield against the pain and uncertainty that loomed over us. My mother continued to hold our family together with unwavering dedication and optimism. We weathered the storms, our bond growing stronger with each passing day. Despite the distance and the hardships they faced, the love and care between our parents never wavered.

My mother stood as a testament to the resilience of the human spirit and the power of love to conquer even the most challenging of circumstances.

Through our story, our family demonstrated that no distance, no obstacle, and no wall could ever dim the flame of love that burned brightly within our hearts. As we stood together—united in our resolve and strength—we served as a shining example of the enduring power of family: a beacon of hope in a world that often seemed dark and unforgiving.

In the midst of societal challenges and global tragedies, I find solace in the stories of humanity and kindness that my parents embodied. Their love for each other and for their children served as the foundation of our family, nurturing a sense of unity and compassion that transcended boundaries. Through their acts of selflessness, they painted a vivid picture of humanity, a rare and precious commodity in a world often marred by strife and conflict.

In sharp contrast, I think of my friends, Abel and Nebiyu—two individuals from broken homes, haunted by the absence of a complete family. Overwhelmed by their own demons, they could barely muster the strength to care for themselves, let alone help others.

As they grew older, the adversities of their upbringing became ever more apparent. Lacking parental guidance and hope, they struggled to find their place in the world, often getting into trouble and seeking solace in the wrong places. Despite the divergence in their paths, both Abel and Nebiyu entered adulthood without any meaningful education. The weight of their past traumas and the absence of parental support began to take its toll. Consumed by anger and resentment towards their absent parents, they spiralled into a cycle of self-destructive behaviours—unable to break free from the shadows of their familial past. As they faced the harsh realities of their upbringing, it became clear that no amount of material wealth or external success could fill the void left by the absence of a united parental front.

Their stories served as a stark reminder of the importance of parental love and guidance in shaping a child's future. Abel and Nebiyu's failures highlighted the enduring truth that children, regardless of their circumstances, need a home filled with parental love to thrive and succeed, paving the way for a brighter future for generations to come.

Our own daughters, Delia and Rakieb, now teenagers, grew up without the loving care of their grandparents after their untimely deaths and the ongoing political and travel barriers in Eritrea.

Though physical distance separated them, we made sure to instil the values of family, culture, resilience, and love in our children through storytelling and frequent contact that bridged the gap between us. Through tales of Eritrea's rich history and the struggles of its people, we painted a vivid picture of their heritage and the importance of unity and strength in the face of adversity.

My wife, Helen, and I knew that telling our children the truth about their ancestral country's current affairs required a delicate balance of honesty and hope, always ensuring that our storytelling style was age-appropriate to maintain its emotional impact. As Delia and Rakieb grew older, they carried with them the lessons we had imparted—the importance of family, the resilience of the Eritrean people, and the belief in a better future. Despite the challenges we faced, our children thrived, guided by the values we had instilled in them and the strength of their familial and cultural bond.

Despite our busy modern lives, we sit with our children daily, continuing the tradition of familyhood and storytelling that has been passed down through generations. Together, we listen to tales of courage, faith, and the enduring power of love—a legacy that my own family would forever carry on, ensuring that our children and grandchildren have the full advantage of growing up with a strong sense of identity and belonging, even in the face of adversity.

In the heart of an ongoing struggle for freedom and peace in the Horn of Africa region, I have made it my life's mission to support the underprivileged through my professional work and personal initiatives. Every step I take is guided by the unwavering inspiration instilled in me by my parents, who were the epitome of selflessness and generosity.

As I navigate the busy streets of life, I carry with me the memories of my childhood, a time when my parents taught me the value of lending a helping hand to those in need. Their dedication to uplifting the lives of others left an indelible mark on my soul, shaping me into the compassionate person I am today. The act of giving back and paying it forward not only brings me immense joy but also provides me with a guilt-free conscience, knowing that I am making a tangible difference in the world.

Despite the challenges and adversities that surround me, I remain steadfast in my commitment to making a difference, one small act of kindness at a time. The stories of my parents' unwavering love and dedication continue to fuel my spirit, propelling me forward in my mission to elevate the lives of those in need. As I listen to the voices of the marginalized and disenfranchised, I am reminded of the power of humanity to overcome even the greatest of obstacles.

In a world that often prioritises power and politics over people, I stand as a beacon of hope and compassion—a testament to the enduring legacy of my parents' selflessness. With each smile I bring to the faces of the underprivileged, I carry forward the torch of humanity, lighting the way for a brighter and more inclusive future for all. As I look to the challenges that lie ahead, I know that my parents' love and the guidance I received from my community will always be with me, a source of strength and inspiration in my quest to make the world a better place.

The harrowing experiences still faced by those fleeing their homelands in search of safety and stability—the faces of young Eritrean and Ethiopian refugees, their eyes reflecting both resilience and vulnerability—and the psychological and physical damage they suffer during their dangerous journeys through scorching deserts and violent seas, serve as a stark reminder of the endlessly harsh realities of the Horn of Africa region. The ongoing political unrest and ethnic tensions, coupled with the recurring devastating wars that loom every decade in the region, continue to claim millions of lives, casting a shadow of fear and uncertainty over the land.

This highlights the urgent need for compassion and inclusivity among both ordinary citizens and those in positions of power.

In the Horn of Africa, a gripping, continuous tale still unfolds, echoing the legacy of power and its toxic hold on nations. The shadows of authoritarian decisions loom large, casting a dark cloud over the land. The Derg, with its iron grip on governance, made a fateful move, reshuffling farmers like pawns on a perilous chessboard. The consequences of this unilateral action reverberate through time, serving as a cautionary tale of the dangers of disregarding expert counsel.

My father, at the heart of some of the region's humanitarian projects, foresaw the brewing tempest long before the winds of change swept across the land. His voice, a beacon of reason amidst the chaos, warned of the dangers of mixing tribes with deep-rooted connections to their ancestral lands. But his words, laden with wisdom, fell on deaf ears, drowned out by the sirens of power.

Now, as the story unfolds four decades later, Ethiopia finds itself on a treacherous path, teetering on the brink of ethnic strife and violence. The clash between the original landowners in Oromia and displaced settlers echoes with the cries of a nation torn asunder. The once-fertile lands now bear witness to a tragic chaos of bloodshed and upheaval, as the ghosts of past decisions haunt the present.

Amidst this turmoil, a chorus of voices rises—the experts, the humanitarian workers, the unsung heroes whose wisdom could steer the ship away from the precipice. Yet their counsel is cast aside, deemed a threat by those who wield power as a weapon. In their quest for control, politicians sow the seeds of conflict, perpetuating a cycle of violence under the guise of false claims over borders and ports.

Similarly, in Eritrea—a nation trapped between the shadows of a painful past and the uncertain grip of a militaristic regime—the sun continues to rise over a landscape scarred by the echoes of lost dreams and unfulfilled promises.

The people of Eritrea, resilient and determined, find themselves ensnared in a web of oppression and despair woven by those in power. The ex-rebel government, once hailed as heroes of independence, now stands as a barrier to progress, suffocating the voices of intellectuals and visionaries who yearn to shape a brighter future.

In the desolate stretches of the Saharan desert, young Eritreans embark on perilous journeys, crossing treacherous seas in overcrowded boats, seeking a glimmer of hope on distant shores. Their longing for a better tomorrow echoes through the winds, a poignant reminder of a nation adrift, yearning to reclaim its place among the community of nations.

Amidst the rugged terrain and dusty streets, the youth of Eritrea walk a path fraught with sacrifice and suffering. The relentless drumbeat of military conscription echoes through the valleys, robbing the young of their freedom and potential, turning the land into a ghost town as its brightest minds flee in search of hope beyond the borders.

On screens around the world, Eritreans have become the face of a refugee crisis—a stark reminder of the price paid for freedom that remains elusive. The once-vibrant society, rich in human and natural resources, now languishes in the shadows, earning itself the grim title of the 'North Korea of Africa,' a beacon of despair in a world that is moving towards progress.

As waves of uncertainty and conflict still wash over the region, casting permanent shadows of war between Eritrea and Ethiopia, the people bear the burden of leaders blinded by selfish ambition and short-sightedness. Lives lost in the name of freedom cry out for change, for a new dawn where peace and prosperity can reign.

As the sun sets over the troubled land, casting a golden glow over a landscape scarred by conflict and strife, the promise of a brighter future flickers like a distant beacon. In the hearts of the people, a flame of resilience still burns, a spark of hope that one day, against all odds, the shadows of war will give way to the light of lasting peace and prosperity.

As the narrative unfolds, a stark truth emerges: unless the voices of reason and expertise are heeded, the region will remain ensnared in a web of perpetual unrest. The fate of a generation hangs in the balance, their stories etched in the headlines of a world grappling with bloodshed and poverty, all contributing to the wider refugee crisis and human misery. Only through unity with those who offer guidance and adherence to international norms can these lands find peace, and its youth reclaim their future from the shadows of strife.

Blurb

In the heart of a land plagued by centuries-old conflicts and ever-evolving political turmoil, the story of Yosief's family unfolded like a chapter of resilience and fortitude amidst the chaos that engulfed their lives. Our story was woven with threads of love, unwavering courage, and resilience—born from the shadows of political turmoil and natural upheavals that had long plagued our land.

At the helm of our family stood a dedicated humanitarian father—my father, Yosief—whose unwavering commitment to alleviating the suffering of his fellow humans knew no bounds. Despite the constant socio-political unrest that gripped the region, he stood as a beacon of hope, tirelessly working to bring about change amidst a landscape fraught with natural calamities, power struggles, and uncertainty that continue to haunt the region.

By his side stood his beloved wife, my mother Hewan—a woman of quiet strength and boundless love. Together, they raised five boys in a world where survival often meant navigating the treacherous waters of hardship and adversity. Hewan, a pillar of support to her husband, managed the household with grace and fortitude, instilling in her sons the values of compassion and resilience that would go on to shape our destinies.

As power shifted with alarming speed in the volatile political and military landscape of Ethiopia and Eritrea, my family found itself thrust into the eye of the storm. My mother, the matriarch of our family, bore the weight of unexplained health predicaments that seemed to mirror the tumultuous state of the world around us. Yet, with unwavering strength and wisdom, she stood as a pillar of protection for her husband and children, shielding us from the evils that threatened to consume our existence.

The tale of my family is a poignant narrative that transcends mere survival in the face of adversity. It is a story of resilience and unity, of holding on to the core values and traditions that defined our familial and cultural heritage. Through the lens of our struggles, the essence of familial bonds emerged as the beacon of hope in a world often engulfed in darkness.

Amidst the backdrop of long imprisonments, assassination attempts, and the harrowing realities of living under a communist regime in the 80s and 90s, my family's journey epitomised the resilience of the human spirit. Moments of joy and laughter intertwined with the raw human suffering that marked our existence, painting a vivid tapestry of the human experience in its most unfiltered and poignant form.

Through the trials and tribulations that tested our resolve, my family rose from the ashes of despair, embodying the indomitable spirit that defined our heritage. Our story became a testament to the enduring power of love, unity, and the unbreakable bond that held us together through the darkest of times. In a world where uncertainty loomed large, our tale stood as a beacon of hope in a sea of despair, a symbol of the strength of the human will.

As we, the children, grew, our family faced many stormy ups and downs, often separated by external forces beyond our control. Despite the challenges and separations, our hearts remained united, bound by a love that transcended distance and time.

We, the children of revolution, inherited our parents' sense of purpose and justice, determined to follow in their footsteps as champions for the marginalised and oppressed. We possessed a natural gift for diplomacy and empathy, bridging divides and fostering unity where others saw only discord.

Together, my family weathered countless trials, leaning on each other for strength and support. Our home, a sanctuary amidst a world in turmoil, was filled with warmth, adventure, and laughter—a refuge from the harsh realities we faced outside its walls. Yet, amidst the struggles and triumphs, there were moments of unexplained events, marked by mystery and culture, that left us wondering about the forces that shaped our destinies. We often spoke of a supernatural being watching over us, guiding our paths in ways that defied rational explanation.

And so, the story of our extraordinary family unfolds—a tapestry woven with threads of love, courage, and resilience. Through the joys and adversities, the trials and triumphs, we remained united in heart and spirit, a testament to the enduring power of family bonds in the face of hardship and uncertainty. Our destiny, like a river, was sometimes calm, other times tumultuous. Evictions and hunger became unwelcome companions as we navigated the harsh realities of life.

Yet, even in the darkest of times, our unwavering resolve and unity shone brightly. Instead of succumbing to despair, we extended a helping hand to those in similar plight, spreading hope like wildfire in our community.

Each time the storm seemed never-ending, fate smiled upon us. A twist of destiny led us from a grand palace, surrounded by opulence and luxury, to a squalid home without amenities and food. It was as if we had walked through the gates of a fairy tale, leaving behind the shadows of our past.

Amidst the glitz and glamour, my family never forgot our roots or the struggles we had faced. We continued to share our newfound blessings with those in need, our hearts overflowing with empathy and kindness.

In this rollercoaster of life, we learned that destiny is a mysterious force, ever-changing and unpredictable. Through the highs and lows, we remained a beacon of light, inspiring others to persevere in the face of adversity.

And so, my family's tale transcended riches and poverty, power and oppression—showcasing the strength of resilience, compassion, and the enduring spirit of a family bound by love.

We, Amiche a formidable force in human and machine, remain in history as symbols of strength and purpose carrying the weight of joy and despair in a fast changing times.

We are the icons of power and resilience that shaped the face of East Africa by sacrificing our blood to keep the delicate balances in a land marked by recurrent conflict and political ignorance.

www.ingramcontent.com/pod-product-compliance
Lightning Source LLC
Chambersburg PA
CBHW081612100526
44590CB00021B/3414